TREATS

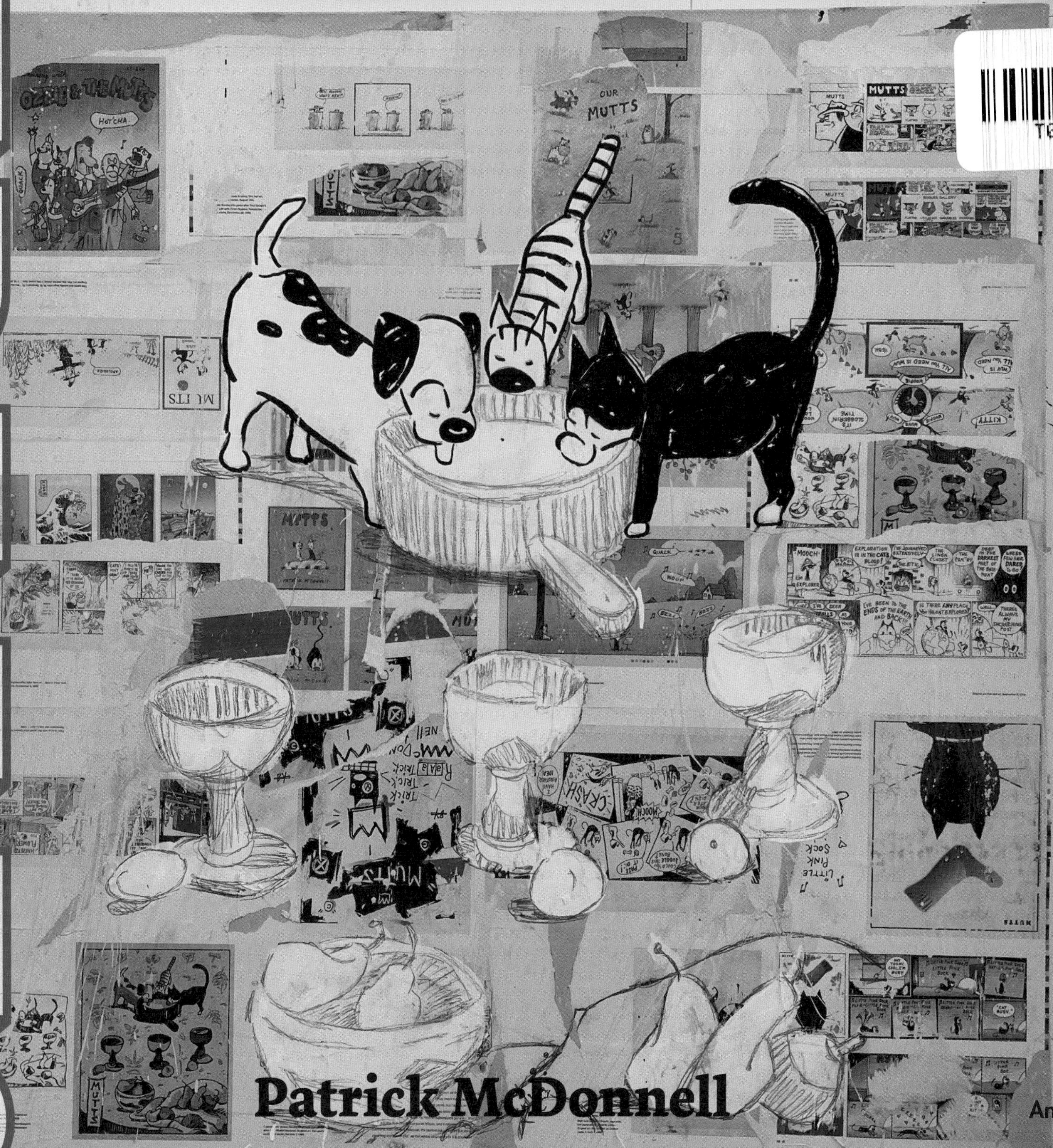

Patrick McDonnell

Andrews McMeel
PUBLISHING®

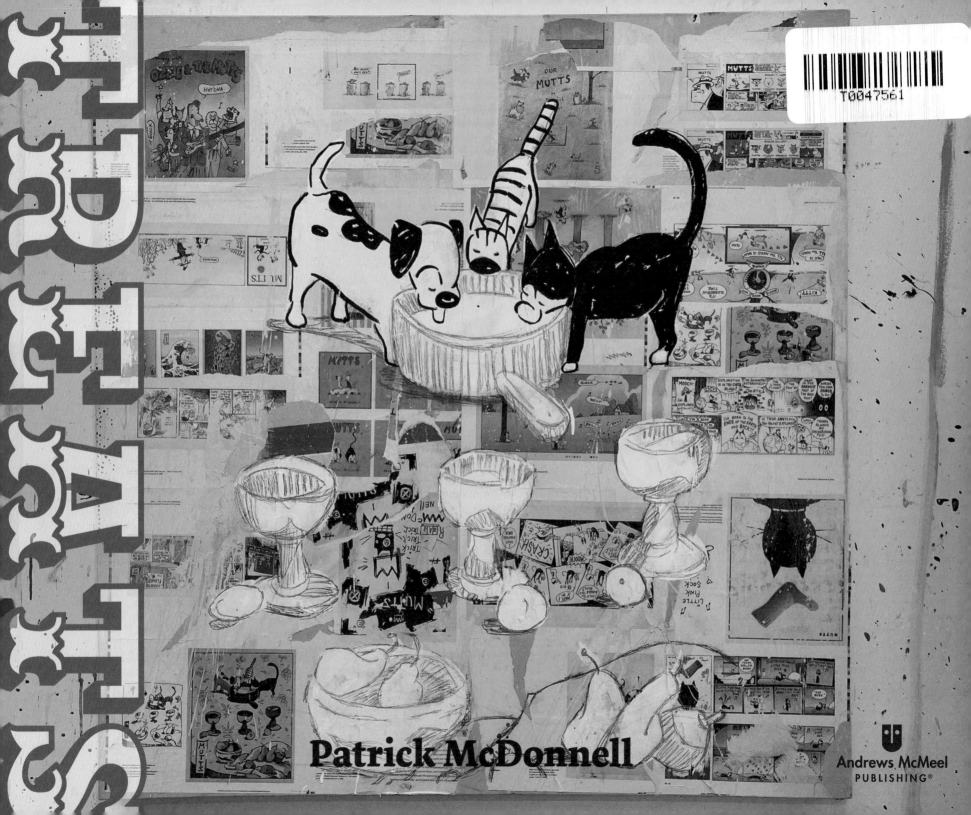

Other Books by Patrick McDonnell

Mutts

Cats and Dogs: Mutts II

More Shtuff: Mutts III

Yesh!: Mutts IV

Our Mutts: Five

A Little Look-See: Mutts VI

What Now: Mutts VII

I Want to Be the Kitty: Mutts VIII

Dog-Eared: Mutts IX

Who Let the Cat Out: Mutts X

Everyday Mutts

Animal Friendly

Call of the Wild

Stop and Smell the Roses

Earl & Mooch

Our Little Kat King

Bonk

A Shtinky Little Christmas

Cat Crazy

Living the Dream

Playtime

Year of Yesh

#LoveMutts

You've Got Those Wild Eyes Again, Mooch

Hot Dogs, Hot Cats

Mutts: Walking Home

Mutts Moments

Mutts Sundays

Sunday Mornings

Sunday Afternoons

Sunday Evenings

Mutts is distributed internationally by King Features Syndicate, Inc. For information, write to King Features Syndicate, Inc., 300 West Fifty-Seventh Street, New York, New York 10019, or visit www.KingFeatures.com.

Treats: A Mutts Treasury copyright © 2024 by Patrick McDonnell. All rights reserved. Printed in China. No part of this book may be used or reproduced in any manner whatsoever without written permission except in the case of reprints in the context of reviews.

Andrews McMeel Publishing, a division of Andrews McMeel Universal, 1130 Walnut Street, Kansas City, Missouri 64106

24 25 26 27 28 POA 10 9 8 7 6 5 4 3 2 1

ISBN: 978-1-5248-8093-4

Library of Congress Control Number: 2023944334

Printed on recycled paper.

Mutts can be found on the Internet at **www.muttscomics.com**

Cover design by Patrick McDonnell and Nicole Tramontana.
Cover painting inspired by Paul Gaugin's 1888 painting Still Life with Three Puppies.

MUTTS
OOO
EARL,
LISTEN...

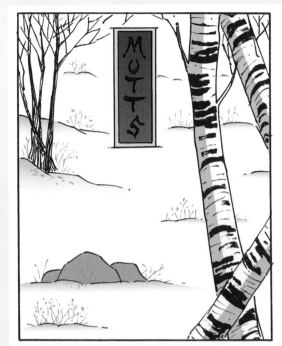

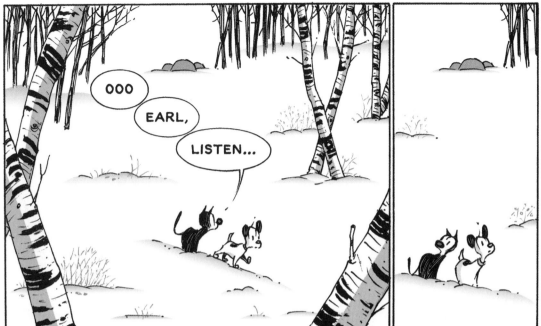

TREATS

Treats is a collection of MUTTS comic strips from the year I took a six-month sabbatical. This allowed me to work on the book *Heart To Heart: A Conversation on Love and Hope for Our Precious Planet*, a collaboration with His Holiness the Dalai Lama. For that portion of the year, I personally chose some of my favorite classic MUTTS from the past to run in the newspapers. These "best of" strips are presented here as well. So, this is a book of new treats (Mooch adds a musical soundtrack to his life; tales of Earl as a puppy) and old treats (Prospero the cat wizard sends Earl back in time, Mooch meets Santa's helper, "Kitten Claws").

Shnack time!

—PATRICK

SHWEET!

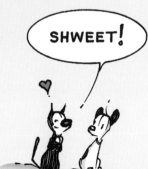

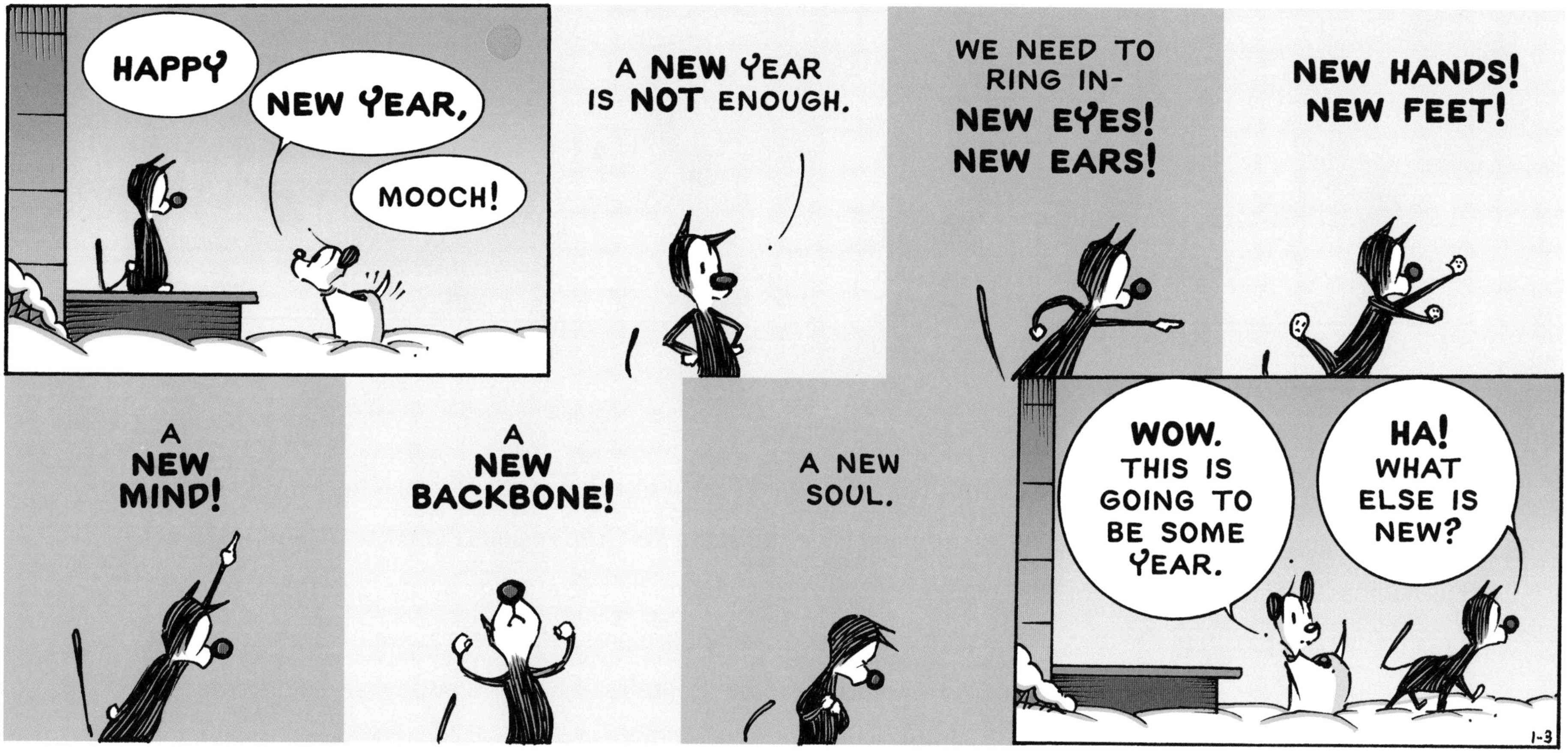
HAPPY
NEW YEAR,
MOOCH!
A NEW YEAR IS NOT ENOUGH.
WE NEED TO RING IN-
NEW EYES! NEW EARS!
NEW HANDS! NEW FEET!
A NEW MIND!
A NEW BACKBONE!
A NEW SOUL.
WOW. THIS IS GOING TO BE SOME YEAR.
HA! WHAT ELSE IS NEW?
1-3

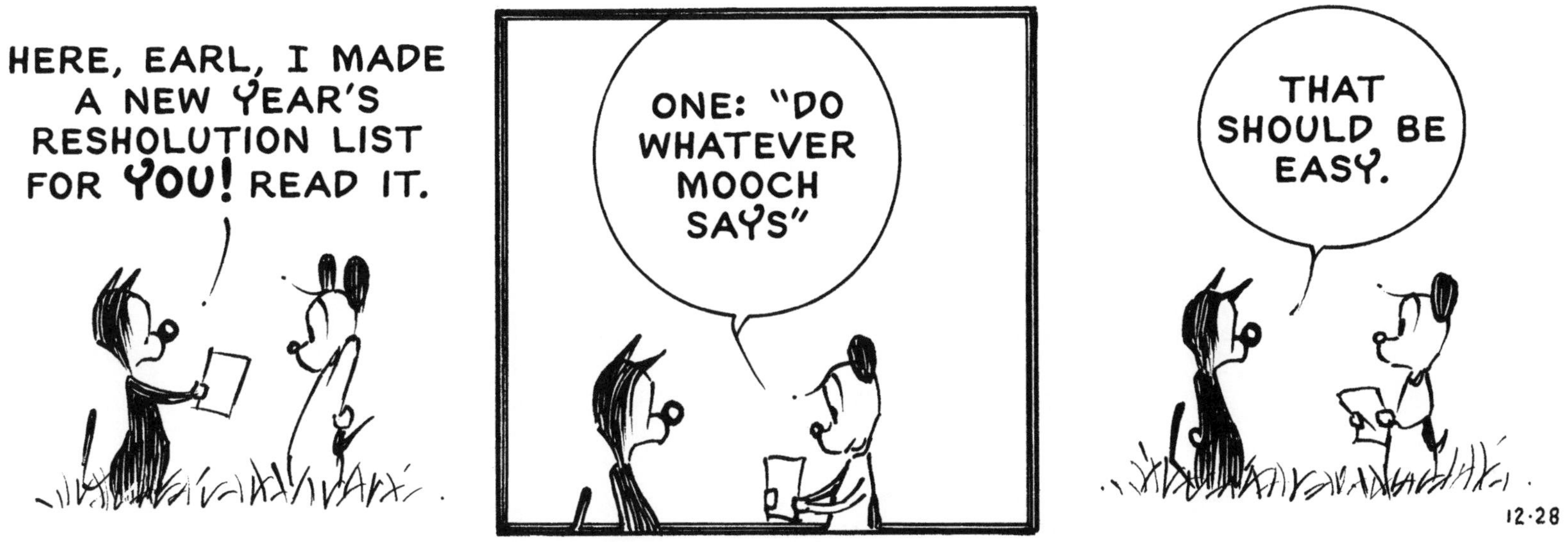
HERE, EARL, I MADE A NEW YEAR'S RESHOLUTION LIST FOR YOU! READ IT.
ONE: "DO WHATEVER MOOCH SAYS"
THAT SHOULD BE EASY.
12·28

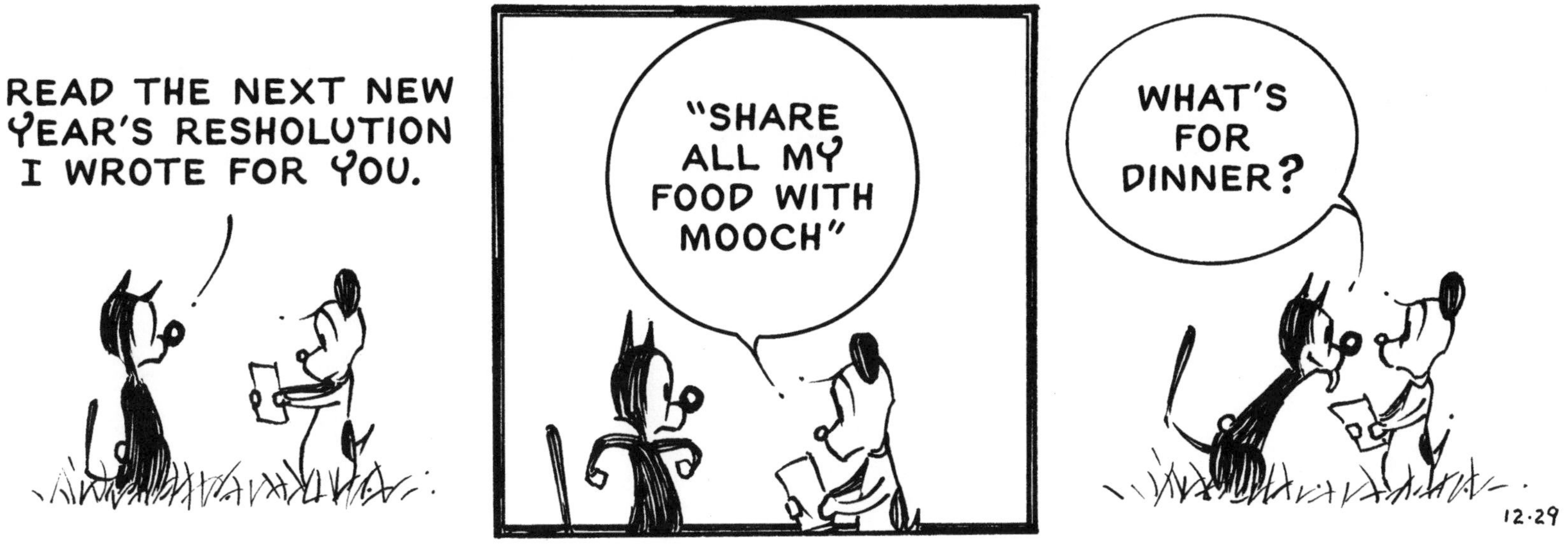
READ THE NEXT NEW YEAR'S RESHOLUTION I WROTE FOR YOU.
"SHARE ALL MY FOOD WITH MOOCH"
WHAT'S FOR DINNER?
12·29

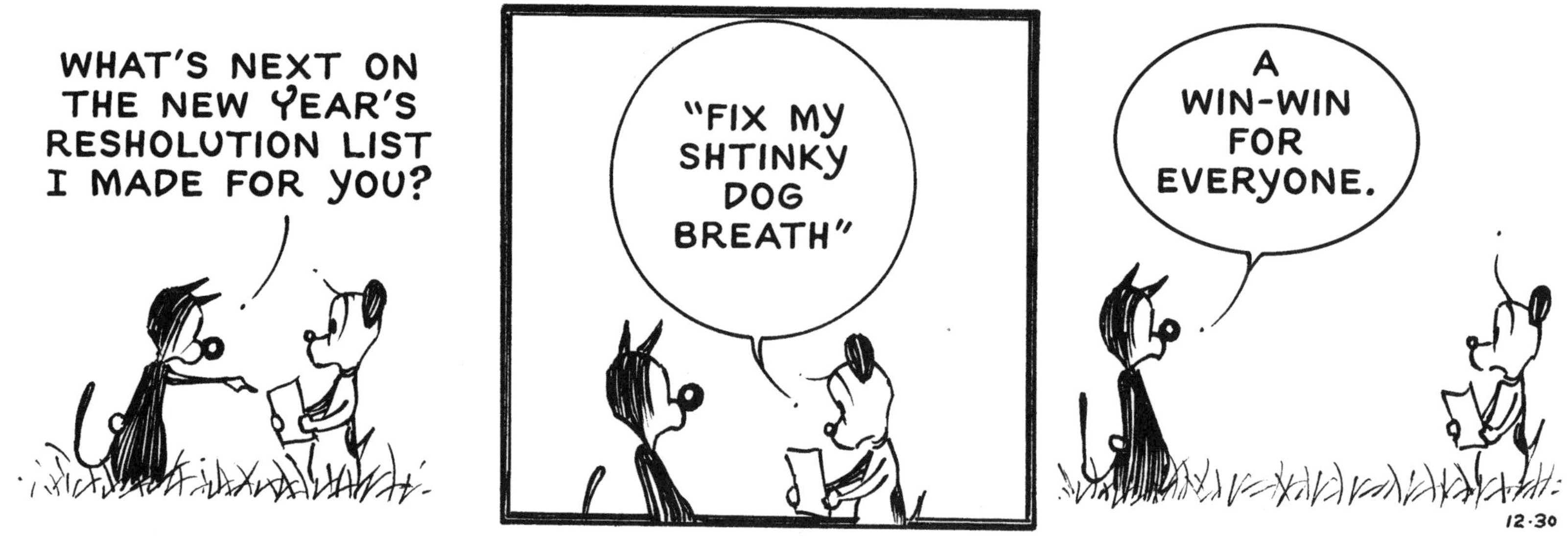
WHAT'S NEXT ON THE NEW YEAR'S RESHOLUTION LIST I MADE FOR YOU?
"FIX MY SHTINKY DOG BREATH"
A WIN-WIN FOR EVERYONE.
12·30

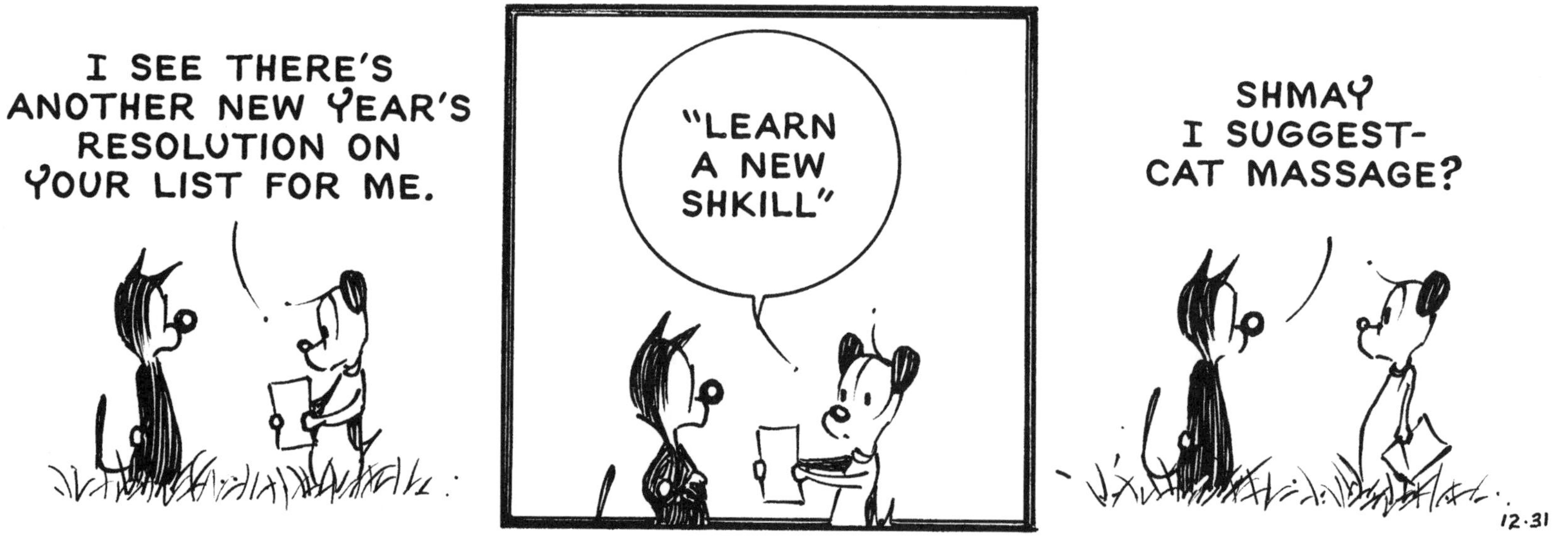
I SEE THERE'S ANOTHER NEW YEAR'S RESOLUTION ON YOUR LIST FOR ME.
"LEARN A NEW SHKILL"
SHMAY I SUGGEST-CAT MASSAGE?
12·31

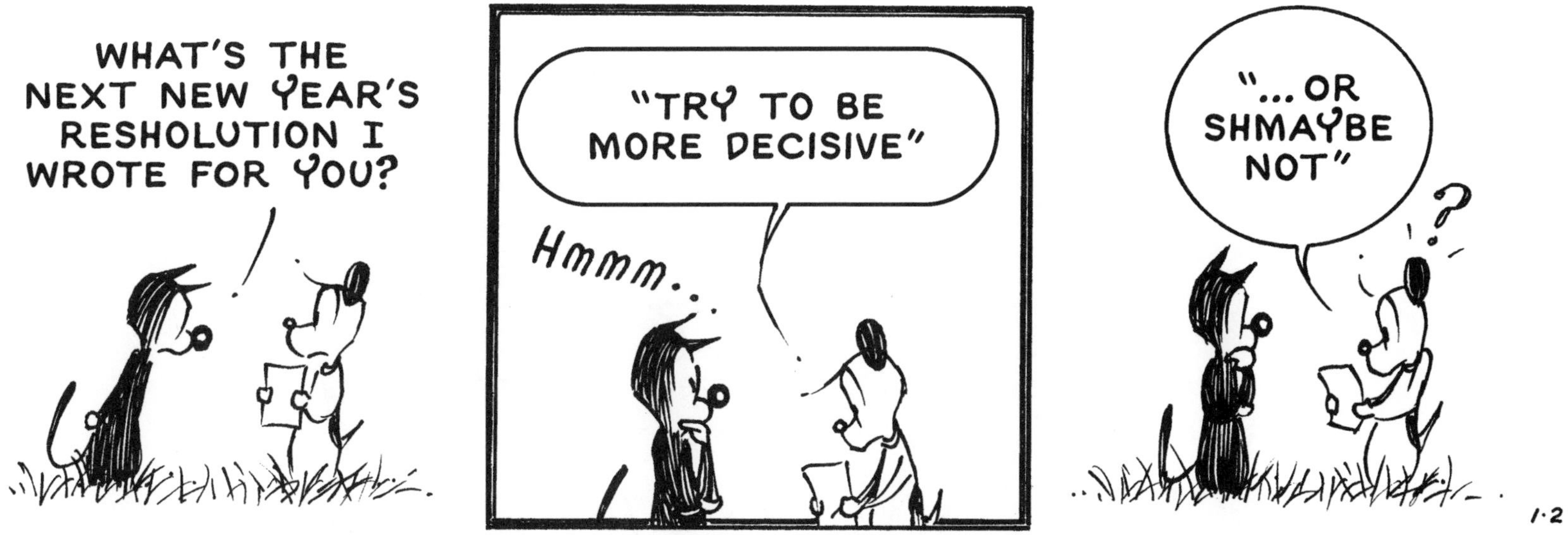
WHAT'S THE NEXT NEW YEAR'S RESHOLUTION I WROTE FOR YOU?
Hmmm...
"TRY TO BE MORE DECISIVE"
"...OR SHMAYBE NOT"
?
1·2

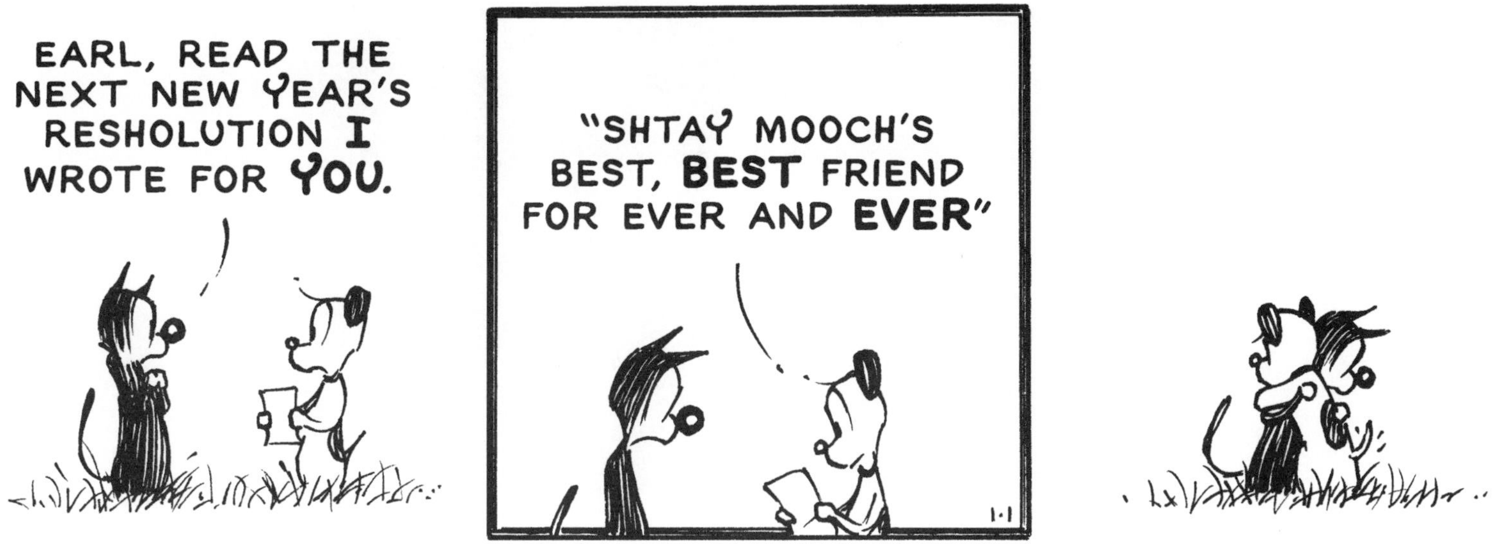
EARL, READ THE NEXT NEW YEAR'S RESHOLUTION **I** WROTE FOR **YOU**.
"SHTAY MOOCH'S BEST, **BEST** FRIEND FOR EVER AND **EVER**"
1·1

MUTTS

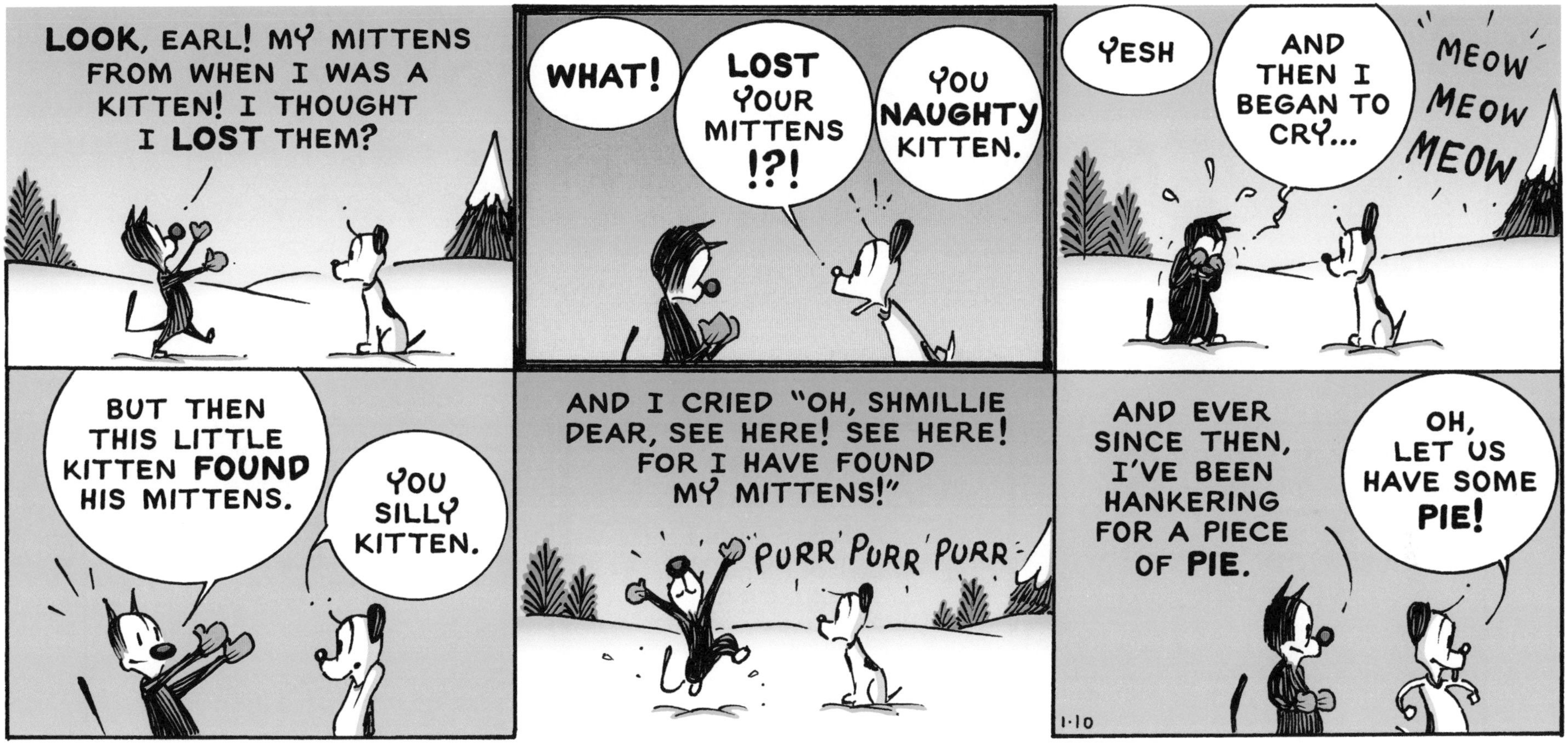
LOOK, EARL! MY MITTENS FROM WHEN I WAS A KITTEN! I THOUGHT I LOST THEM?
WHAT!
LOST YOUR MITTENS !?!
YOU NAUGHTY KITTEN.
YESH
AND THEN I BEGAN TO CRY...
MEOW MEOW MEOW
BUT THEN THIS LITTLE KITTEN FOUND HIS MITTENS.
YOU SILLY KITTEN.
AND I CRIED "OH, SHMILLIE DEAR, SEE HERE! SEE HERE! FOR I HAVE FOUND MY MITTENS!"
PURR PURR PURR
AND EVER SINCE THEN, I'VE BEEN HANKERING FOR A PIECE OF PIE.
OH, LET US HAVE SOME PIE!
1·10

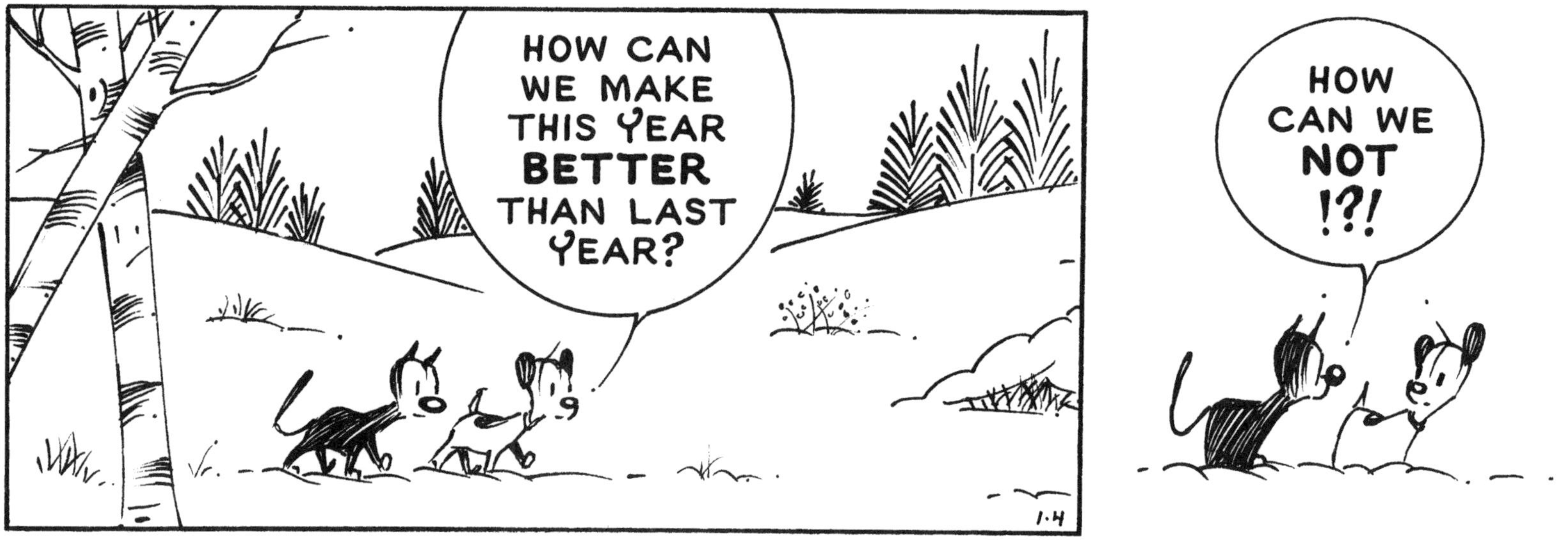
HOW CAN WE MAKE THIS YEAR **BETTER** THAN LAST YEAR?
HOW CAN WE **NOT !?!**
1·4

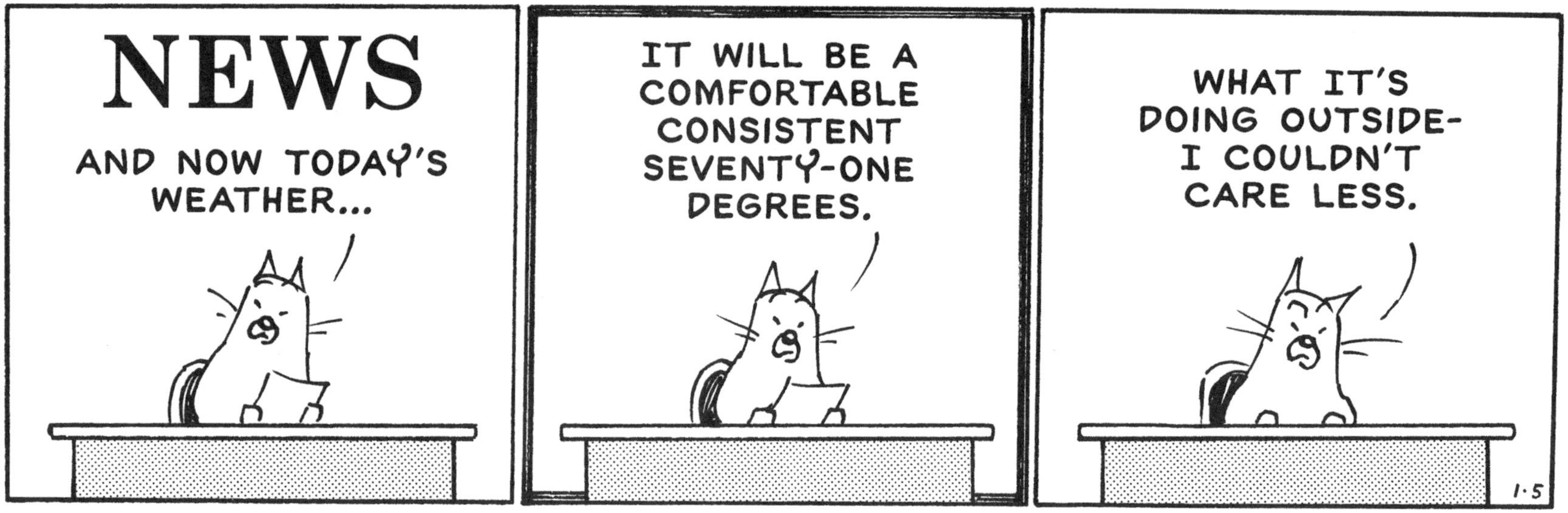
NEWS
AND NOW TODAY'S WEATHER...
IT WILL BE A COMFORTABLE CONSISTENT SEVENTY-ONE DEGREES.
WHAT IT'S DOING OUTSIDE- I COULDN'T CARE LESS.
1·5

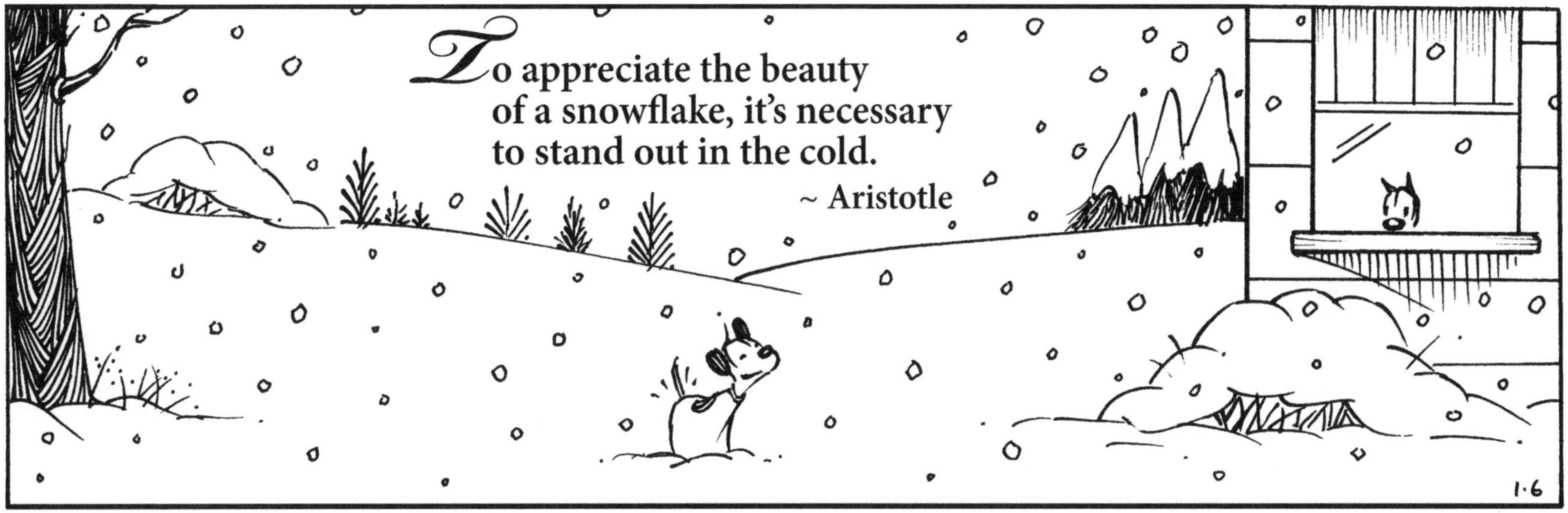
To appreciate the beauty of a snowflake, it's necessary to stand out in the cold.
~ Aristotle
1·6

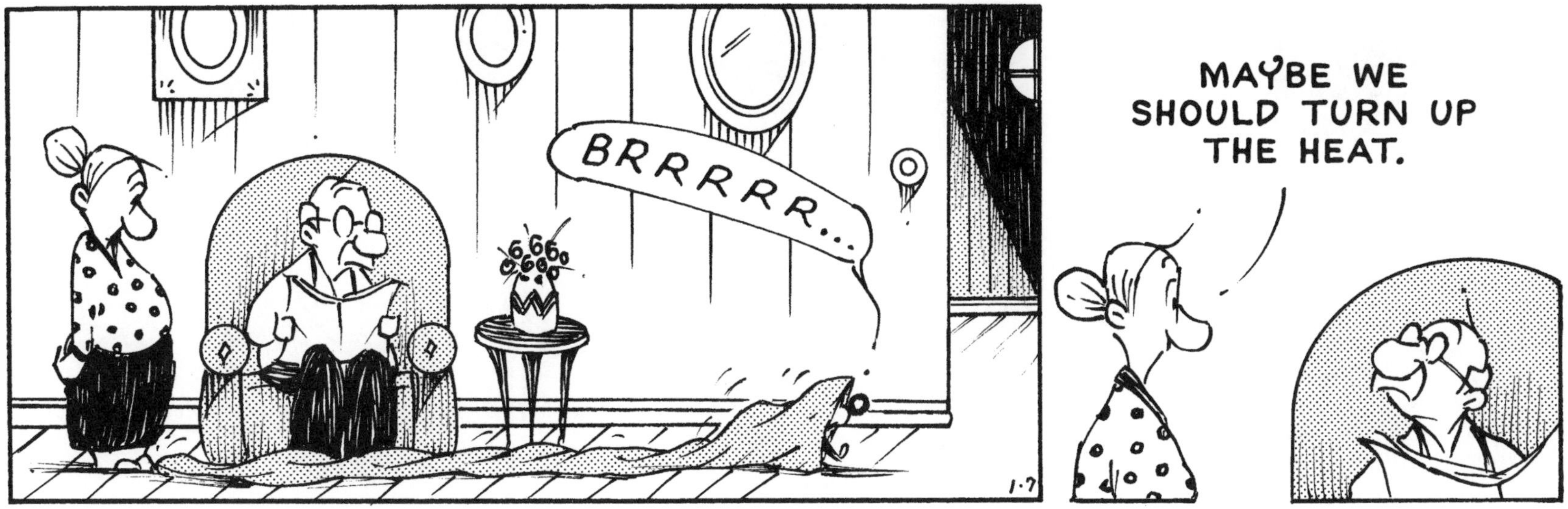
BRRRRRR...
1·7
MAYBE WE SHOULD TURN UP THE HEAT.

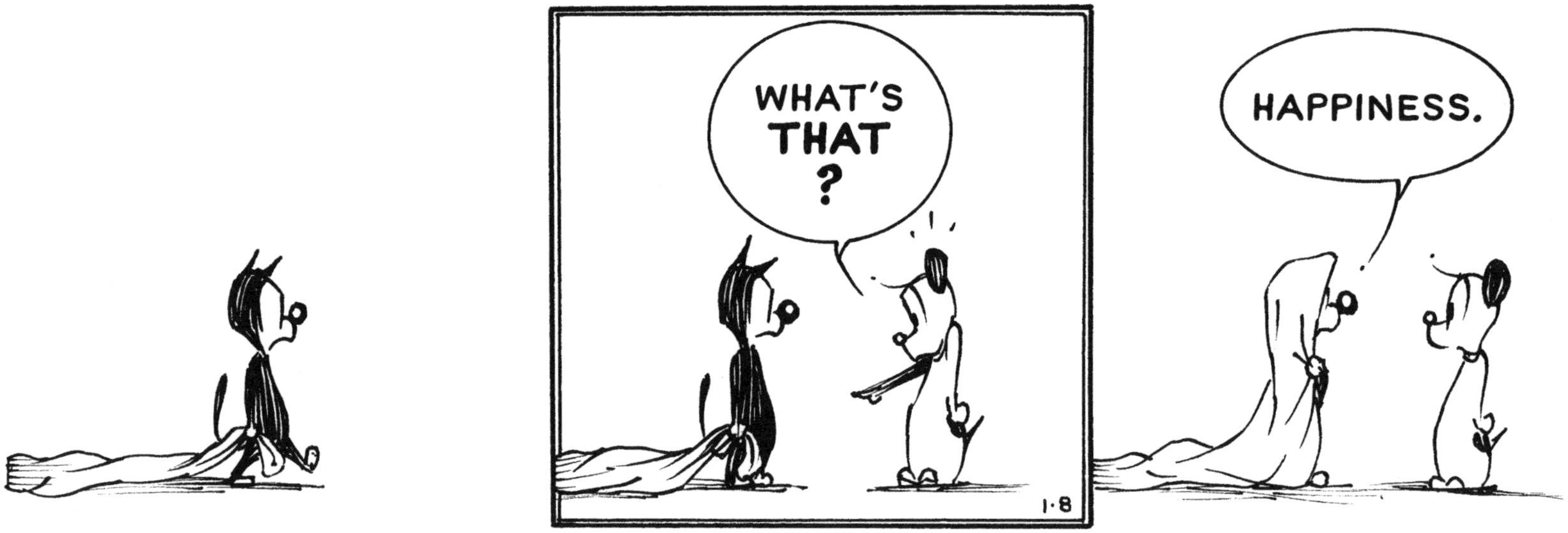
WHAT'S THAT ?
HAPPINESS.
1·8

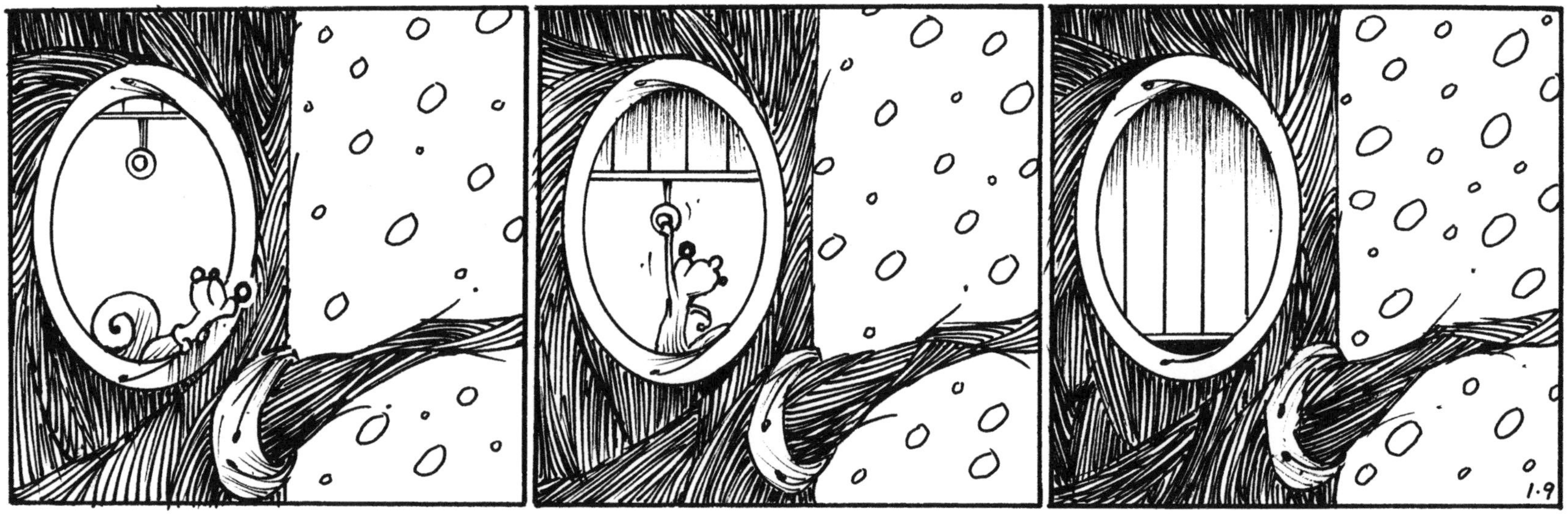
1·9

MUTTS

Patrick McDonnell

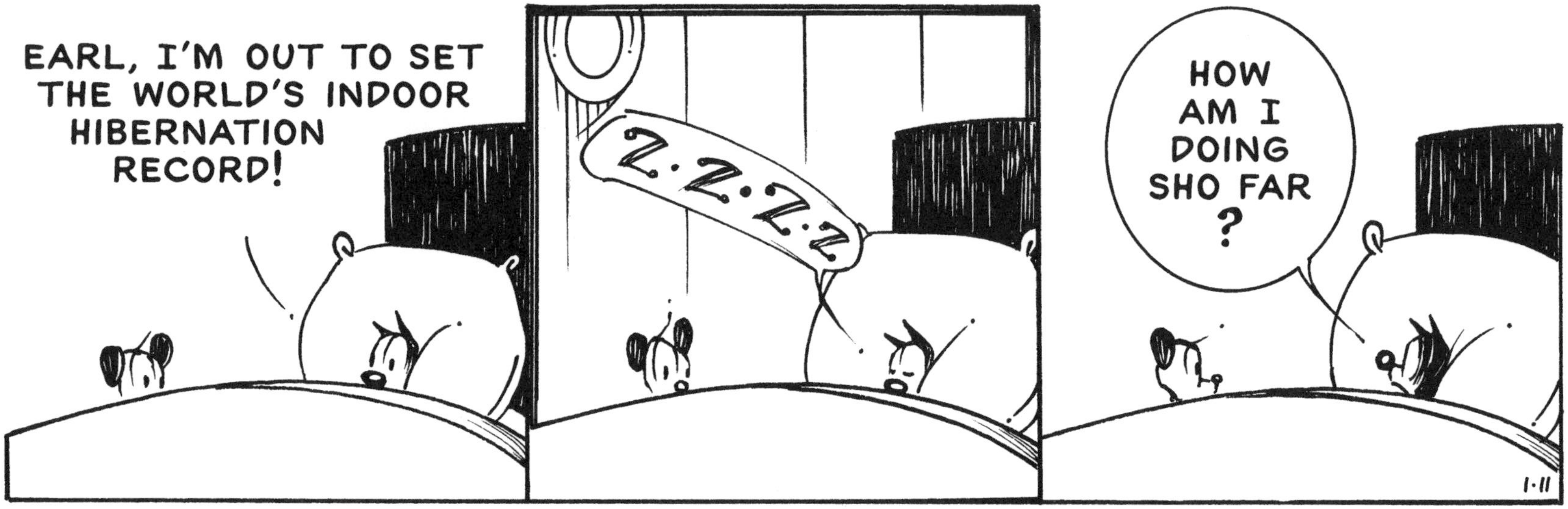
EARL, I'M OUT TO SET THE WORLD'S INDOOR HIBERNATION RECORD!
Z.Z.Z.Z
HOW AM I DOING SHO FAR?
1·11

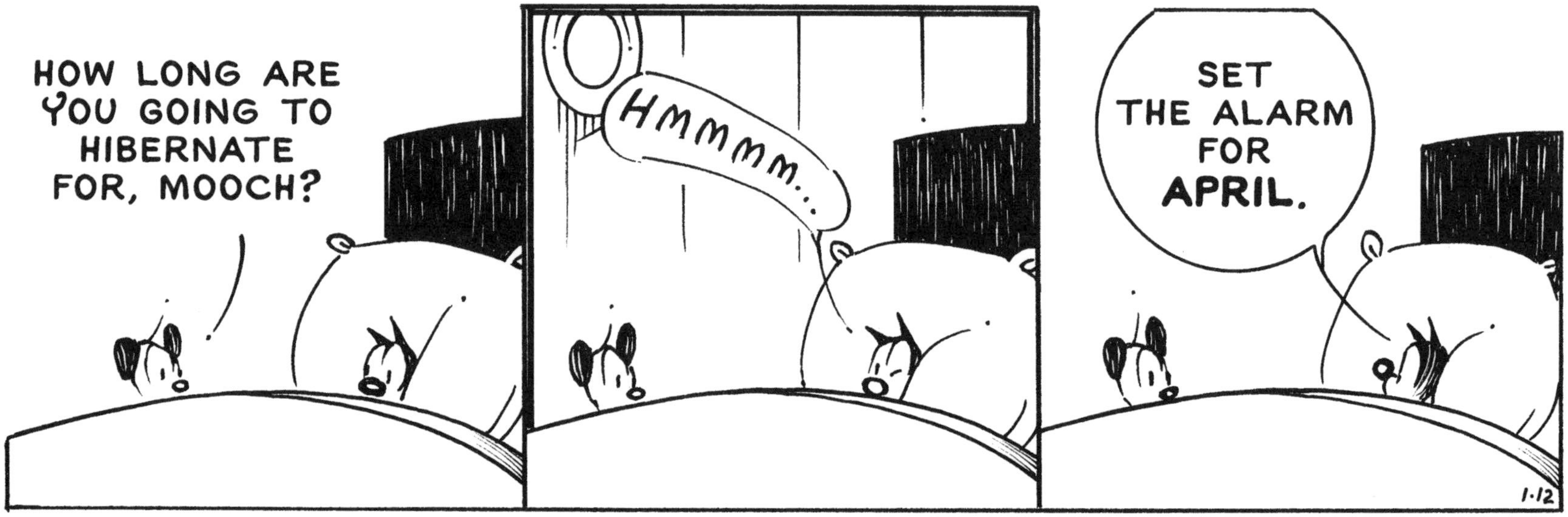
HOW LONG ARE YOU GOING TO HIBERNATE FOR, MOOCH?
HMMMM...
SET THE ALARM FOR **APRIL.**
1·12

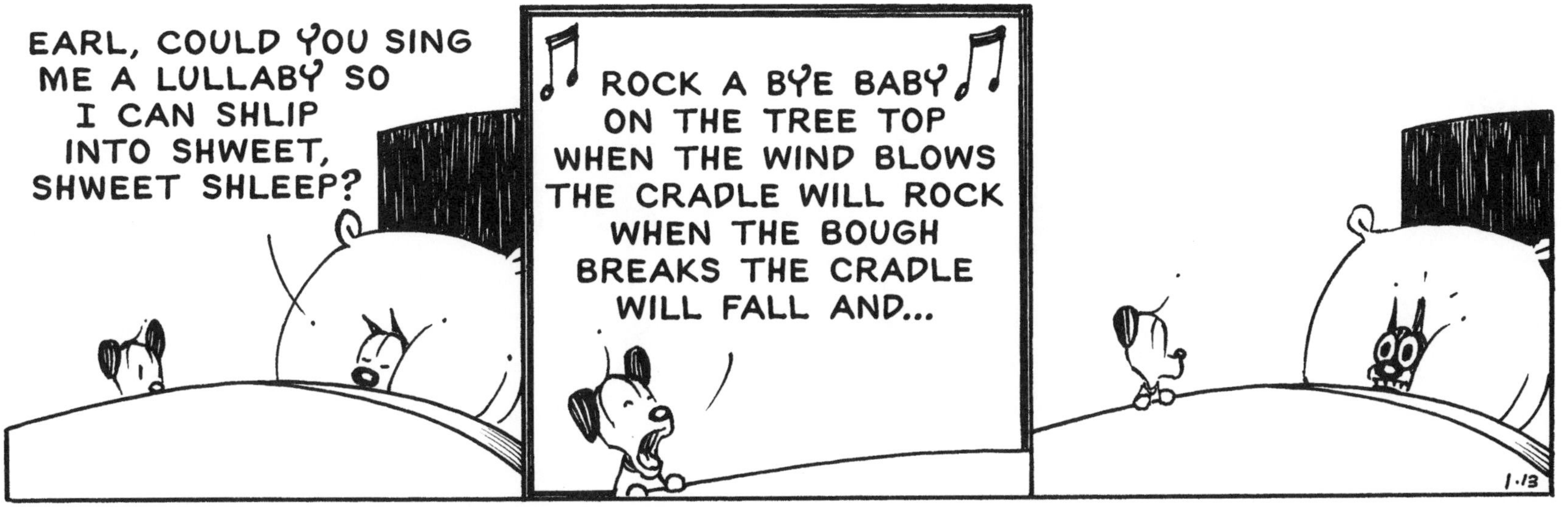
EARL, COULD YOU SING ME A LULLABY SO I CAN SHLIP INTO SHWEET, SHWEET SHLEEP?
ROCK A BYE BABY ON THE TREE TOP WHEN THE WIND BLOWS THE CRADLE WILL ROCK WHEN THE BOUGH BREAKS THE CRADLE WILL FALL AND...
1.13

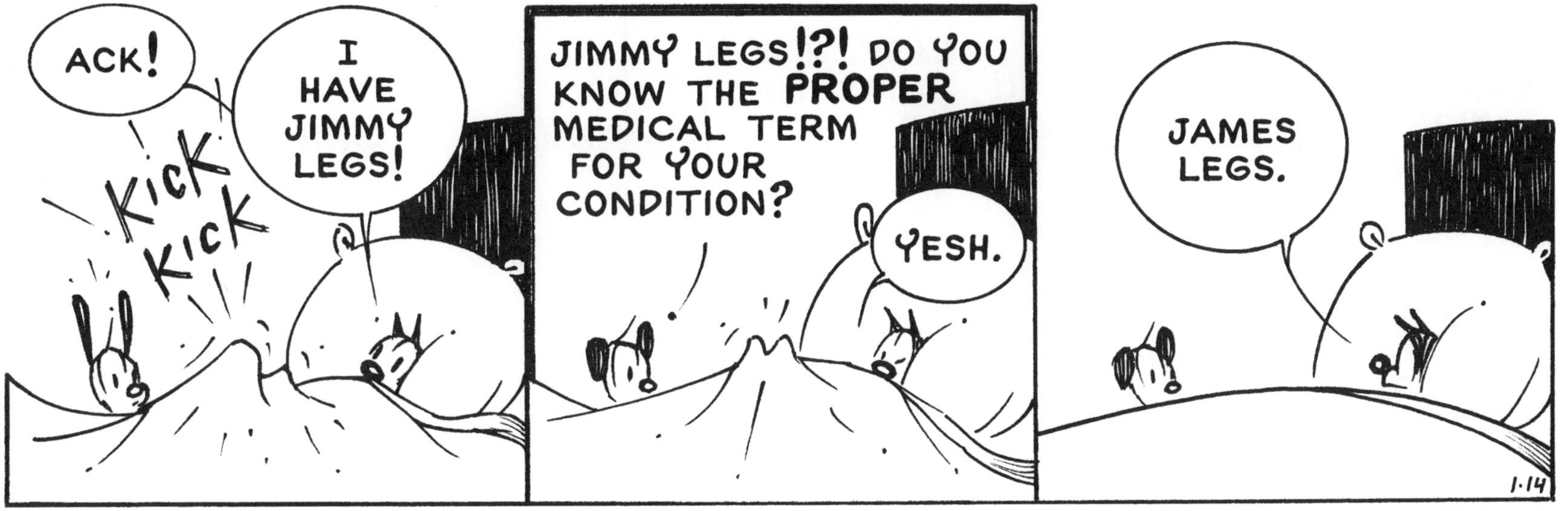
ACK!
I HAVE JIMMY LEGS!
KICK KICK
JIMMY LEGS!?! DO YOU KNOW THE **PROPER** MEDICAL TERM FOR YOUR CONDITION?
YESH.
JAMES LEGS.
1.14

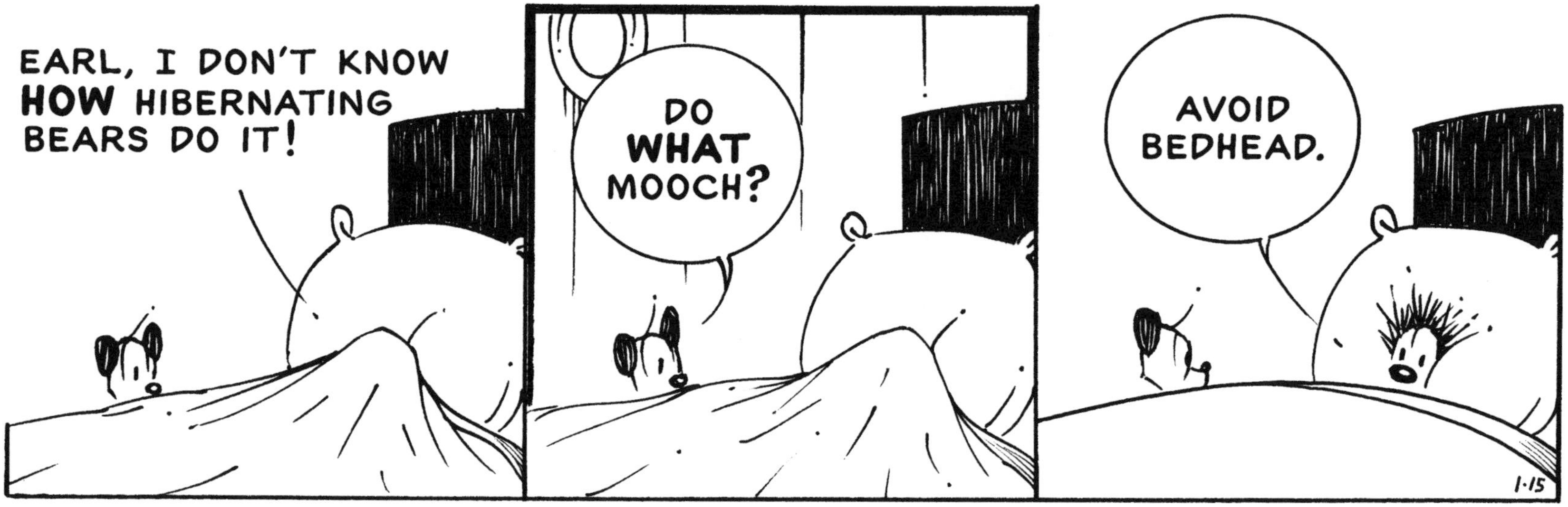
EARL, I DON'T KNOW **HOW** HIBERNATING BEARS DO IT!
DO **WHAT** MOOCH?
AVOID BEDHEAD.
1·15

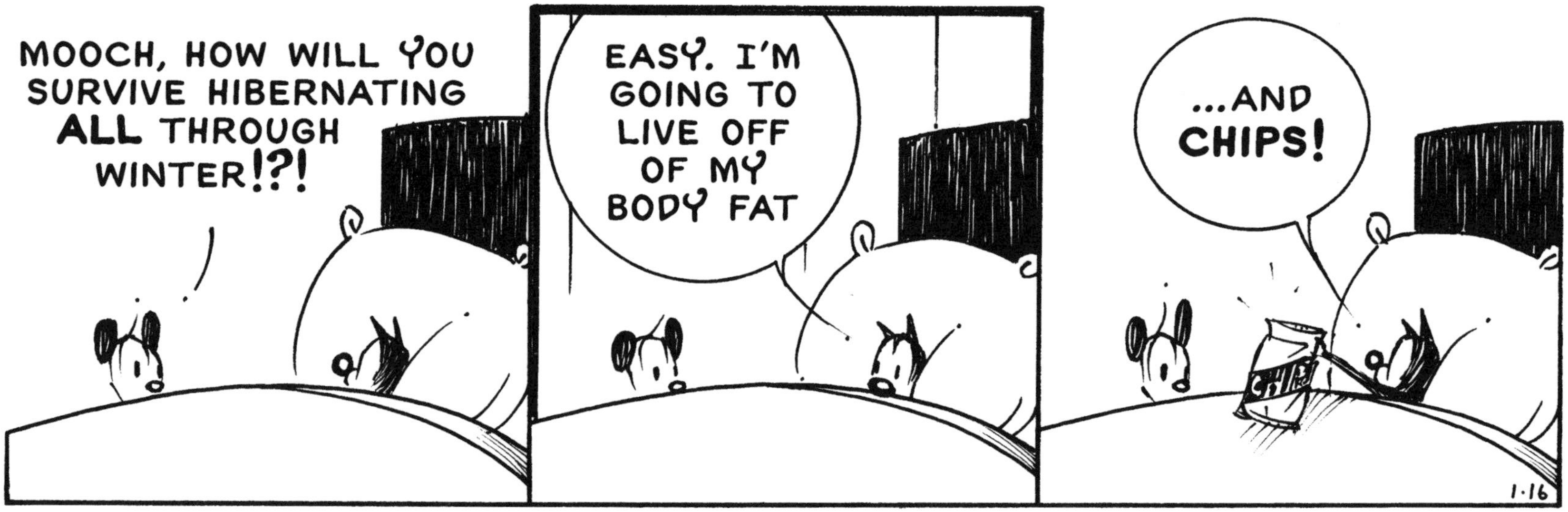
MOOCH, HOW WILL YOU SURVIVE HIBERNATING **ALL** THROUGH WINTER!?!
EASY. I'M GOING TO LIVE OFF OF MY BODY FAT
...AND **CHIPS!**
1·16

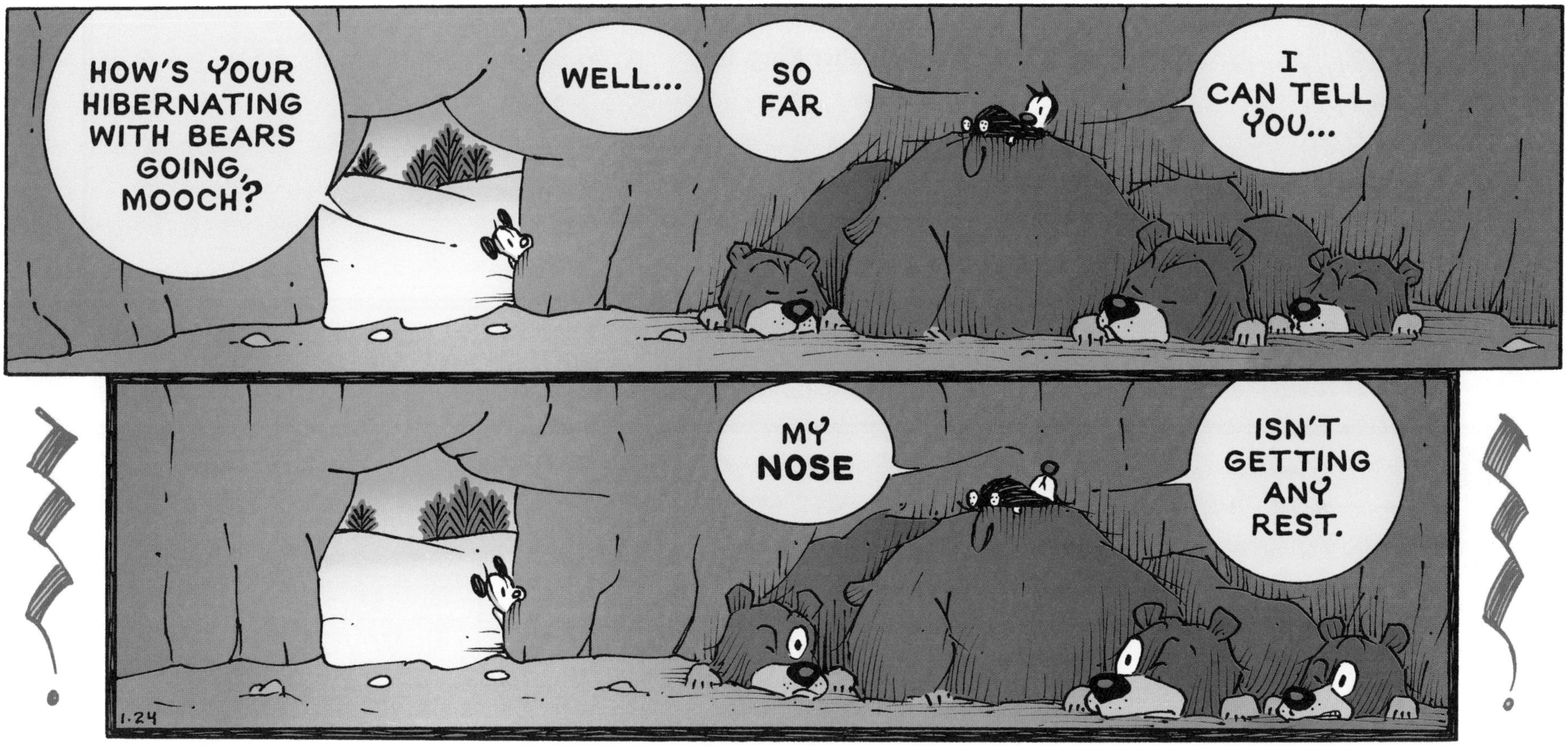
HOW'S YOUR HIBERNATING WITH BEARS GOING, MOOCH?
WELL...
SO FAR
I CAN TELL YOU...
MY **NOSE**
ISN'T GETTING ANY REST.
1·24

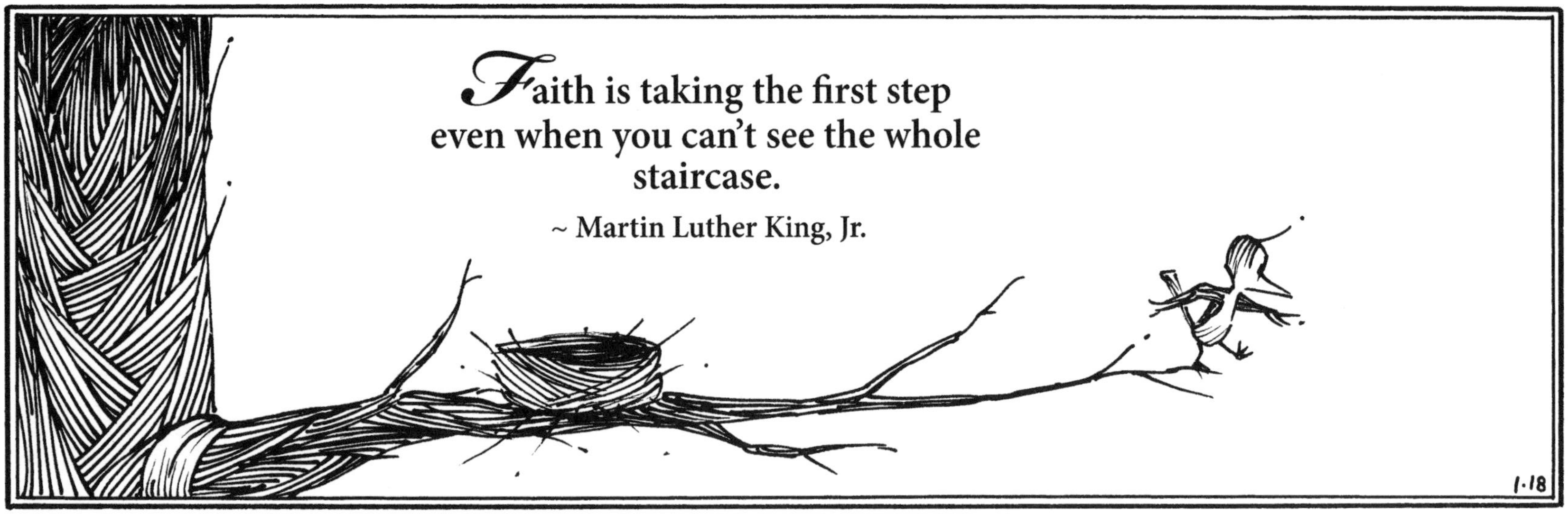
Faith is taking the first step even when you can't see the whole staircase.
~ Martin Luther King, Jr.
1.18

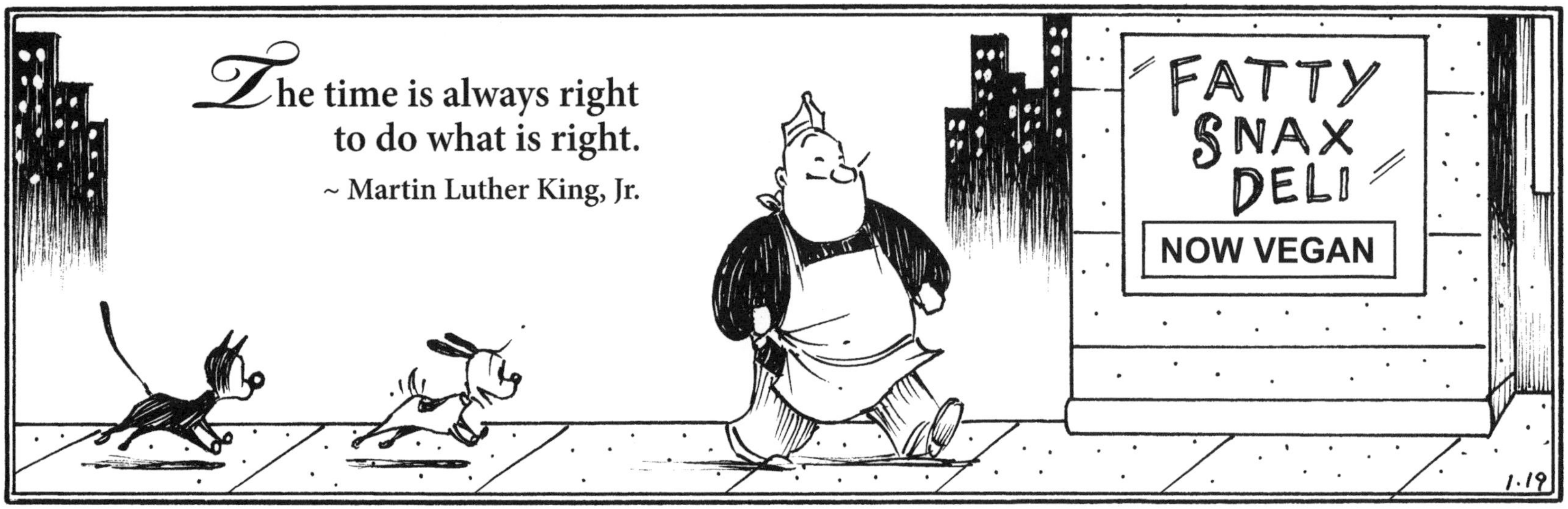
The time is always right to do what is right.
~ Martin Luther King, Jr.
FATTY SNAX DELI
NOW VEGAN
1.19

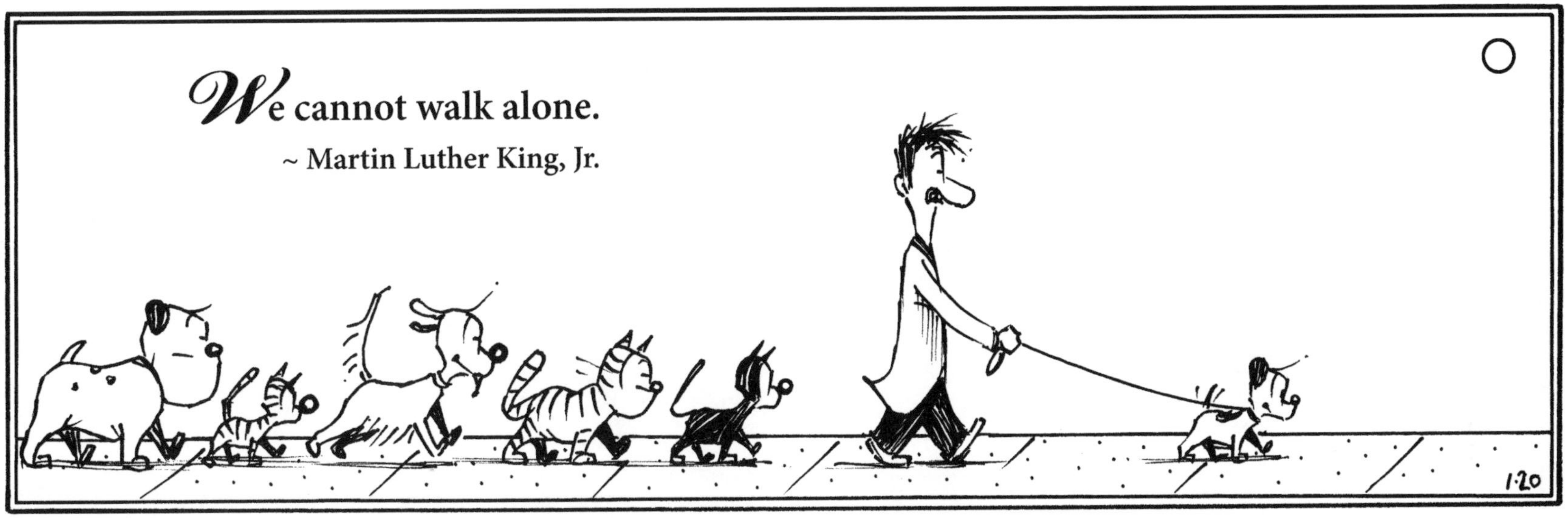
We cannot walk alone.
~ Martin Luther King, Jr.
1·20

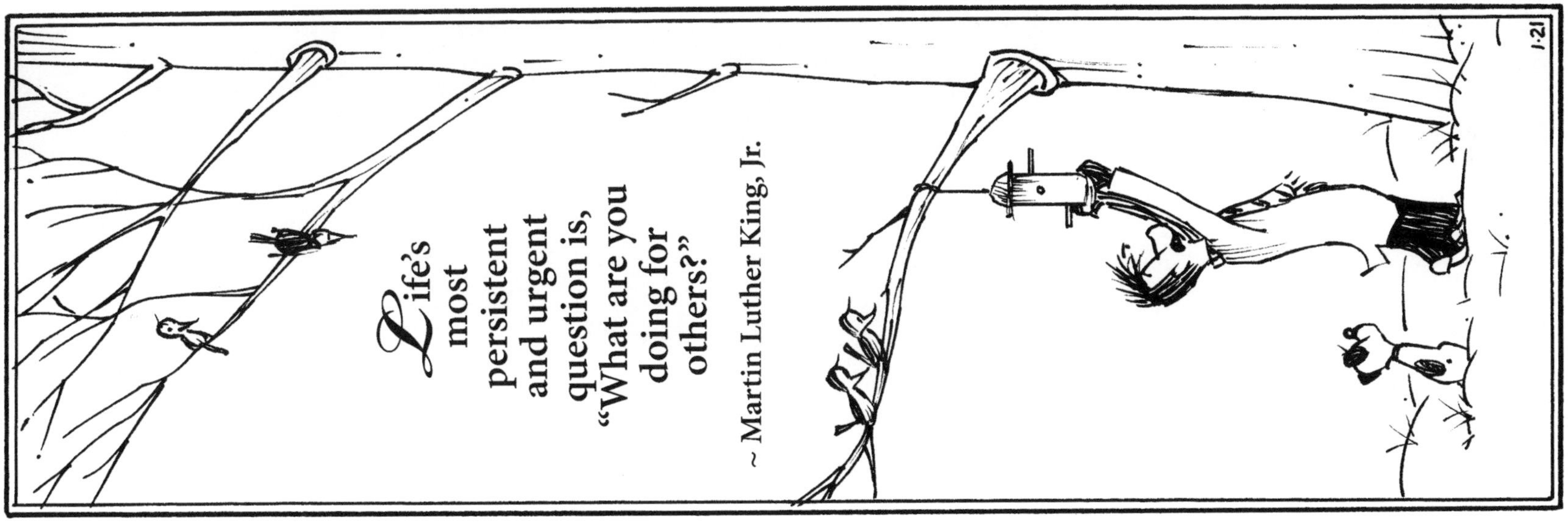
1·21
Life's most persistent and urgent question is, "What are you doing for others?"
~ Martin Luther King, Jr.

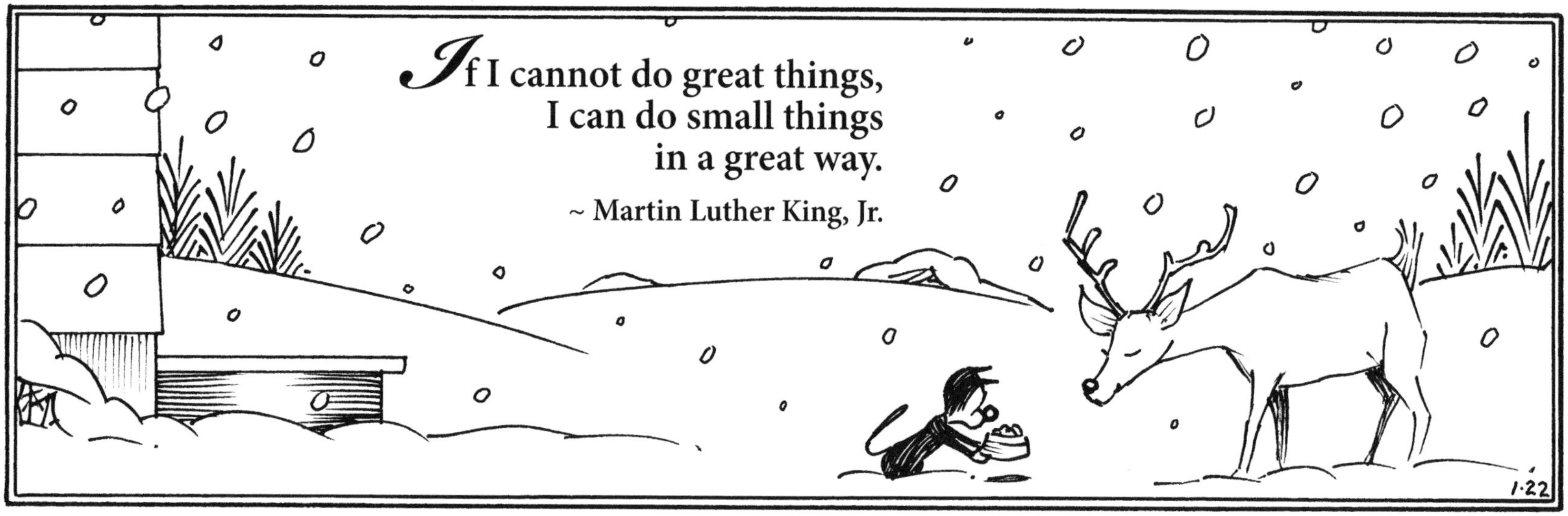
If I cannot do great things,
I can do small things
in a great way.
~ Martin Luther King, Jr.
1·22

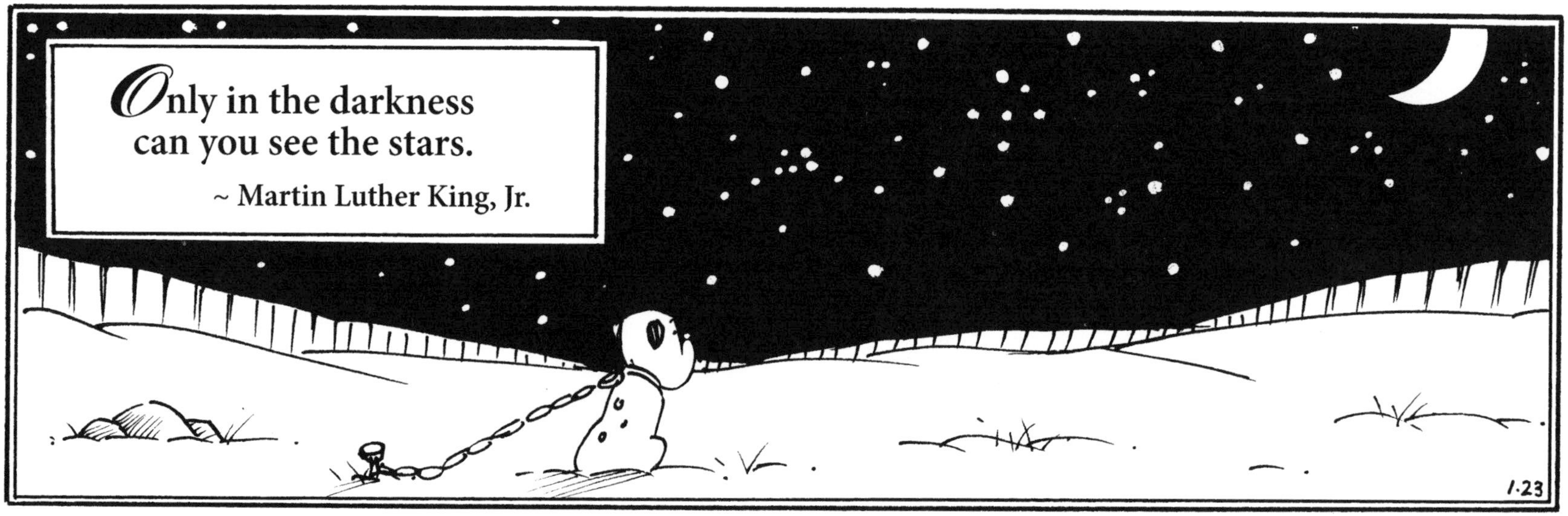
Only in the darkness
can you see the stars.
~ Martin Luther King, Jr.
1·23

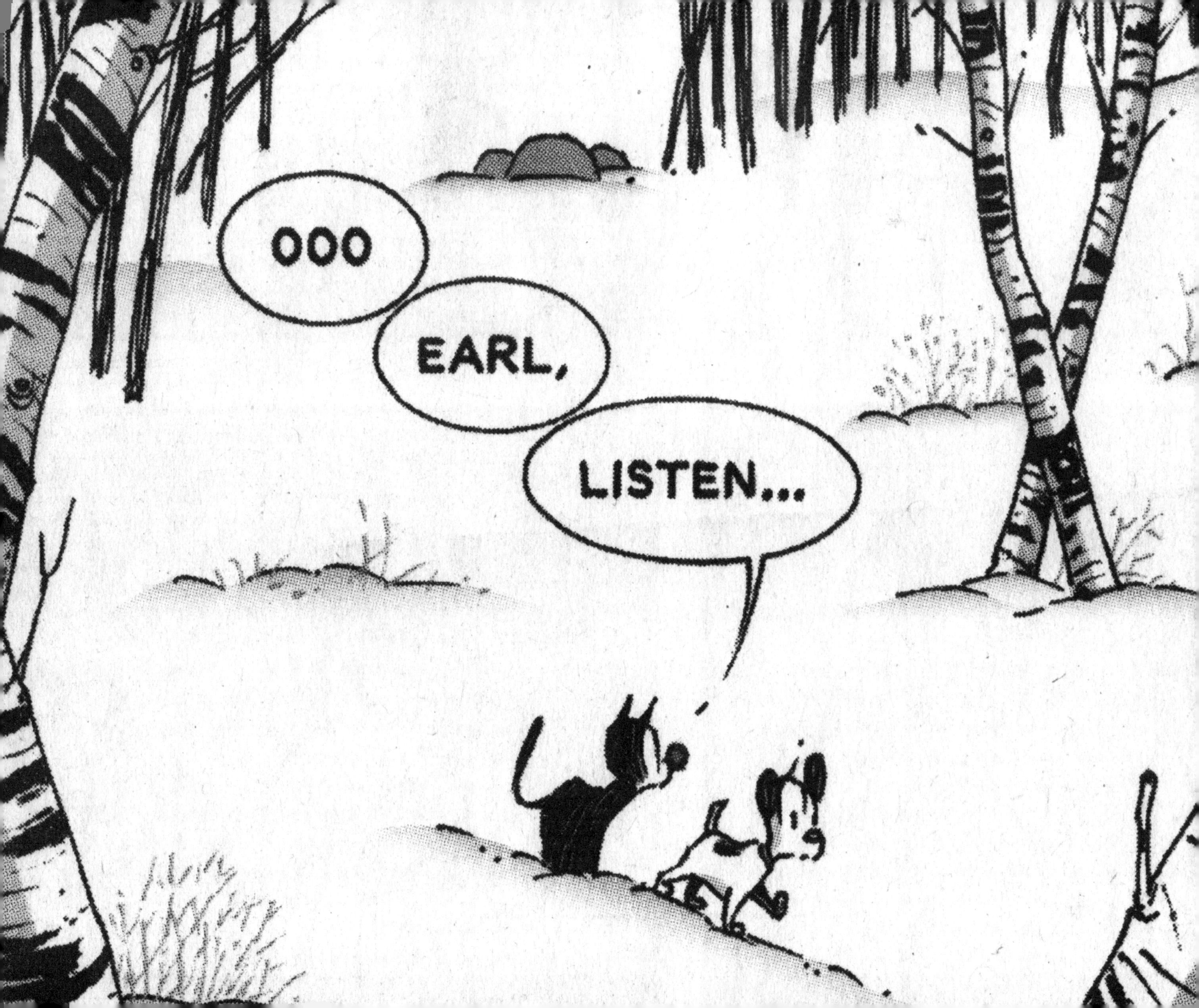
OOO
EARL,
LISTEN...

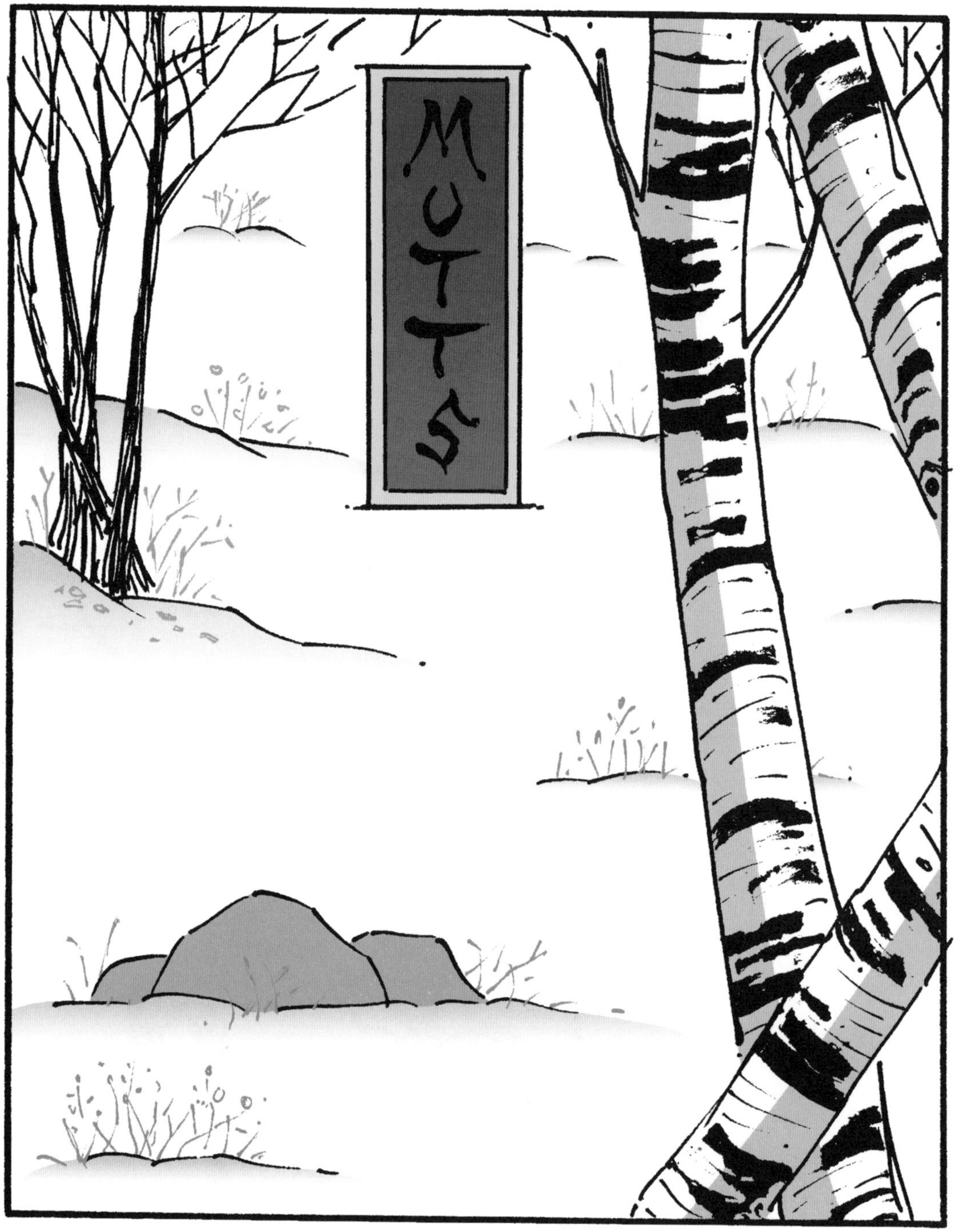
MUTTS

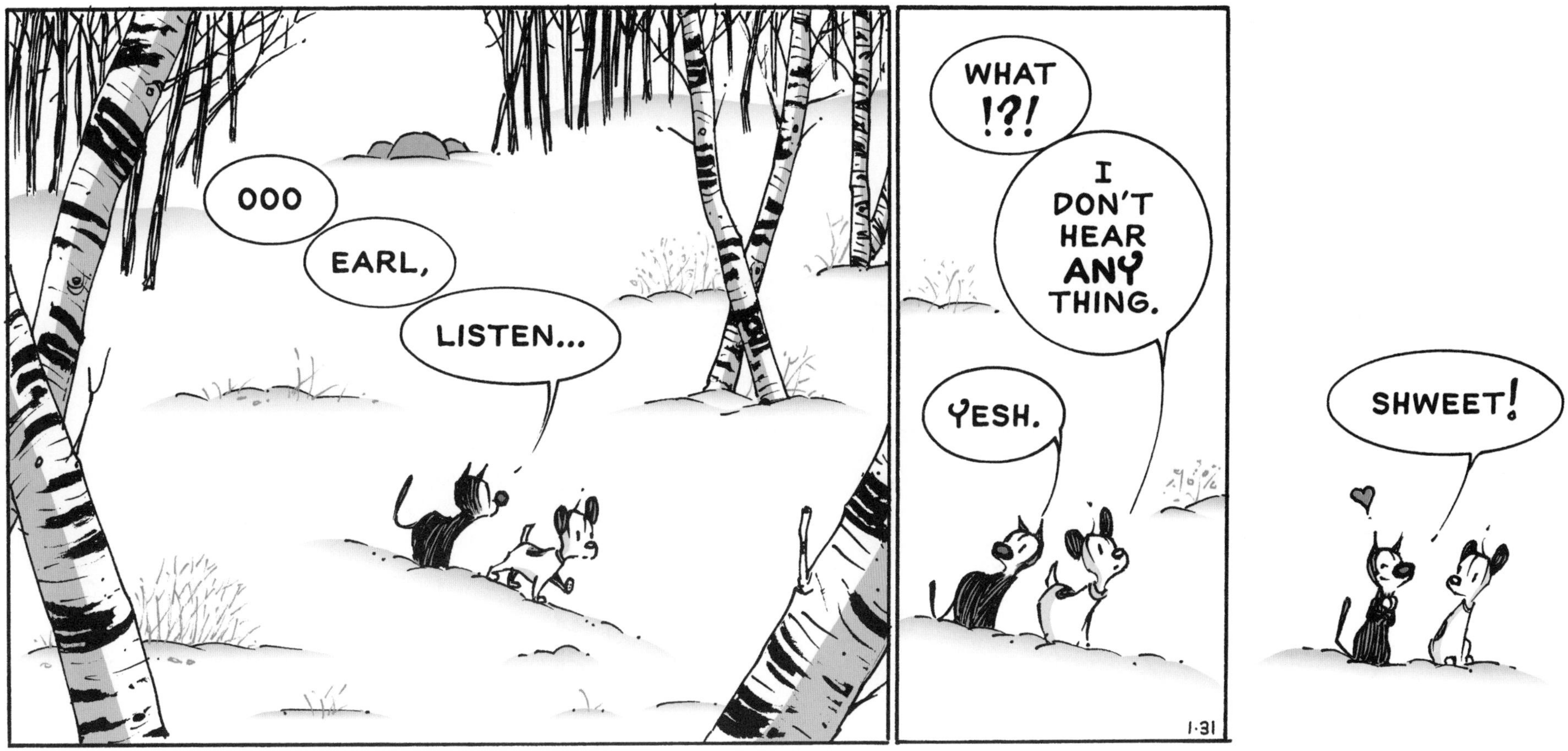
OOO
EARL,
LISTEN...
WHAT !?!
I DON'T HEAR ANY THING.
YESH.
SHWEET!
1·31

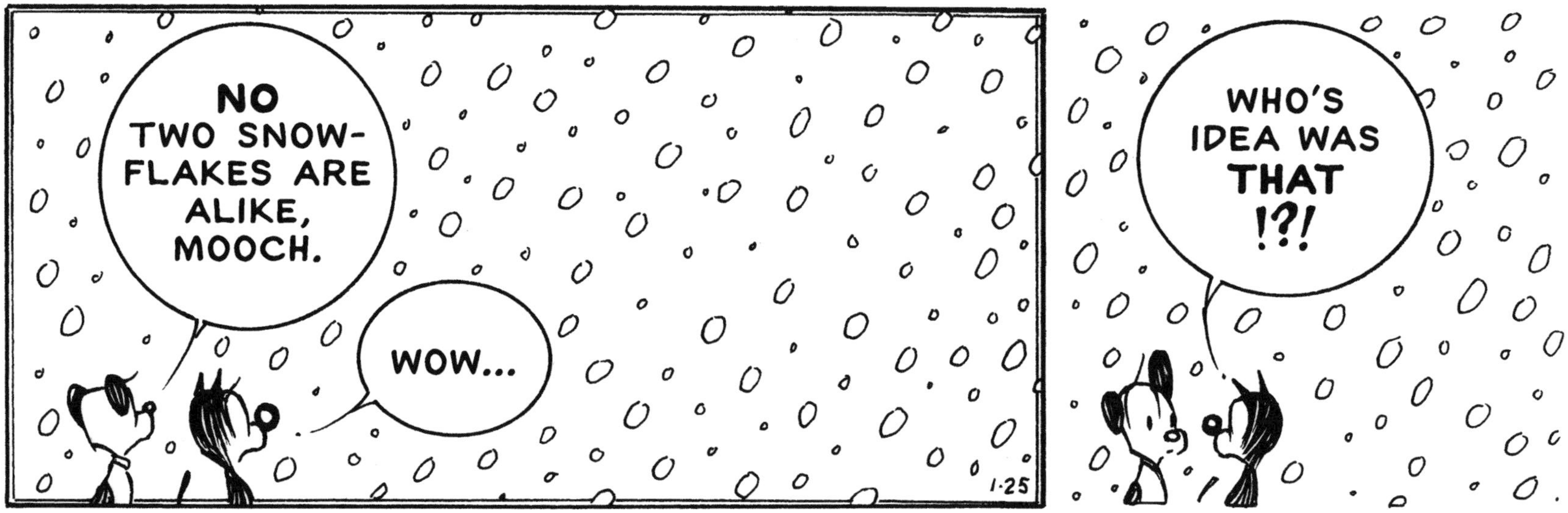

NO TWO SNOW-FLAKES ARE ALIKE, MOOCH.
WOW...
1·25
WHO'S IDEA WAS THAT !?!

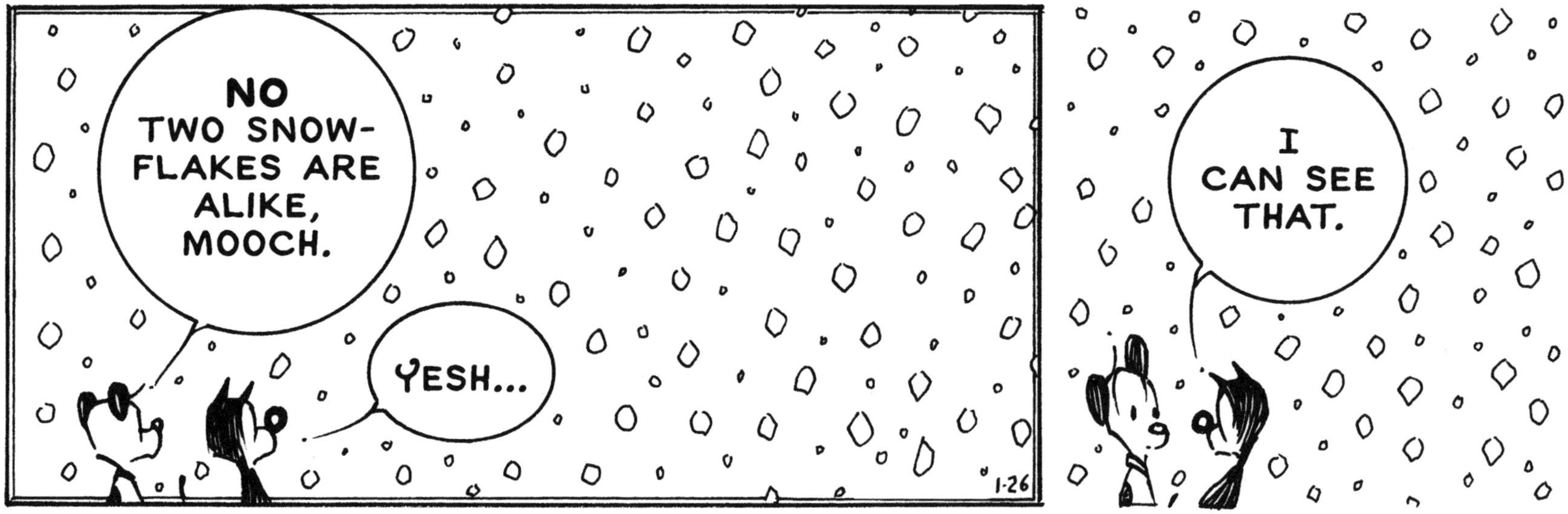

NO TWO SNOW-FLAKES ARE ALIKE, MOOCH.
YESH...
1·26
I CAN SEE THAT.

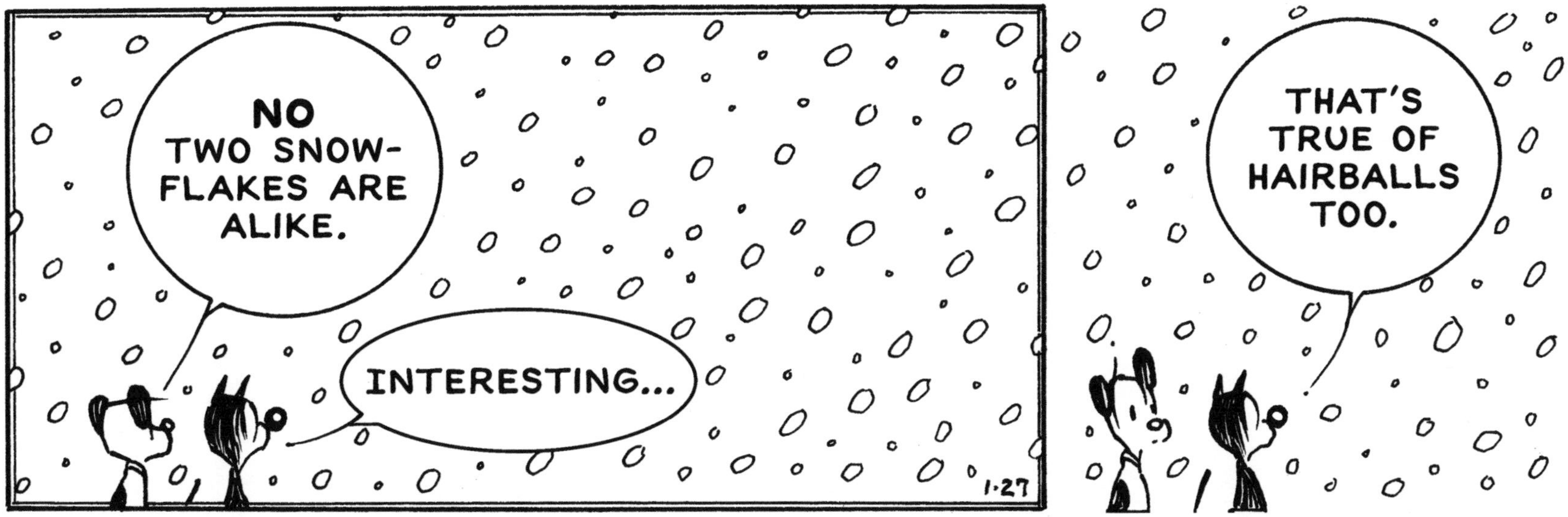
NO TWO SNOW-FLAKES ARE ALIKE.
INTERESTING...
1·27
THAT'S TRUE OF HAIRBALLS TOO.

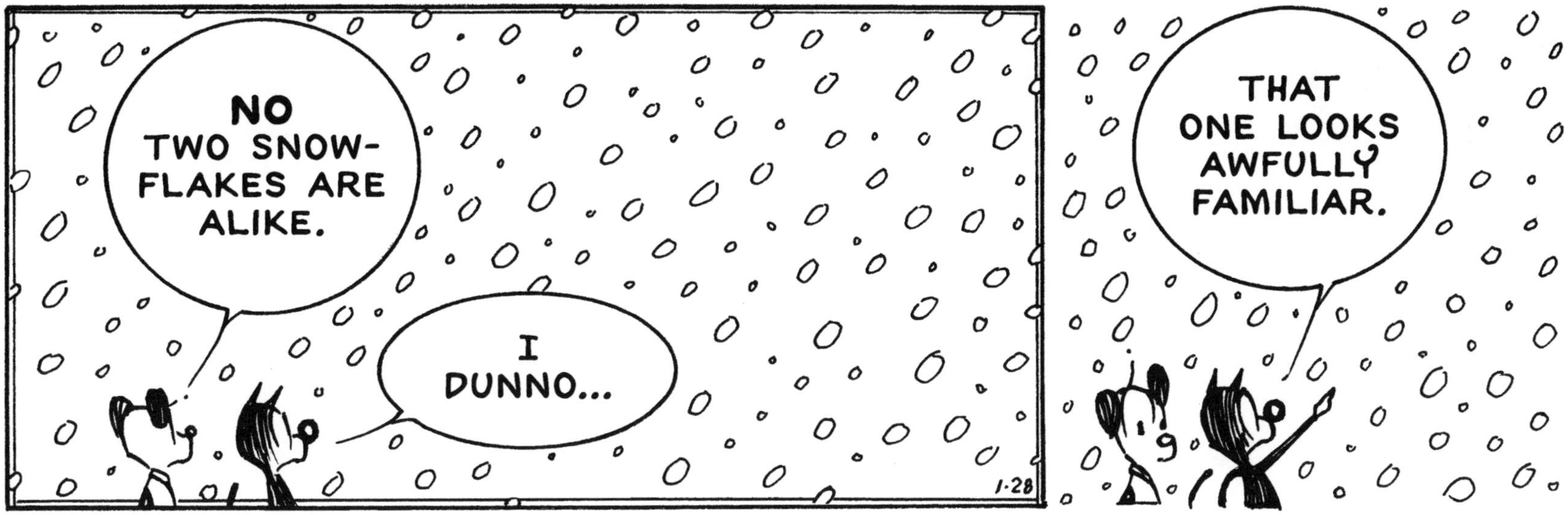
NO TWO SNOW-FLAKES ARE ALIKE.
I DUNNO...
1·28
THAT ONE LOOKS AWFULLY FAMILIAR.

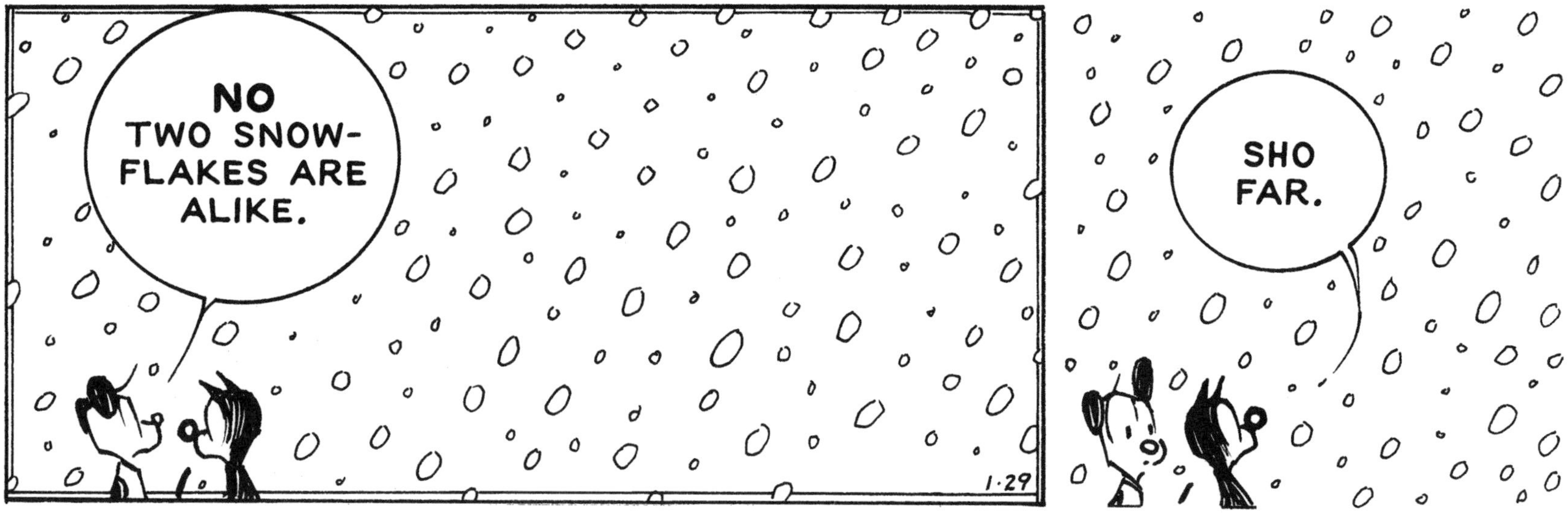
NO TWO SNOW-FLAKES ARE ALIKE.
1·29
SHO FAR.

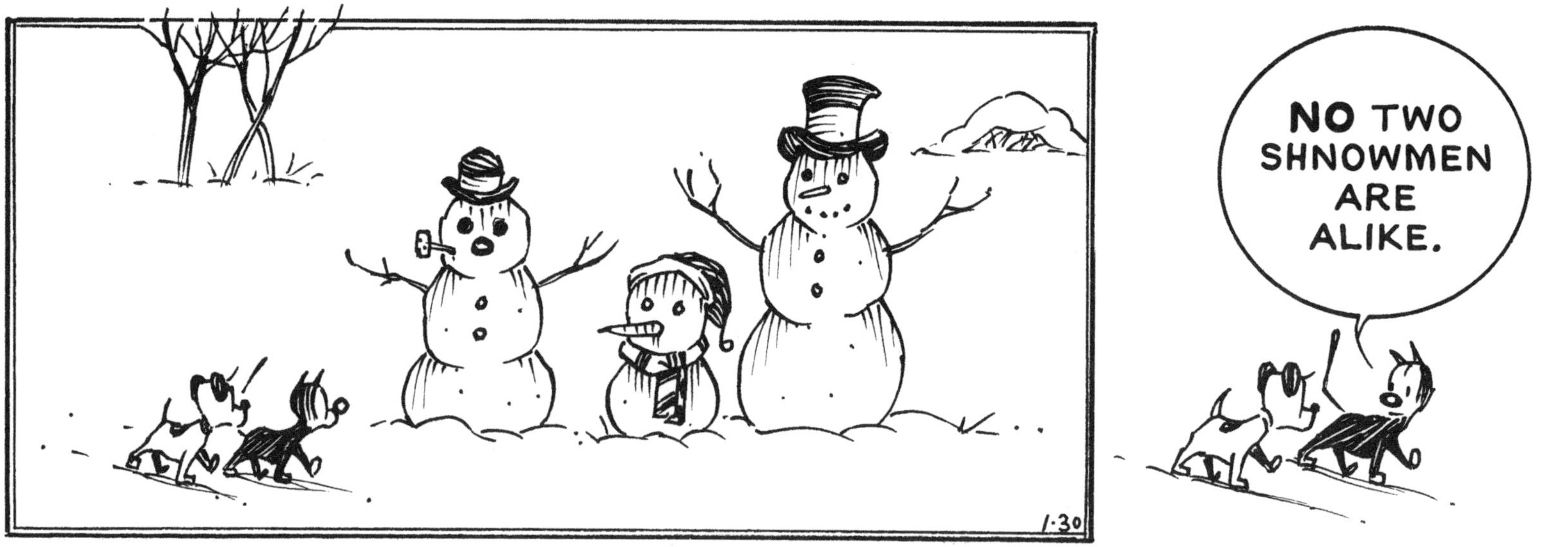
1·30
NO TWO SHNOWMEN ARE ALIKE.

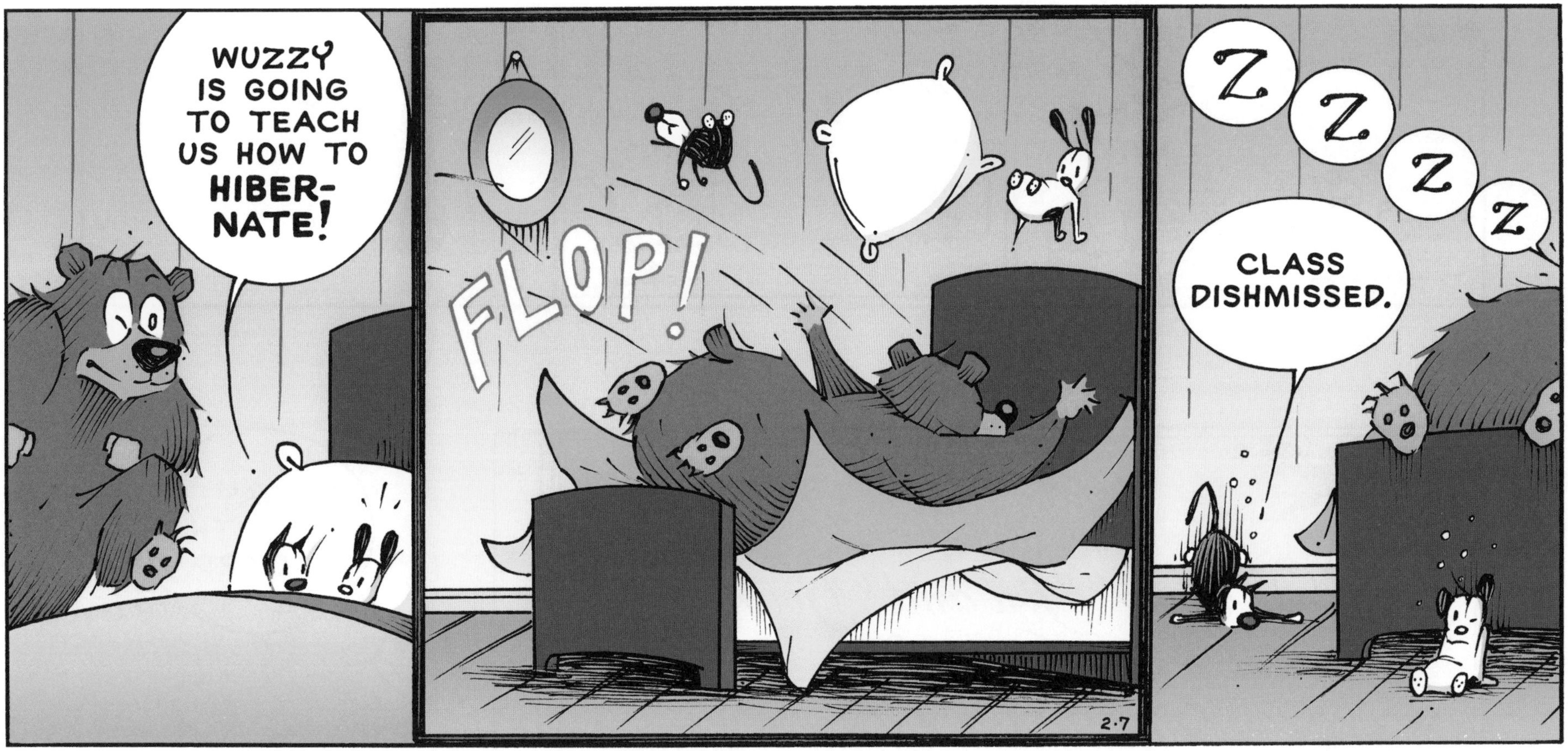
WUZZY IS GOING TO TEACH US HOW TO **HIBER-NATE!**
FLOP!
2·7
Z Z Z Z
CLASS DISHMISSED.

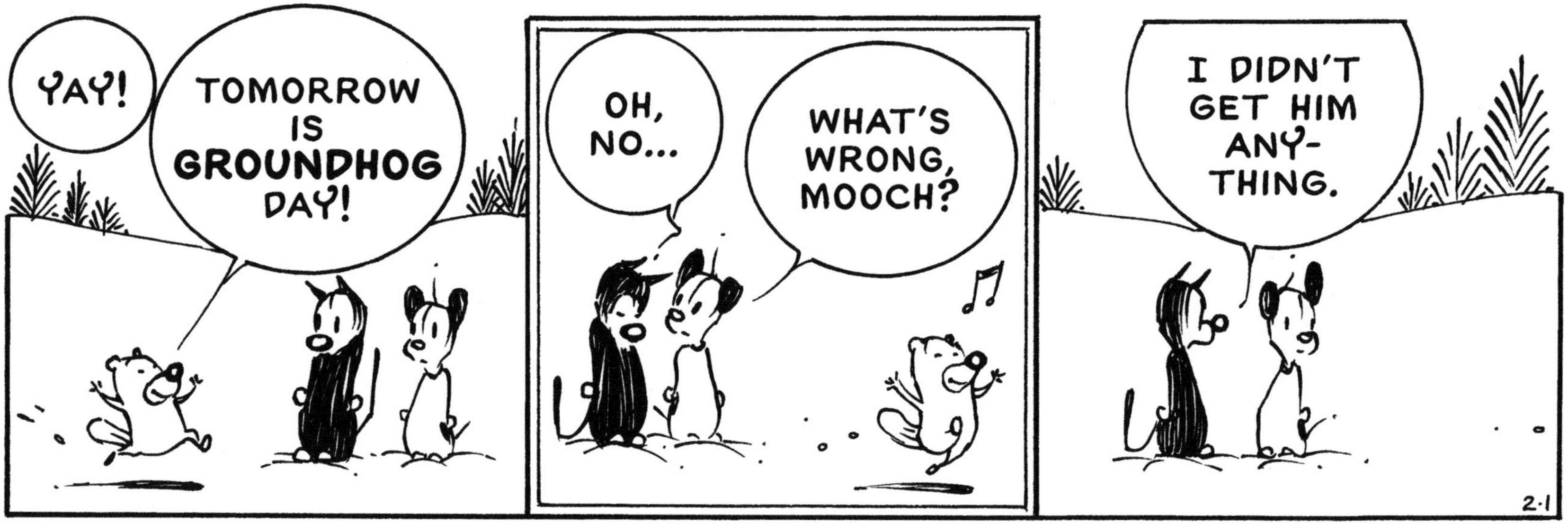
YAY!
TOMORROW IS GROUNDHOG DAY!
OH, NO...
WHAT'S WRONG, MOOCH?
I DIDN'T GET HIM ANY-THING.
2·1

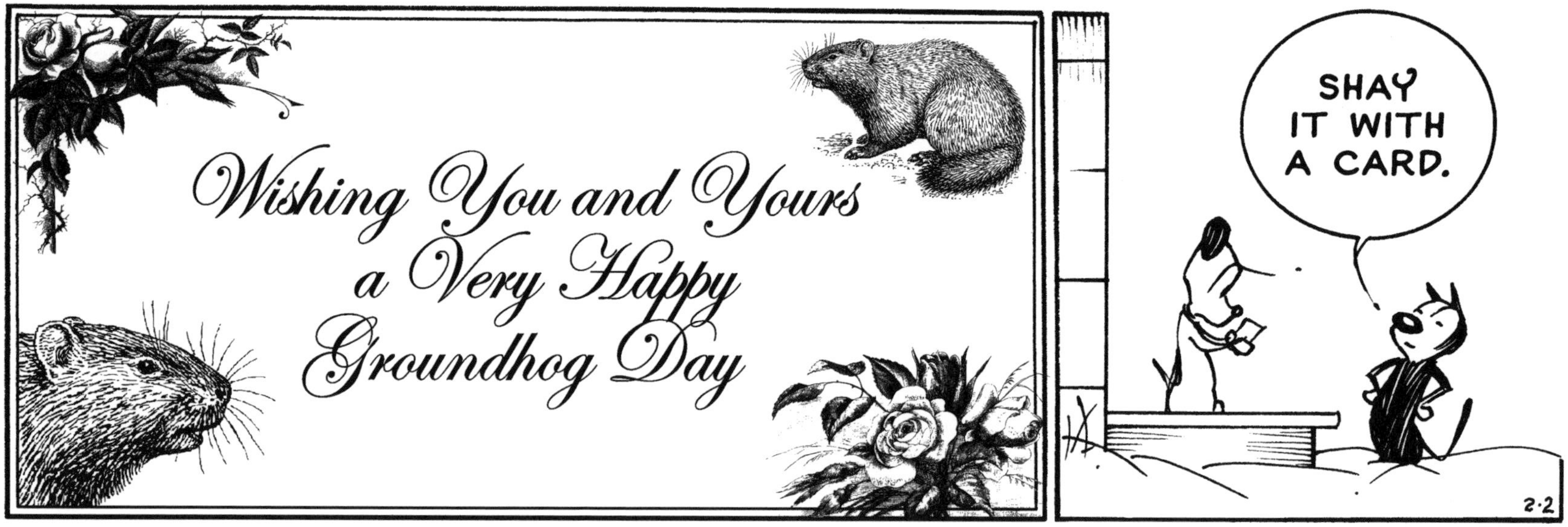
Wishing You and Yours a Very Happy Groundhog Day
SHAY IT WITH A CARD.
2·2

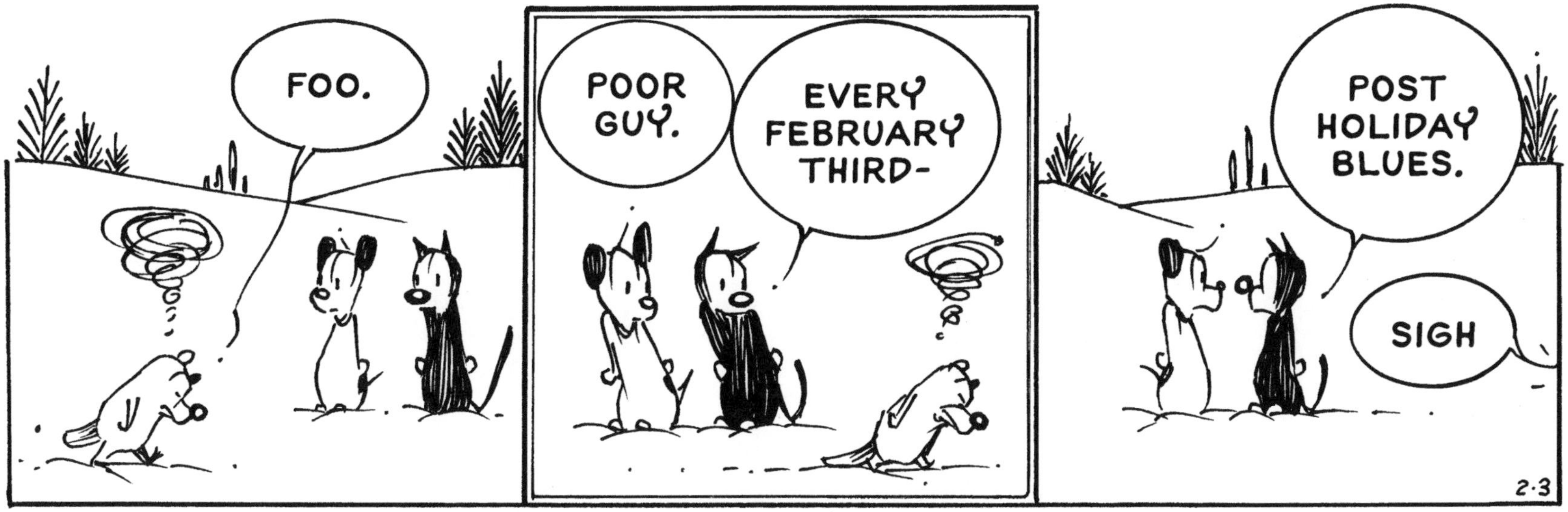
FOO.
POOR GUY.
EVERY FEBRUARY THIRD-
POST HOLIDAY BLUES.
SIGH
2·3

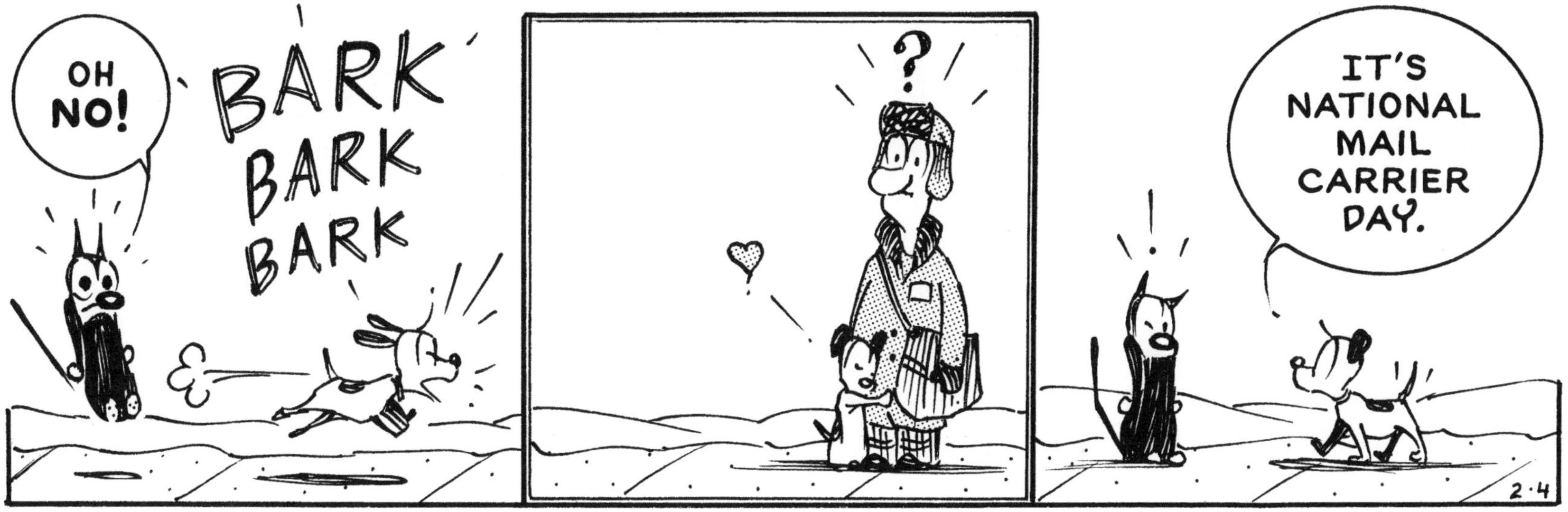
OH NO!
BARK BARK BARK
?
IT'S NATIONAL MAIL CARRIER DAY.
2·4

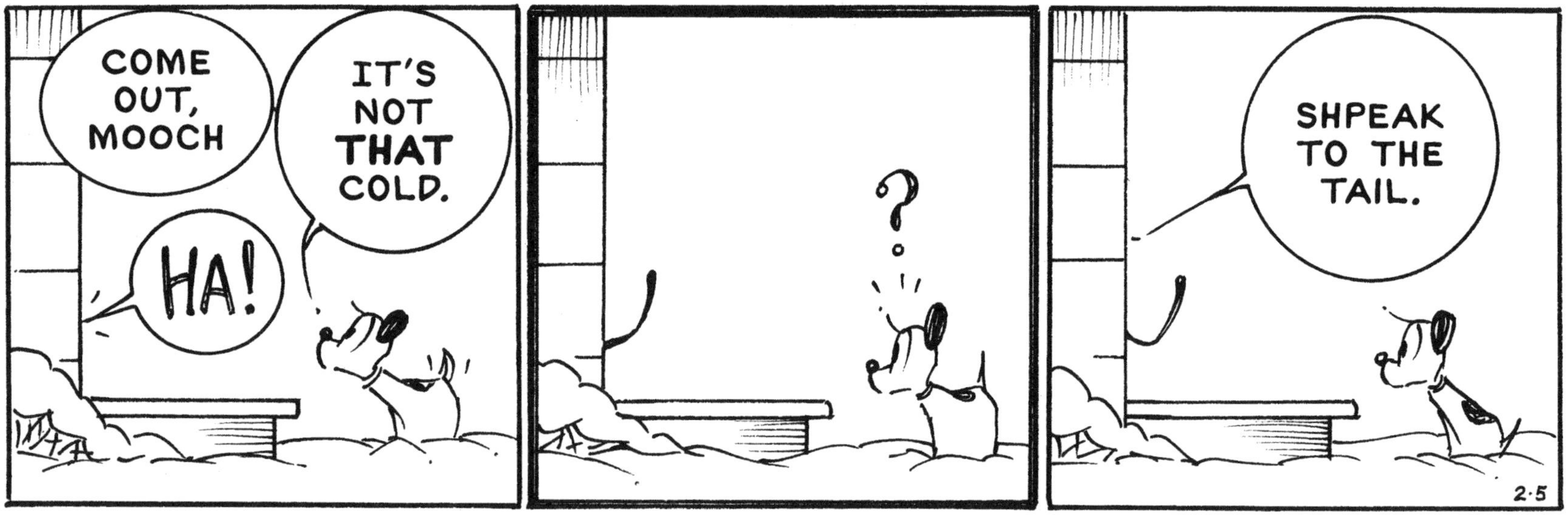
COME OUT, MOOCH
HA!
IT'S NOT THAT COLD.
?
SHPEAK TO THE TAIL.
2·5

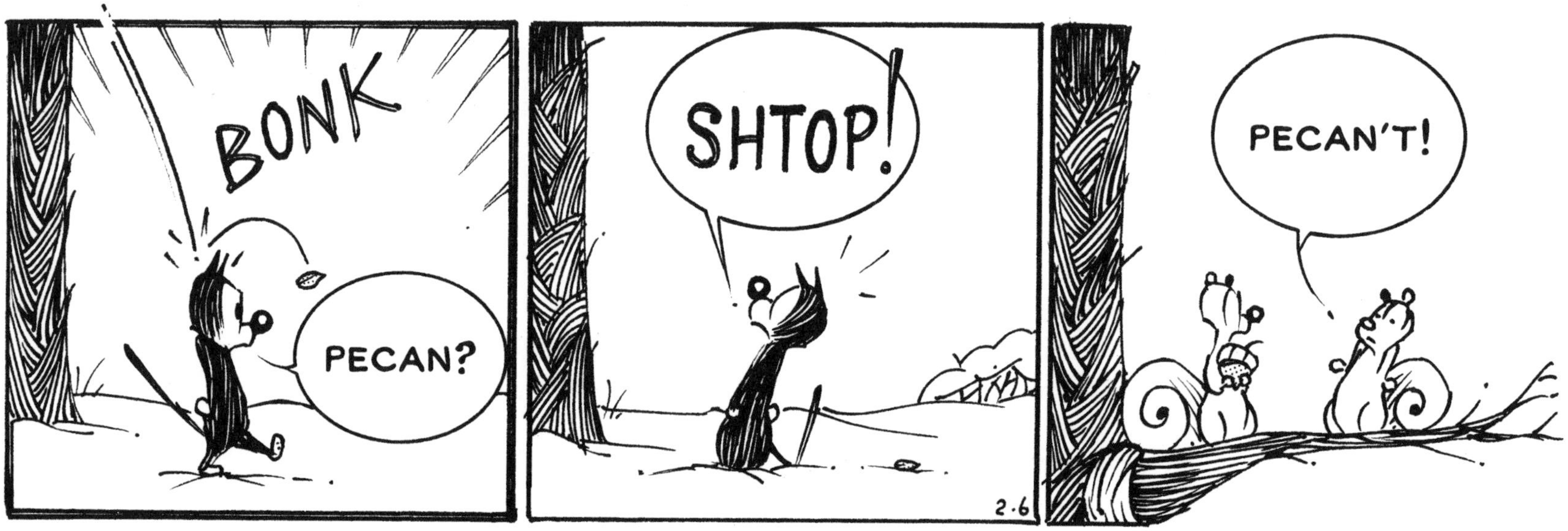
BONK
PECAN?
SHTOP!
2·6
PECAN'T!

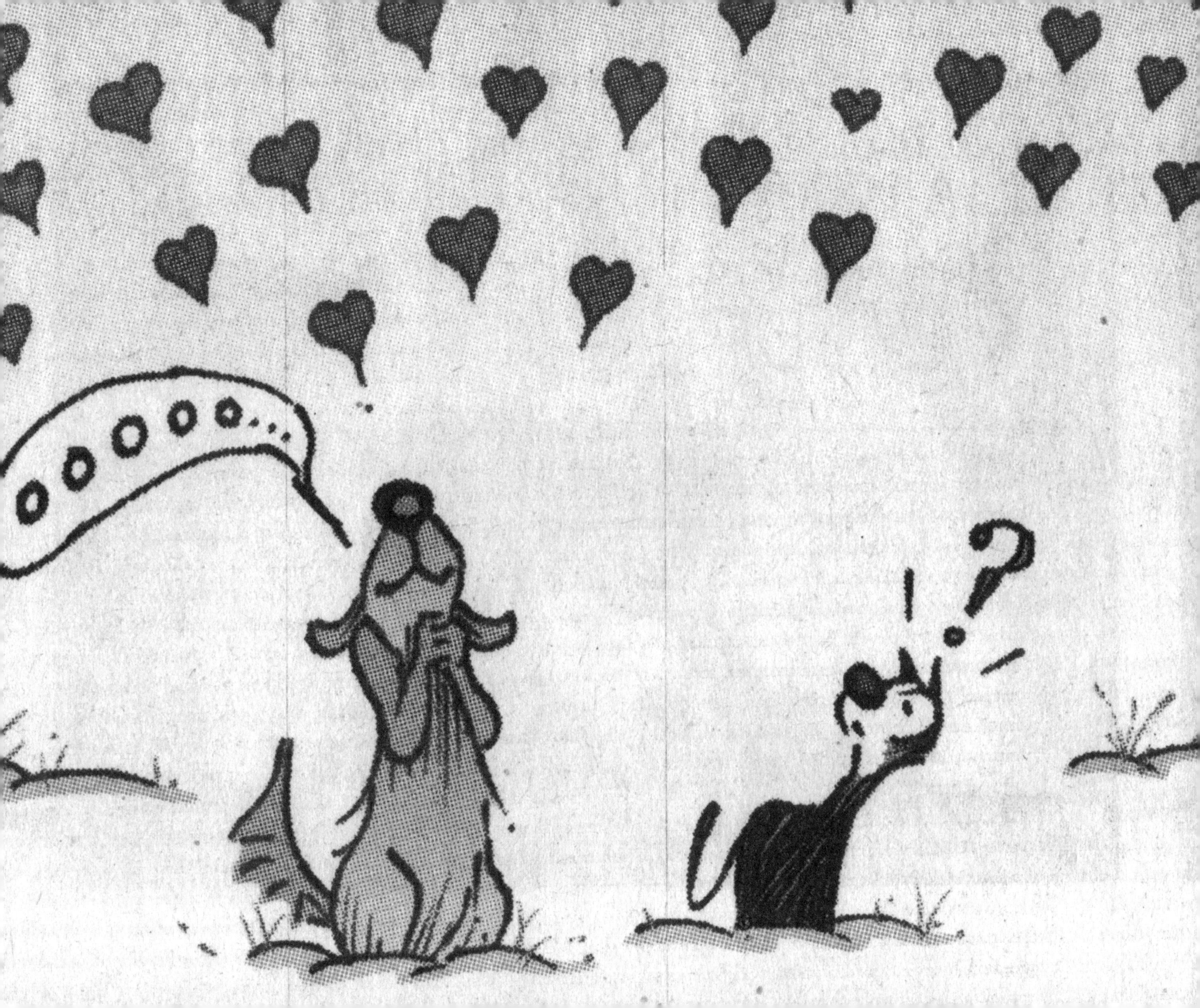
OOOOOO....

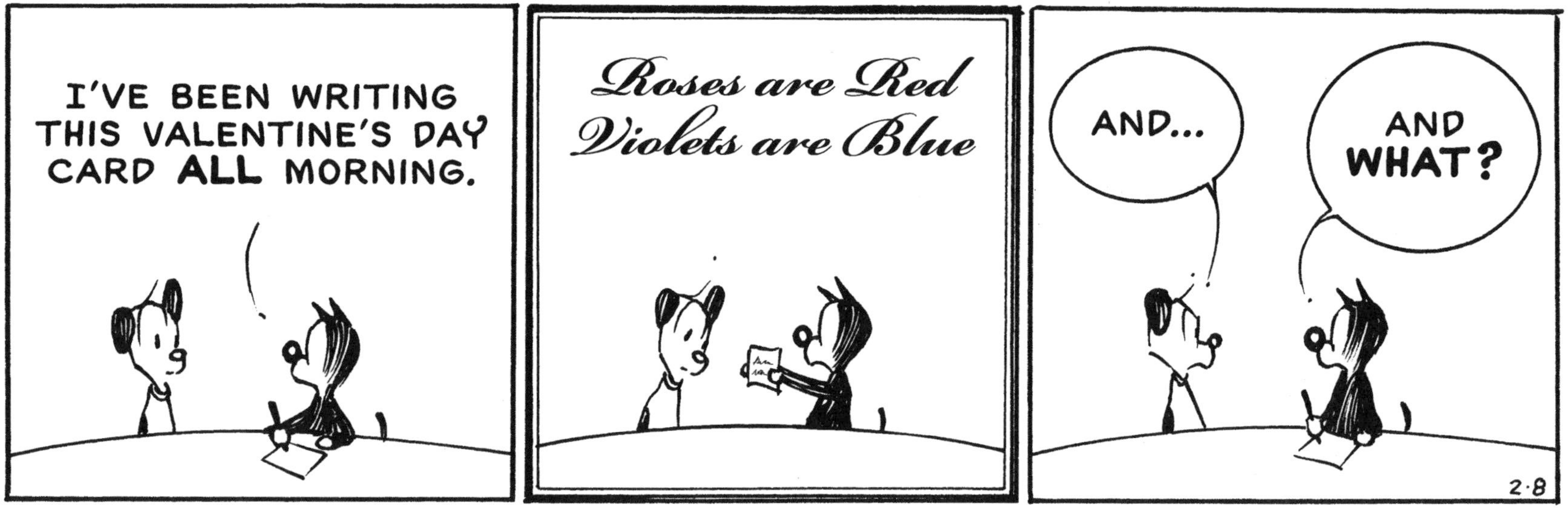
I'VE BEEN WRITING THIS VALENTINE'S DAY CARD ALL MORNING.
Roses are Red
Violets are Blue
AND...
AND WHAT?
2·8

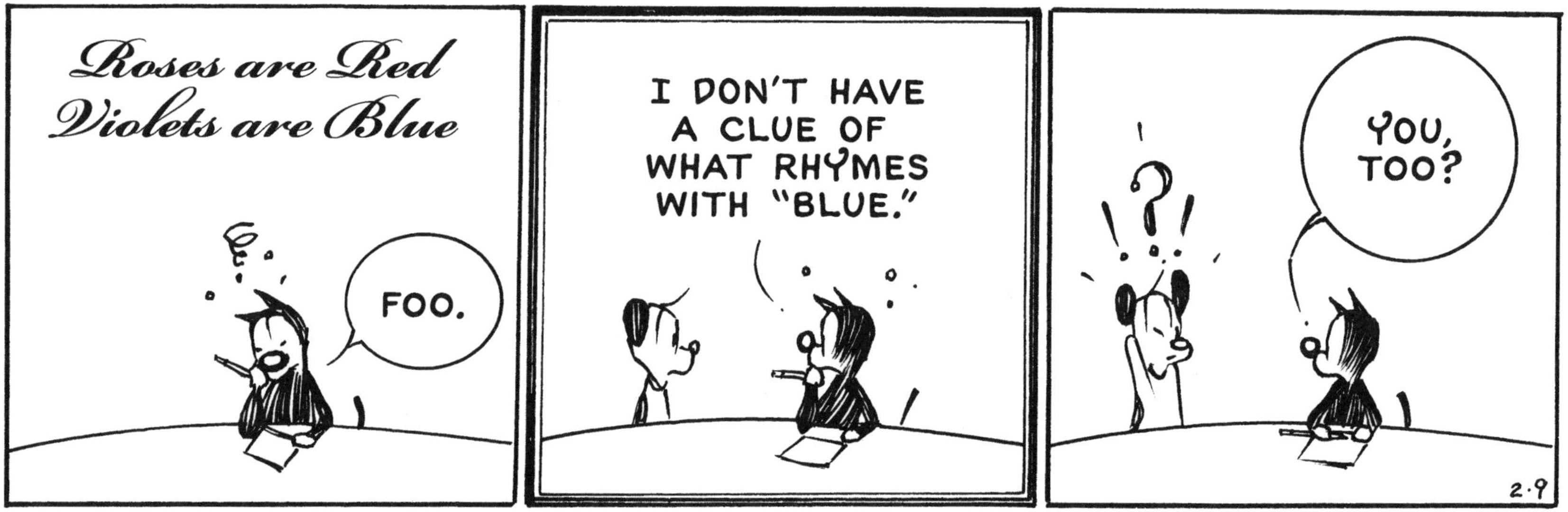
Roses are Red
Violets are Blue
FOO.
I DON'T HAVE A CLUE OF WHAT RHYMES WITH "BLUE."
YOU, TOO?
2·9

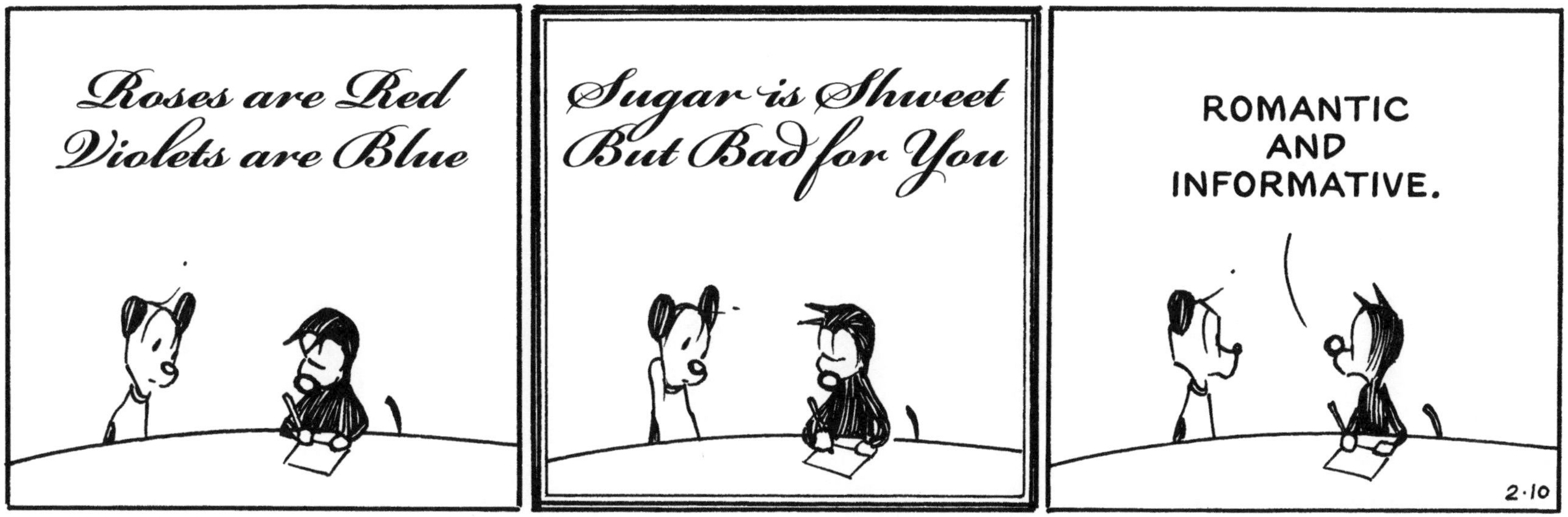
Roses are Red
Violets are Blue
Sugar is Shweet
But Bad for You
ROMANTIC AND INFORMATIVE.
2·10

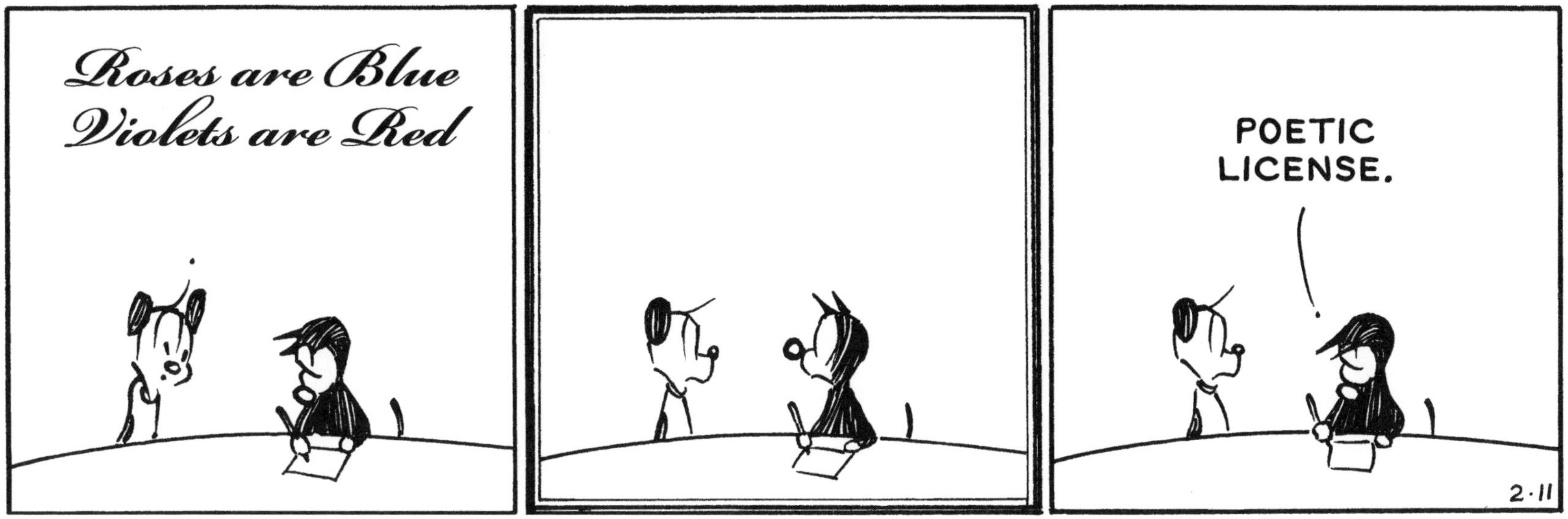
Roses are Blue
Violets are Red
POETIC LICENSE.
2·11

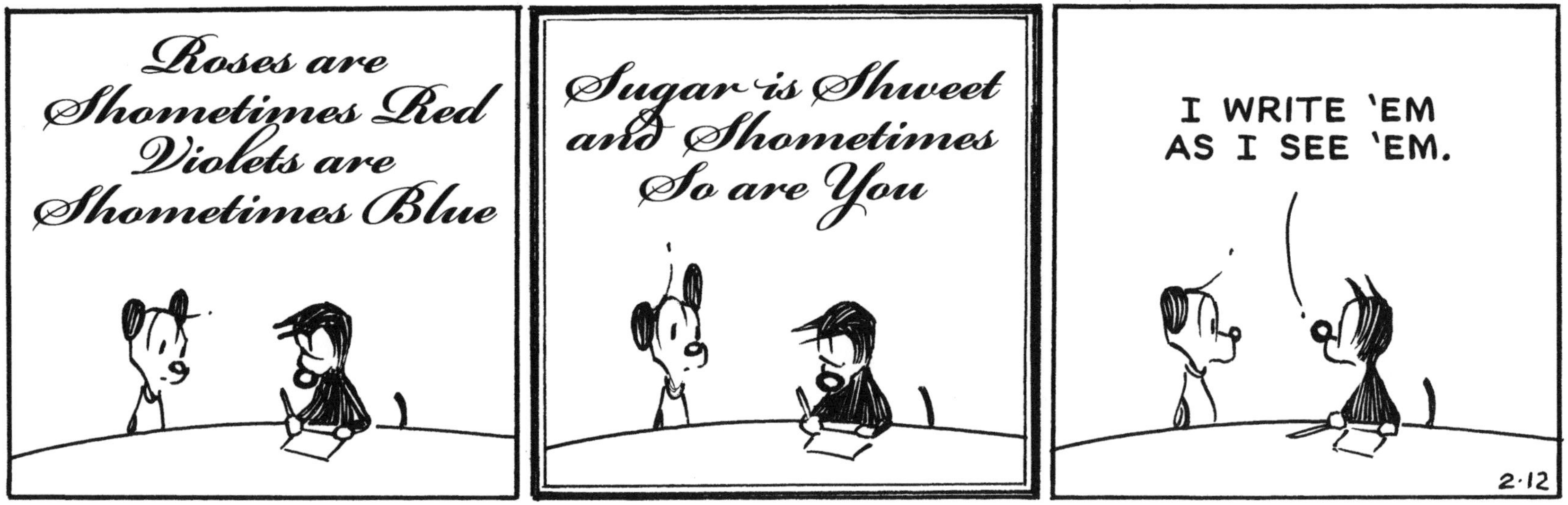
Roses are Shometimes Red Violets are Shometimes Blue
Sugar is Shweet and Shometimes So are You
I WRITE 'EM AS I SEE 'EM.
2·12

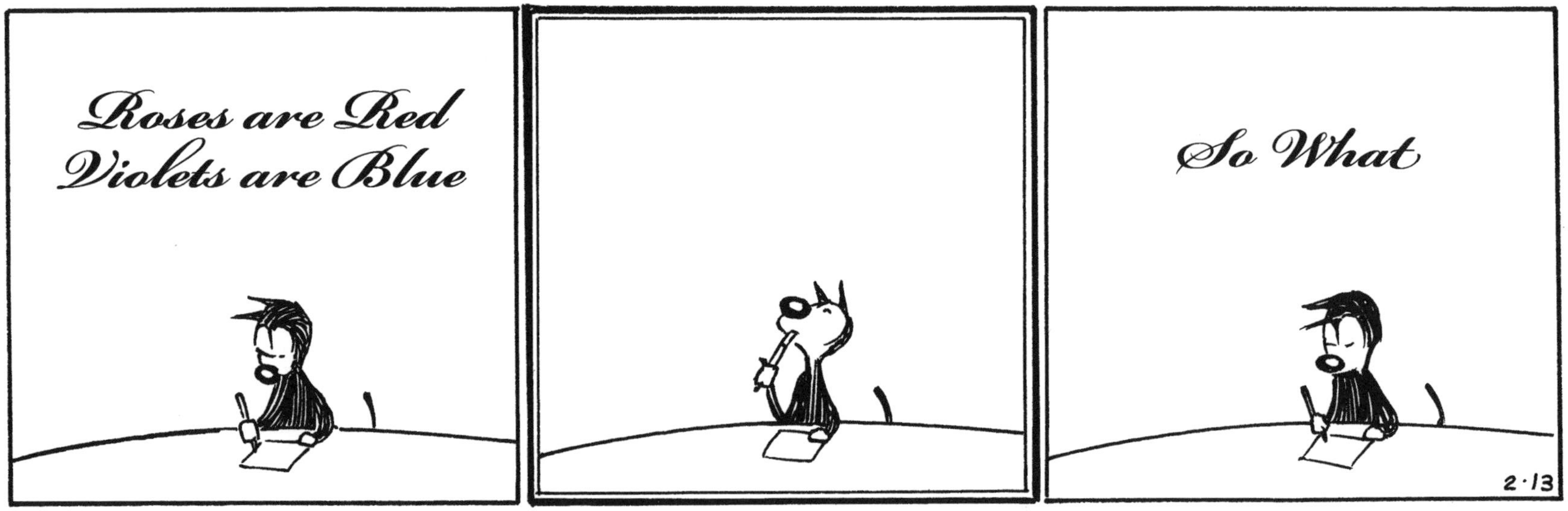
Roses are Red Violets are Blue
So What
2·13

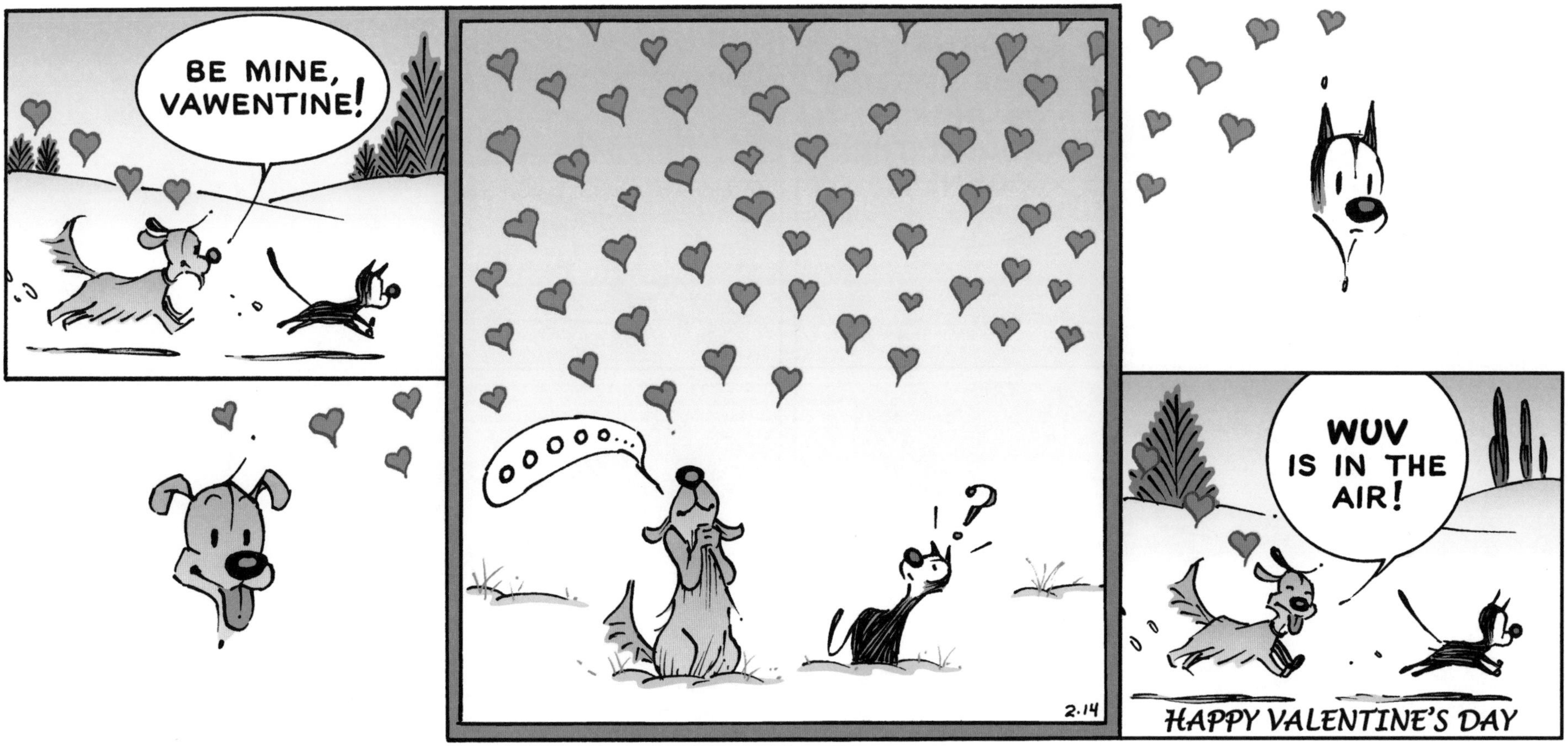
BE MINE, VAWENTINE!
OOOOO...
2.14
WUV IS IN THE AIR!
HAPPY VALENTINE'S DAY

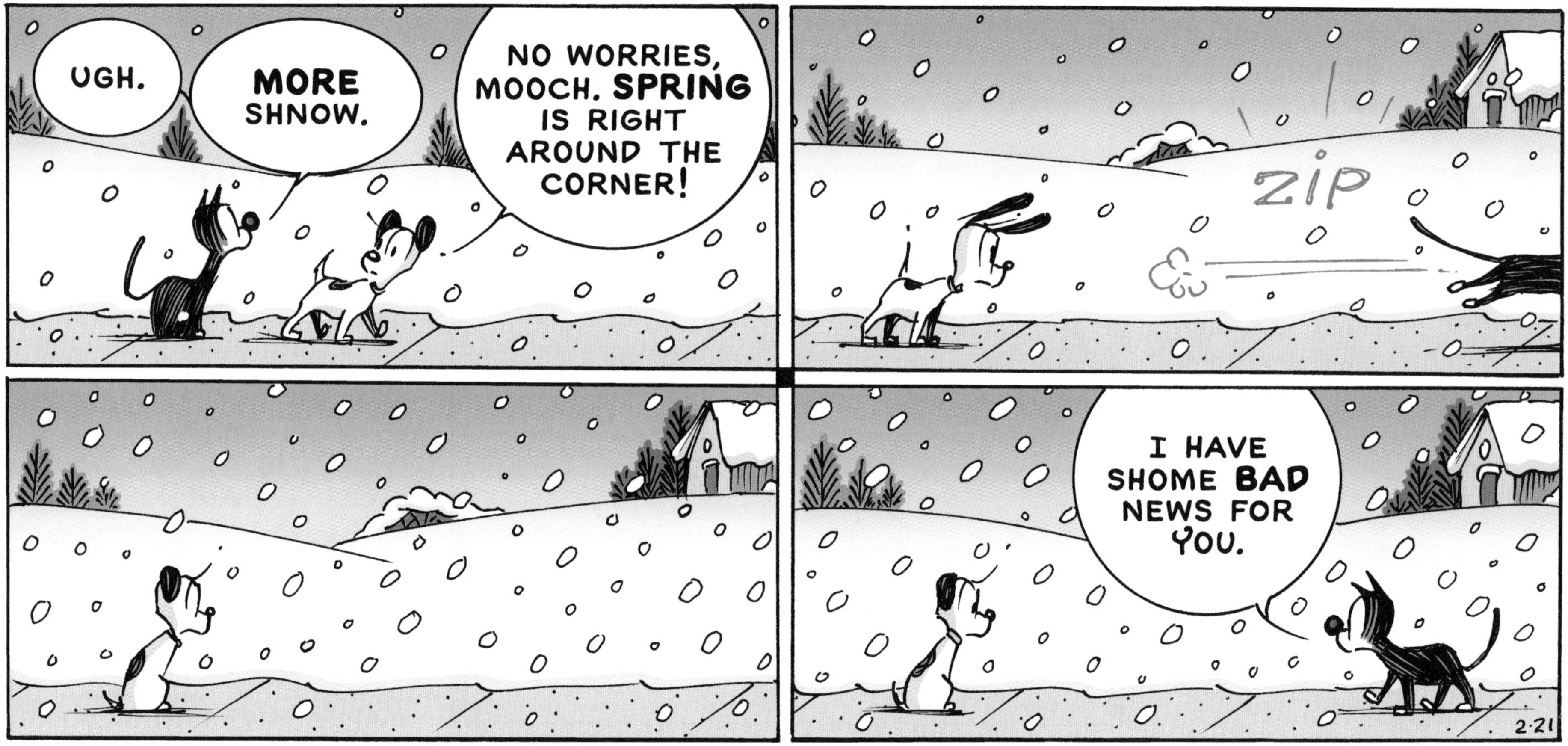
UGH.
MORE SHNOW.
NO WORRIES, MOOCH. SPRING IS RIGHT AROUND THE CORNER!
ZIP
I HAVE SHOME BAD NEWS FOR YOU.
2·21

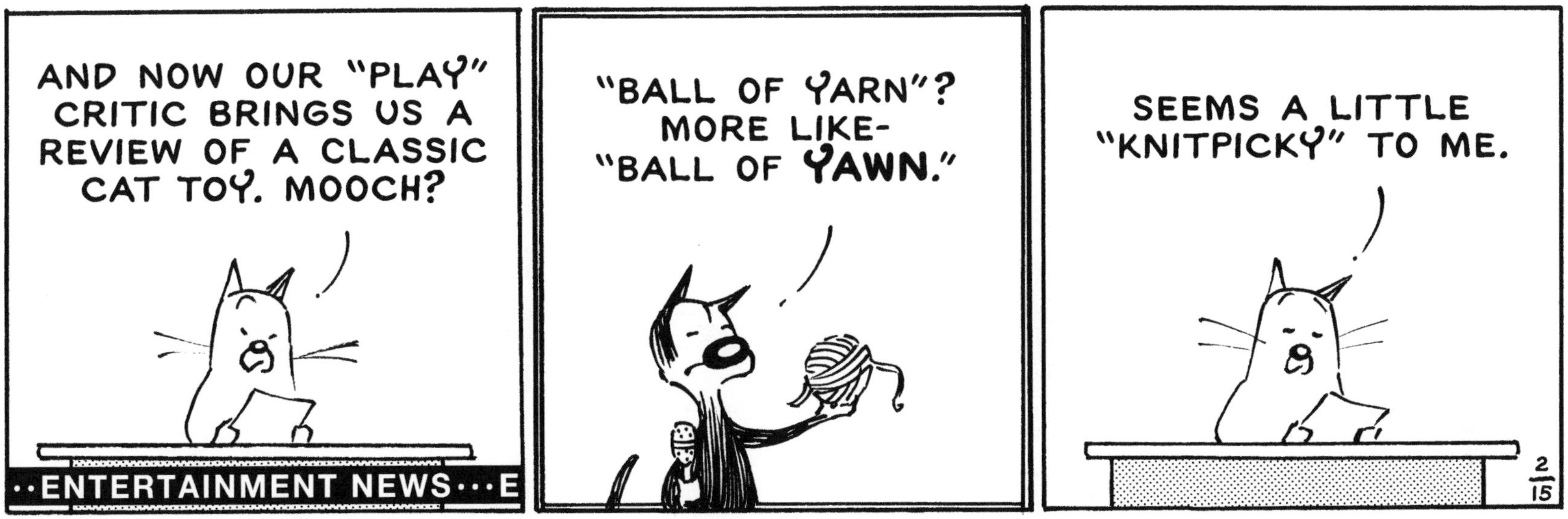
AND NOW OUR "PLAY" CRITIC BRINGS US A REVIEW OF A CLASSIC CAT TOY. MOOCH?
ENTERTAINMENT NEWS
"BALL OF YARN"? MORE LIKE- "BALL OF YAWN."
SEEMS A LITTLE "KNITPICKY" TO ME.
2/15

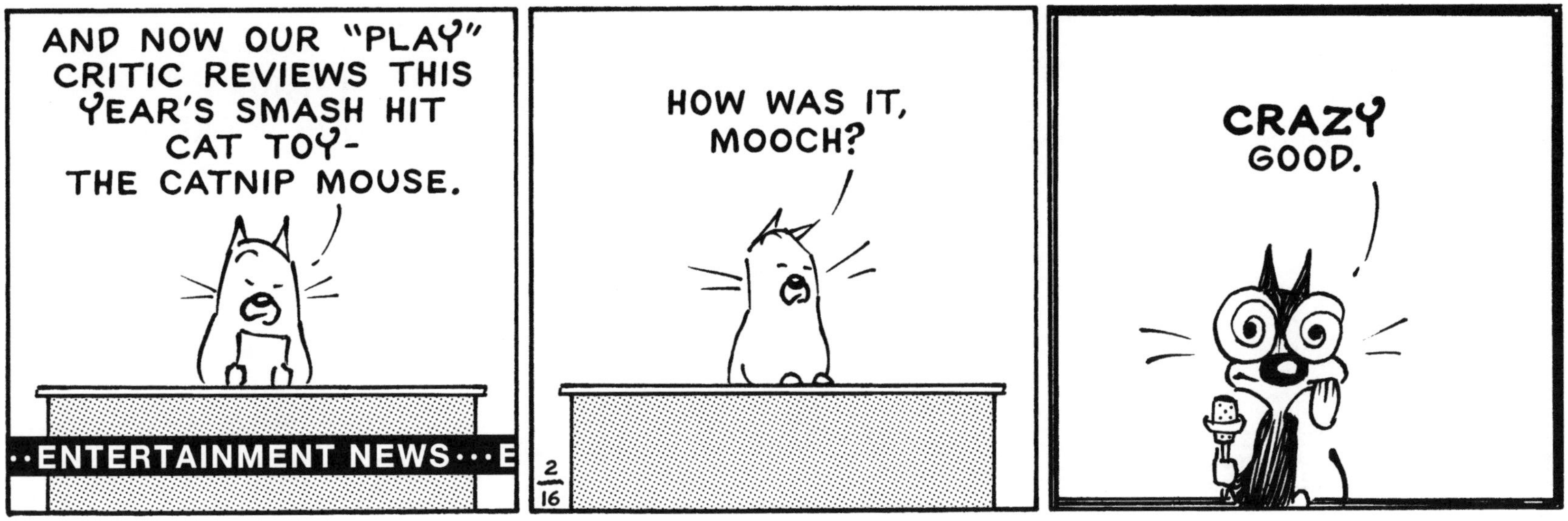
AND NOW OUR "PLAY" CRITIC REVIEWS THIS YEAR'S SMASH HIT CAT TOY- THE CATNIP MOUSE.
ENTERTAINMENT NEWS
HOW WAS IT, MOOCH?
2/16
CRAZY GOOD.

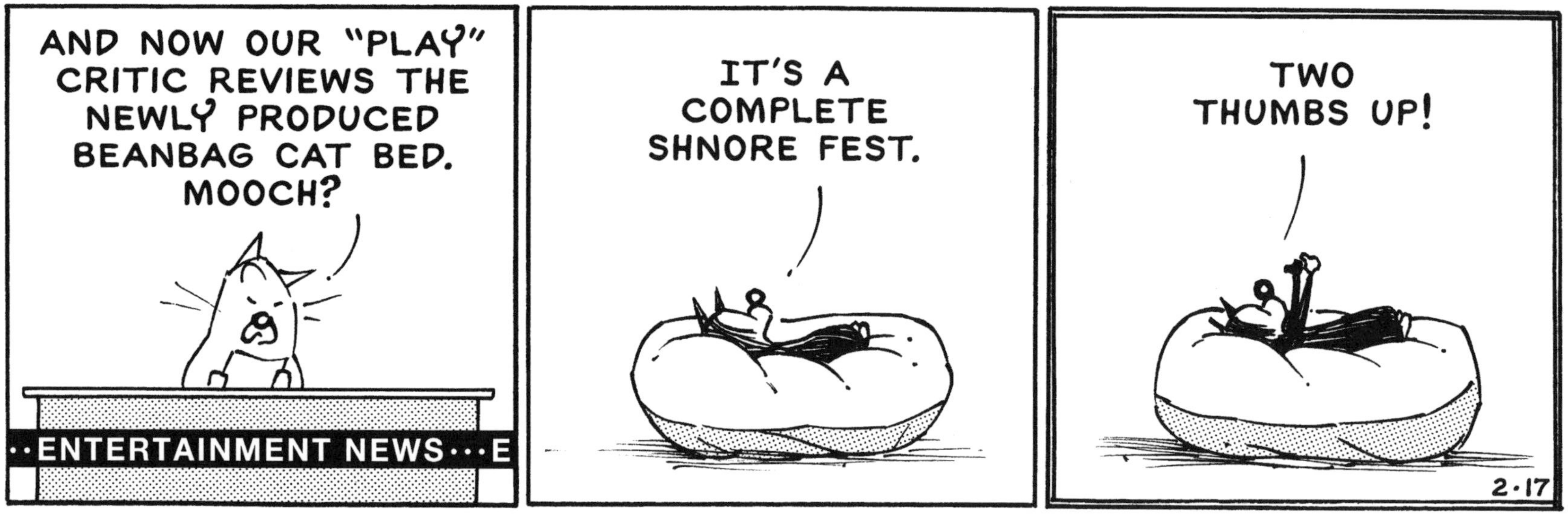
AND NOW OUR "PLAY" CRITIC REVIEWS THE NEWLY PRODUCED BEANBAG CAT BED. MOOCH?
ENTERTAINMENT NEWS
IT'S A COMPLETE SHNORE FEST.
TWO THUMBS UP!
2·17

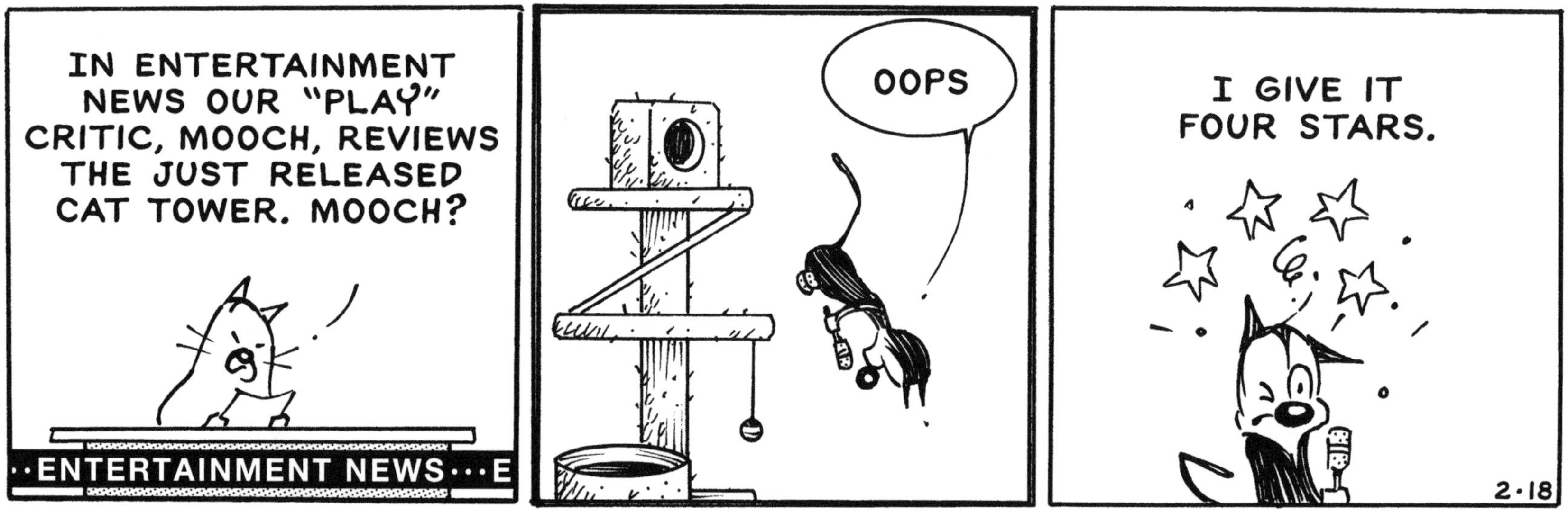
IN ENTERTAINMENT NEWS OUR "PLAY" CRITIC, MOOCH, REVIEWS THE JUST RELEASED CAT TOWER. MOOCH?
ENTERTAINMENT NEWS
OOPS
I GIVE IT FOUR STARS.
2·18

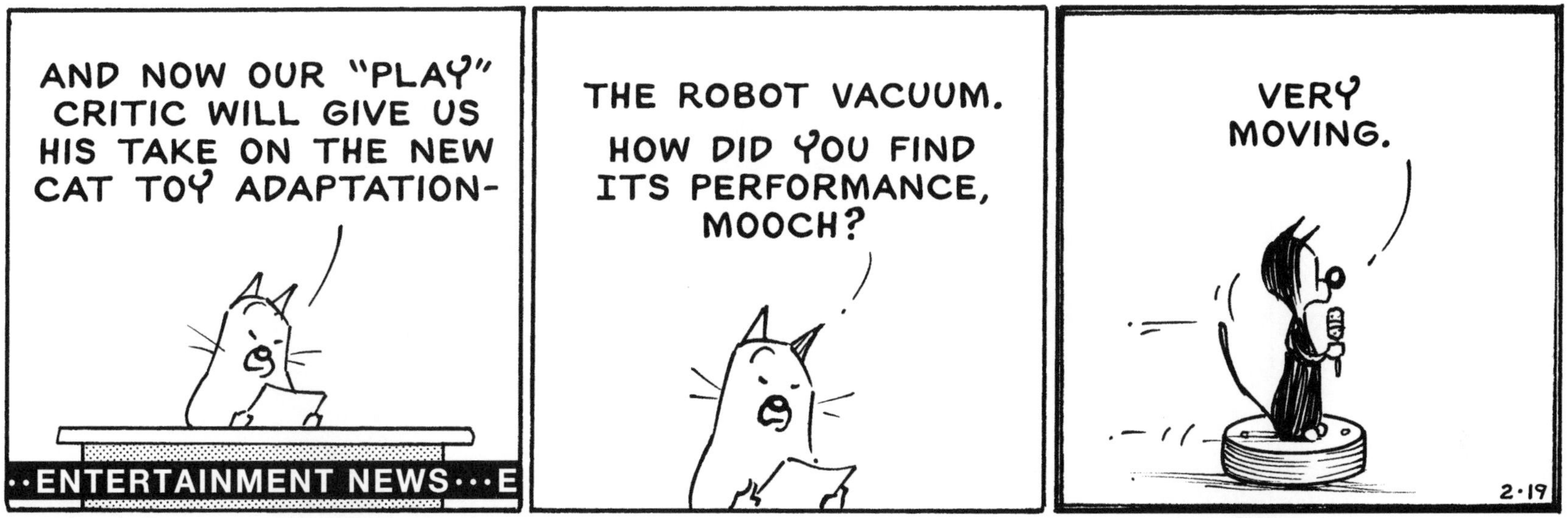
AND NOW OUR "PLAY" CRITIC WILL GIVE US HIS TAKE ON THE NEW CAT TOY ADAPTATION-
••ENTERTAINMENT NEWS•••E
THE ROBOT VACUUM.
HOW DID YOU FIND ITS PERFORMANCE, MOOCH?
VERY MOVING.
2•19

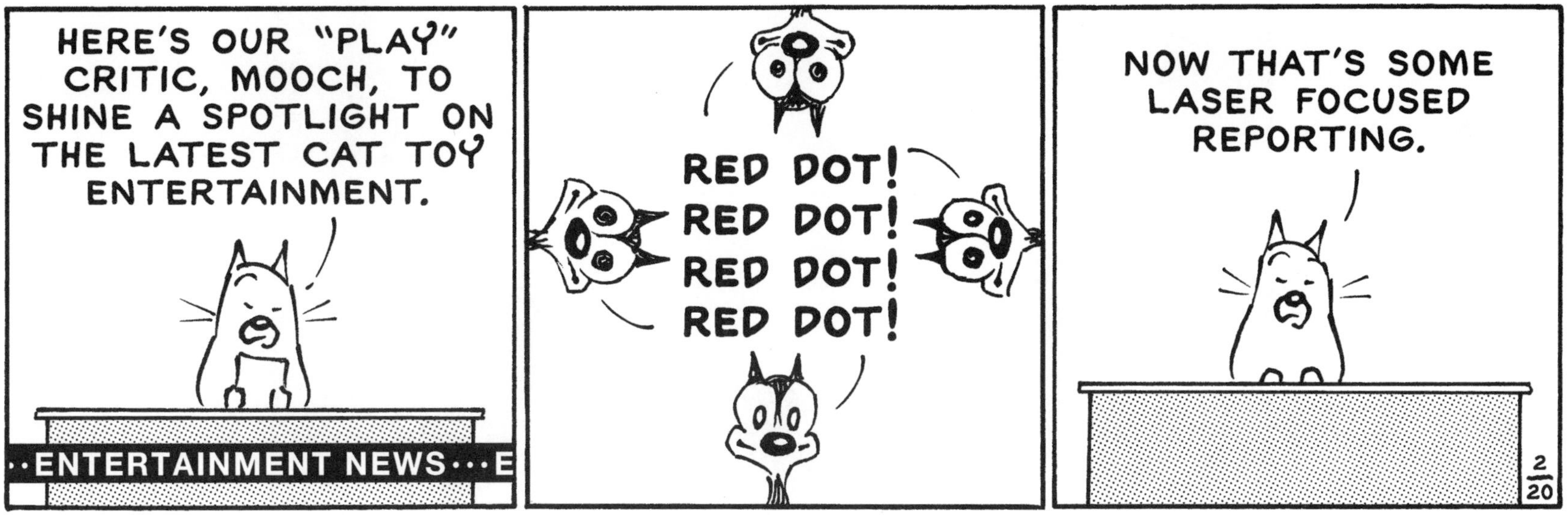
HERE'S OUR "PLAY" CRITIC, MOOCH, TO SHINE A SPOTLIGHT ON THE LATEST CAT TOY ENTERTAINMENT.
••ENTERTAINMENT NEWS•••E
RED DOT!
RED DOT!
RED DOT!
RED DOT!
NOW THAT'S SOME LASER FOCUSED REPORTING.
2/20

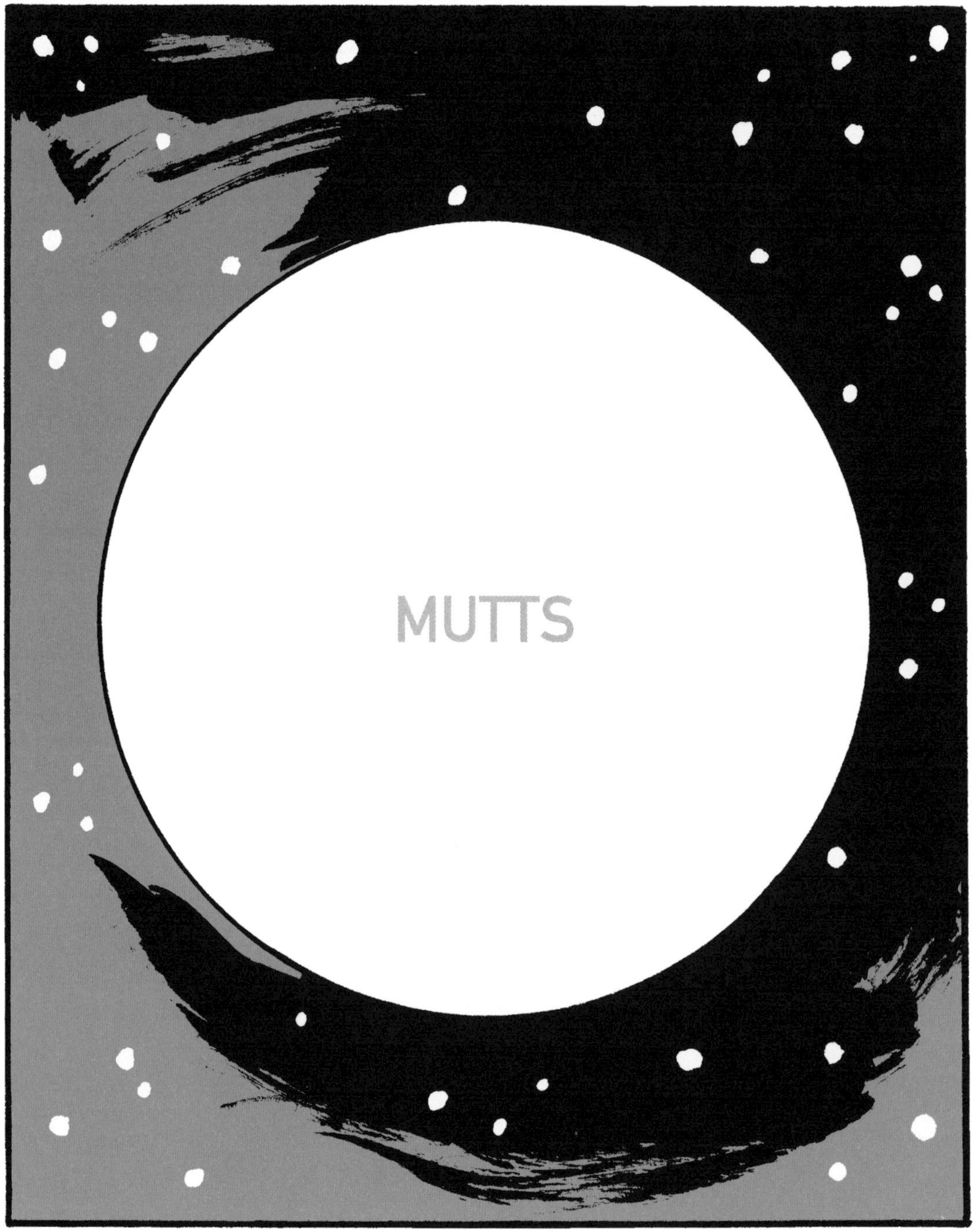
MUTTS

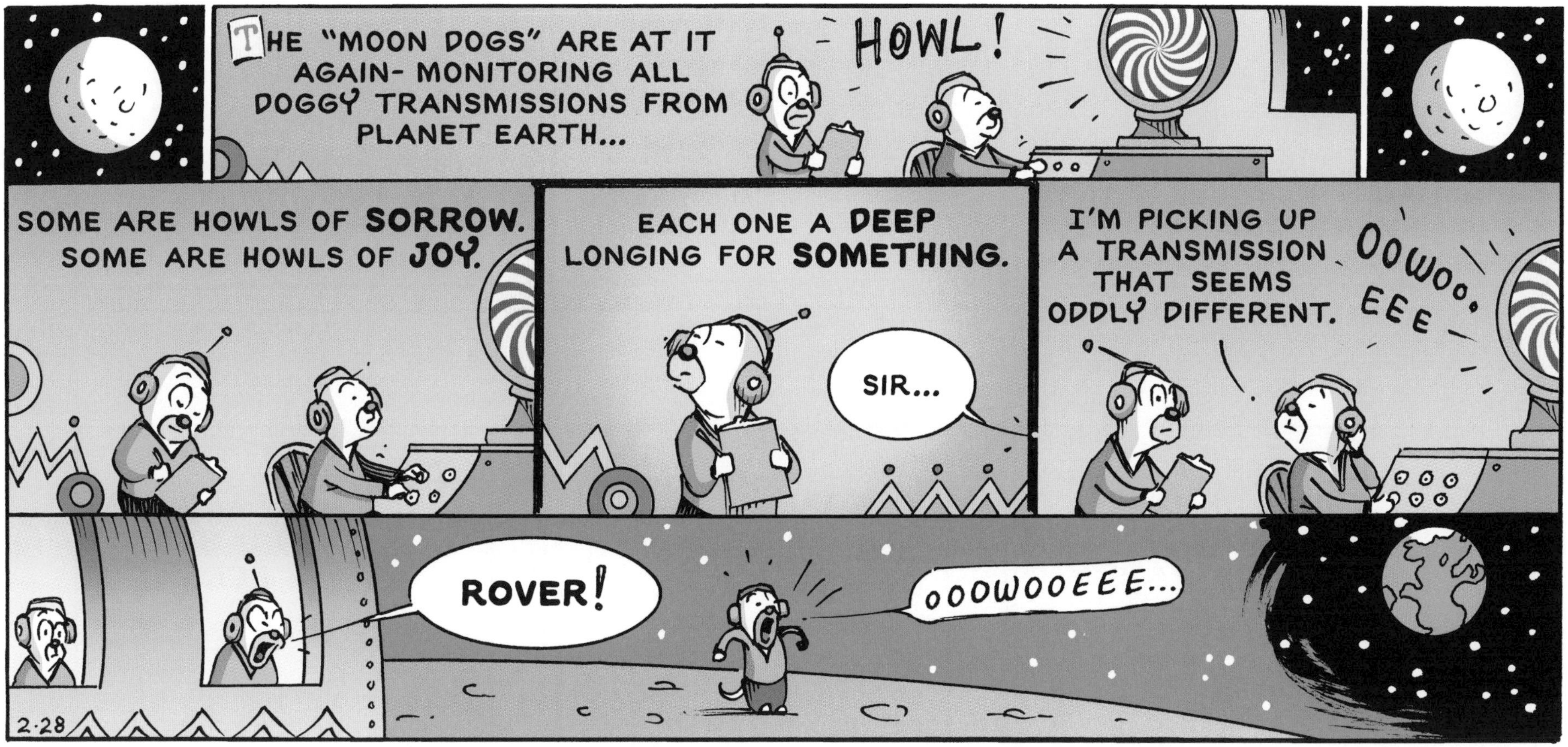
THE "MOON DOGS" ARE AT IT AGAIN- MONITORING ALL DOGGY TRANSMISSIONS FROM PLANET EARTH...
HOWL!
SOME ARE HOWLS OF SORROW. SOME ARE HOWLS OF JOY.
EACH ONE A DEEP LONGING FOR SOMETHING.
SIR...
I'M PICKING UP A TRANSMISSION THAT SEEMS ODDLY DIFFERENT.
OOWOOO EEE
ROVER!
OOOWOOEEE...
2·28

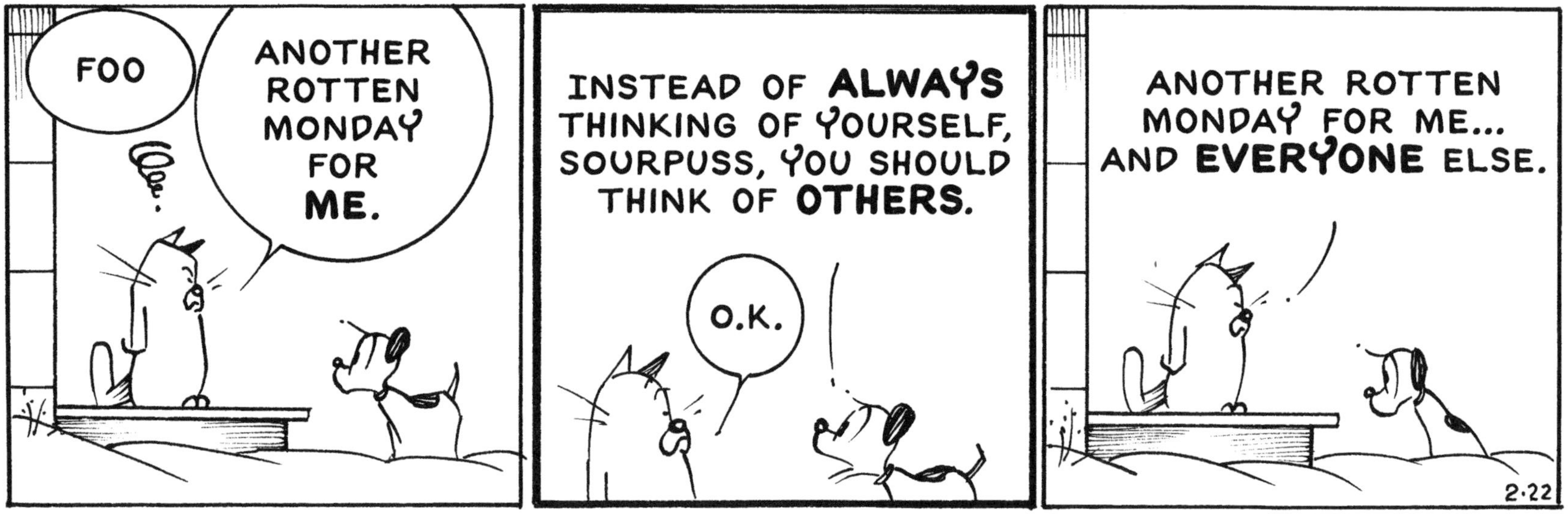
FOO
ANOTHER ROTTEN MONDAY FOR ME.
INSTEAD OF ALWAYS THINKING OF YOURSELF, SOURPUSS, YOU SHOULD THINK OF OTHERS.
O.K.
ANOTHER ROTTEN MONDAY FOR ME... AND EVERYONE ELSE.
2·22

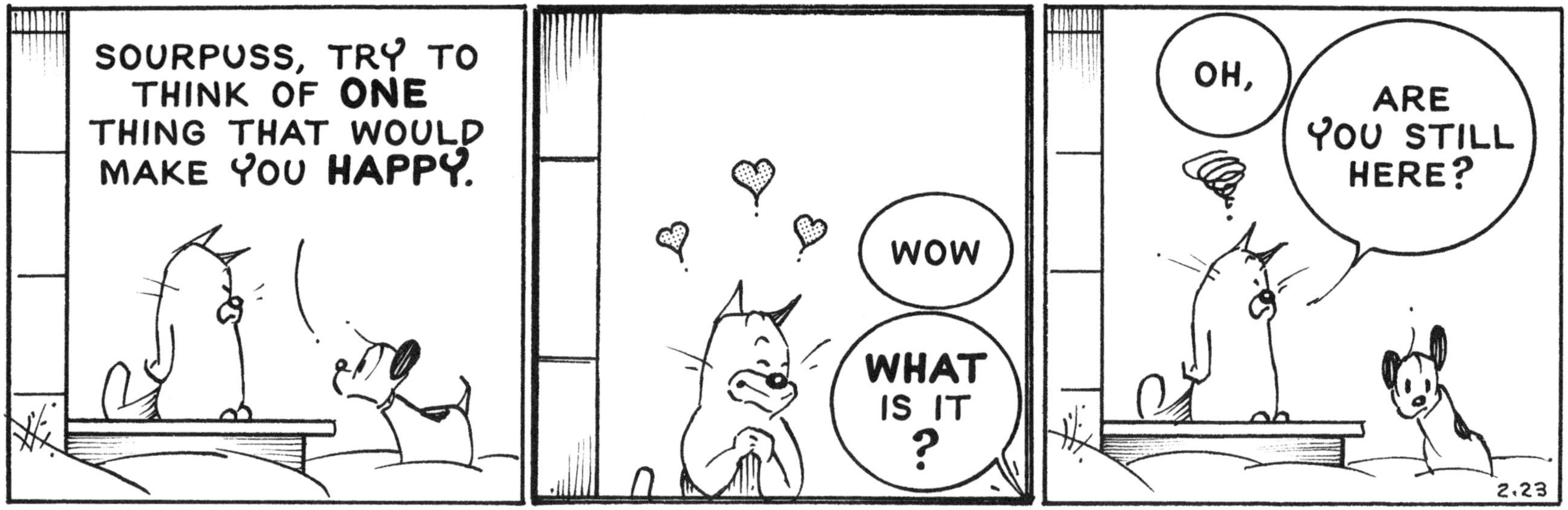
SOURPUSS, TRY TO THINK OF ONE THING THAT WOULD MAKE YOU HAPPY.
WOW
WHAT IS IT ?
OH,
ARE YOU STILL HERE?
2·23

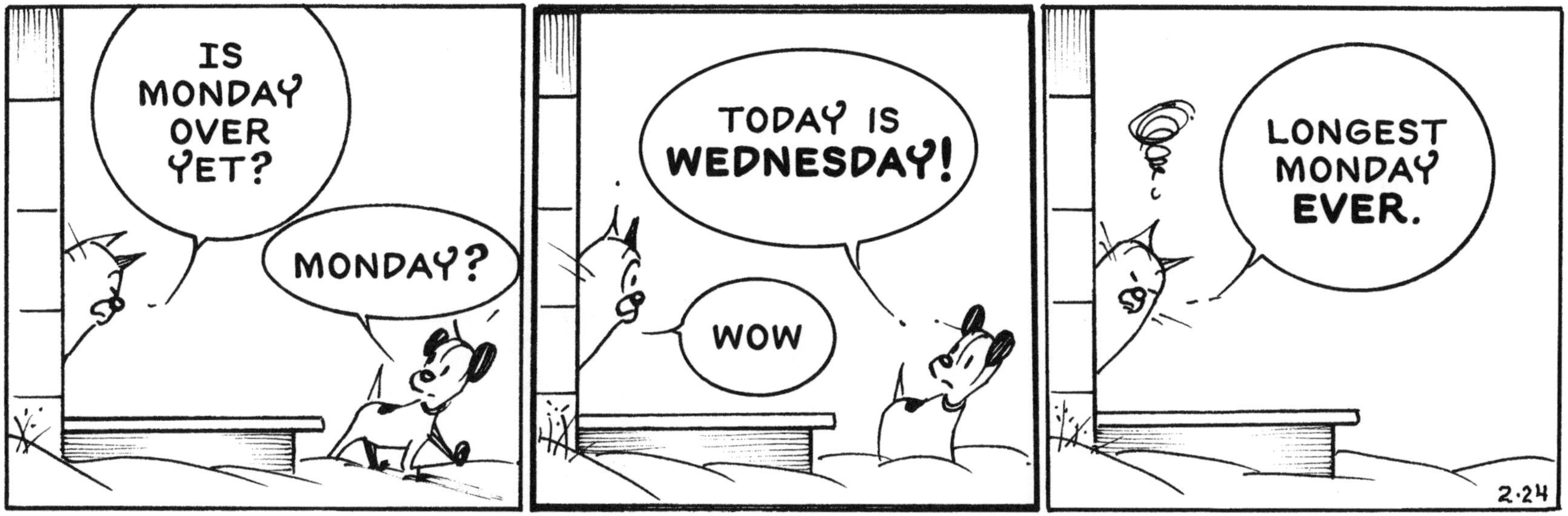
IS MONDAY OVER YET?
MONDAY?
TODAY IS **WEDNESDAY!**
WOW
LONGEST MONDAY **EVER.**
2·24

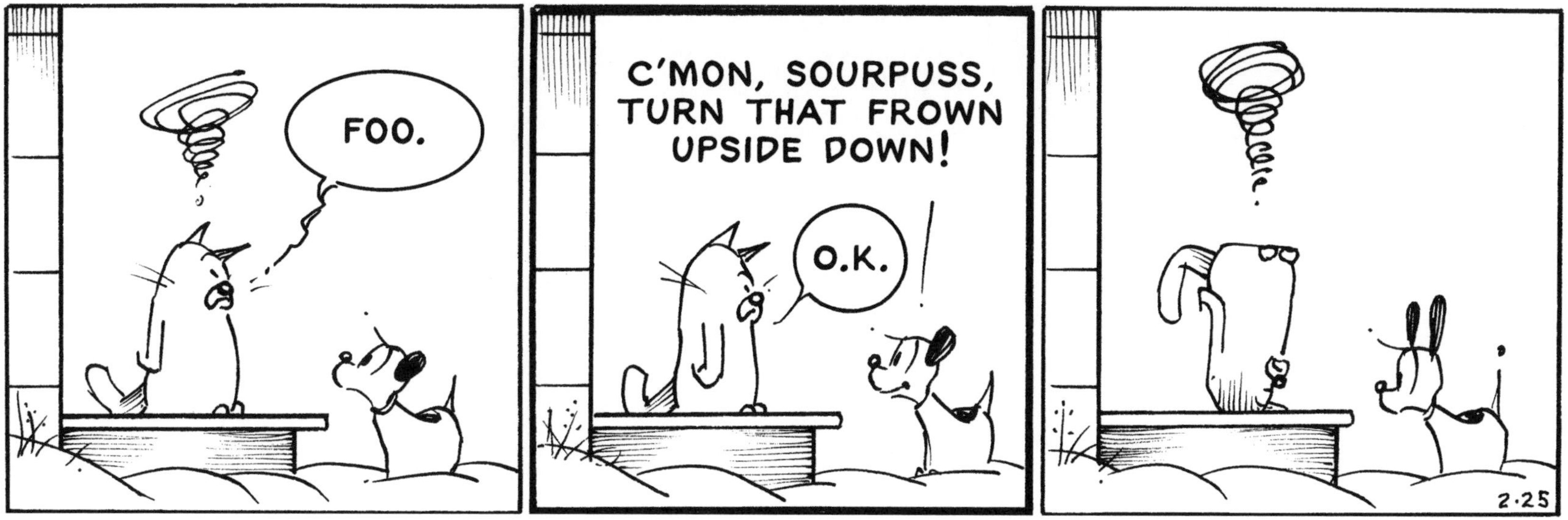
FOO.
C'MON, SOURPUSS, TURN THAT FROWN UPSIDE DOWN!
O.K.
2·25

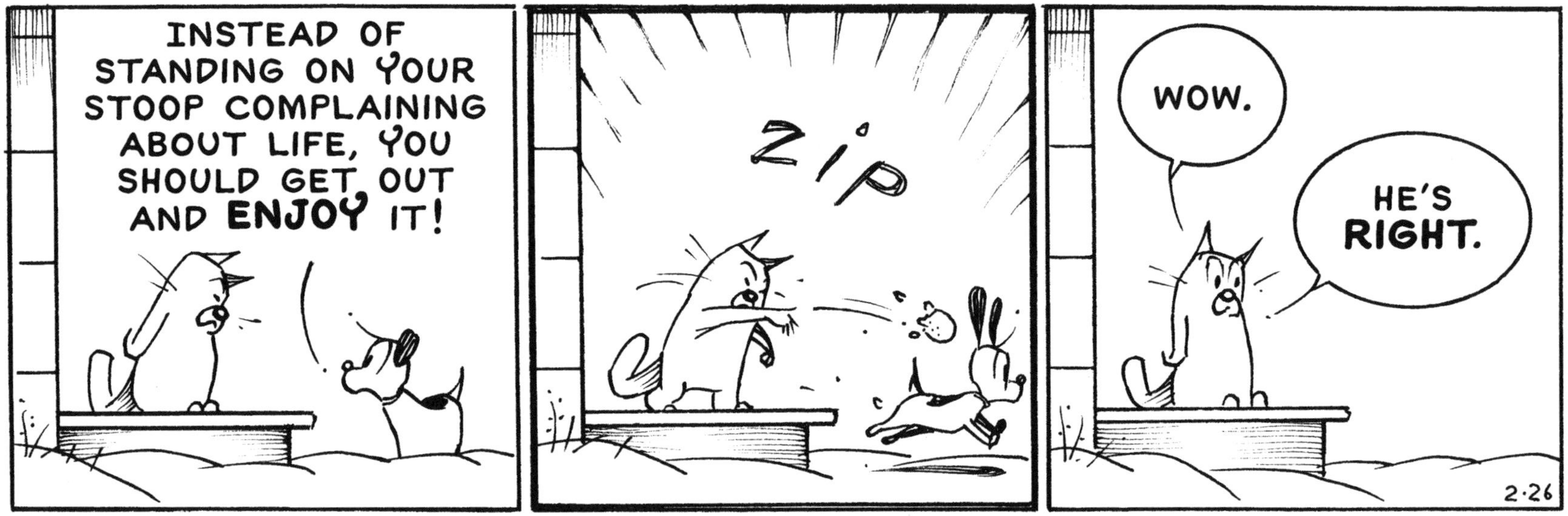
INSTEAD OF STANDING ON YOUR STOOP COMPLAINING ABOUT LIFE, YOU SHOULD GET OUT AND **ENJOY** IT!
ZIP
WOW.
HE'S **RIGHT.**
2·26

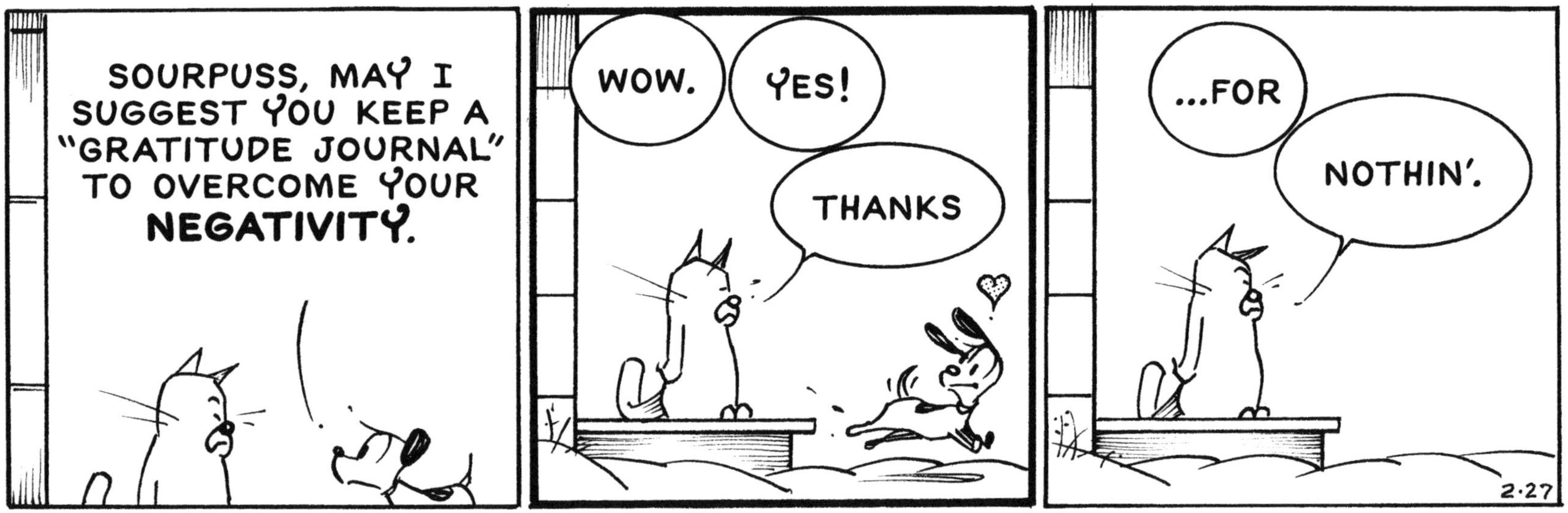
SOURPUSS, MAY I SUGGEST YOU KEEP A "GRATITUDE JOURNAL" TO OVERCOME YOUR **NEGATIVITY.**
WOW.
YES!
THANKS
...FOR
NOTHIN'.
2·27

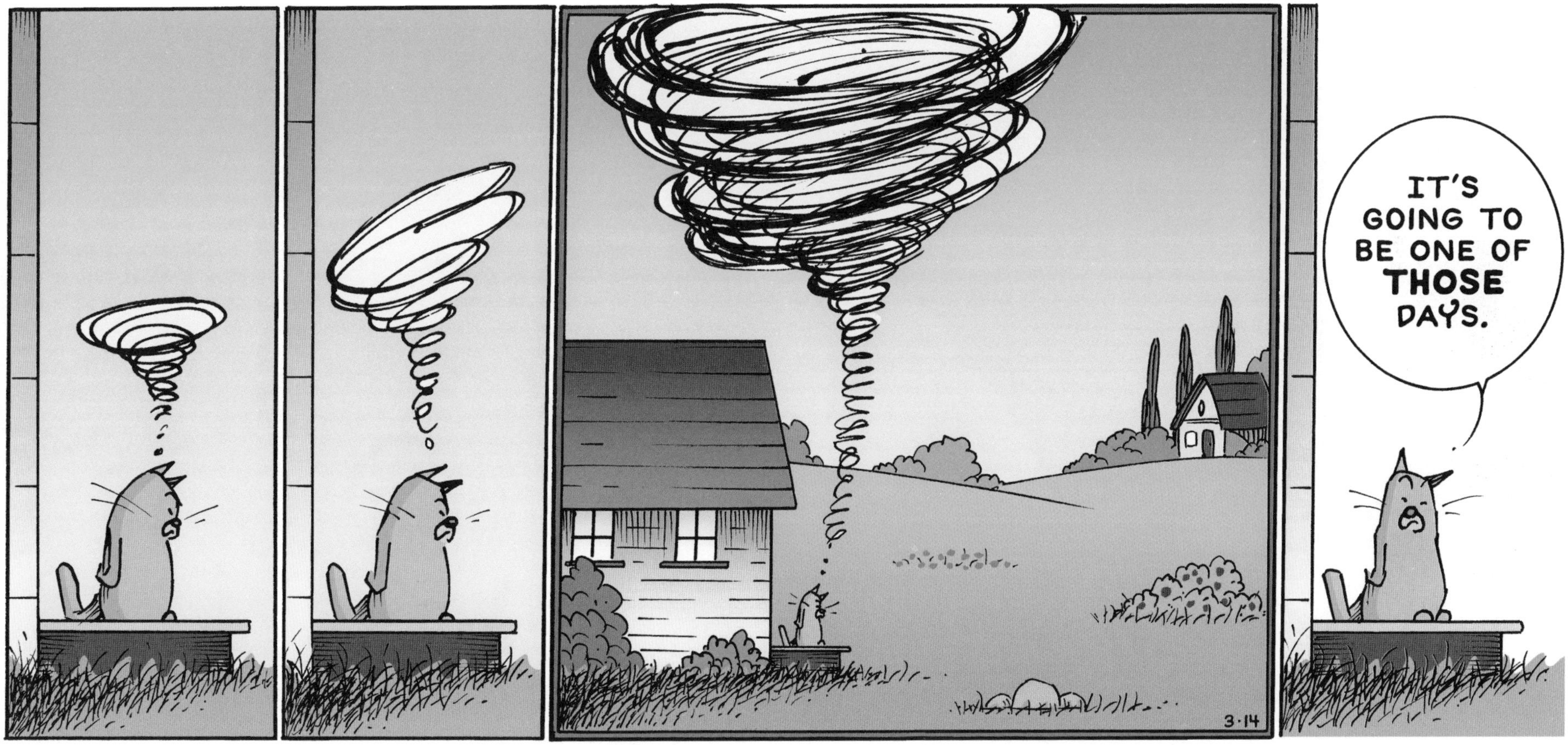
IT'S GOING TO BE ONE OF **THOSE** DAYS.
3·14

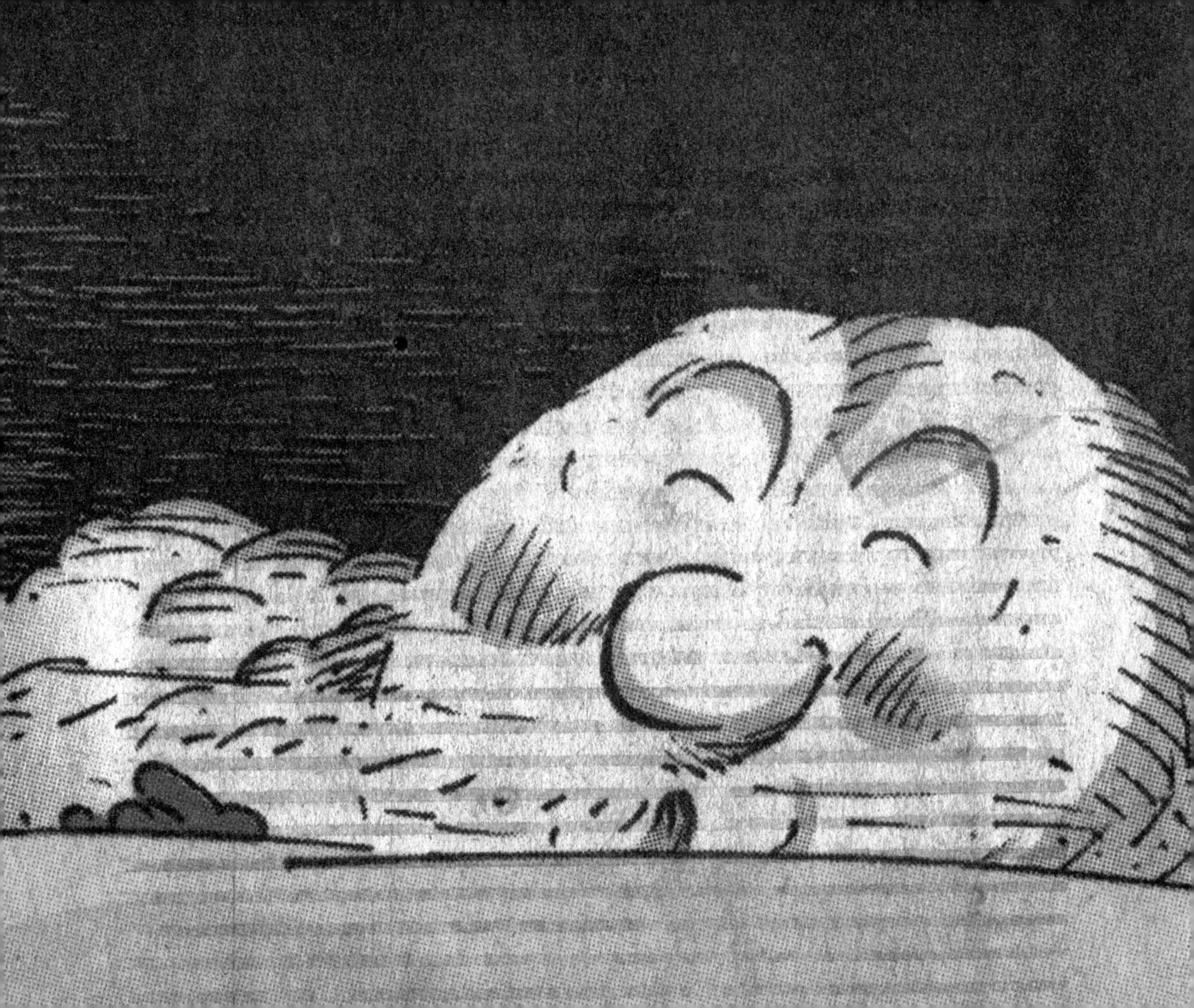

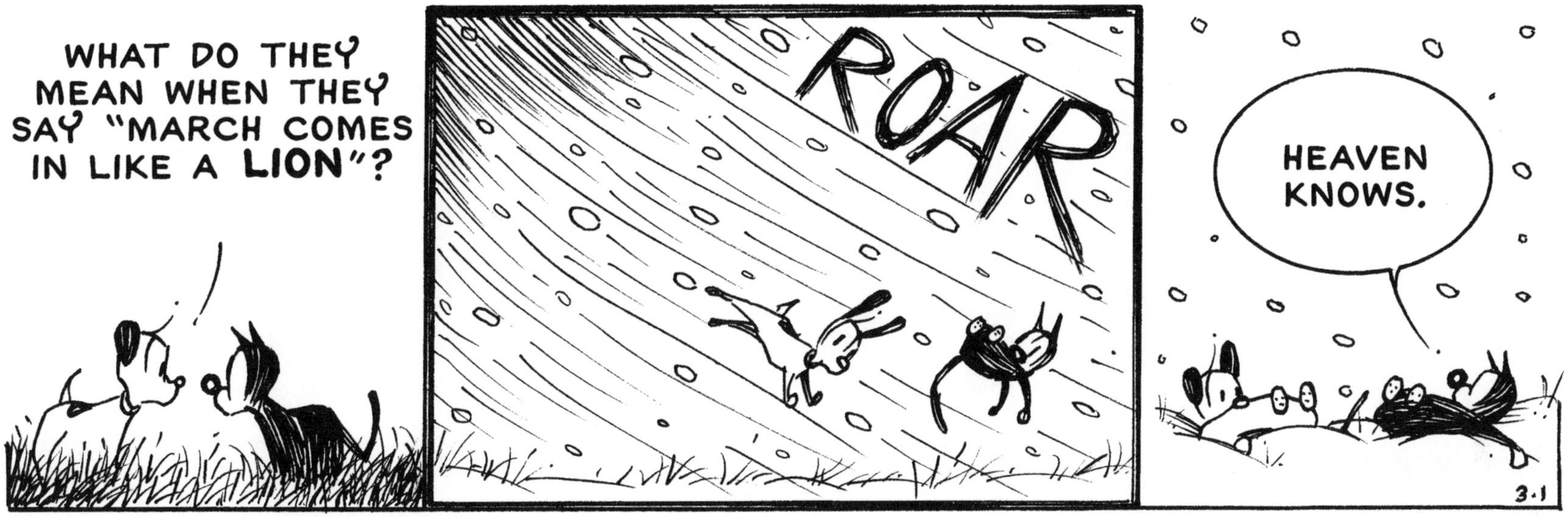
WHAT DO THEY MEAN WHEN THEY SAY "MARCH COMES IN LIKE A **LION**"?
ROAR
HEAVEN KNOWS.
3·1

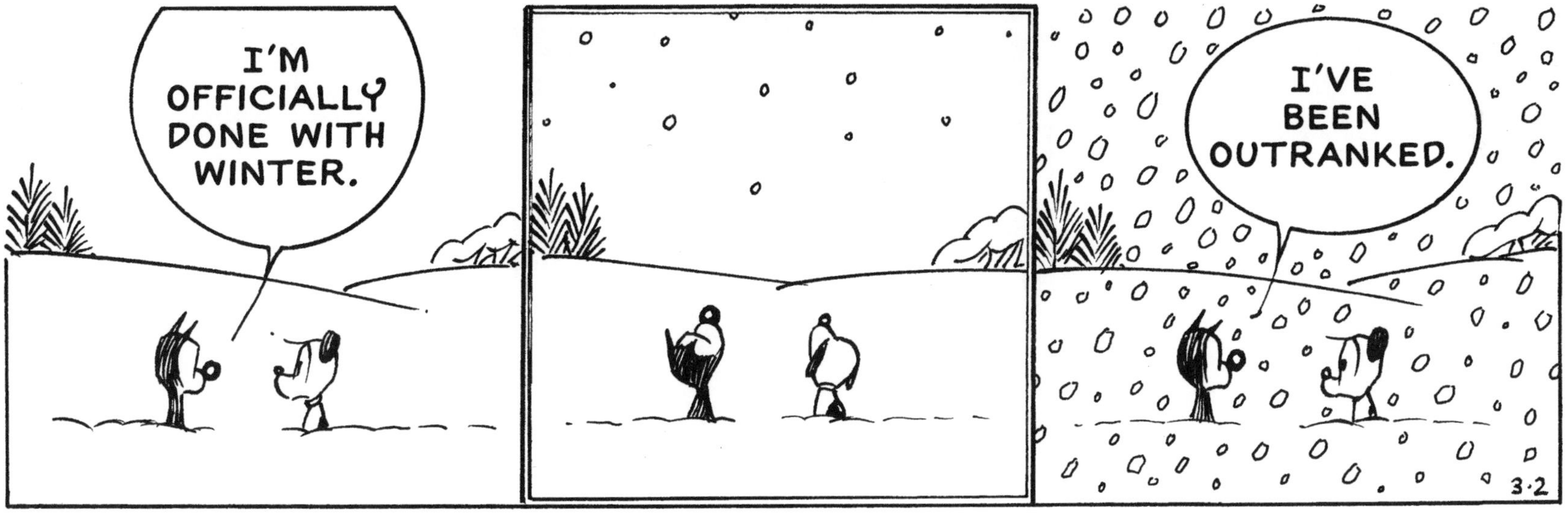
I'M OFFICIALLY DONE WITH WINTER.
I'VE BEEN OUTRANKED.
3·2

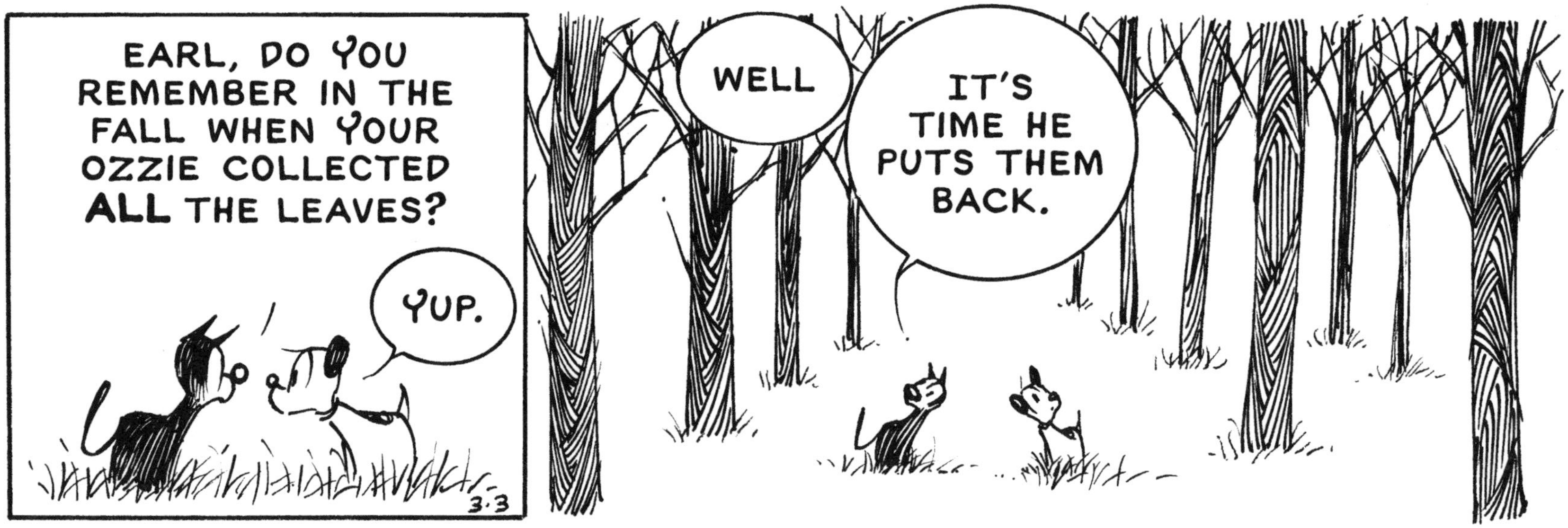
EARL, DO YOU REMEMBER IN THE FALL WHEN YOUR OZZIE COLLECTED ALL THE LEAVES?
YUP.
3·3
WELL
IT'S TIME HE PUTS THEM BACK.

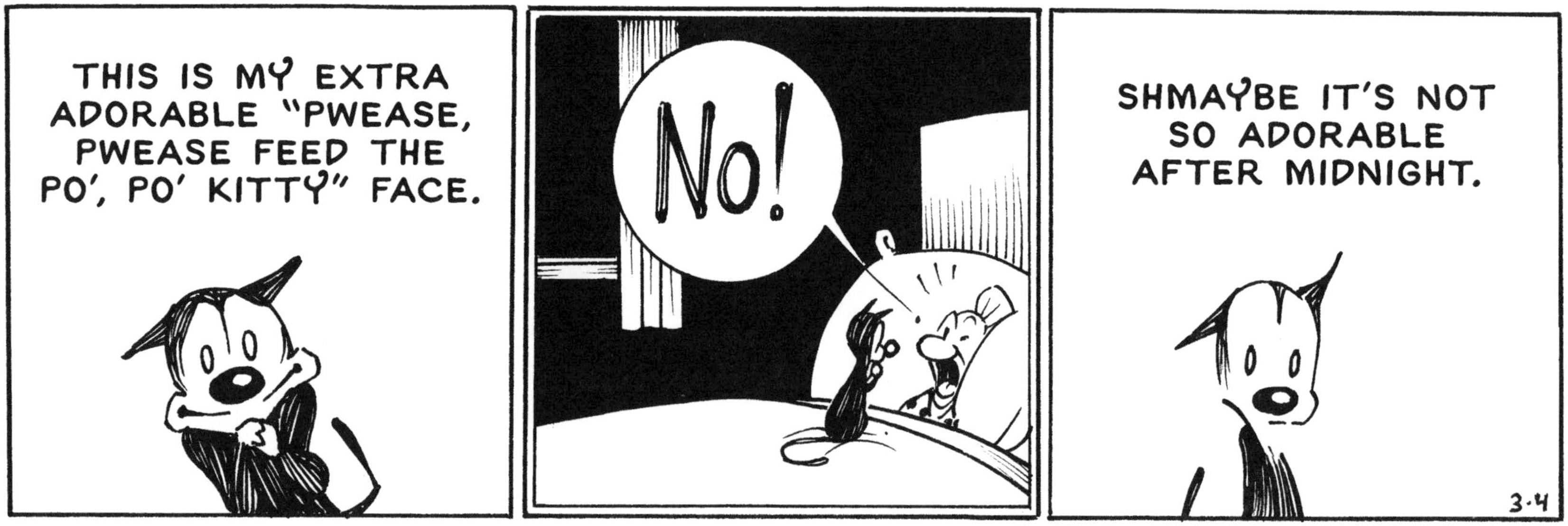
THIS IS MY EXTRA ADORABLE "PWEASE, PWEASE FEED THE PO', PO' KITTY" FACE.
No!
SHMAYBE IT'S NOT SO ADORABLE AFTER MIDNIGHT.
3·4

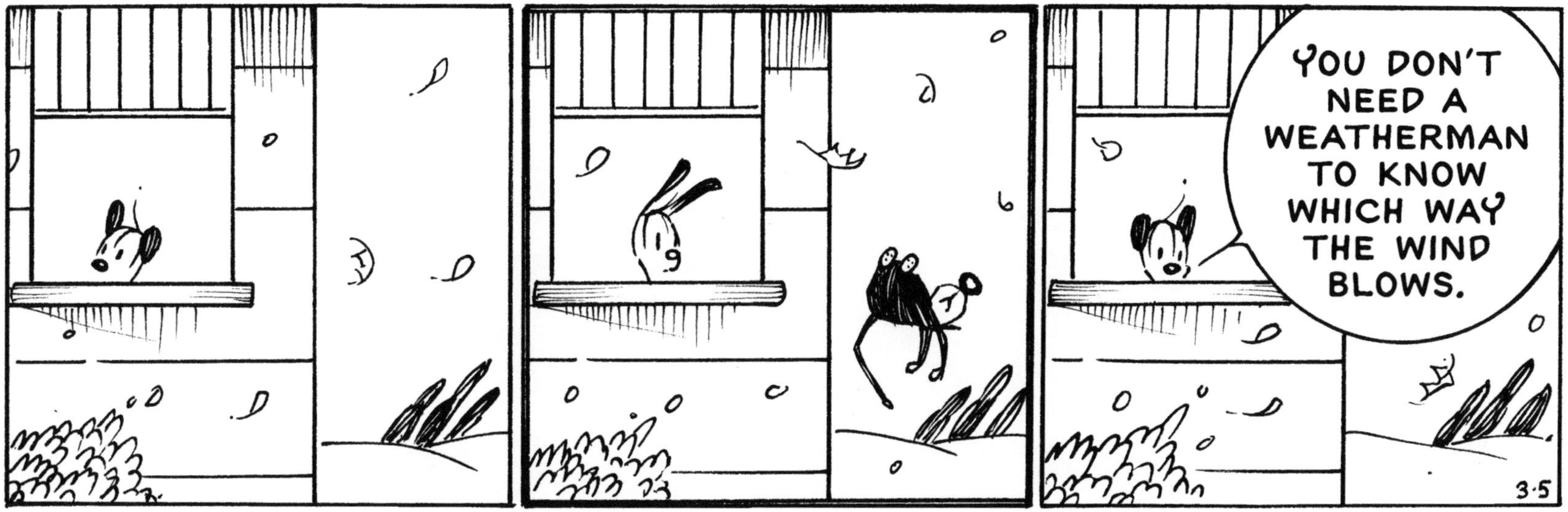
YOU DON'T NEED A WEATHERMAN TO KNOW WHICH WAY THE WIND BLOWS.
3·5

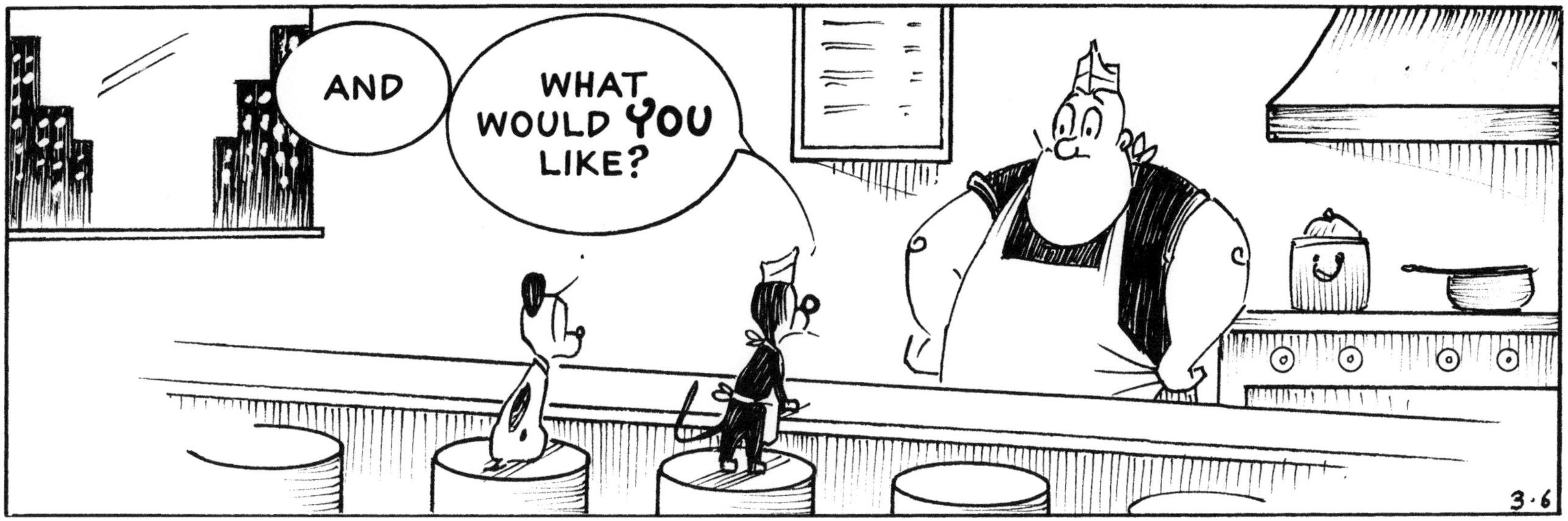
AND
WHAT WOULD YOU LIKE?
3·6

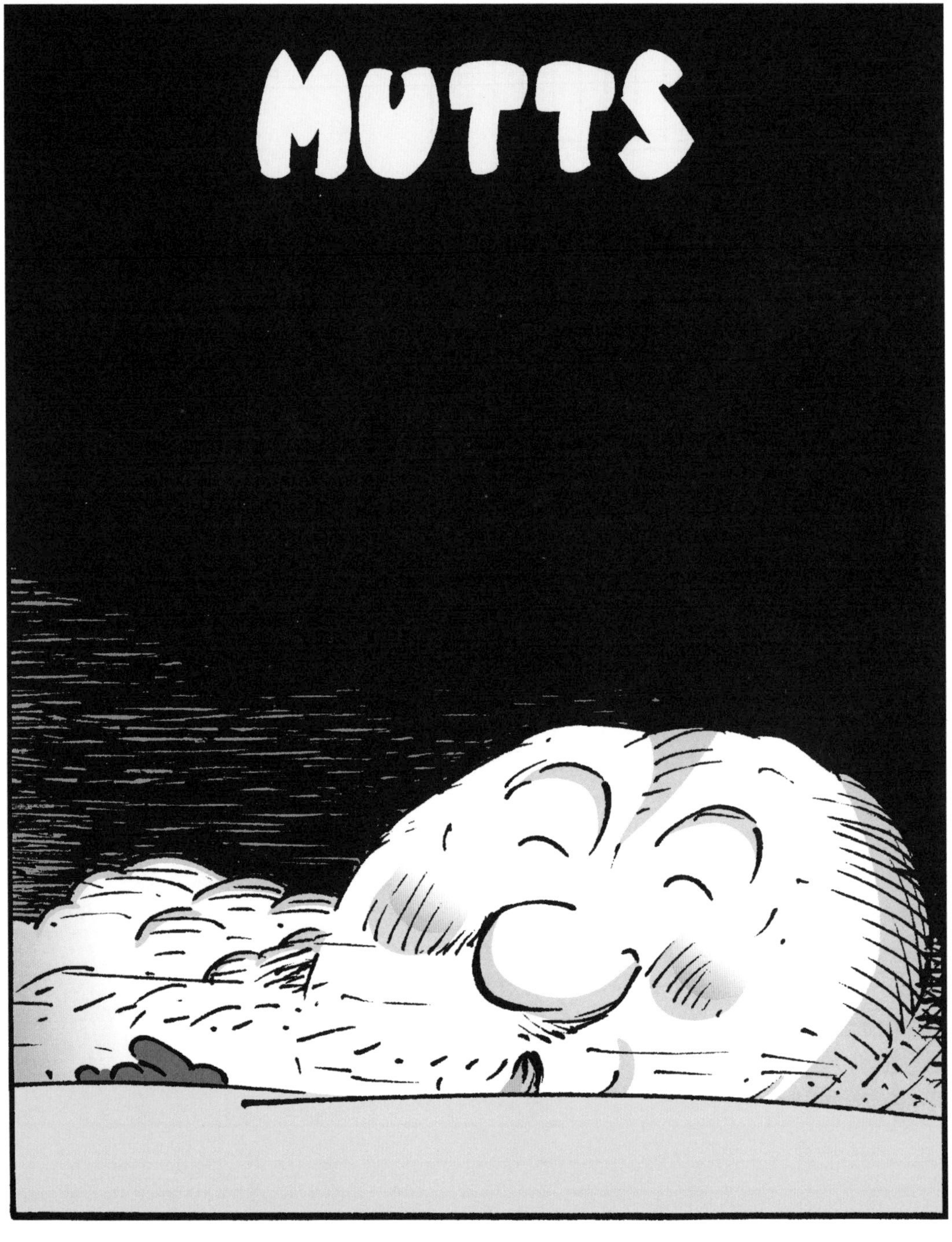
MUTTS

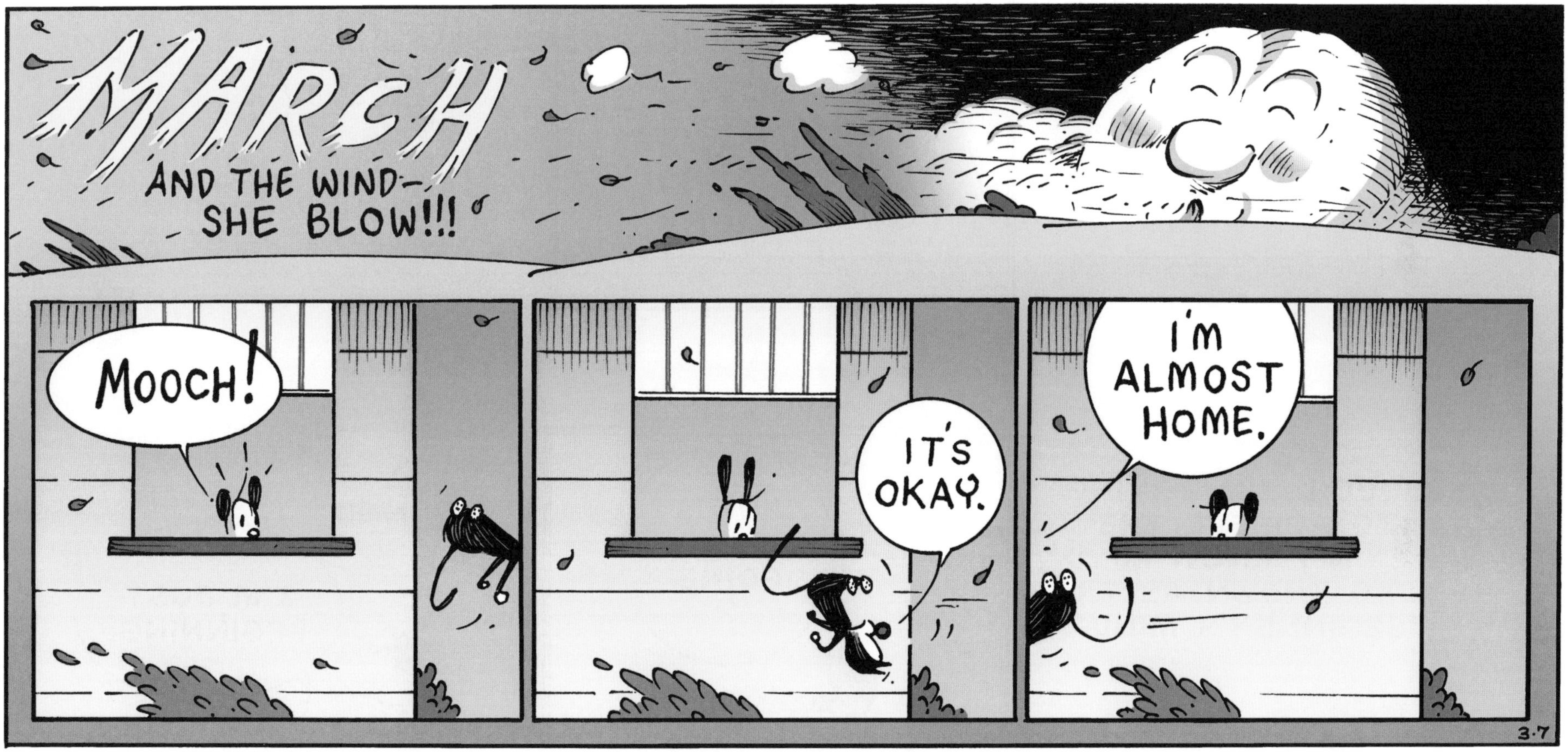
MARCH
AND THE WIND-SHE BLOW!!!
MOOCH!
IT'S OKAY.
I'M ALMOST HOME.
3·7

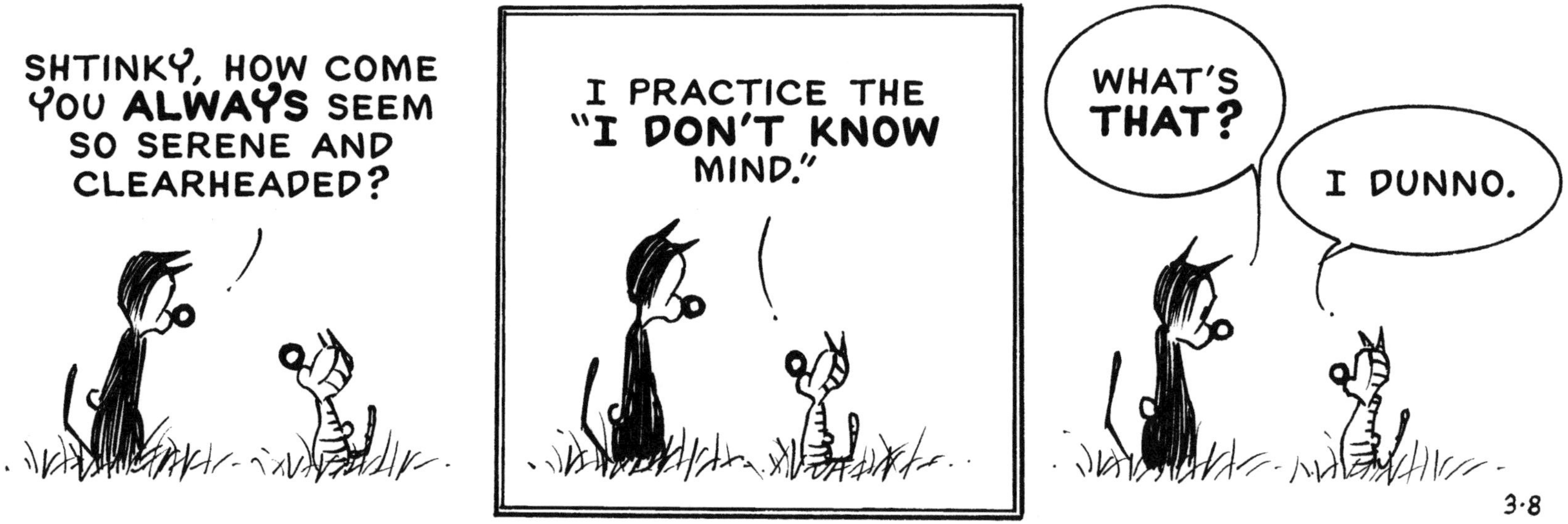
SHTINKY, HOW COME YOU **ALWAYS** SEEM SO SERENE AND CLEARHEADED?
I PRACTICE THE **"I DON'T KNOW** MIND."
WHAT'S **THAT?**
I DUNNO.
3·8

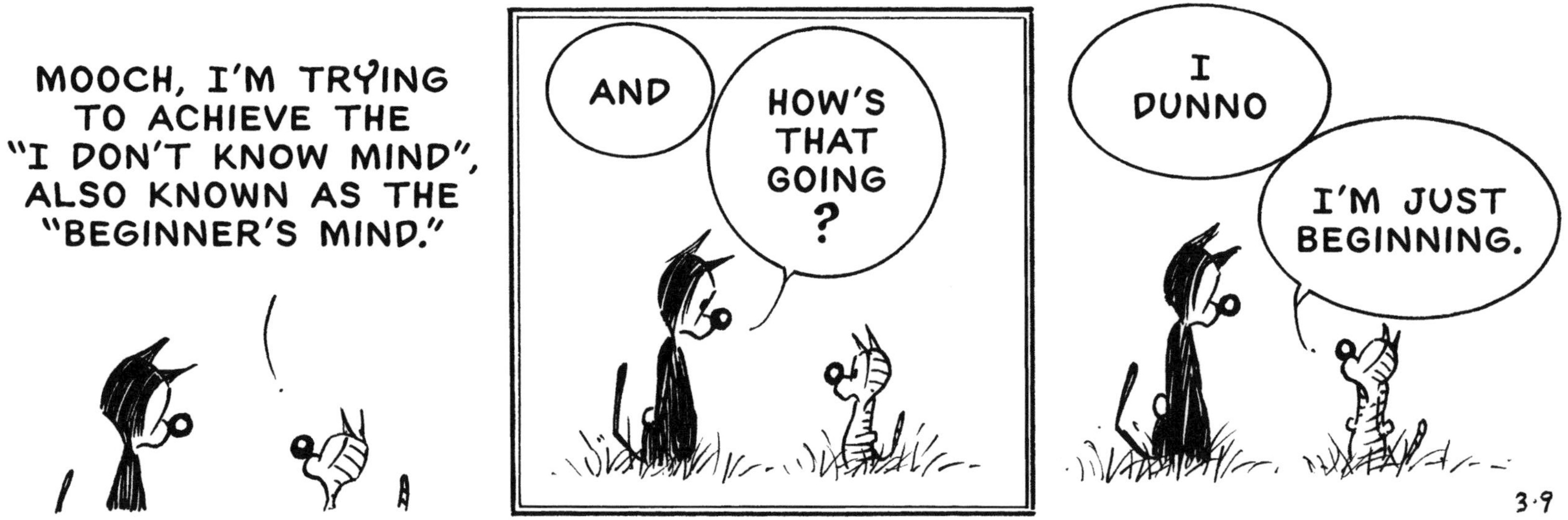
MOOCH, I'M TRYING TO ACHIEVE THE "I DON'T KNOW MIND", ALSO KNOWN AS THE "BEGINNER'S MIND."
AND
HOW'S THAT GOING ?
I DUNNO
I'M JUST BEGINNING.
3·9

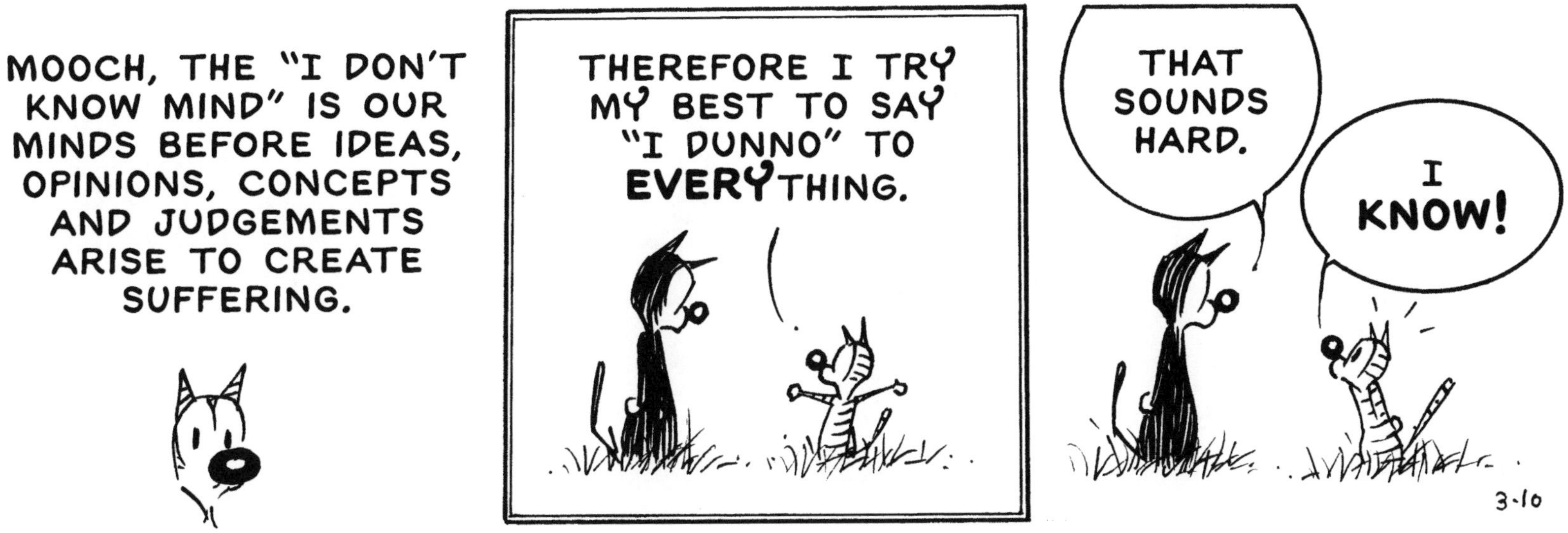
MOOCH, THE "I DON'T KNOW MIND" IS OUR MINDS BEFORE IDEAS, OPINIONS, CONCEPTS AND JUDGEMENTS ARISE TO CREATE SUFFERING.
THEREFORE I TRY MY BEST TO SAY "I DUNNO" TO EVERYTHING.
THAT SOUNDS HARD.
I KNOW!
3-10

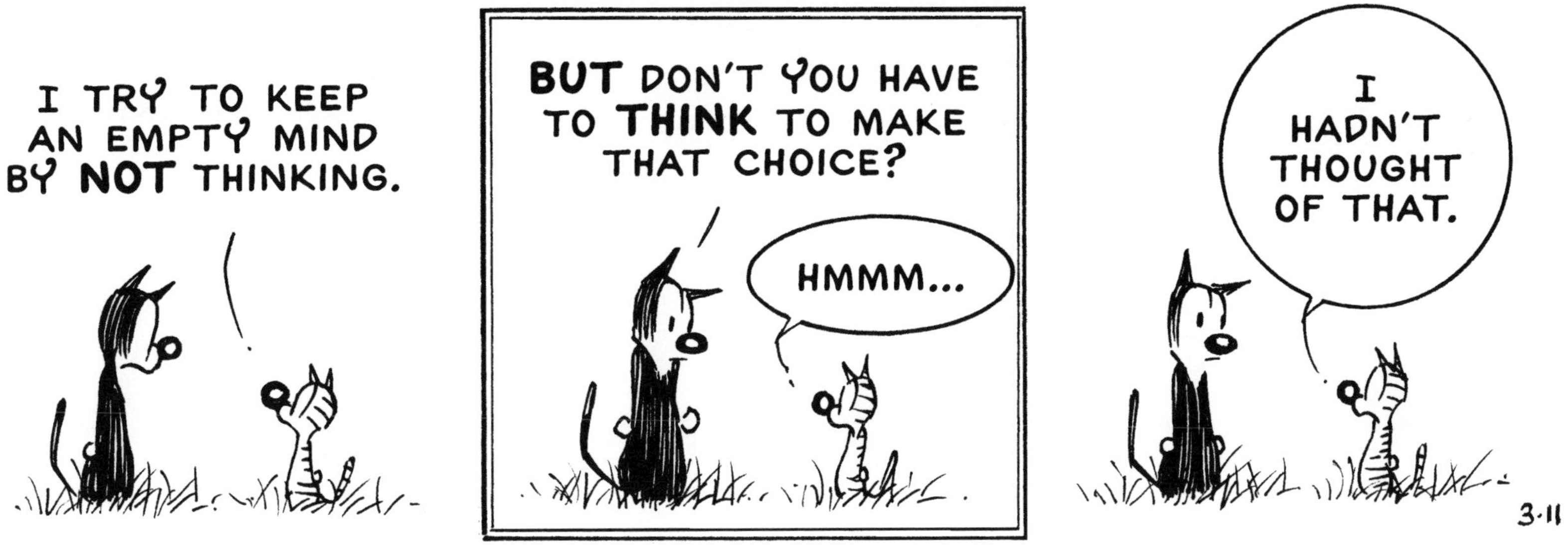
I TRY TO KEEP AN EMPTY MIND BY NOT THINKING.
BUT DON'T YOU HAVE TO THINK TO MAKE THAT CHOICE?
HMMM...
I HADN'T THOUGHT OF THAT.
3-11

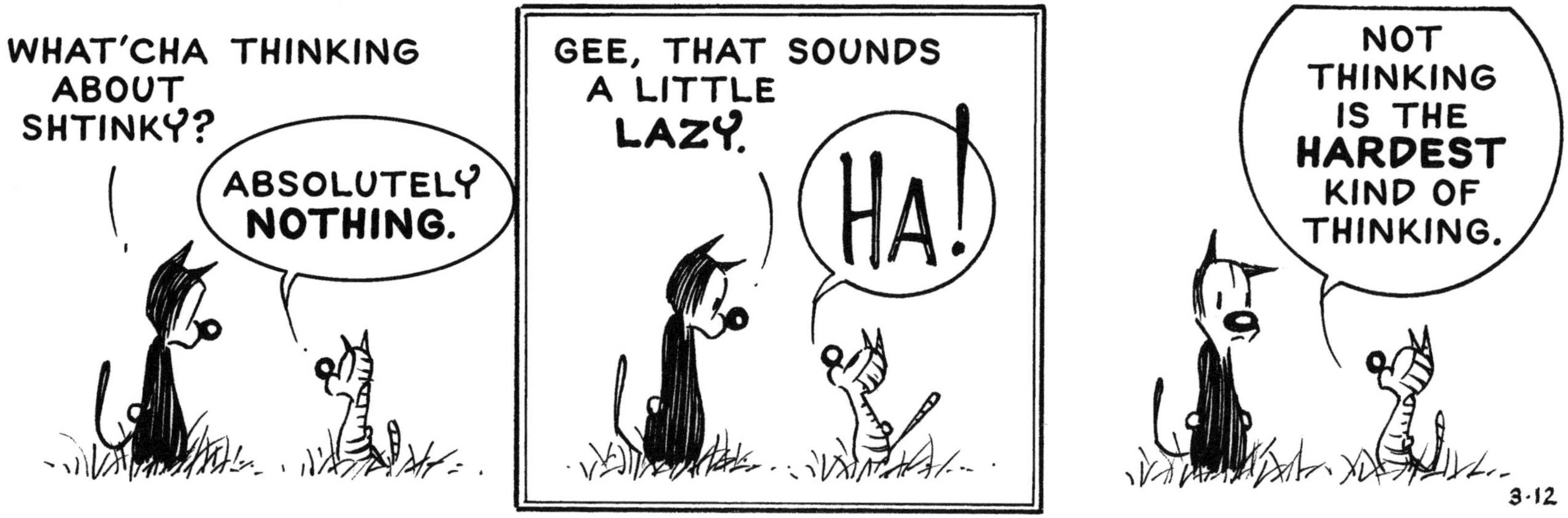
WHAT'CHA THINKING ABOUT SHTINKY?
ABSOLUTELY NOTHING.
GEE, THAT SOUNDS A LITTLE LAZY.
HA!
NOT THINKING IS THE HARDEST KIND OF THINKING.
3·12

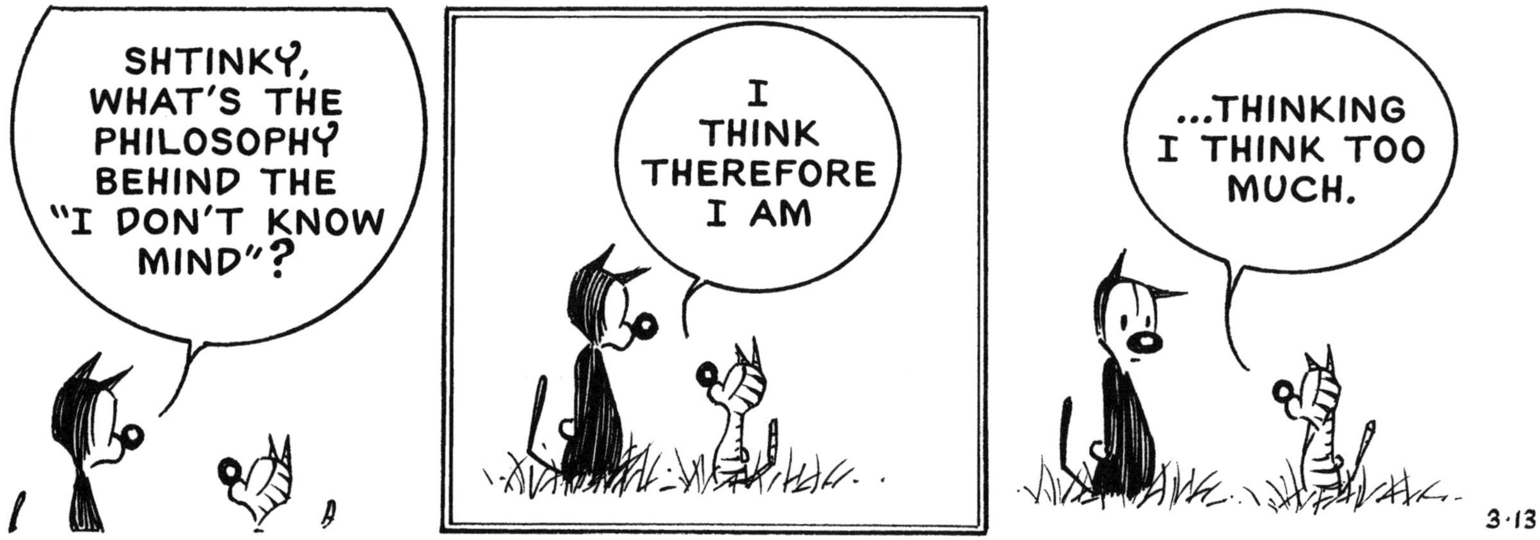
SHTINKY, WHAT'S THE PHILOSOPHY BEHIND THE "I DON'T KNOW MIND"?
I THINK THEREFORE I AM
...THINKING I THINK TOO MUCH.
3·13

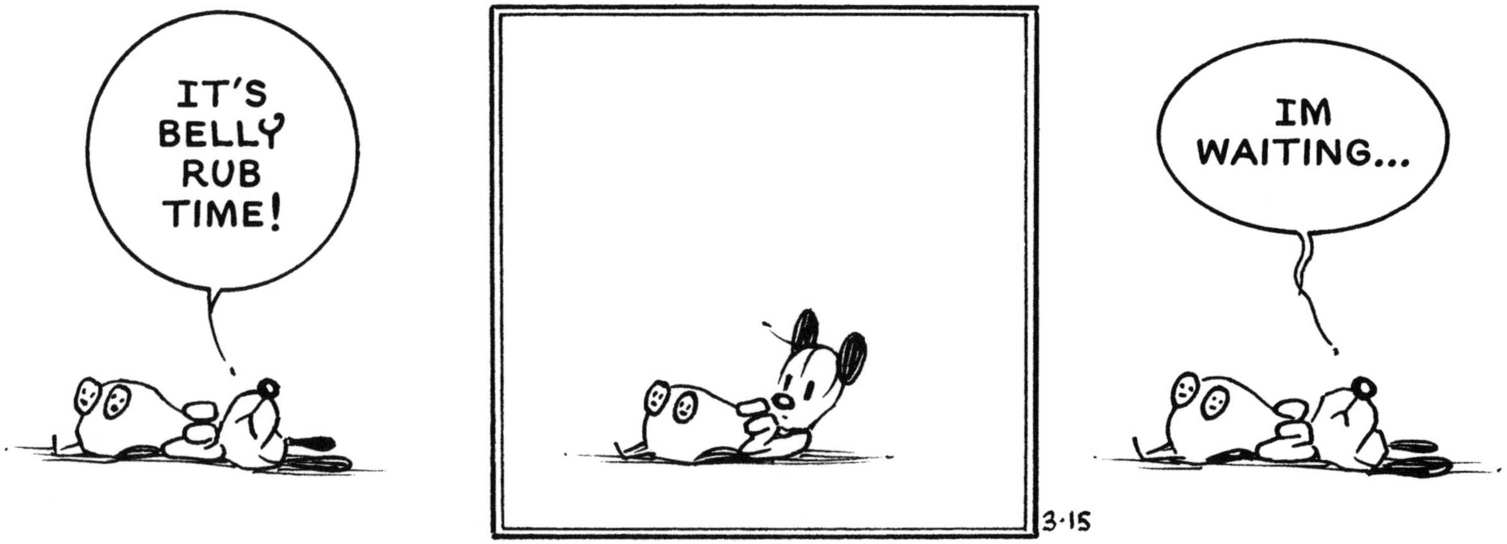
IT'S BELLY RUB TIME!
IM WAITING...
3·15

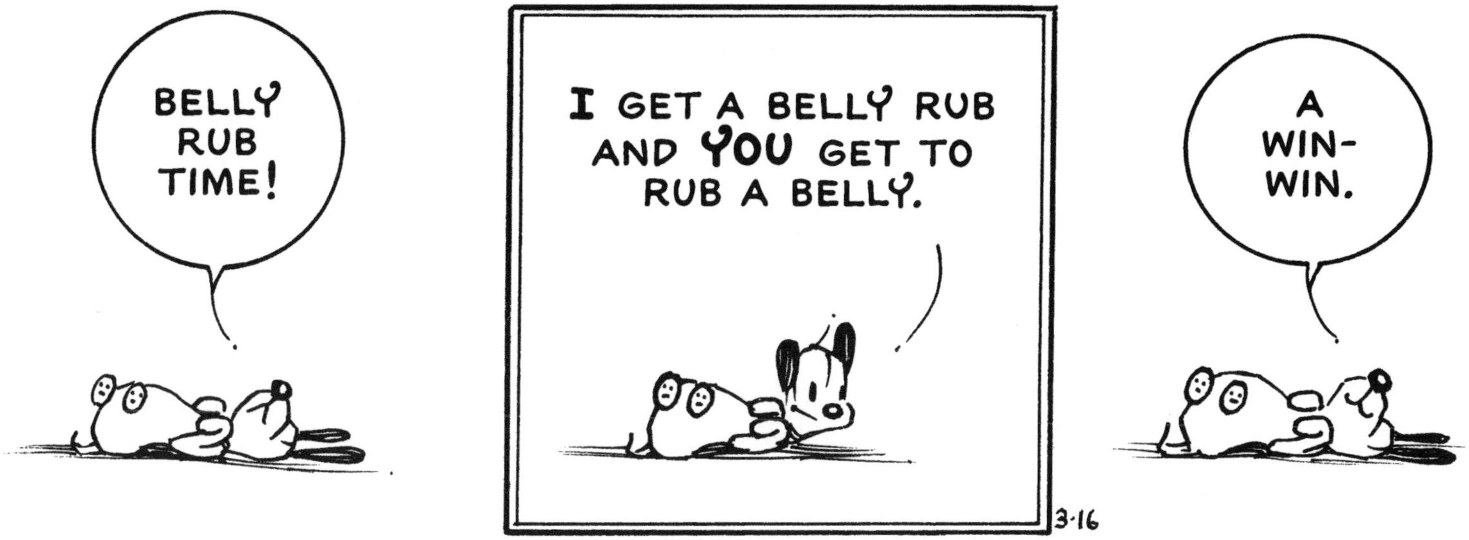
BELLY RUB TIME!
I GET A BELLY RUB AND YOU GET TO RUB A BELLY.
A WIN-WIN.
3·16

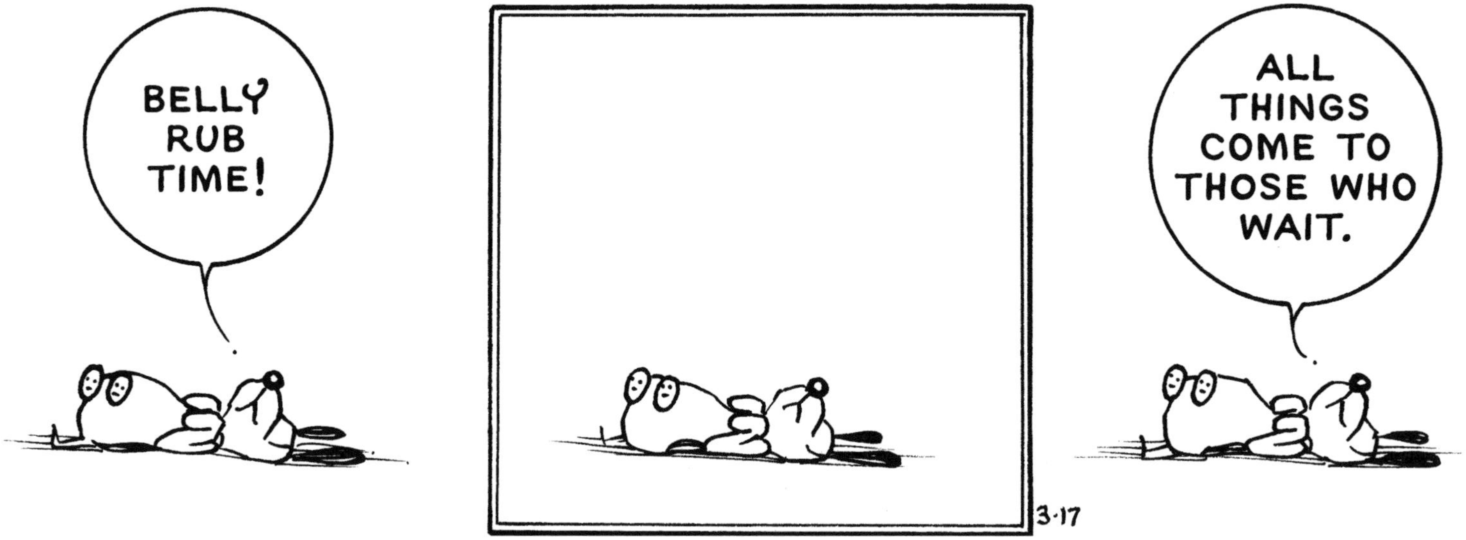
BELLY RUB TIME!
ALL THINGS COME TO THOSE WHO WAIT.
3-17

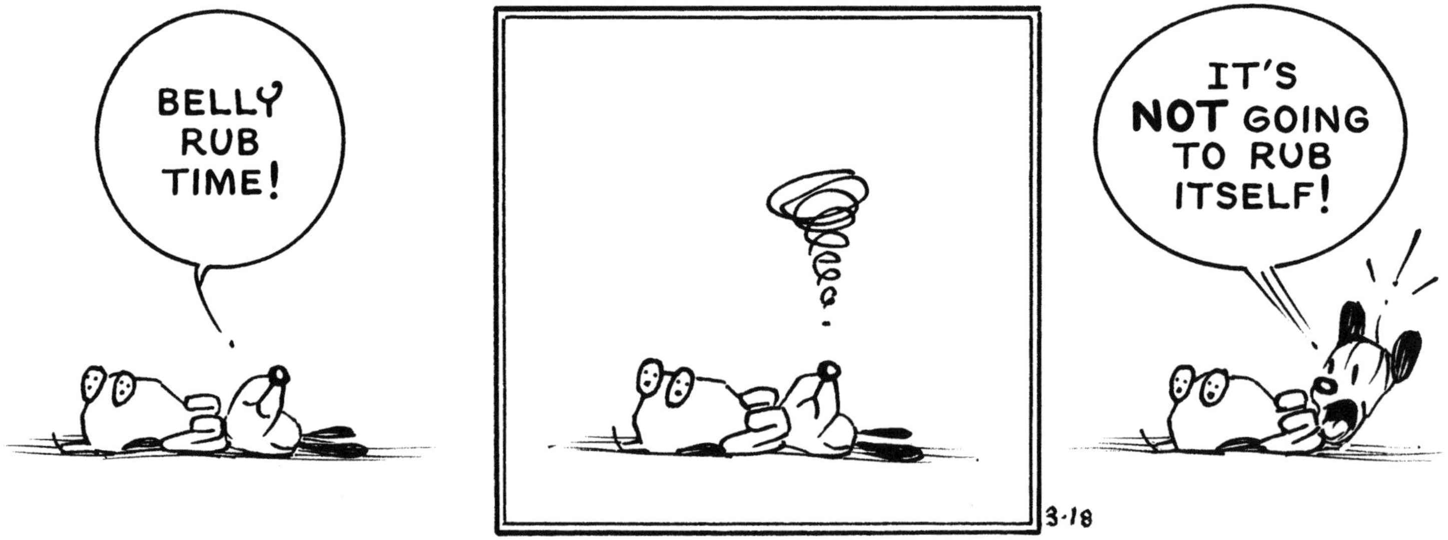
BELLY RUB TIME!
IT'S **NOT** GOING TO RUB ITSELF!
3-18

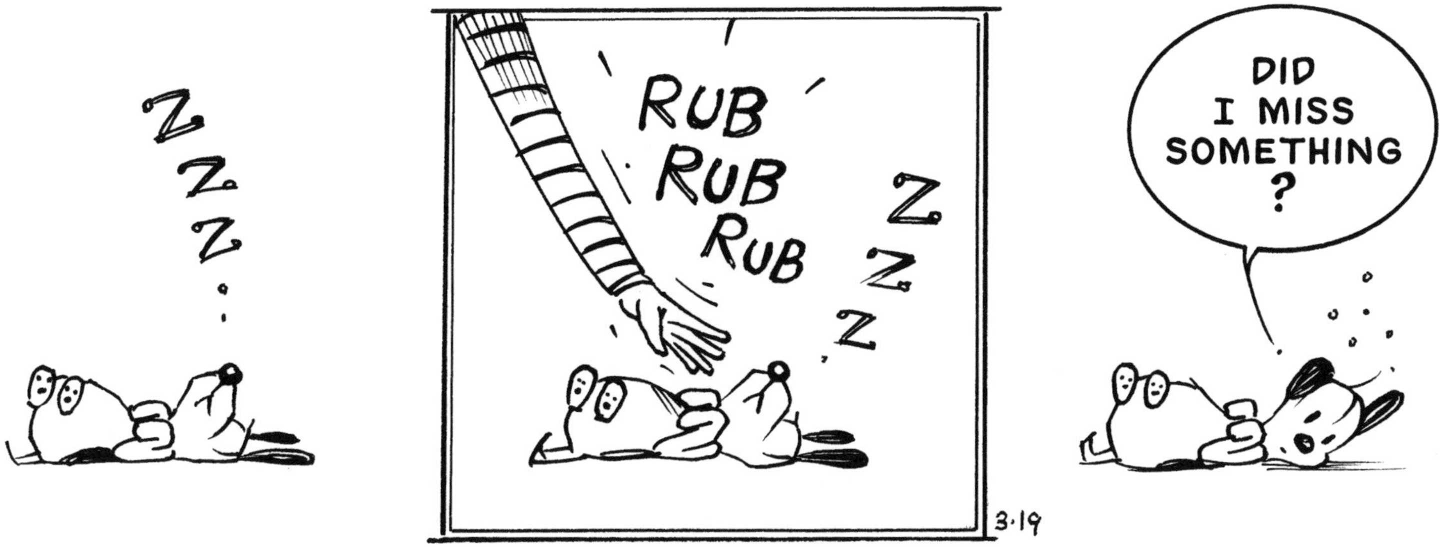
Z
Z
Z
RUB
RUB
RUB
Z
Z
Z
DID I MISS SOMETHING?
3·19

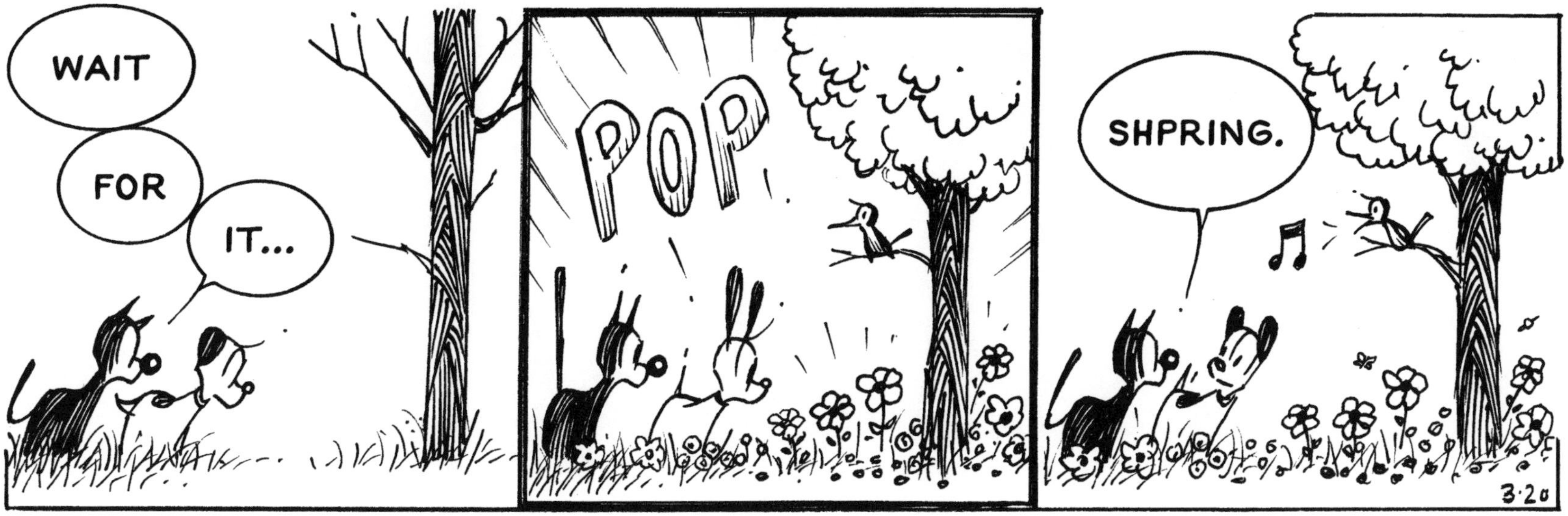
WAIT
FOR
IT...
POP
SHPRING.
3·20

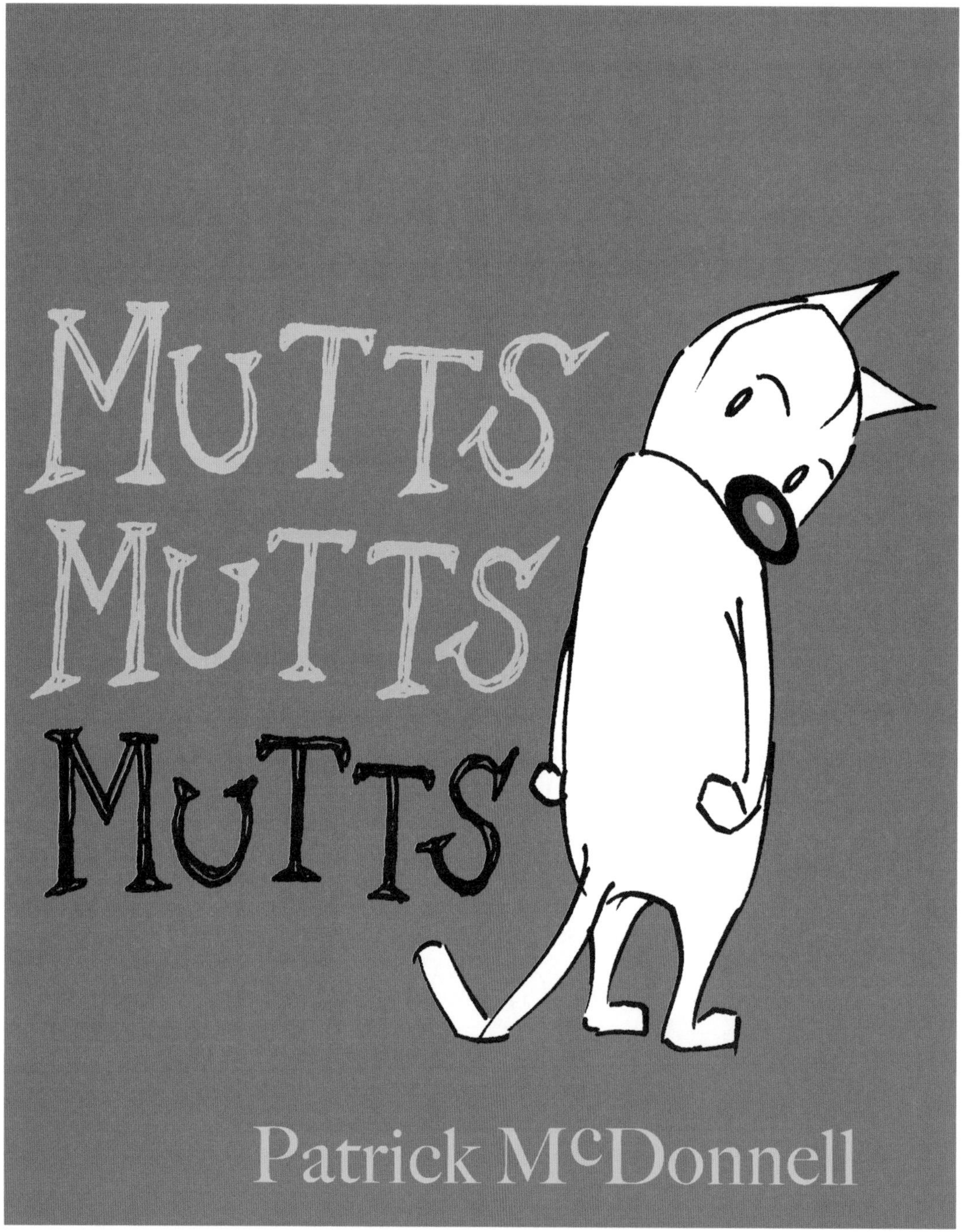
MUTTS
MUTTS
MUTTS
Patrick McDonnell

A DANCE
TO SHPRING

TO REBIRTH

TO REGROWTH

TO
REJUVENATION

TO
RENEWAL

TO...
TO...

FOO...

I FORGOT WHAT
I WAS DANCING
ABOUT...

OH, WELL...

I'LL JUST
SHTART OVER.

3·21

59

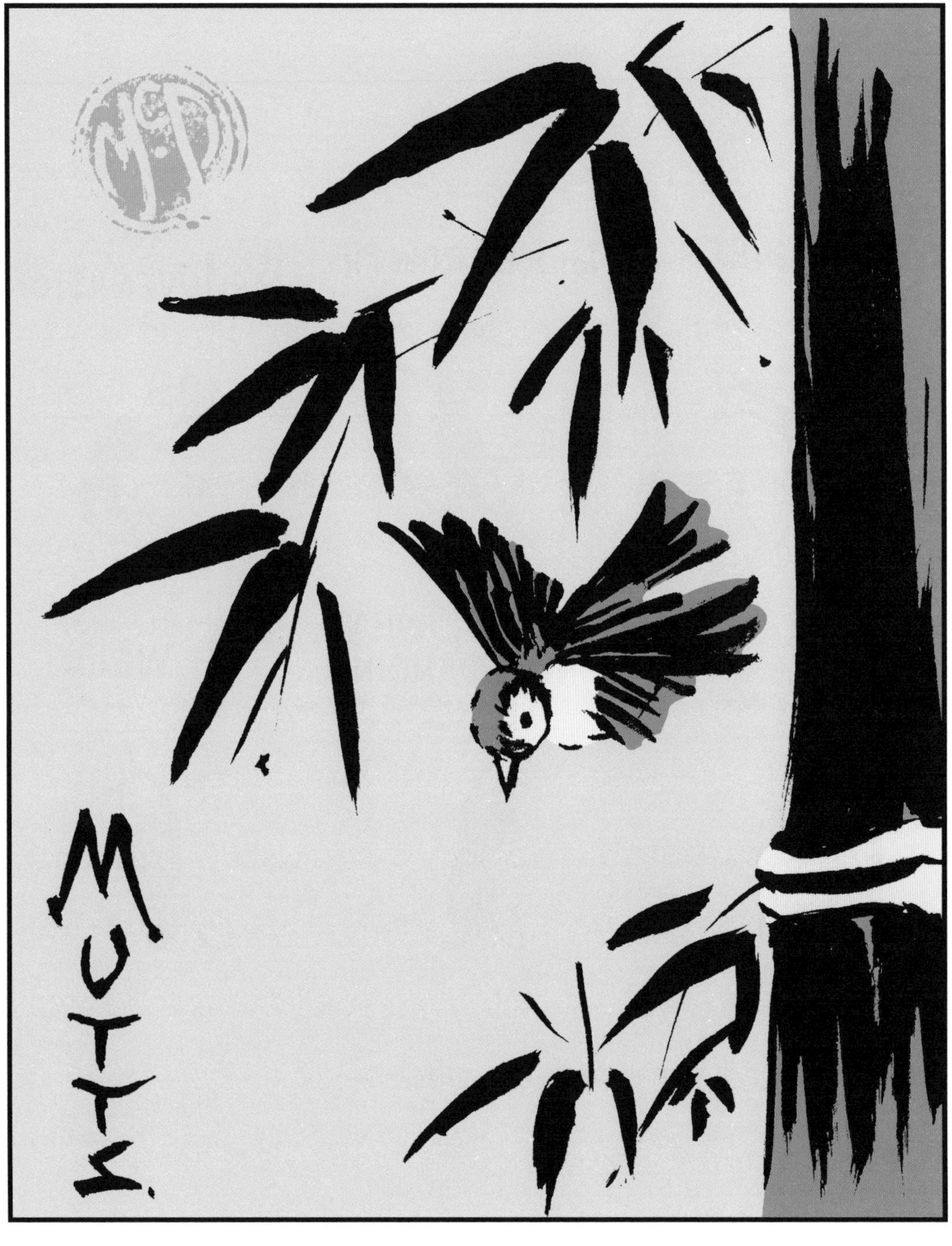
MUTTS

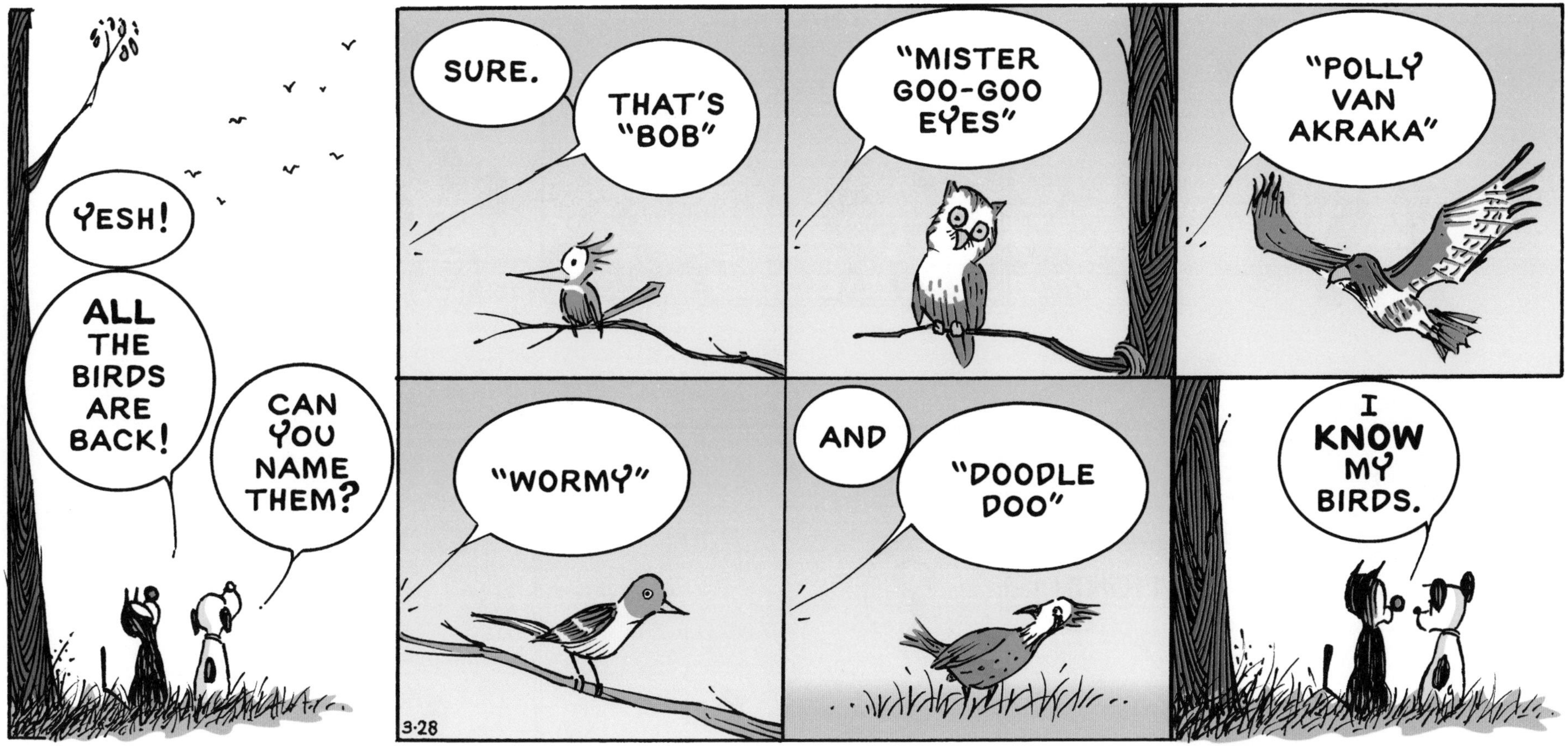
YESH!
ALL THE BIRDS ARE BACK!
CAN YOU NAME THEM?
SURE.
THAT'S "BOB"
"MISTER GOO-GOO EYES"
"POLLY VAN AKRAKA"
"WORMY"
AND
"DOODLE DOO"
I KNOW MY BIRDS.
3·28

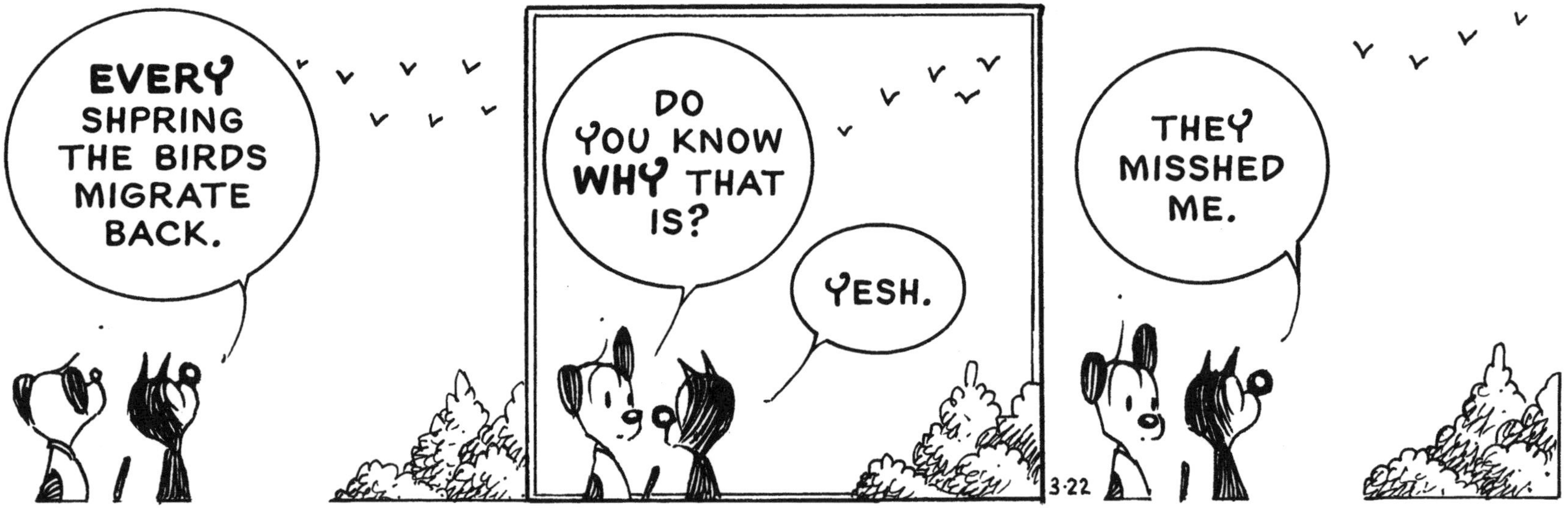
EVERY SHPRING THE BIRDS MIGRATE BACK.
DO YOU KNOW WHY THAT IS?
YESH.
3·22
THEY MISSHED ME.

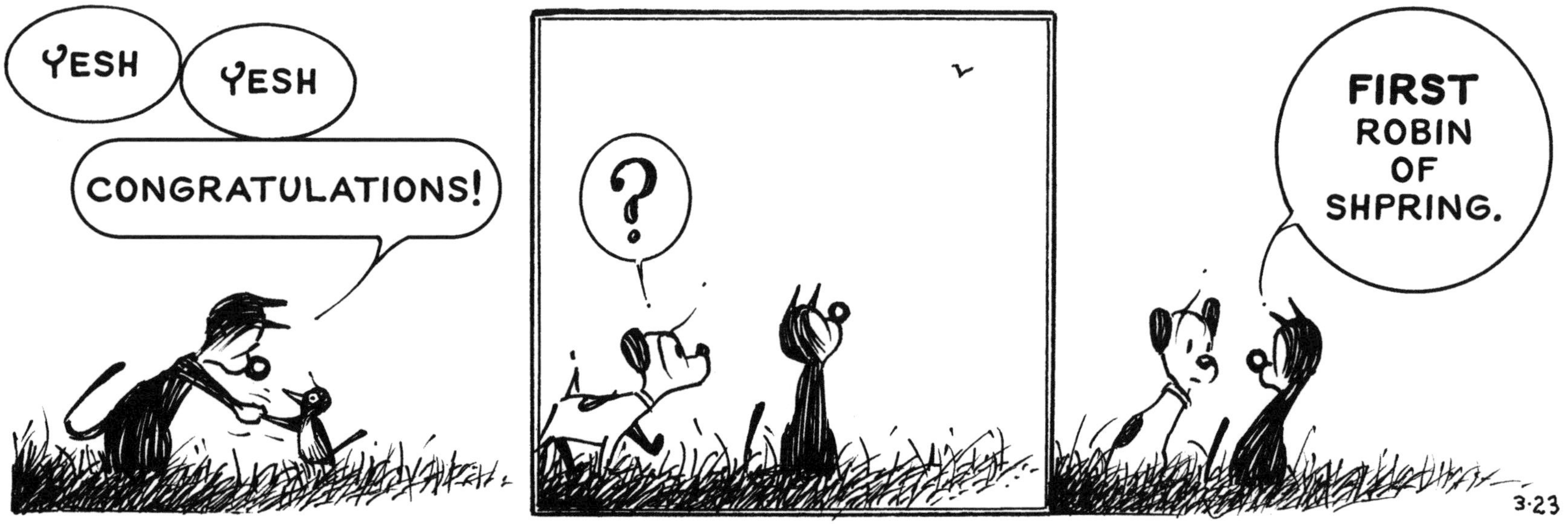
YESH
YESH
CONGRATULATIONS!
?
FIRST ROBIN OF SHPRING.
3·23

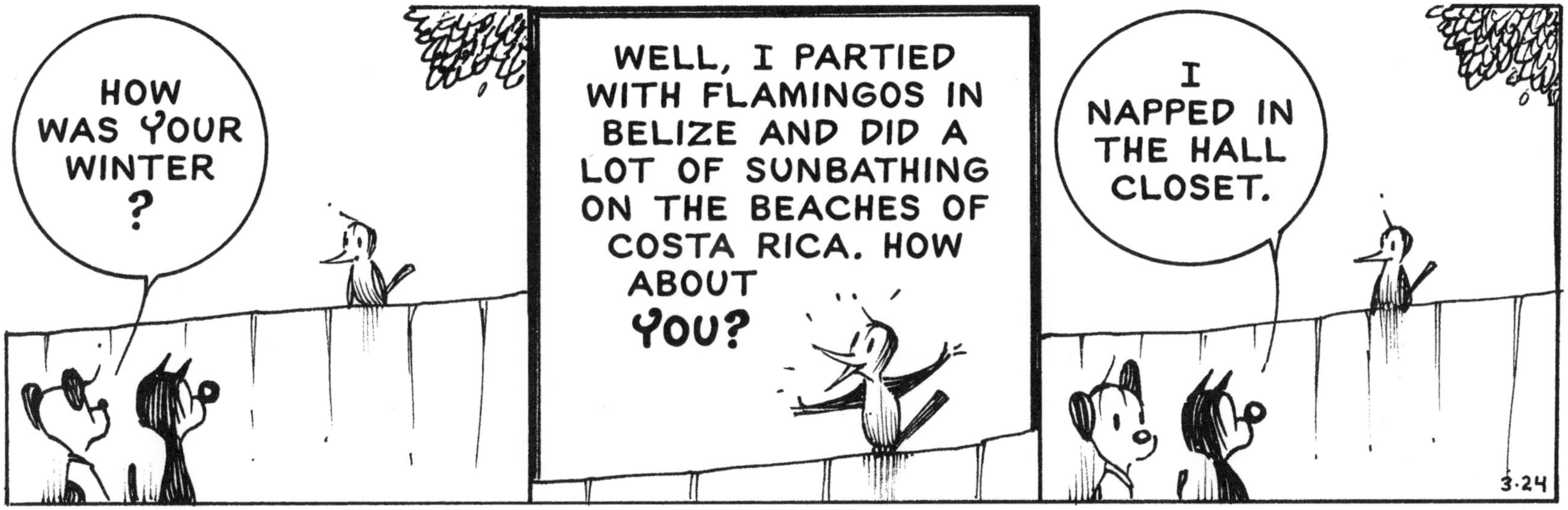
HOW WAS YOUR WINTER ?
WELL, I PARTIED WITH FLAMINGOS IN BELIZE AND DID A LOT OF SUNBATHING ON THE BEACHES OF COSTA RICA. HOW ABOUT **YOU?**
I NAPPED IN THE HALL CLOSET.
3·24

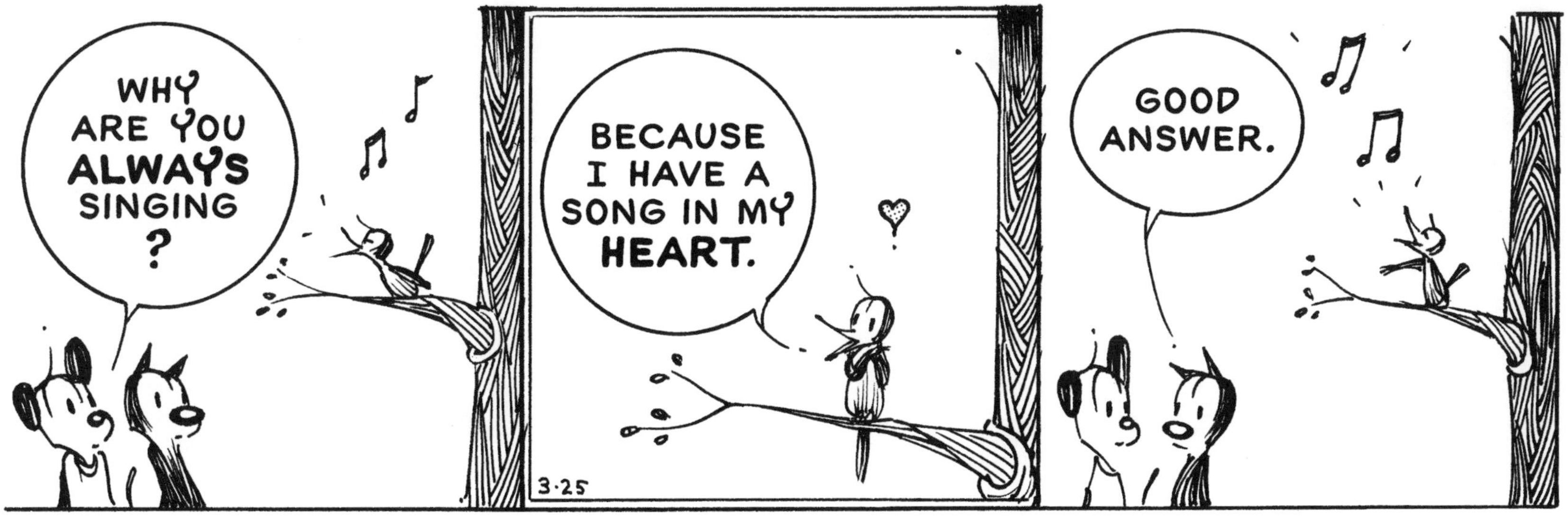
WHY ARE YOU **ALWAYS** SINGING ?
BECAUSE I HAVE A SONG IN MY **HEART.**
3·25
GOOD ANSWER.

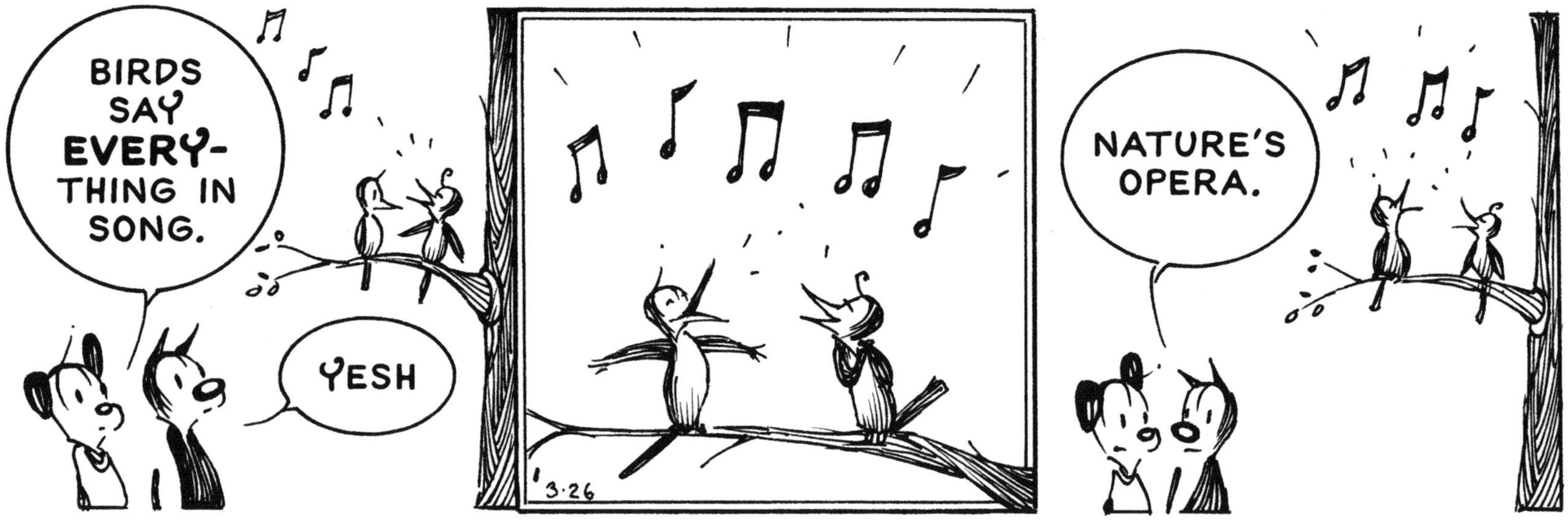
BIRDS SAY EVERY-THING IN SONG.
YESH
NATURE'S OPERA.
3·26

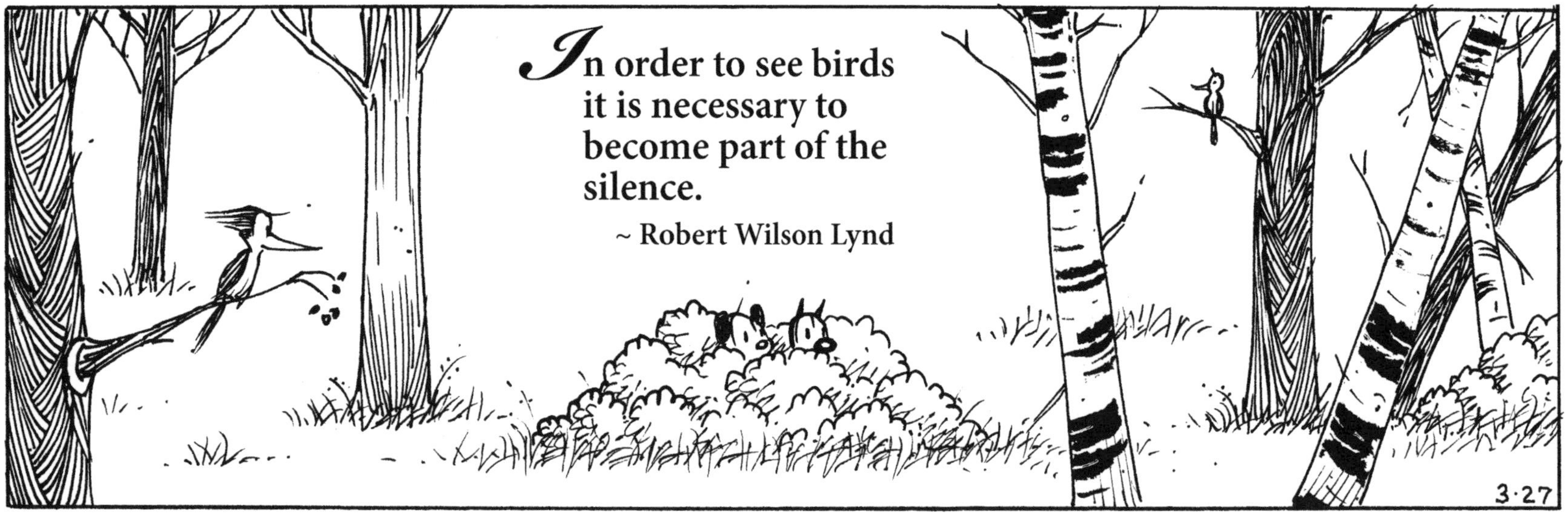
In order to see birds it is necessary to become part of the silence.
~ Robert Wilson Lynd
3·27

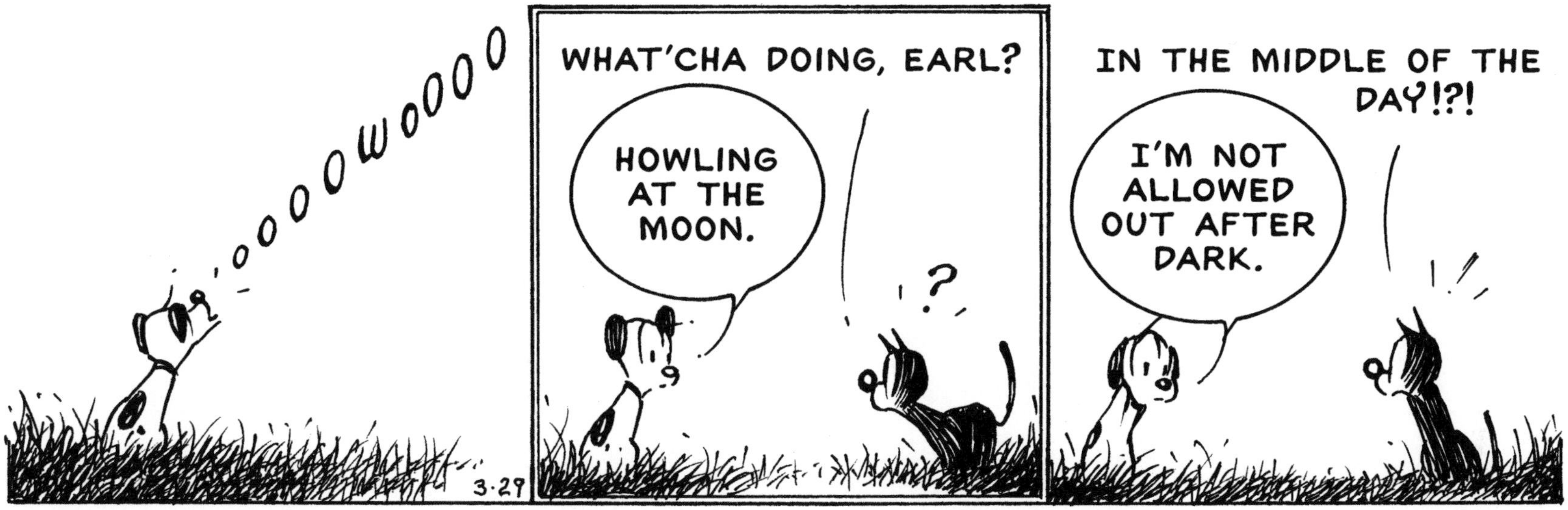

...OOOOOWOOOOO
WHAT'CHA DOING, EARL?
HOWLING AT THE MOON.
IN THE MIDDLE OF THE DAY!?!
I'M NOT ALLOWED OUT AFTER DARK.
3·29

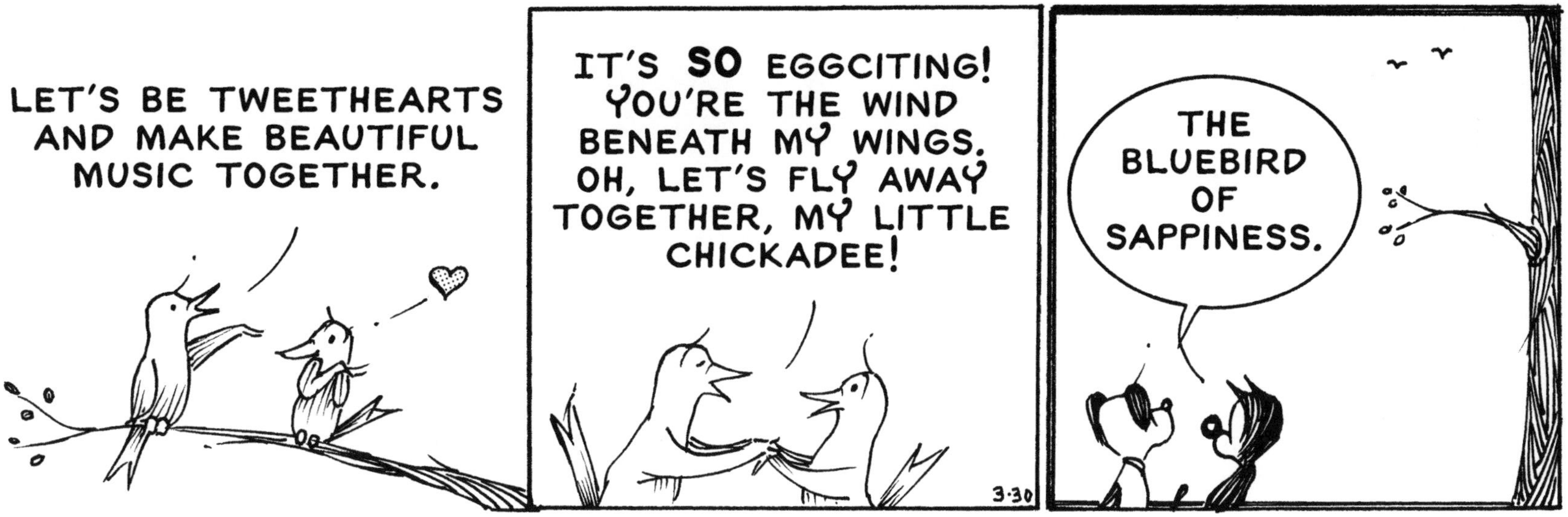

LET'S BE TWEETHEARTS AND MAKE BEAUTIFUL MUSIC TOGETHER.
IT'S **SO** EGGCITING! YOU'RE THE WIND BENEATH MY WINGS. OH, LET'S FLY AWAY TOGETHER, MY LITTLE CHICKADEE!
3·30
THE BLUEBIRD OF SAPPINESS.

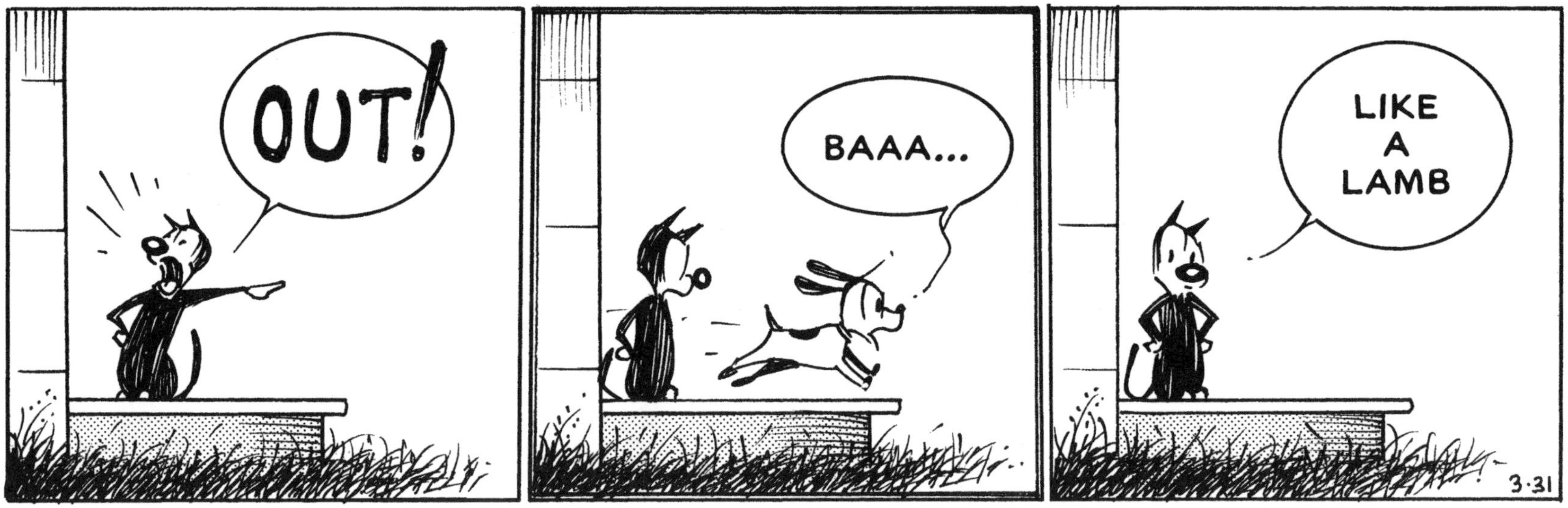
OUT!
BAAA...
LIKE A LAMB
3·31

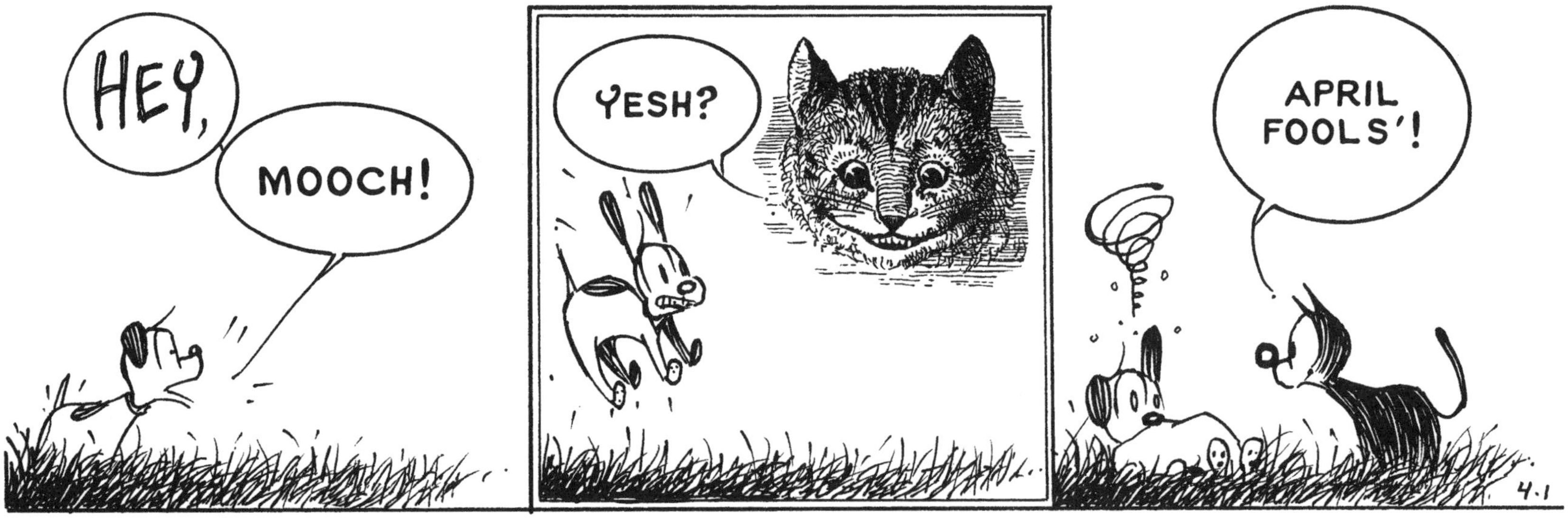
HEY,
MOOCH!
YESH?
APRIL FOOLS'!
4·1

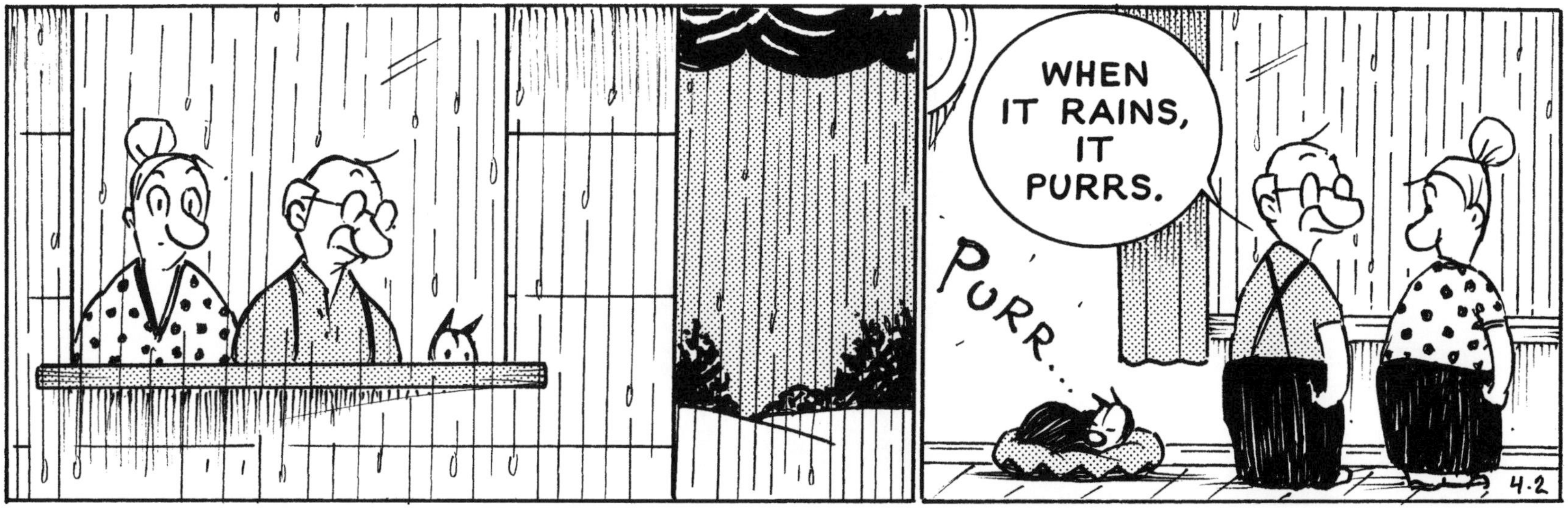
WHEN IT RAINS, IT PURRS.
PURR....
4·2

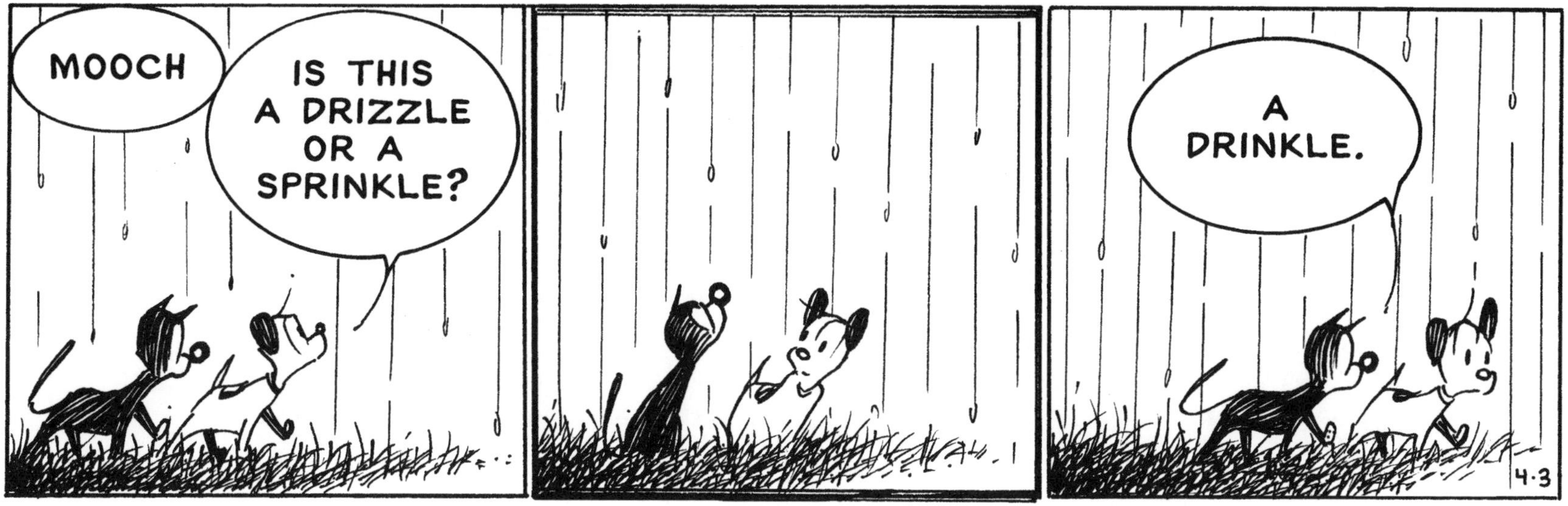
MOOCH
IS THIS A DRIZZLE OR A SPRINKLE?
A DRINKLE.
4·3

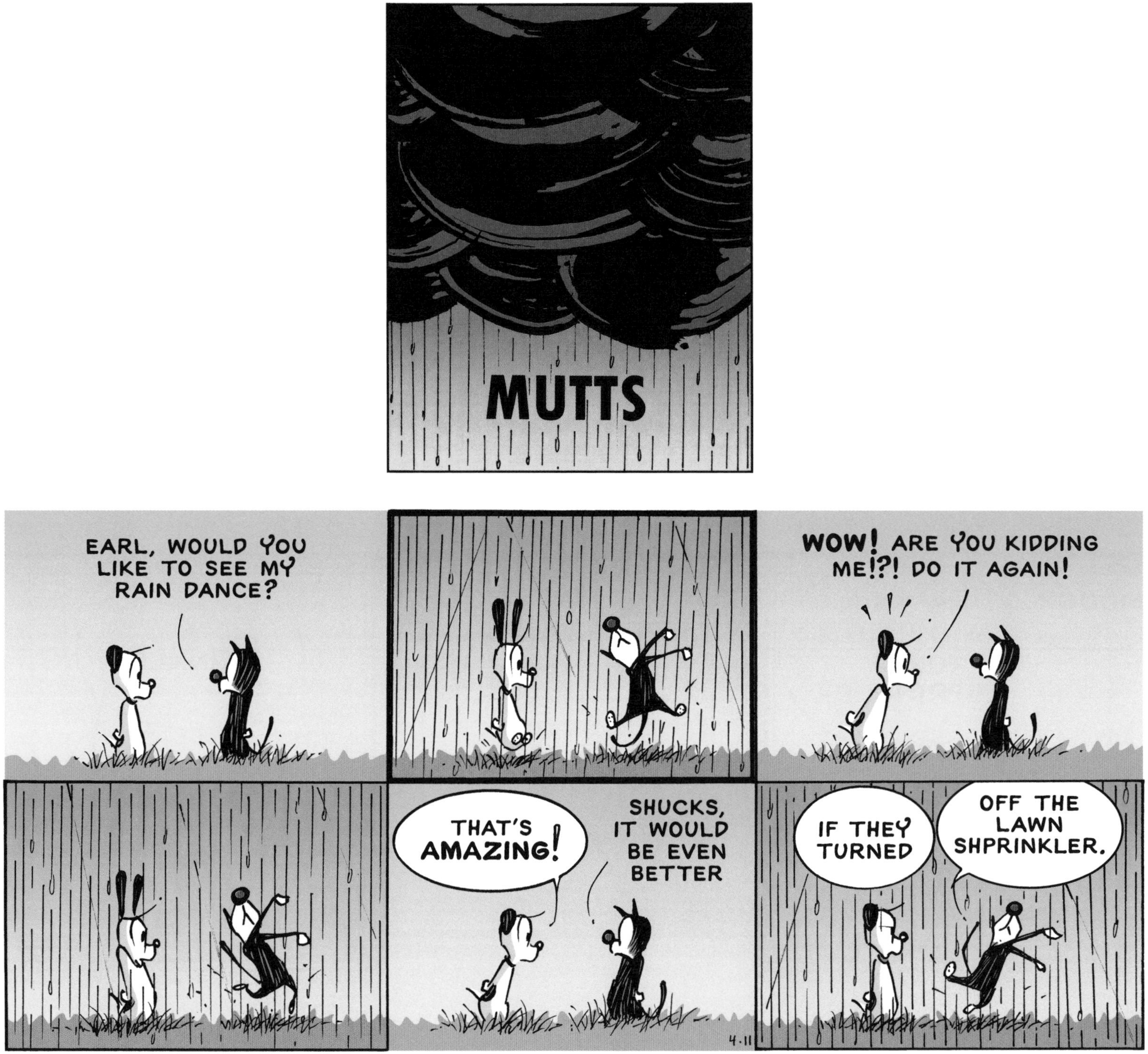
MUTTS
EARL, WOULD YOU LIKE TO SEE MY RAIN DANCE?
WOW! ARE YOU KIDDING ME!?! DO IT AGAIN!
THAT'S AMAZING!
SHUCKS, IT WOULD BE EVEN BETTER
IF THEY TURNED
OFF THE LAWN SHPRINKLER.
4·11

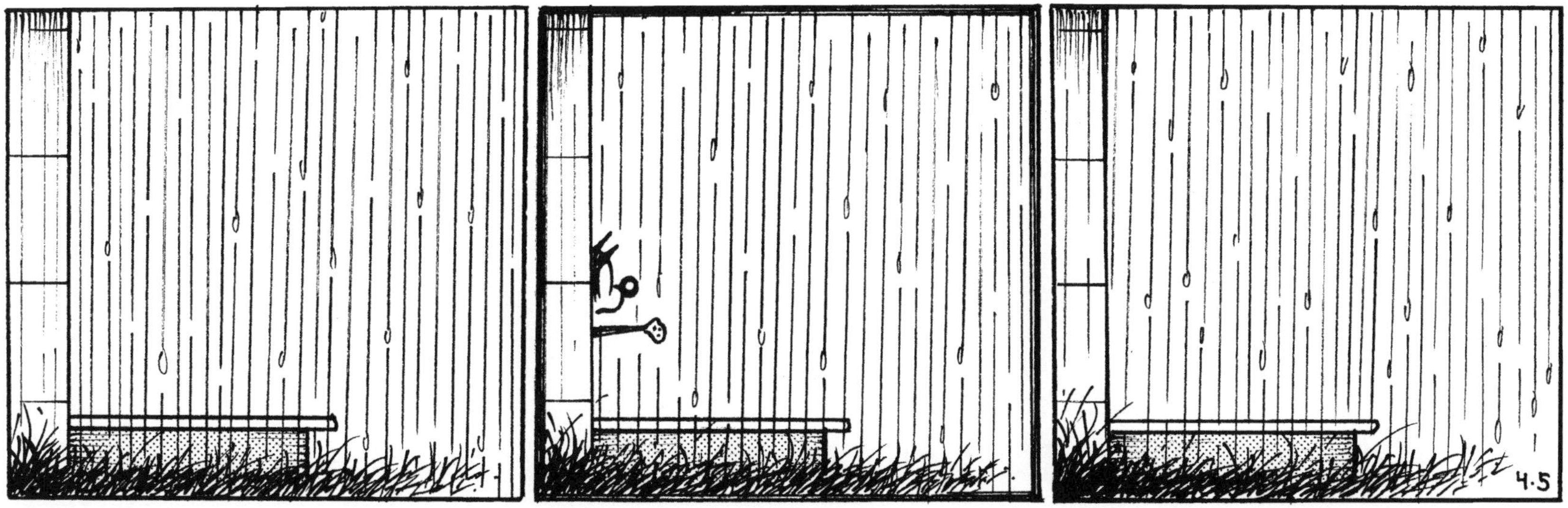
4·5

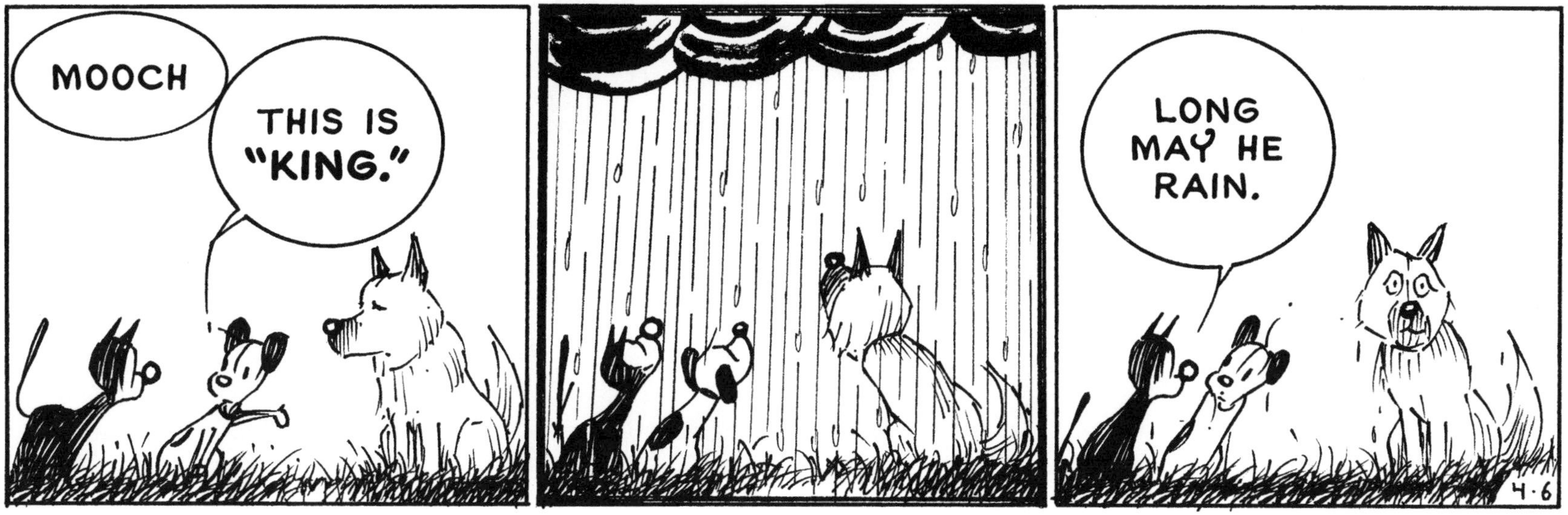
MOOCH
THIS IS "KING."
LONG MAY HE RAIN.
4·6

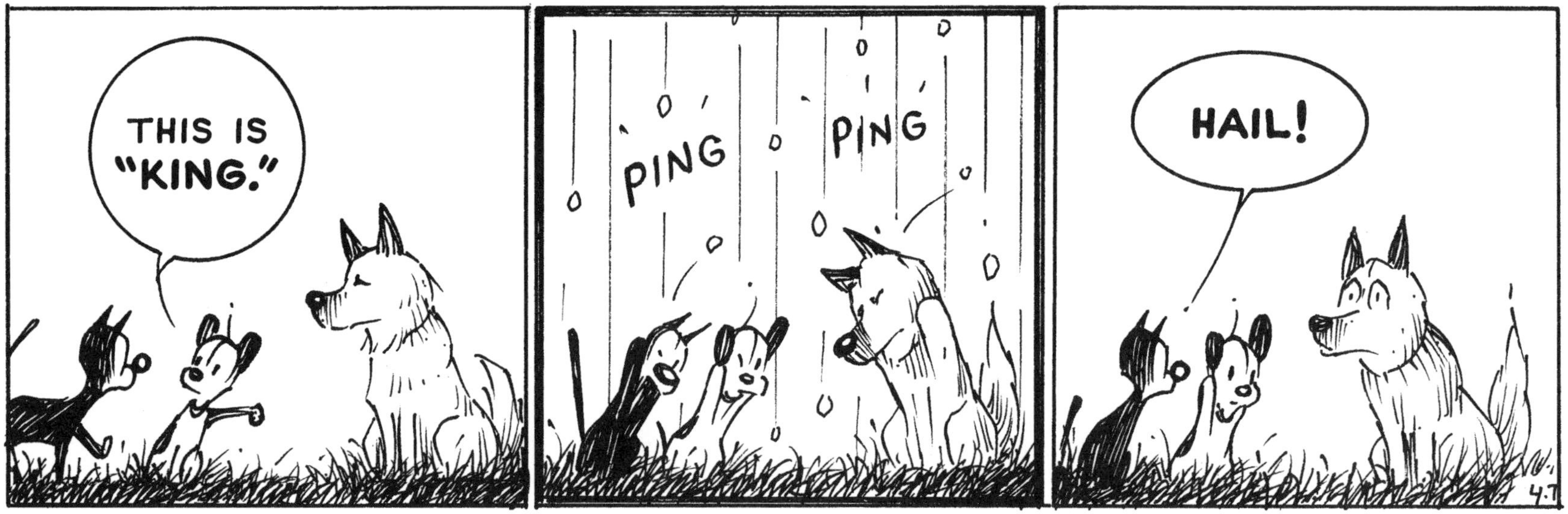
THIS IS "KING."
PING PING
HAIL!
4.7

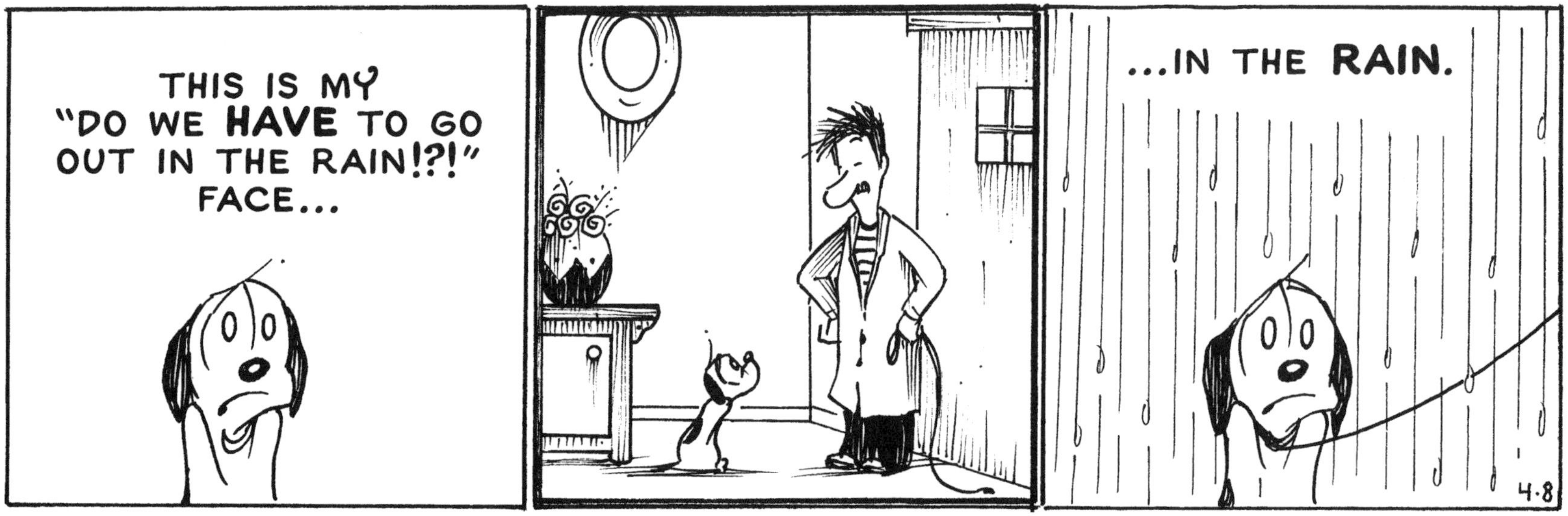
THIS IS MY "DO WE HAVE TO GO OUT IN THE RAIN!?!" FACE...
...IN THE RAIN.
4.8

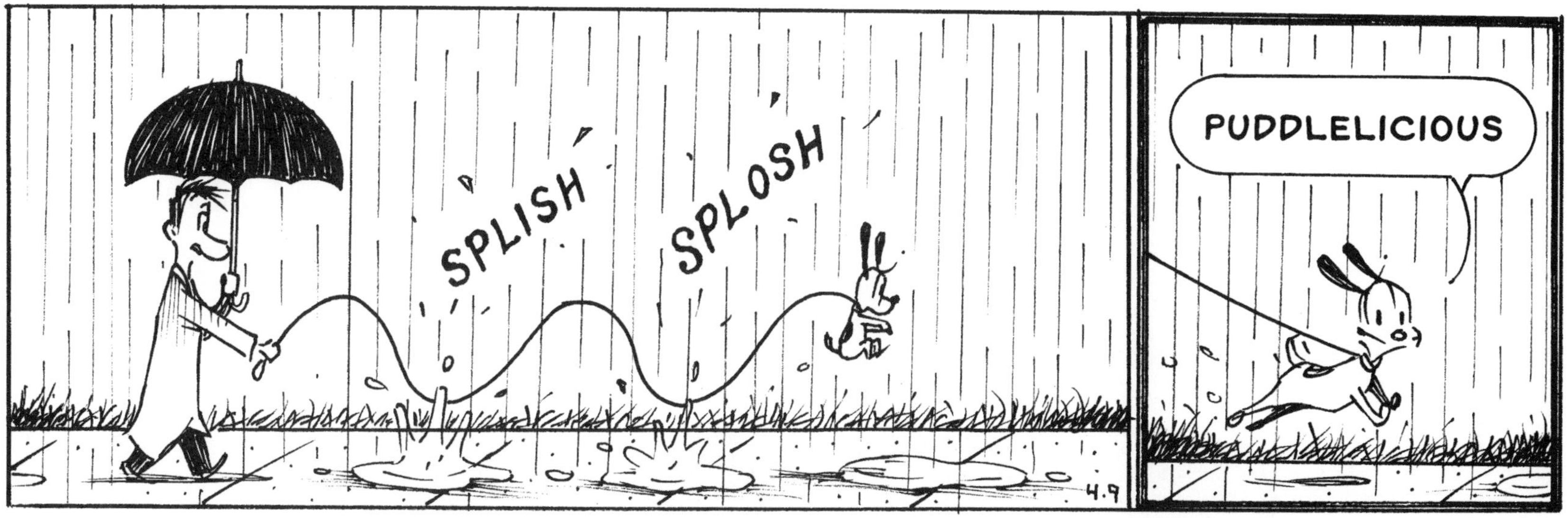
SPLISH
SPLOSH
4.9
PUDDLELICIOUS

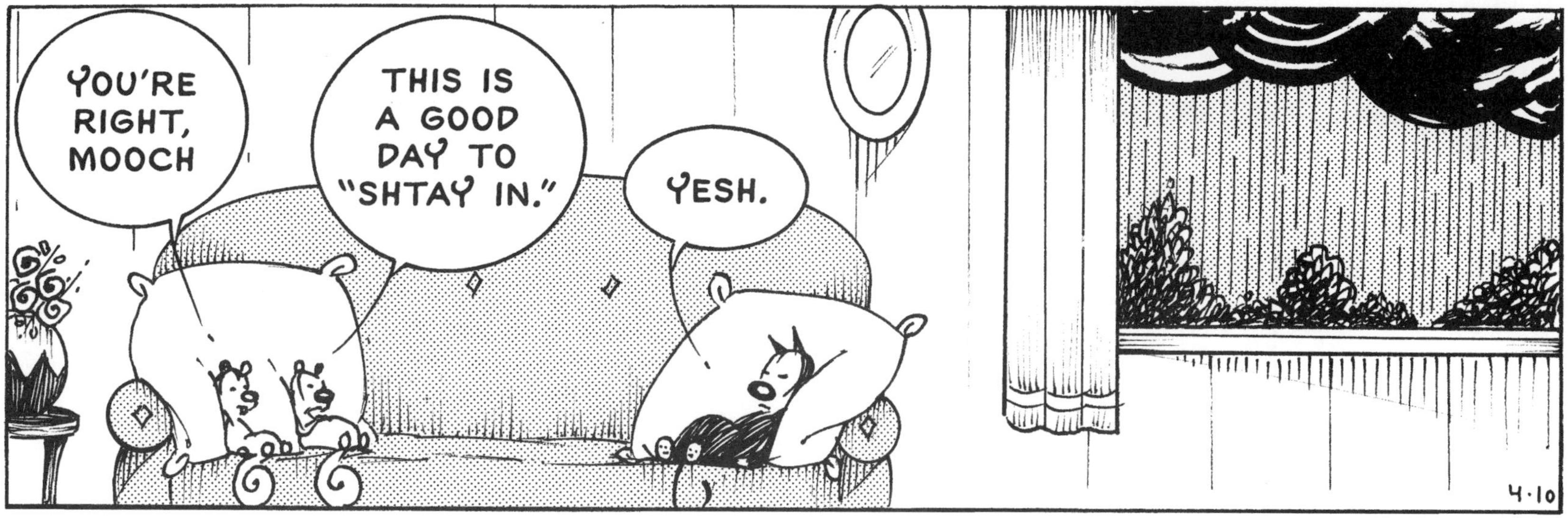
YOU'RE RIGHT, MOOCH
THIS IS A GOOD DAY TO "SHTAY IN."
YESH.
4.10

SOMETHING ELSE-
MUTTS

By Patrick McDonnell

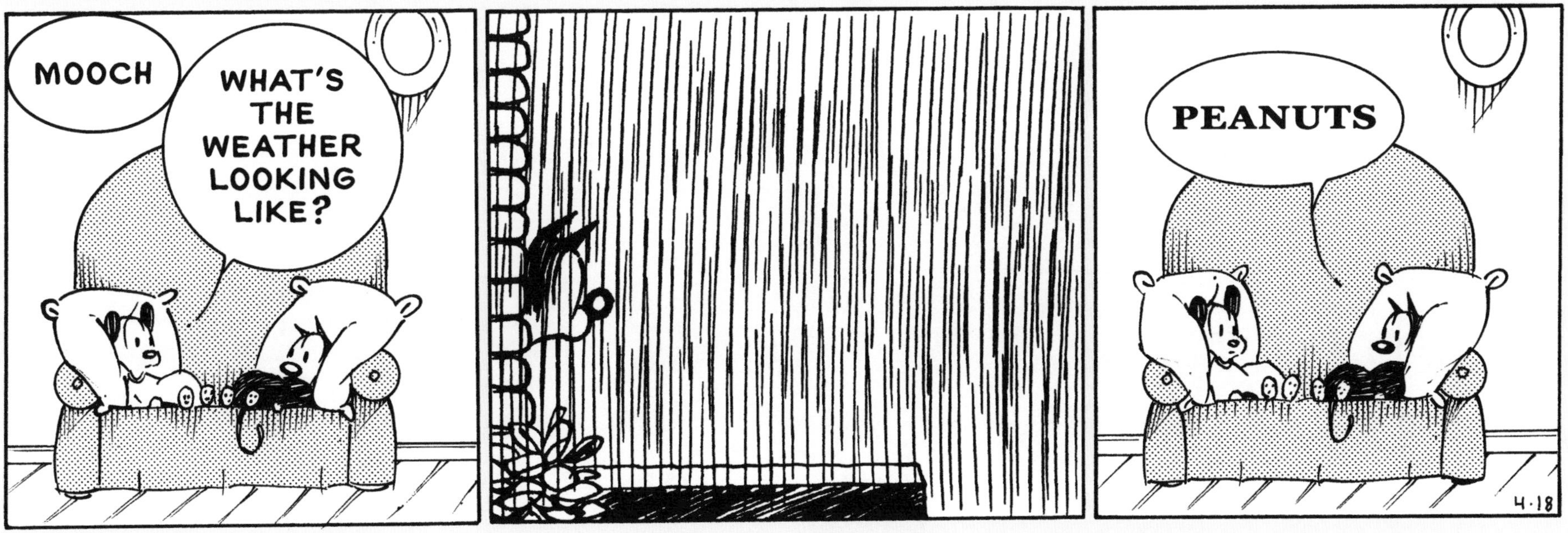
MOOCH
WHAT'S THE WEATHER LOOKING LIKE?
PEANUTS
4·18

MUTTS

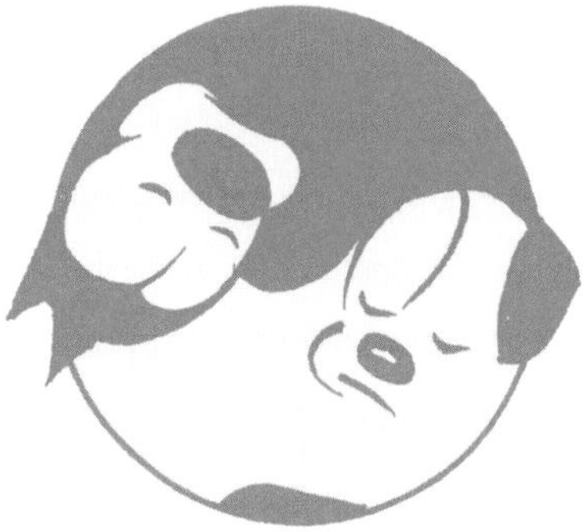

PATRICK McDONNELL

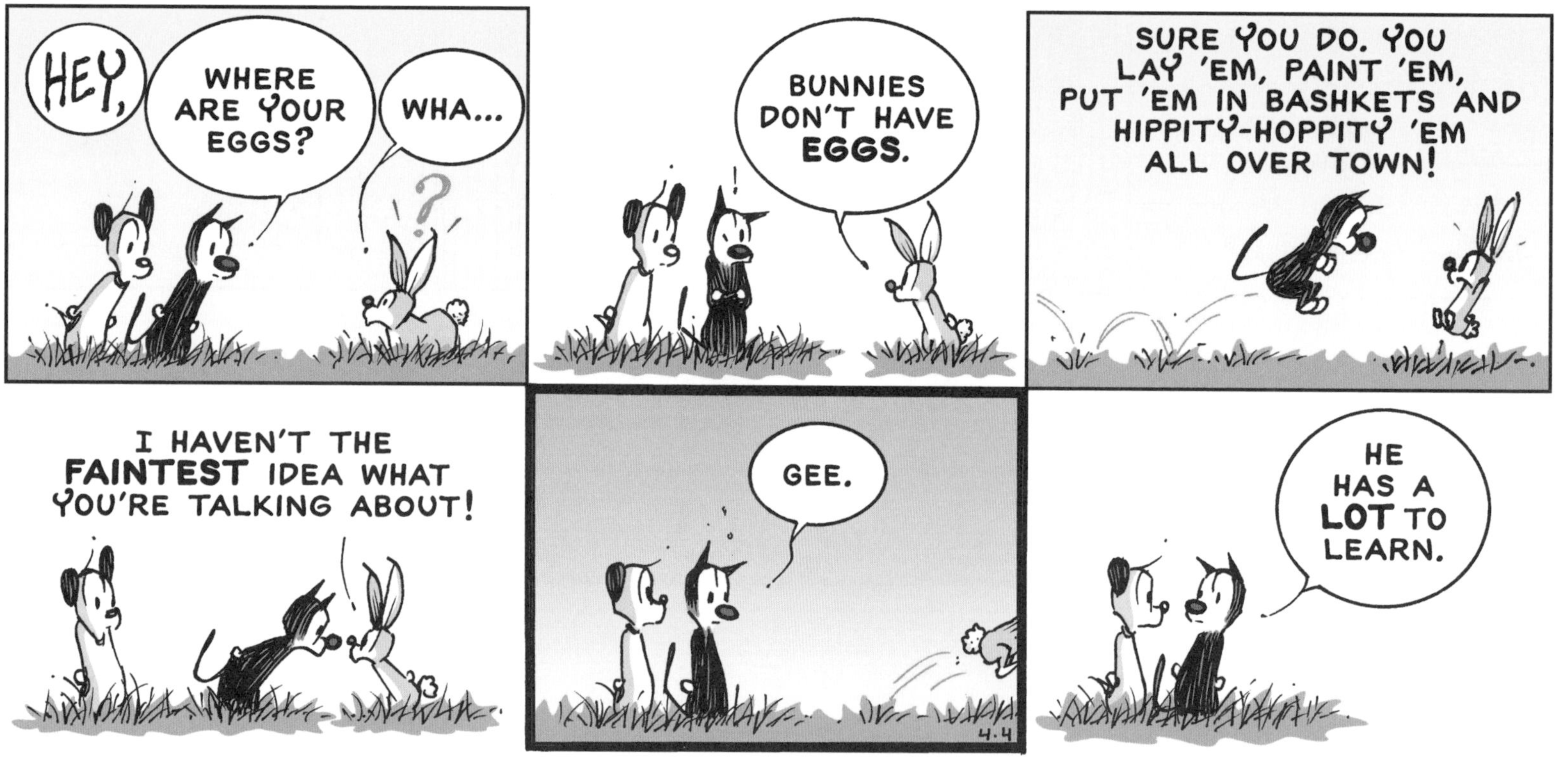
HEY,
WHERE ARE YOUR EGGS?
WHA...
BUNNIES DON'T HAVE EGGS.
SURE YOU DO. YOU LAY 'EM, PAINT 'EM, PUT 'EM IN BASHKETS AND HIPPITY-HOPPITY 'EM ALL OVER TOWN!
I HAVEN'T THE FAINTEST IDEA WHAT YOU'RE TALKING ABOUT!
GEE.
4.4
HE HAS A LOT TO LEARN.

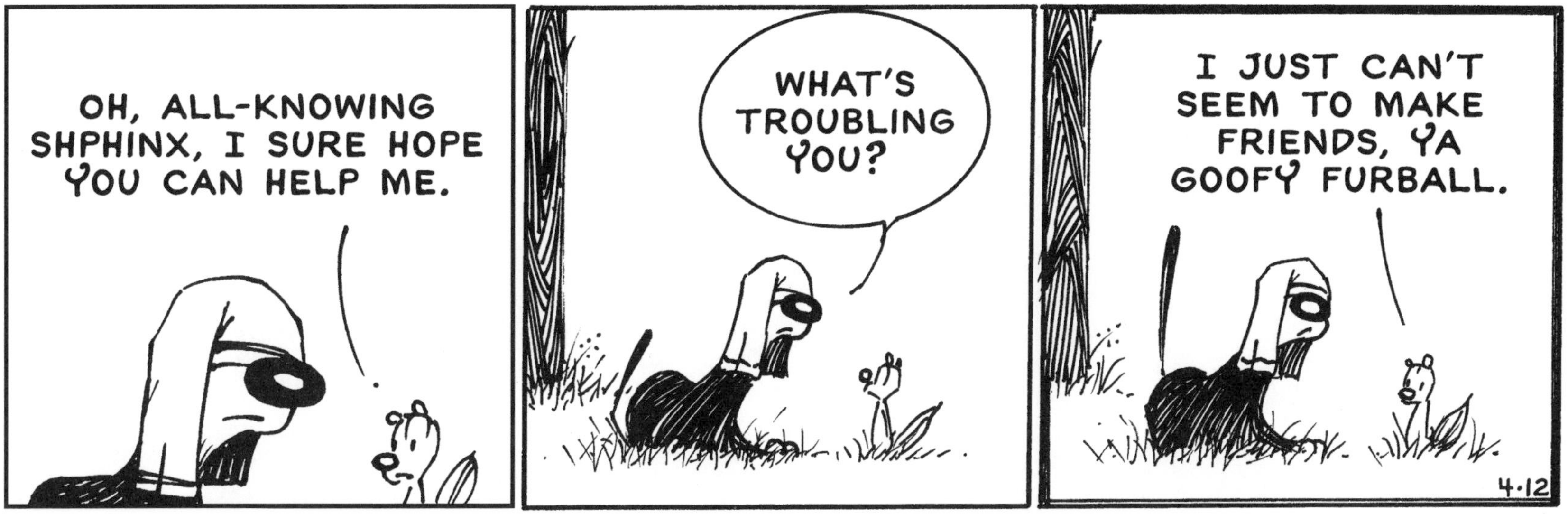
OH, ALL-KNOWING SHPHINX, I SURE HOPE YOU CAN HELP ME.
WHAT'S TROUBLING YOU?
I JUST CAN'T SEEM TO MAKE FRIENDS, YA GOOFY FURBALL.
4·12

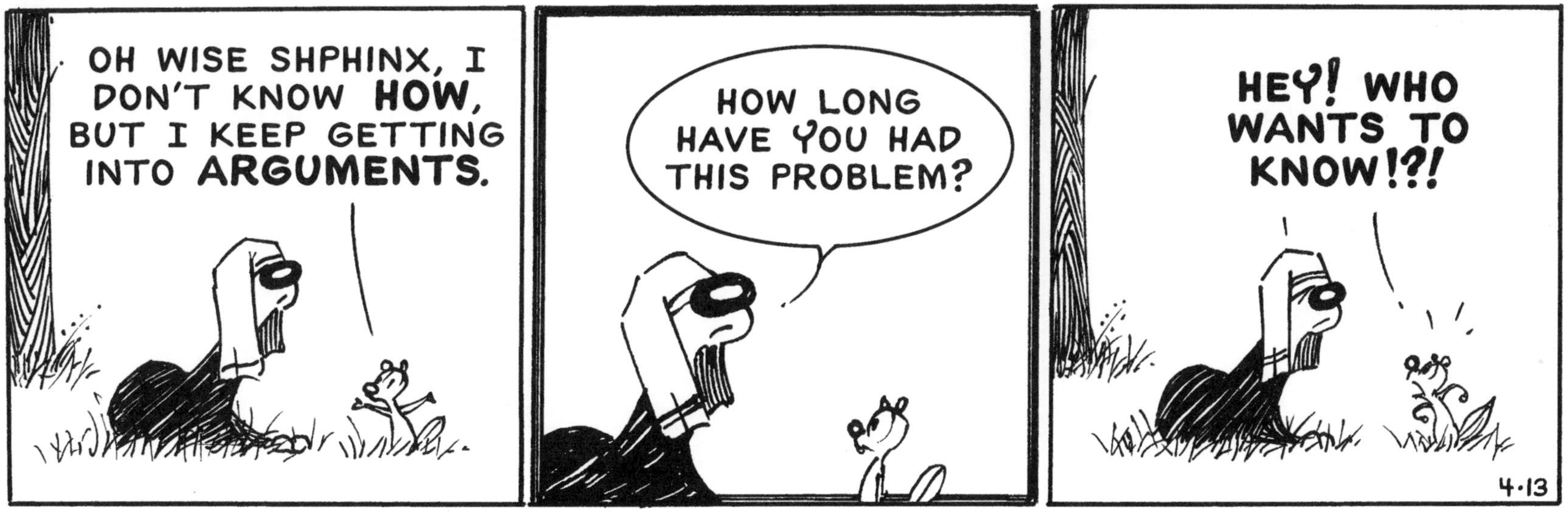
OH WISE SHPHINX, I DON'T KNOW **HOW**, BUT I KEEP GETTING INTO **ARGUMENTS**.
HOW LONG HAVE YOU HAD THIS PROBLEM?
HEY! WHO WANTS TO KNOW!?!
4·13

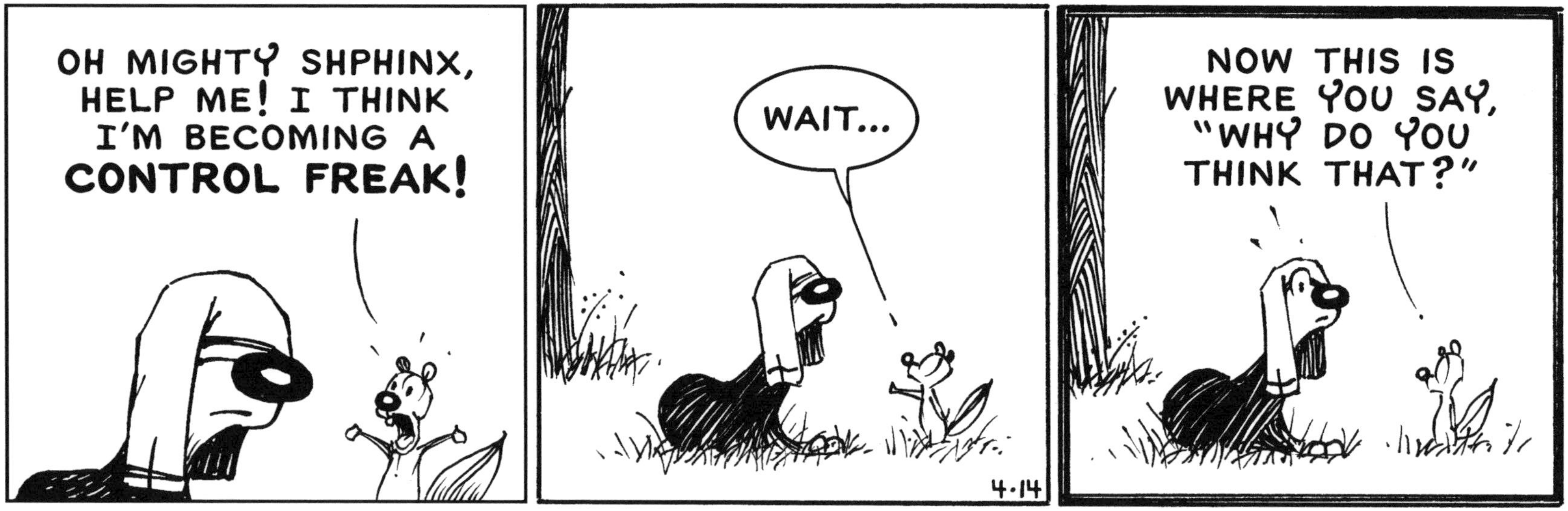
OH MIGHTY SHPHINX, HELP ME! I THINK I'M BECOMING A **CONTROL FREAK!**
WAIT...
NOW THIS IS WHERE YOU SAY, "WHY DO YOU THINK THAT?"
4·14

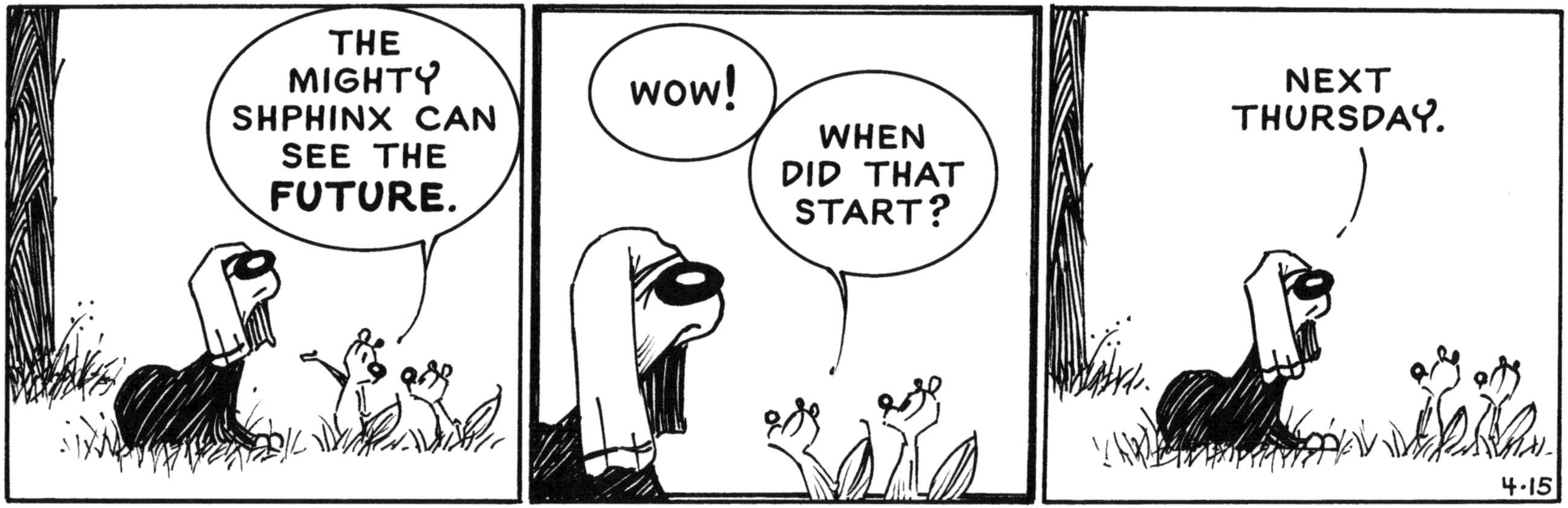
THE MIGHTY SHPHINX CAN SEE THE **FUTURE.**
WOW!
WHEN DID THAT START?
NEXT THURSDAY.
4·15

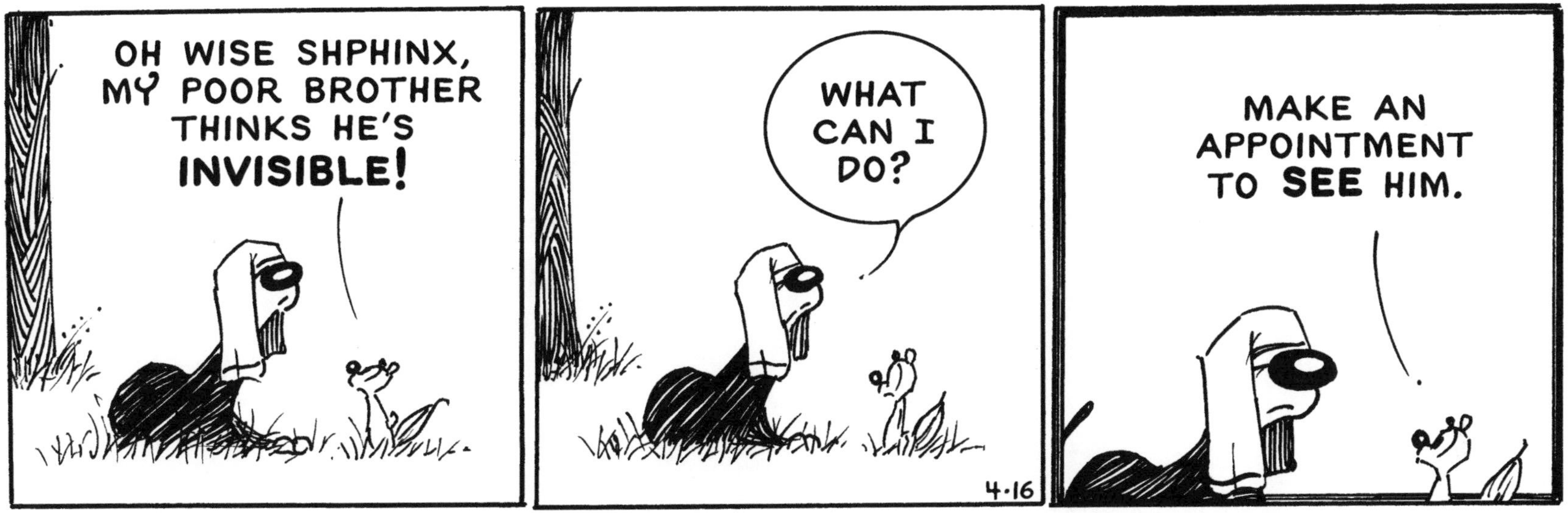
OH WISE SHPHINX, MY POOR BROTHER THINKS HE'S **INVISIBLE!**
WHAT CAN I DO?
4·16
MAKE AN APPOINTMENT TO **SEE** HIM.

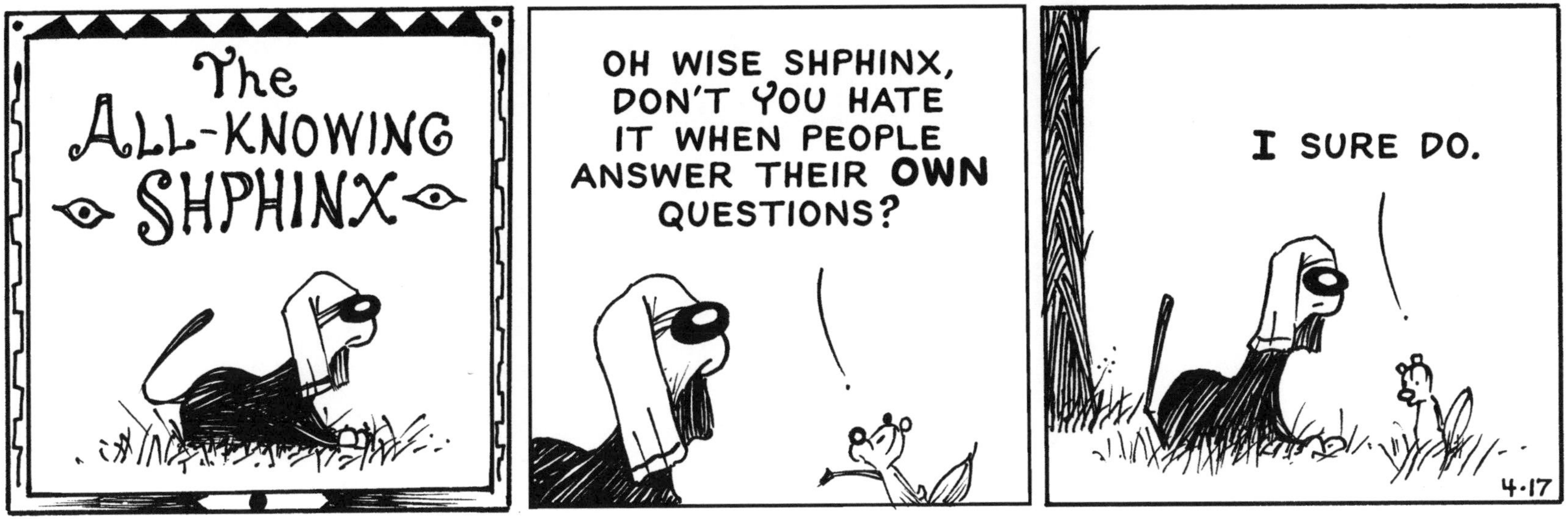
The ALL-KNOWING SHPHINX
OH WISE SHPHINX, DON'T YOU HATE IT WHEN PEOPLE ANSWER THEIR **OWN** QUESTIONS?
I SURE DO.
4·17

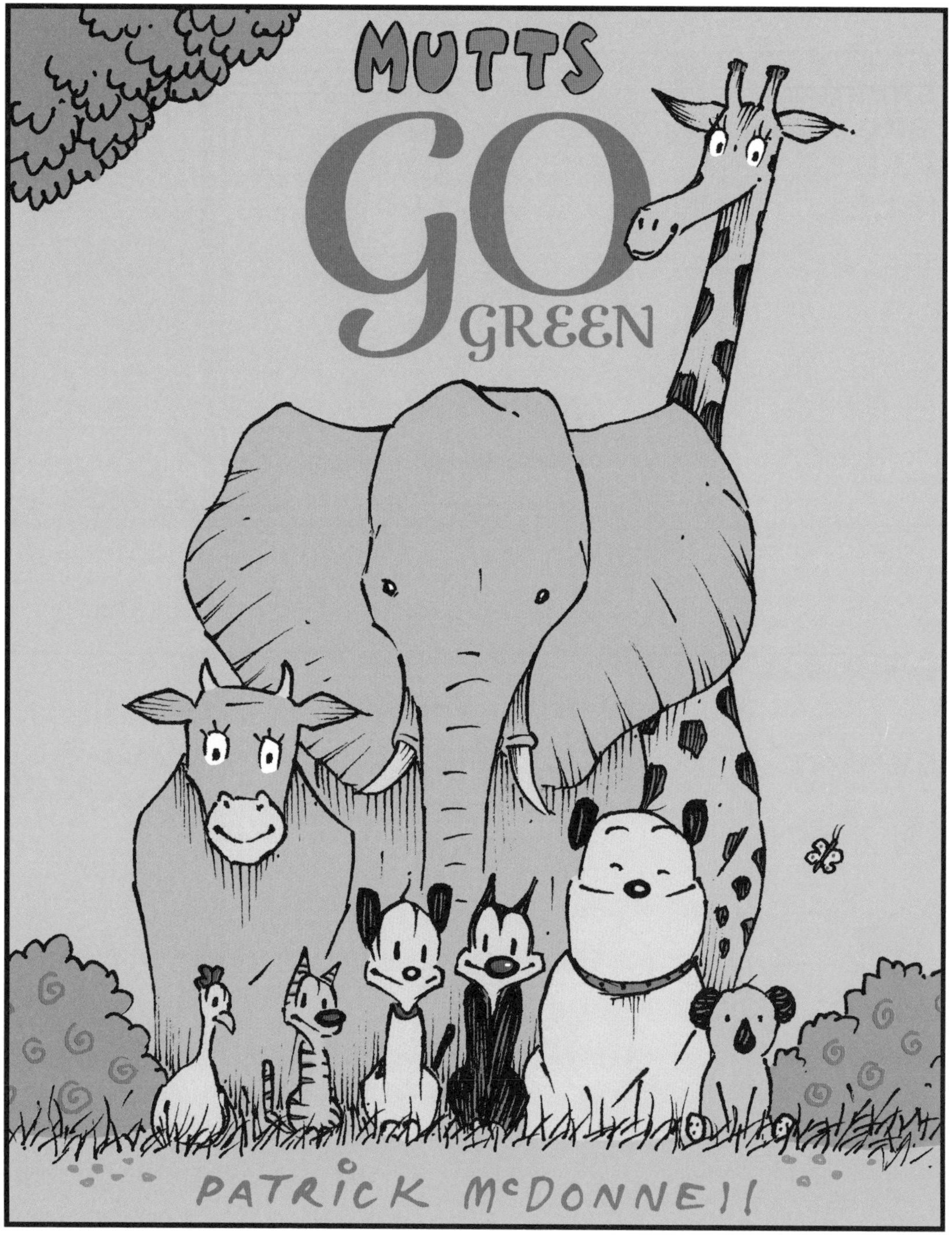
MUTTS
GO
GREEN
PATRICK McDONNELL

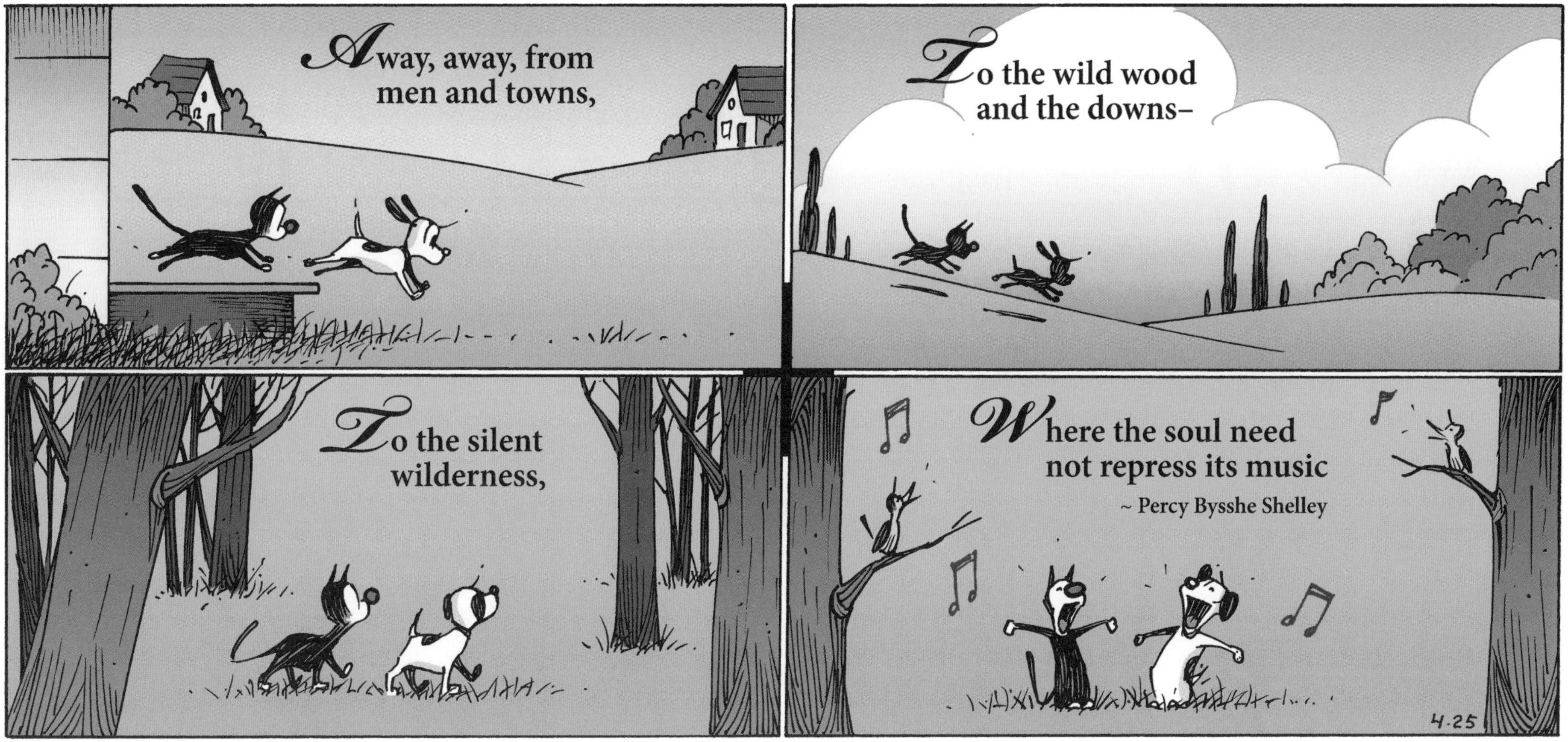
Away, away, from men and towns,
To the wild wood and the downs-
To the silent wilderness,
Where the soul need not repress its music
~ Percy Bysshe Shelley
4.25

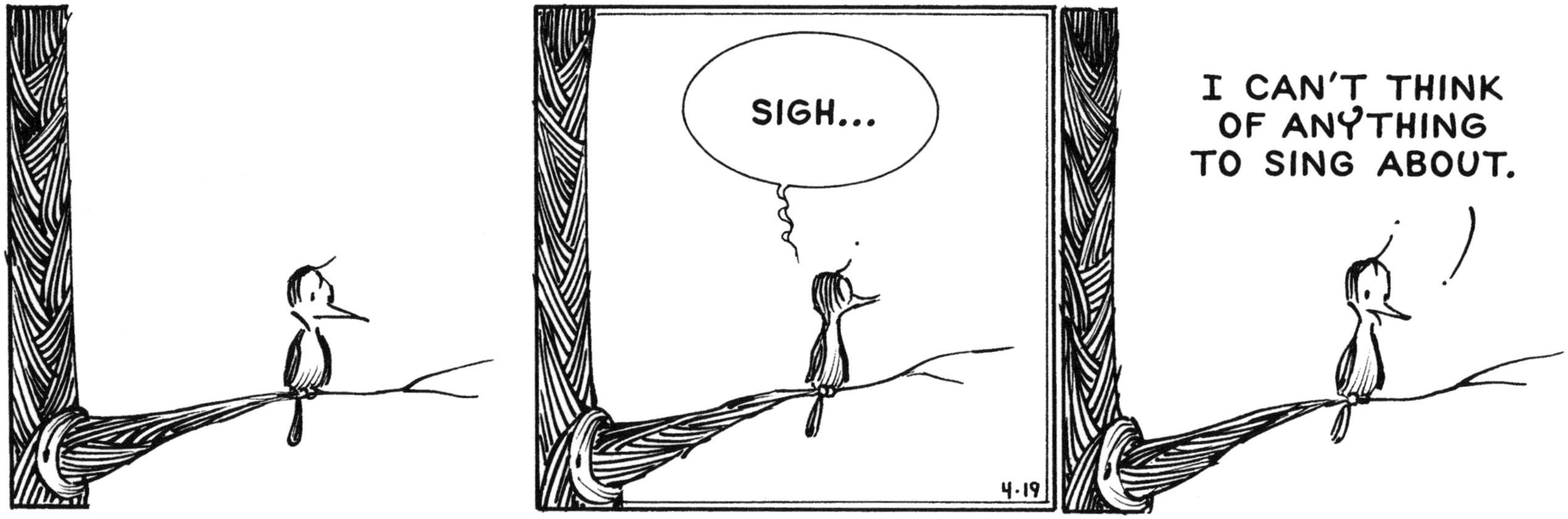
SIGH...
I CAN'T THINK OF ANYTHING TO SING ABOUT.
4·19

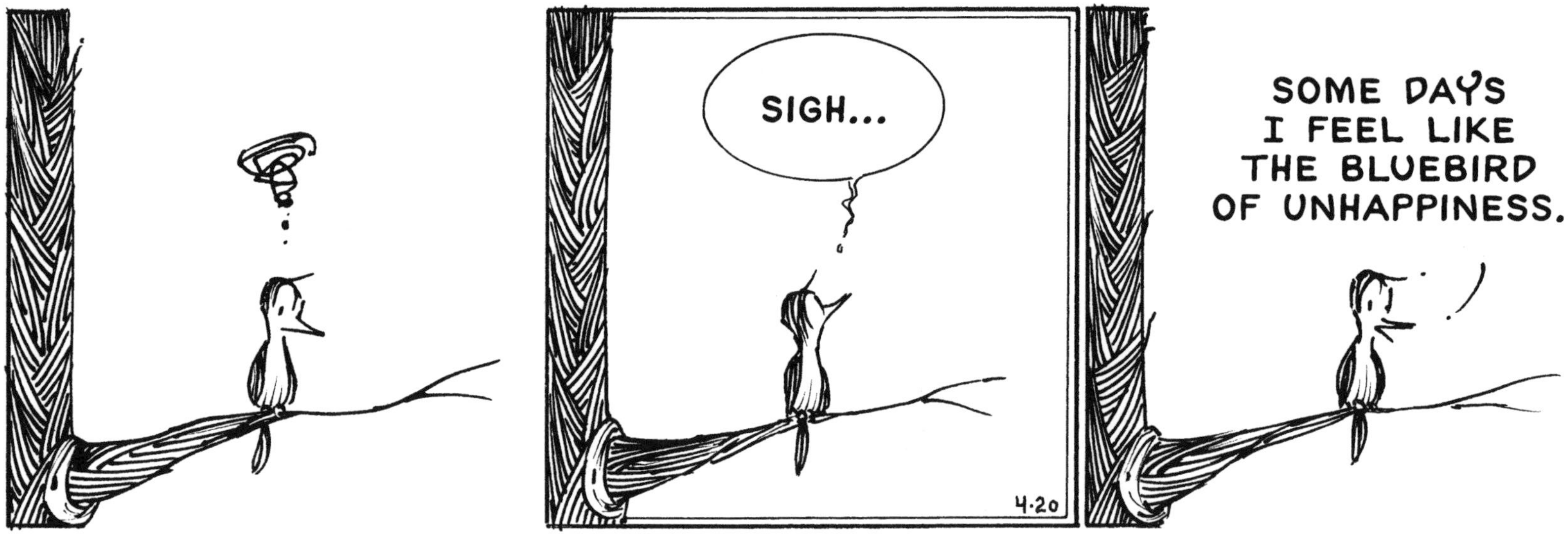
SIGH...
SOME DAYS I FEEL LIKE THE BLUEBIRD OF UNHAPPINESS.
4·20

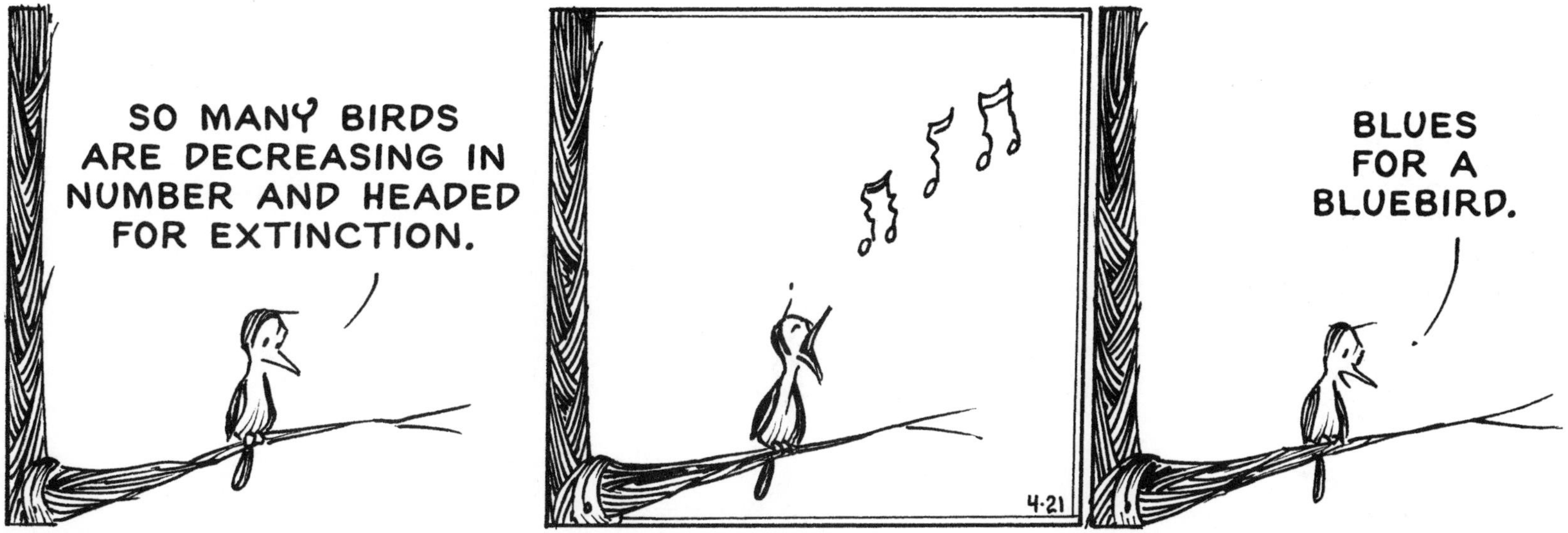
SO MANY BIRDS ARE DECREASING IN NUMBER AND HEADED FOR EXTINCTION.
4·21
BLUES FOR A BLUEBIRD.

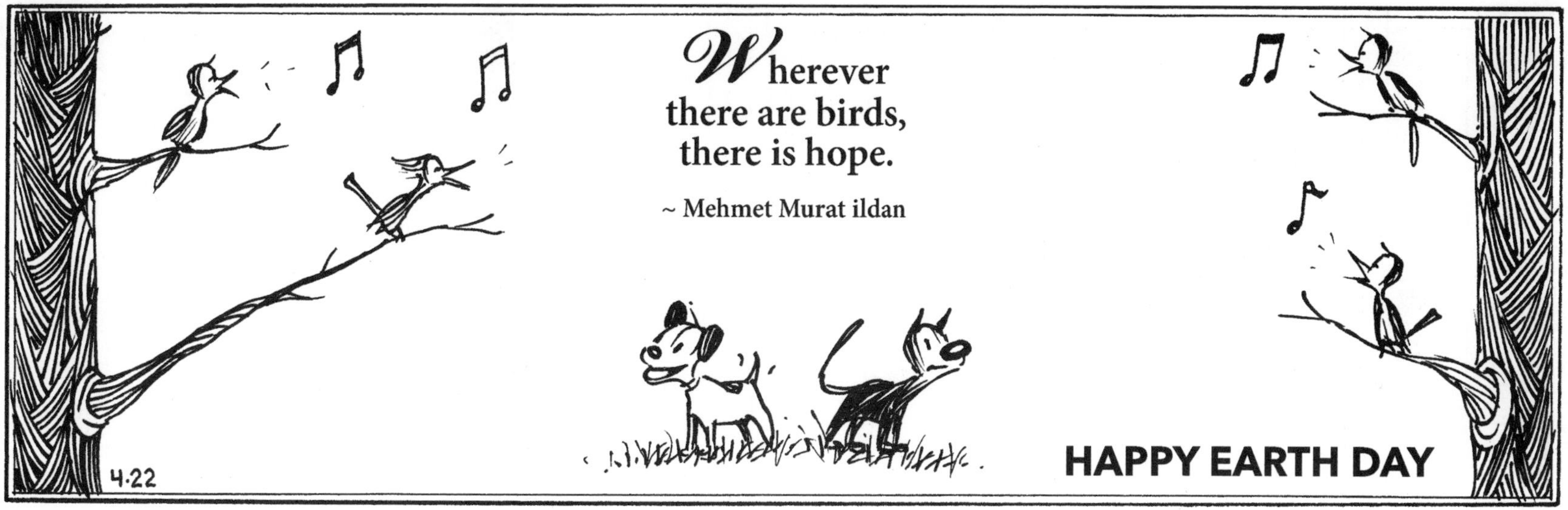
Wherever there are birds, there is hope.
~ Mehmet Murat ildan
4·22
HAPPY EARTH DAY

WITH STRONG CONSERVATION EFFORTS **MANY** BIRDS CAN BE **SAVED** FROM EXTINCTION. WE **MUST** PREVAIL!

4.23

PREACHING TO THE CHOIR.

MUSIC FOR A RAINY DAY.

4.24

To the wild wood
and the downs—

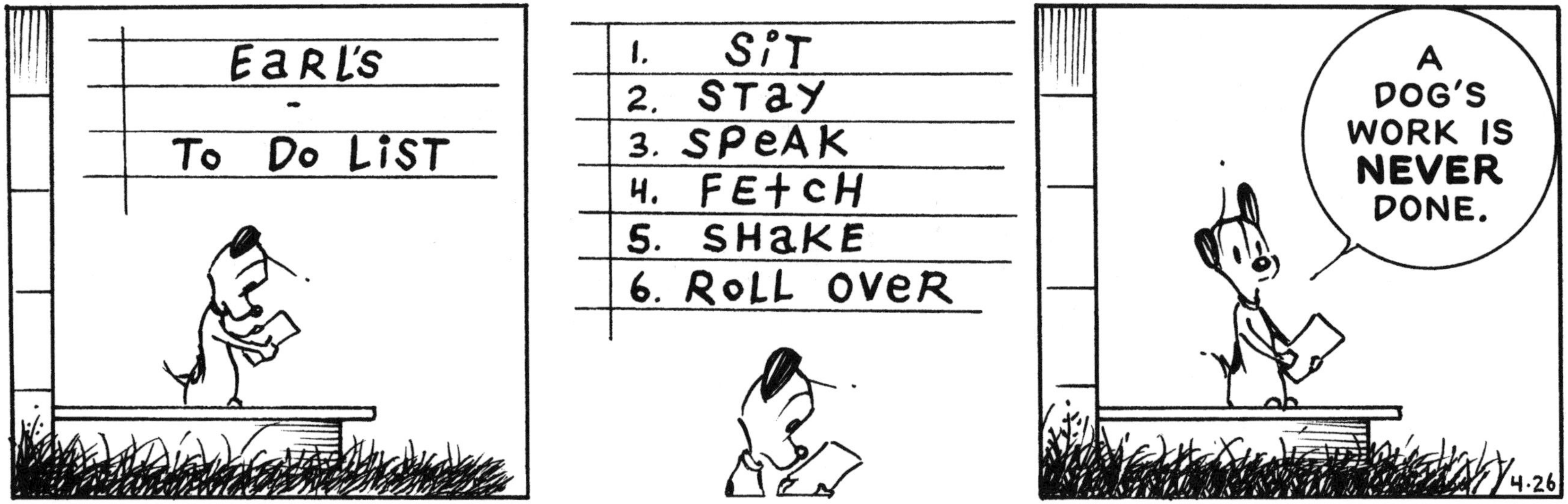
EarL's
-
To Do LisT
1. SiT
2. STay
3. SPeAK
4. FEtcH
5. SHaKE
6. RoLL OVeR
A DOG'S WORK IS **NEVER** DONE.
4·26

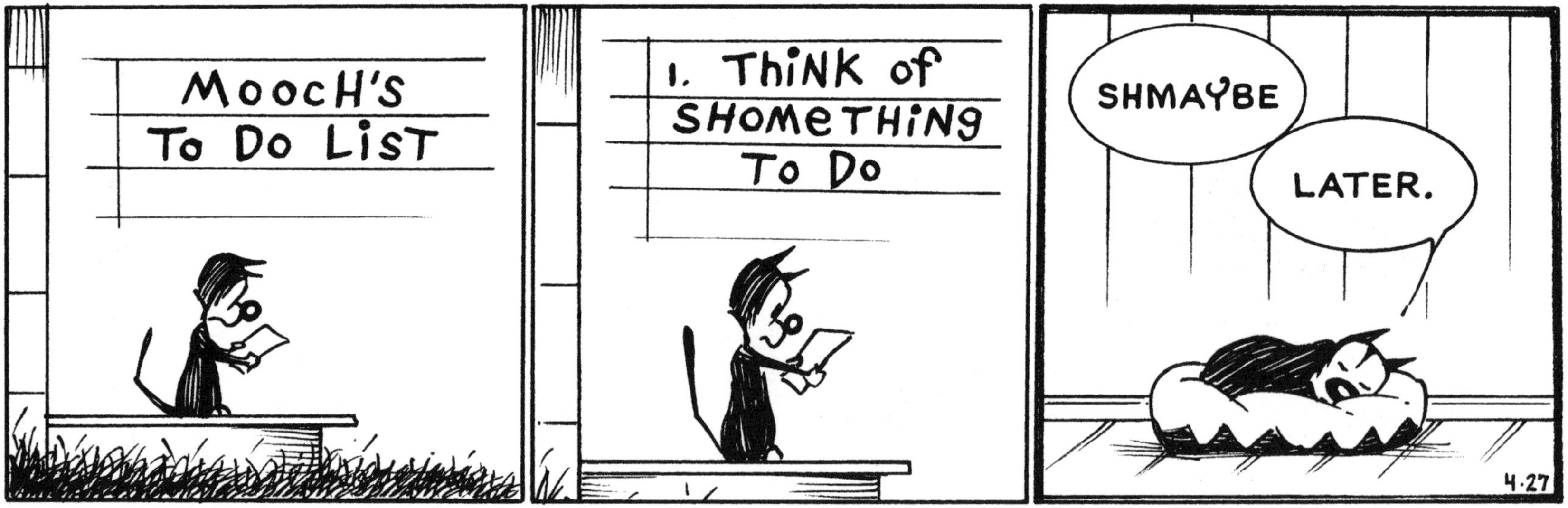
MoocH's
To Do LisT
1. ThiNK of SHOMeTHiNg To Do
SHMAYBE
LATER.
4·27

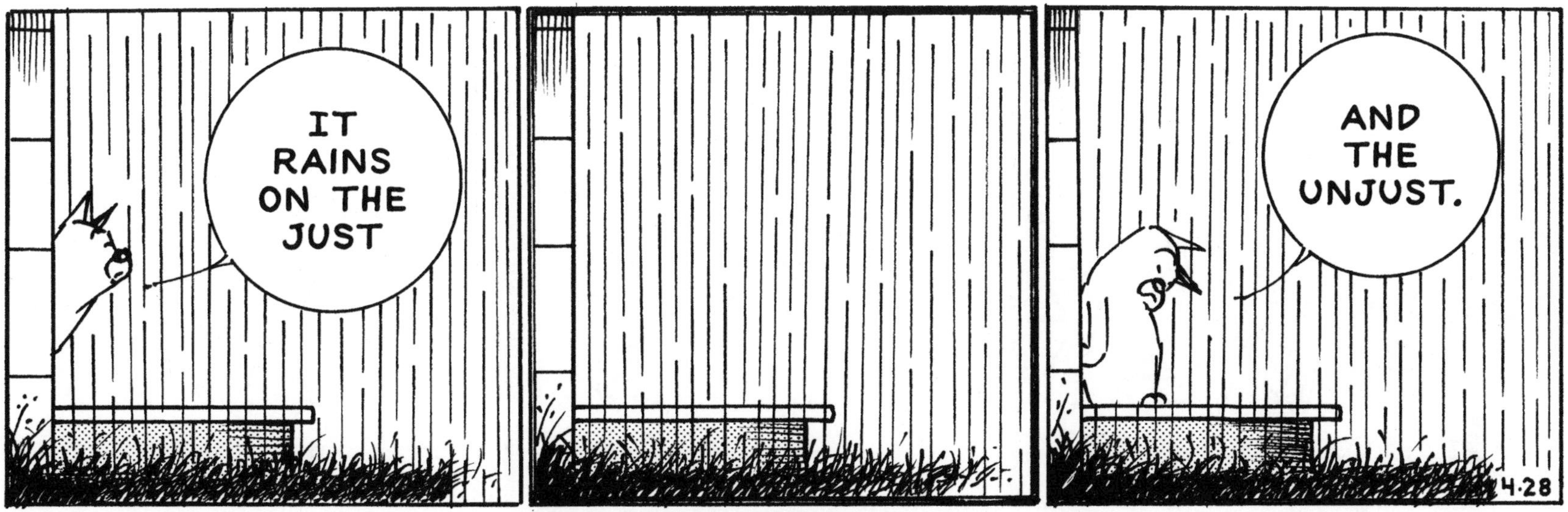
IT RAINS ON THE JUST
AND THE UNJUST.
4·28

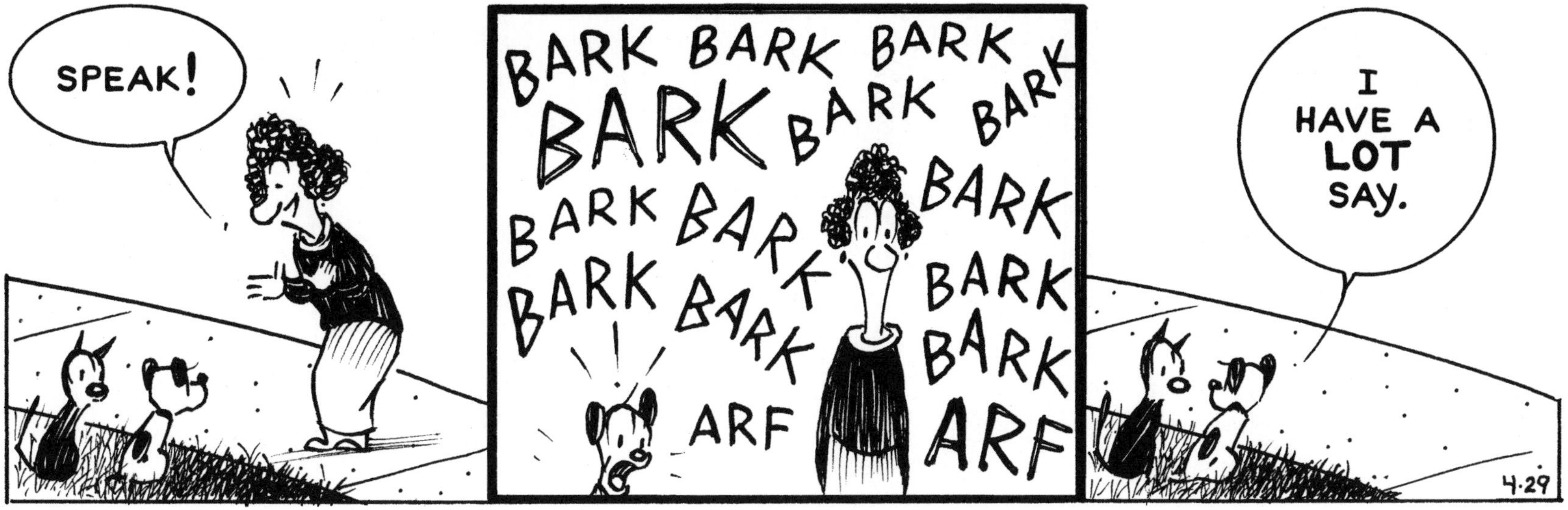
SPEAK!
BARK BARK BARK
BARK BARK BARK
BARK BARK BARK
BARK BARK BARK
BARK BARK BARK
ARF ARF
I HAVE A LOT SAY.
4·29

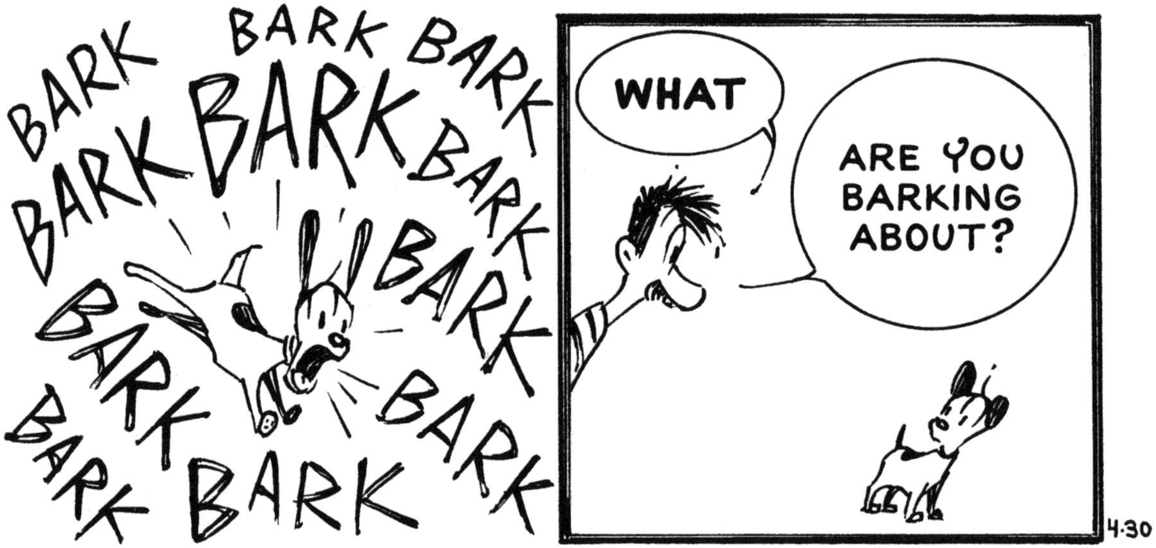
BARK BARK BARK BARK BARK BARK BARK BARK BARK BARK BARK BARK BARK BARK
WHAT
ARE YOU BARKING ABOUT?
EVERYTHING.
4·30

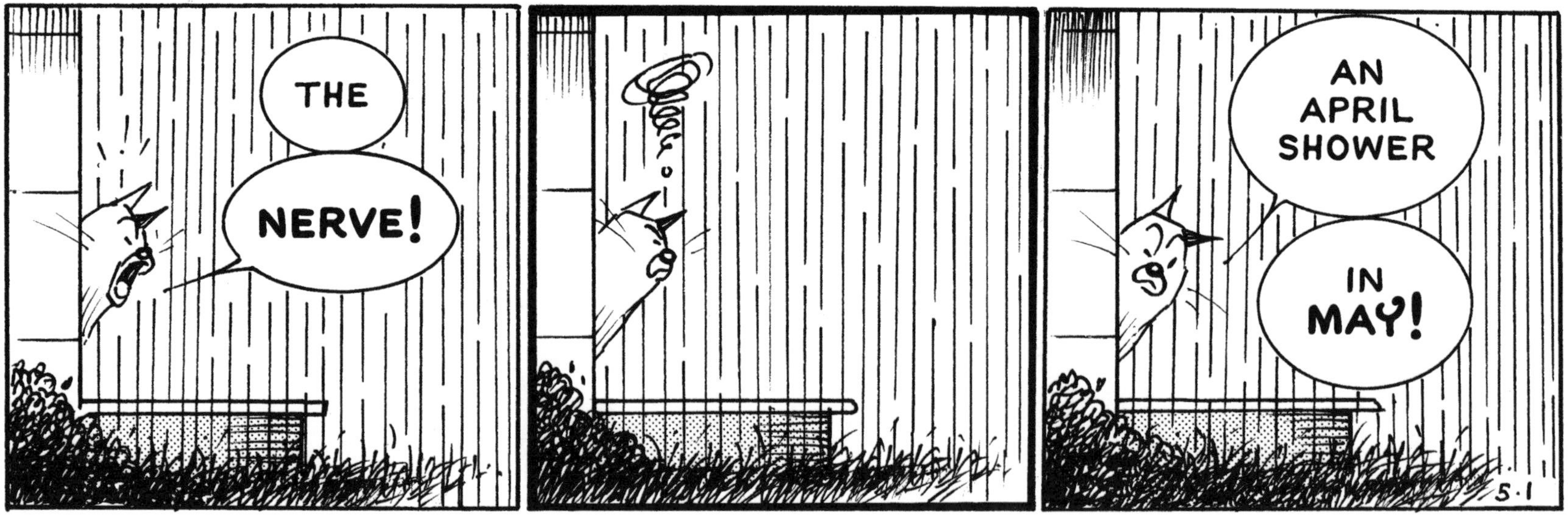
THE
NERVE!
AN APRIL SHOWER
IN MAY!
5·1

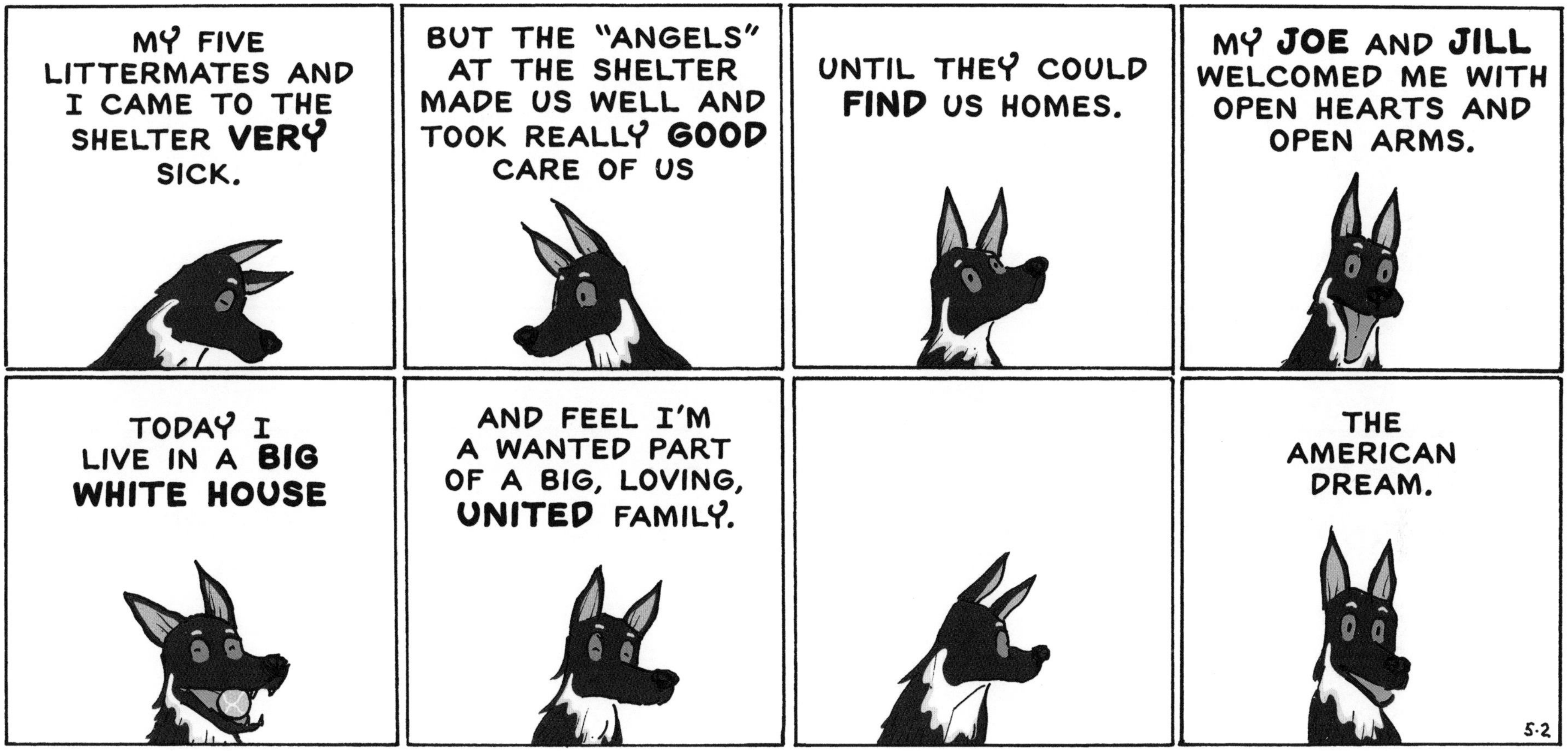
MY FIVE LITTERMATES AND I CAME TO THE SHELTER **VERY** SICK.
BUT THE "ANGELS" AT THE SHELTER MADE US WELL AND TOOK REALLY **GOOD** CARE OF US
UNTIL THEY COULD **FIND** US HOMES.
MY **JOE** AND **JILL** WELCOMED ME WITH OPEN HEARTS AND OPEN ARMS.
TODAY I LIVE IN A **BIG WHITE HOUSE**
AND FEEL I'M A WANTED PART OF A BIG, LOVING, **UNITED** FAMILY.
THE AMERICAN DREAM.
5·2

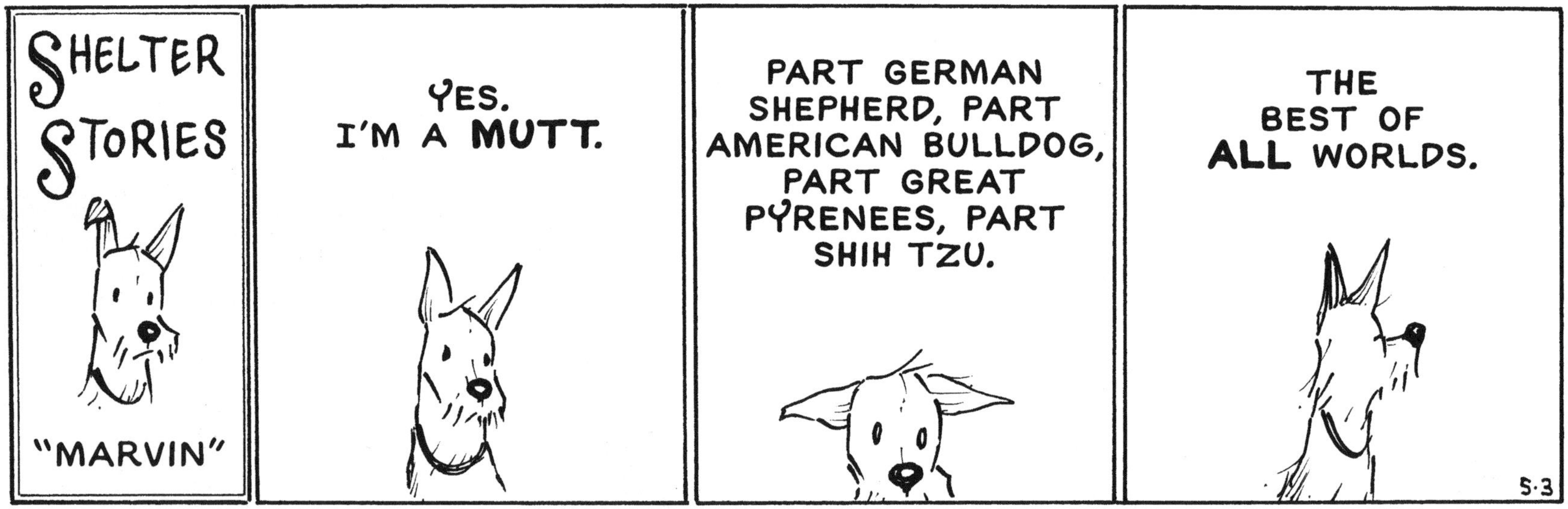
SHELTER STORIES
"MARVIN"
YES. I'M A MUTT.
PART GERMAN SHEPHERD, PART AMERICAN BULLDOG, PART GREAT PYRENEES, PART SHIH TZU.
THE BEST OF ALL WORLDS.
5·3

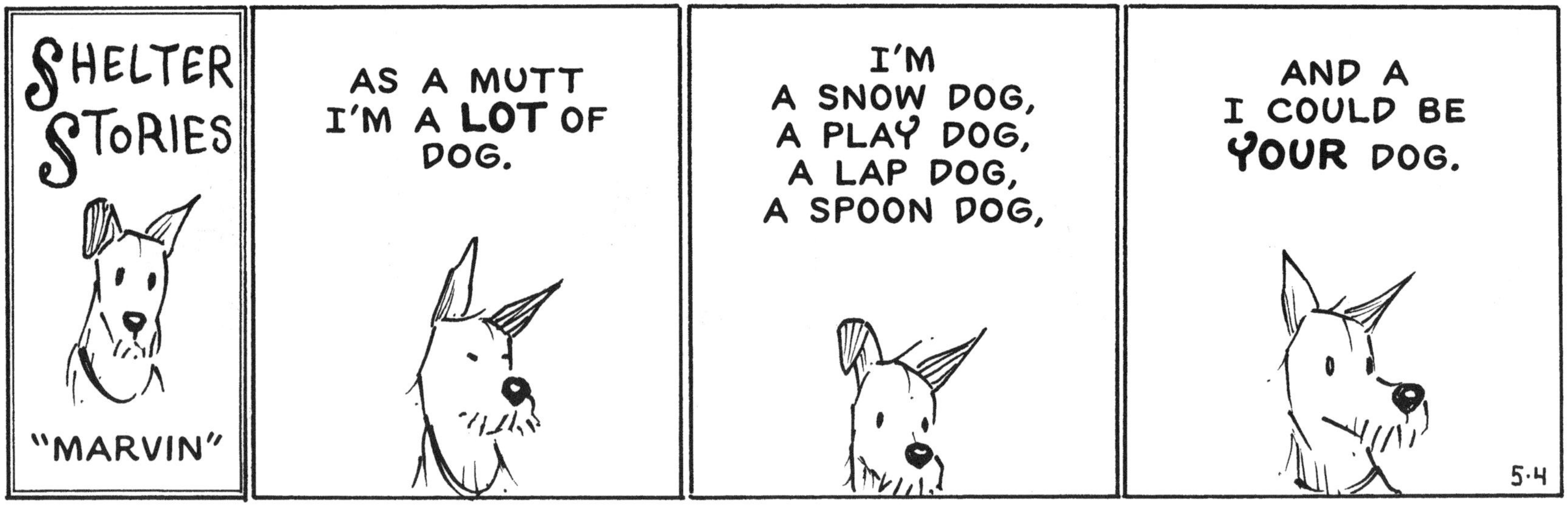
SHELTER STORIES
"MARVIN"
AS A MUTT I'M A LOT OF DOG.
I'M A SNOW DOG, A PLAY DOG, A LAP DOG, A SPOON DOG,
AND A I COULD BE YOUR DOG.
5·4

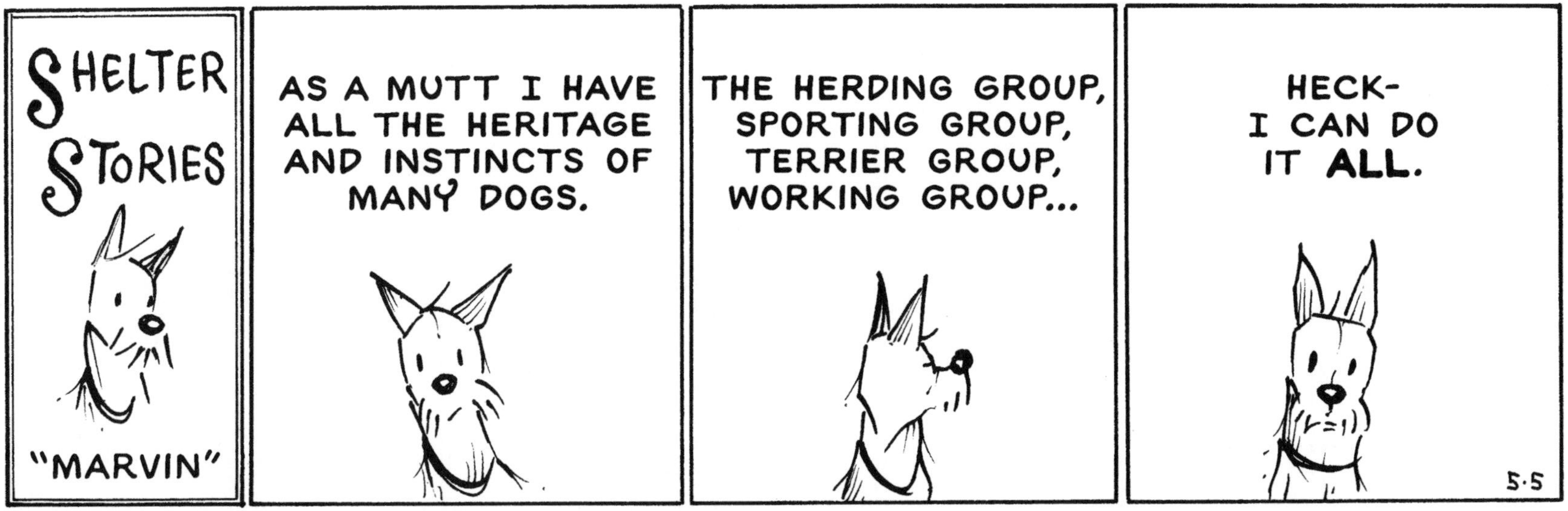
SHELTER STORIES
"MARVIN"
AS A MUTT I HAVE ALL THE HERITAGE AND INSTINCTS OF MANY DOGS.
THE HERDING GROUP, SPORTING GROUP, TERRIER GROUP, WORKING GROUP...
HECK- I CAN DO IT **ALL**.
5·5

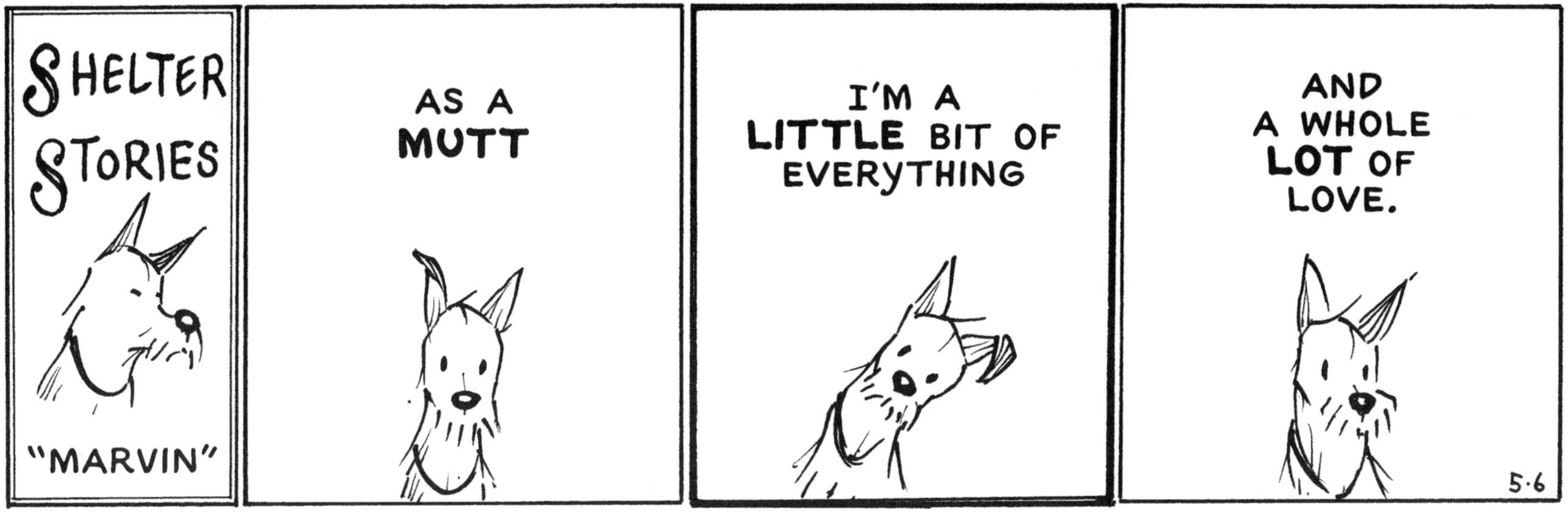
SHELTER STORIES
"MARVIN"
AS A **MUTT**
I'M A **LITTLE** BIT OF EVERYTHING
AND A WHOLE **LOT** OF LOVE.
5·6

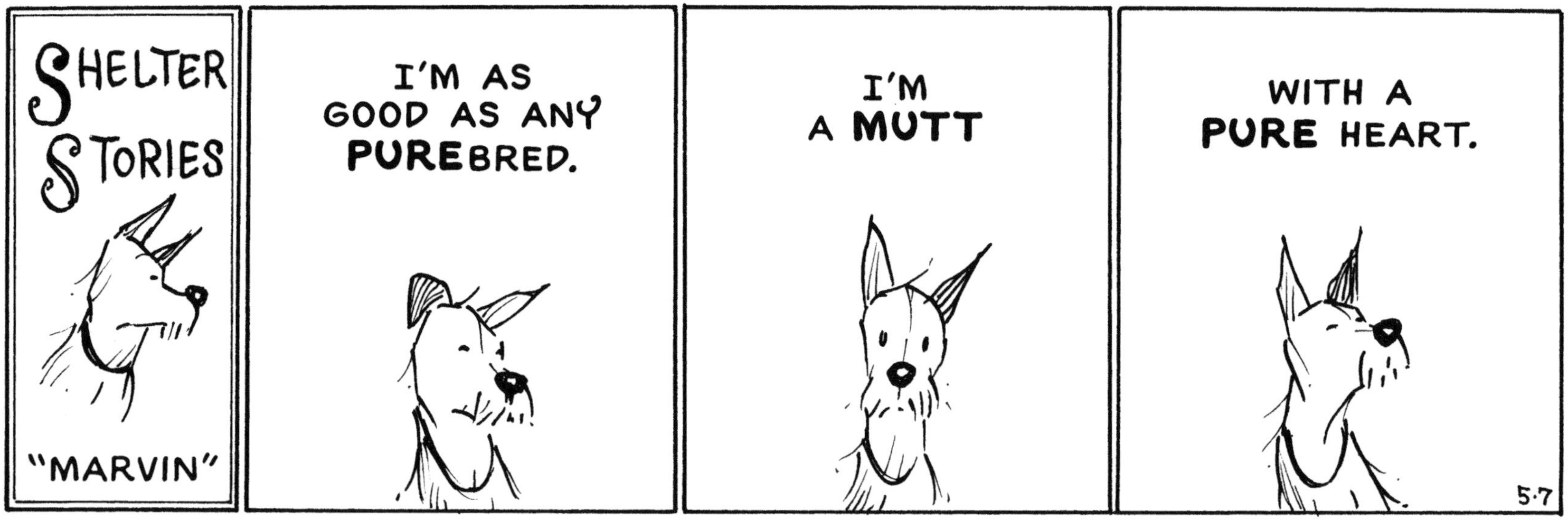
SHELTER STORIES
"MARVIN"
I'M AS GOOD AS ANY PUREBRED.
I'M A MUTT
WITH A PURE HEART.
5·7

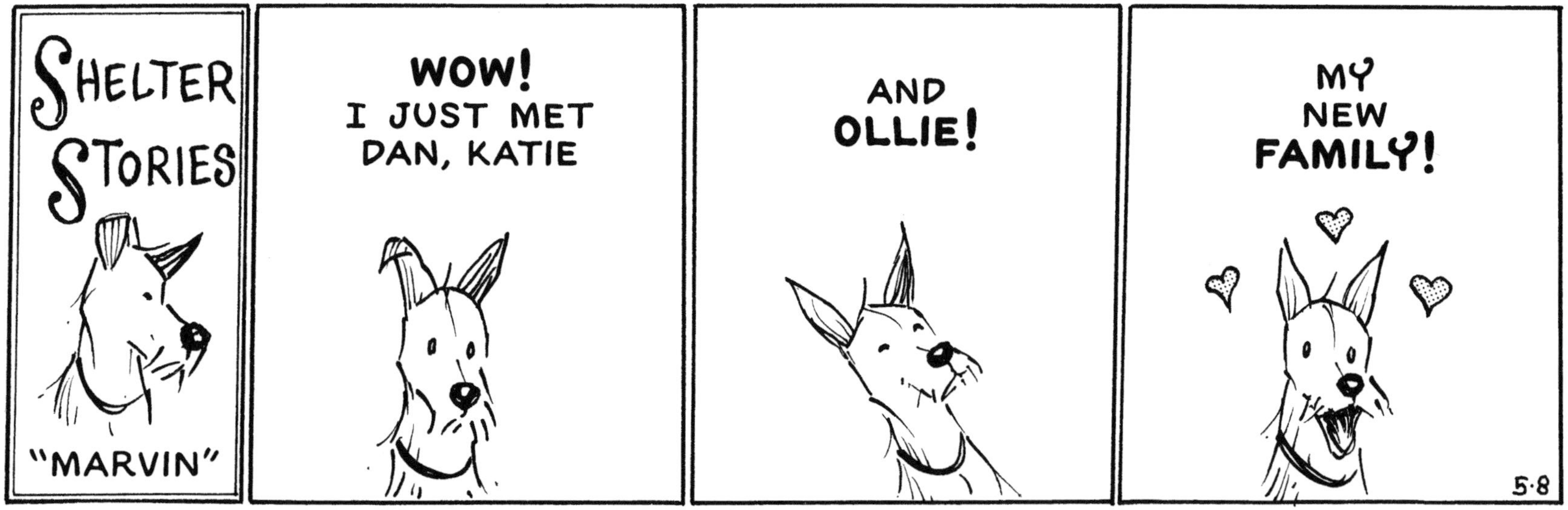
SHELTER STORIES
"MARVIN"
WOW! I JUST MET DAN, KATIE
AND OLLIE!
MY NEW FAMILY!
5·8

MUTTS

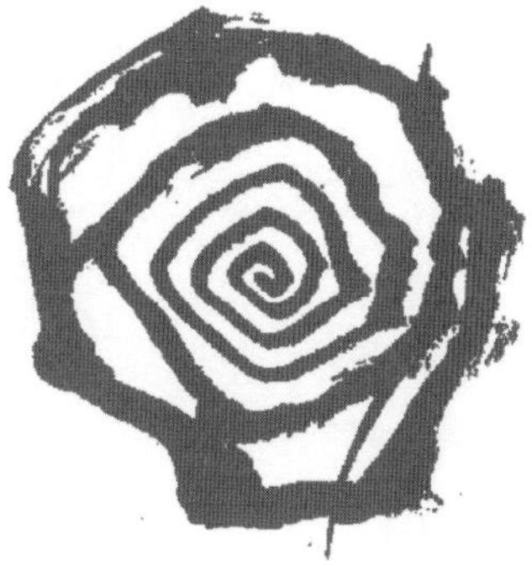

• PATRICK McDONNELL •

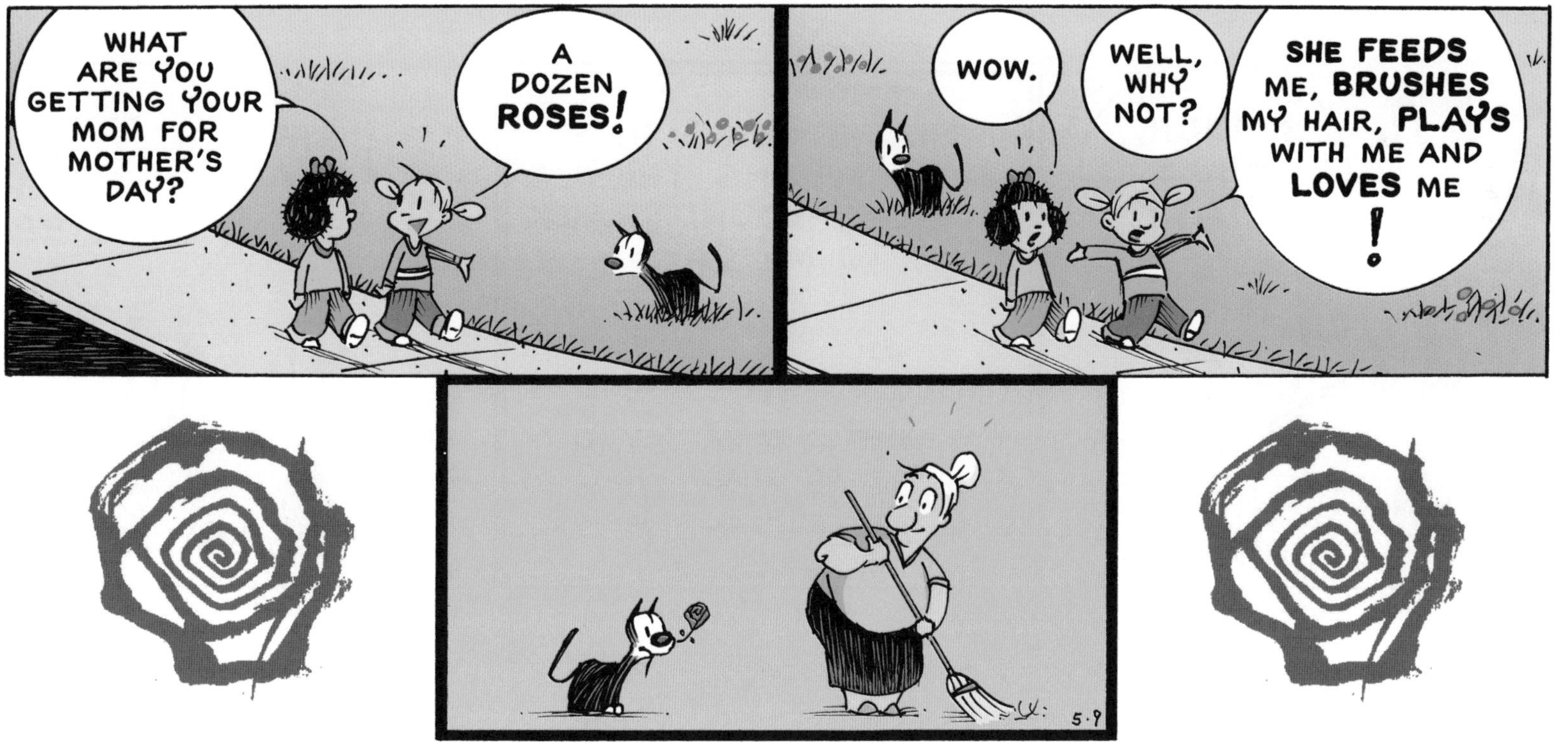
WHAT ARE YOU GETTING YOUR MOM FOR MOTHER'S DAY?
A DOZEN ROSES!
WOW.
WELL, WHY NOT?
SHE FEEDS ME, BRUSHES MY HAIR, PLAYS WITH ME AND LOVES ME !
5·9

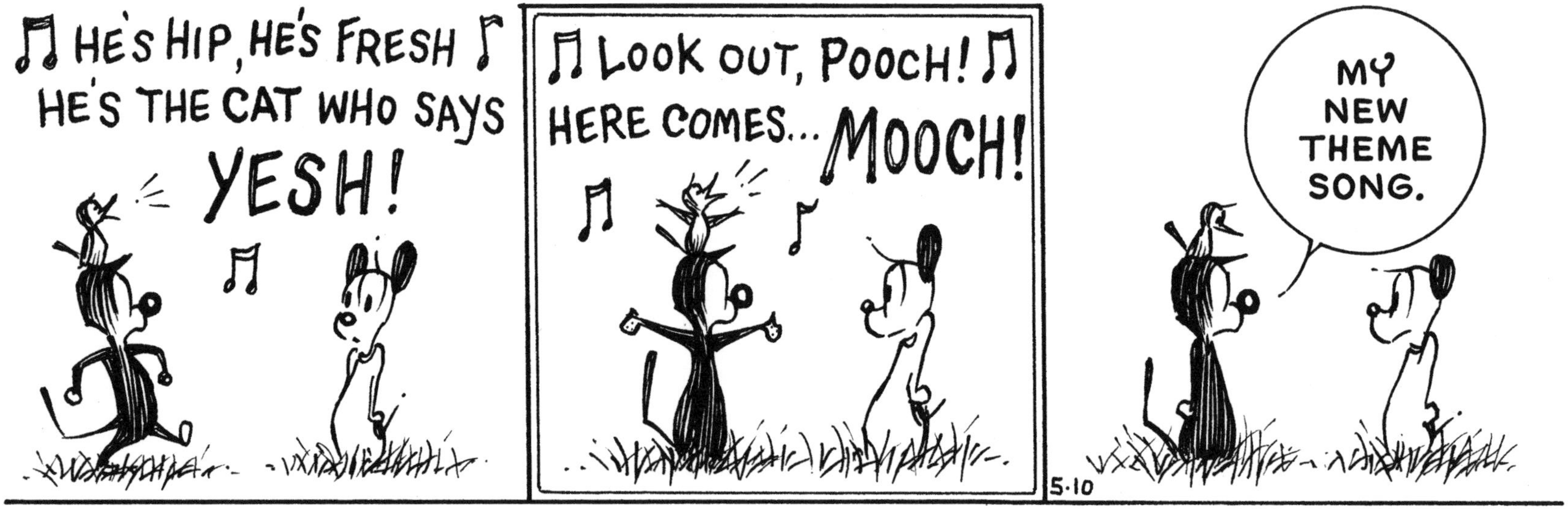
HE'S HIP, HE'S FRESH
HE'S THE CAT WHO SAYS
YESH!
LOOK OUT, POOCH!
HERE COMES... MOOCH!
MY NEW THEME SONG.
5·10

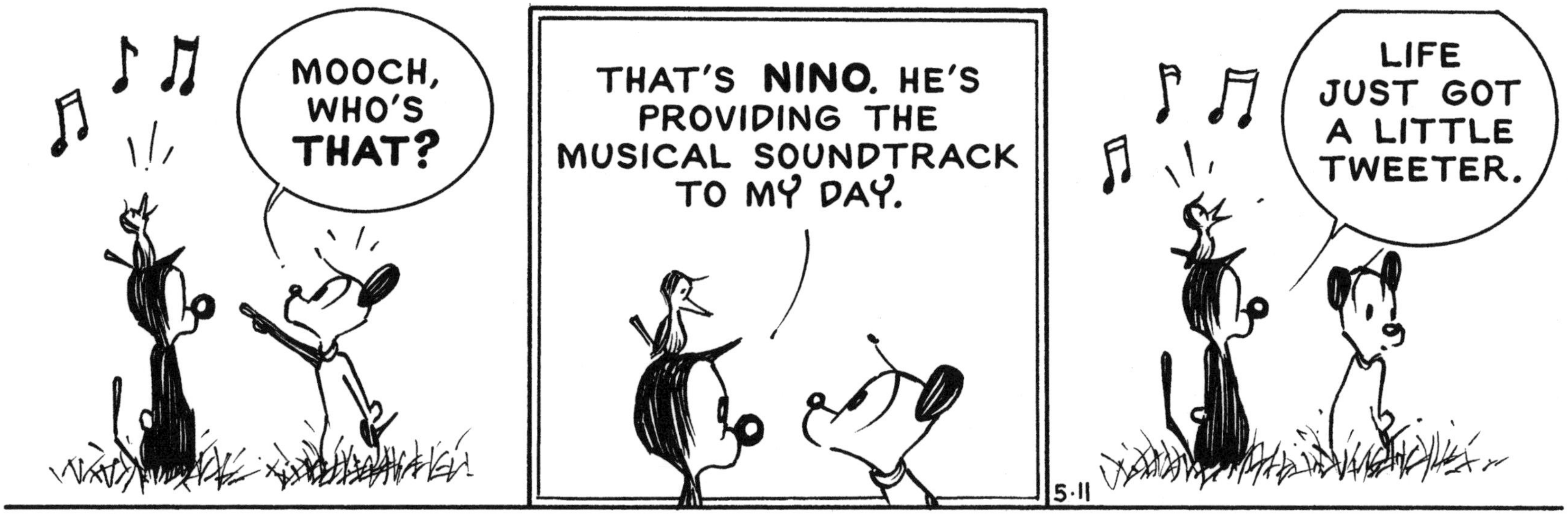
MOOCH, WHO'S THAT?
THAT'S NINO. HE'S PROVIDING THE MUSICAL SOUNDTRACK TO MY DAY.
LIFE JUST GOT A LITTLE TWEETER.
5·11

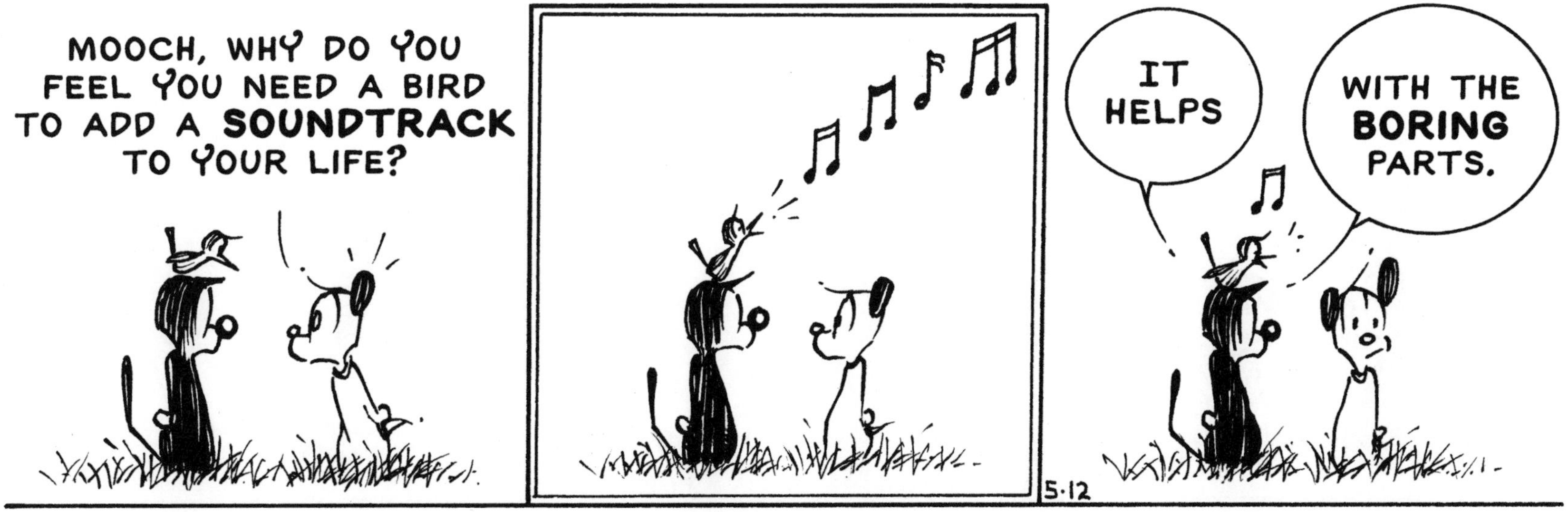
MOOCH, WHY DO YOU FEEL YOU NEED A BIRD TO ADD A **SOUNDTRACK** TO YOUR LIFE?
IT HELPS
WITH THE **BORING** PARTS.
5·12

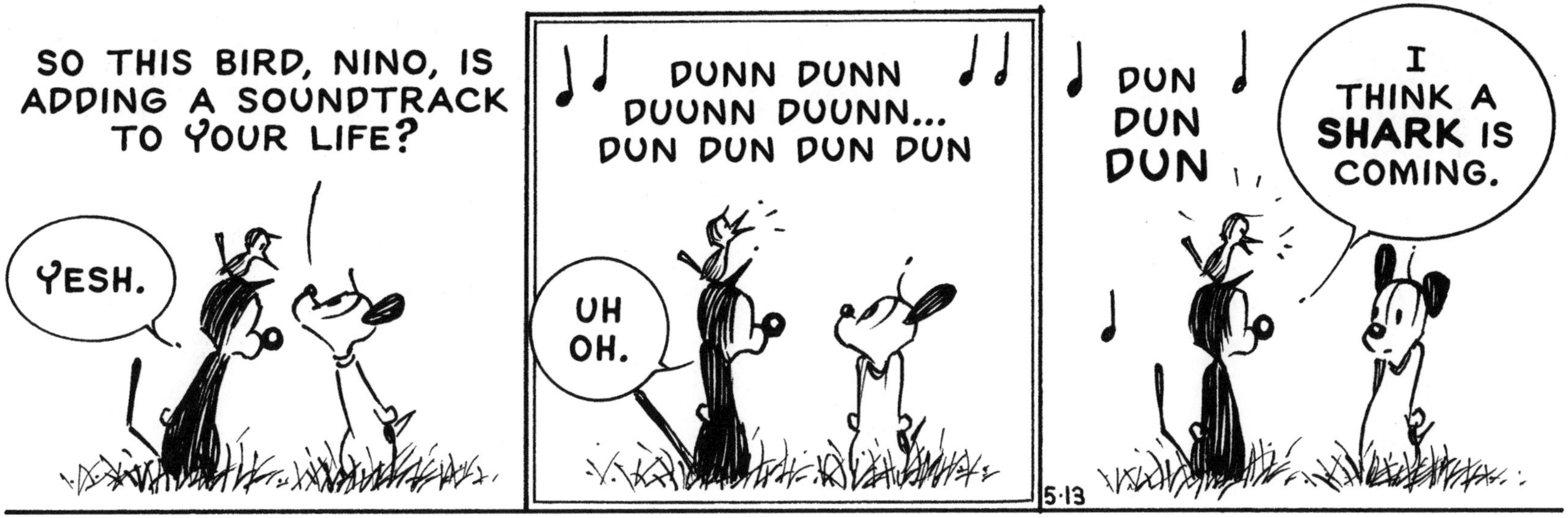
SO THIS BIRD, NINO, IS ADDING A SOUNDTRACK TO YOUR LIFE?
YESH.
DUNN DUNN DUUNN DUUNN... DUN DUN DUN DUN
UH OH.
DUN DUN DUN
I THINK A **SHARK** IS COMING.
5·13

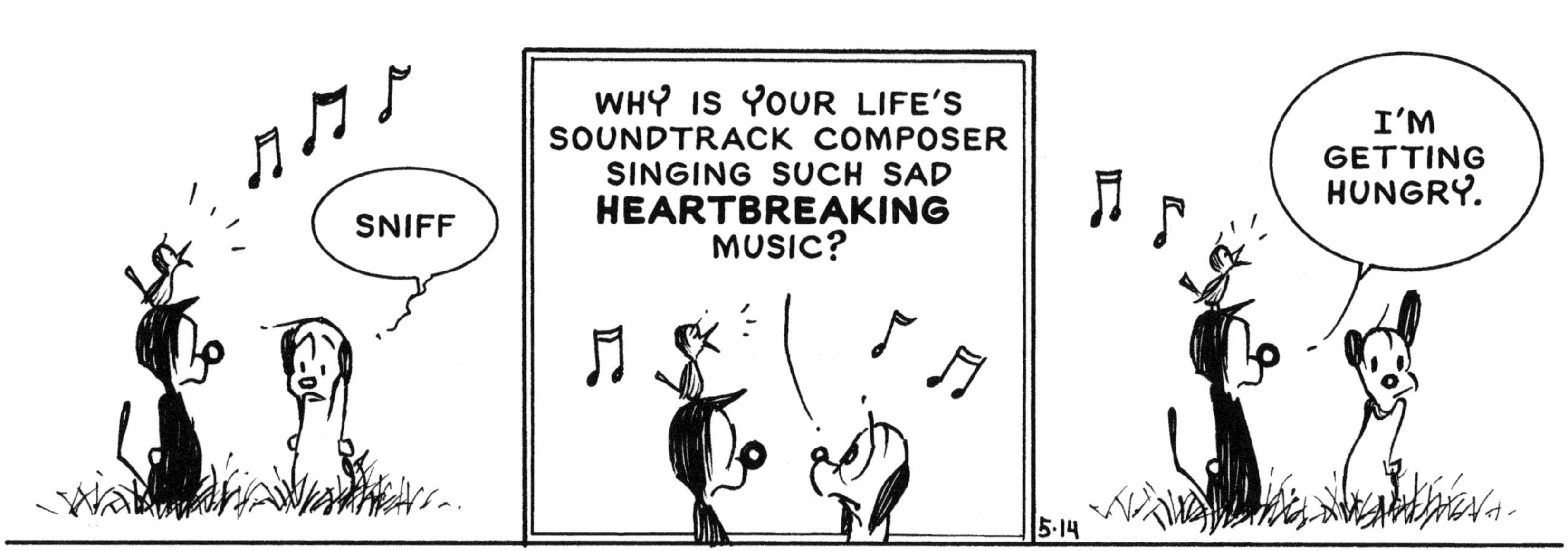
SNIFF
WHY IS YOUR LIFE'S SOUNDTRACK COMPOSER SINGING SUCH SAD **HEARTBREAKING** MUSIC?
5·14
I'M GETTING HUNGRY.

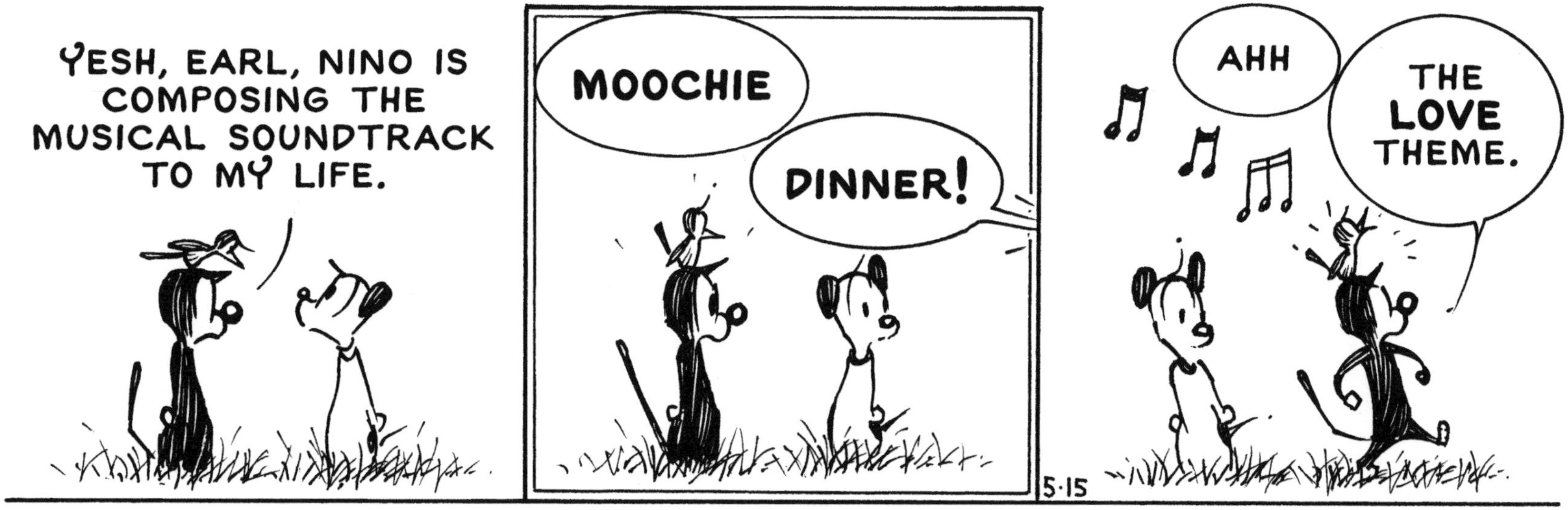
YESH, EARL, NINO IS COMPOSING THE MUSICAL SOUNDTRACK TO MY LIFE.
MOOCHIE
DINNER!
5·15
AHH
THE **LOVE** THEME.

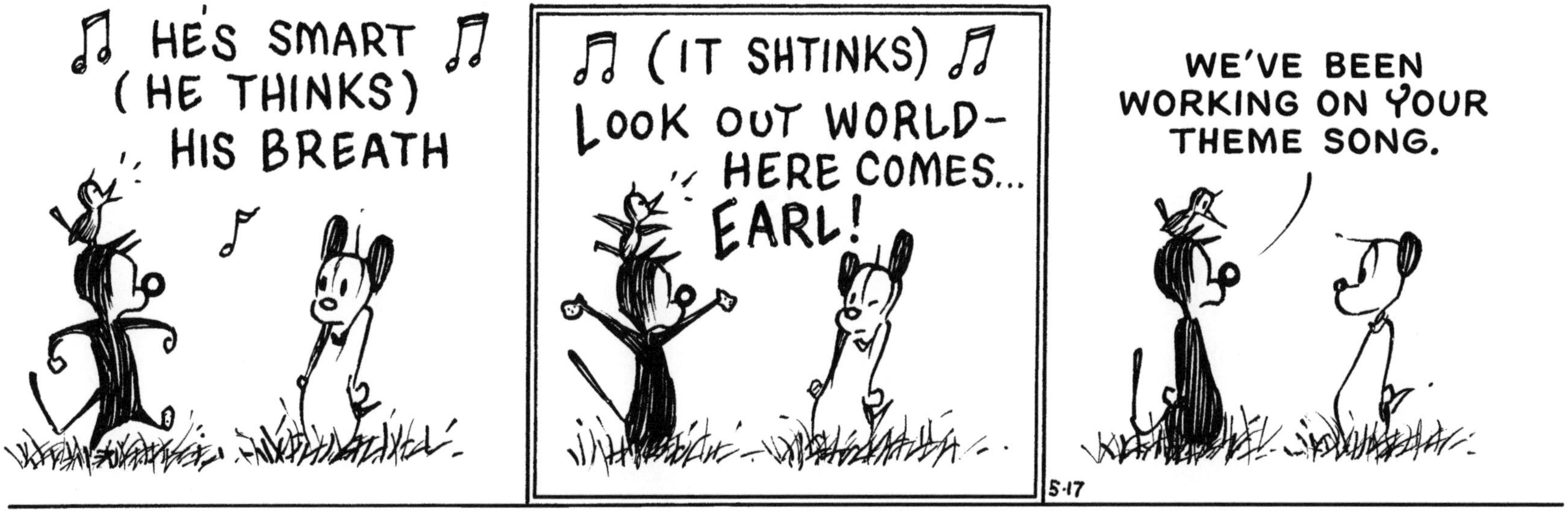
♫ HE'S SMART ♫ (HE THINKS) HIS BREATH
♫ (IT SHTINKS) ♫ LOOK OUT WORLD- HERE COMES... EARL!
WE'VE BEEN WORKING ON YOUR THEME SONG.
5·17

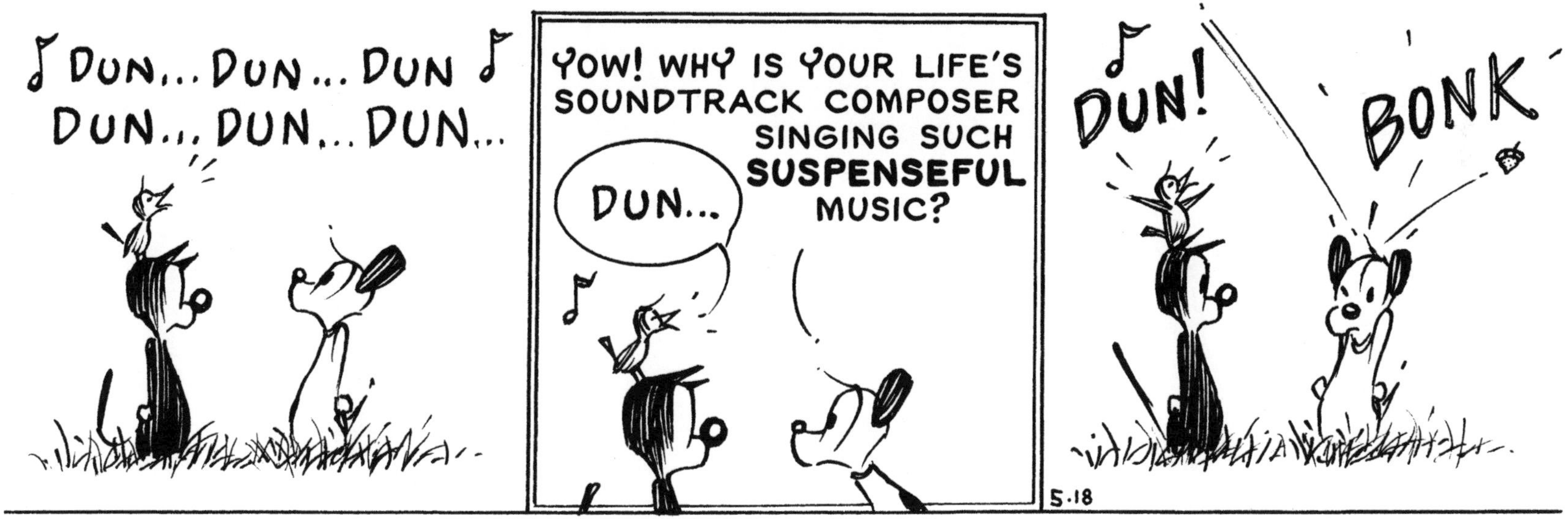
DUN... DUN... DUN DUN... DUN... DUN...
YOW! WHY IS YOUR LIFE'S SOUNDTRACK COMPOSER SINGING SUCH **SUSPENSEFUL** MUSIC?
DUN...
DUN!
BONK
5·18

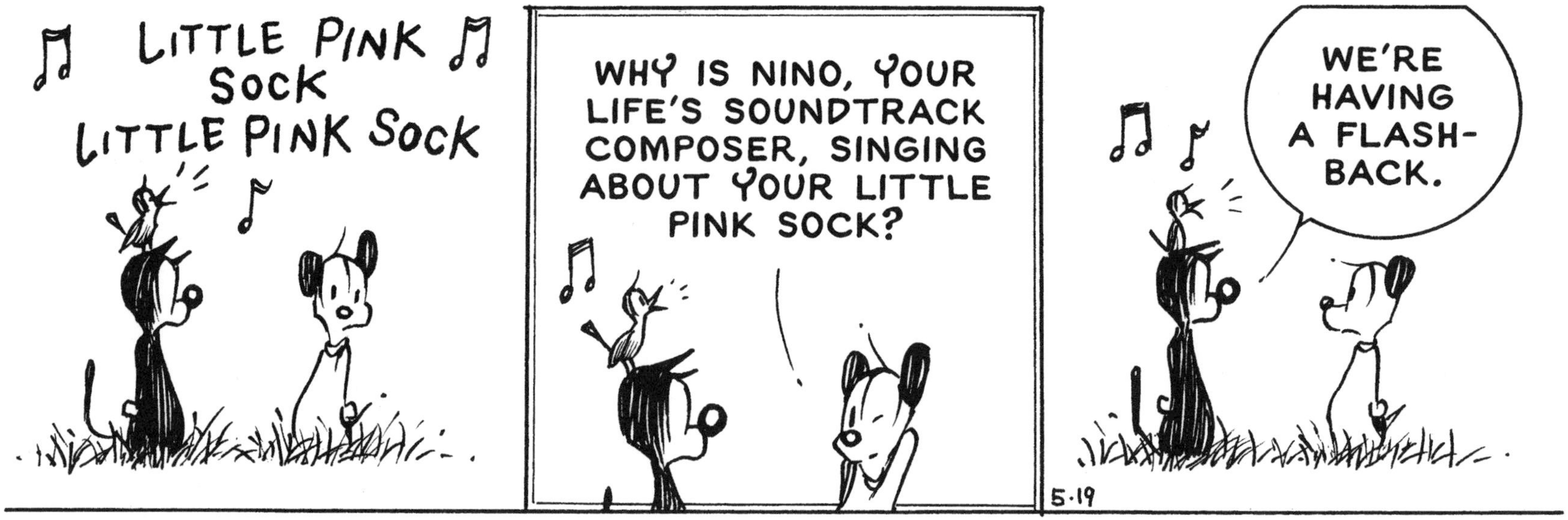
LITTLE PINK SOCK
LITTLE PINK SOCK
WHY IS NINO, YOUR LIFE'S SOUNDTRACK COMPOSER, SINGING ABOUT YOUR LITTLE PINK SOCK?
WE'RE HAVING A FLASH-BACK.
5·19

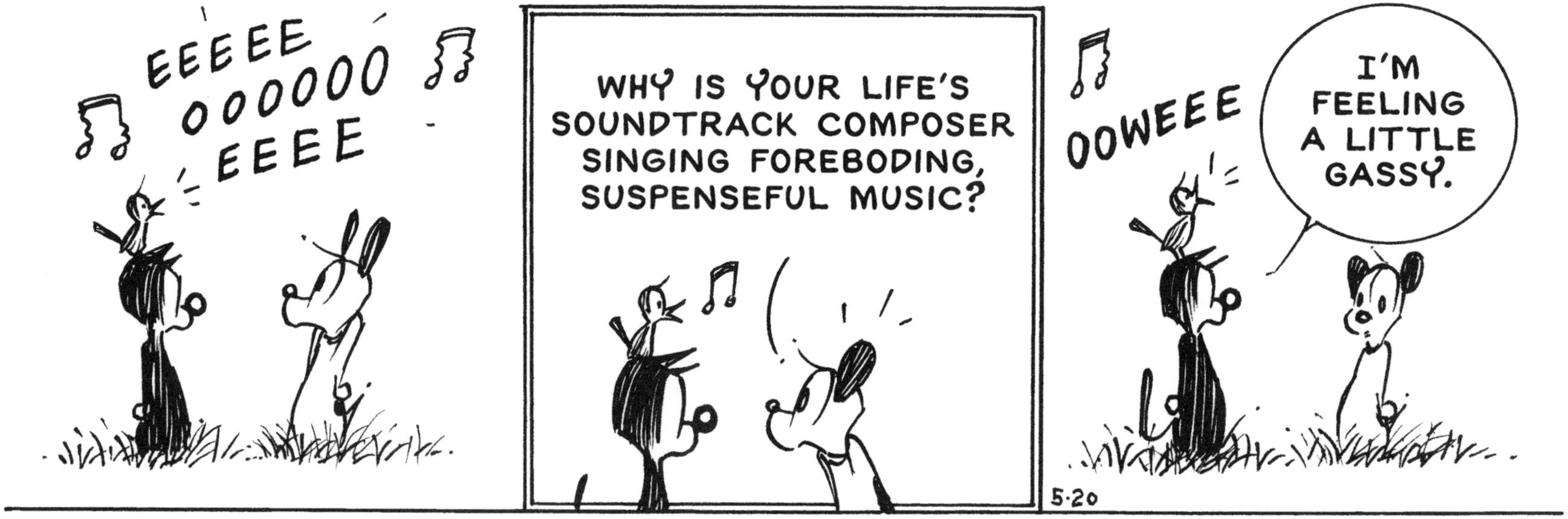
EEEEE OOOOOO EEEE
WHY IS YOUR LIFE'S SOUNDTRACK COMPOSER SINGING FOREBODING, SUSPENSEFUL MUSIC?
OOWEEE
I'M FEELING A LITTLE GASSY.
5·20

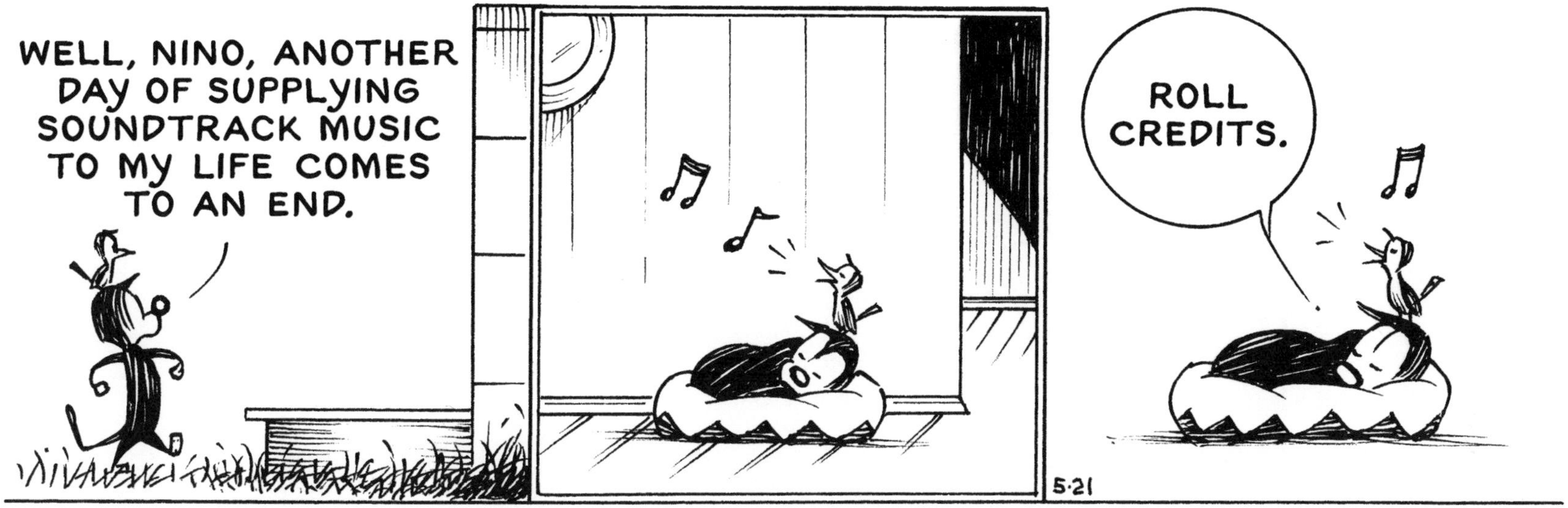
WELL, NINO, ANOTHER DAY OF SUPPLYING SOUNDTRACK MUSIC TO MY LIFE COMES TO AN END.
ROLL CREDITS.
5·21

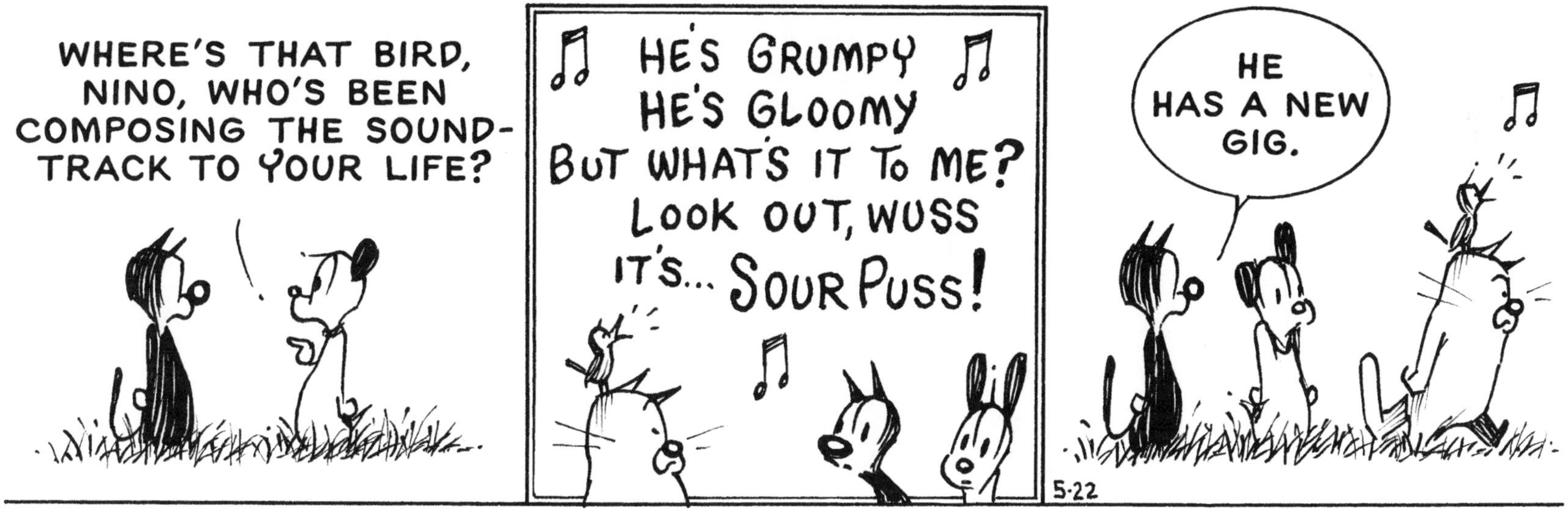
WHERE'S THAT BIRD, NINO, WHO'S BEEN COMPOSING THE SOUND-TRACK TO YOUR LIFE?
HE'S GRUMPY
HE'S GLOOMY
BUT WHAT'S IT TO ME?
LOOK OUT, WUSS
IT'S... SOUR PUSS!
HE HAS A NEW GIG.
5·22

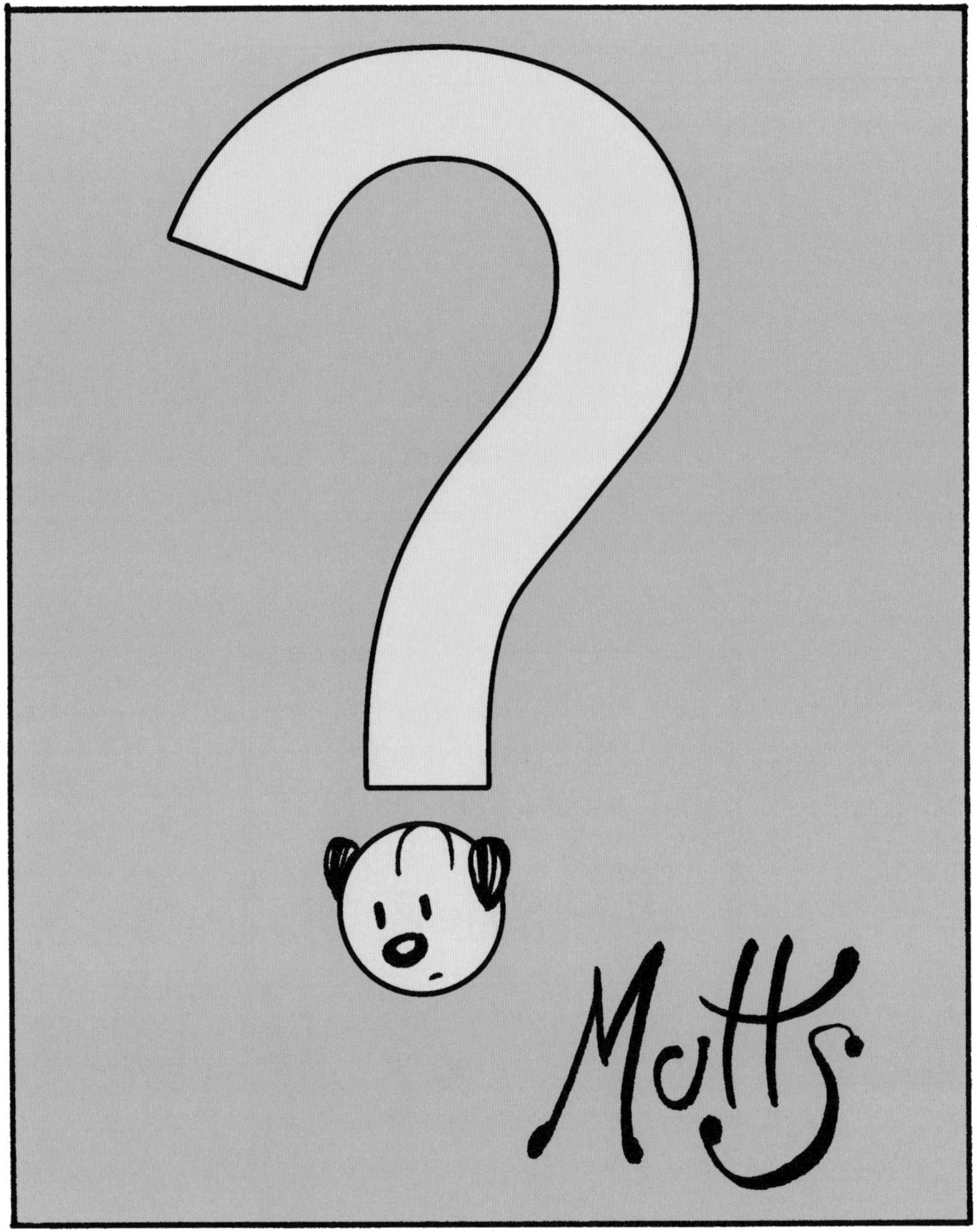
Mutts

? FOOLISH HUMAN QUESTIONS ?

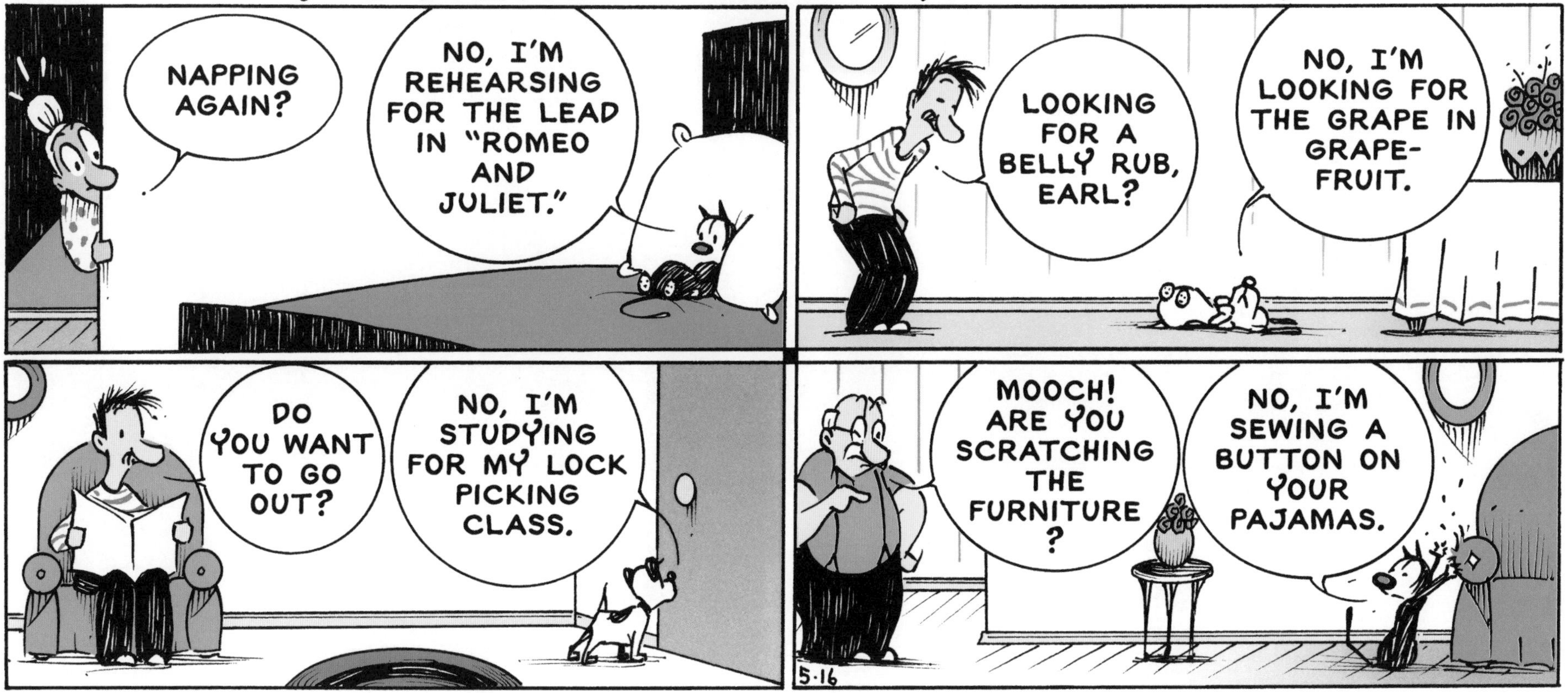

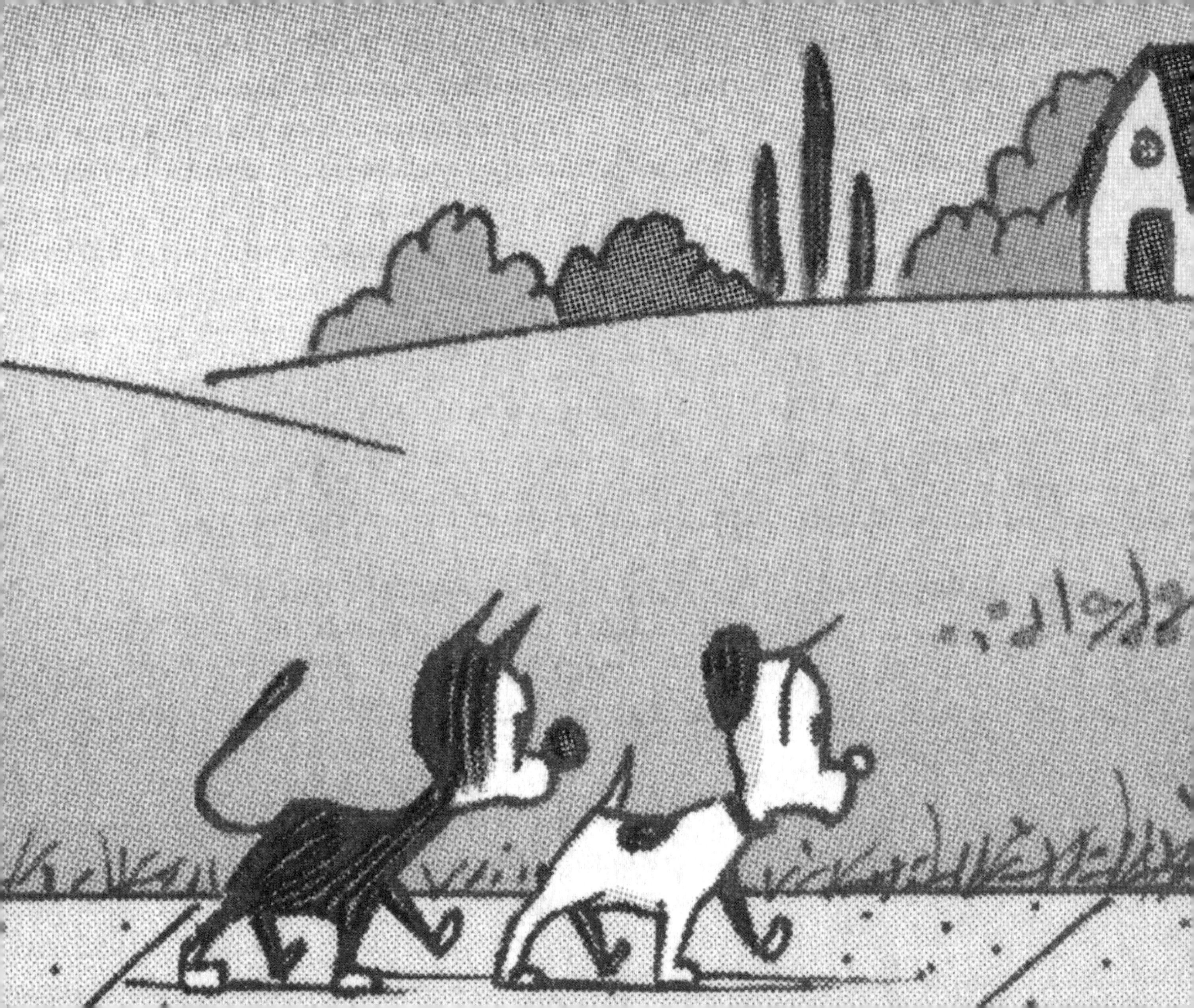

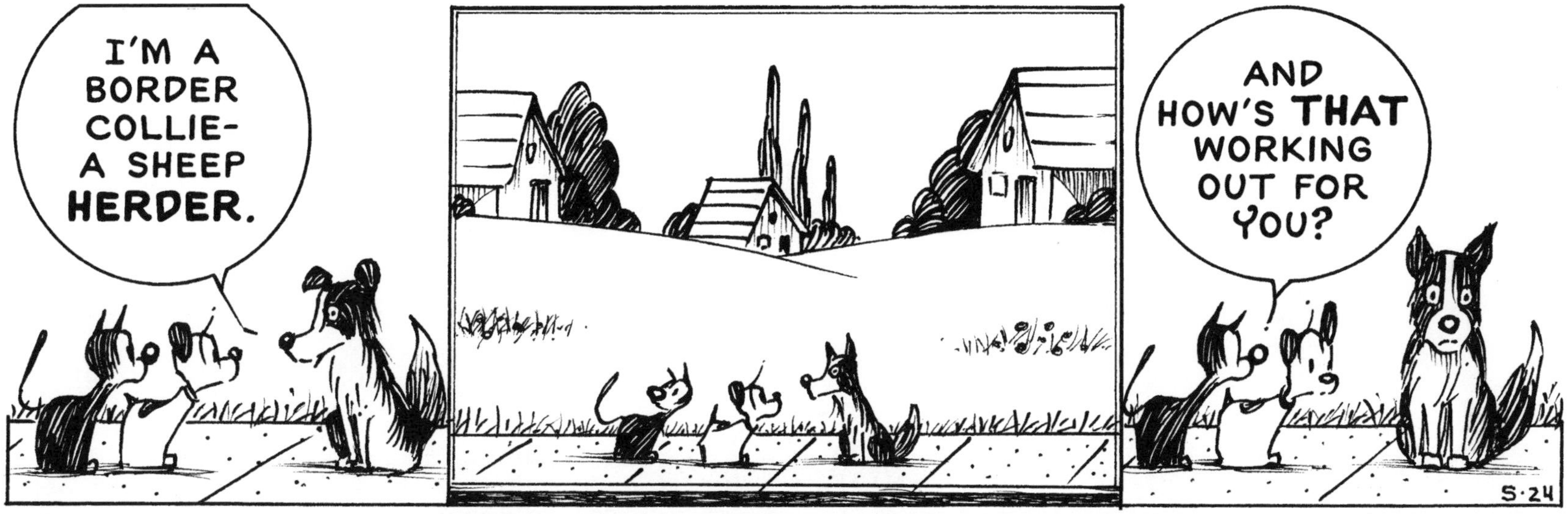
I'M A BORDER COLLIE- A SHEEP HERDER.
AND HOW'S THAT WORKING OUT FOR YOU?
5·24

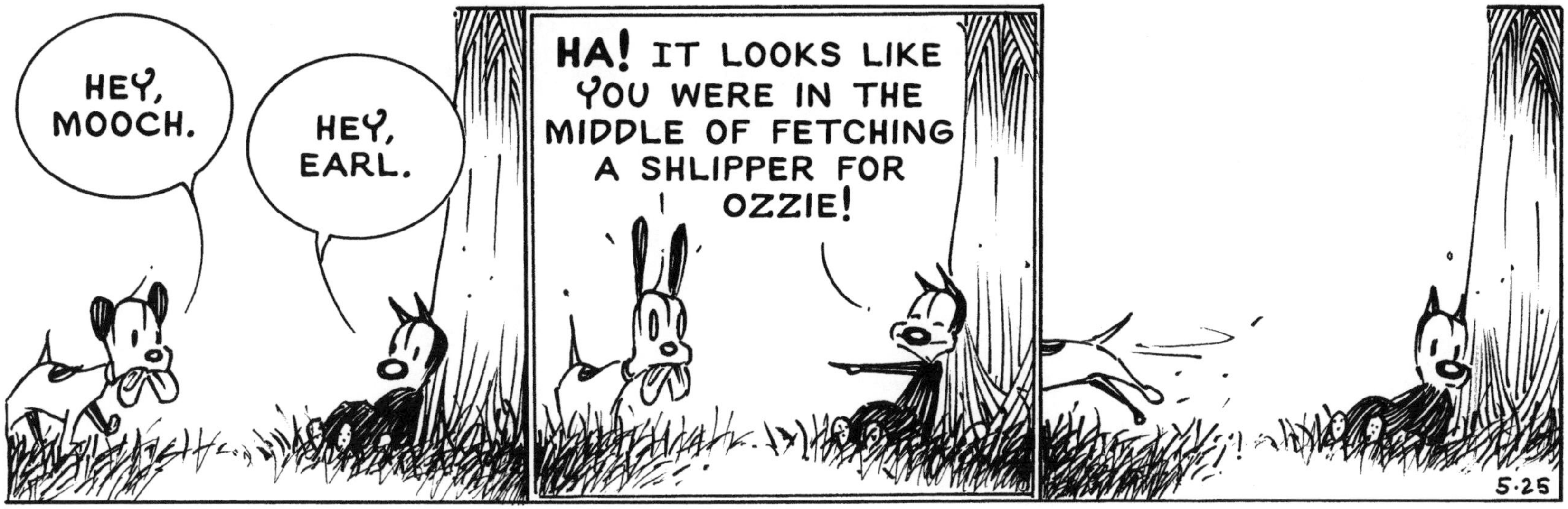
HEY, MOOCH.
HEY, EARL.
HA! IT LOOKS LIKE YOU WERE IN THE MIDDLE OF FETCHING A SHLIPPER FOR OZZIE!
5·25

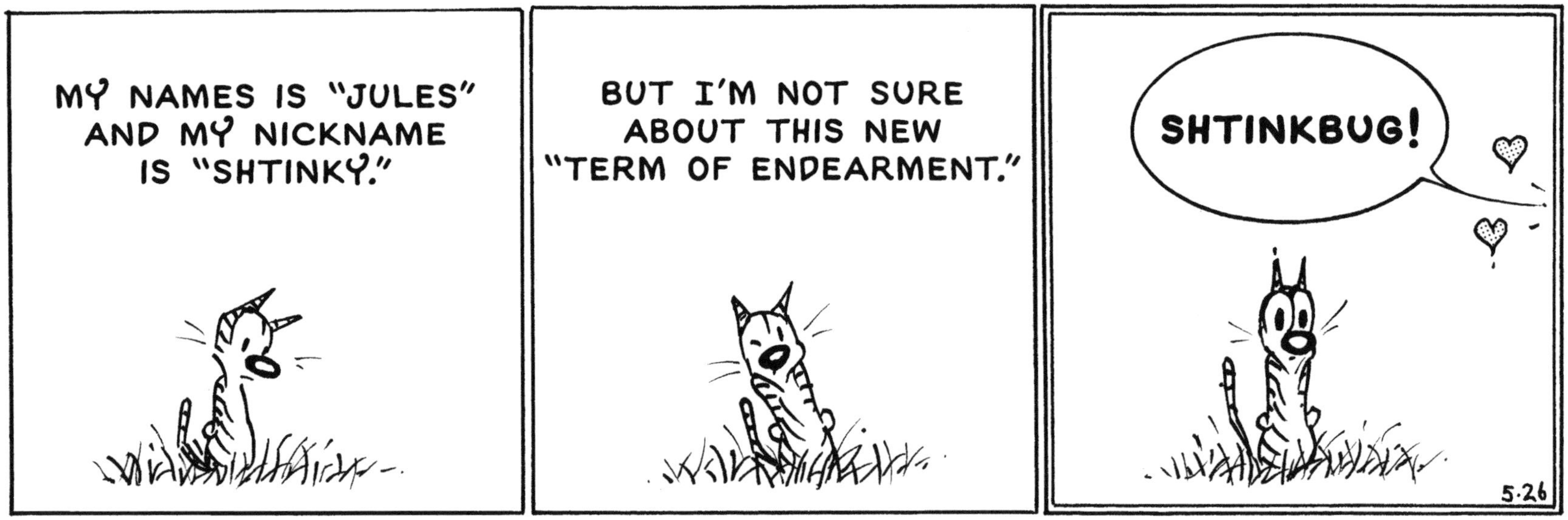
MY NAMES IS "JULES" AND MY NICKNAME IS "SHTINKY."
BUT I'M NOT SURE ABOUT THIS NEW "TERM OF ENDEARMENT."
SHTINKBUG!
5·26

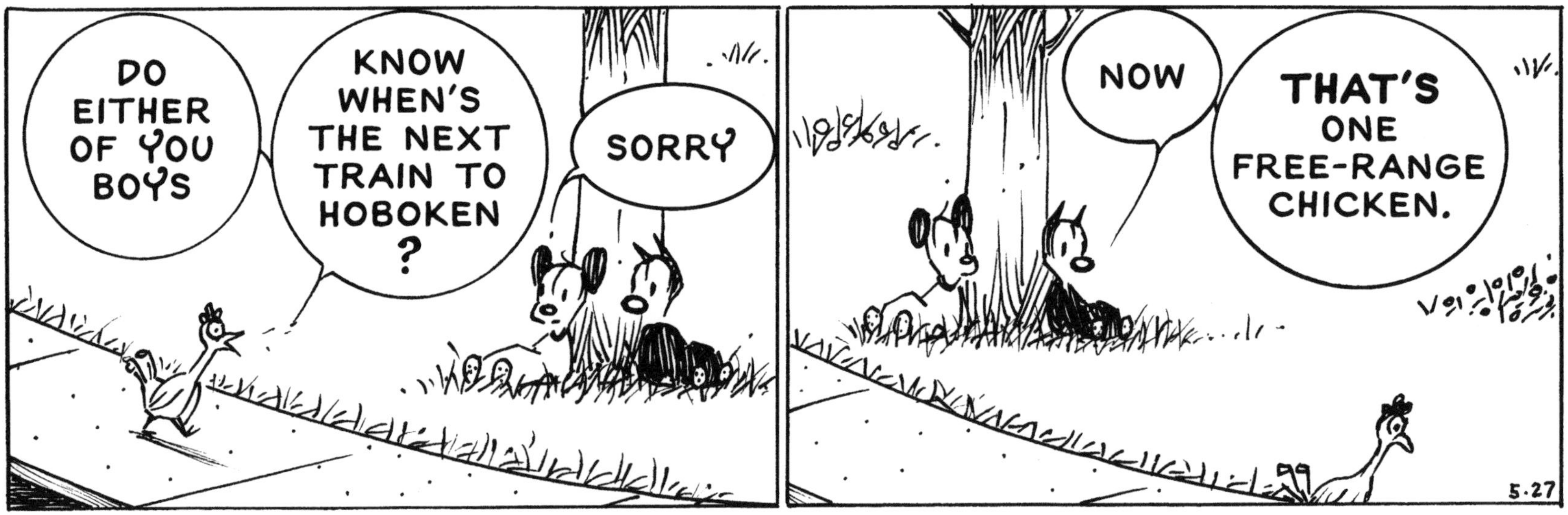
DO EITHER OF YOU BOYS
KNOW WHEN'S THE NEXT TRAIN TO HOBOKEN ?
SORRY
NOW
THAT'S ONE FREE-RANGE CHICKEN.
5·27

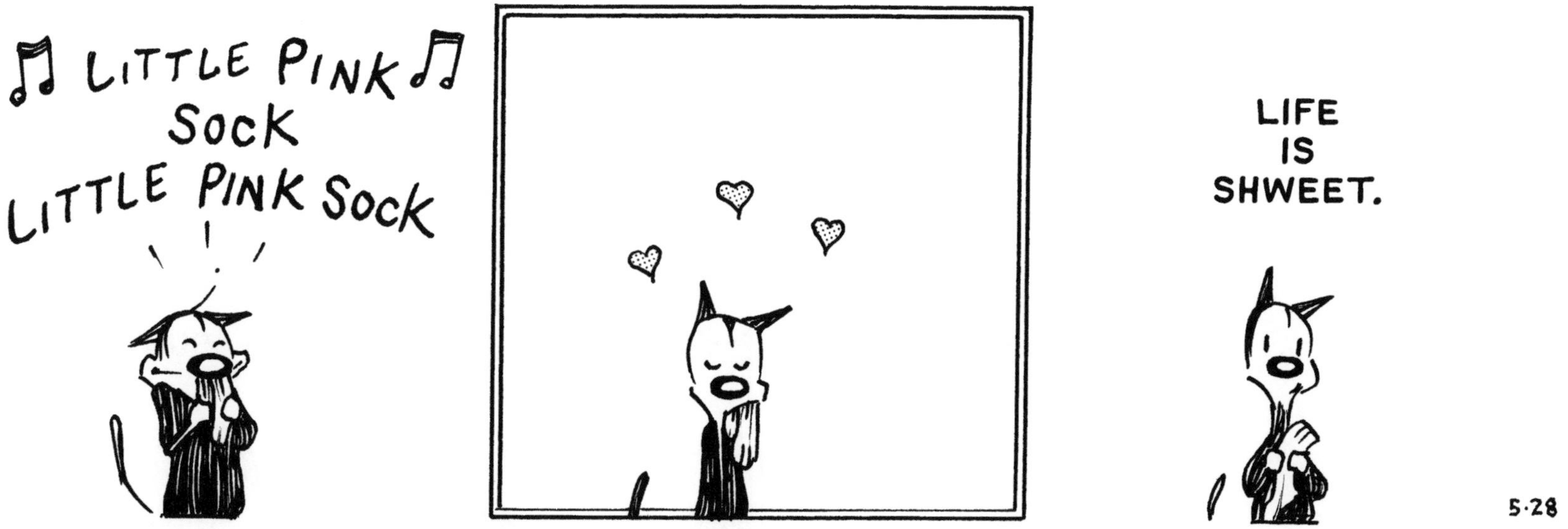
♫ LITTLE PINK ♫ SOCK LITTLE PINK SOCK
LIFE IS SHWEET.
5·28

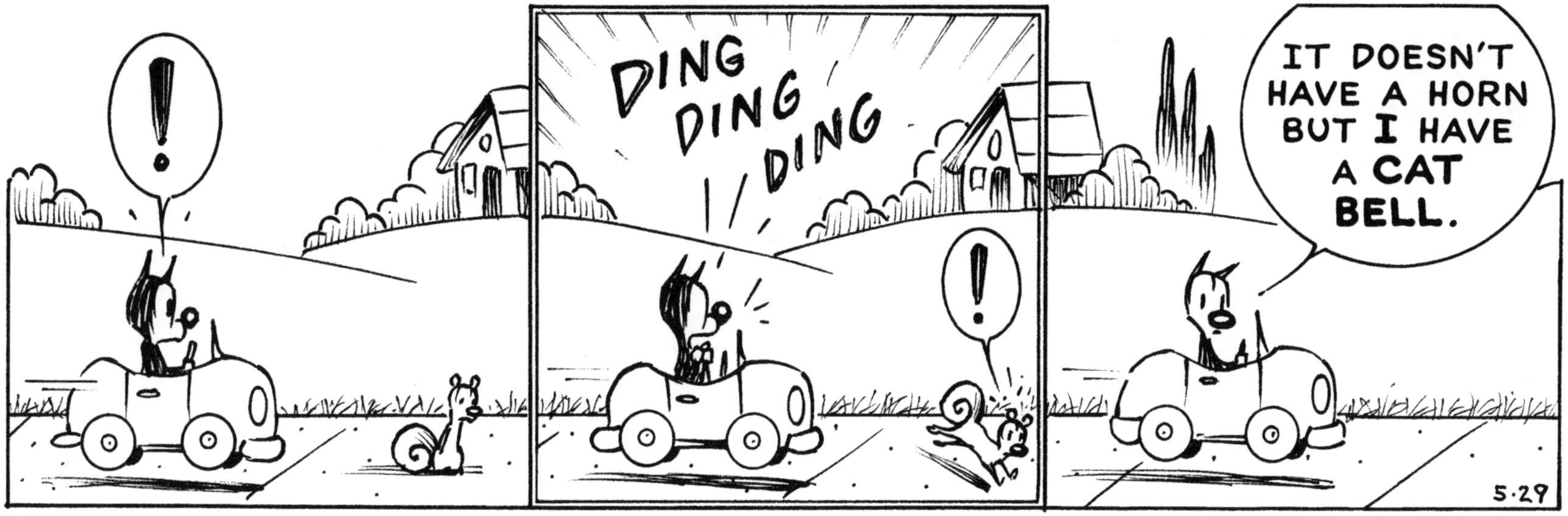
!
DING DING DING
!
IT DOESN'T HAVE A HORN BUT I HAVE A CAT BELL.
5·29

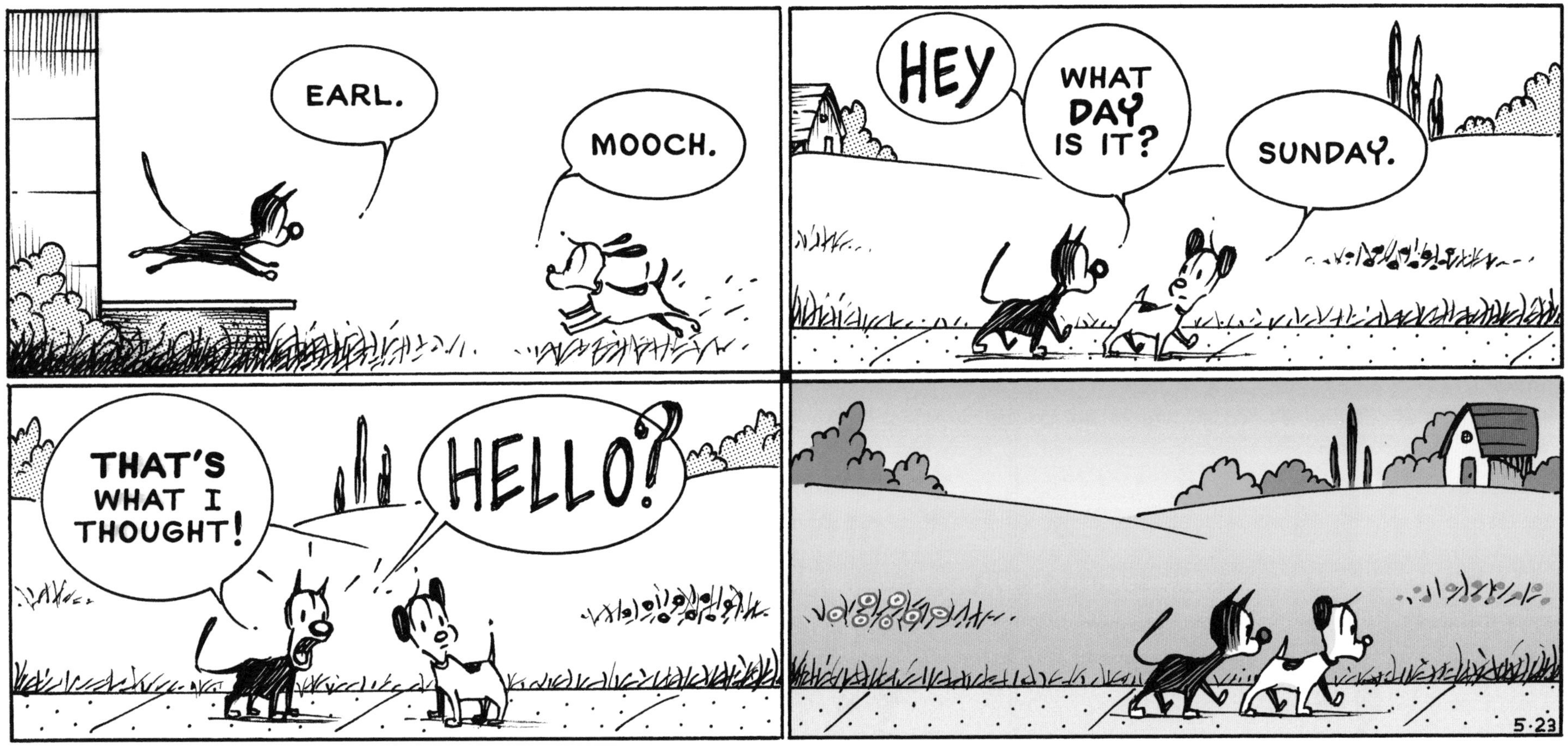
EARL.
MOOCH.
HEY
WHAT DAY IS IT?
SUNDAY.
THAT'S WHAT I THOUGHT!
HELLO?
5·23

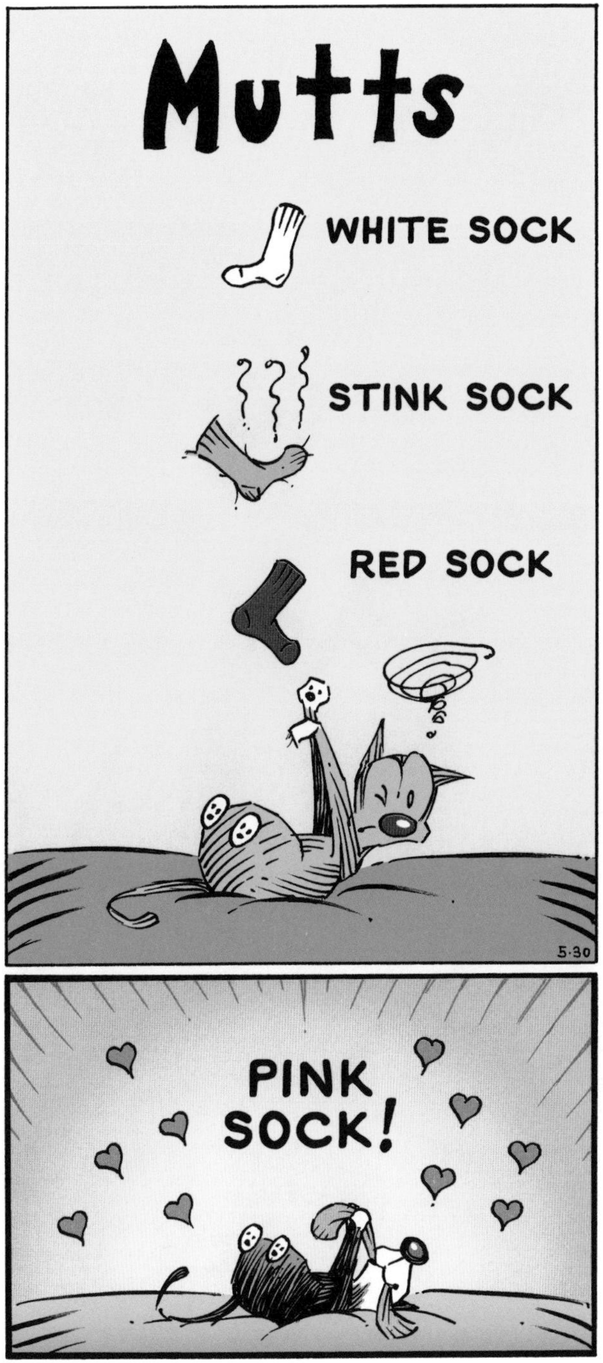
Mutts
WHITE SOCK
STINK SOCK
RED SOCK
5·30
PINK SOCK!

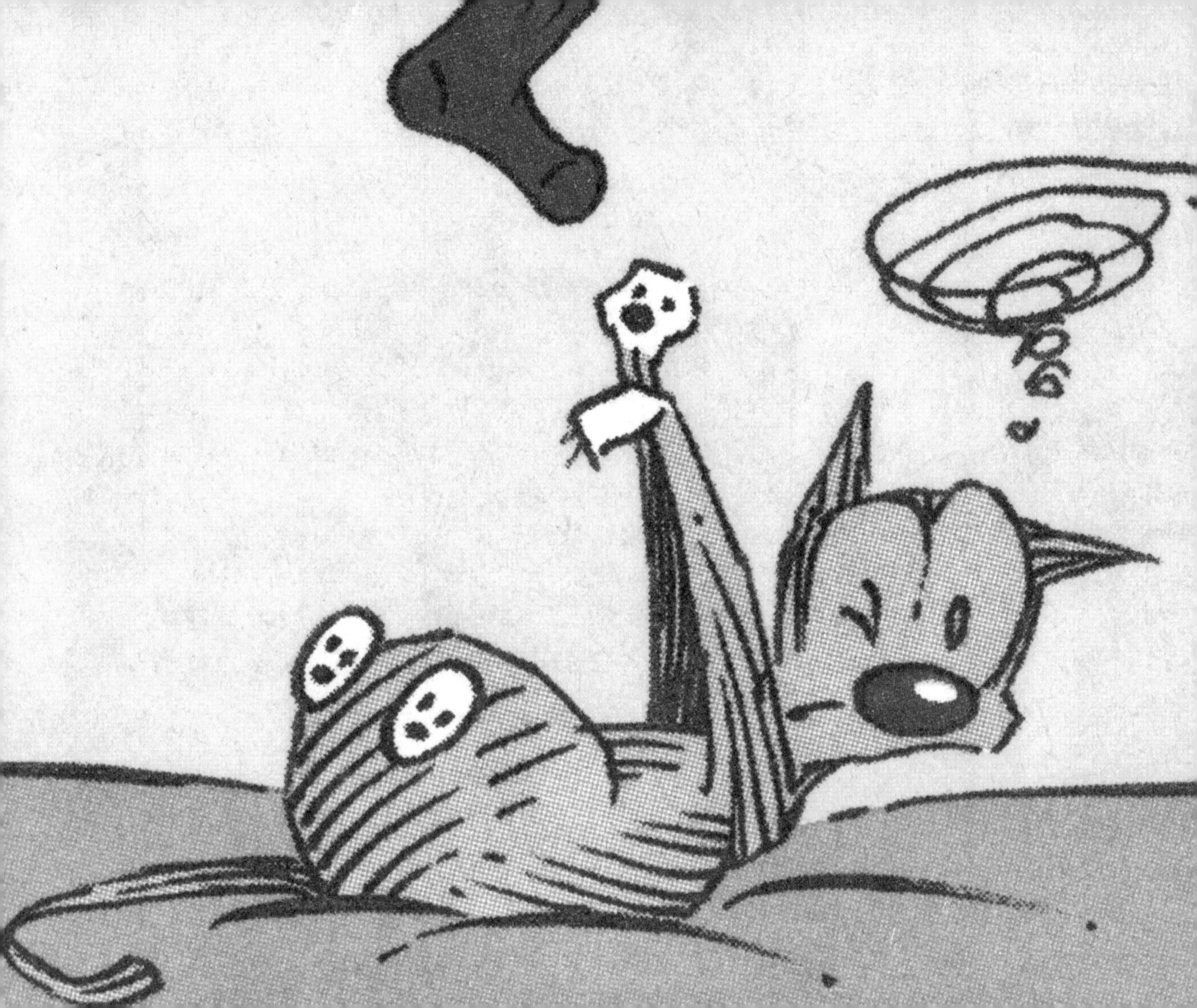

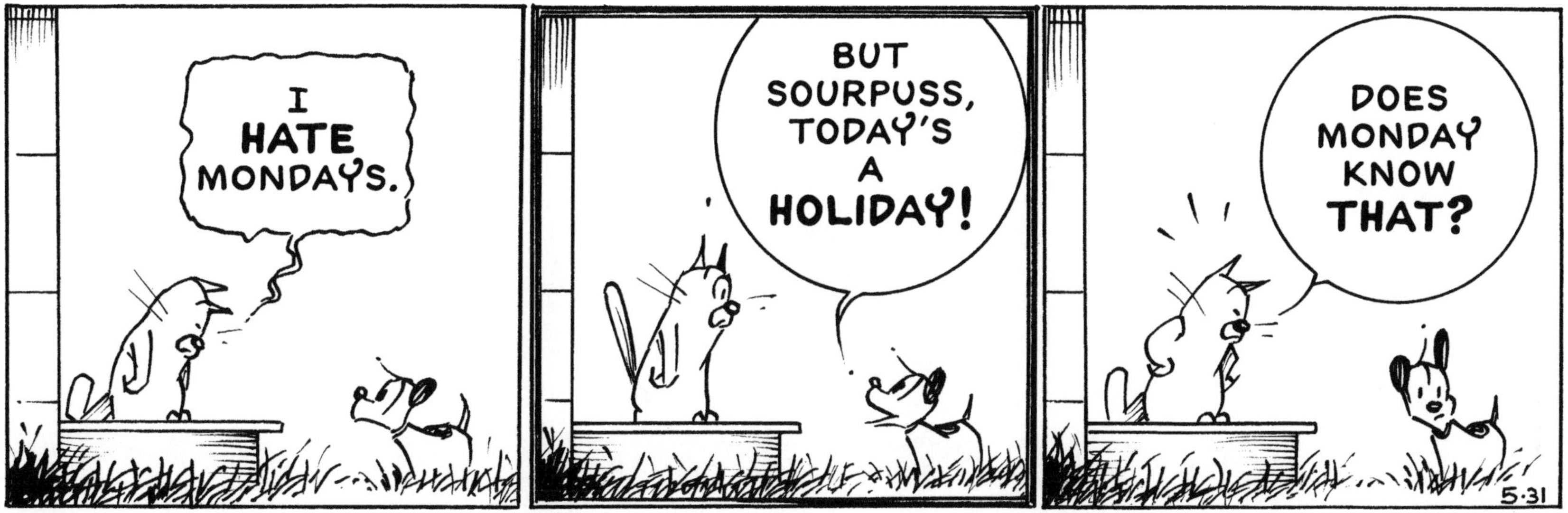
I HATE MONDAYS.
BUT SOURPUSS, TODAY'S A HOLIDAY!
DOES MONDAY KNOW THAT?
5·31

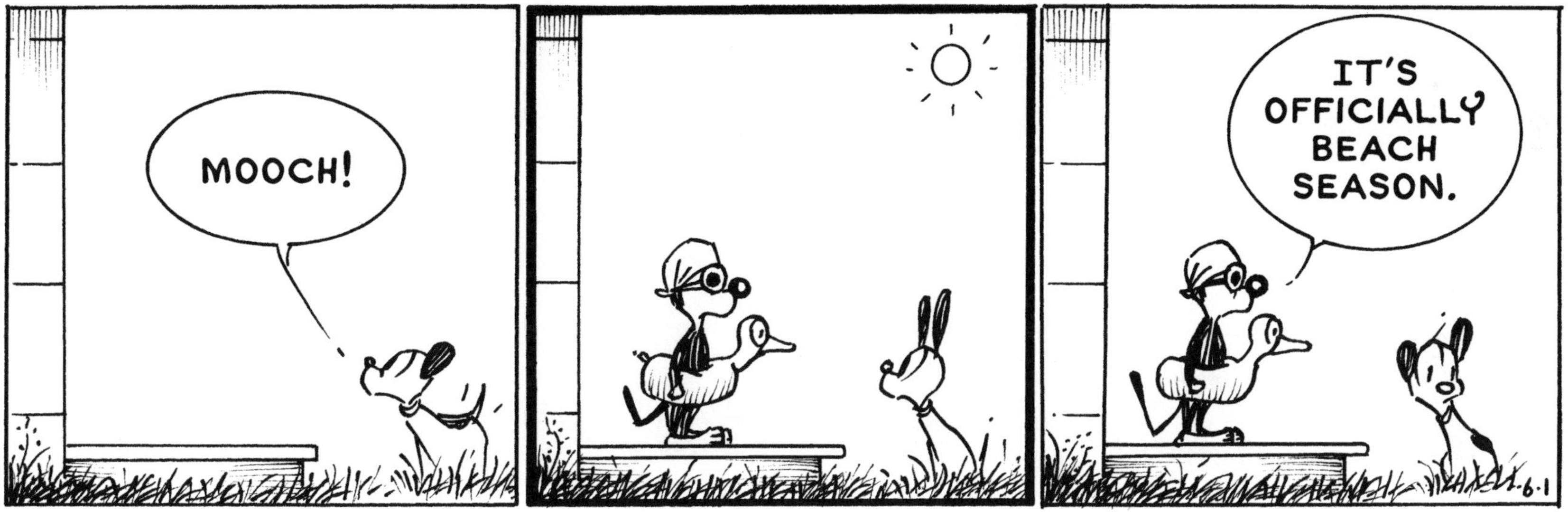
MOOCH!
IT'S OFFICIALLY BEACH SEASON.
6·1

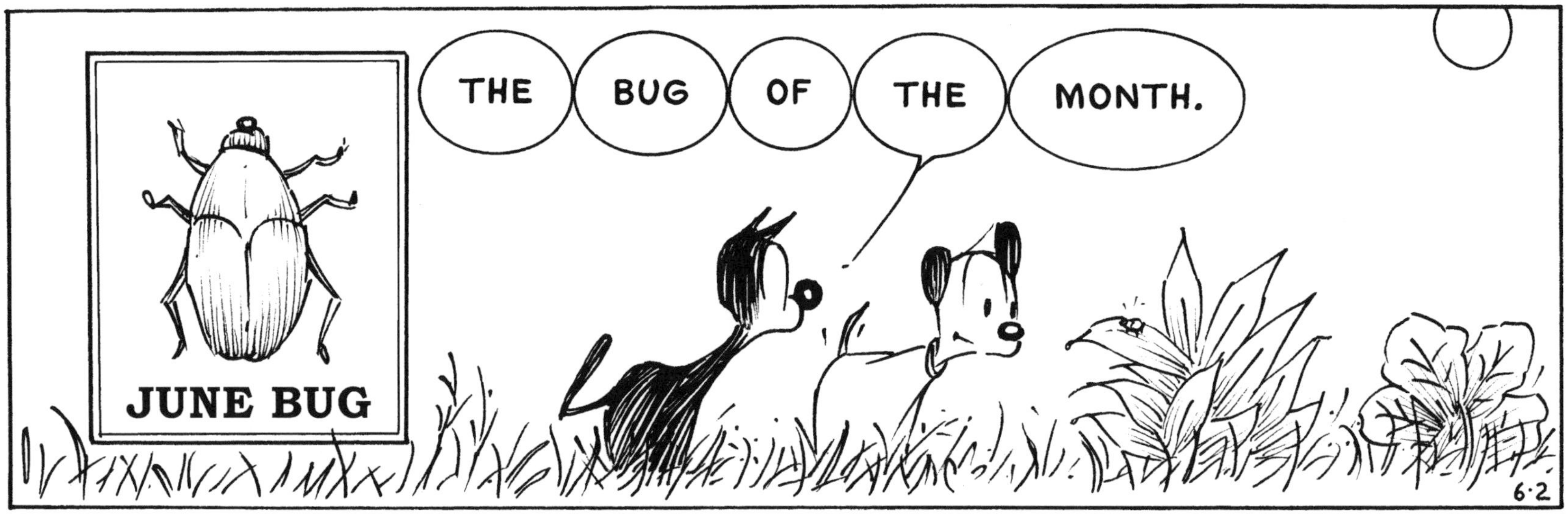
JUNE BUG
THE
BUG
OF
THE
MONTH.
6·2

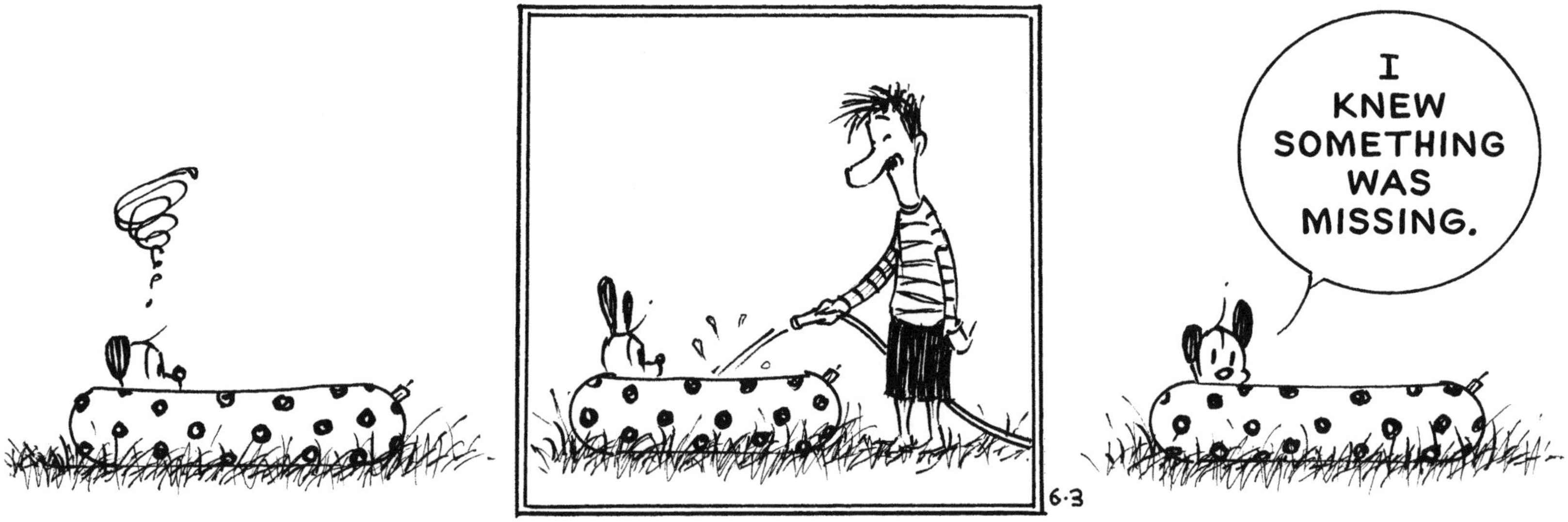
6·3
I KNEW SOMETHING WAS MISSING.

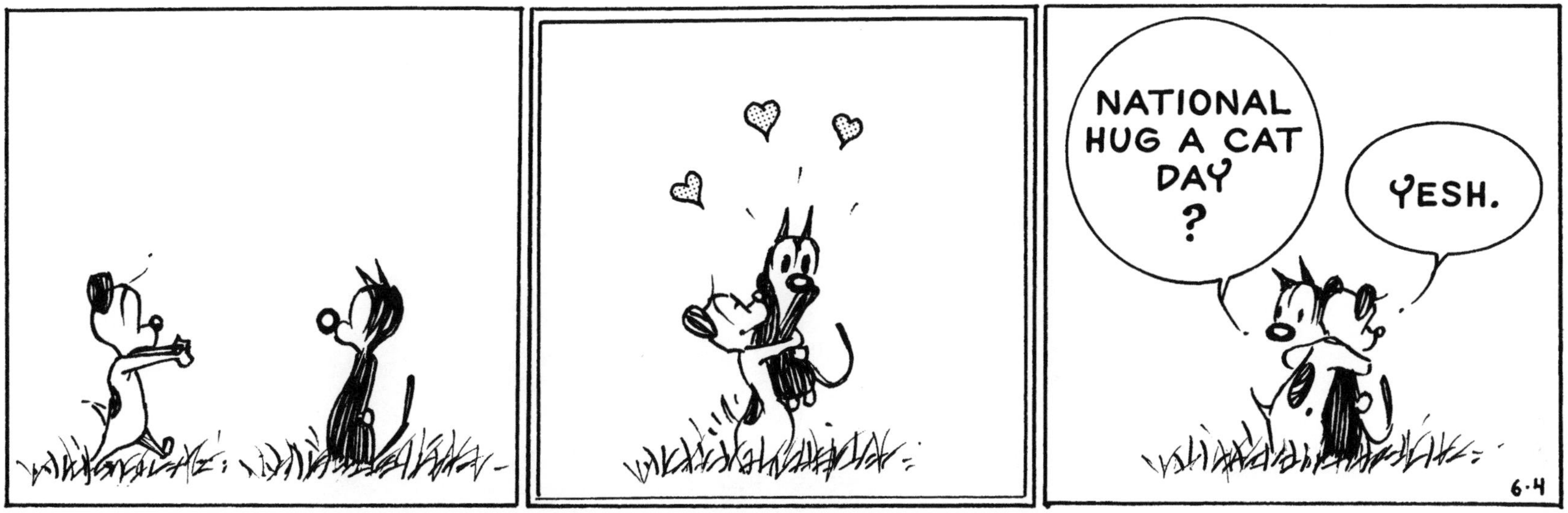
NATIONAL HUG A CAT DAY ?
YESH.
6·4

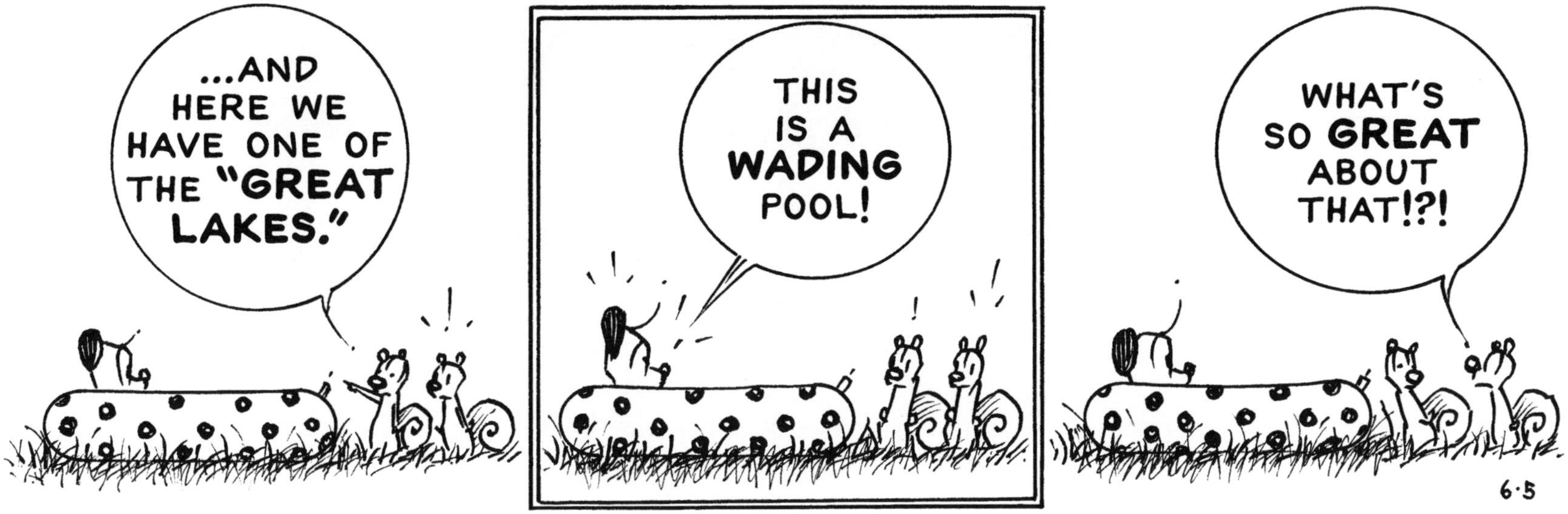
...AND HERE WE HAVE ONE OF THE "GREAT LAKES."
THIS IS A WADING POOL!
WHAT'S SO GREAT ABOUT THAT!?!
6·5

THE MUTTS

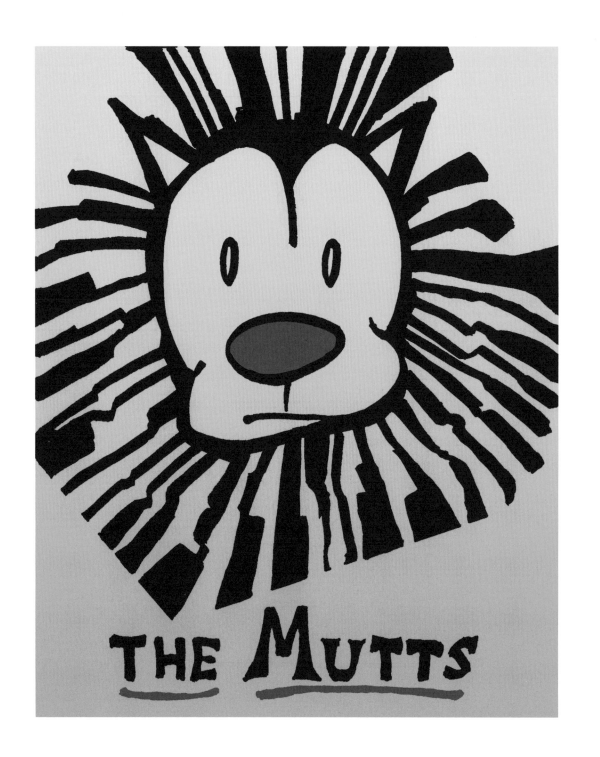

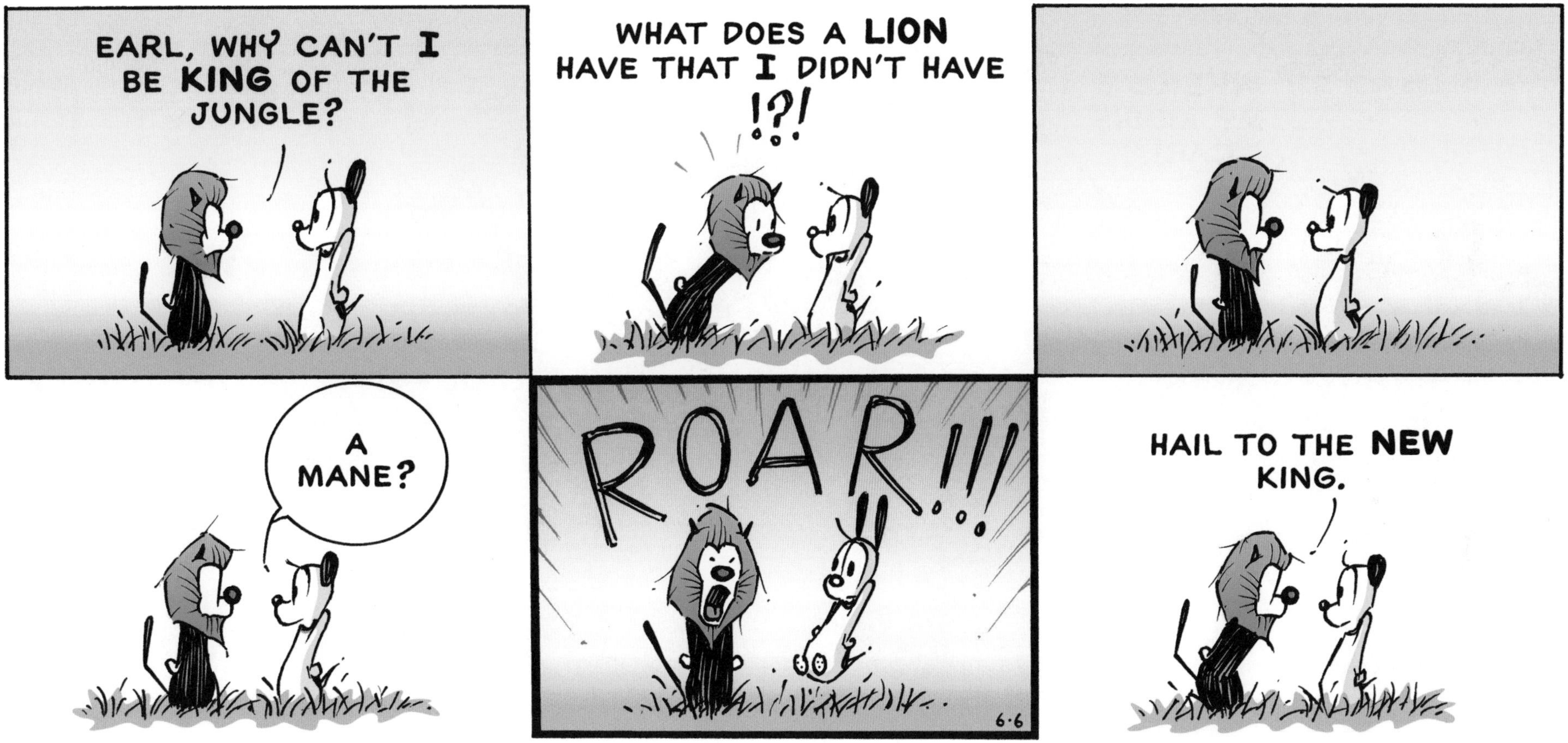
EARL, WHY CAN'T I BE KING OF THE JUNGLE?
WHAT DOES A LION HAVE THAT I DIDN'T HAVE !?!
A MANE?
ROAR!!!
6·6
HAIL TO THE NEW KING.

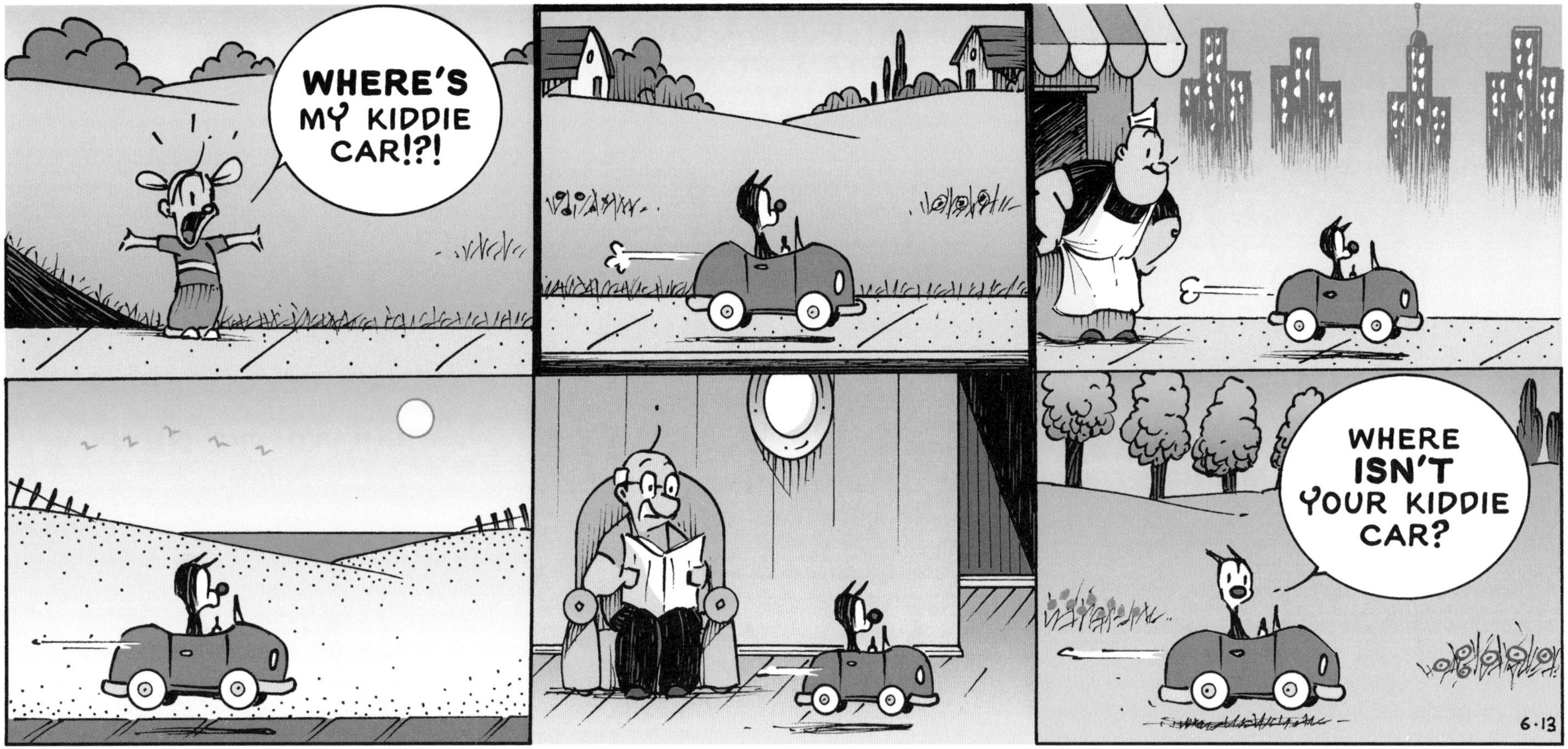
WHERE'S MY KIDDIE CAR!?!
WHERE ISN'T YOUR KIDDIE CAR?
6·13

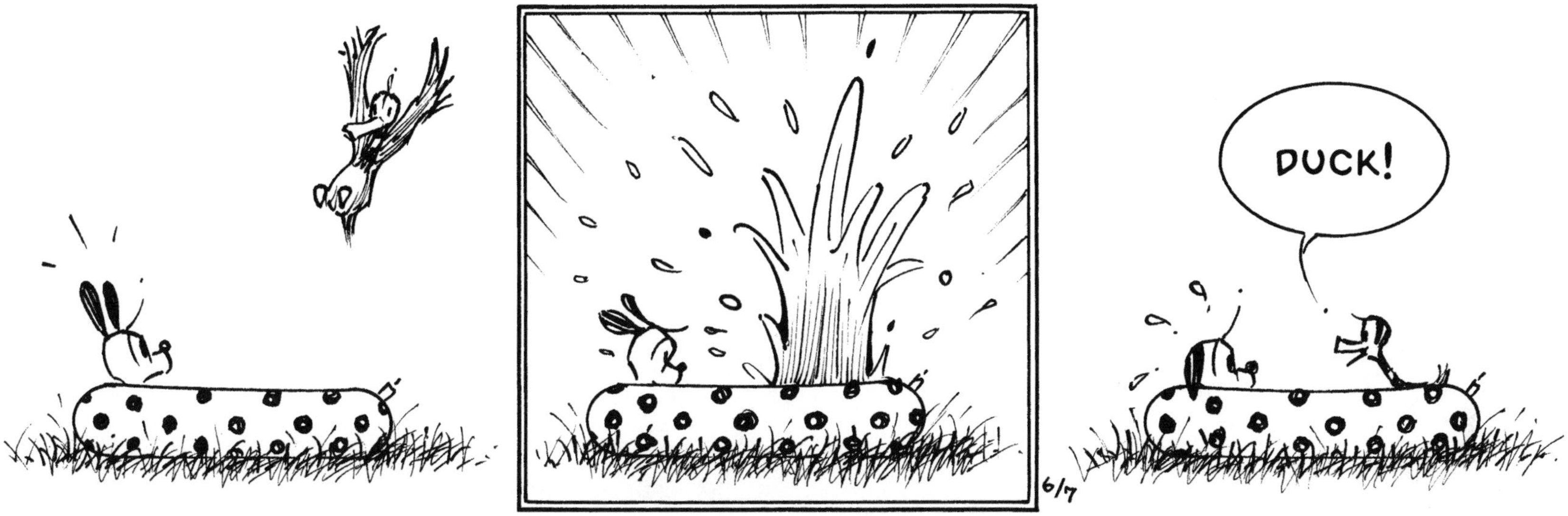
DUCK!
6/7

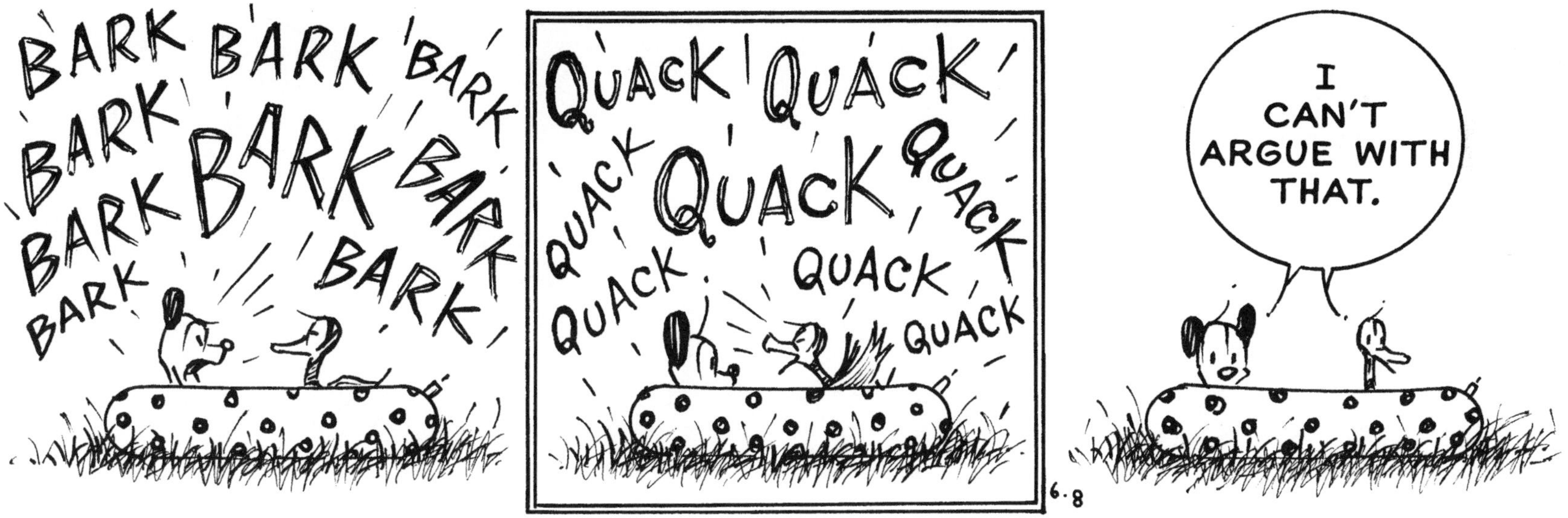
BARK BARK BARK
BARK
BARK BARK BARK
BARK BARK
BARK
QUACK QUACK
QUACK QUACK QUACK
QUACK QUACK QUACK
I CAN'T ARGUE WITH THAT.
6.8

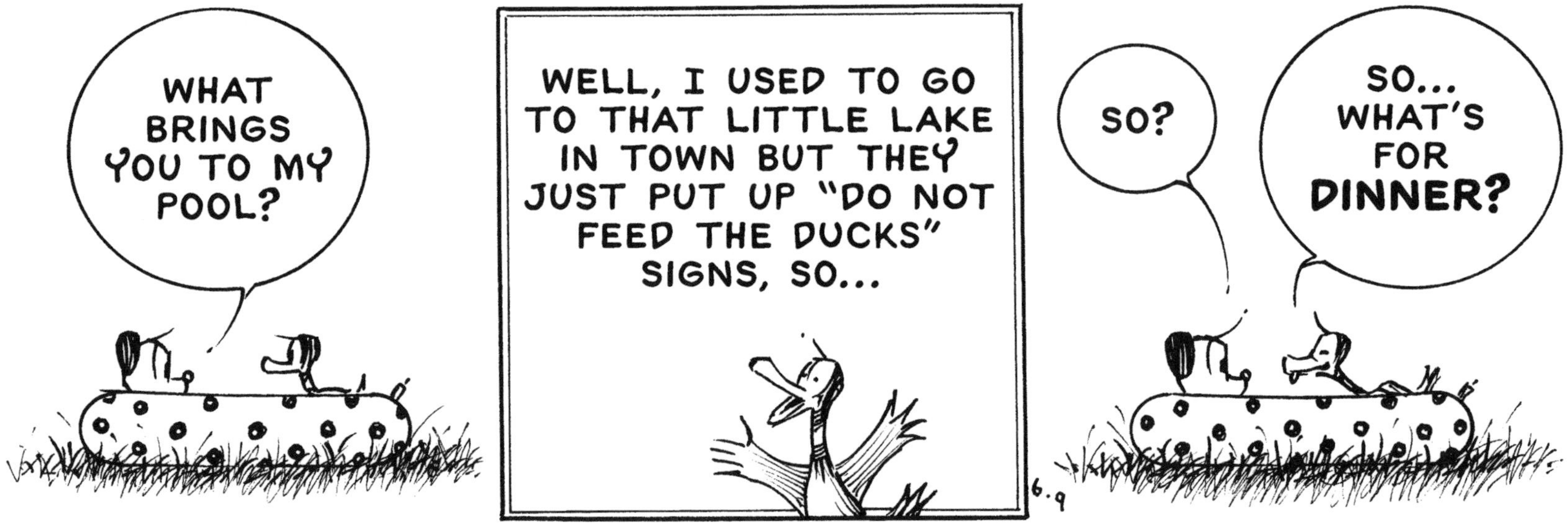
WHAT BRINGS YOU TO MY POOL?
WELL, I USED TO GO TO THAT LITTLE LAKE IN TOWN BUT THEY JUST PUT UP "DO NOT FEED THE DUCKS" SIGNS, SO...
SO?
SO... WHAT'S FOR **DINNER?**
6.9

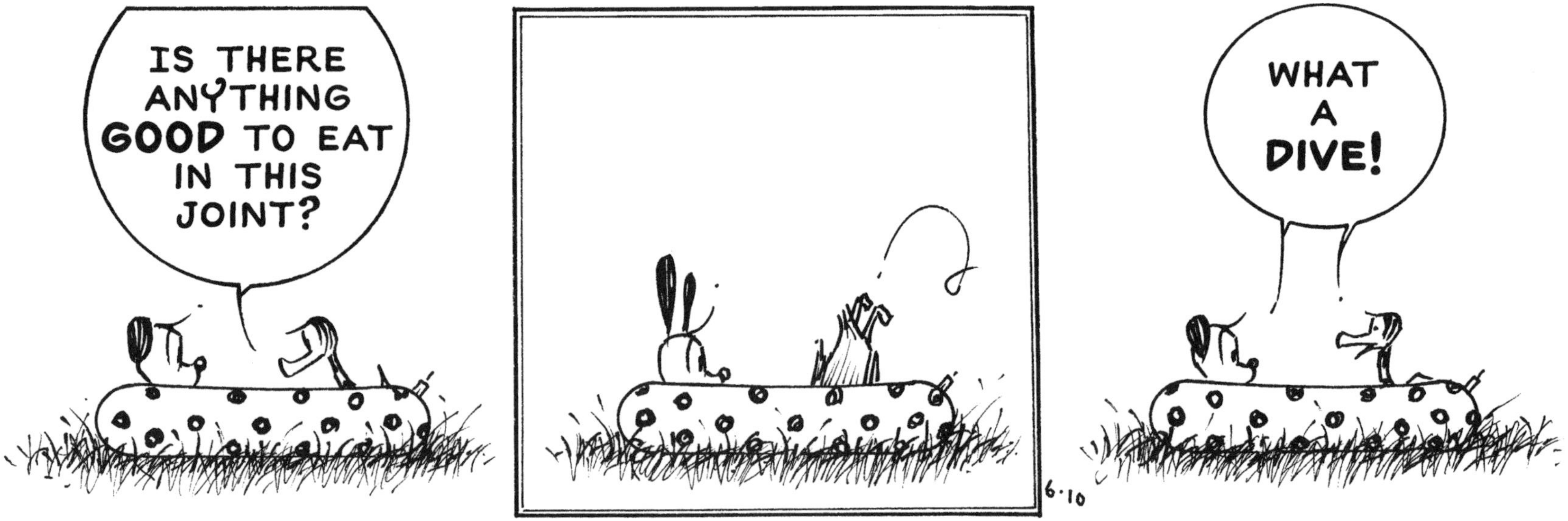
IS THERE ANYTHING **GOOD** TO EAT IN THIS JOINT?
6.10
WHAT A **DIVE!**

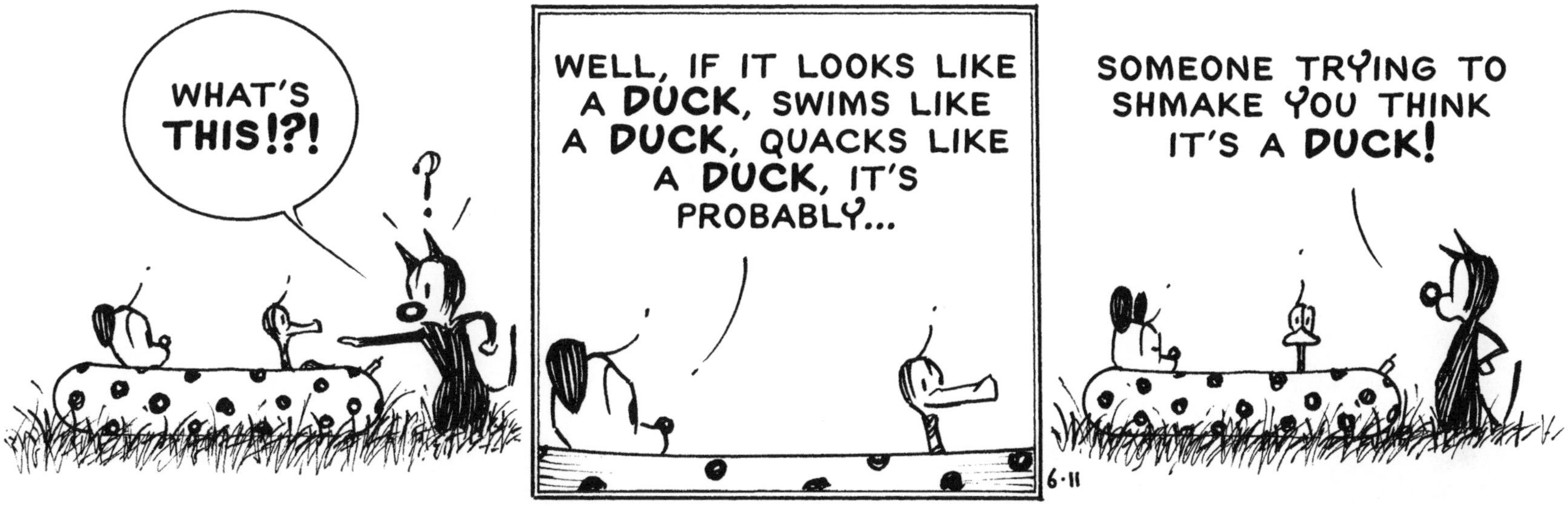
WHAT'S THIS!?!
WELL, IF IT LOOKS LIKE A DUCK, SWIMS LIKE A DUCK, QUACKS LIKE A DUCK, IT'S PROBABLY...
SOMEONE TRYING TO SHMAKE YOU THINK IT'S A DUCK!
6·11

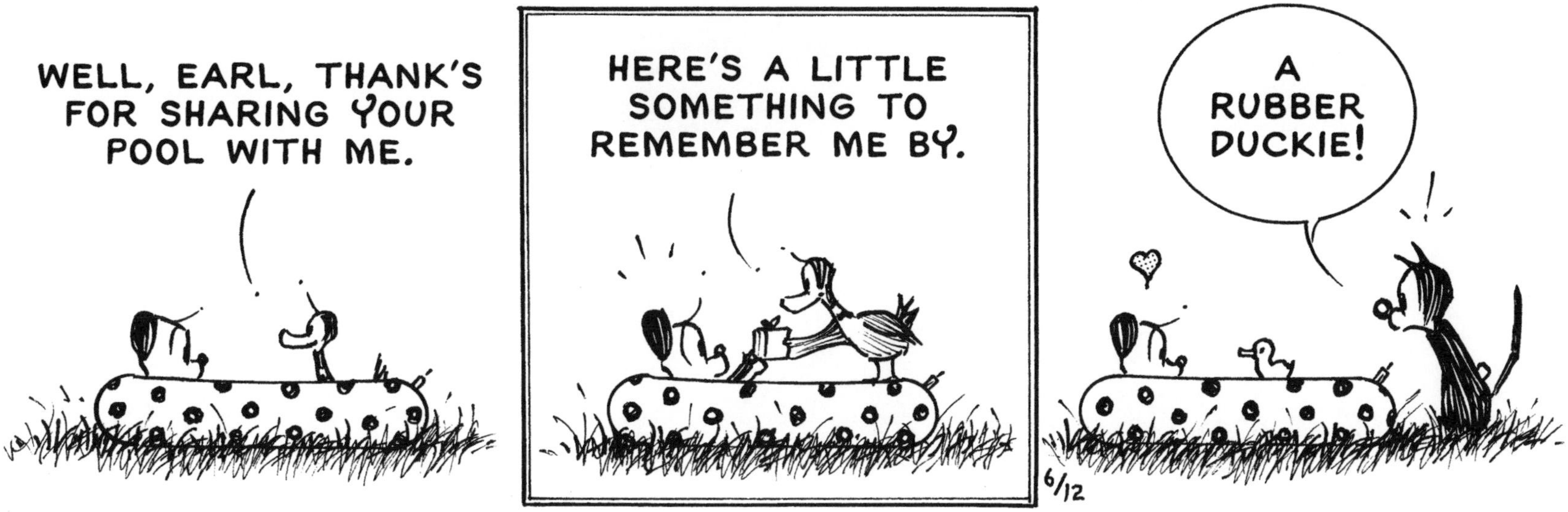
WELL, EARL, THANK'S FOR SHARING YOUR POOL WITH ME.
HERE'S A LITTLE SOMETHING TO REMEMBER ME BY.
A RUBBER DUCKIE!
6/12

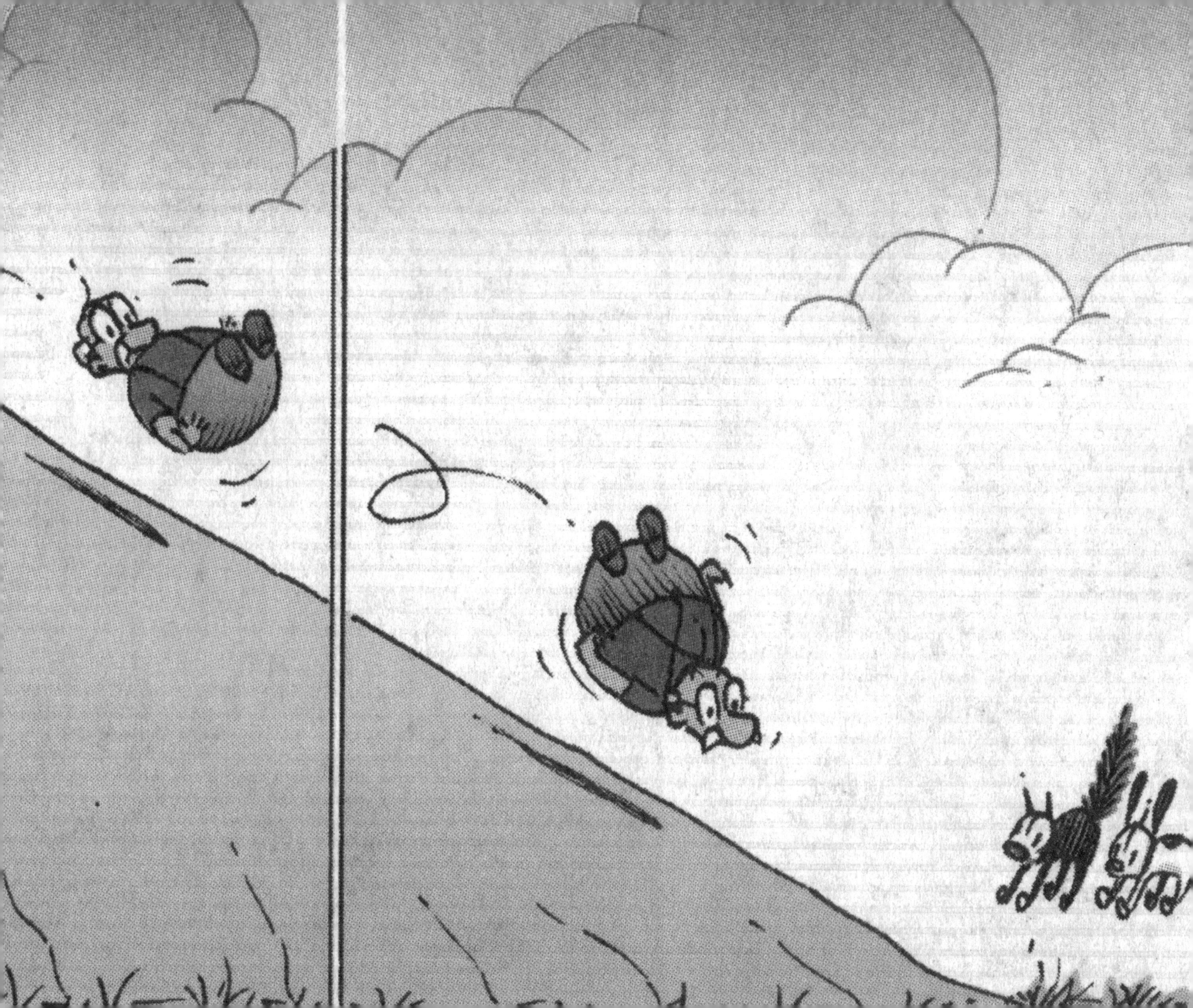

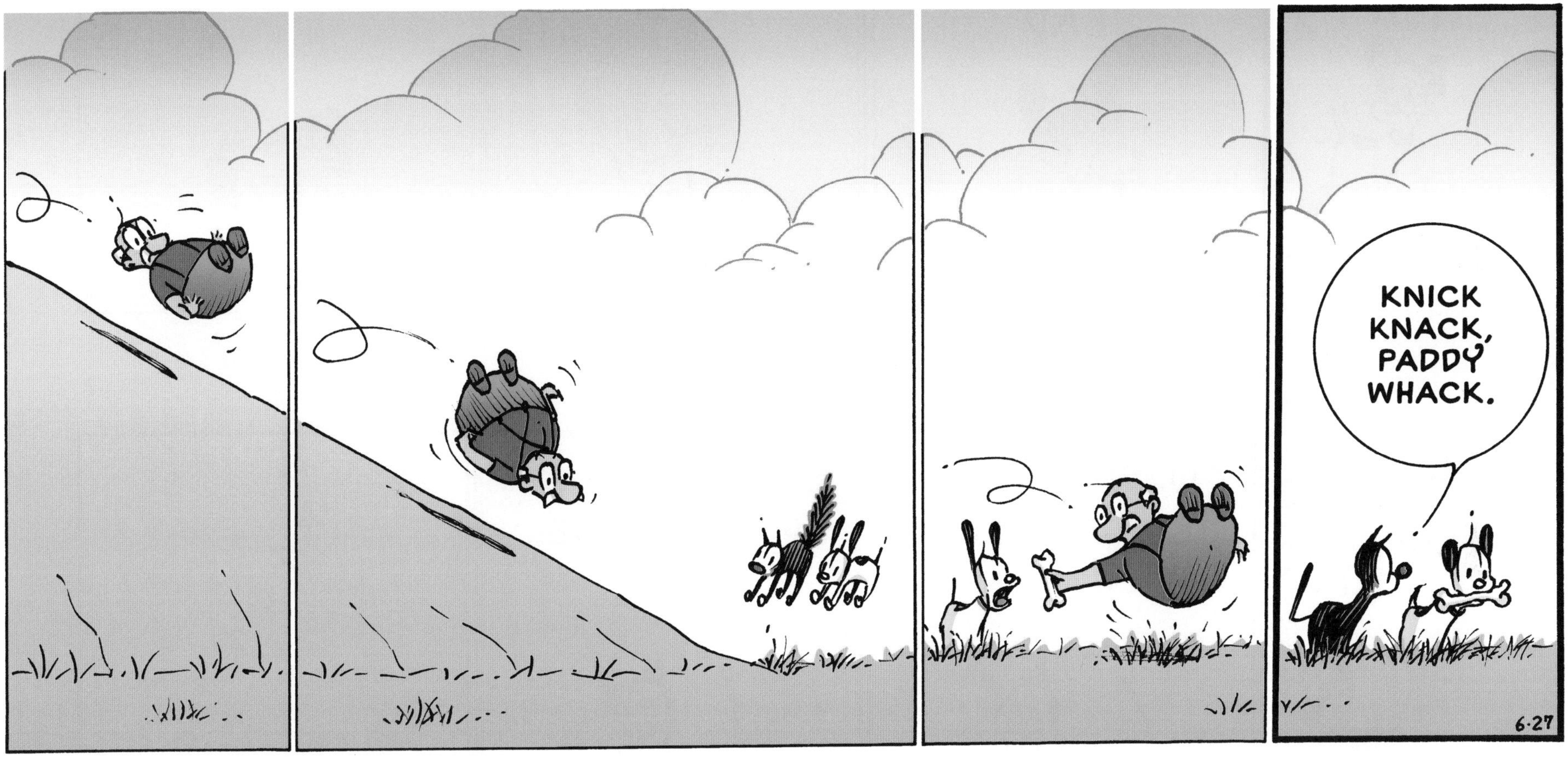
KNICK KNACK, PADDY WHACK.
6·27

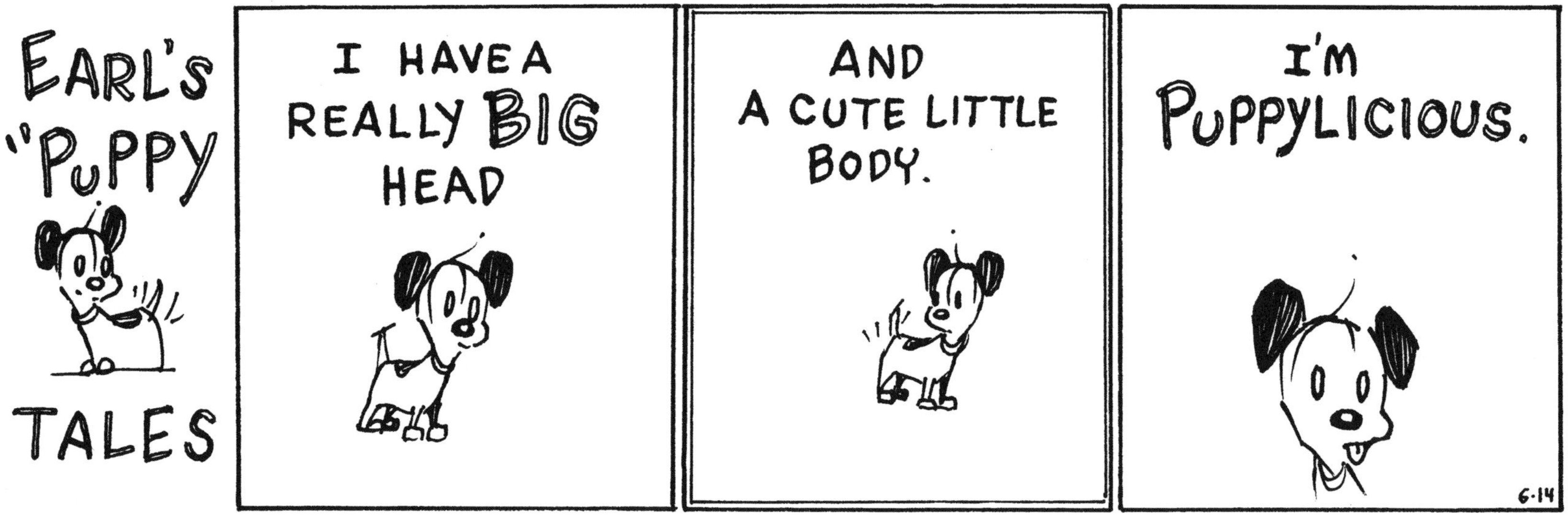
EARL'S "PUPPY TALES
I HAVE A REALLY BIG HEAD
AND A CUTE LITTLE BODY.
I'M PUPPYLICIOUS.
6·14

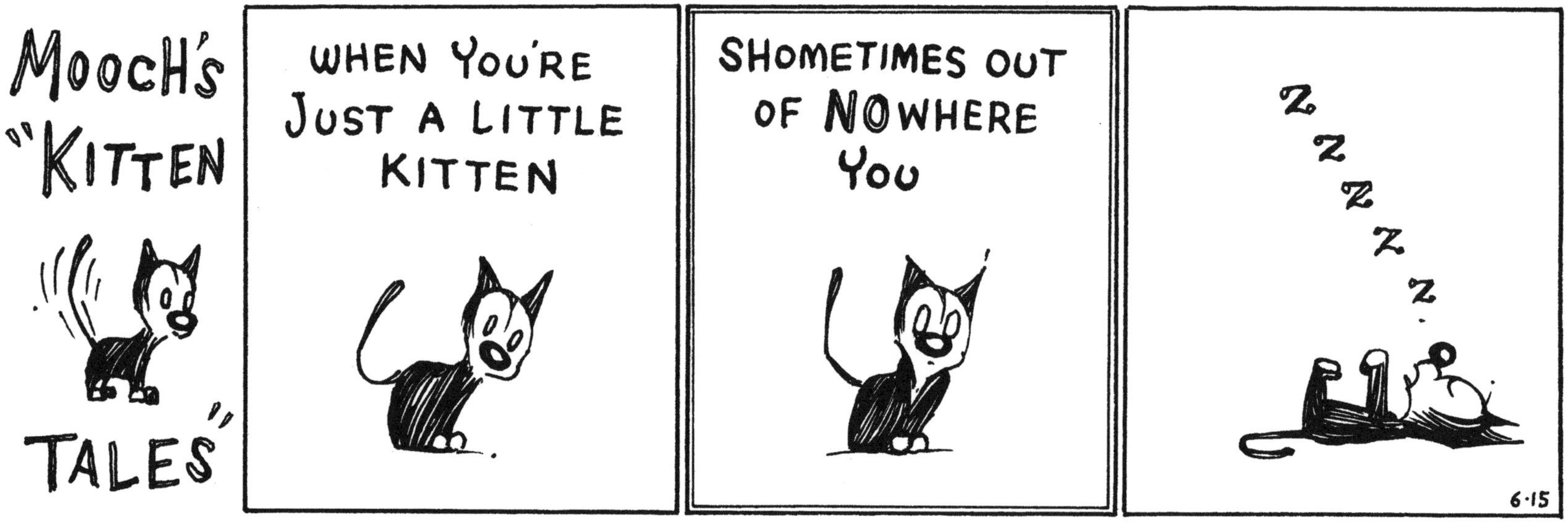
MOOCH'S "KITTEN TALES"
WHEN YOU'RE JUST A LITTLE KITTEN
SHOMETIMES OUT OF NOWHERE YOU
Z Z Z Z Z
6·15

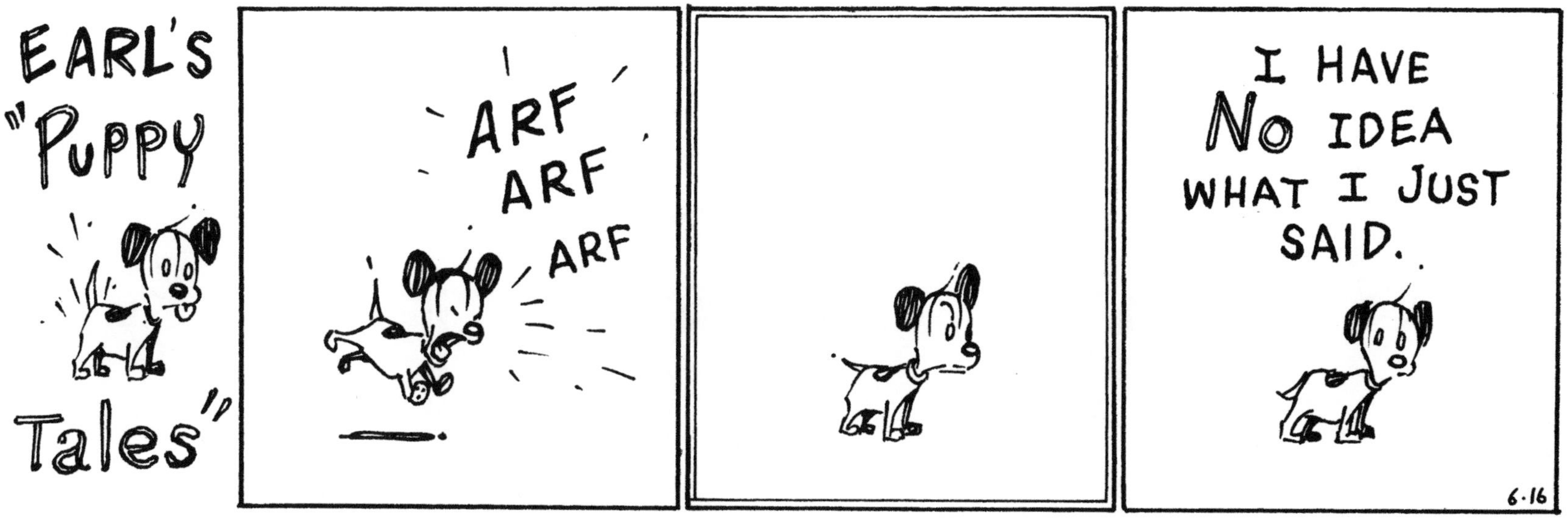
EARL'S "PUPPY TALES"
ARF
ARF
ARF
I HAVE NO IDEA WHAT I JUST SAID.
6·16

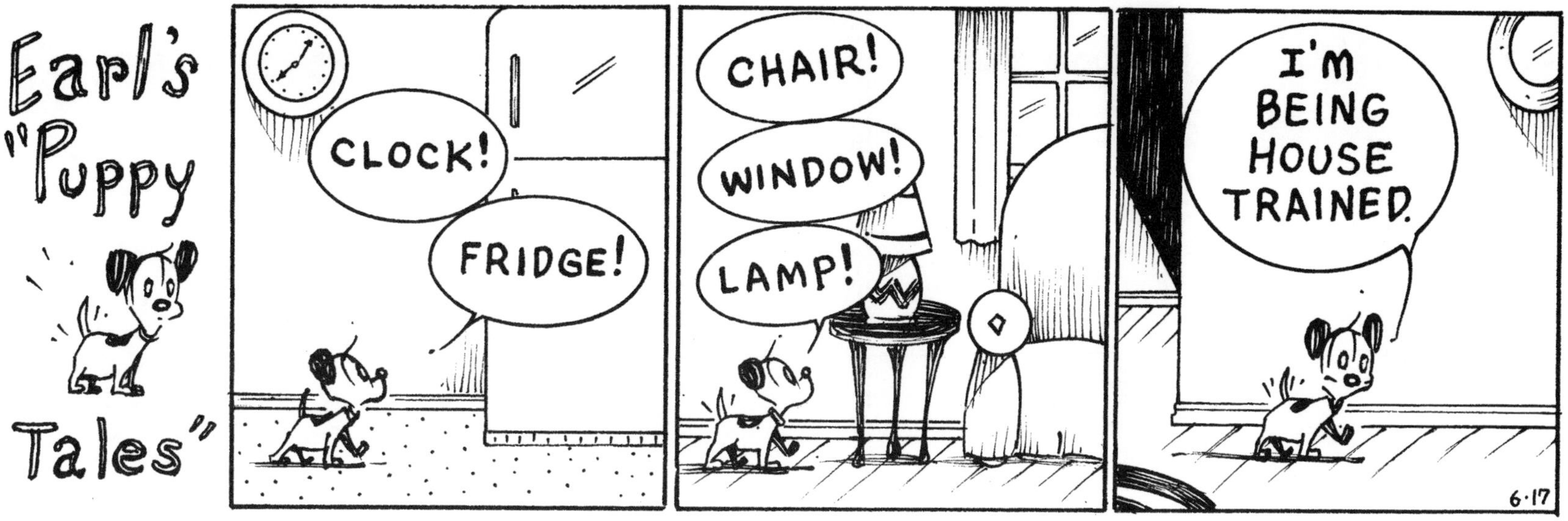
Earl's "Puppy Tales"
CLOCK!
FRIDGE!
CHAIR!
WINDOW!
LAMP!
I'M BEING HOUSE TRAINED.
6·17

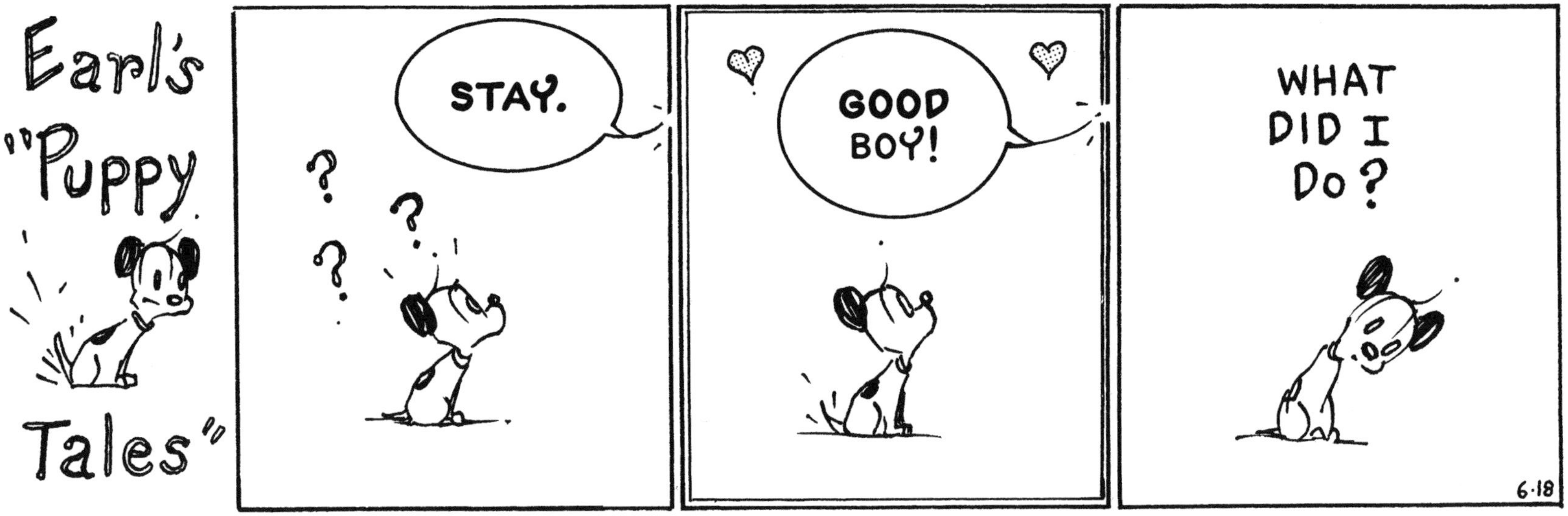
Earl's "Puppy Tales"
STAY.
GOOD BOY!
WHAT DID I DO?
6·18

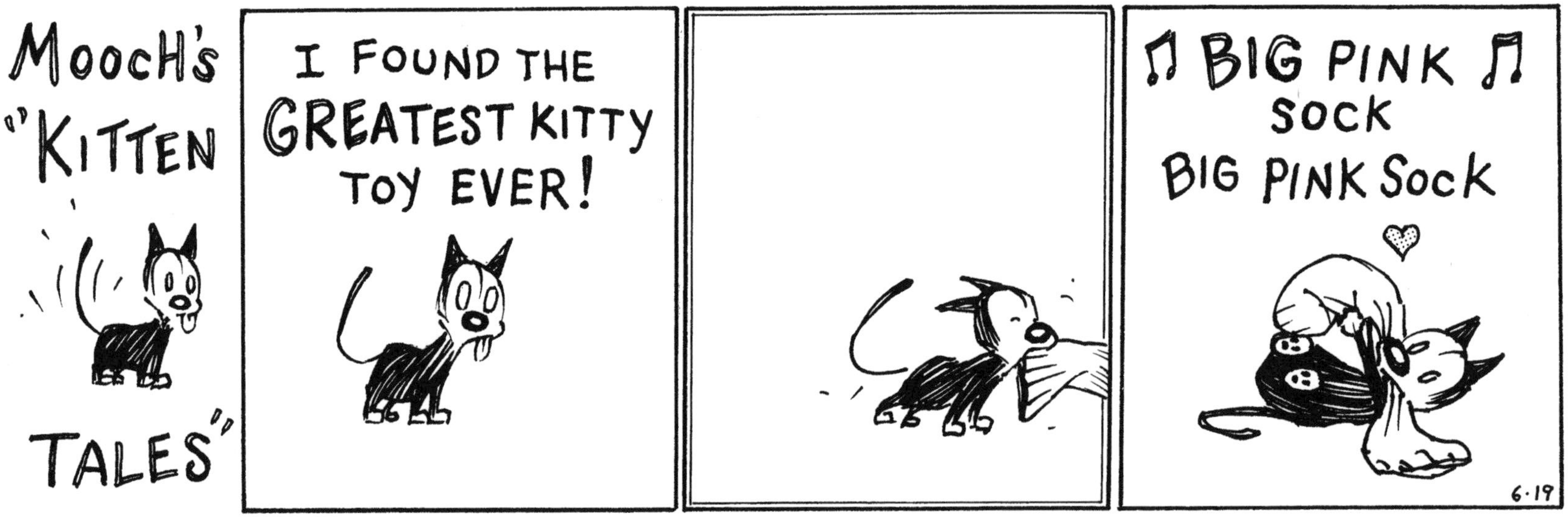
Mooch's "Kitten Tales"
I FOUND THE GREATEST KITTY TOY EVER!
♫ BIG PINK ♫ SOCK
BIG PINK SOCK
6·19

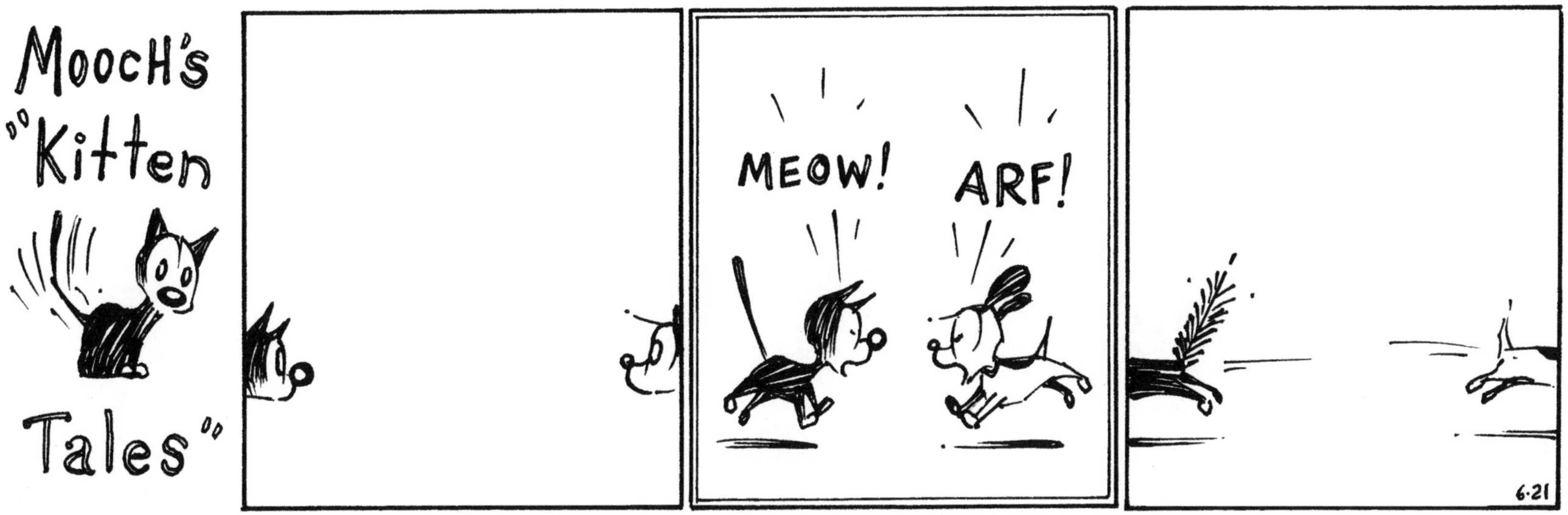
Mooch's "Kitten Tales"
MEOW!
ARF!
6·21

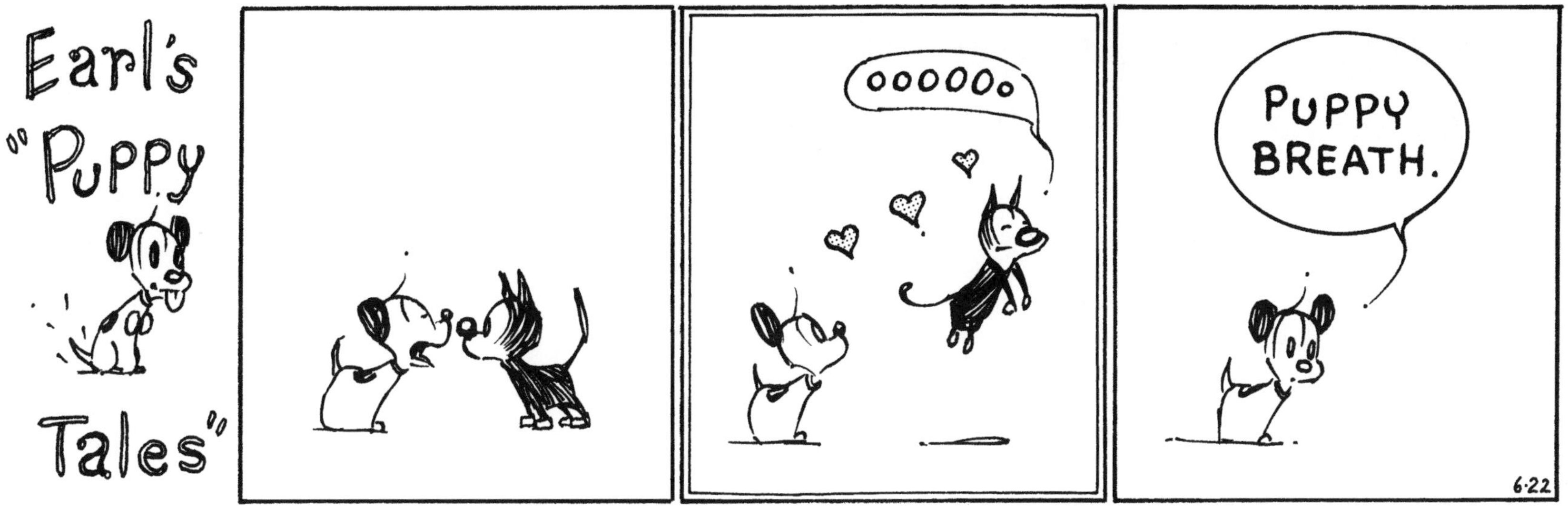
Earl's "Puppy Tales"
oooooo
PUPPY BREATH.
6·22

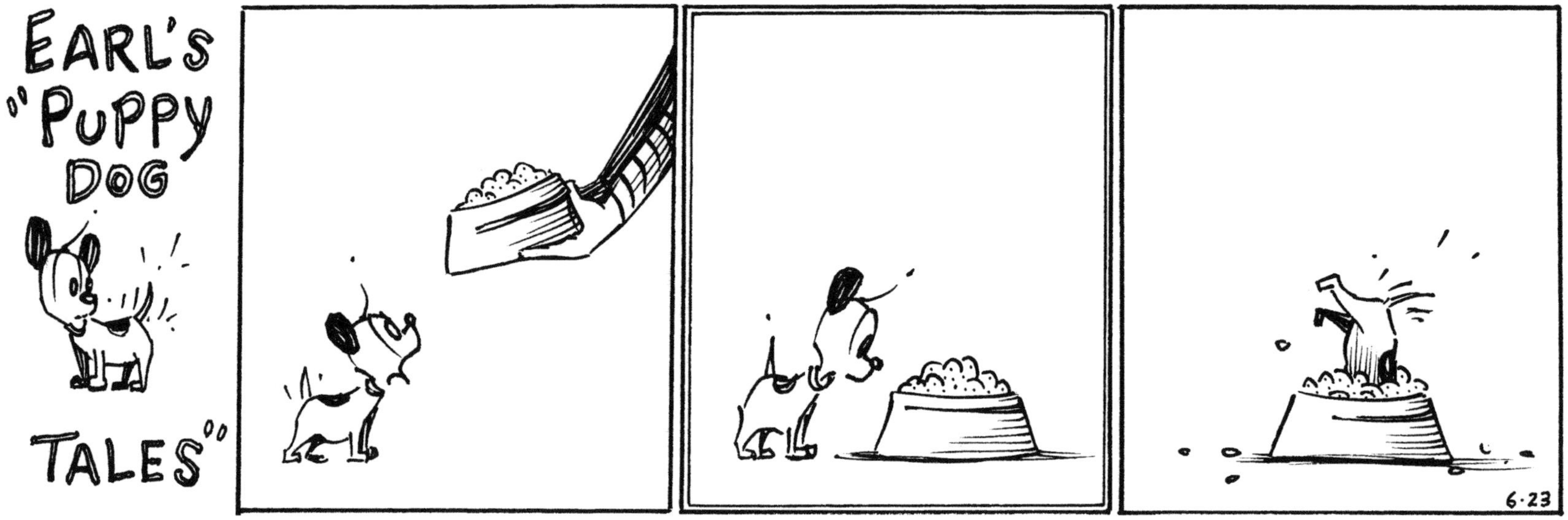
EARL'S "PUPPY DOG TALES"
6·23

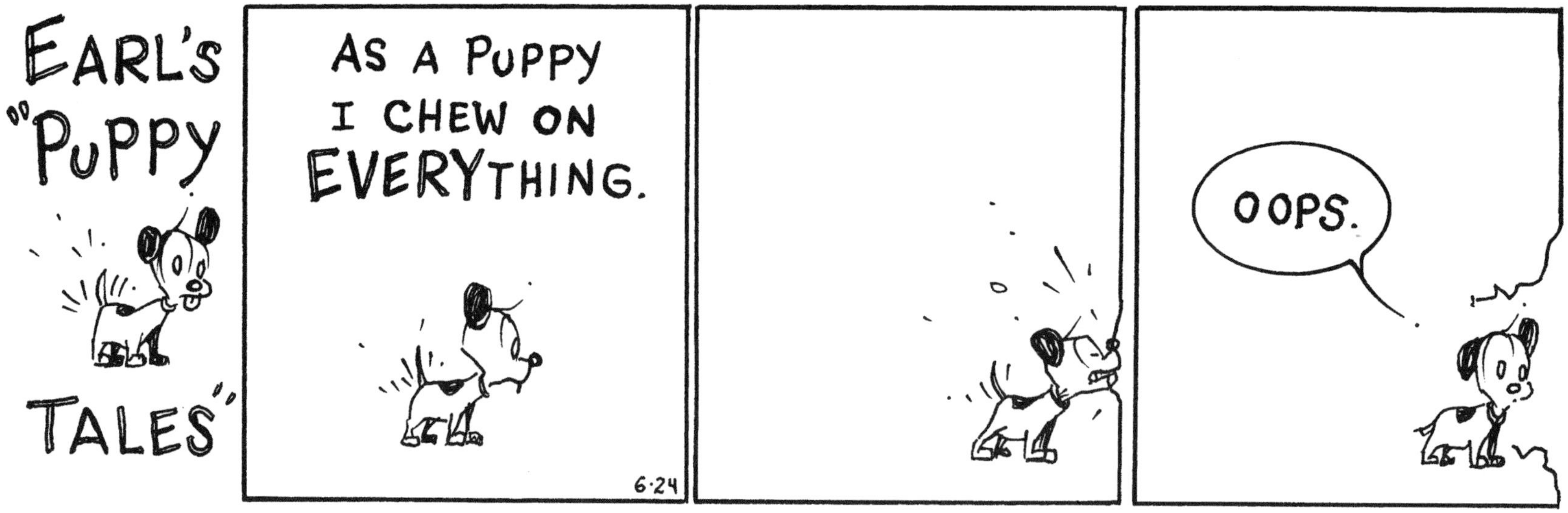
EARL'S "PUPPY TALES"
AS A PUPPY I CHEW ON EVERYTHING.
6·24
OOPS.

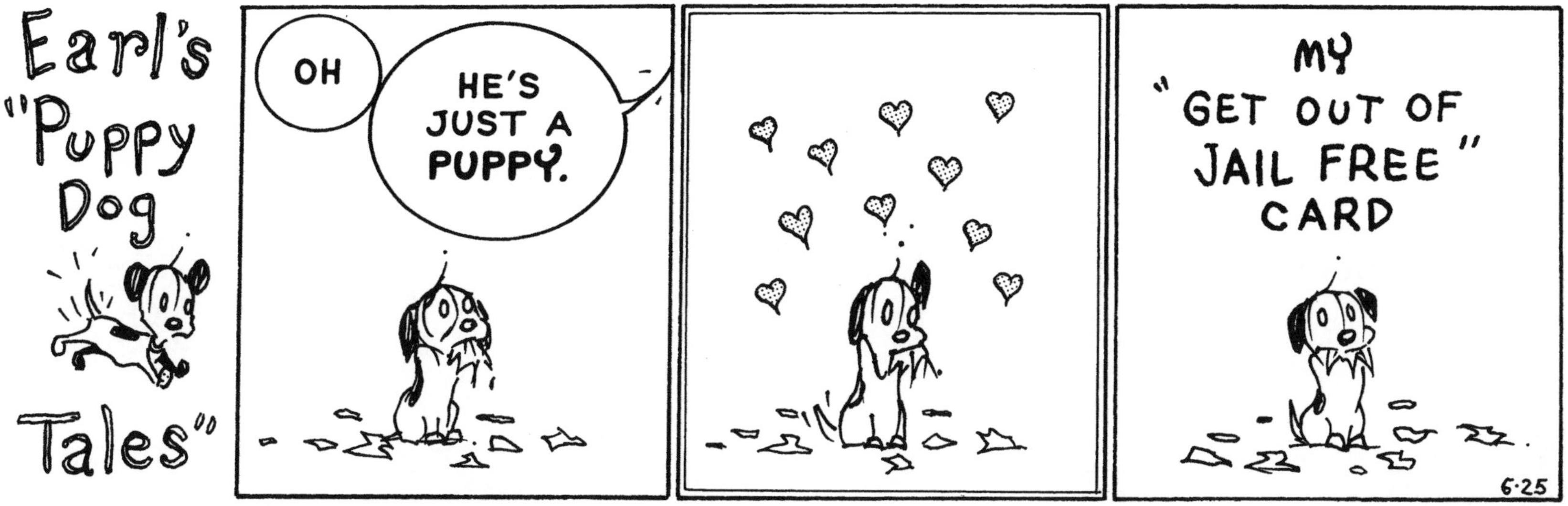
Earl's "Puppy Dog Tales"
OH
HE'S JUST A PUPPY.
MY "GET OUT OF JAIL FREE" CARD
6·25

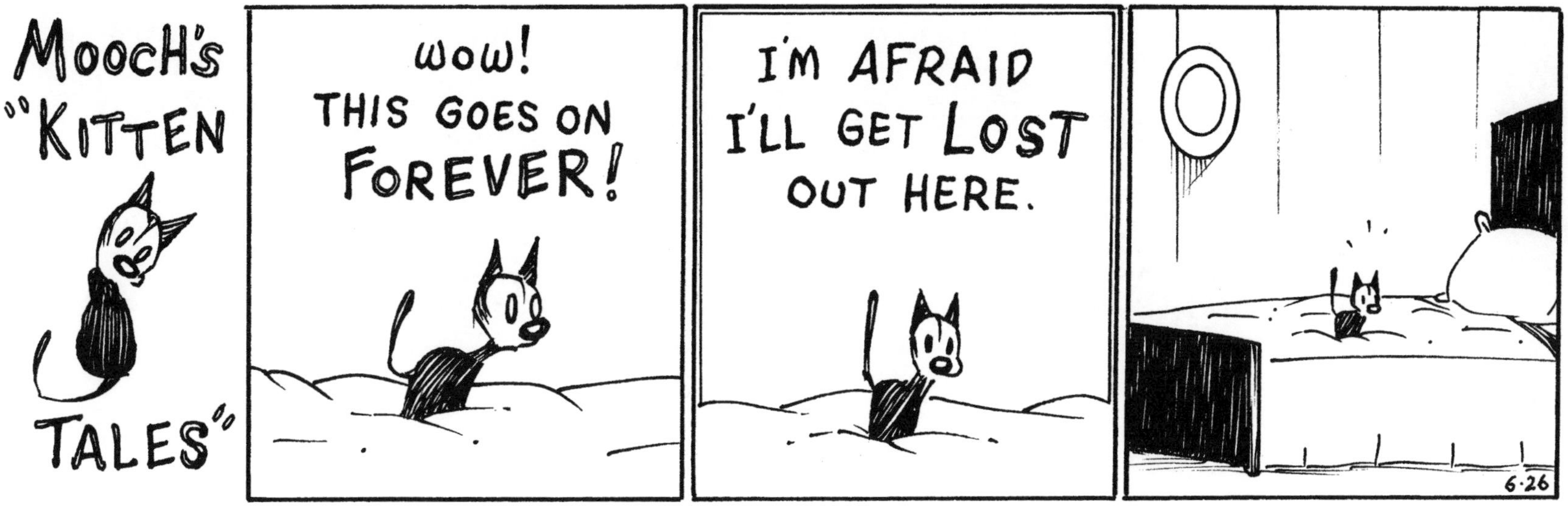
MOOCH'S "KITTEN TALES"
WOW! THIS GOES ON FOREVER!
I'M AFRAID I'LL GET LOST OUT HERE.
6·26

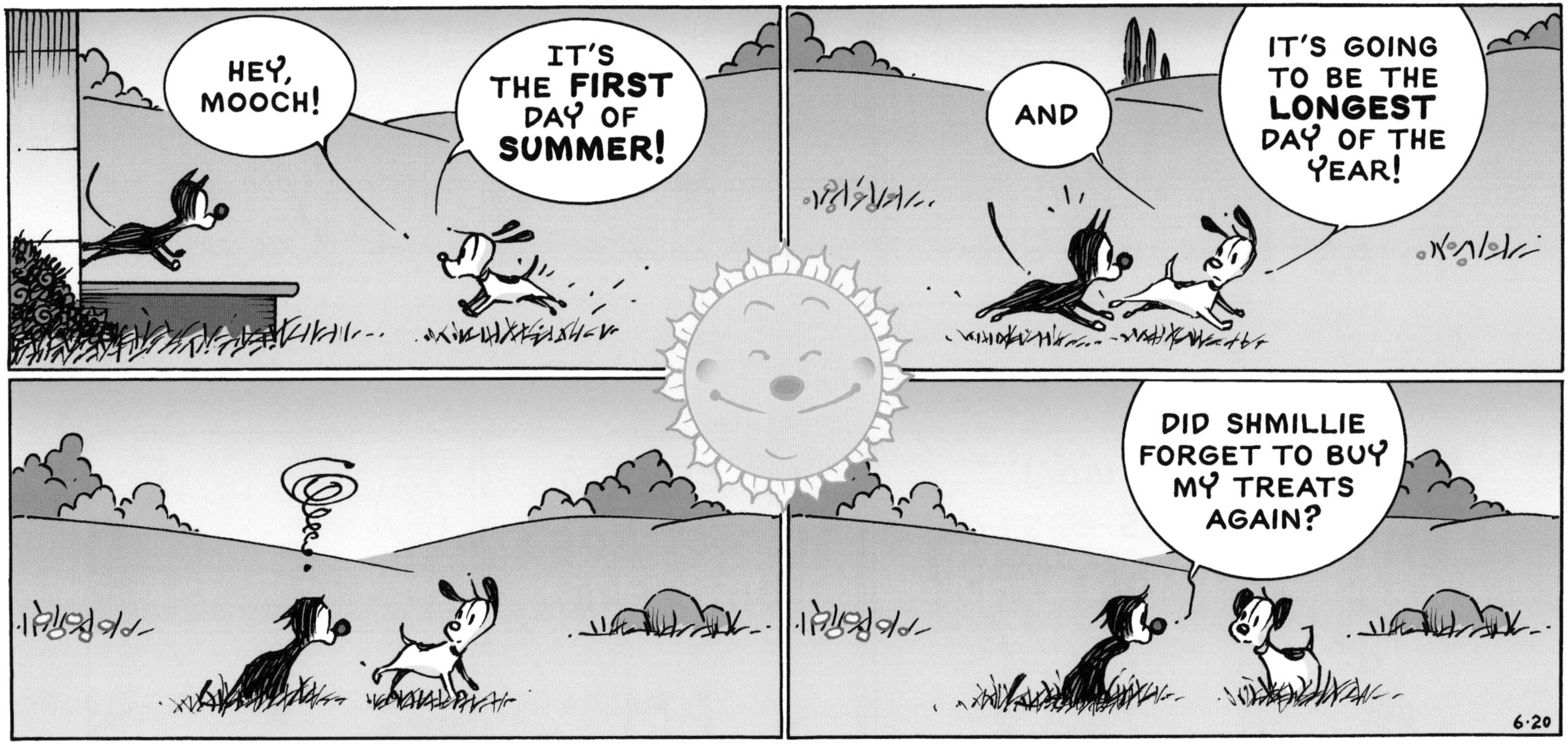
HEY, MOOCH!
IT'S THE FIRST DAY OF SUMMER!
AND
IT'S GOING TO BE THE LONGEST DAY OF THE YEAR!
DID SHMILLIE FORGET TO BUY MY TREATS AGAIN?
6·20

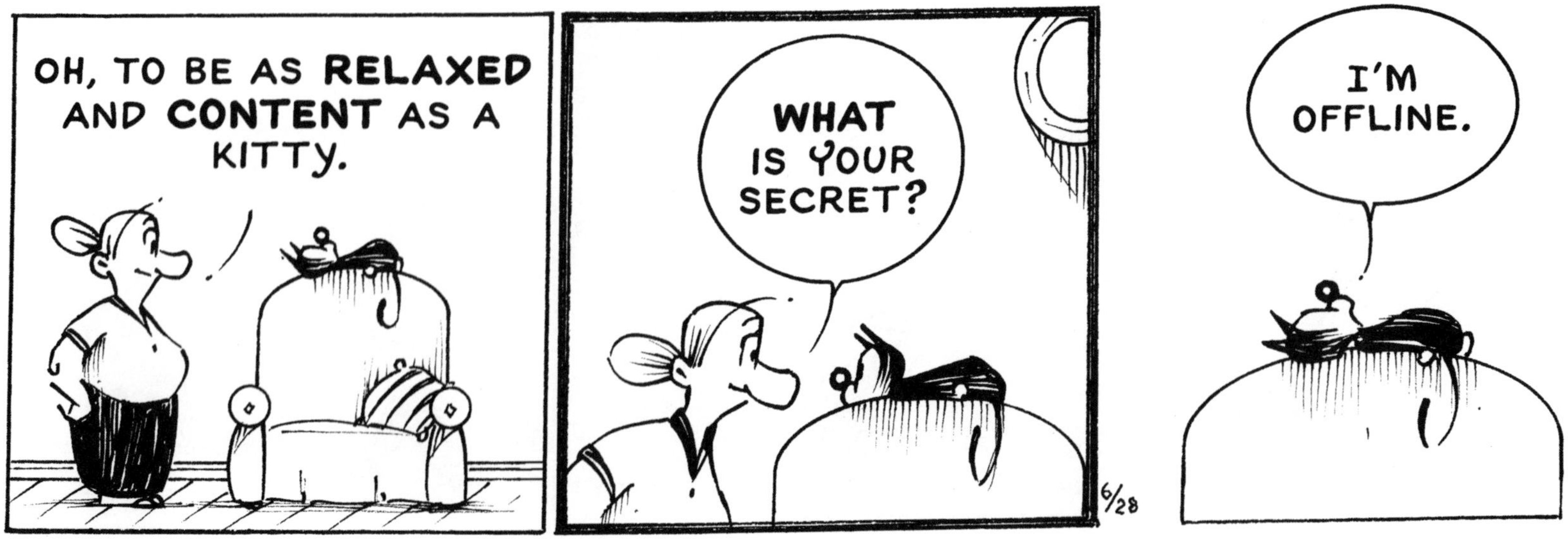
OH, TO BE AS RELAXED AND CONTENT AS A KITTY.
WHAT IS YOUR SECRET?
6/28
I'M OFFLINE.

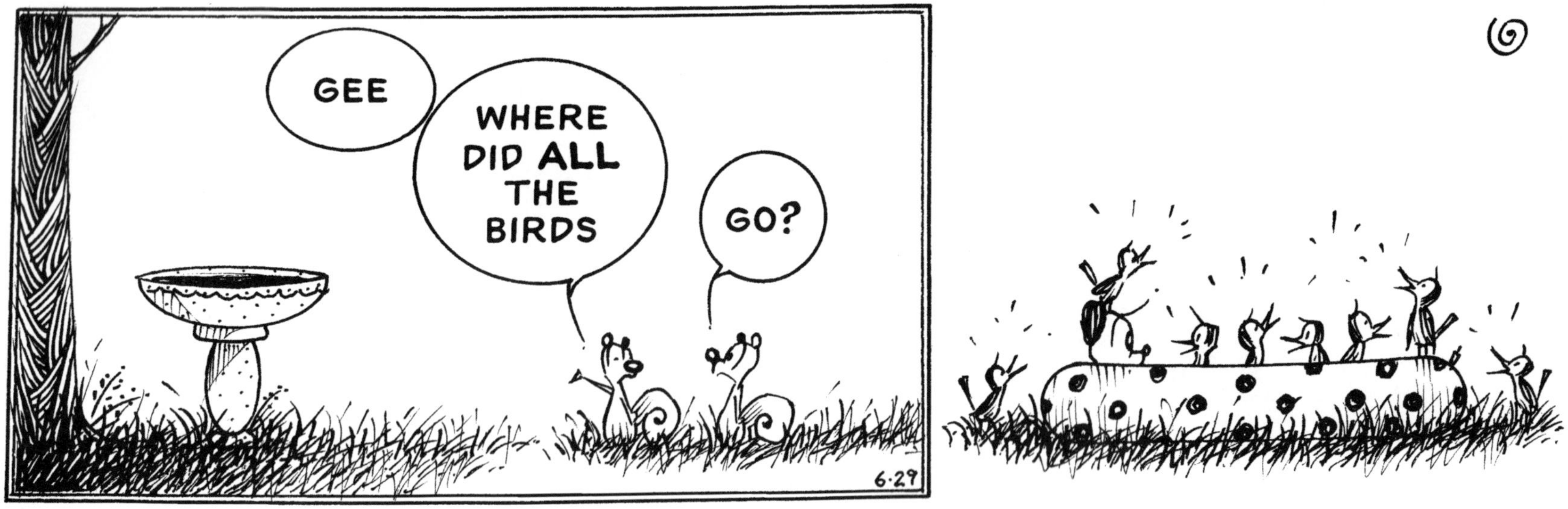
GEE
WHERE DID ALL THE BIRDS
GO?
6·29

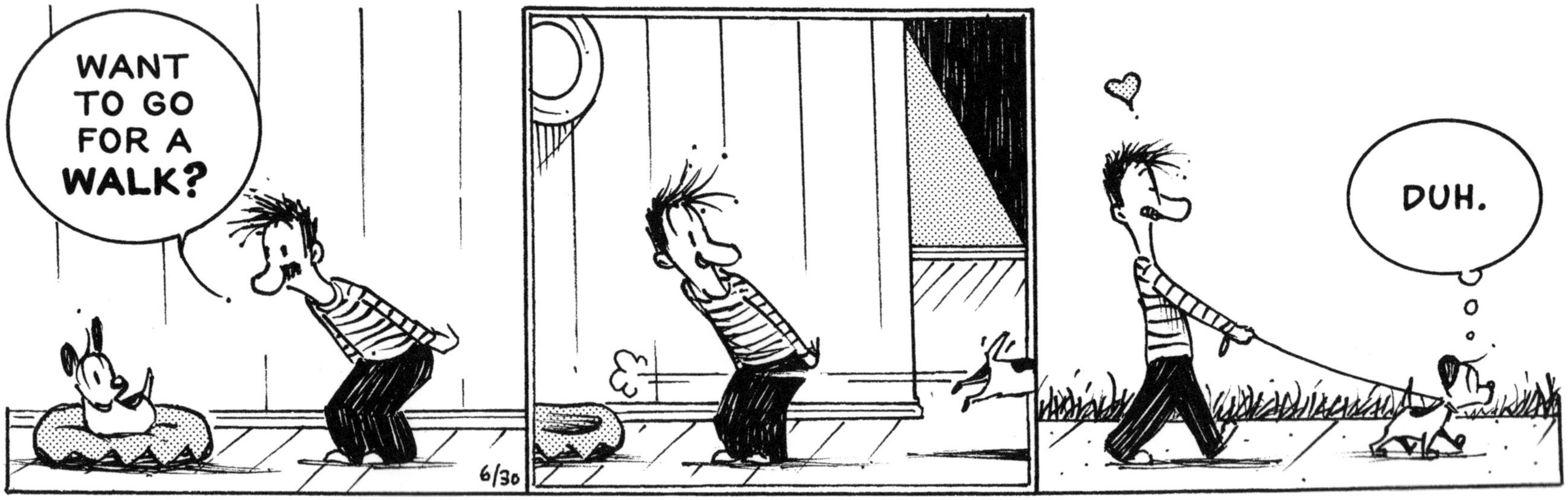
WANT TO GO FOR A WALK?
6/30
DUH.

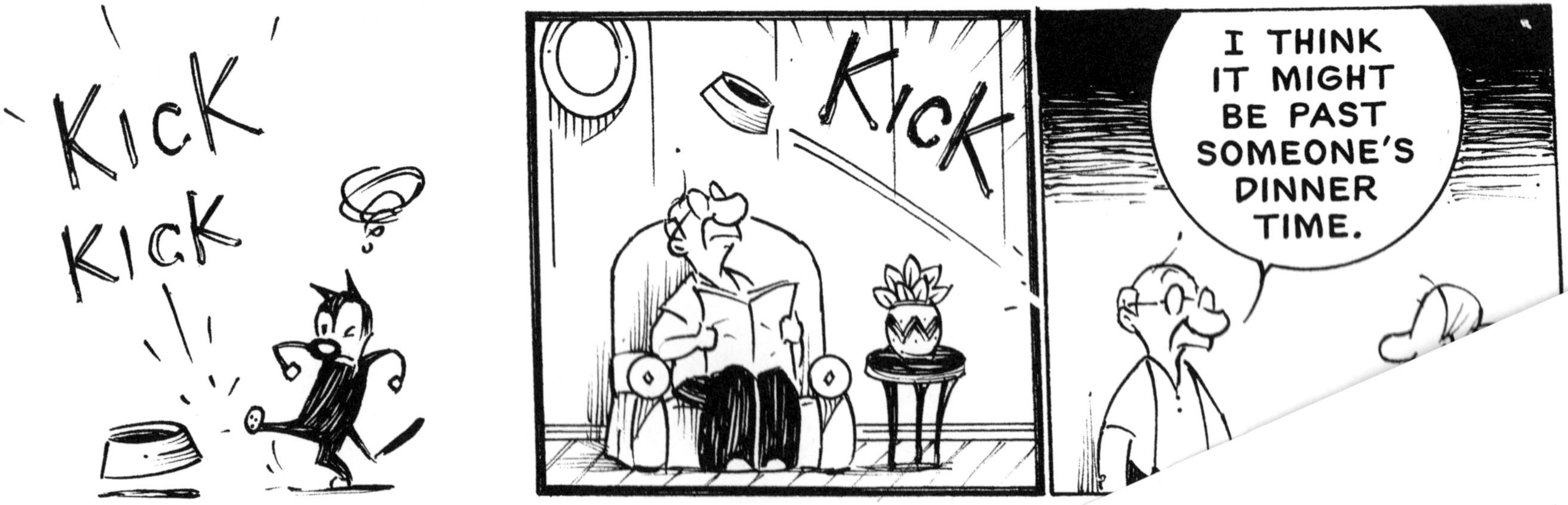
KICK KICK
KICK
I THINK IT MIGHT BE PAST SOMEONE'S DINNER TIME.

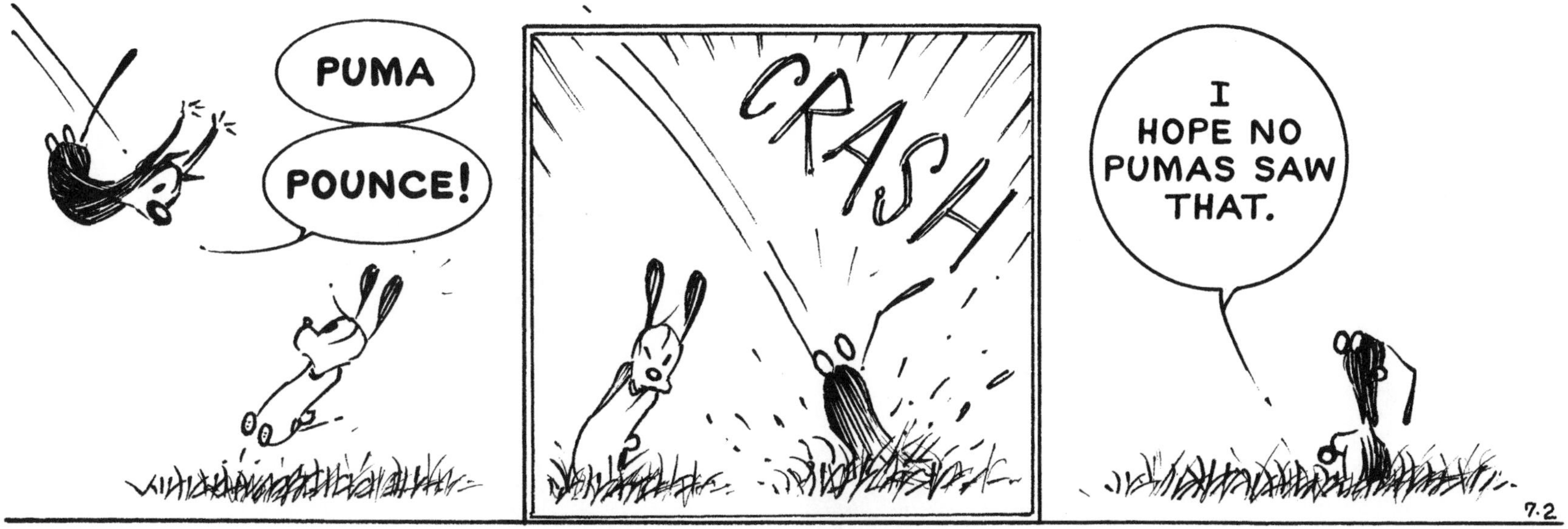
PUMA
POUNCE!
CRASH
I HOPE NO PUMAS SAW THAT.
7.2

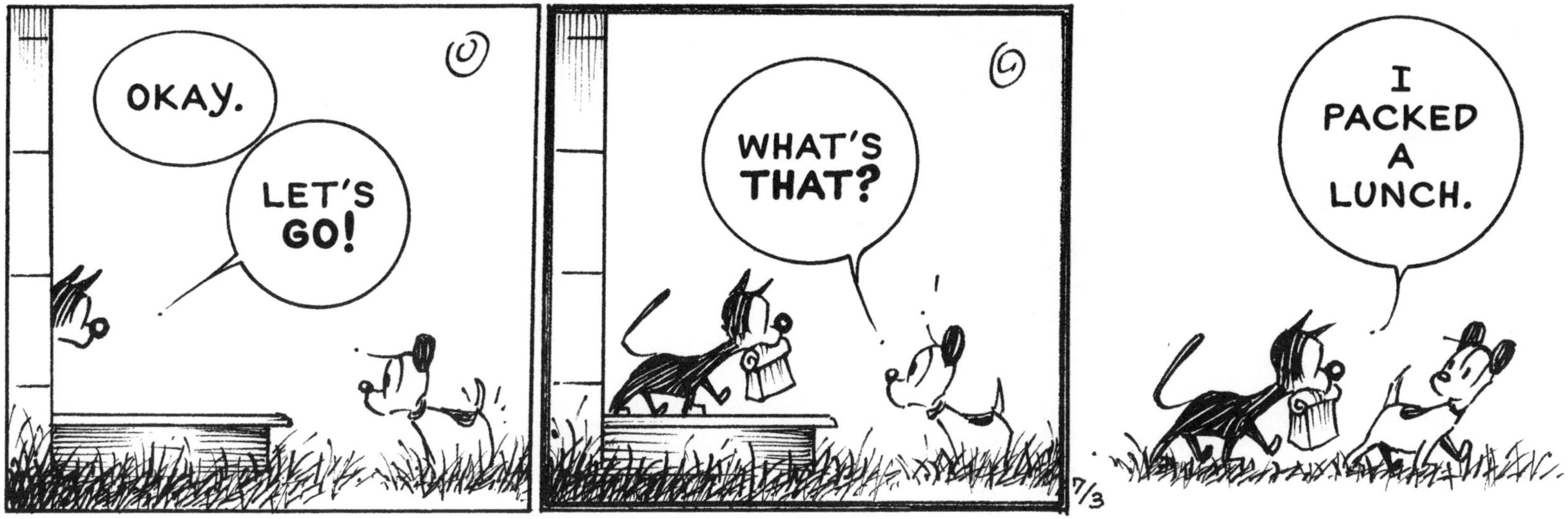
OKAY.
LET'S GO!
WHAT'S THAT?
7/3
I PACKED A LUNCH.

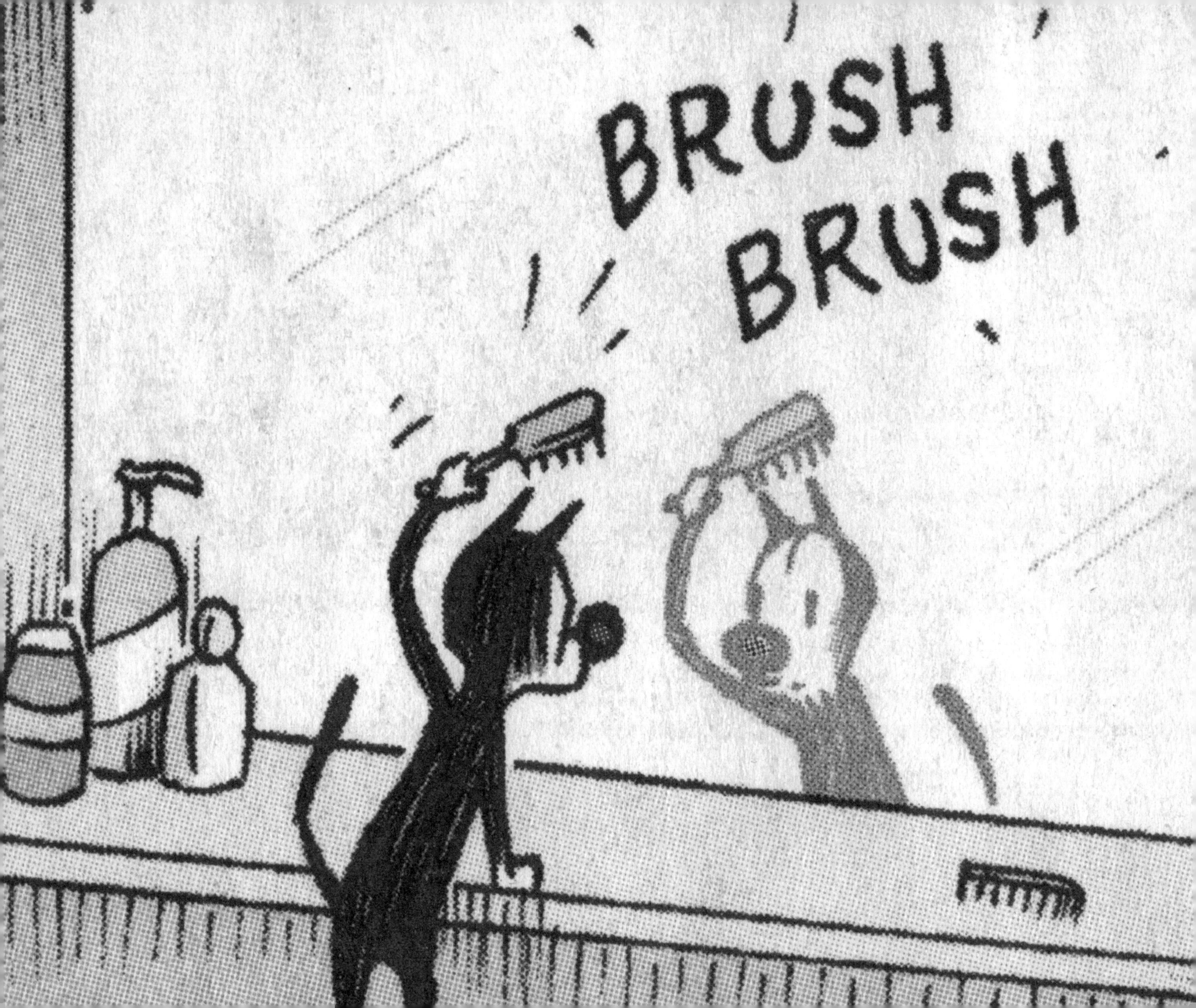
BRUSH
BRUSH

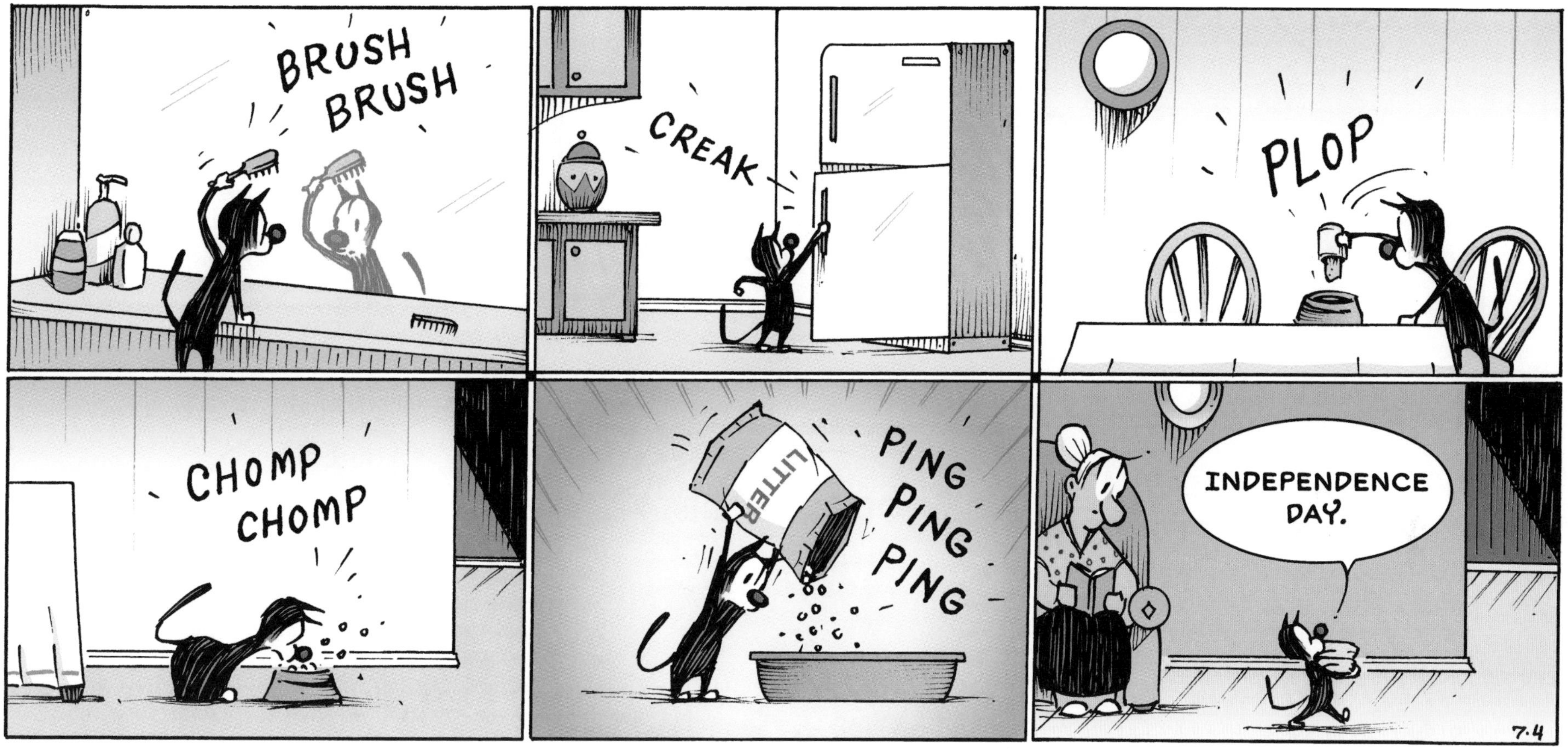
BRUSH
BRUSH
CREAK
PLOP
CHOMP
CHOMP
LITTER
PING
PING
PING
INDEPENDENCE DAY.
7.4

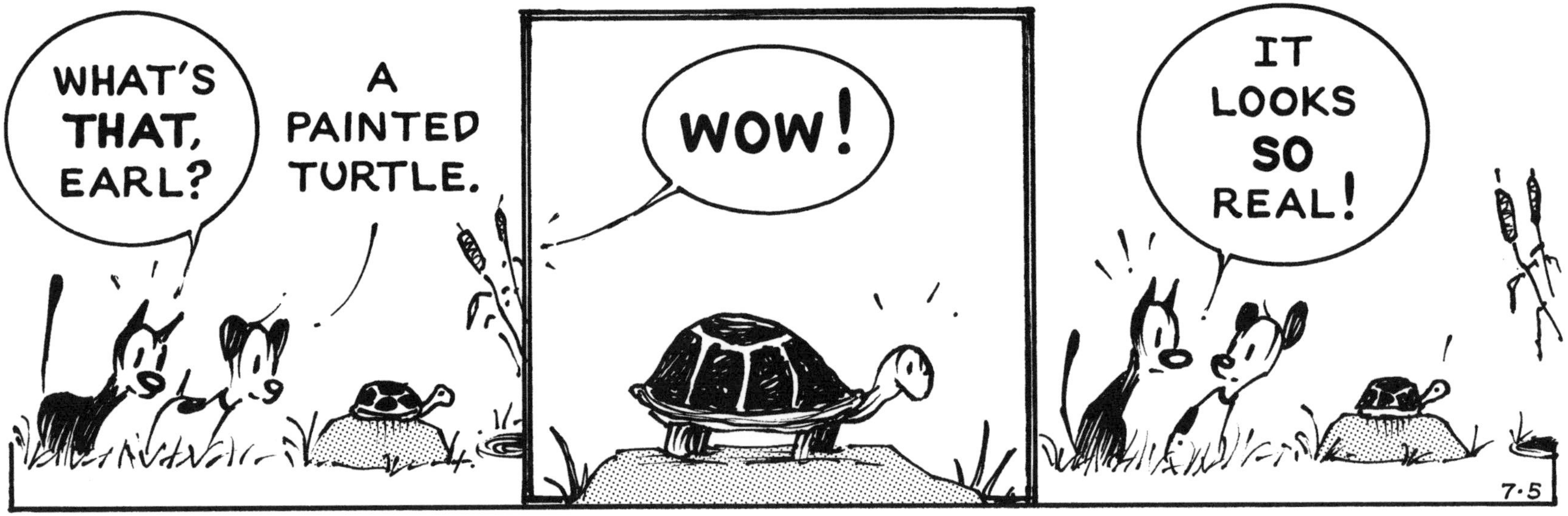
WHAT'S THAT, EARL?
A PAINTED TURTLE.
WOW!
IT LOOKS SO REAL!
7·5

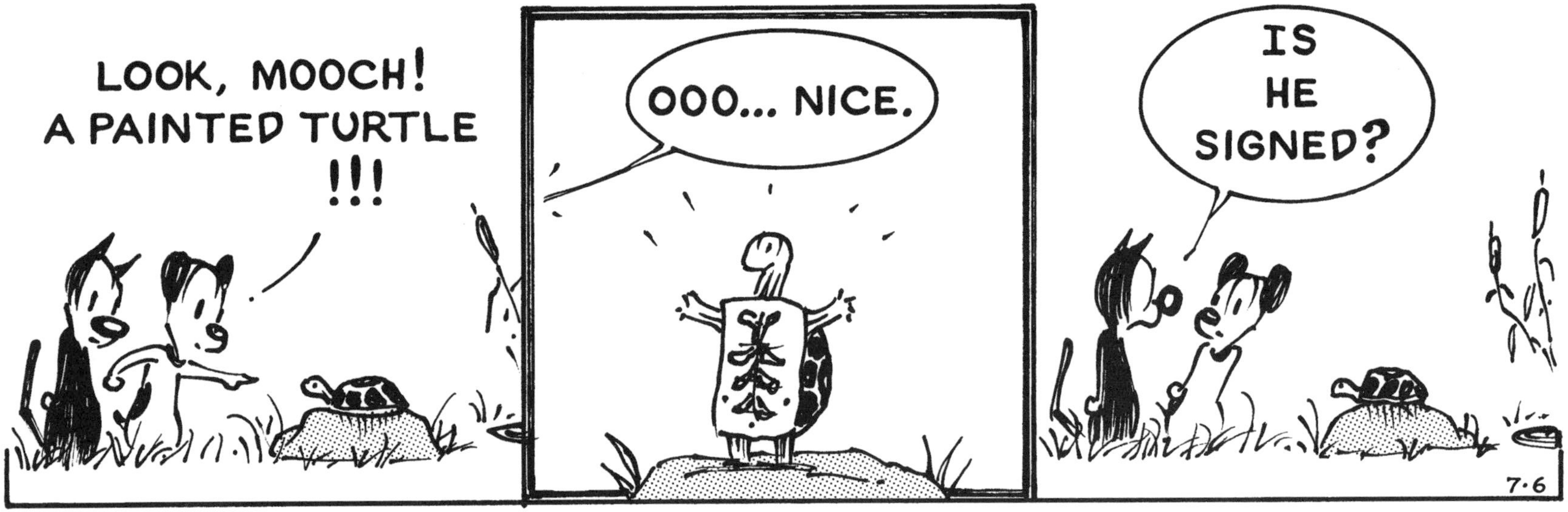
LOOK, MOOCH! A PAINTED TURTLE !!!
OOO... NICE.
IS HE SIGNED?
7·6

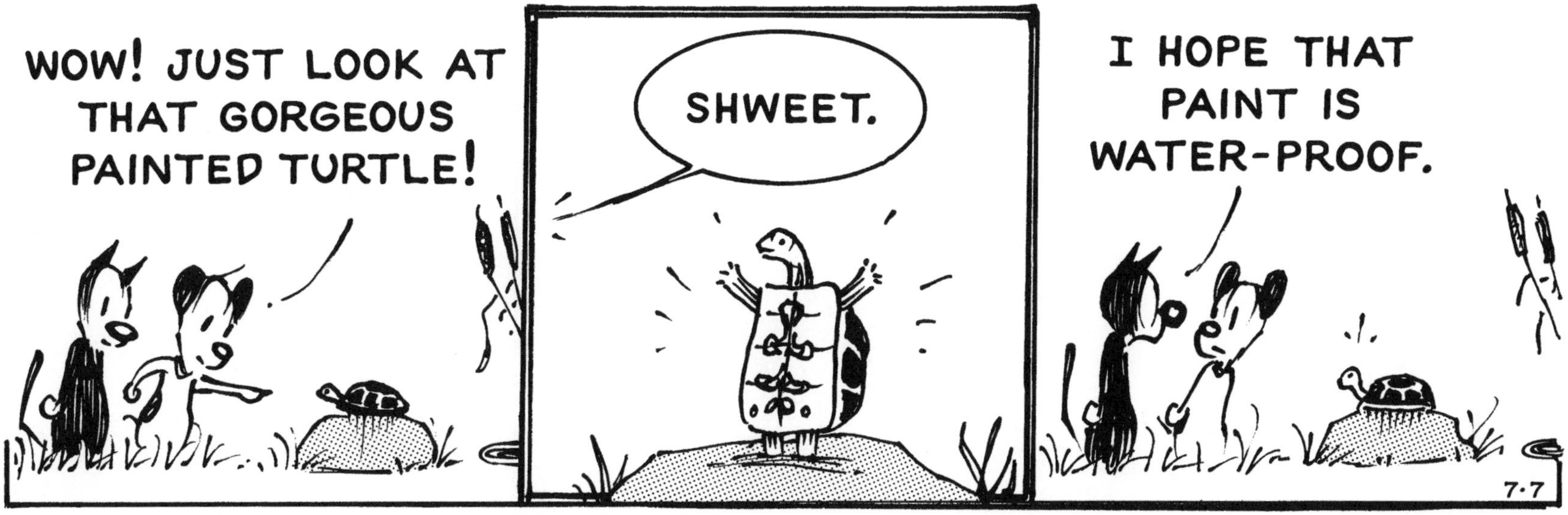
WOW! JUST LOOK AT THAT GORGEOUS PAINTED TURTLE!
SHWEET.
I HOPE THAT PAINT IS WATER-PROOF.
7·7

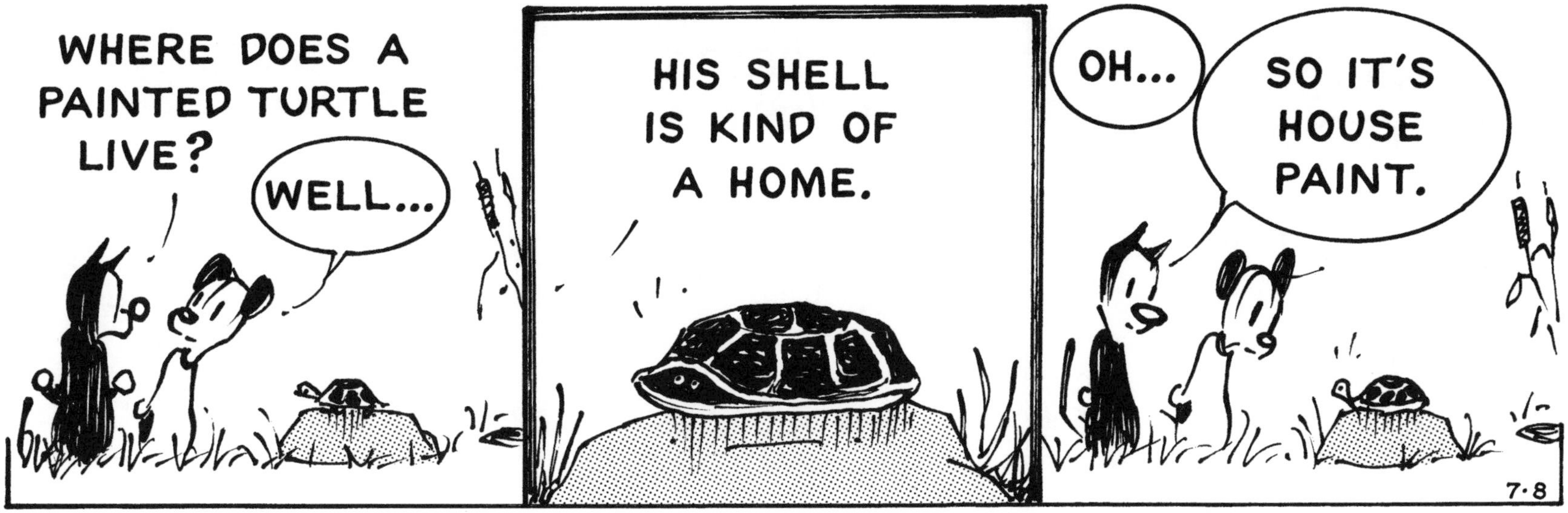
WHERE DOES A PAINTED TURTLE LIVE?
WELL...
HIS SHELL IS KIND OF A HOME.
OH...
SO IT'S HOUSE PAINT.
7·8

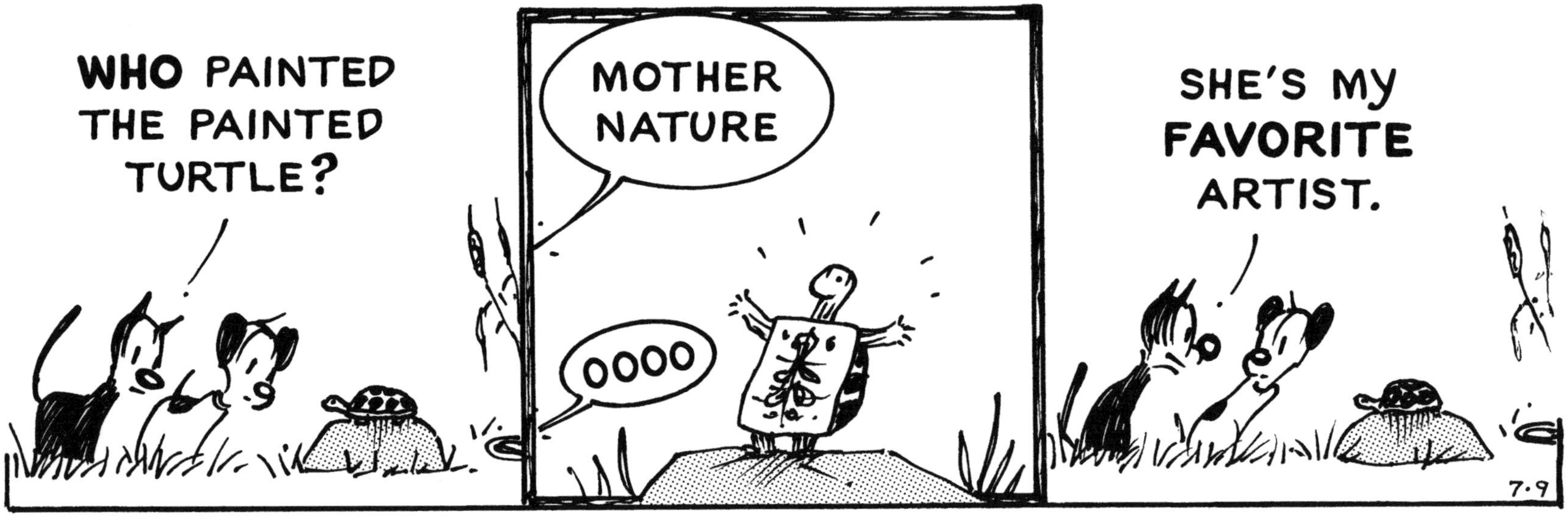
WHO PAINTED THE PAINTED TURTLE?
MOTHER NATURE
OOOO
SHE'S MY FAVORITE ARTIST.
7·9

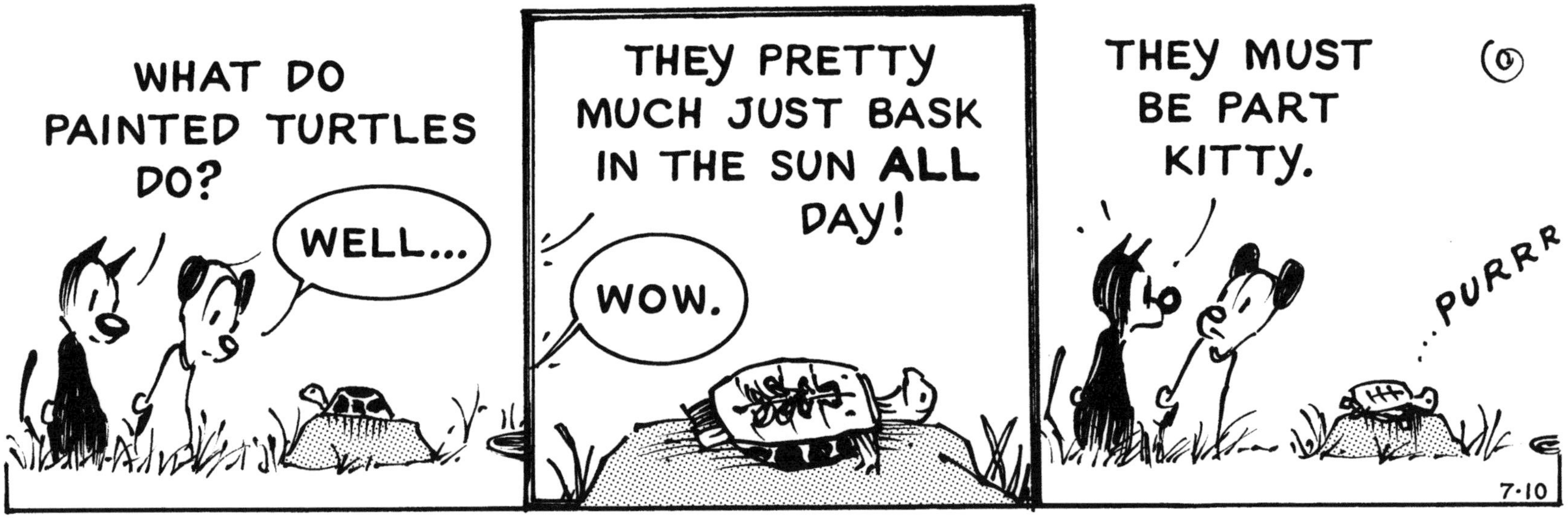
WHAT DO PAINTED TURTLES DO?
WELL...
THEY PRETTY MUCH JUST BASK IN THE SUN ALL DAY!
WOW.
THEY MUST BE PART KITTY.
...PURRR
7·10

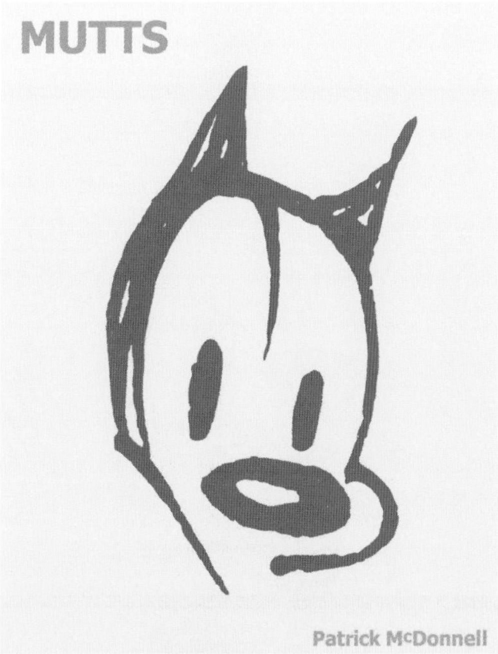
MUTTS
Patrick McDonnell

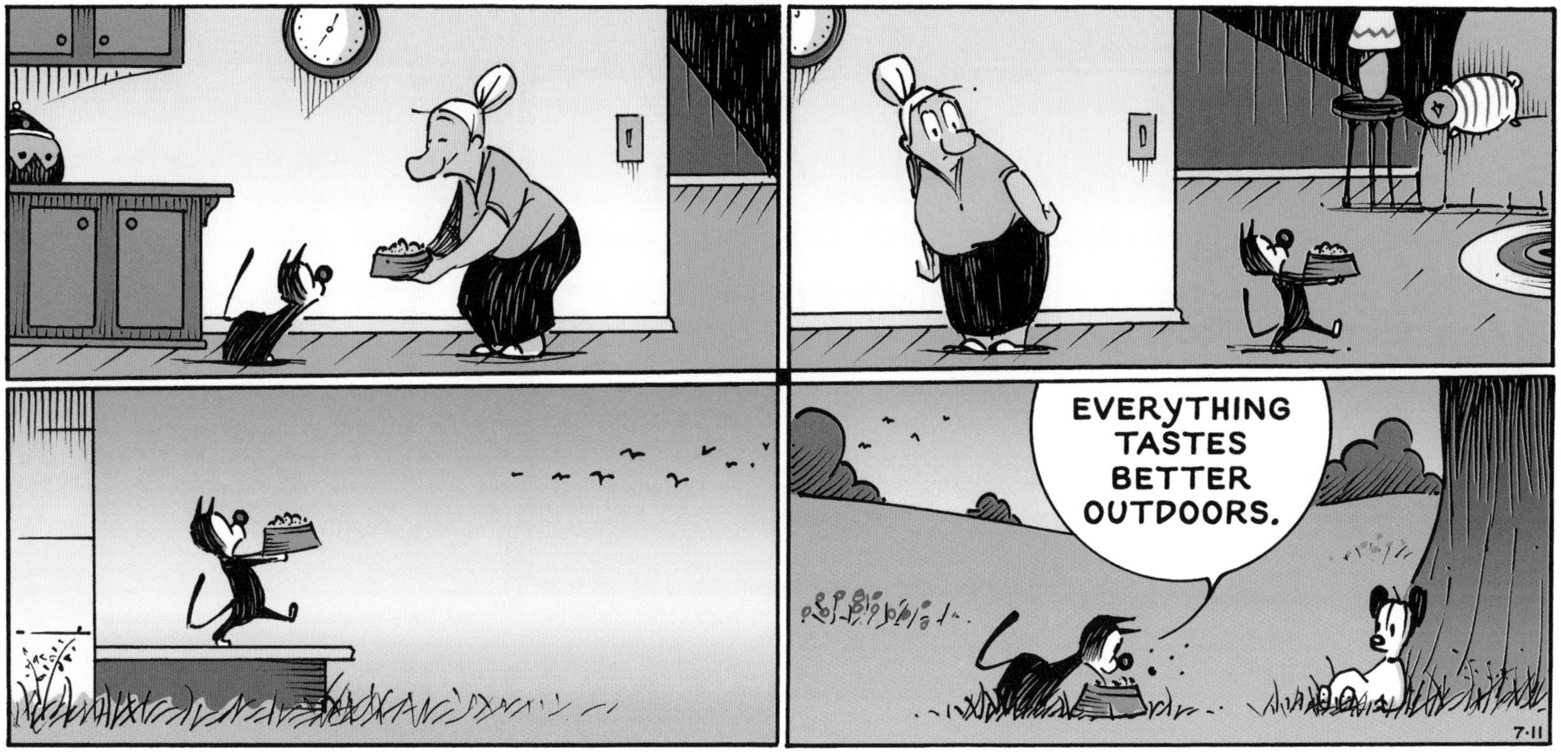
EVERYTHING TASTES BETTER OUTDOORS.
7·11

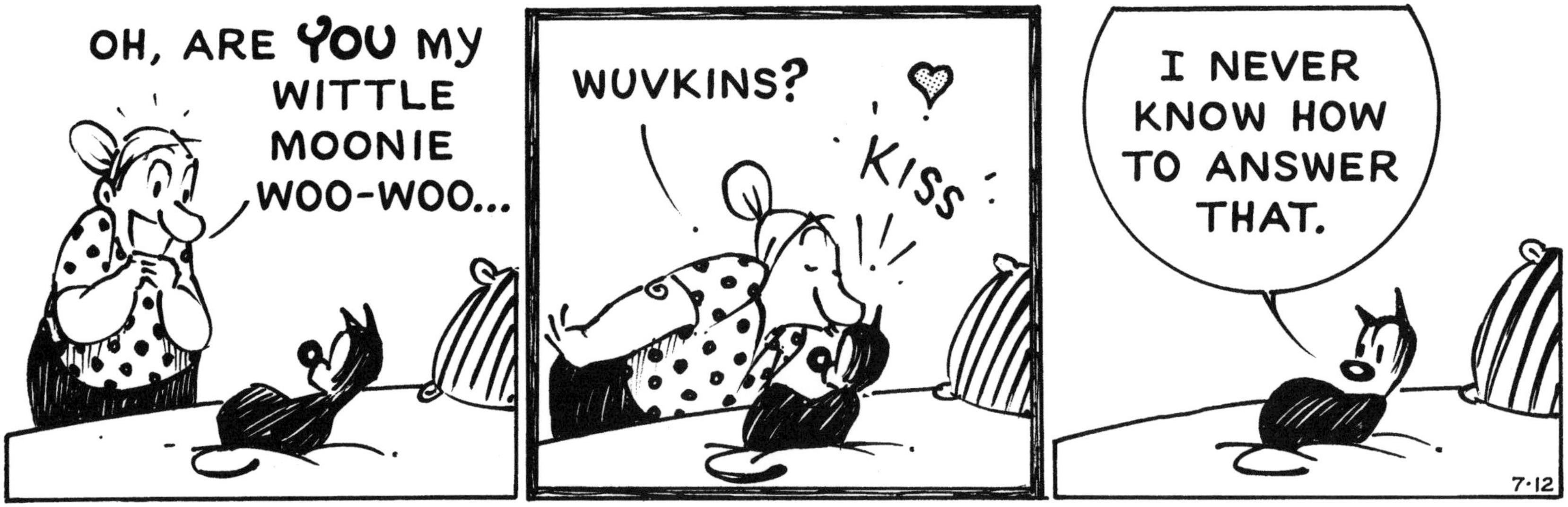
OH, ARE YOU MY WITTLE MOONIE WOO-WOO...
WUVKINS?
KISS
I NEVER KNOW HOW TO ANSWER THAT.
7·12

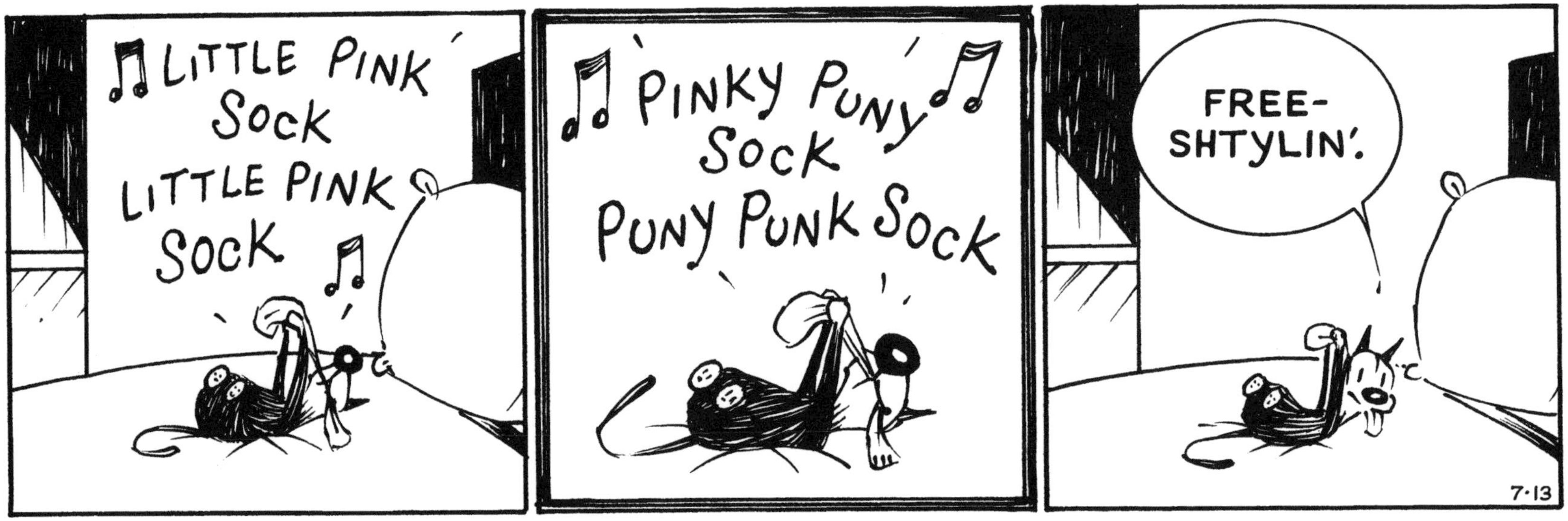
LITTLE PINK SOCK LITTLE PINK SOCK
PINKY PUNY SOCK PUNY PUNK SOCK
FREE-SHTYLIN'.
7·13

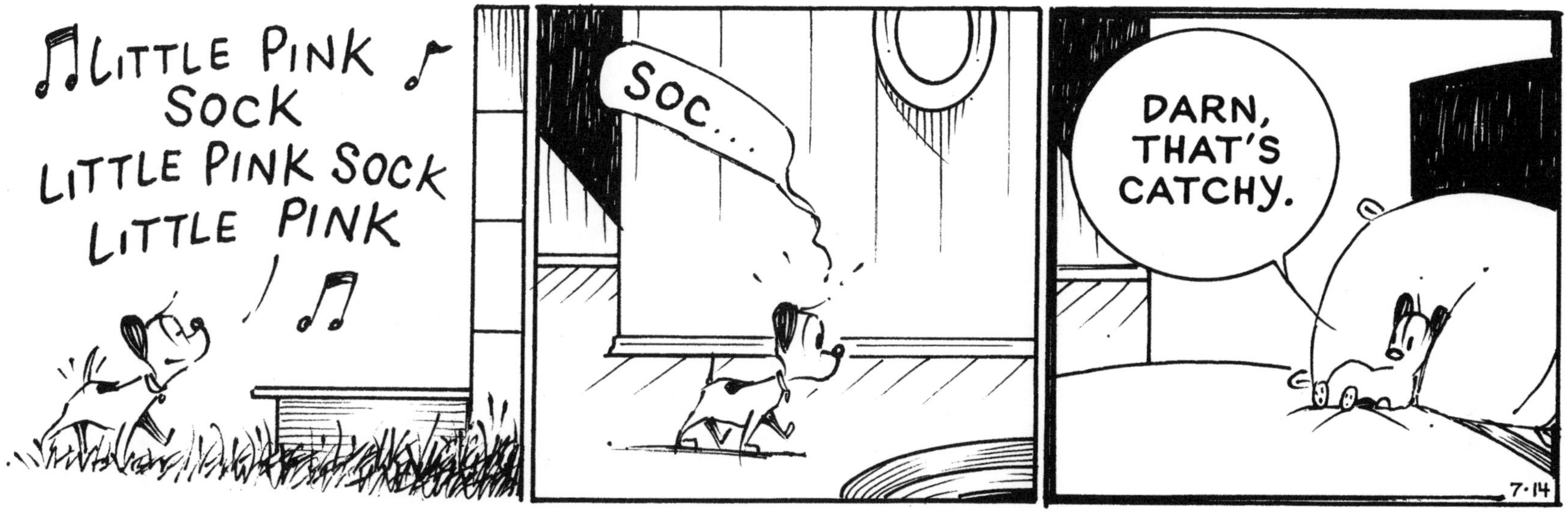
LITTLE PINK SOCK
LITTLE PINK SOCK
LITTLE PINK
SOC...
DARN, THAT'S CATCHY.
7·14

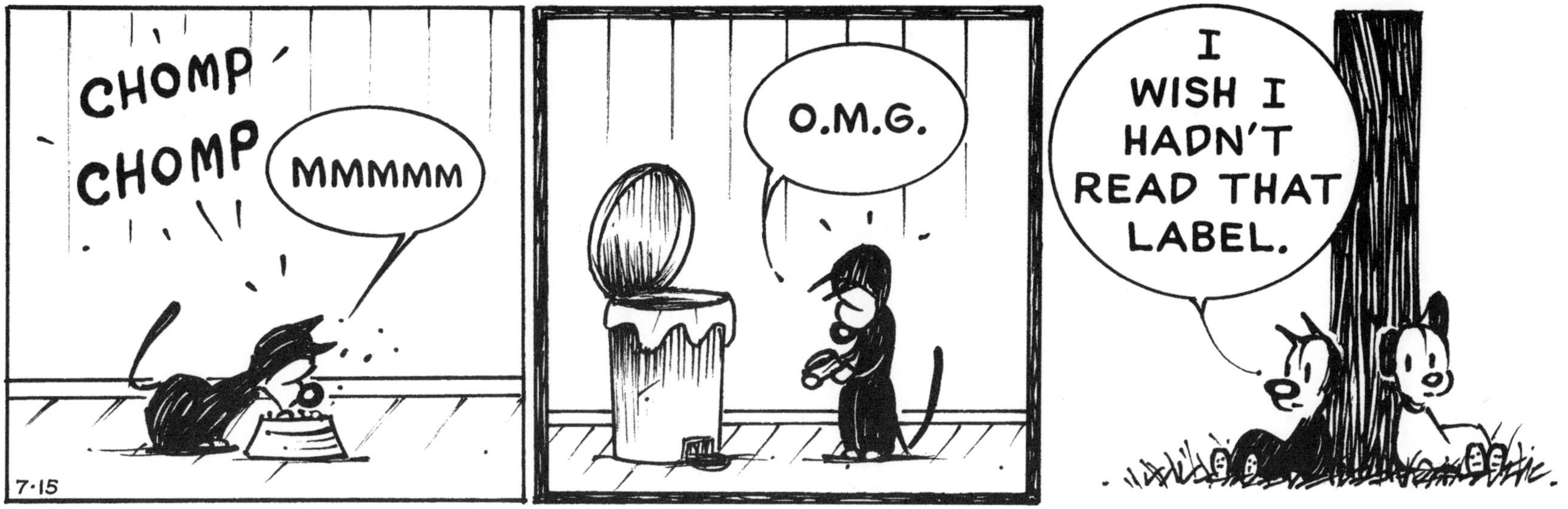
CHOMP
CHOMP
MMMMMM
7·15
O.M.G.
I WISH I HADN'T READ THAT LABEL.

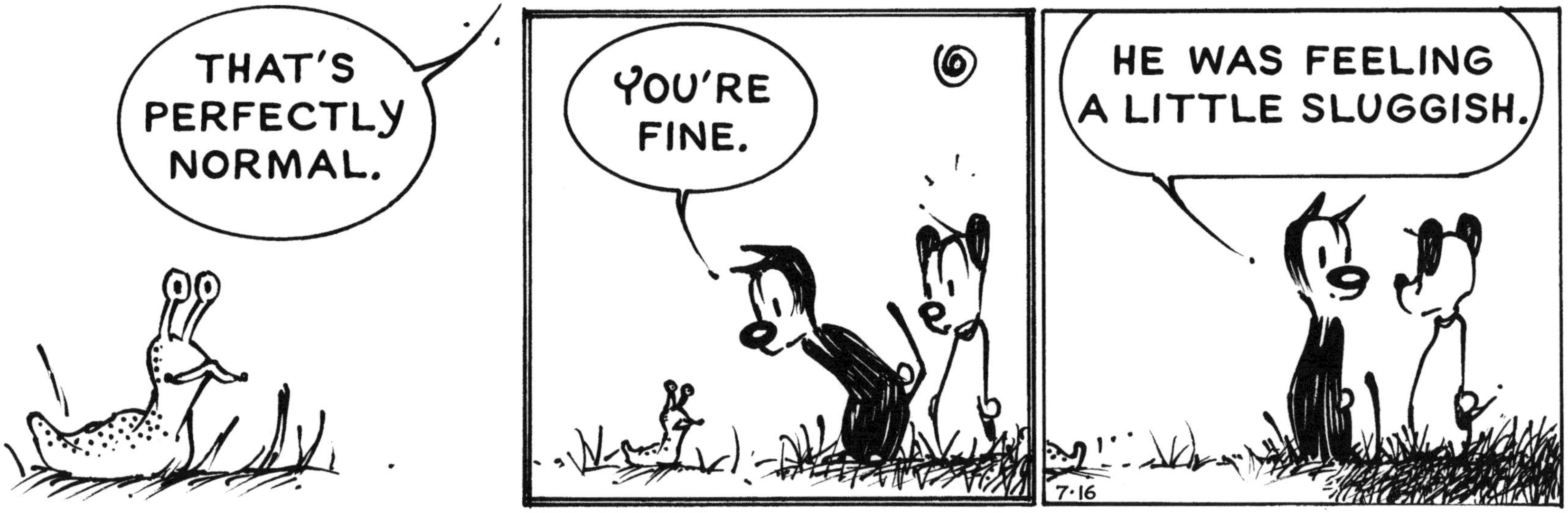
THAT'S PERFECTLY NORMAL.
YOU'RE FINE.
HE WAS FEELING A LITTLE SLUGGISH.
7·16

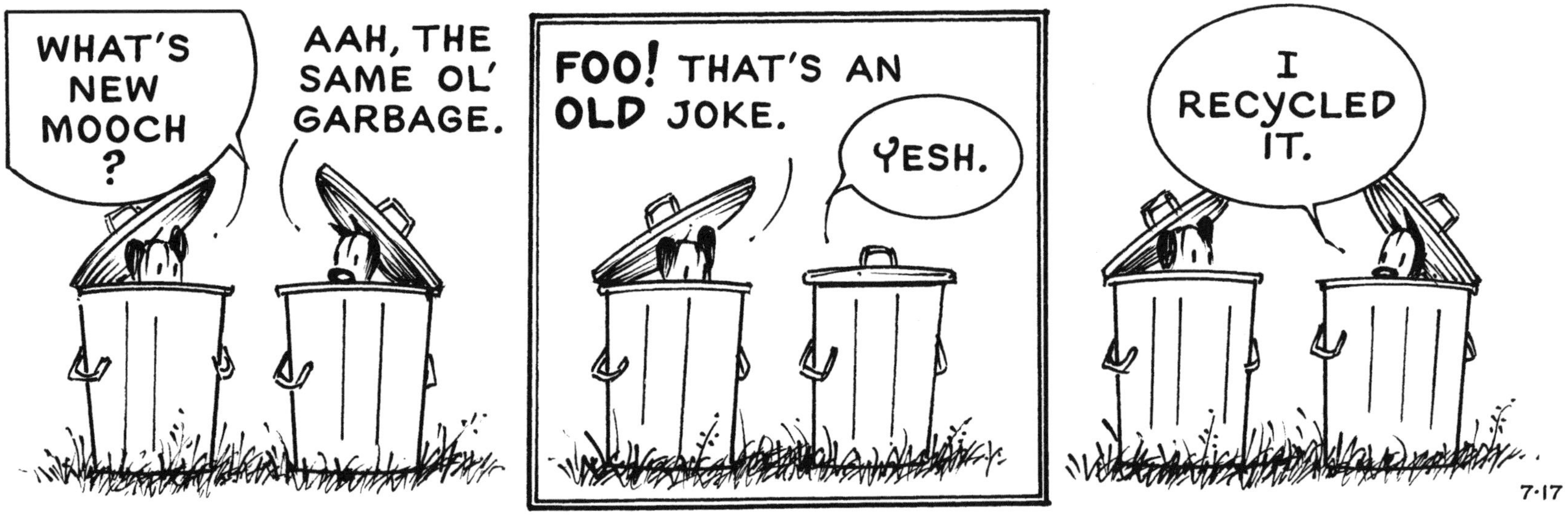
WHAT'S NEW MOOCH ?
AAH, THE SAME OL' GARBAGE.
FOO! THAT'S AN OLD JOKE.
YESH.
I RECYCLED IT.
7·17

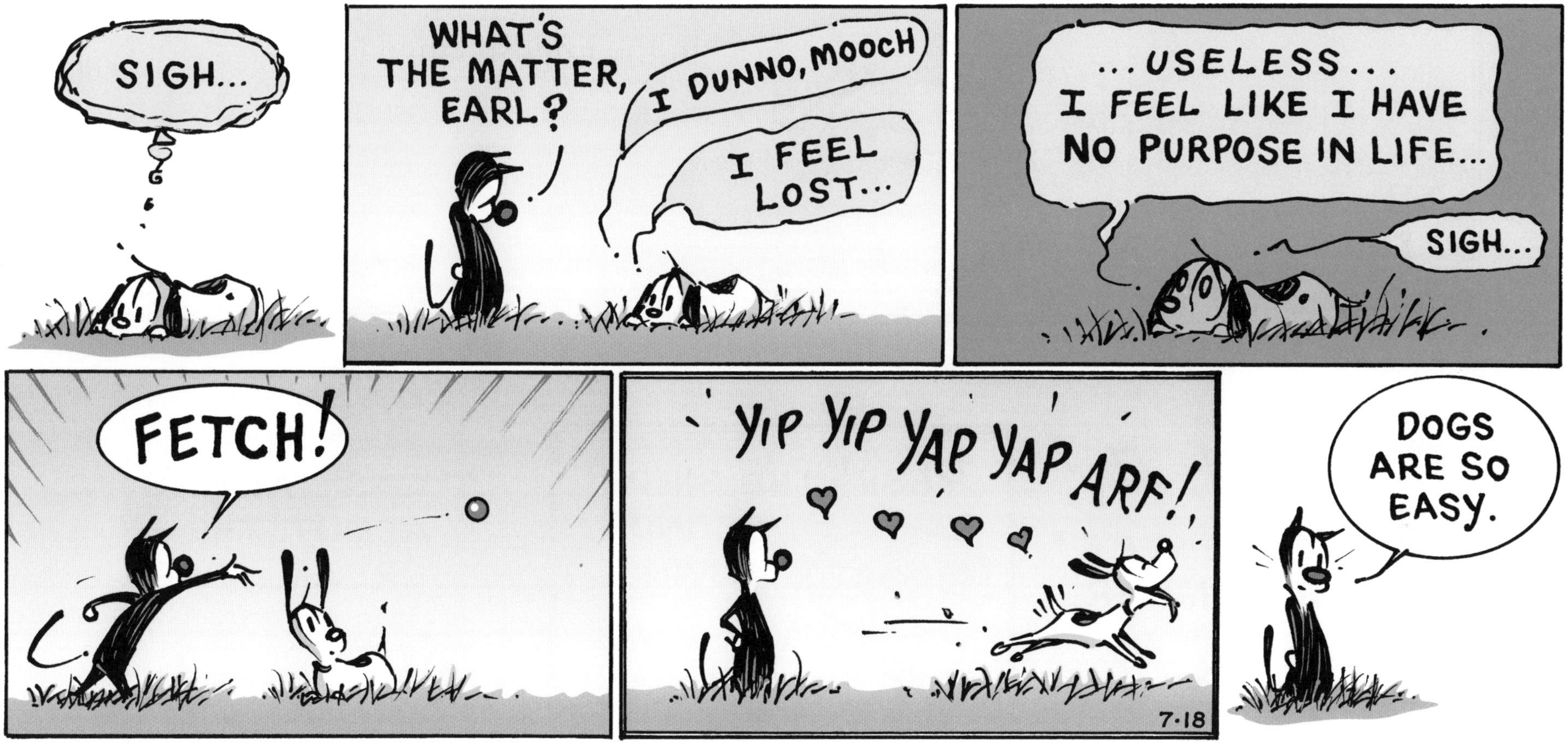
SIGH...
WHAT'S THE MATTER, EARL?
I DUNNO, MOOCH
I FEEL LOST...
...USELESS... I FEEL LIKE I HAVE NO PURPOSE IN LIFE...
SIGH...
FETCH!
YIP YIP YAP YAP ARF!
7·18
DOGS ARE SO EASY.

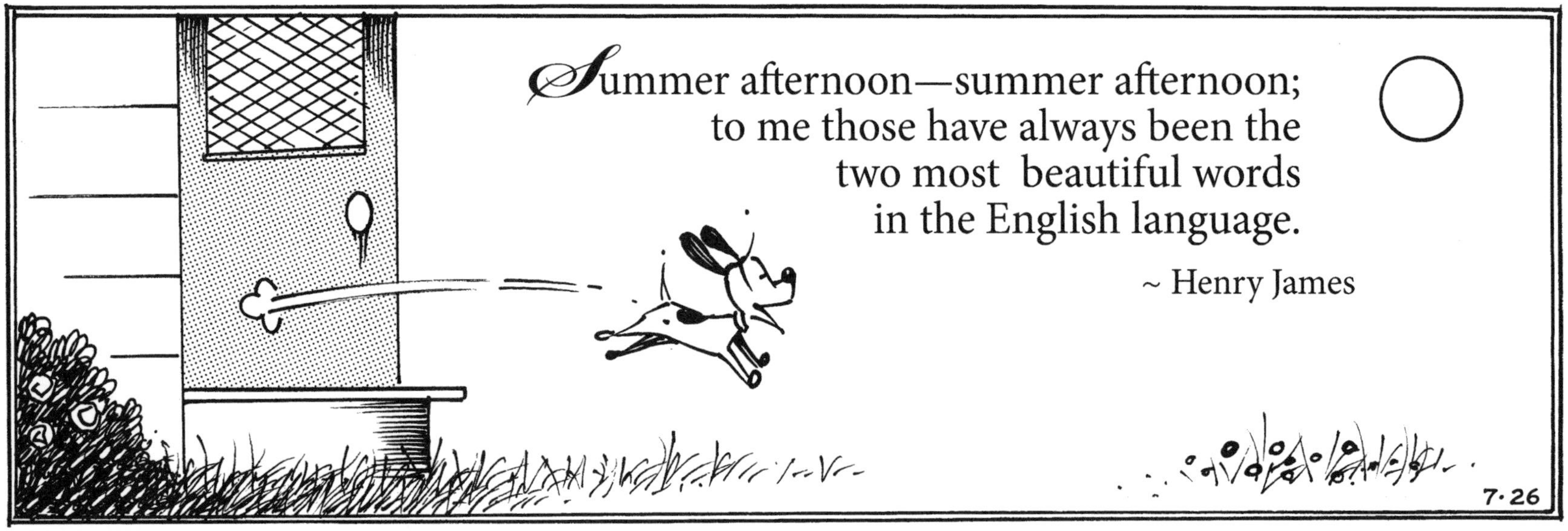
Summer afternoon—summer afternoon;
to me those have always been the
two most beautiful words
in the English language.
~ Henry James
7·26

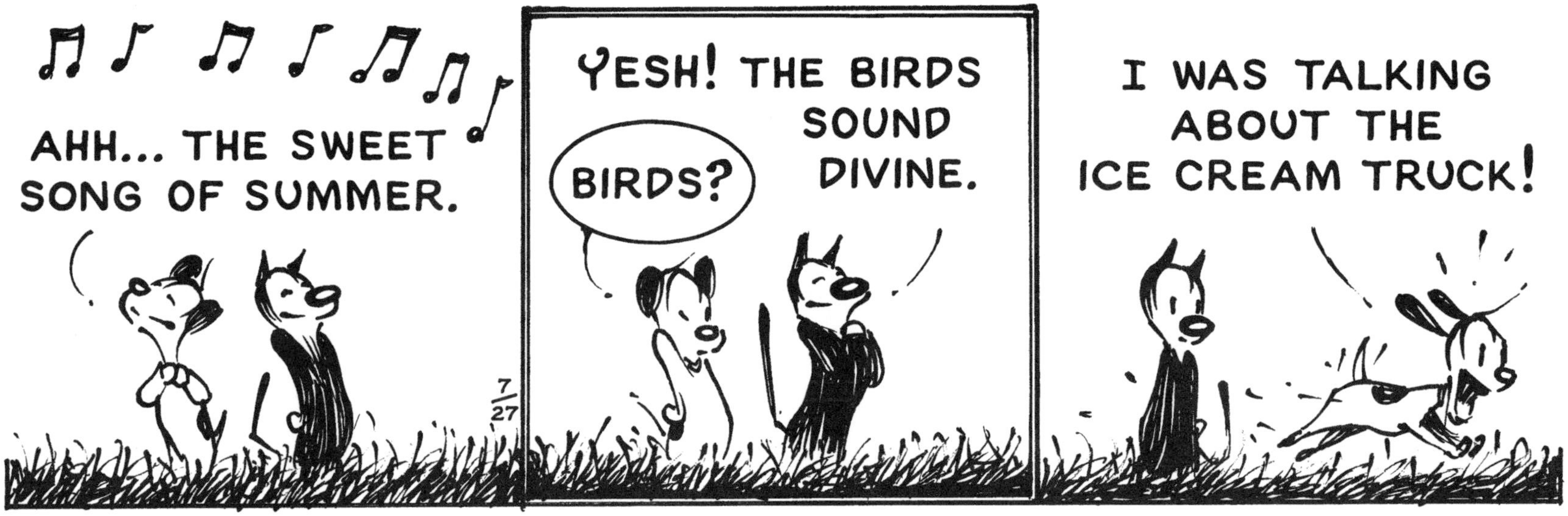
AHH... THE SWEET SONG OF SUMMER.
7/27
YESH! THE BIRDS SOUND DIVINE.
BIRDS?
I WAS TALKING ABOUT THE ICE CREAM TRUCK!

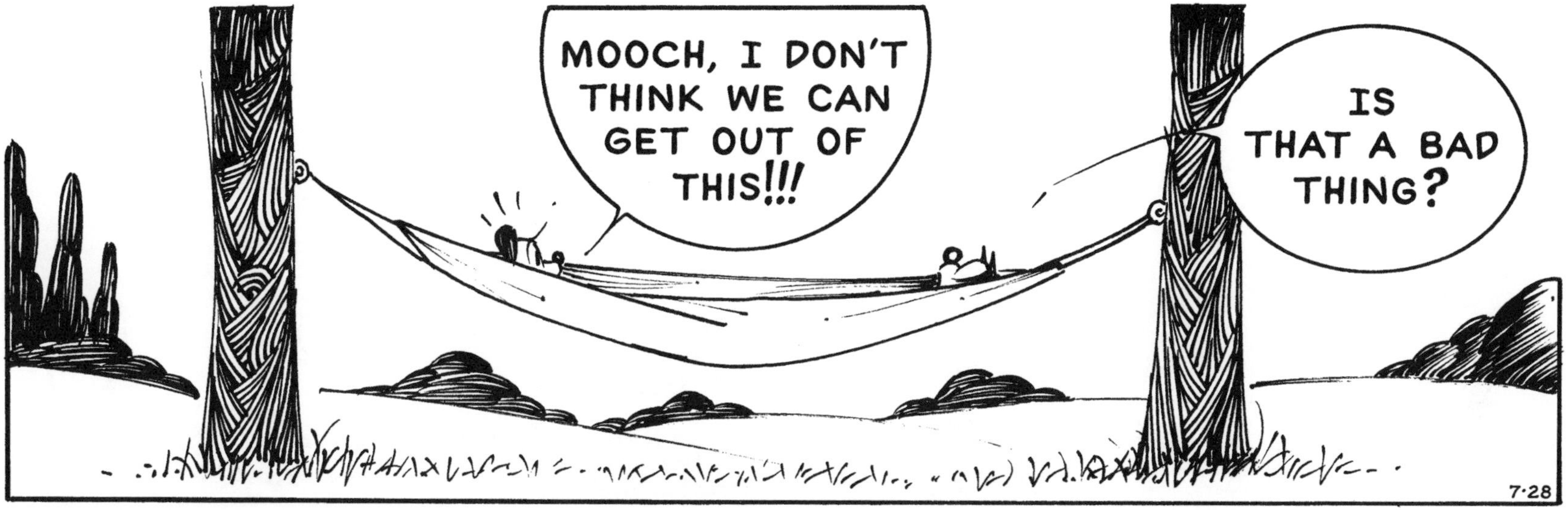
MOOCH, I DON'T THINK WE CAN GET OUT OF THIS!!!
IS THAT A BAD THING?
7·28

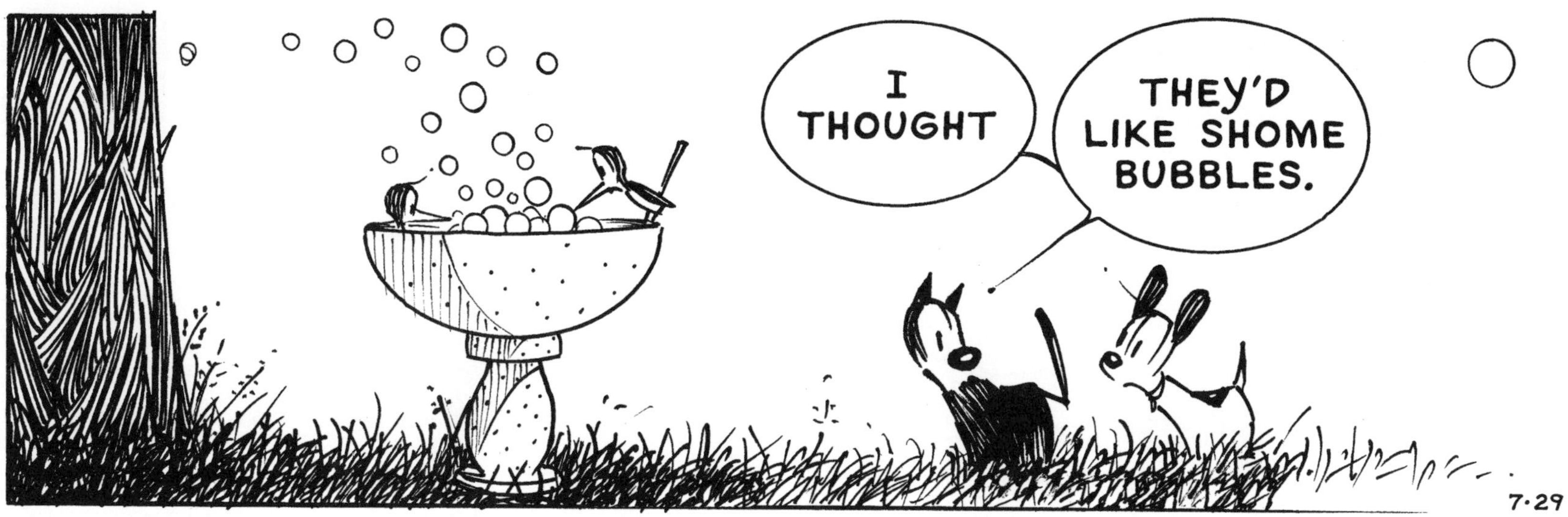
I THOUGHT
THEY'D LIKE SHOME BUBBLES.
7·29

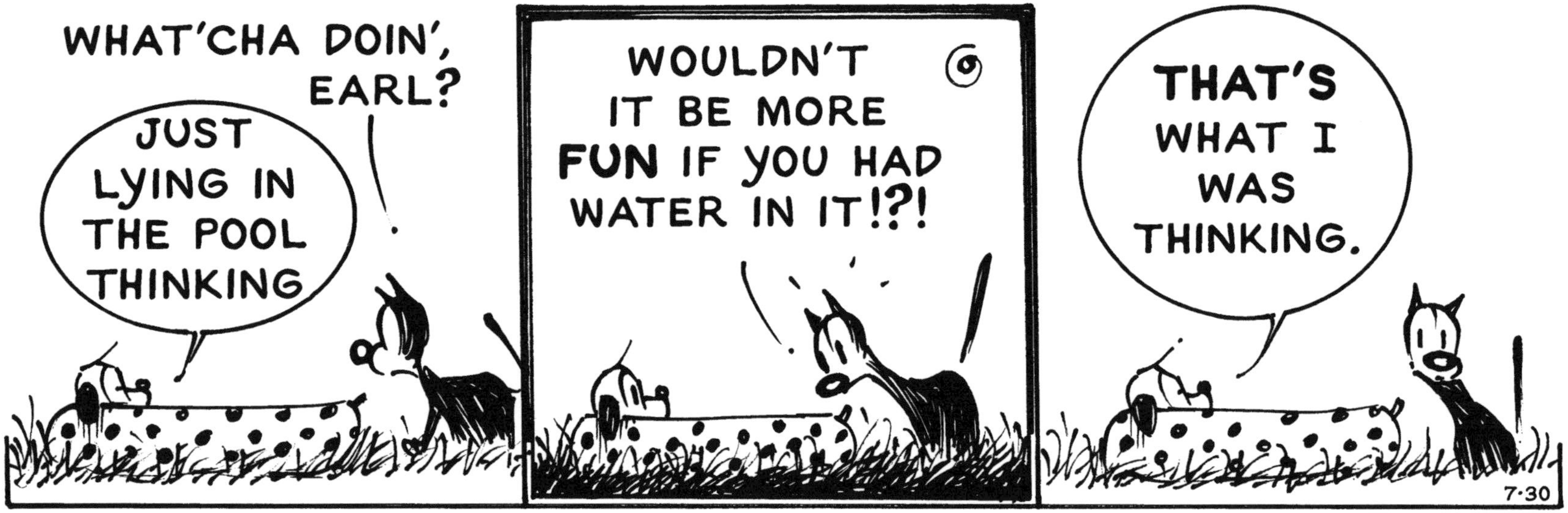
WHAT'CHA DOIN', EARL?
JUST LYING IN THE POOL THINKING
WOULDN'T IT BE MORE FUN IF YOU HAD WATER IN IT!?!
THAT'S WHAT I WAS THINKING.
7·30

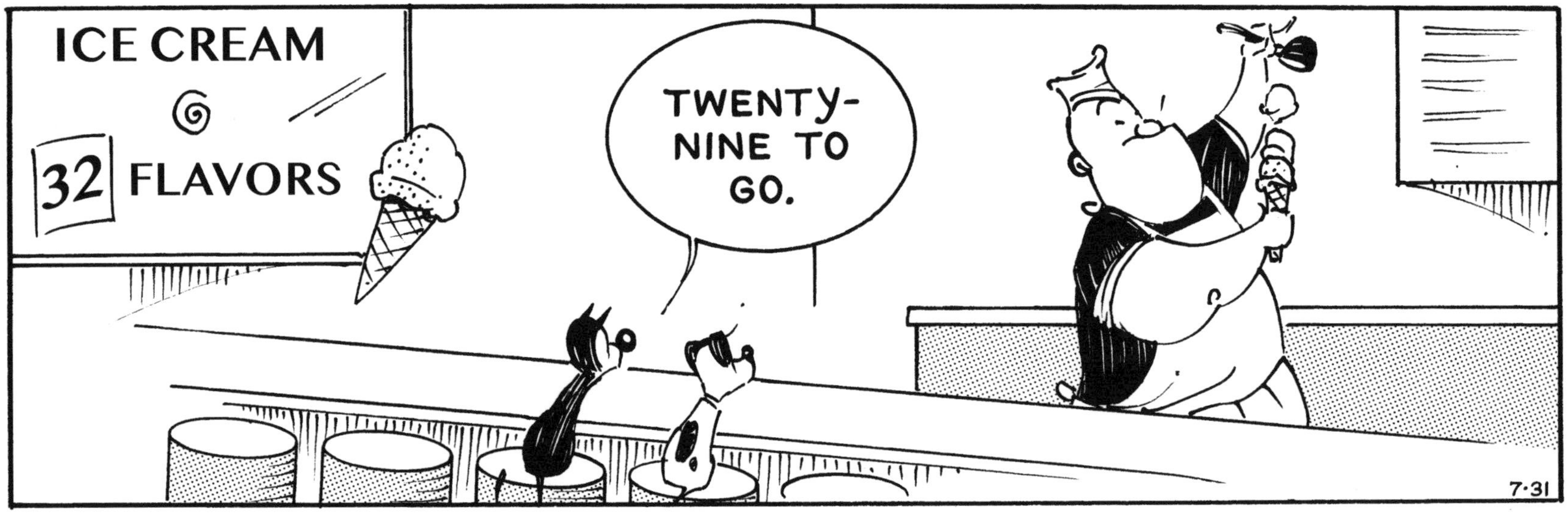
ICE CREAM
32 FLAVORS
TWENTY-NINE TO GO.
7·31

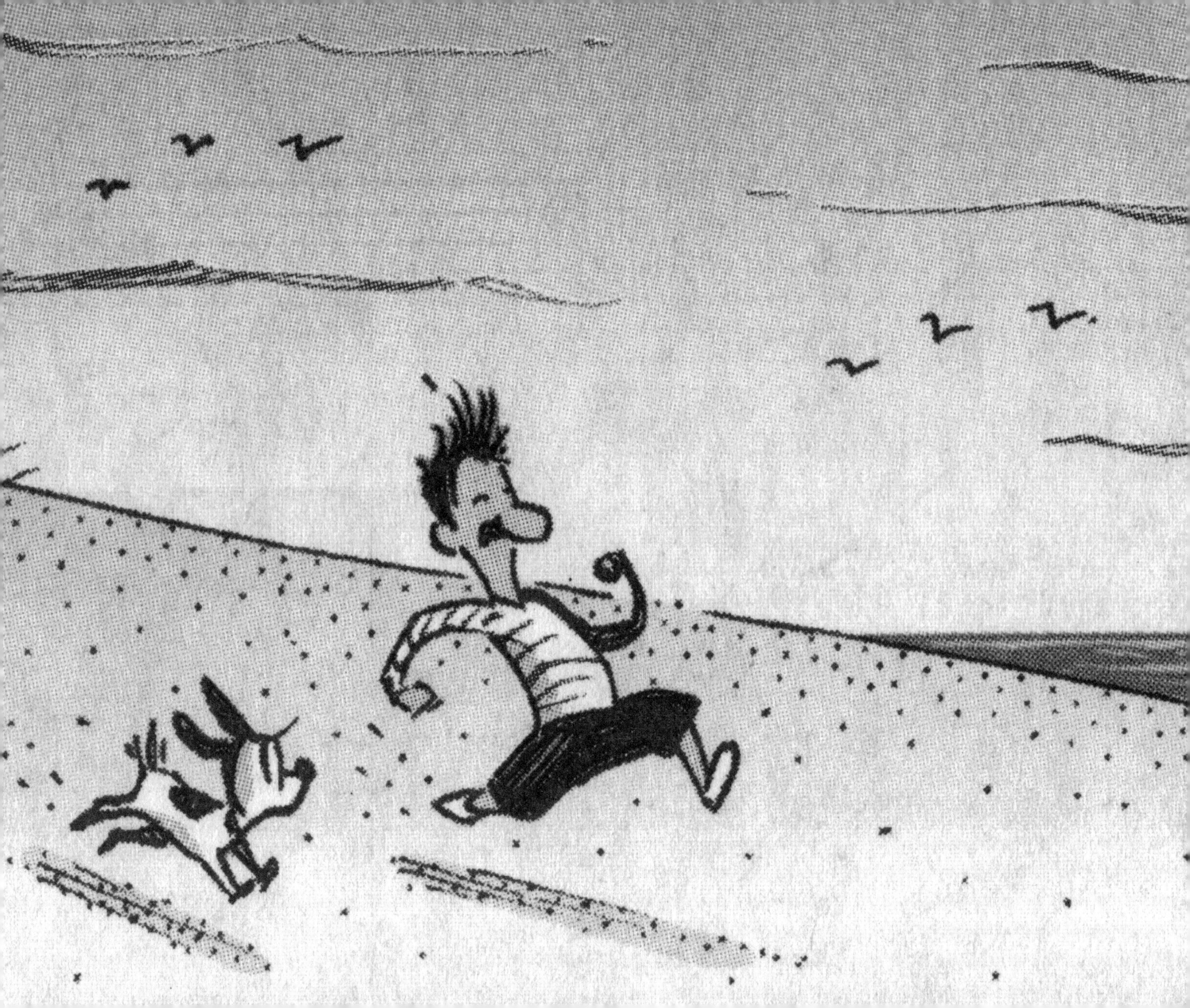

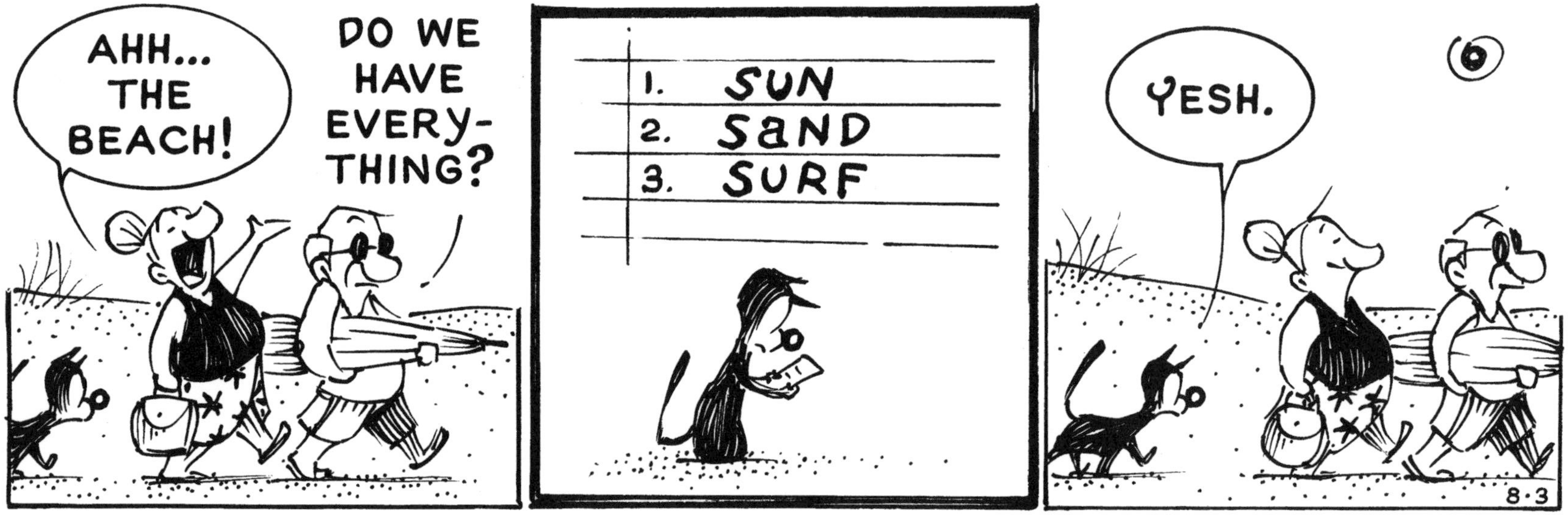
AHH... THE BEACH!
DO WE HAVE EVERY-THING?
1. SUN
2. SAND
3. SURF
YESH.
8·3

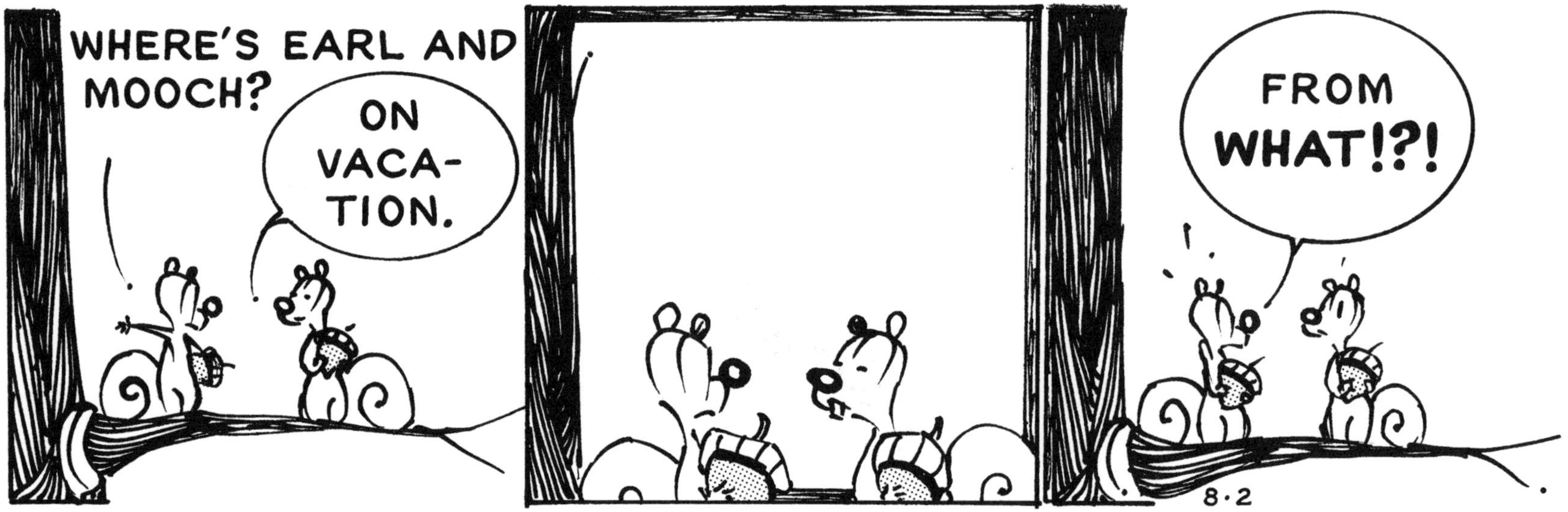
WHERE'S EARL AND MOOCH?
ON VACA-TION.
FROM WHAT!?!
8·2

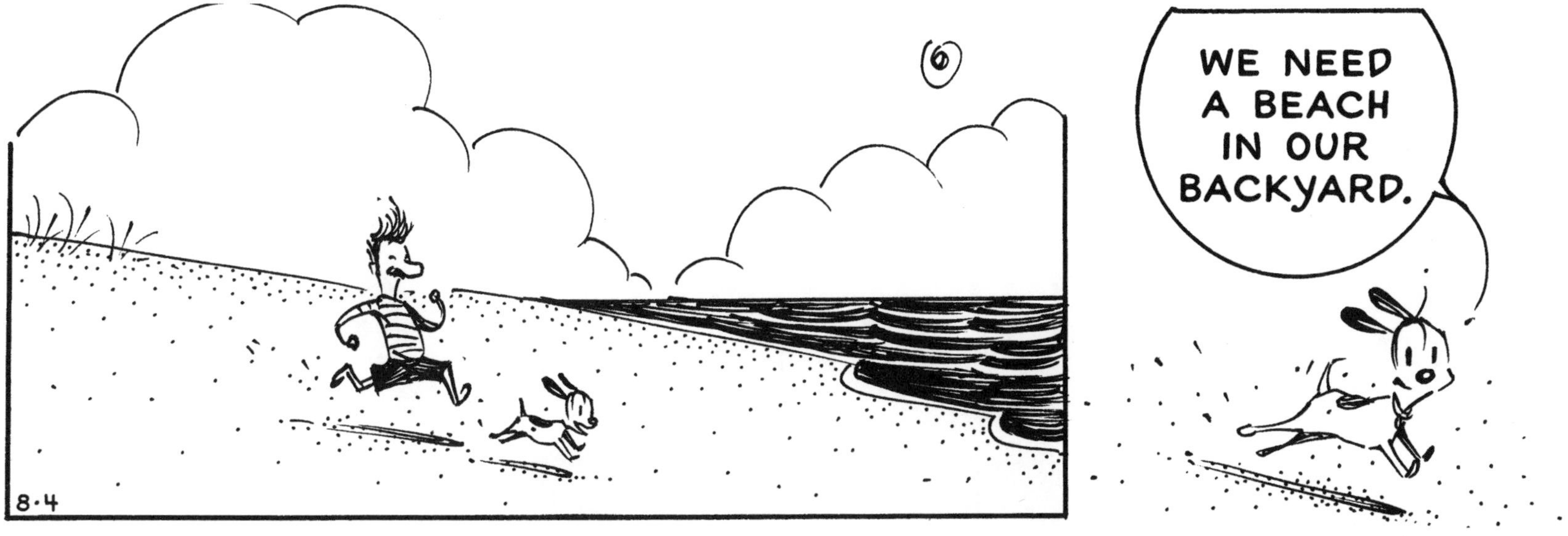
8·4
WE NEED A BEACH IN OUR BACKYARD.

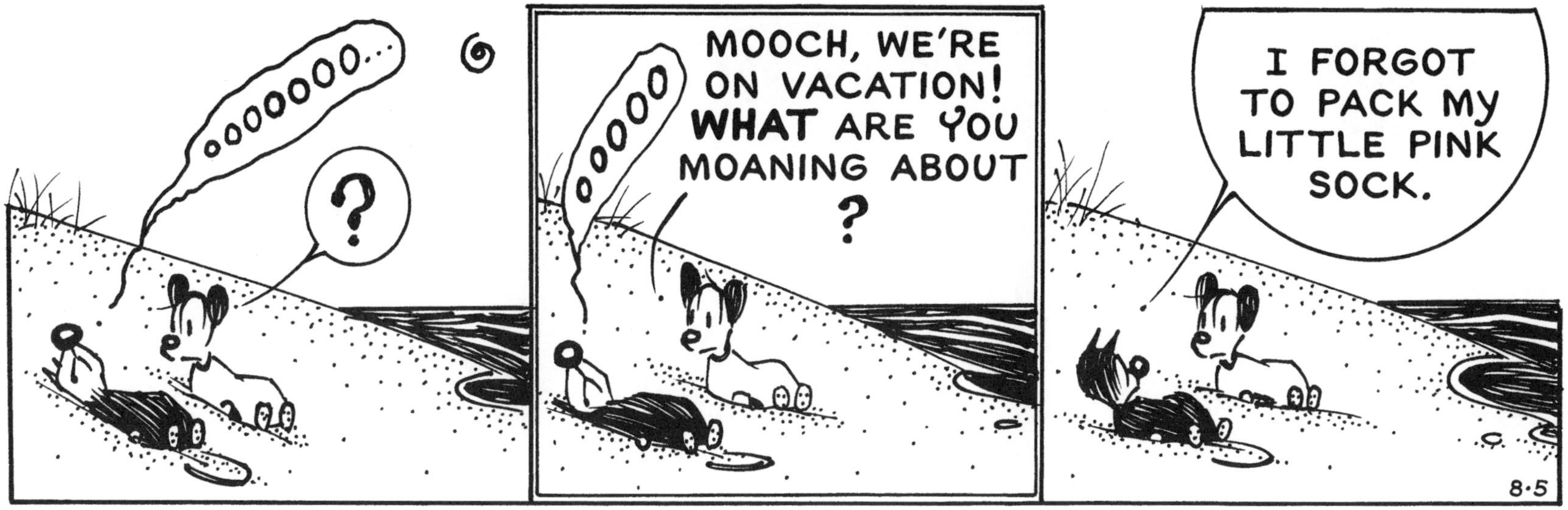
oooooooo...
?
ooooo
MOOCH, WE'RE ON VACATION! **WHAT** ARE YOU MOANING ABOUT ?
I FORGOT TO PACK MY LITTLE PINK SOCK.
8·5

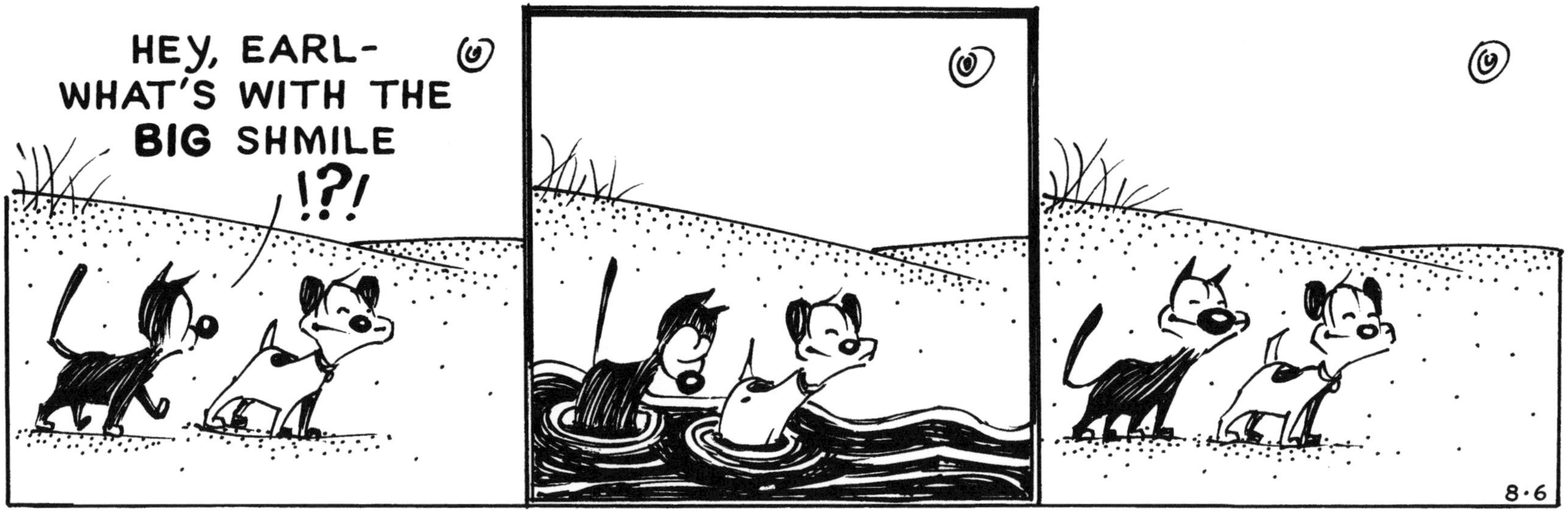
HEY, EARL- WHAT'S WITH THE **BIG** SHMILE
!?!
8·6

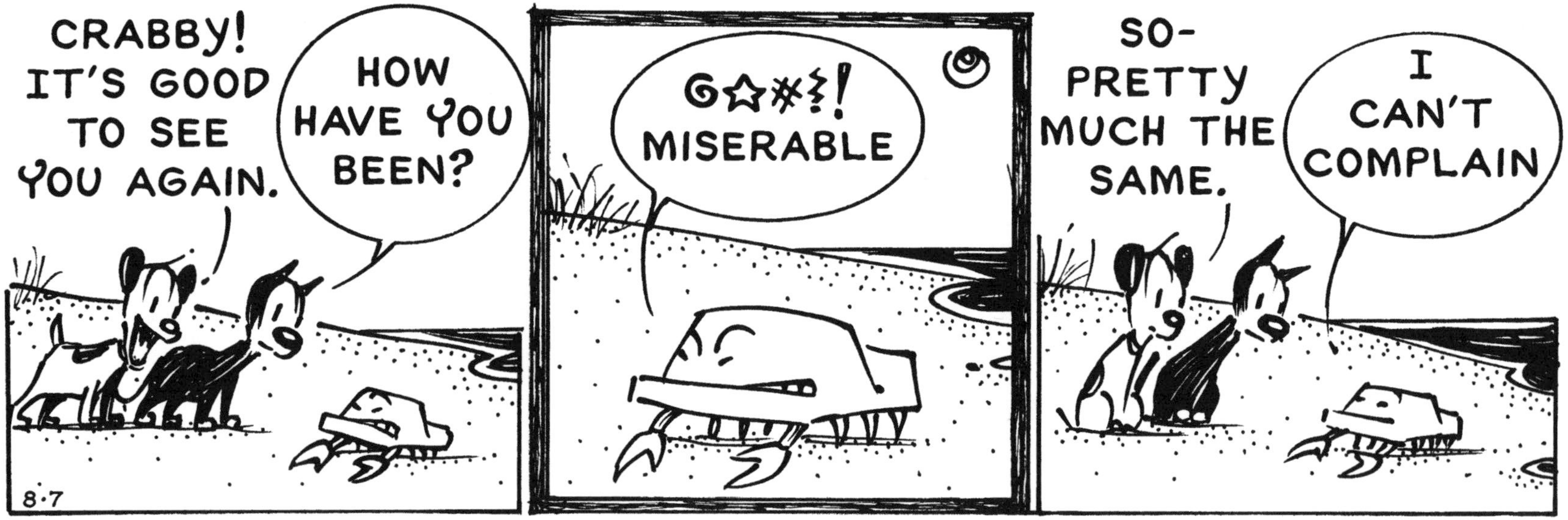
CRABBY! IT'S GOOD TO SEE YOU AGAIN.
HOW HAVE YOU BEEN?
MISERABLE
SO- PRETTY MUCH THE SAME.
I CAN'T COMPLAIN
8·7

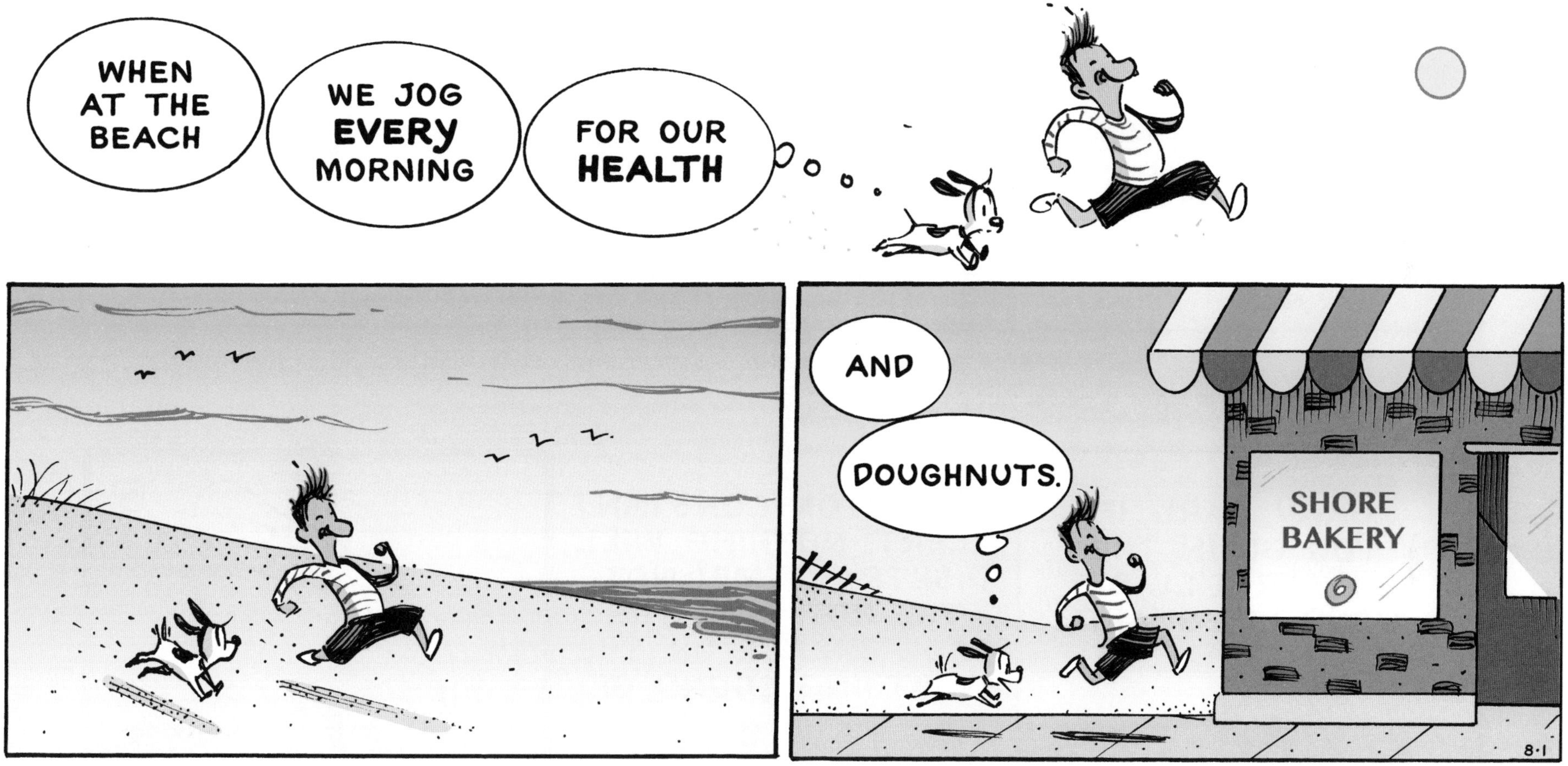
WHEN AT THE BEACH
WE JOG EVERY MORNING
FOR OUR HEALTH
AND
DOUGHNUTS.
SHORE BAKERY
8·1

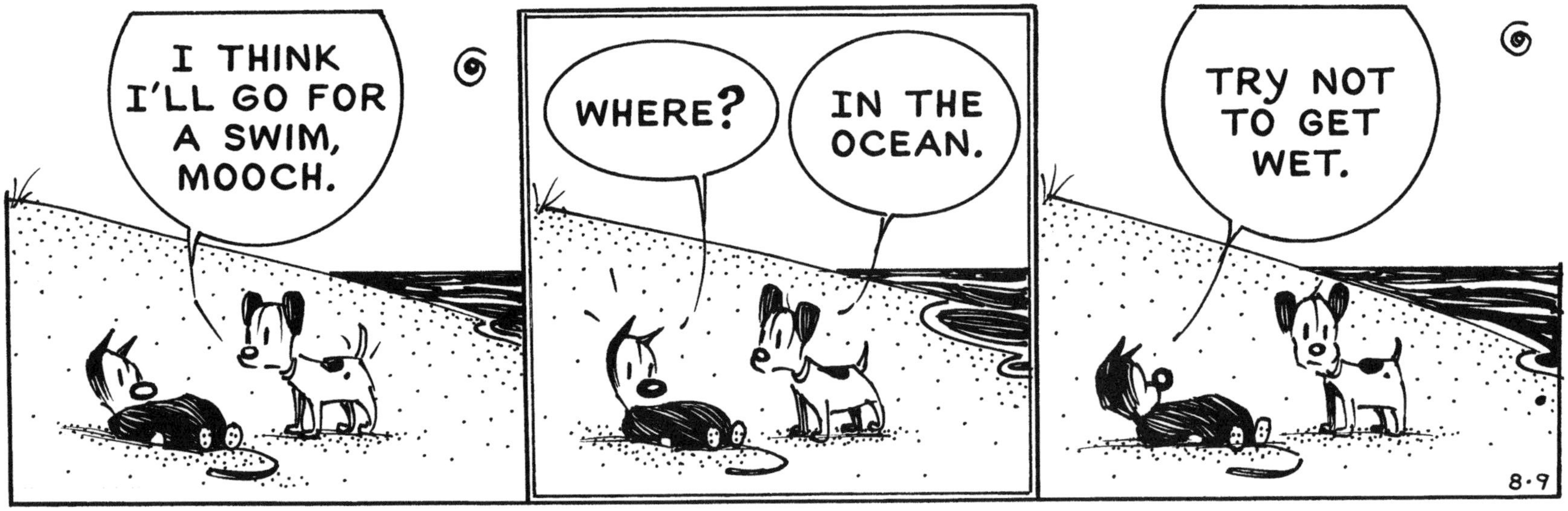
I THINK I'LL GO FOR A SWIM, MOOCH.
WHERE?
IN THE OCEAN.
TRY NOT TO GET WET.
8·9

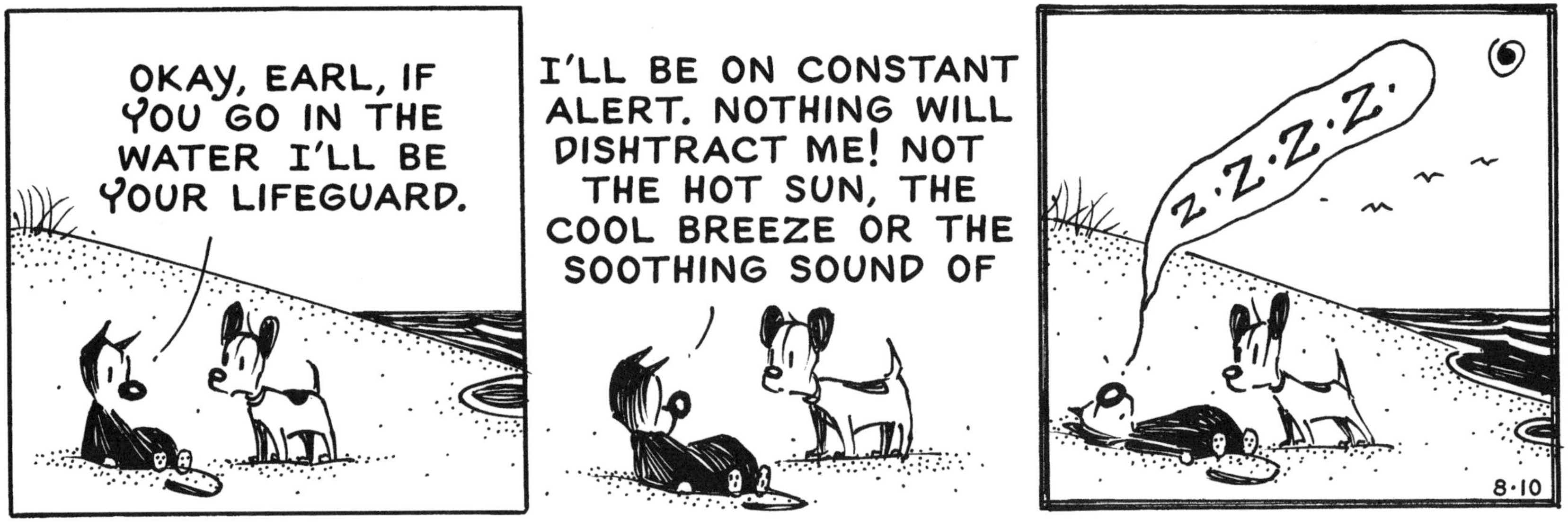
OKAY, EARL, IF YOU GO IN THE WATER I'LL BE YOUR LIFEGUARD.
I'LL BE ON CONSTANT ALERT. NOTHING WILL DISHTRACT ME! NOT THE HOT SUN, THE COOL BREEZE OR THE SOOTHING SOUND OF
Z·Z·Z·Z·Z·
8·10

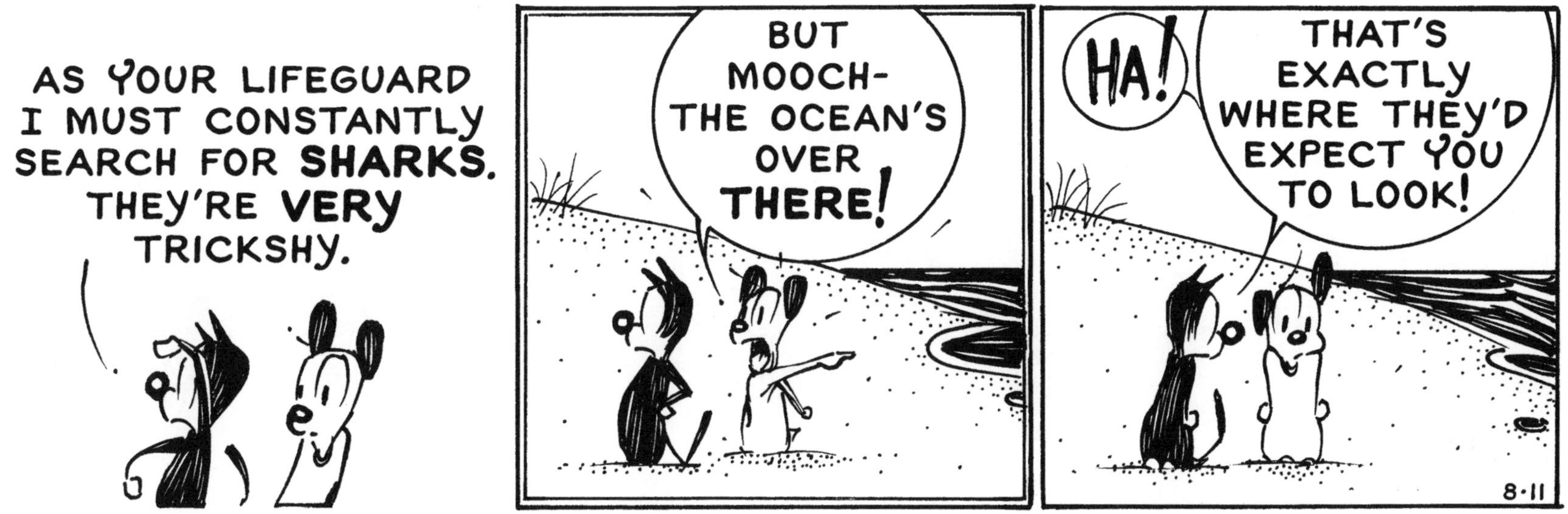
AS YOUR LIFEGUARD I MUST CONSTANTLY SEARCH FOR SHARKS. THEY'RE VERY TRICKSHY.
BUT MOOCH- THE OCEAN'S OVER THERE!
HA!
THAT'S EXACTLY WHERE THEY'D EXPECT YOU TO LOOK!
8·11

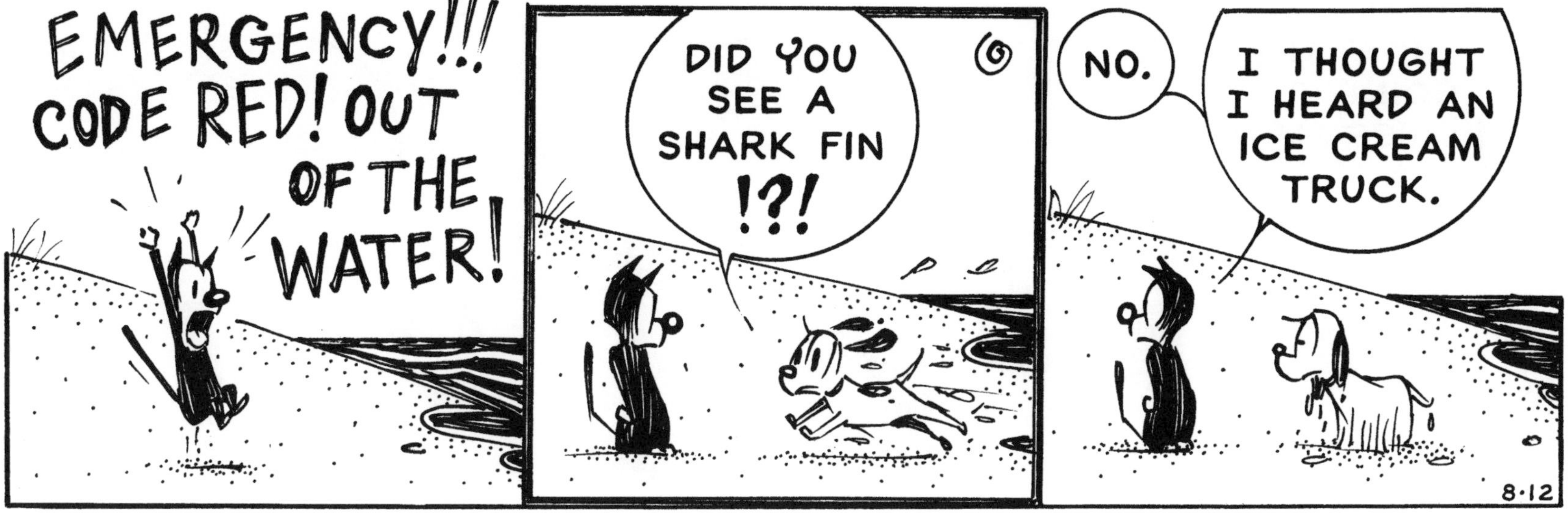
EMERGENCY!!! CODE RED! OUT OF THE WATER!
DID YOU SEE A SHARK FIN !?!
NO.
I THOUGHT I HEARD AN ICE CREAM TRUCK.
8·12

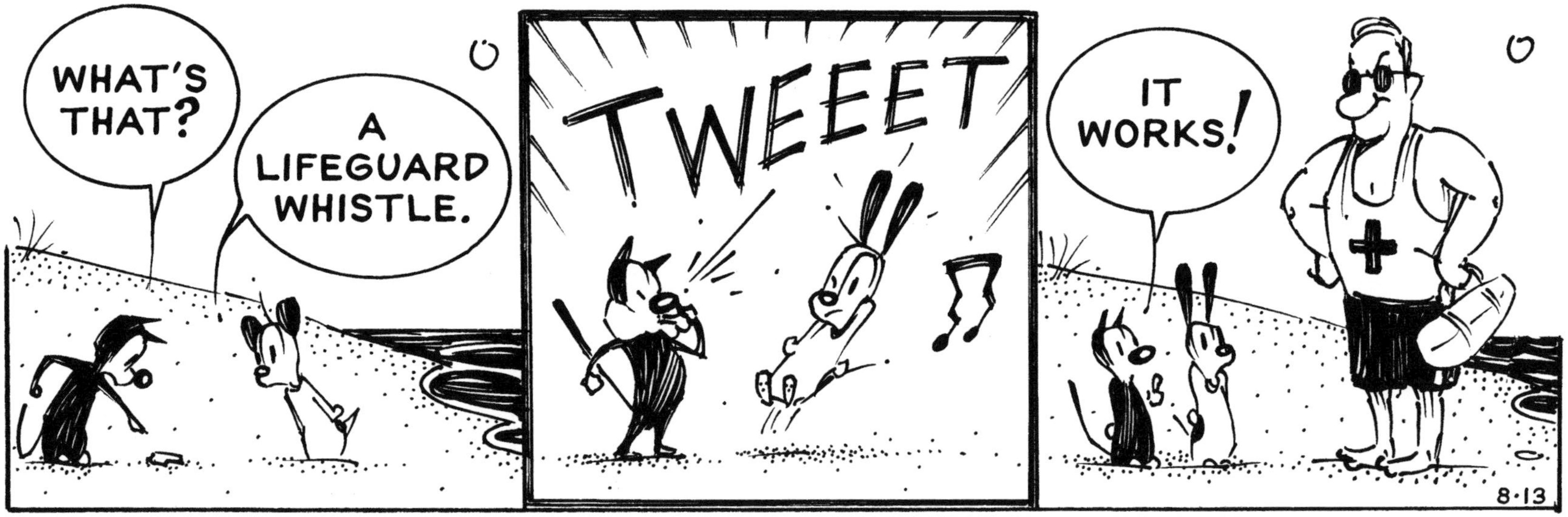
WHAT'S THAT?
A LIFEGUARD WHISTLE.
TWEEET
IT WORKS!
8·13

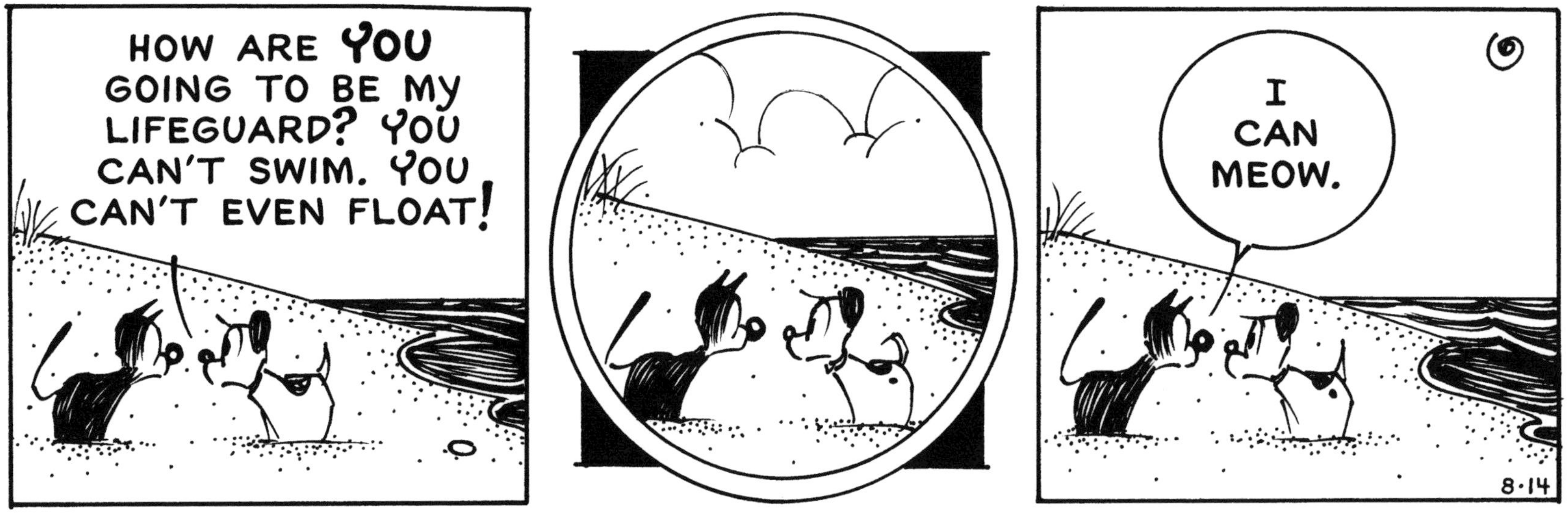
HOW ARE YOU GOING TO BE MY LIFEGUARD? YOU CAN'T SWIM. YOU CAN'T EVEN FLOAT!
I CAN MEOW.
8·14

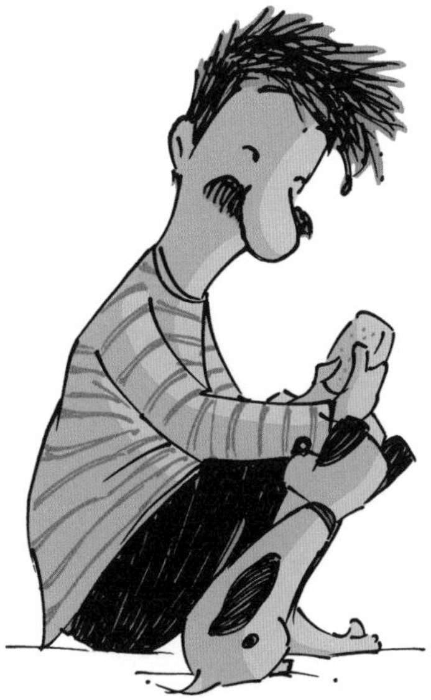

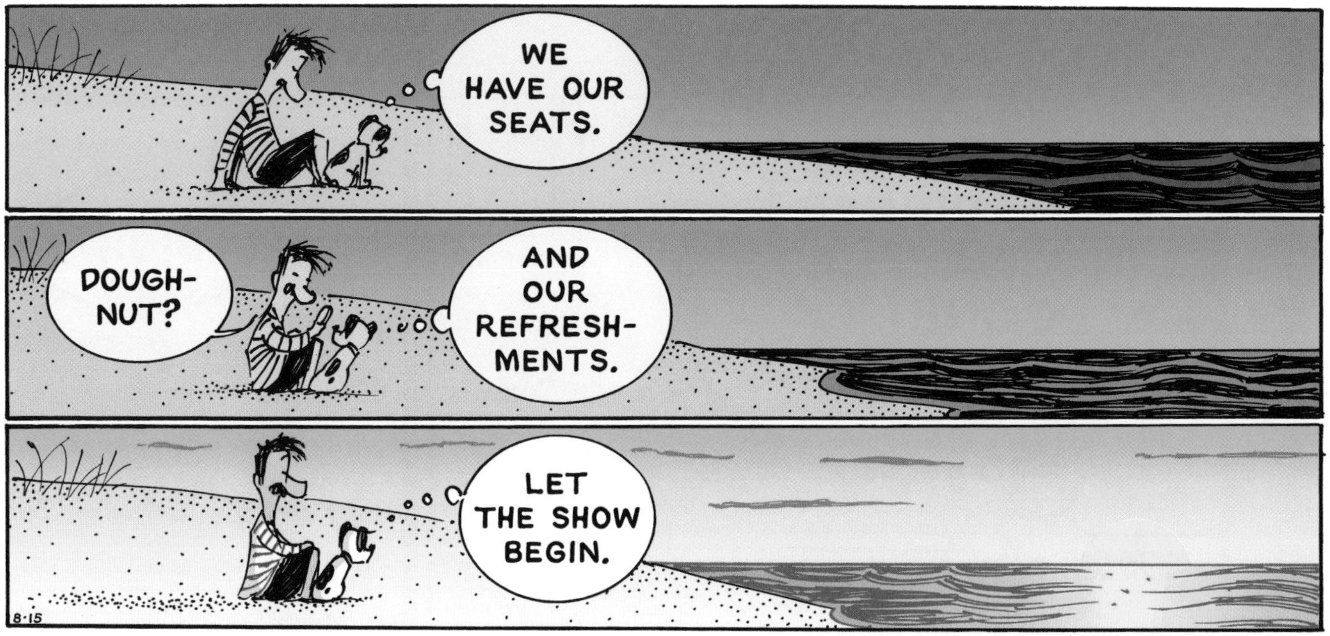

WE HAVE OUR SEATS.
AND OUR REFRESHMENTS.
DOUGHNUT?
LET THE SHOW BEGIN.
8·15

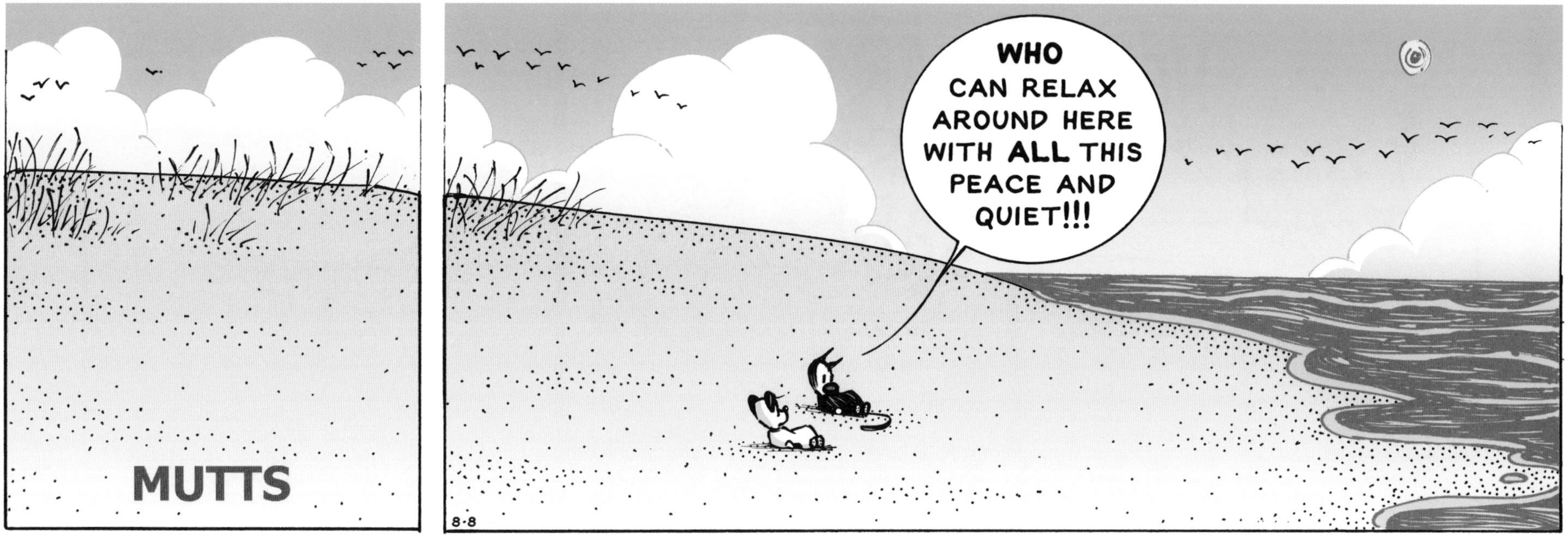

MUTTS
WHO CAN RELAX AROUND HERE WITH ALL THIS PEACE AND QUIET!!!
8·8

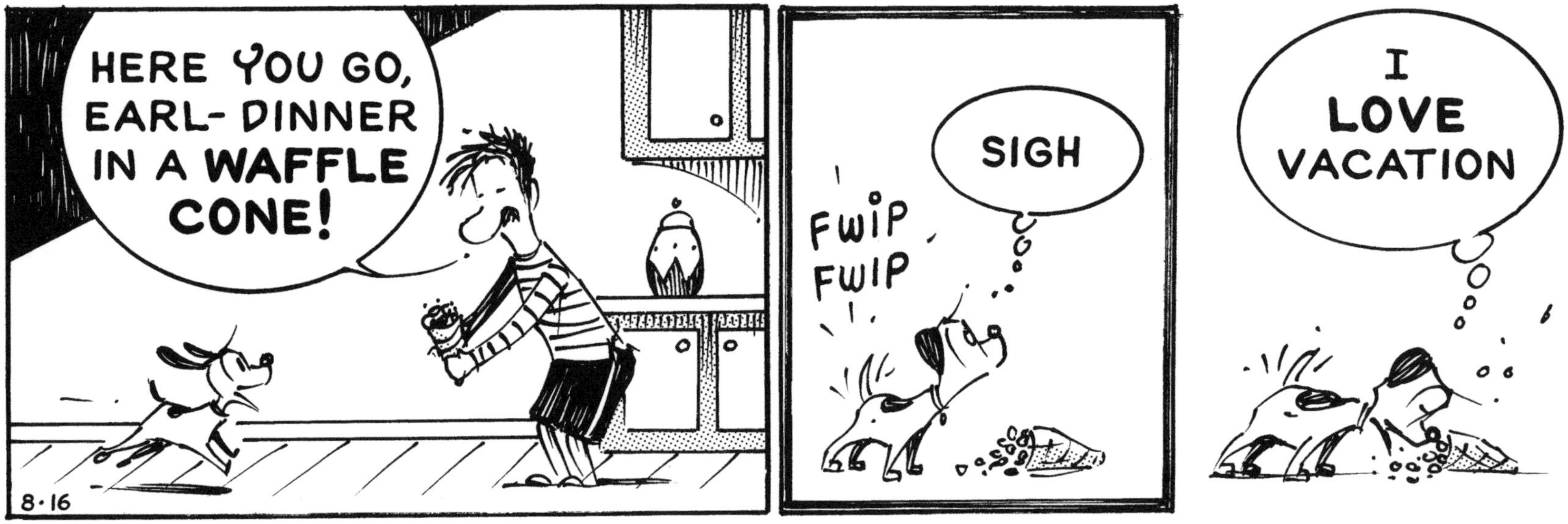
HERE YOU GO, EARL- DINNER IN A **WAFFLE CONE!**
8·16
FWIP FWIP
SIGH
I **LOVE** VACATION

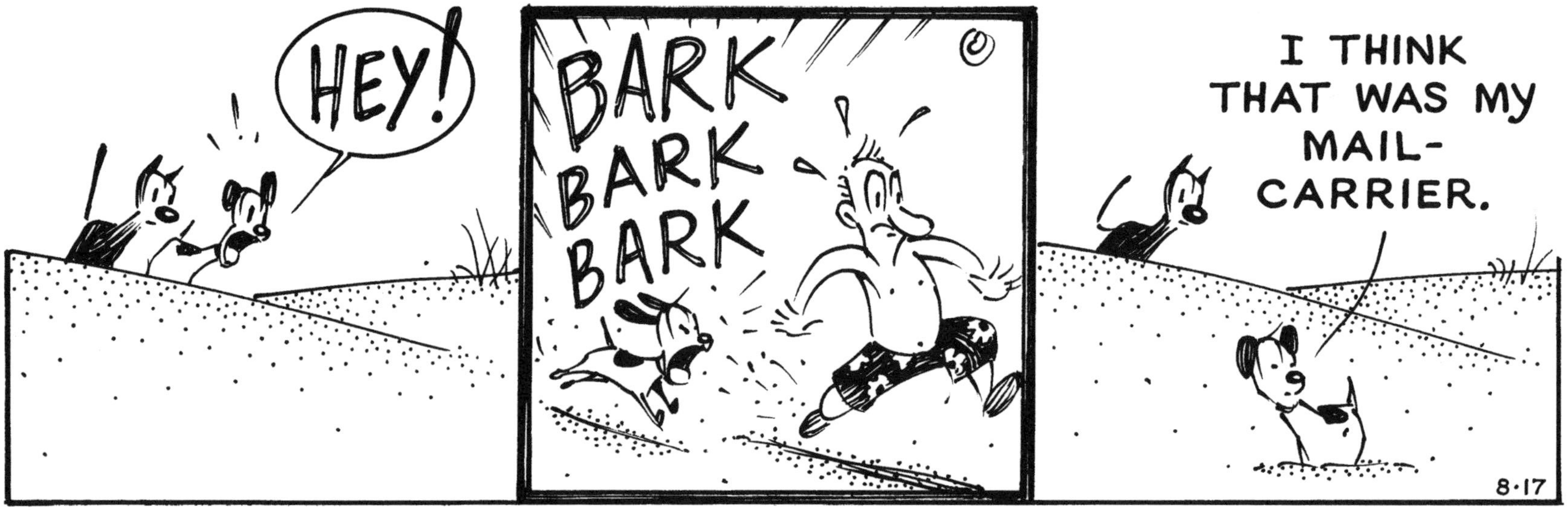
HEY!
BARK BARK BARK
©
I THINK THAT WAS MY MAIL-CARRIER.
8·17

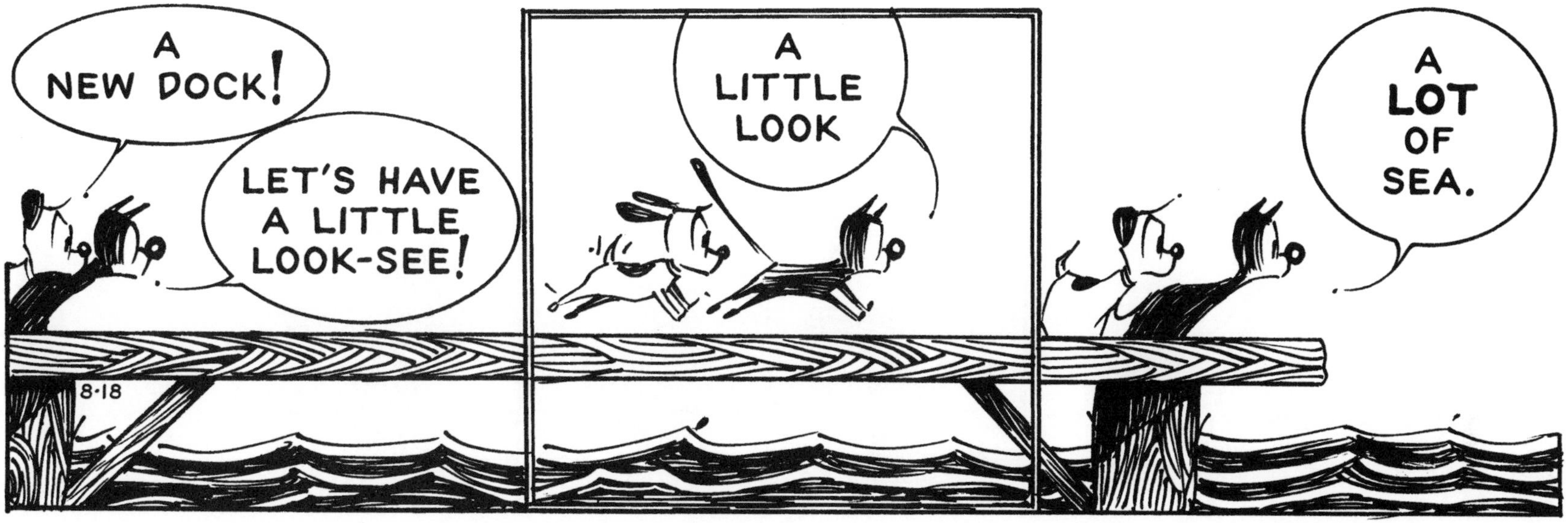
A NEW DOCK!
LET'S HAVE A LITTLE LOOK-SEE!
8·18
A LITTLE LOOK
A LOT OF SEA.

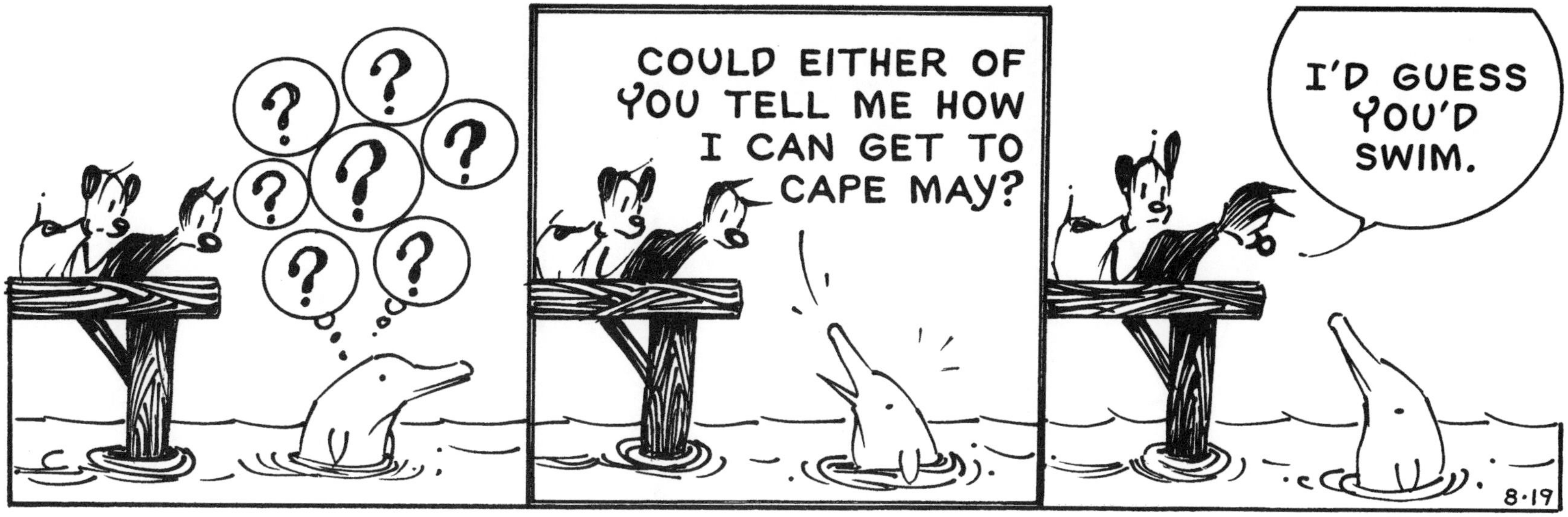
? ? ? ? ? ? ?
COULD EITHER OF YOU TELL ME HOW I CAN GET TO CAPE MAY?
I'D GUESS YOU'D SWIM.
8·19

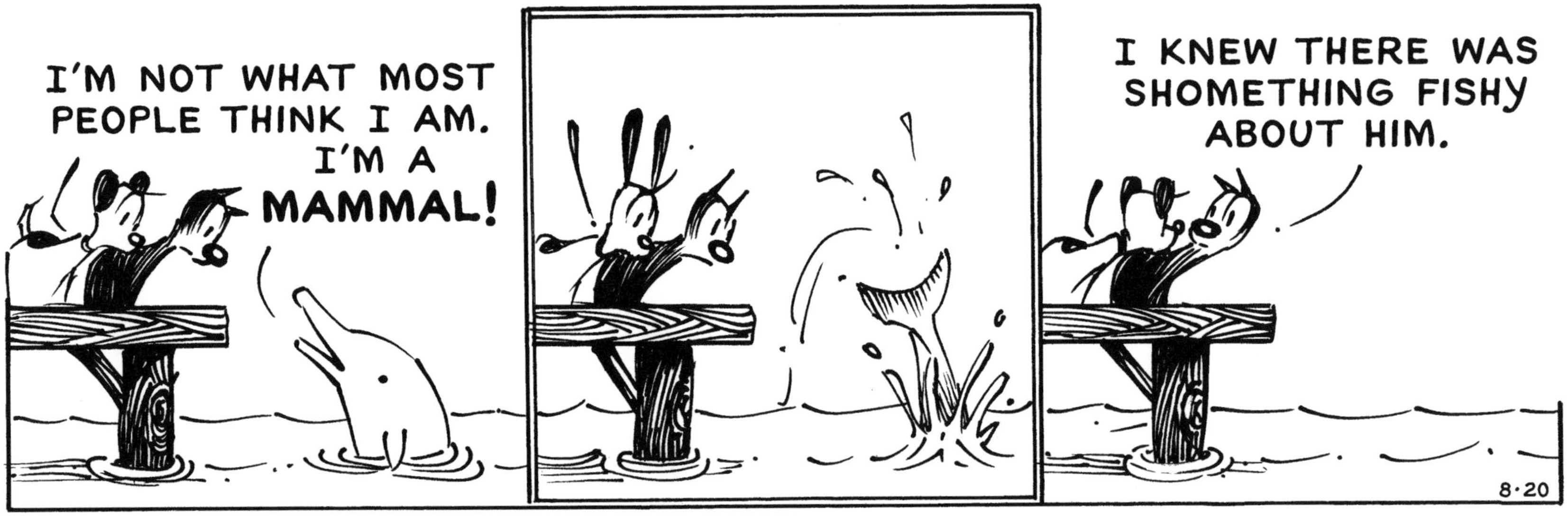
I'M NOT WHAT MOST PEOPLE THINK I AM. I'M A **MAMMAL!**
I KNEW THERE WAS SHOMETHING FISHY ABOUT HIM.
8·20

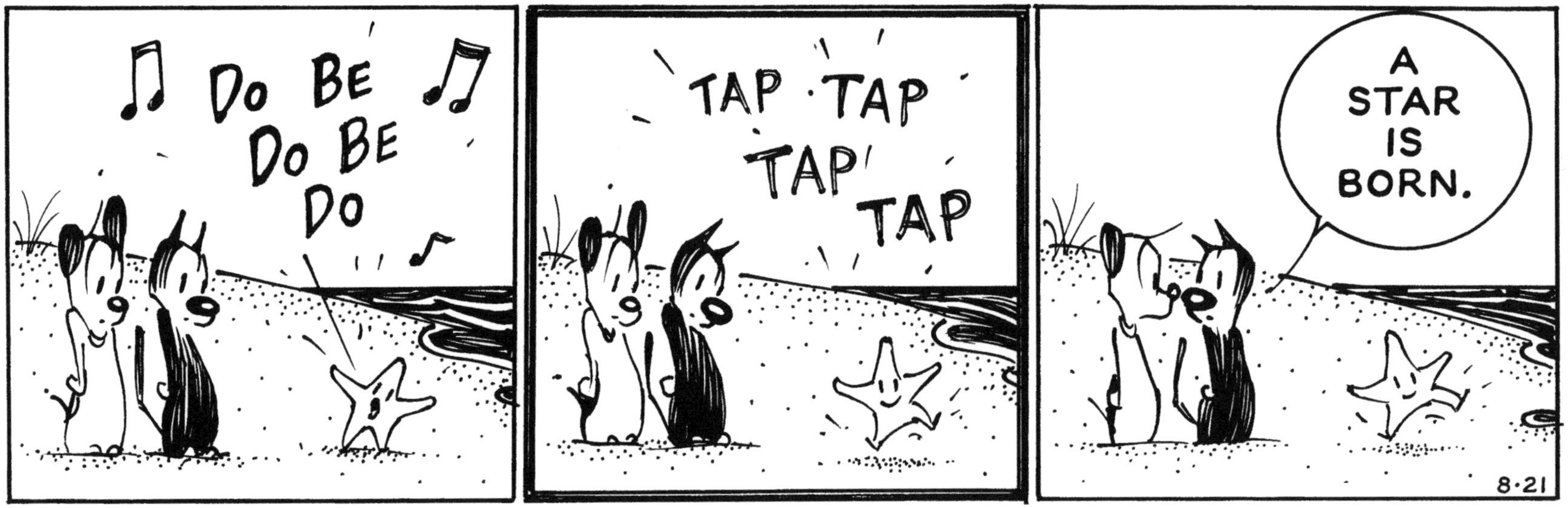
DO BE DO BE DO
TAP TAP TAP TAP
A STAR IS BORN.
8·21

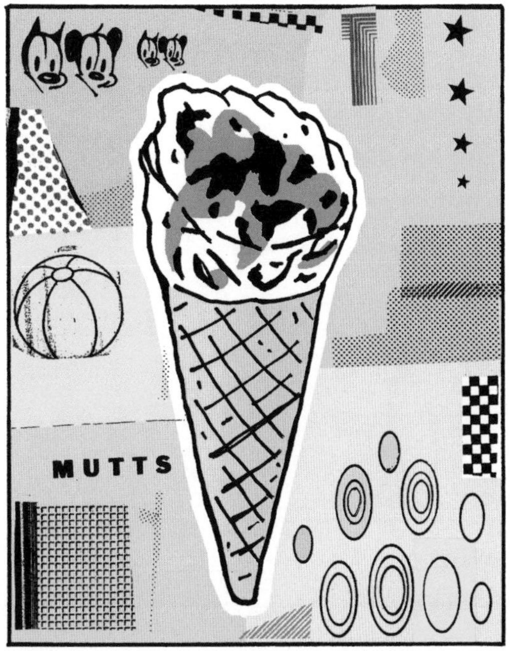
MUTTS

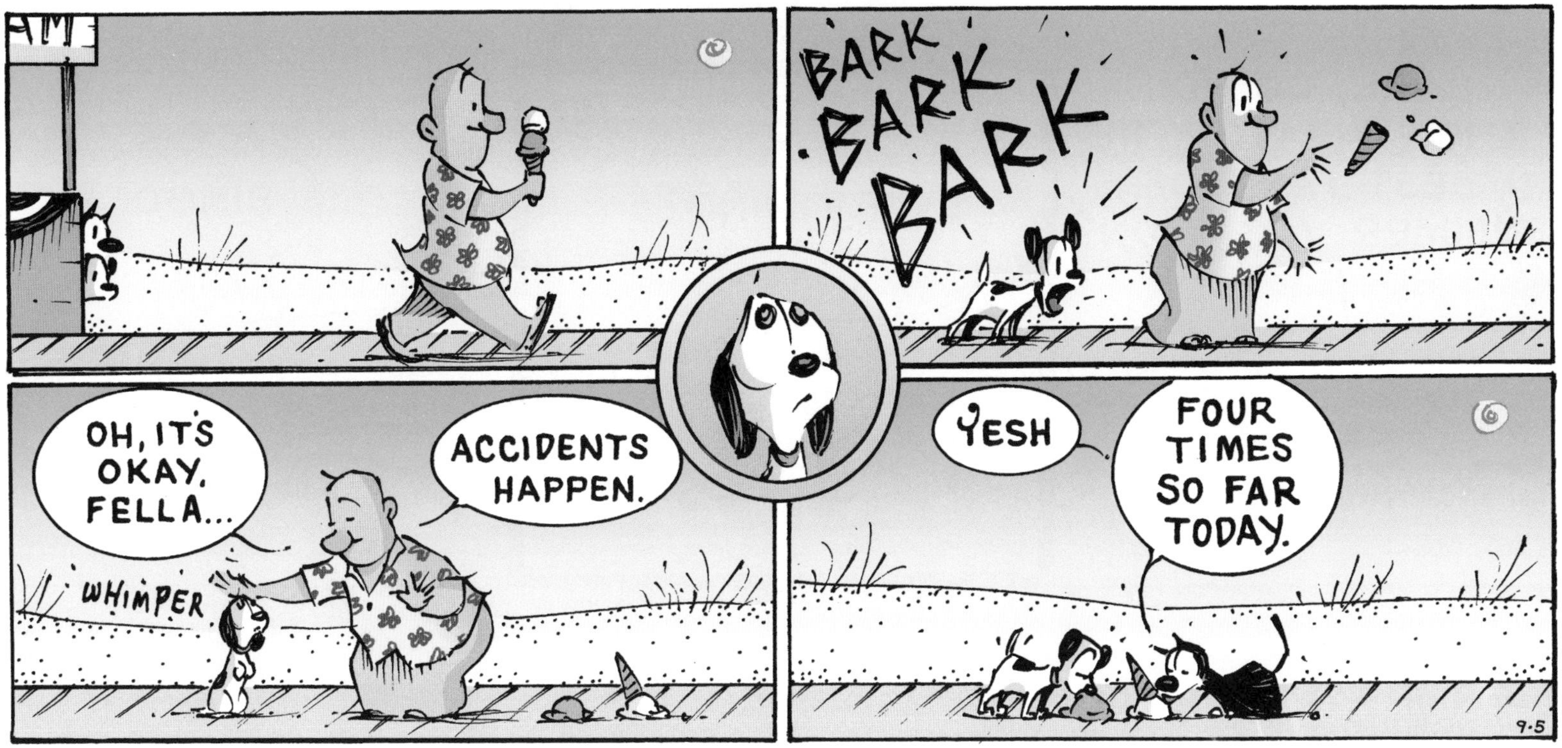
BARK
BARK
BARK
OH, IT'S OKAY, FELLA...
WHIMPER
ACCIDENTS HAPPEN.
YESH
FOUR TIMES SO FAR TODAY.
9·5

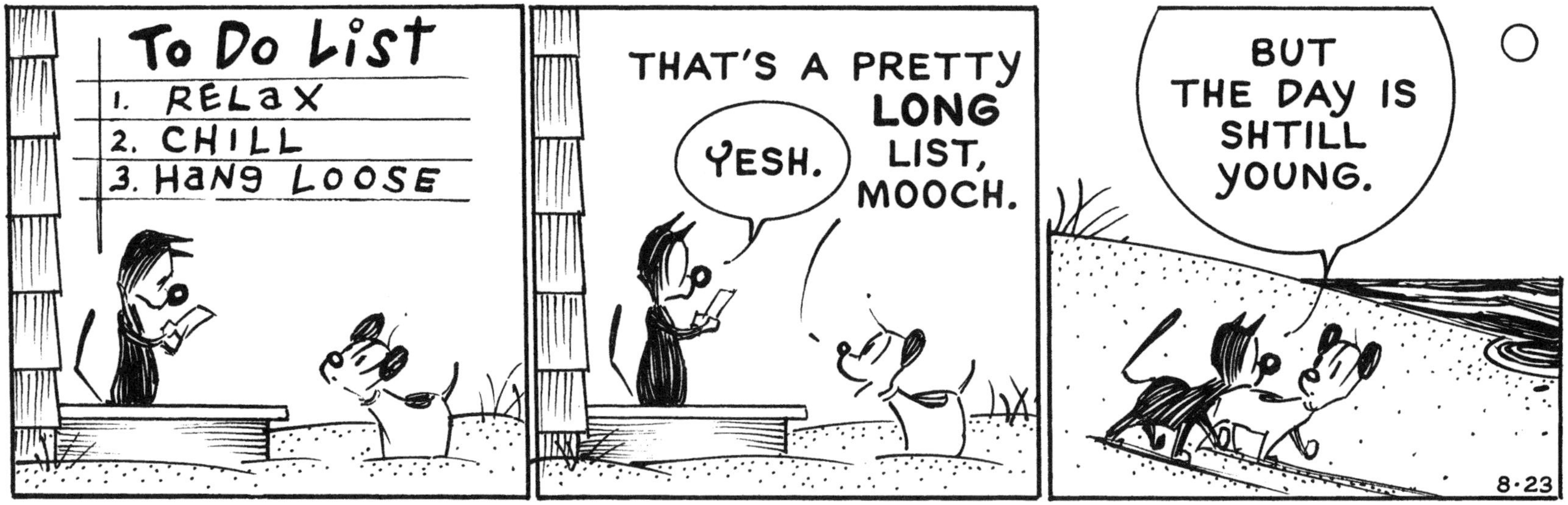
To Do List
1. RELaX
2. CHILL
3. HaNg LOOSE
THAT'S A PRETTY LONG LIST, MOOCH.
YESH.
BUT THE DAY IS SHTILL YOUNG.
8-23

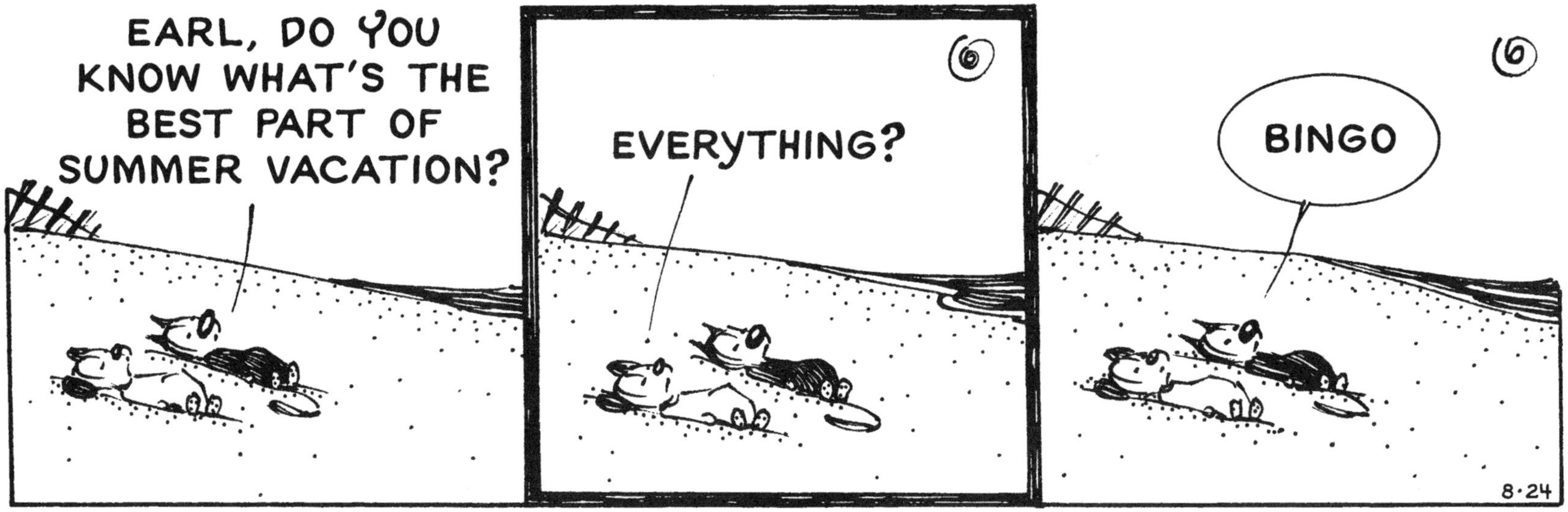
EARL, DO YOU KNOW WHAT'S THE BEST PART OF SUMMER VACATION?
EVERYTHING?
BINGO
8-24

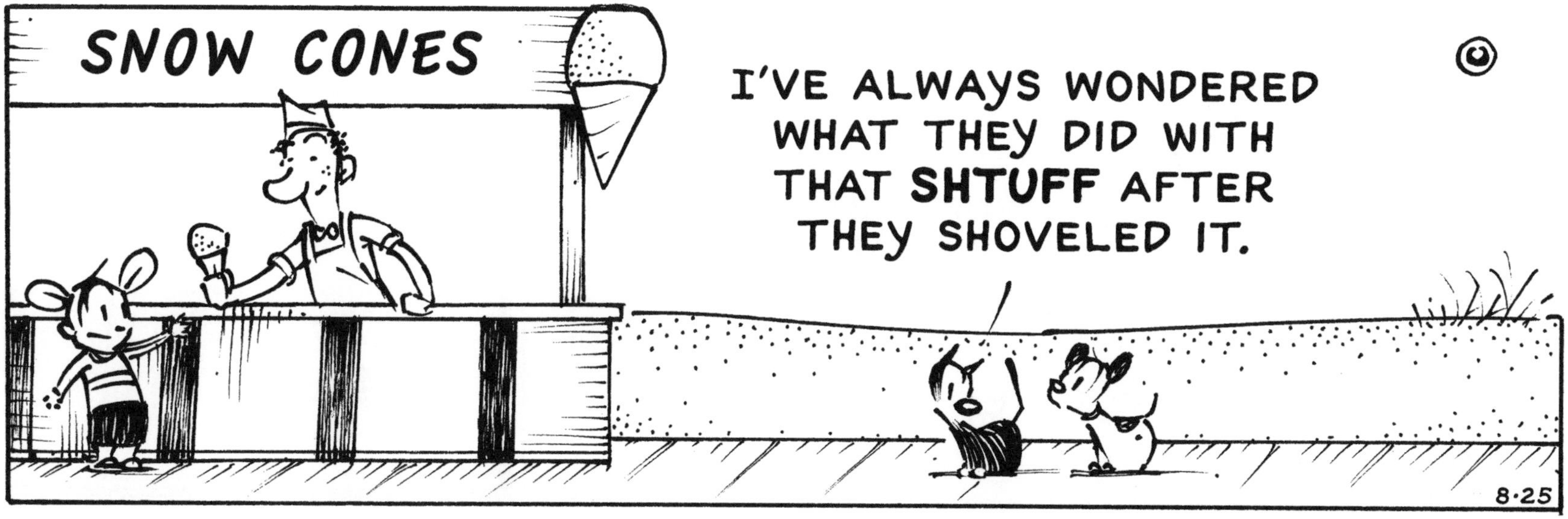
SNOW CONES
I'VE ALWAYS WONDERED WHAT THEY DID WITH THAT SHTUFF AFTER THEY SHOVELED IT.
8·25

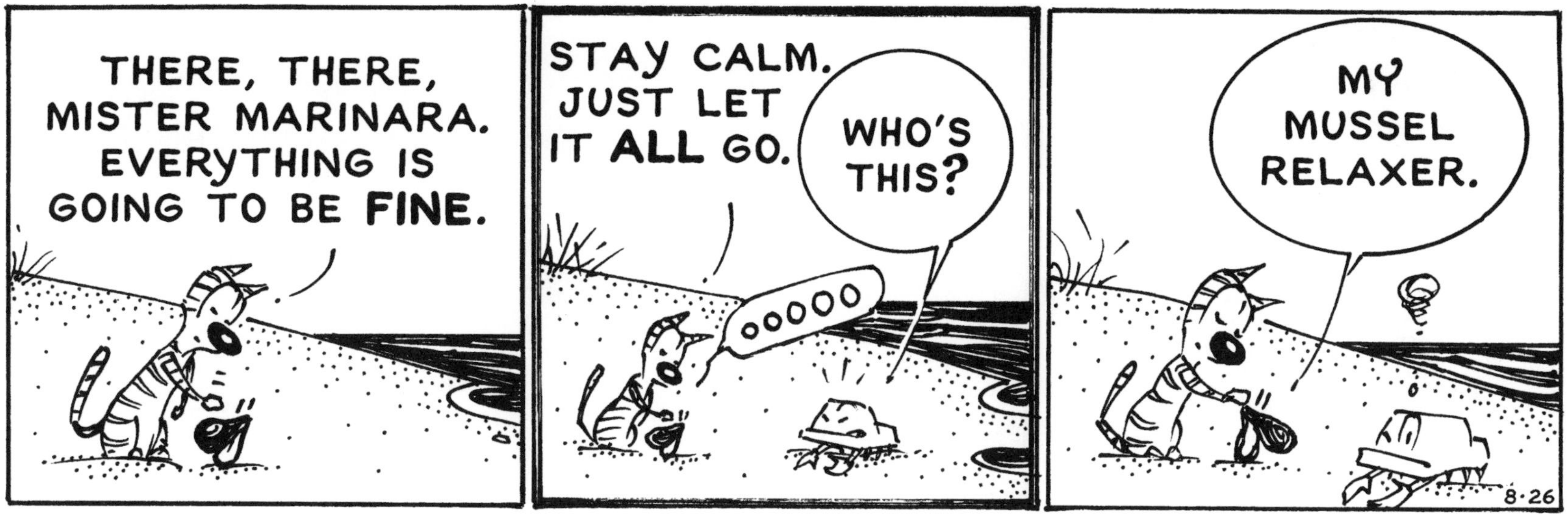
THERE, THERE, MISTER MARINARA. EVERYTHING IS GOING TO BE FINE.
STAY CALM. JUST LET IT ALL GO.
ooooo
WHO'S THIS?
MY MUSSEL RELAXER.
8·26

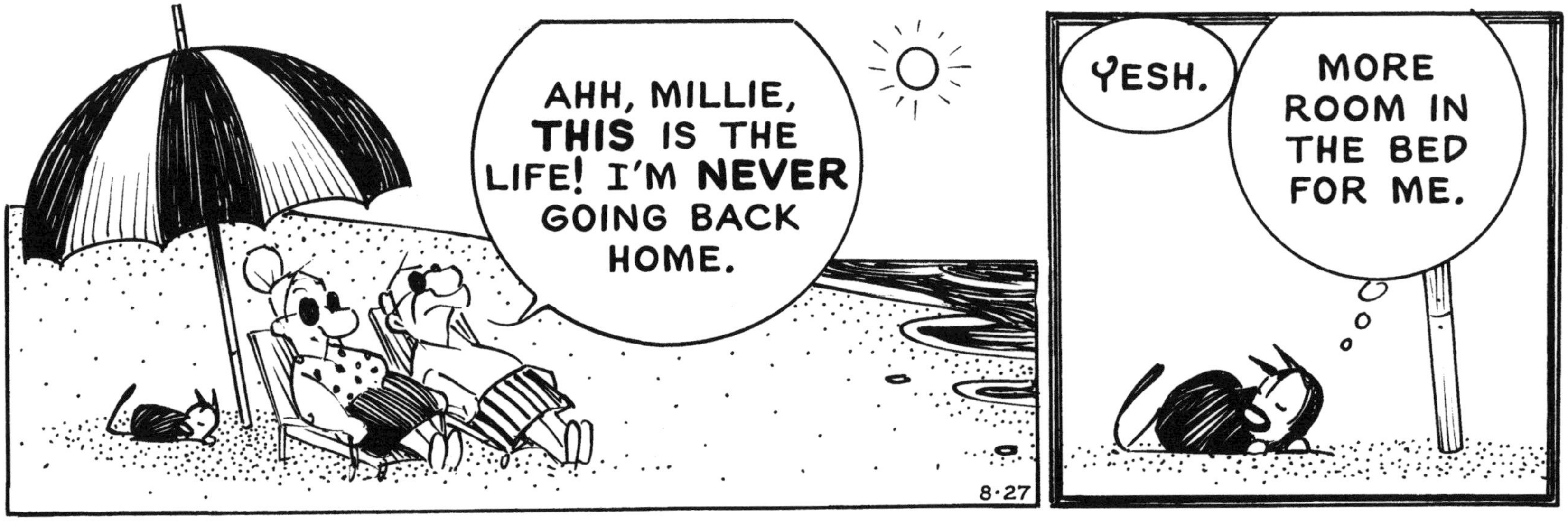
AHH, MILLIE, THIS IS THE LIFE! I'M NEVER GOING BACK HOME.
YESH.
MORE ROOM IN THE BED FOR ME.
8·27

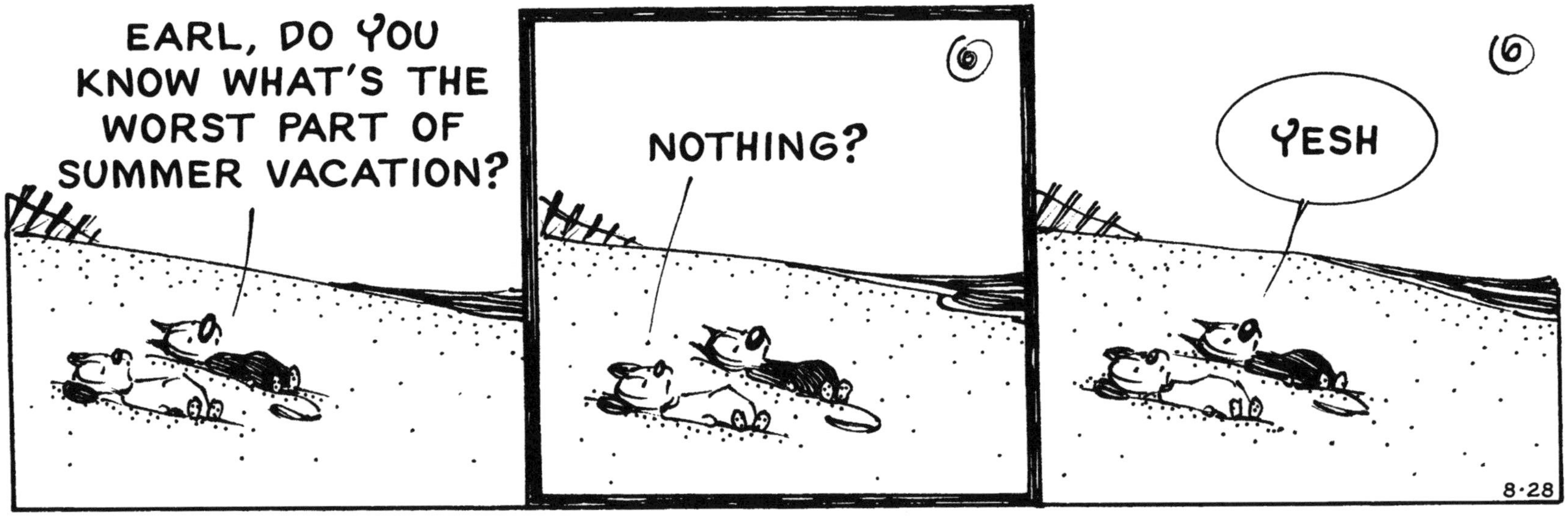
EARL, DO YOU KNOW WHAT'S THE WORST PART OF SUMMER VACATION?
NOTHING?
YESH
8·28

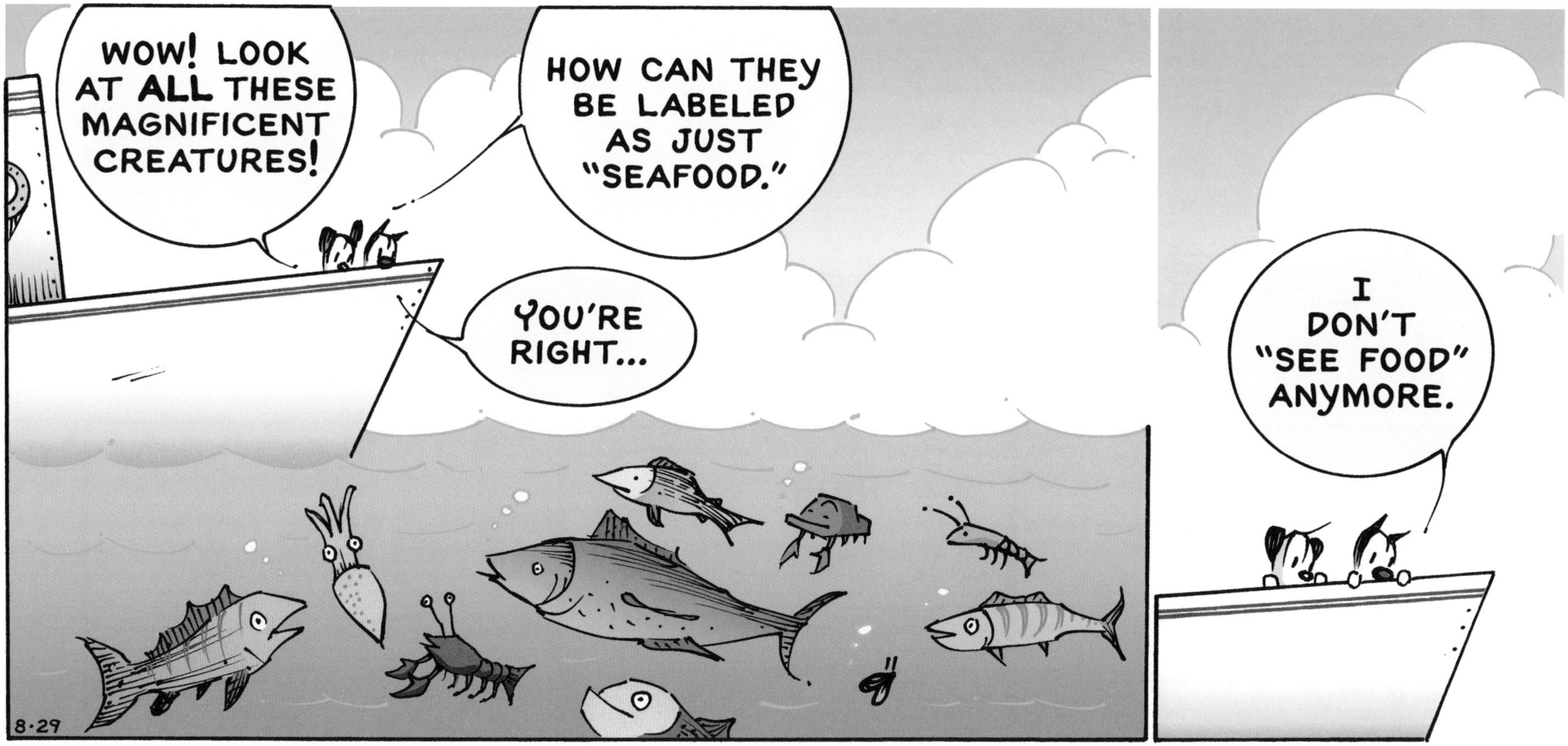
WOW! LOOK AT ALL THESE MAGNIFICENT CREATURES!
HOW CAN THEY BE LABELED AS JUST "SEAFOOD."
YOU'RE RIGHT...
I DON'T "SEE FOOD" ANYMORE.
8·29

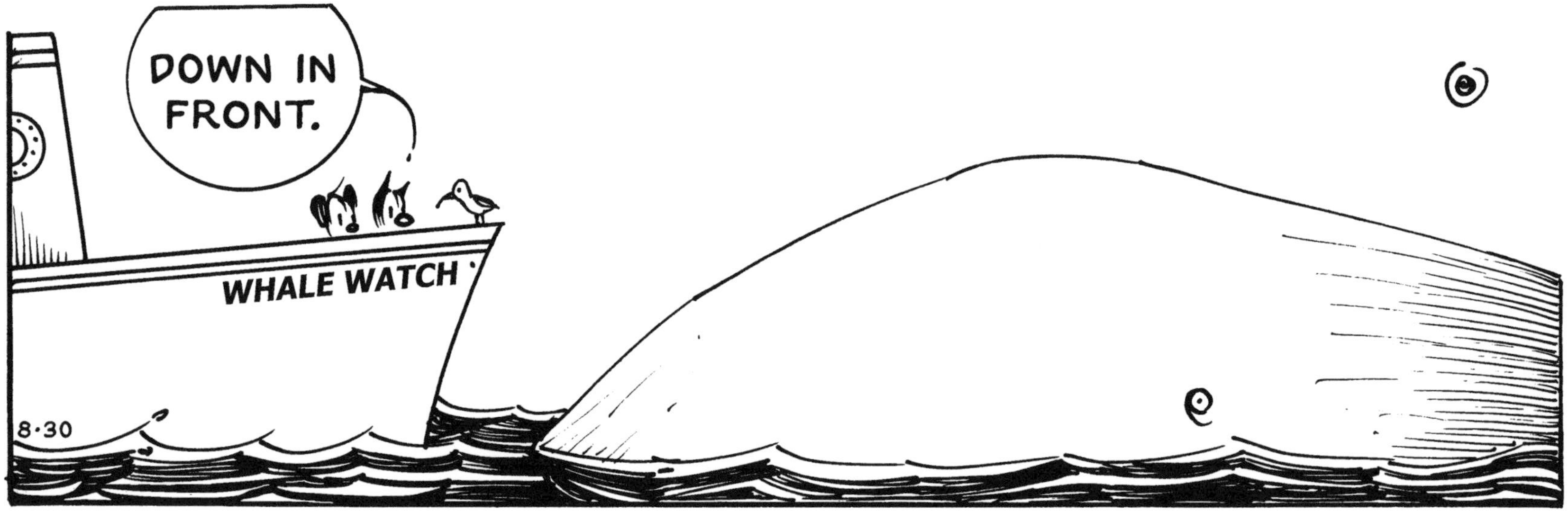
DOWN IN FRONT.
WHALE WATCH
8·30

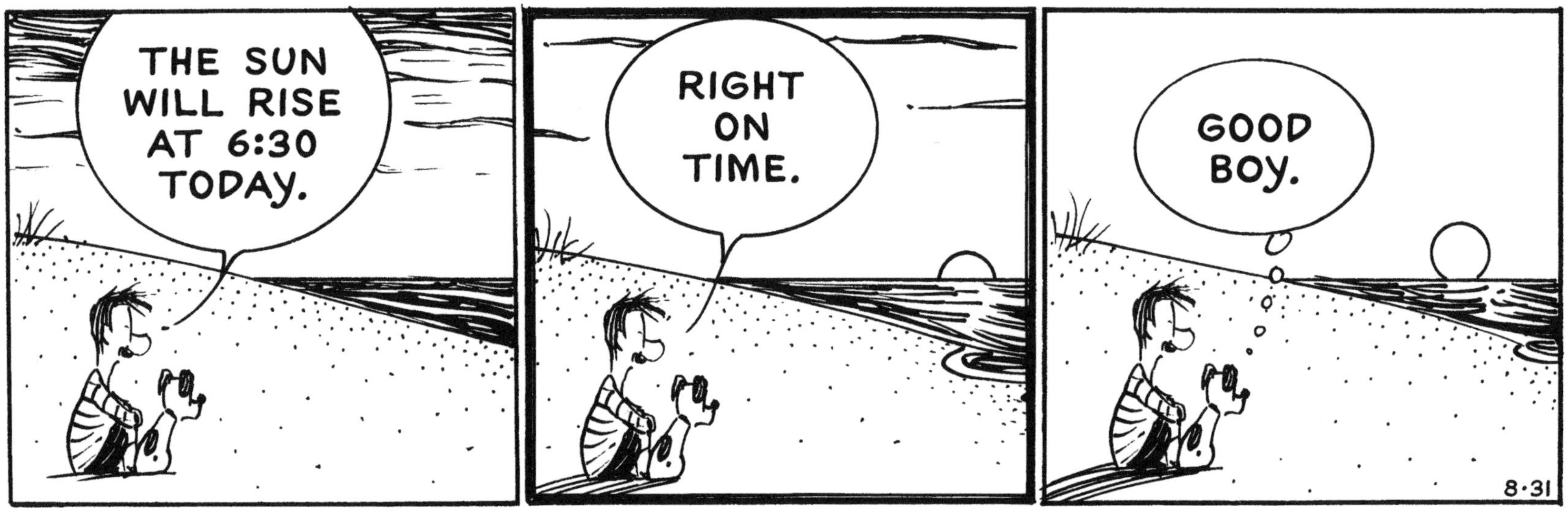
THE SUN WILL RISE AT 6:30 TODAY.
RIGHT ON TIME.
GOOD BOY.
8·31

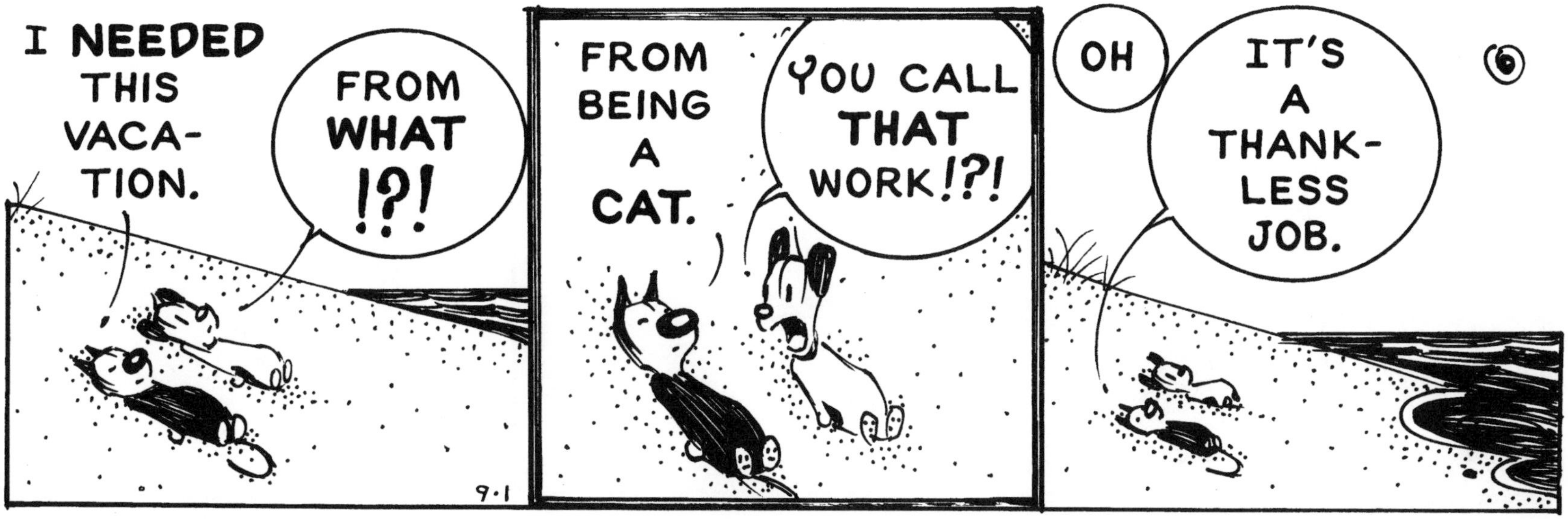
I NEEDED THIS VACA- TION.
FROM WHAT !?!
FROM BEING A CAT.
YOU CALL THAT WORK!?!
OH
IT'S A THANK- LESS JOB.
9·1

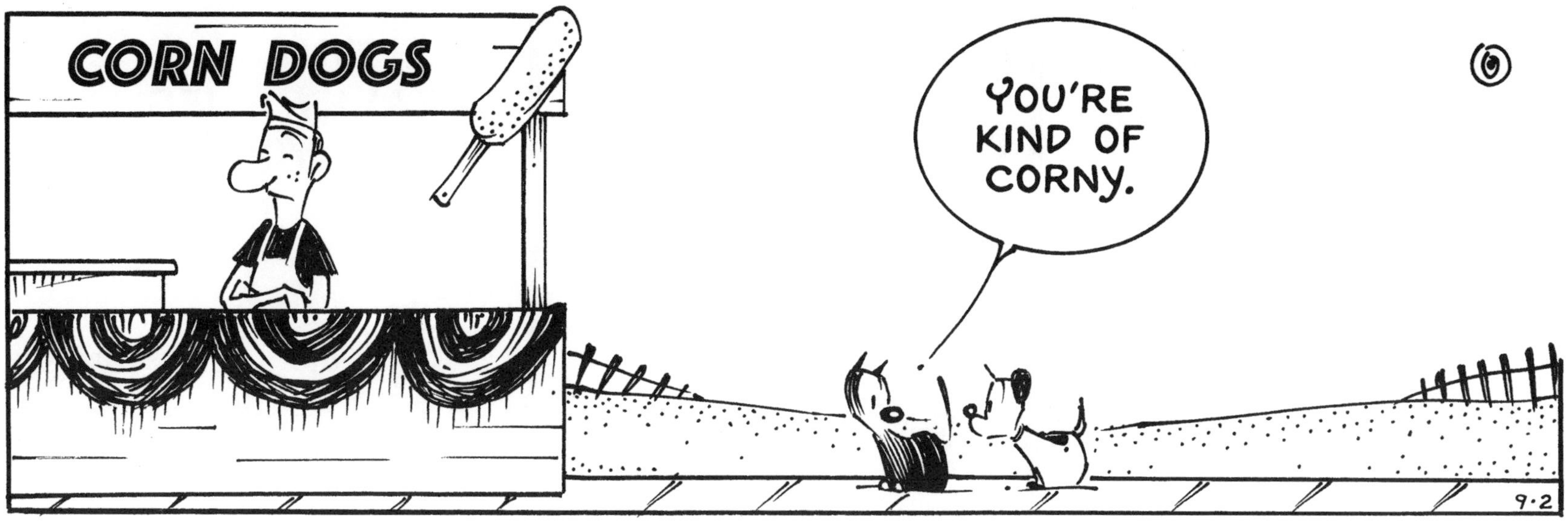
CORN DOGS
YOU'RE KIND OF CORNY.
9·2

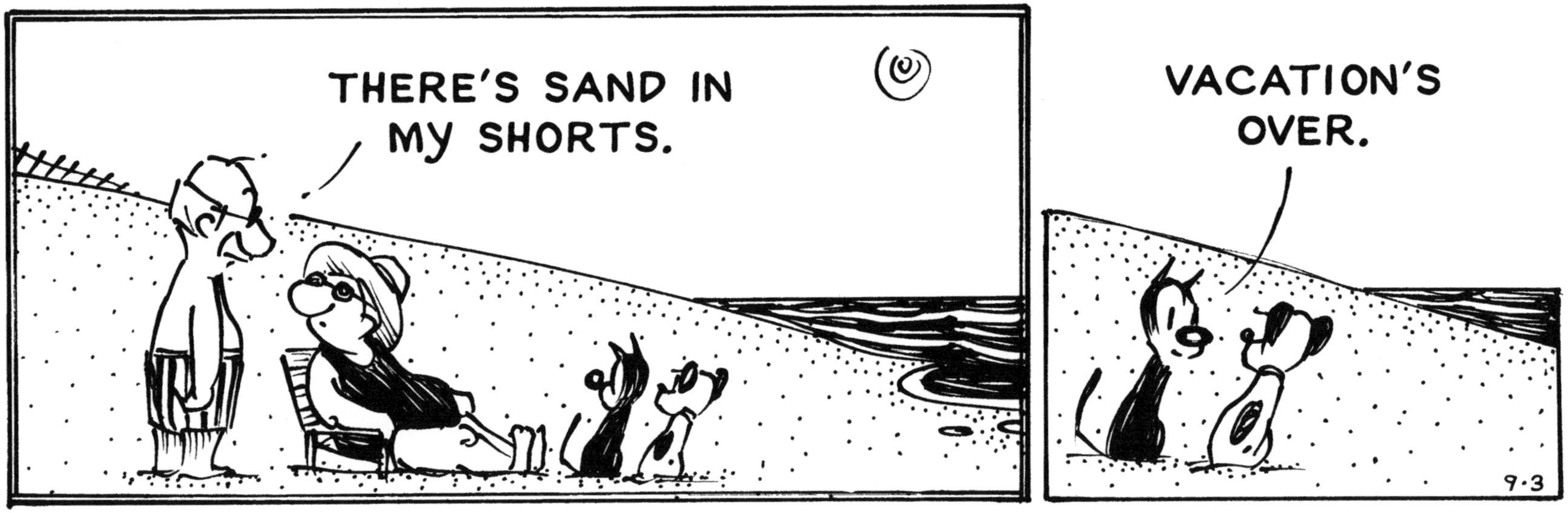
THERE'S SAND IN MY SHORTS.
VACATION'S OVER.
9·3

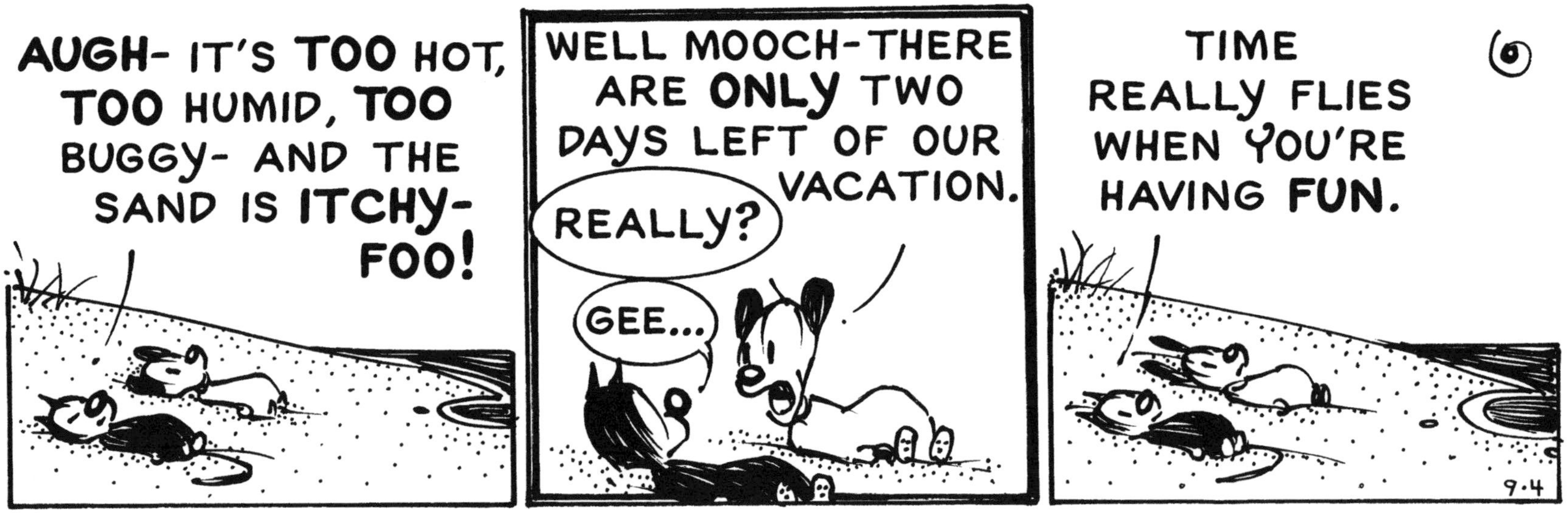
AUGH- IT'S TOO HOT, TOO HUMID, TOO BUGGY- AND THE SAND IS ITCHY-FOO!
WELL MOOCH-THERE ARE ONLY TWO DAYS LEFT OF OUR VACATION.
REALLY?
GEE...
TIME REALLY FLIES WHEN YOU'RE HAVING FUN.
9·4

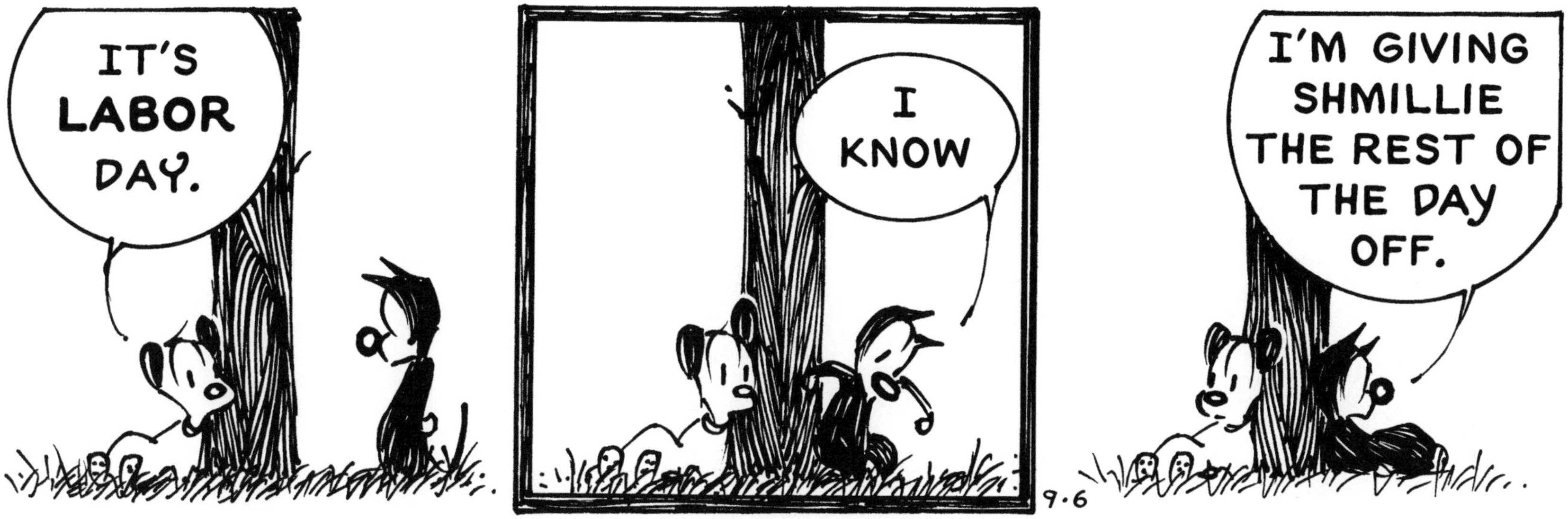
IT'S LABOR DAY.
I KNOW
I'M GIVING SHMILLIE THE REST OF THE DAY OFF.
9·6

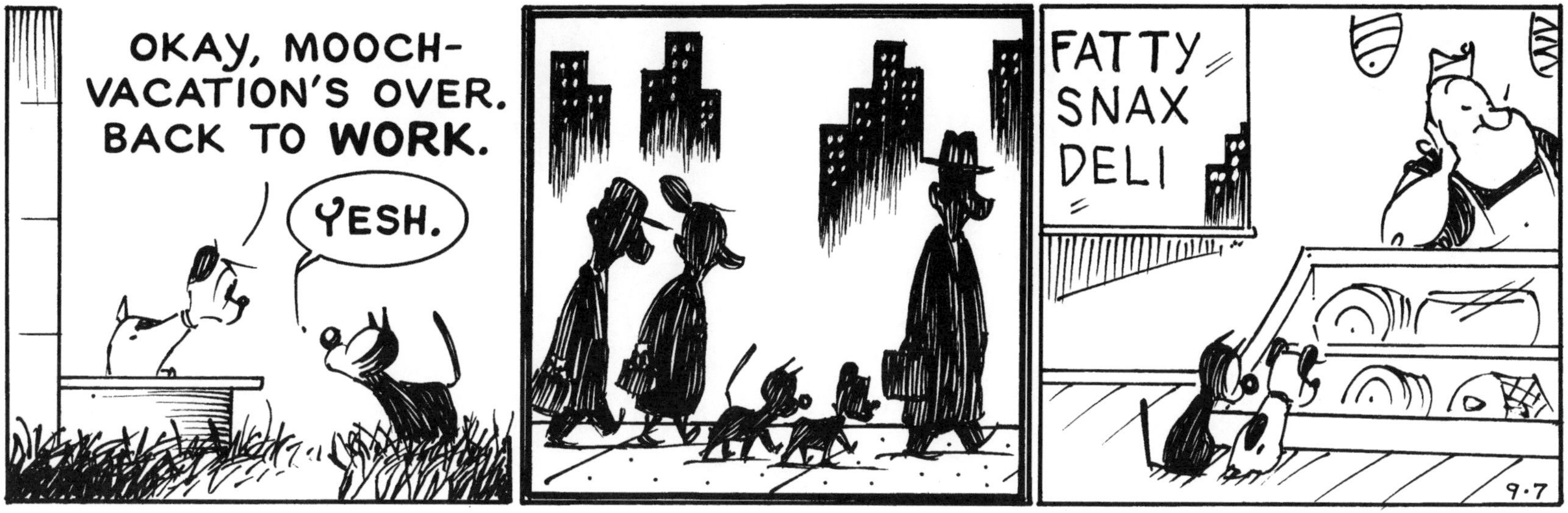
OKAY, MOOCH-VACATION'S OVER. BACK TO WORK.
YESH.
FATTY SNAX DELI
9·7

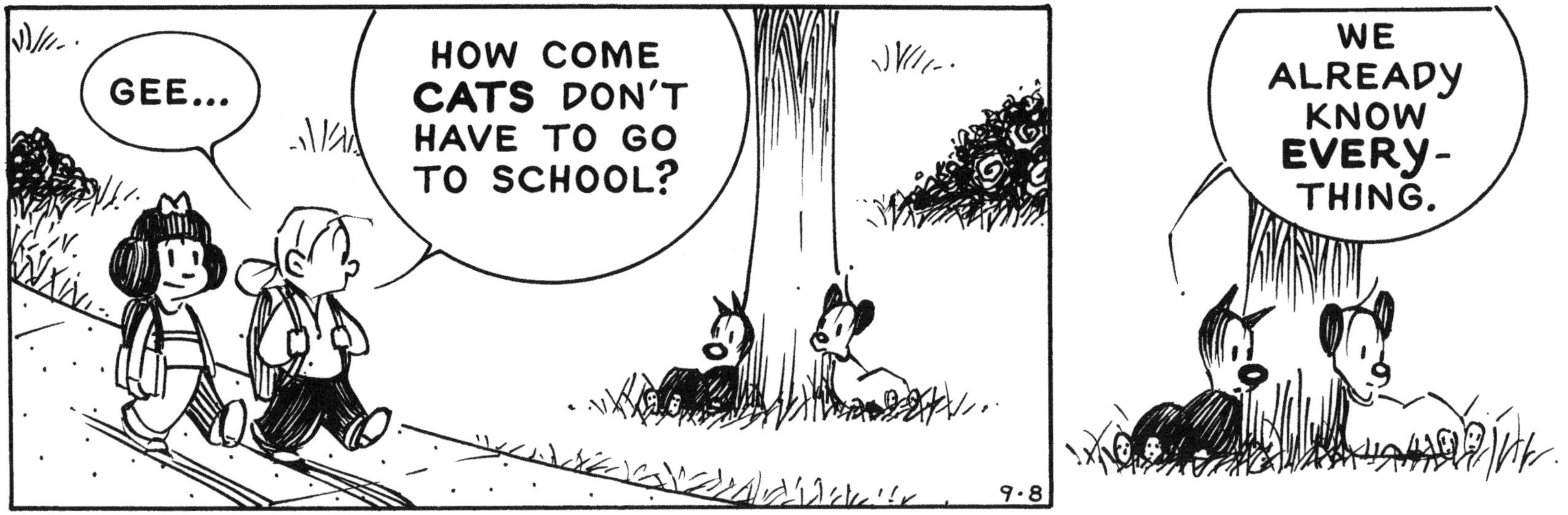
GEE...
HOW COME CATS DON'T HAVE TO GO TO SCHOOL?
9·8
WE ALREADY KNOW EVERY-THING.

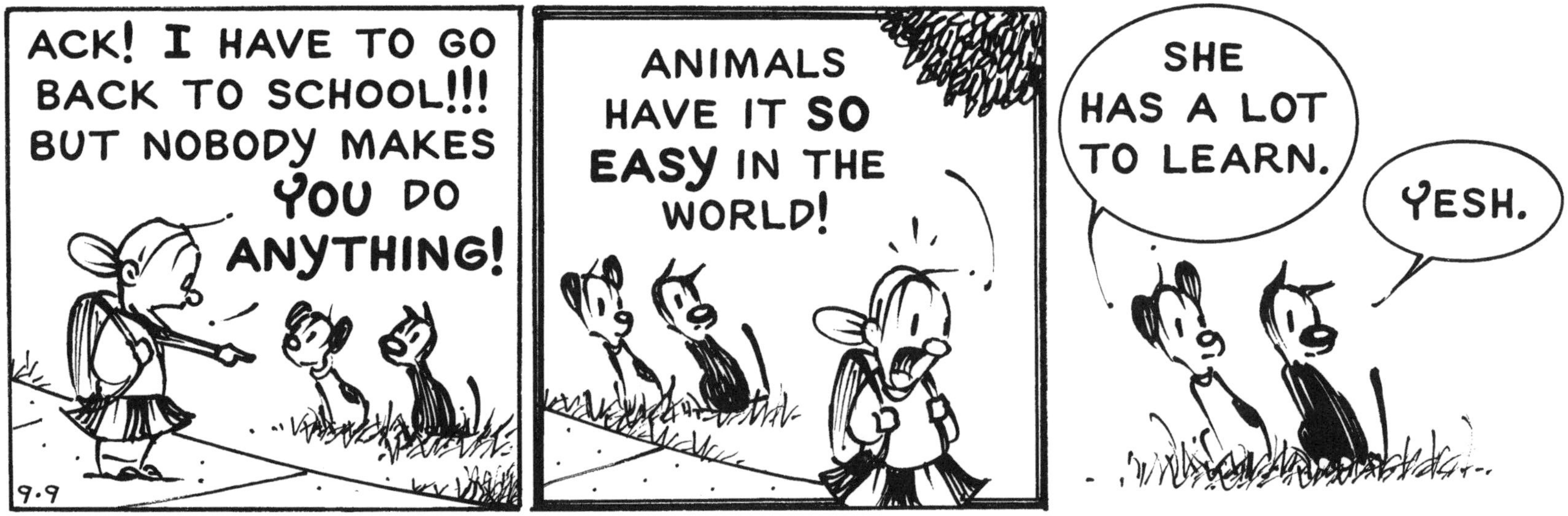
ACK! I HAVE TO GO BACK TO SCHOOL!!! BUT NOBODY MAKES YOU DO ANYTHING!
9·9
ANIMALS HAVE IT SO EASY IN THE WORLD!
SHE HAS A LOT TO LEARN.
YESH.

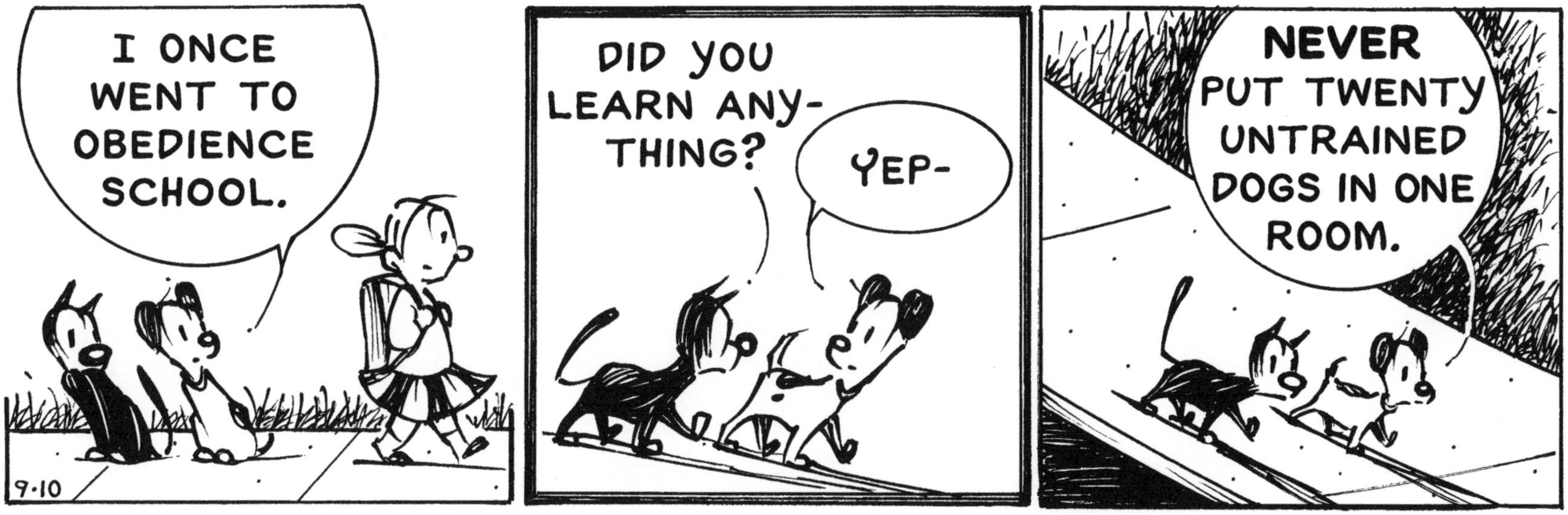
I ONCE WENT TO OBEDIENCE SCHOOL.
9·10
DID YOU LEARN ANY-THING?
YEP-
NEVER PUT TWENTY UNTRAINED DOGS IN ONE ROOM.

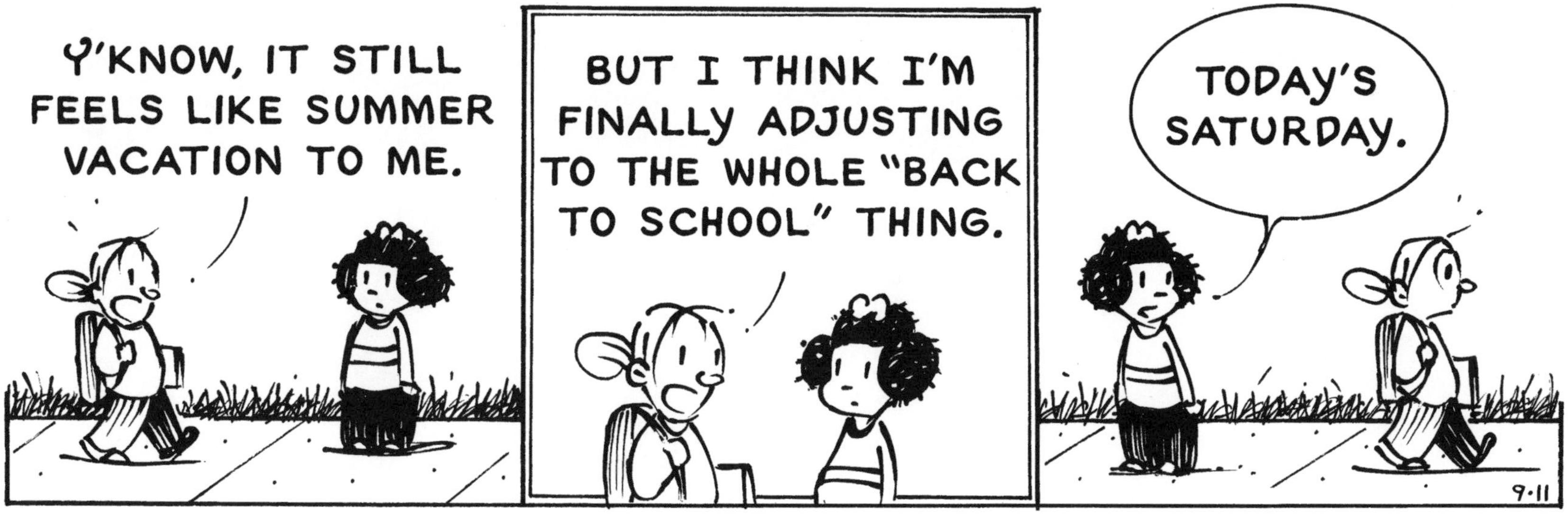
Y'KNOW, IT STILL FEELS LIKE SUMMER VACATION TO ME.
BUT I THINK I'M FINALLY ADJUSTING TO THE WHOLE "BACK TO SCHOOL" THING.
TODAY'S SATURDAY.
9·11

MUTTS
mutts
MUTTS
MUTTS
MUTTS
McD

YES, MA'AM- THE CAT IS MY "SHOW-AND-TELL."
AND WHAT IS HE GOING TO "SHOW" US TODAY?
KOFF · GAK · URK
OOOK
HACK
PITOOO
!
THEN I SHCRATCHED THE TEACHER'S DESK FOR EXTRA CREDIT.
9·12

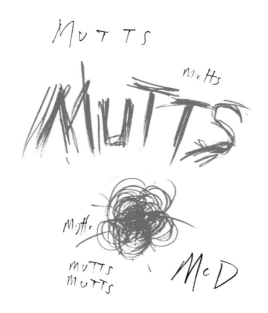

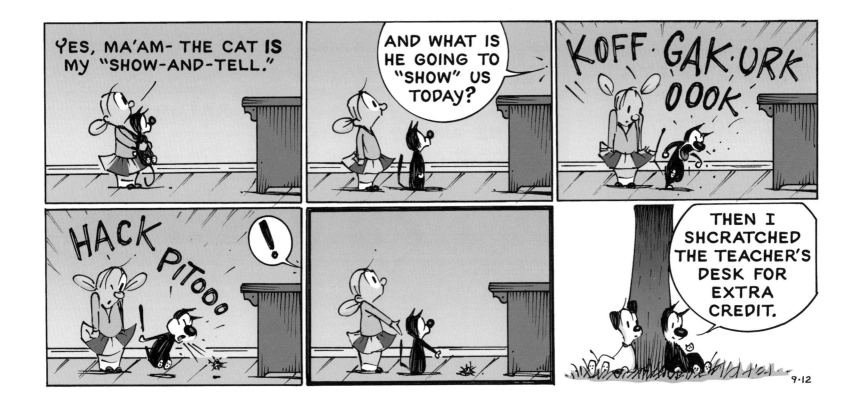

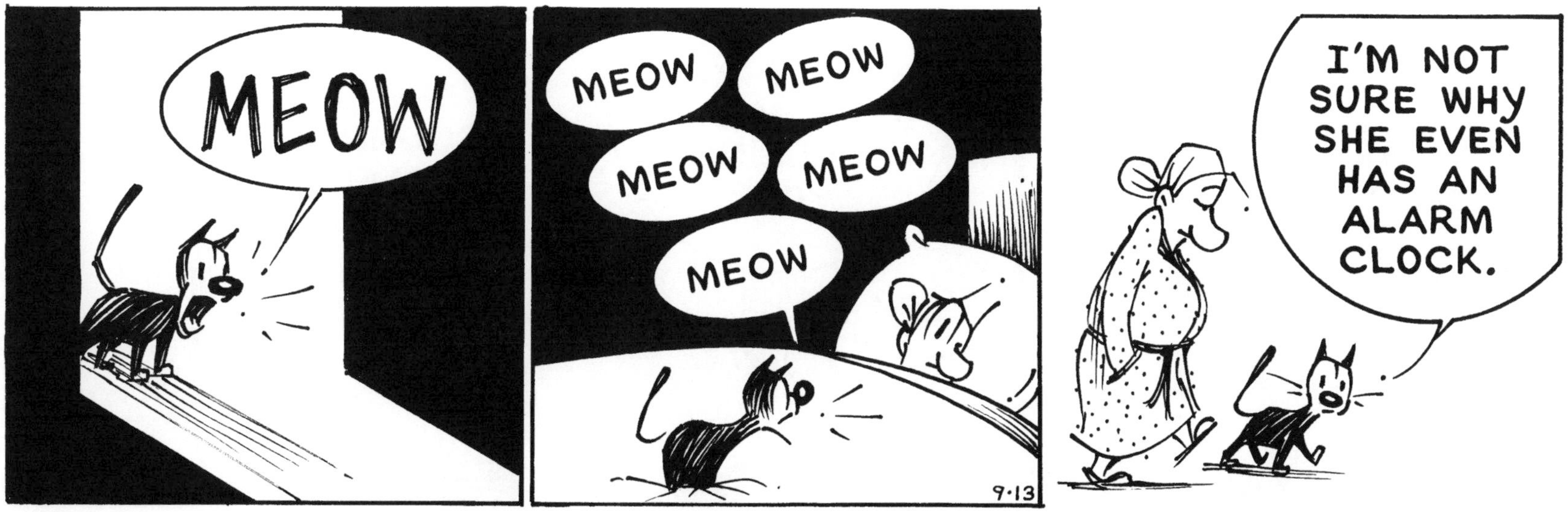
MEOW
MEOW
MEOW
MEOW
MEOW
MEOW
9·13
I'M NOT SURE WHY SHE EVEN HAS AN ALARM CLOCK.

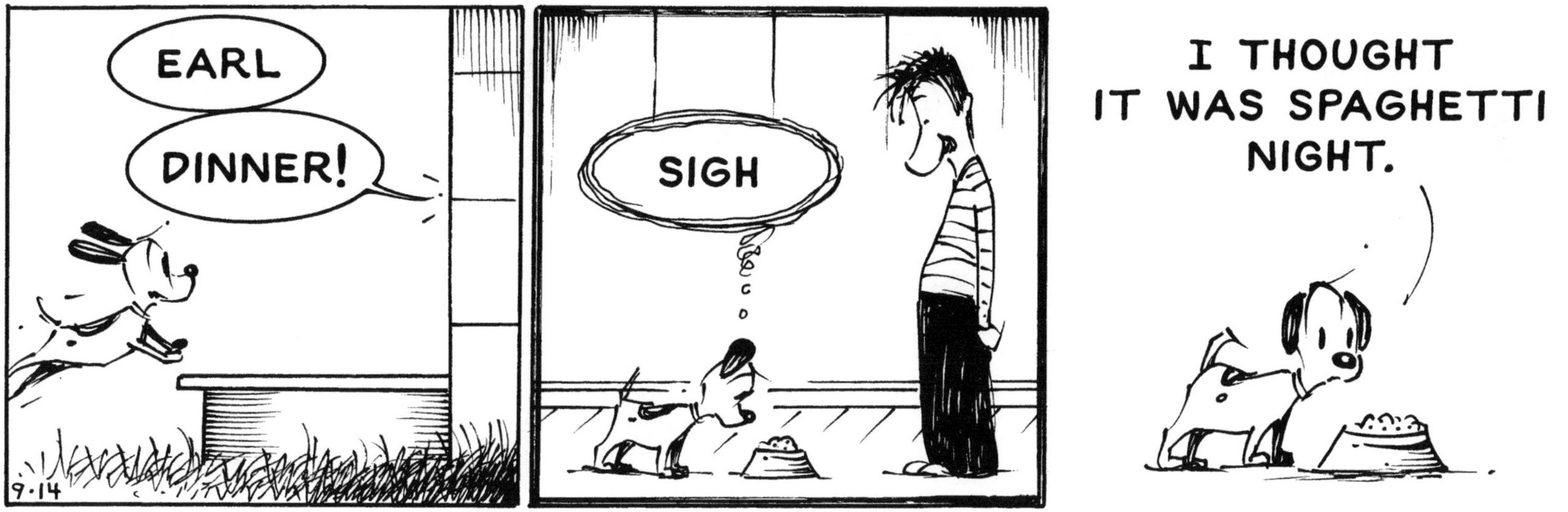
EARL
DINNER!
9·14
SIGH
I THOUGHT IT WAS SPAGHETTI NIGHT.

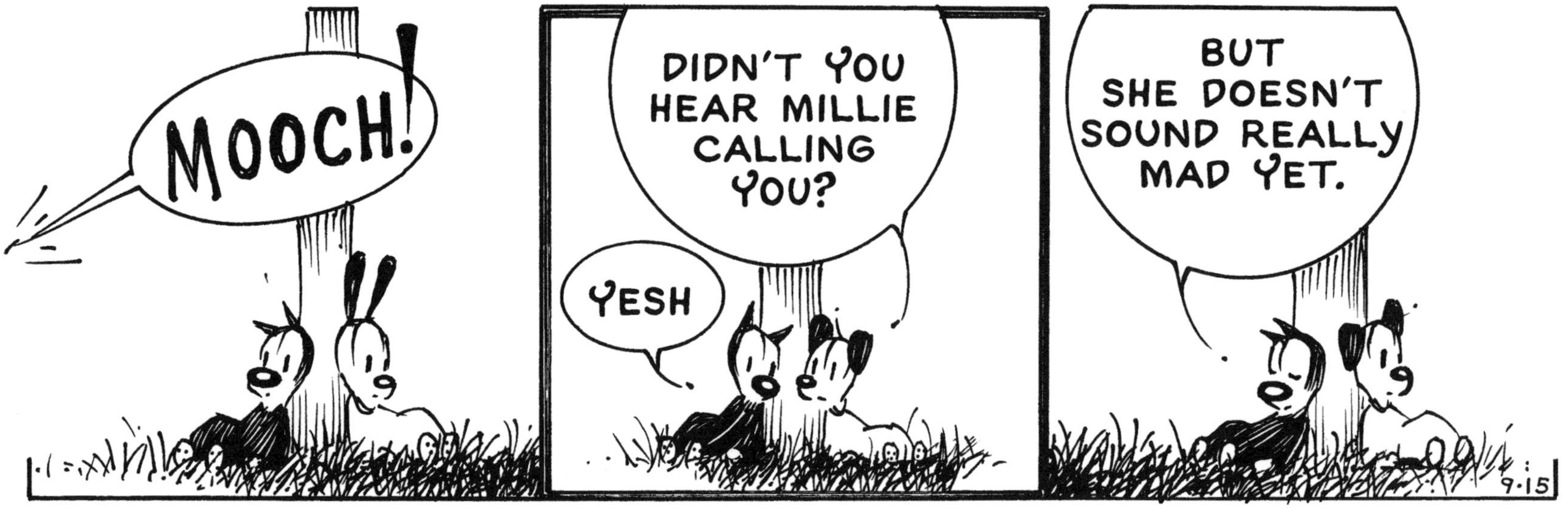
MOOCH!
DIDN'T YOU HEAR MILLIE CALLING YOU?
YESH
BUT SHE DOESN'T SOUND REALLY MAD YET.
9·15

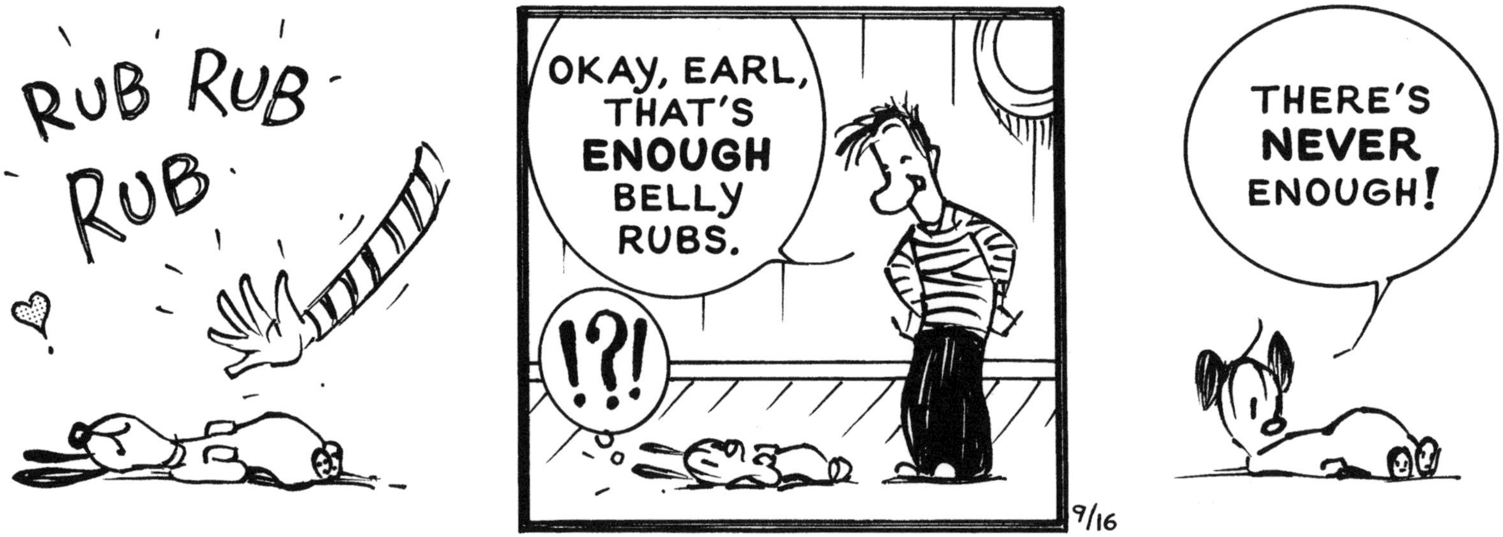
RUB RUB RUB
OKAY, EARL, THAT'S **ENOUGH** BELLY RUBS.
!?!
THERE'S **NEVER** ENOUGH!
9/16

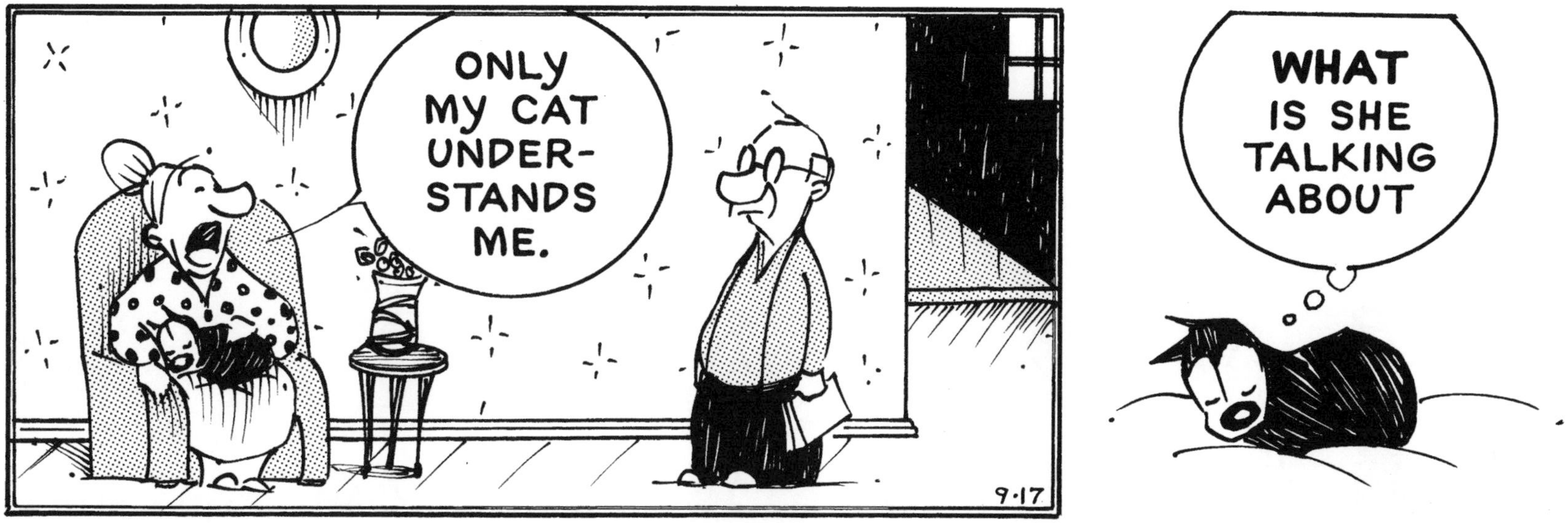
ONLY MY CAT UNDER-STANDS ME.
WHAT IS SHE TALKING ABOUT
9·17

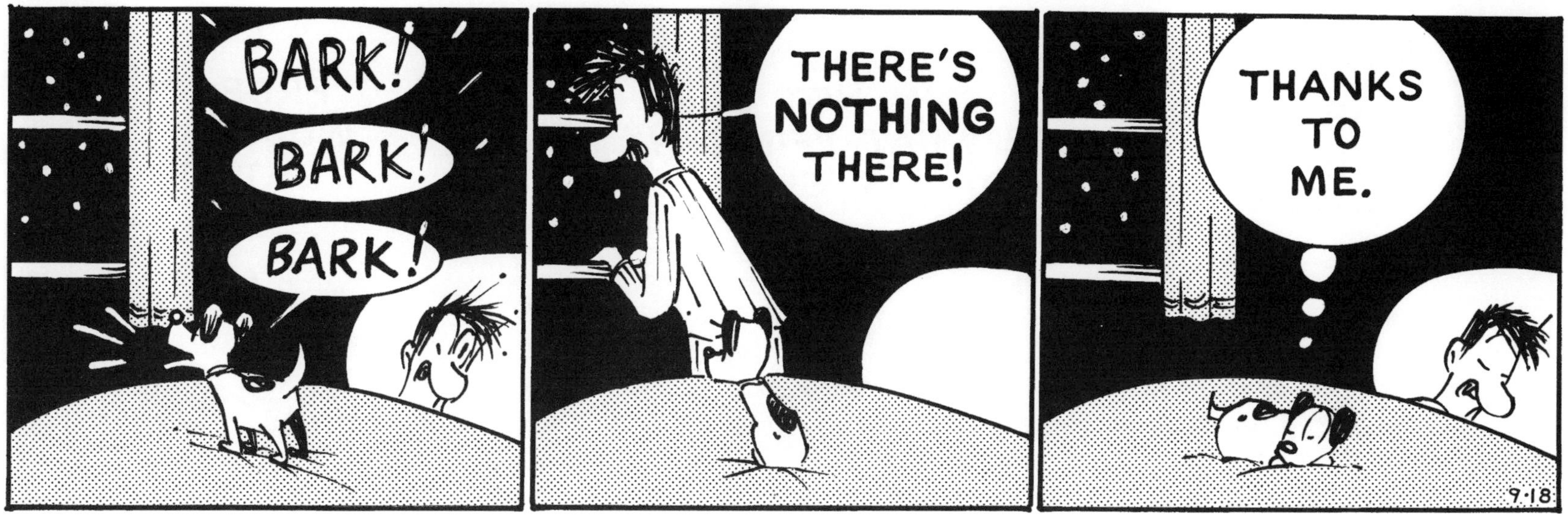
BARK!
BARK!
BARK!
THERE'S NOTHING THERE!
THANKS TO ME.
9·18

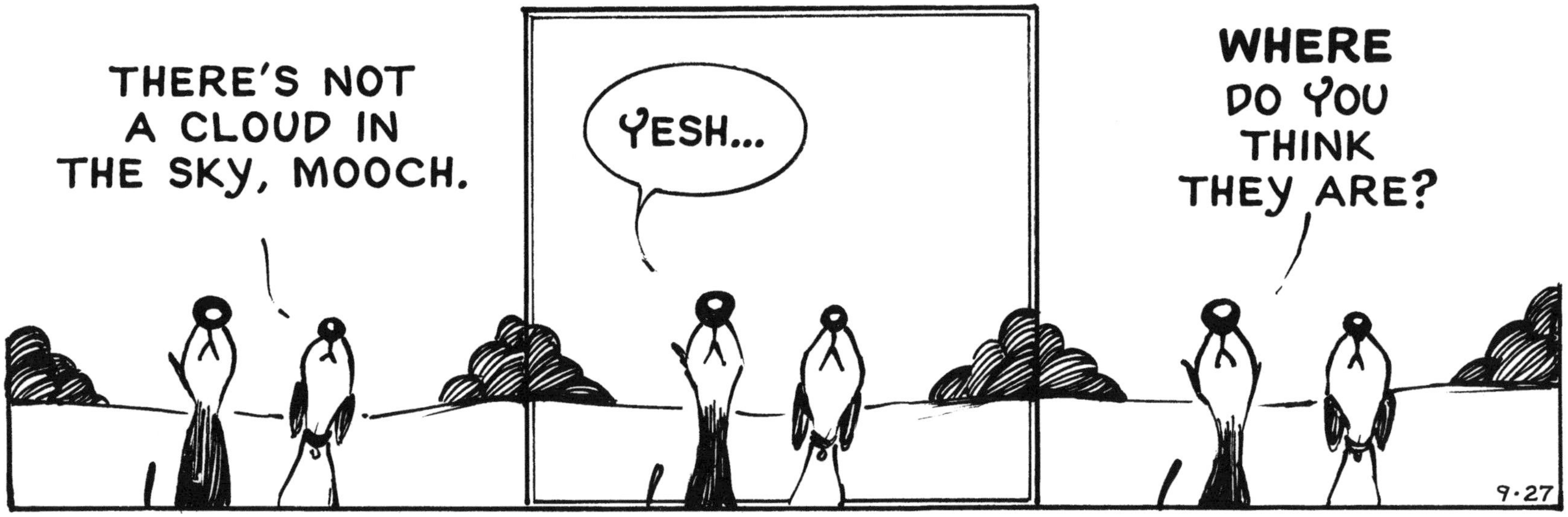
THERE'S NOT A CLOUD IN THE SKY, MOOCH.
YESH...
WHERE DO YOU THINK THEY ARE?
9·27

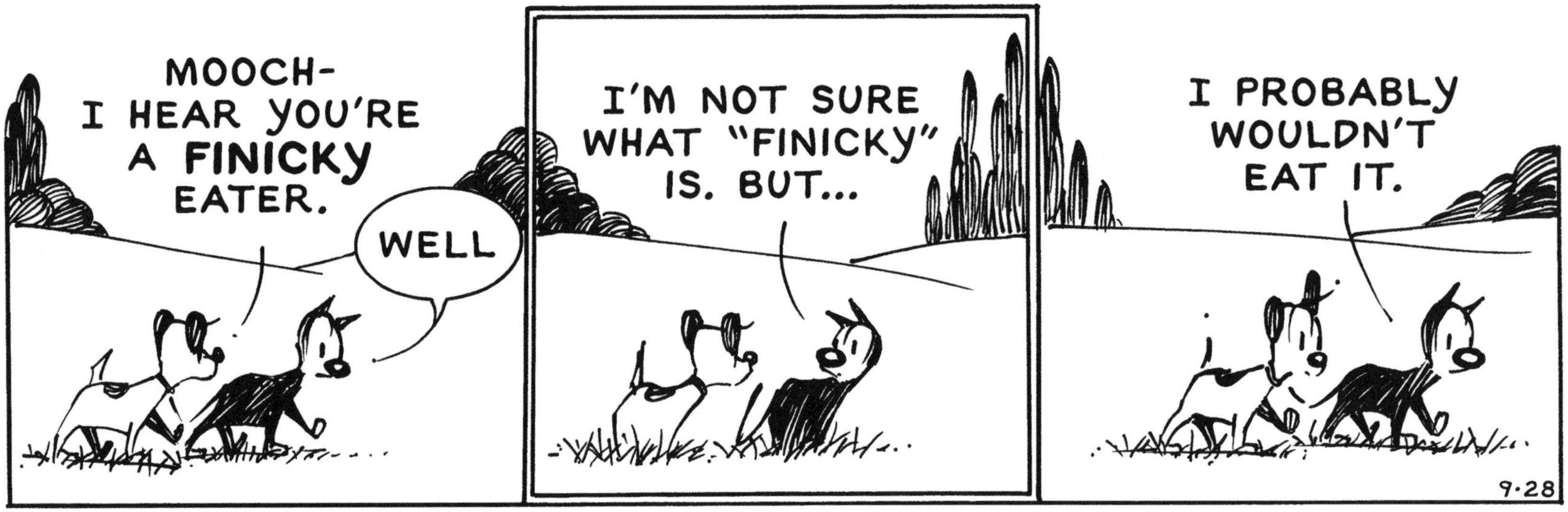
MOOCH- I HEAR YOU'RE A FINICKY EATER.
WELL
I'M NOT SURE WHAT "FINICKY" IS. BUT...
I PROBABLY WOULDN'T EAT IT.
9·28

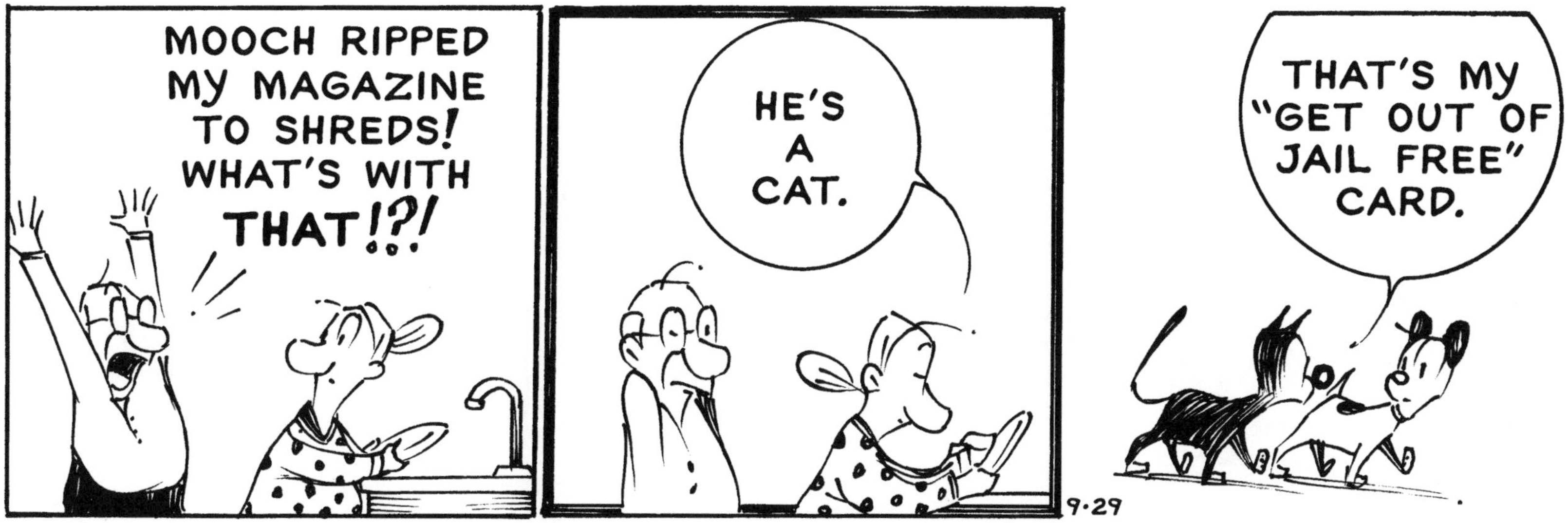
MOOCH RIPPED MY MAGAZINE TO SHREDS! WHAT'S WITH THAT!?!
HE'S A CAT.
THAT'S MY "GET OUT OF JAIL FREE" CARD.
9·29

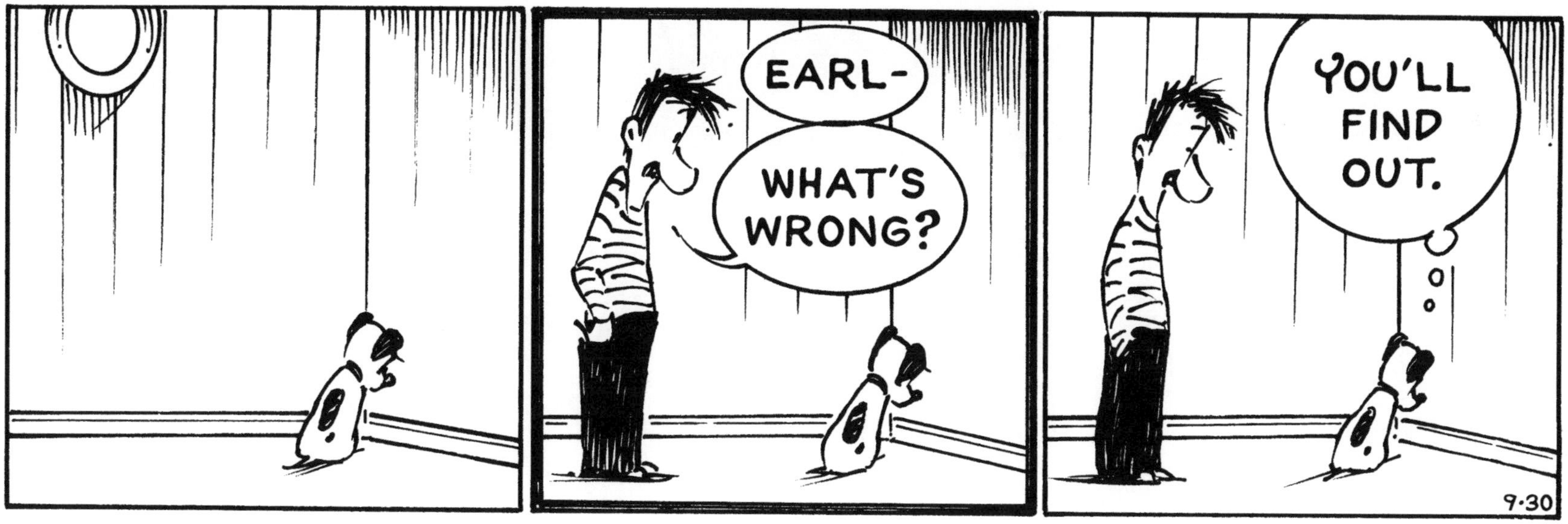
EARL-
WHAT'S WRONG?
YOU'LL FIND OUT.
9·30

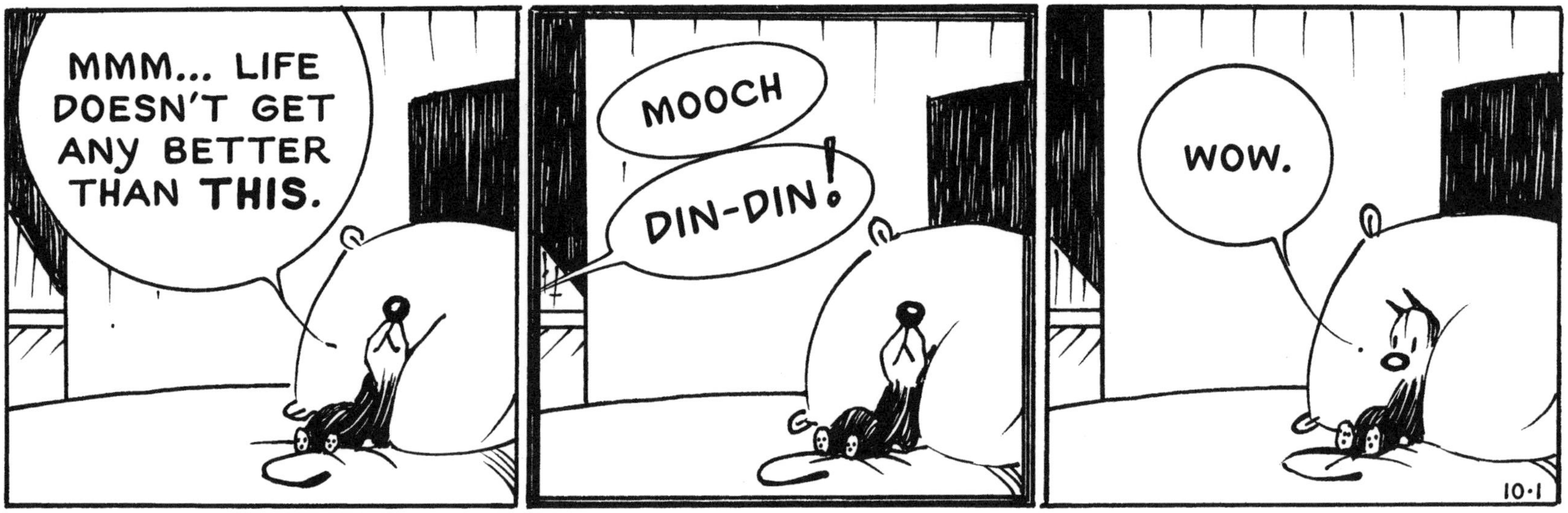
MMM... LIFE DOESN'T GET ANY BETTER THAN THIS.
MOOCH
DIN-DIN!
WOW.
10·1

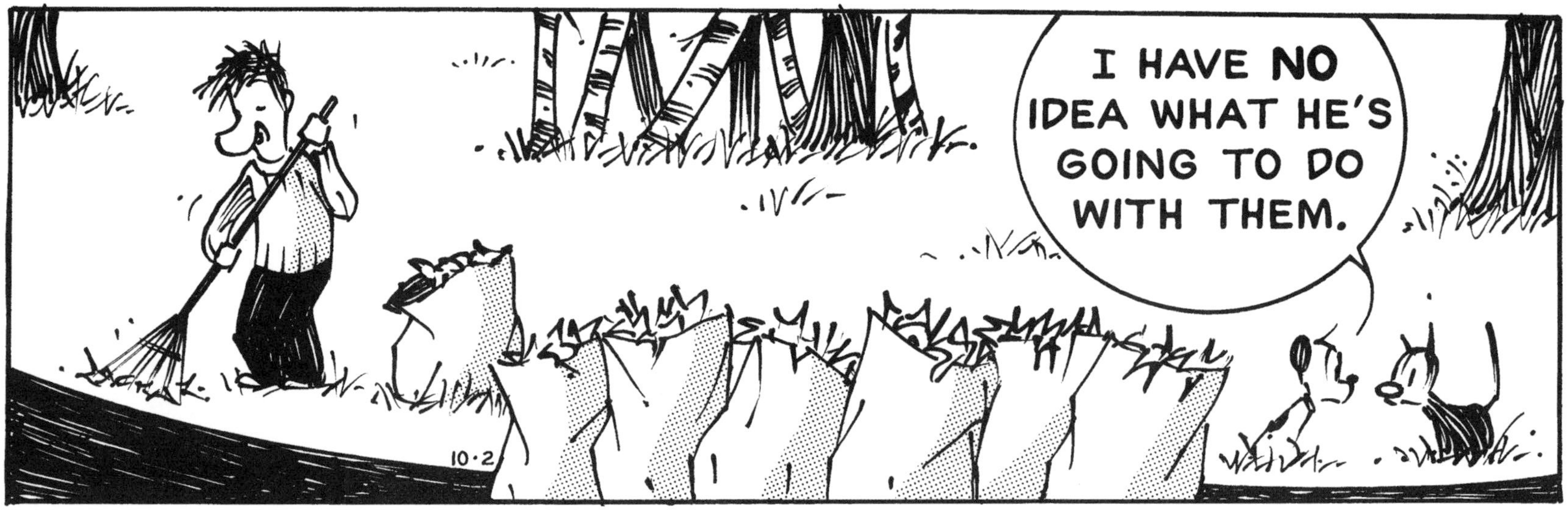
I HAVE NO IDEA WHAT HE'S GOING TO DO WITH THEM.
10·2

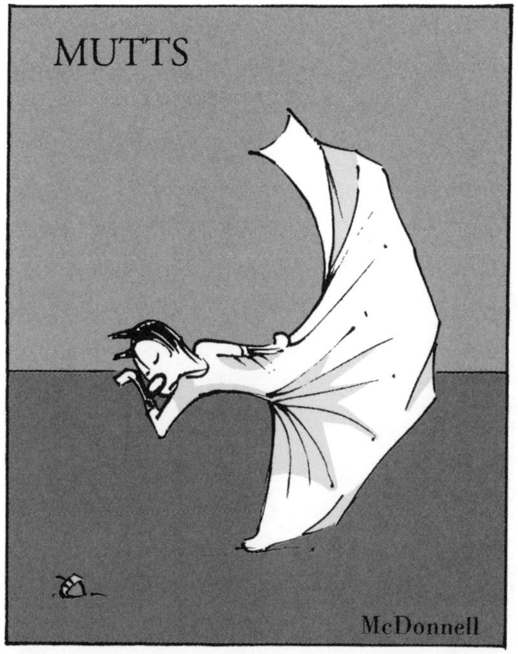
MUTTS
McDonnell

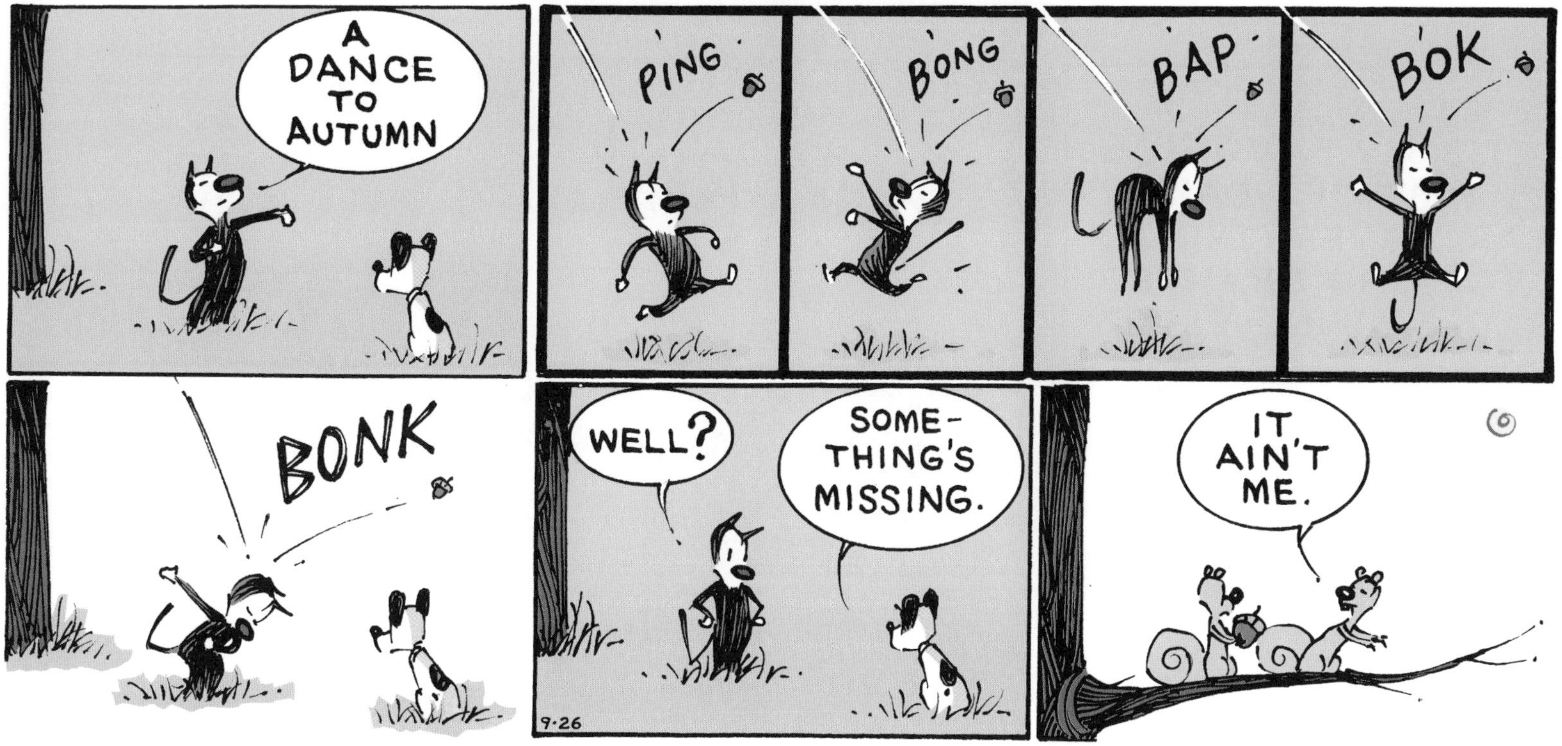
A DANCE TO AUTUMN
PING
BONG
BAP
BOK
BONK
WELL?
SOME-THING'S MISSING.
9·26
IT AIN'T ME.
©

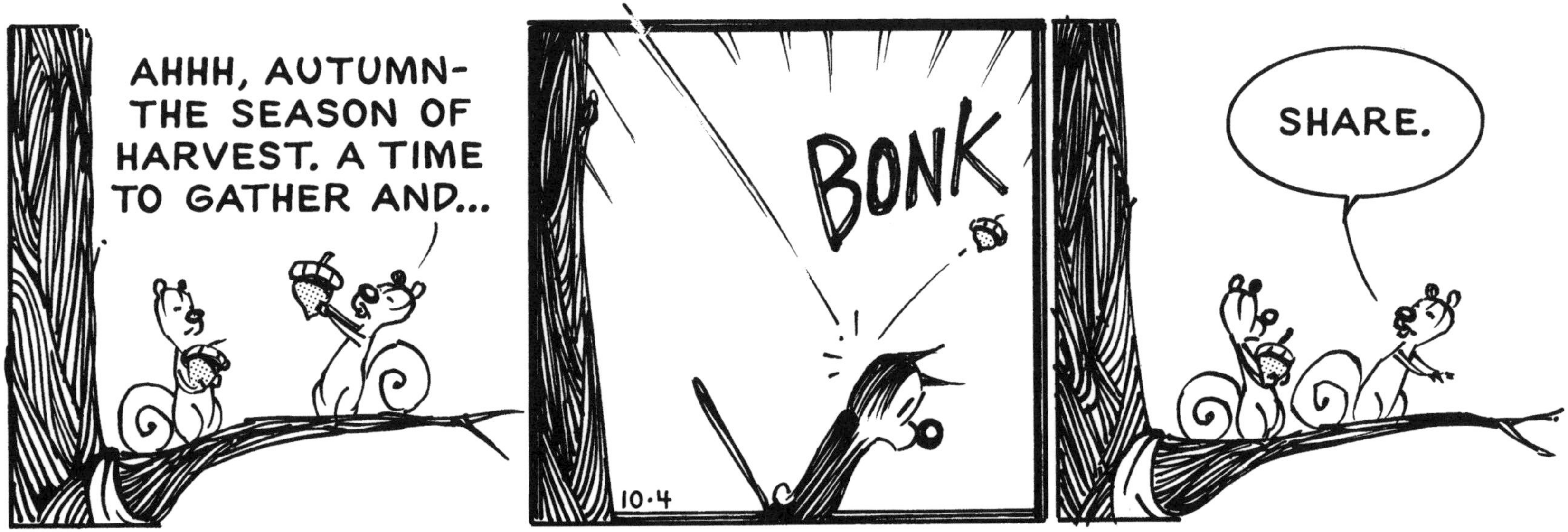
AHHH, AUTUMN- THE SEASON OF HARVEST. A TIME TO GATHER AND...
BONK
10·4
SHARE.

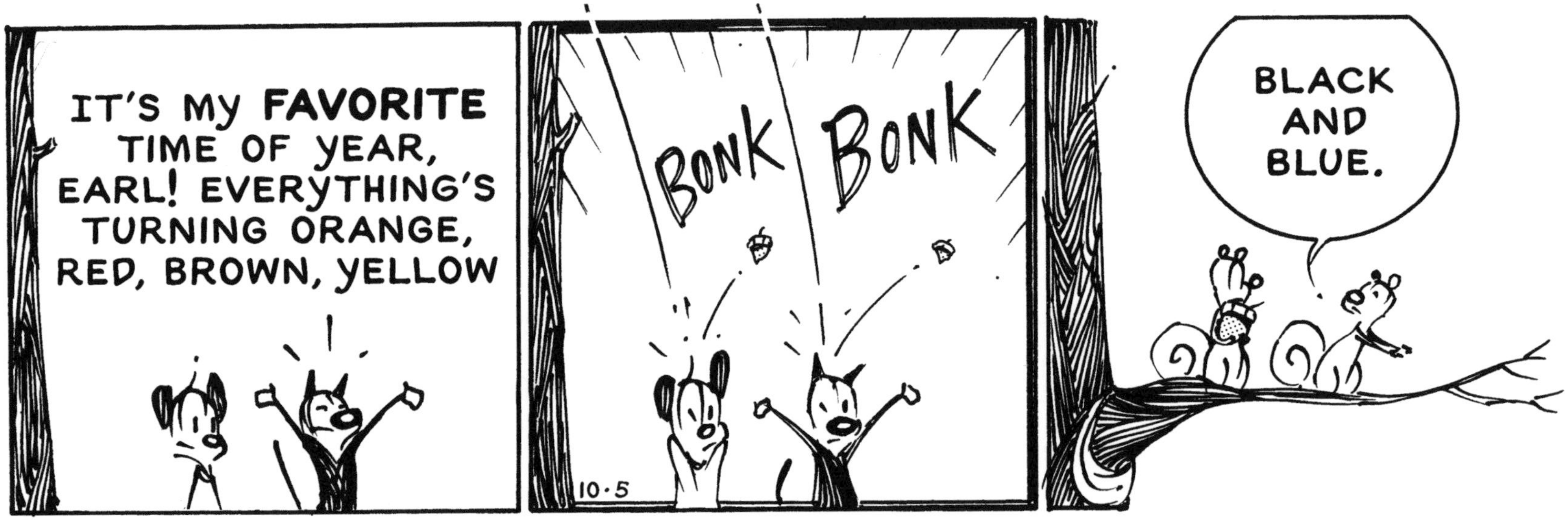
IT'S MY **FAVORITE** TIME OF YEAR, EARL! EVERYTHING'S TURNING ORANGE, RED, BROWN, YELLOW
BONK
BONK
10·5
BLACK AND BLUE.

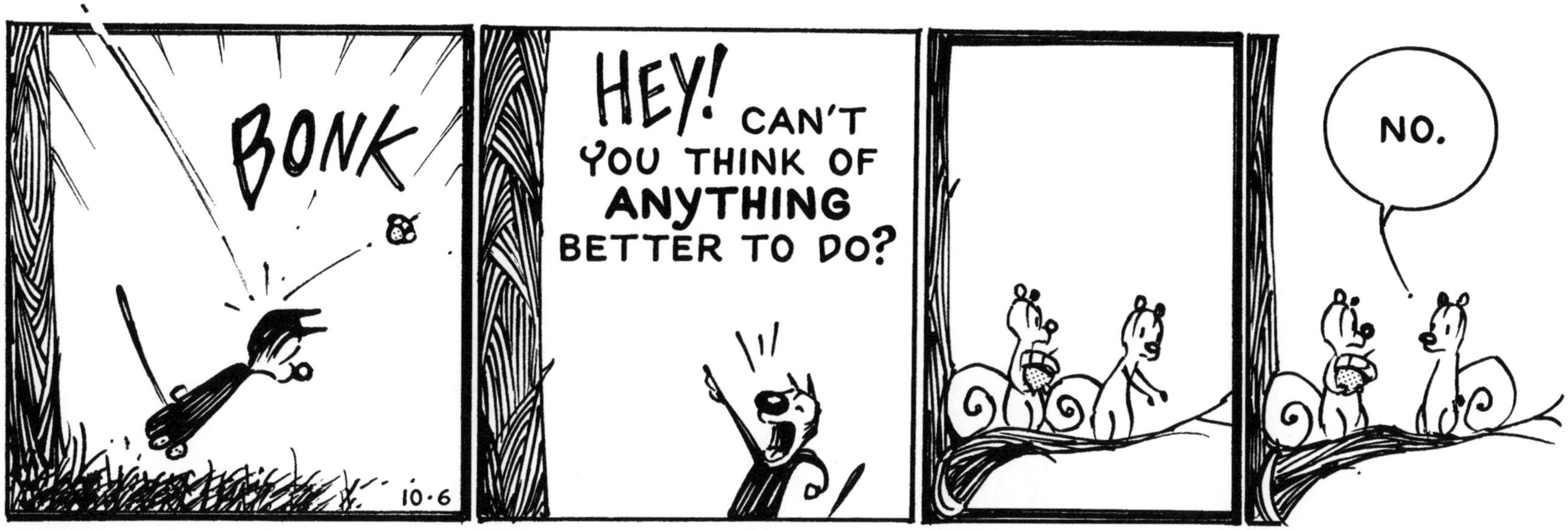
BONK
10·6
HEY! CAN'T YOU THINK OF ANYTHING BETTER TO DO?
NO.

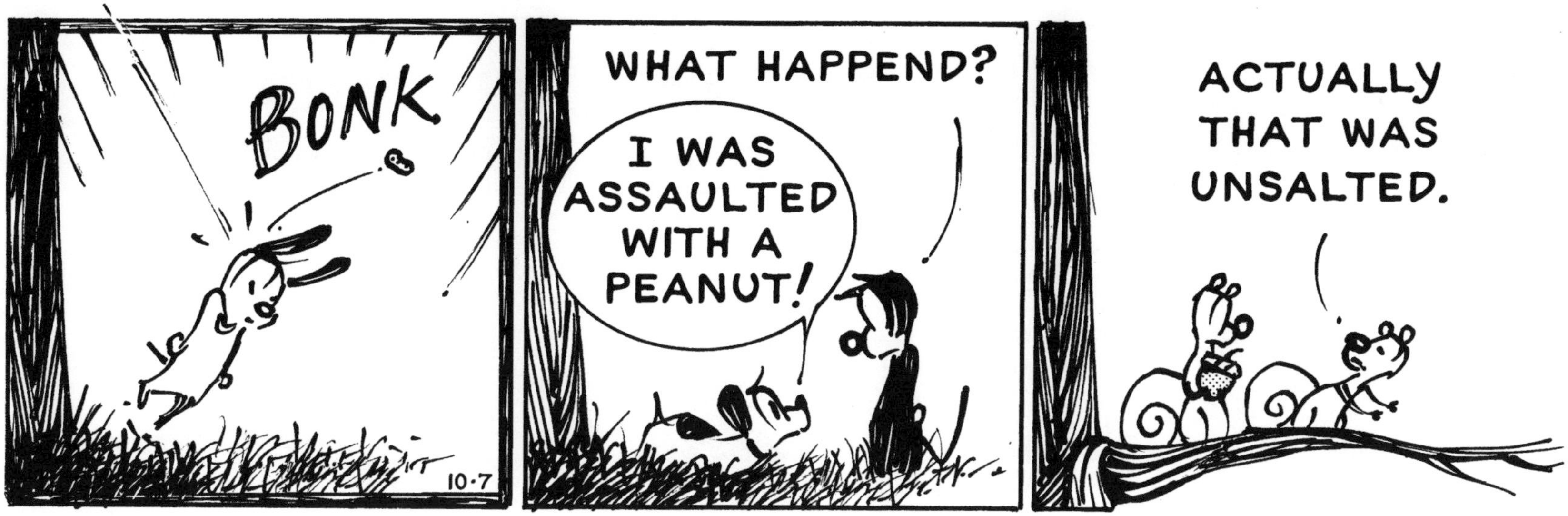
BONK
10·7
WHAT HAPPEND?
I WAS ASSAULTED WITH A PEANUT!
ACTUALLY THAT WAS UNSALTED.

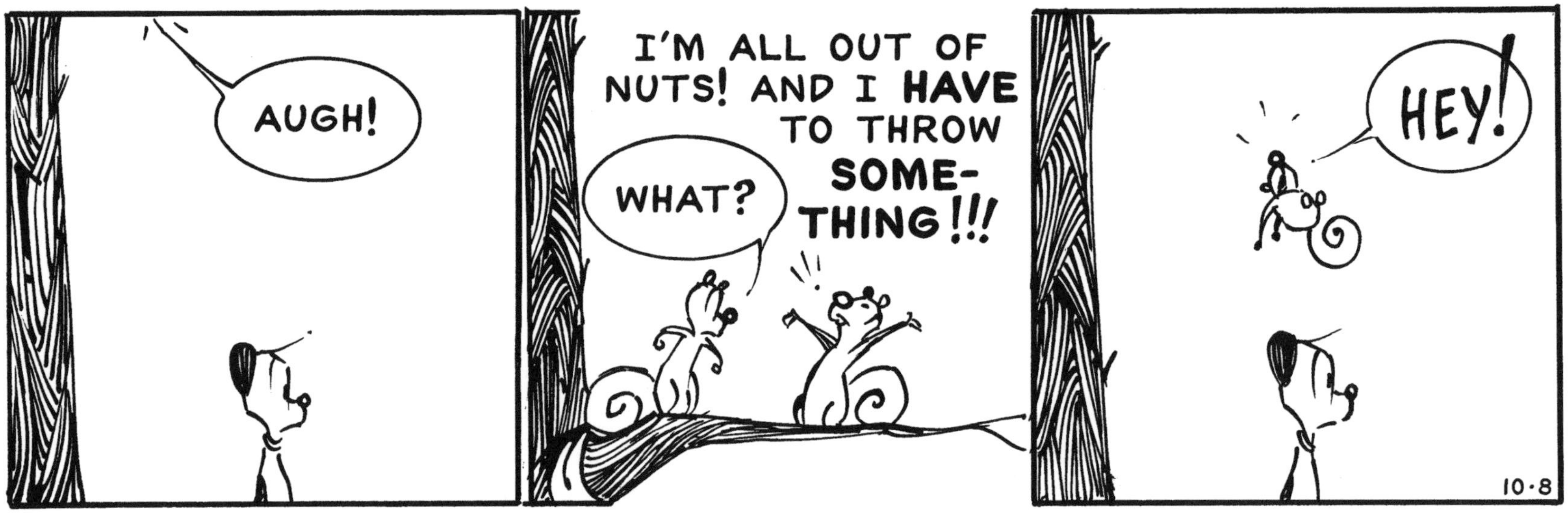
AUGH!
I'M ALL OUT OF NUTS! AND I HAVE TO THROW SOME-THING!!!
WHAT?
HEY!
10·8

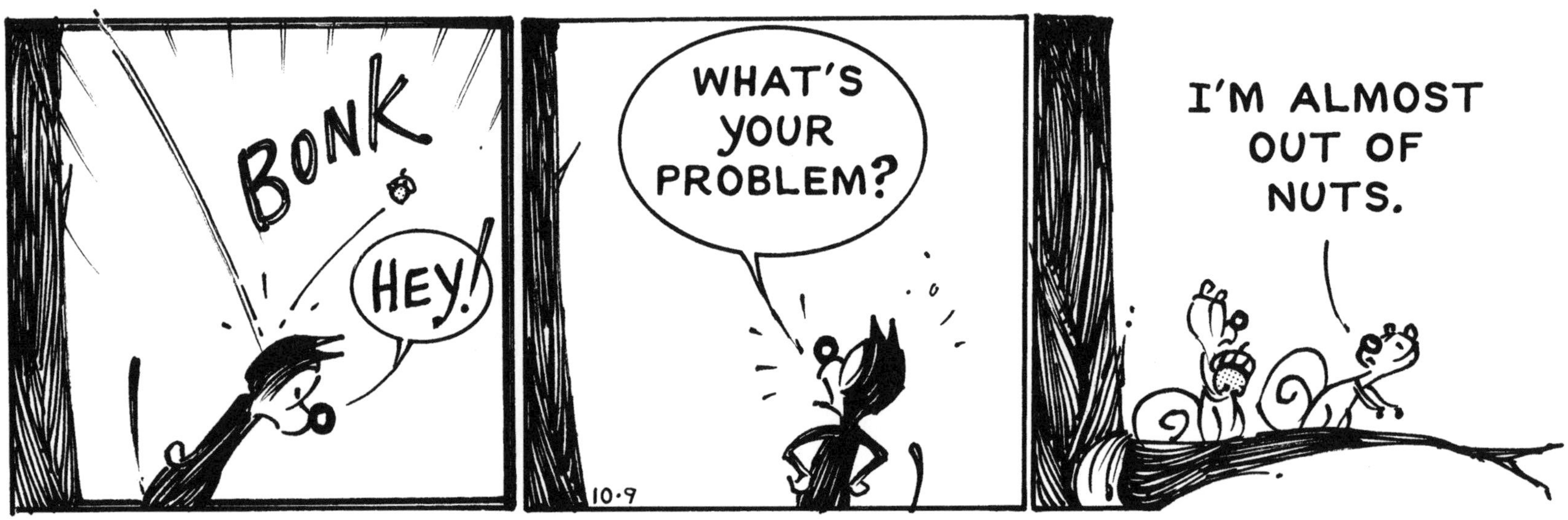
BONK
HEY!
WHAT'S YOUR PROBLEM?
10·9
I'M ALMOST OUT OF NUTS.

MUTTS

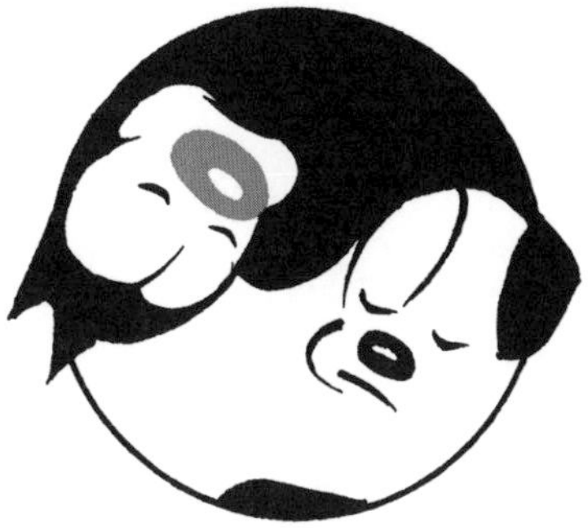

PATRICK M^c^ DONNELL

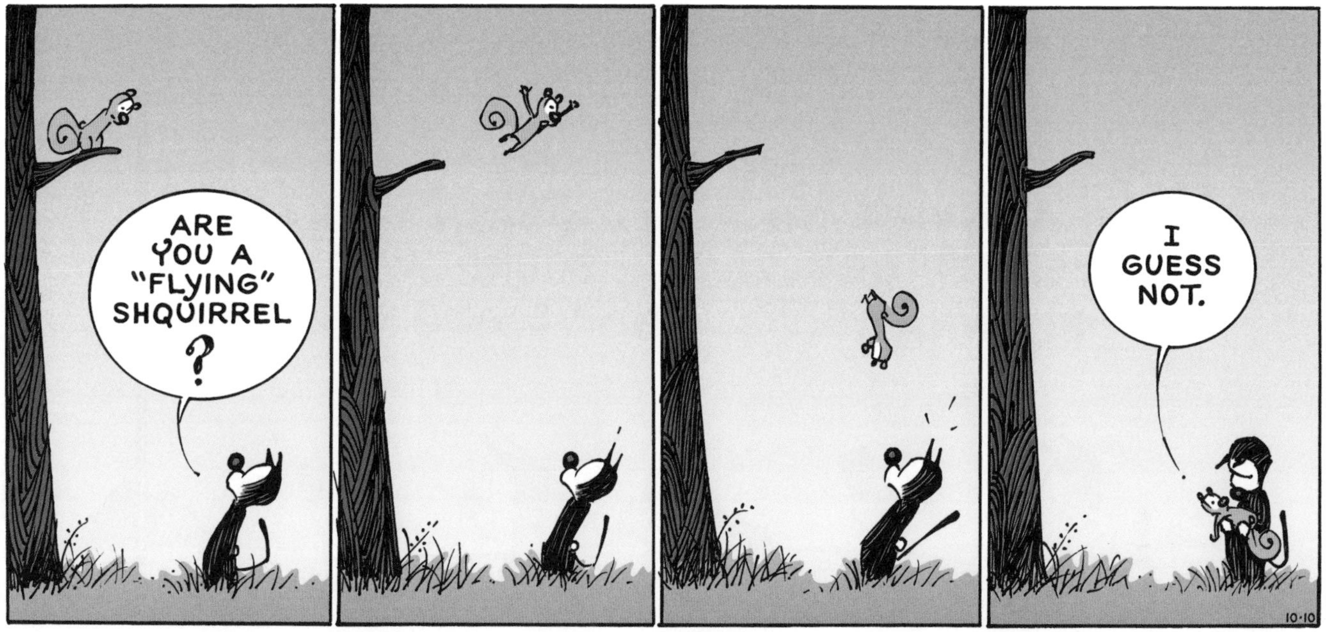
ARE YOU A "FLYING" SHQUIRREL ?
I GUESS NOT.
10·10

MUTTS

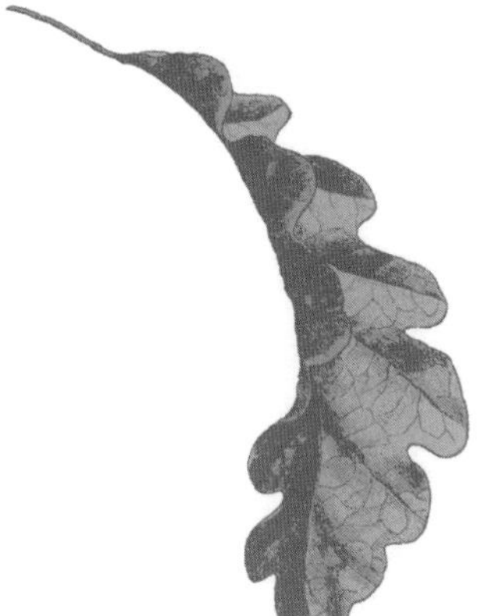

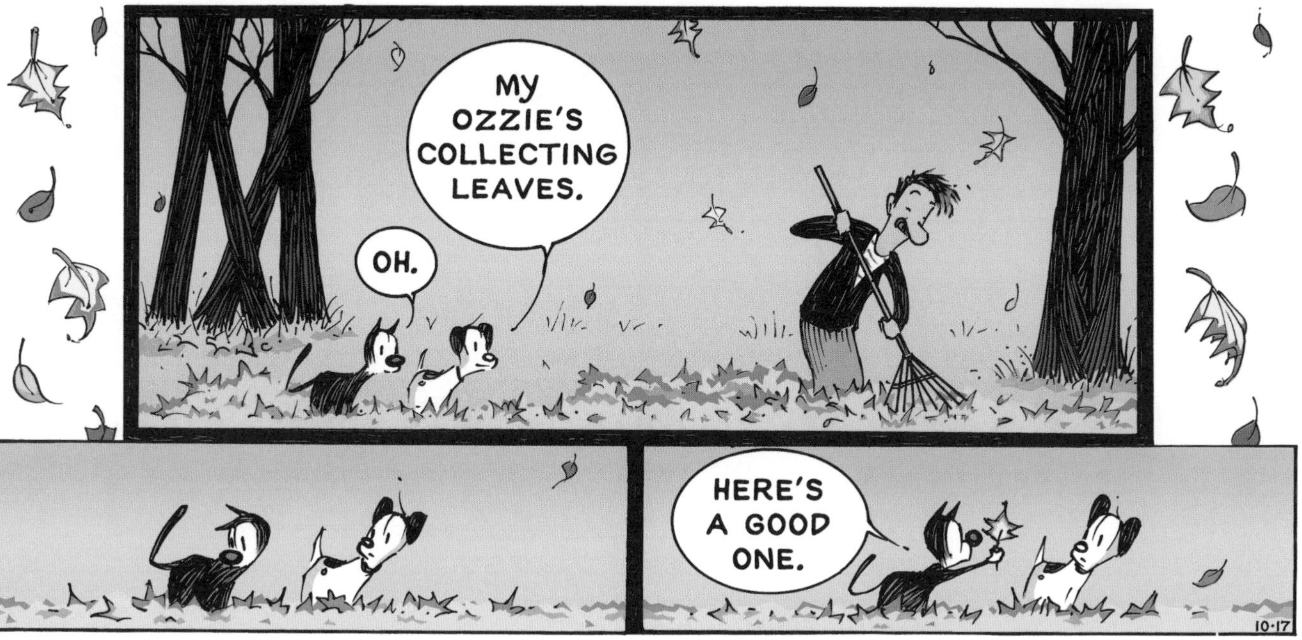
MY OZZIE'S COLLECTING LEAVES.
OH.
HERE'S A GOOD ONE.
10·17

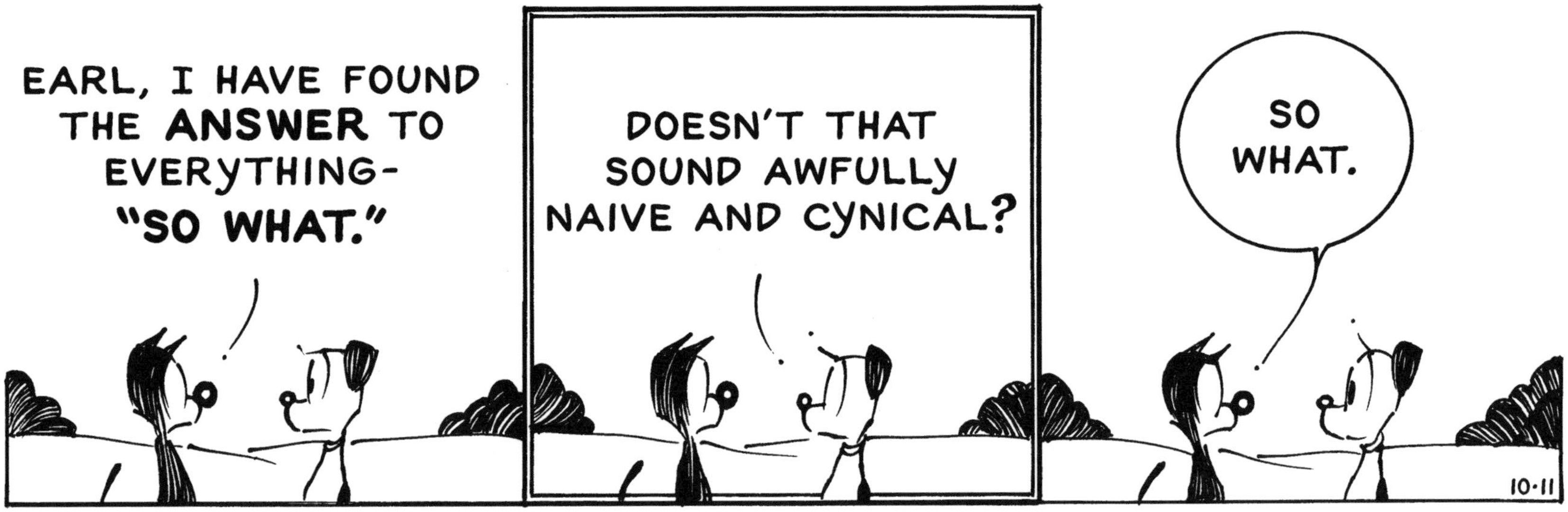
EARL, I HAVE FOUND THE ANSWER TO EVERYTHING- "SO WHAT."
DOESN'T THAT SOUND AWFULLY NAIVE AND CYNICAL?
SO WHAT.
10·11

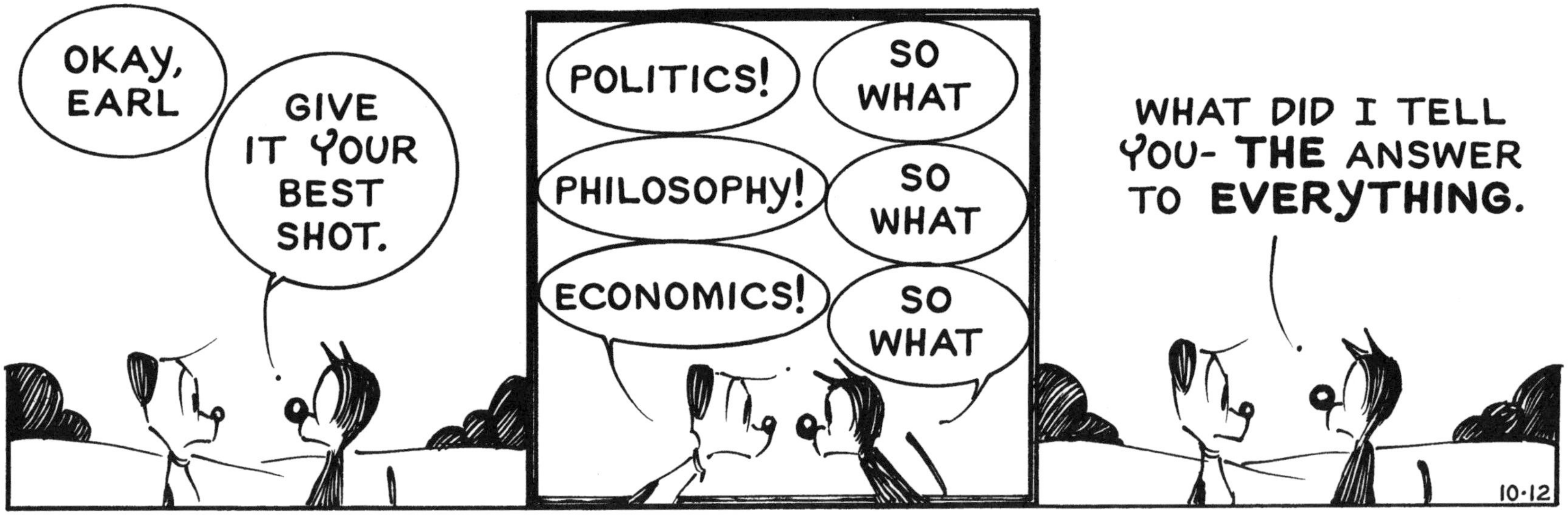
OKAY, EARL
GIVE IT YOUR BEST SHOT.
POLITICS!
SO WHAT
PHILOSOPHY!
SO WHAT
ECONOMICS!
SO WHAT
WHAT DID I TELL YOU- THE ANSWER TO EVERYTHING.
10·12

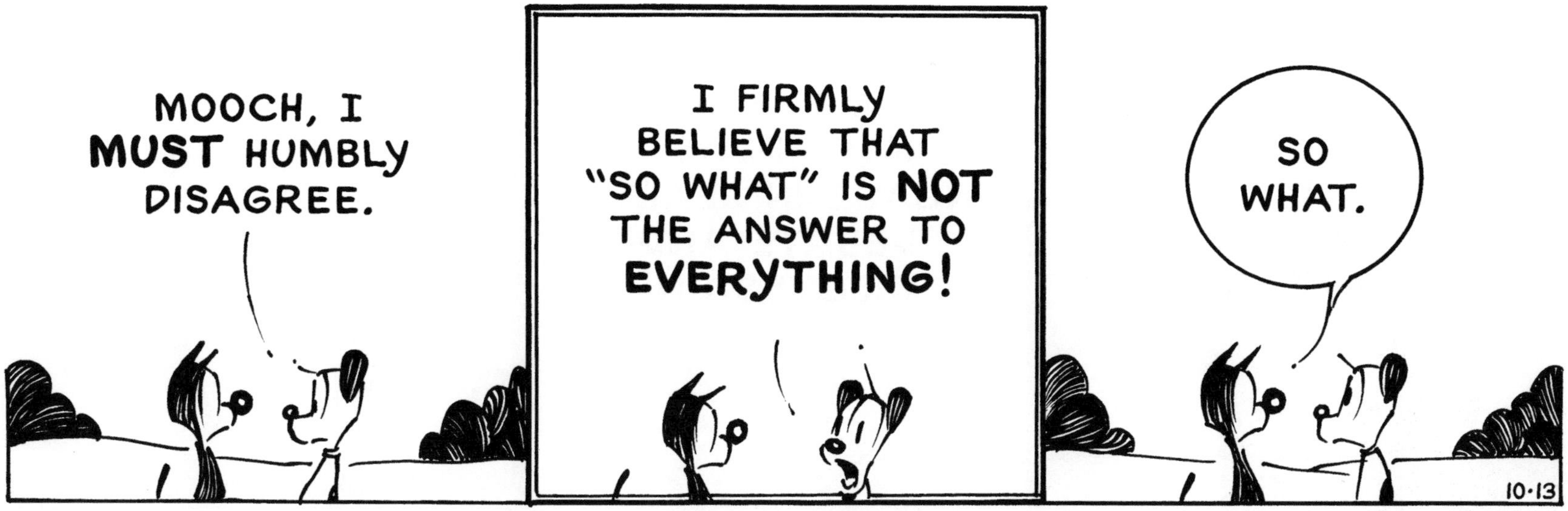
MOOCH, I MUST HUMBLY DISAGREE.
I FIRMLY BELIEVE THAT "SO WHAT" IS NOT THE ANSWER TO EVERYTHING!
SO WHAT.
10·13

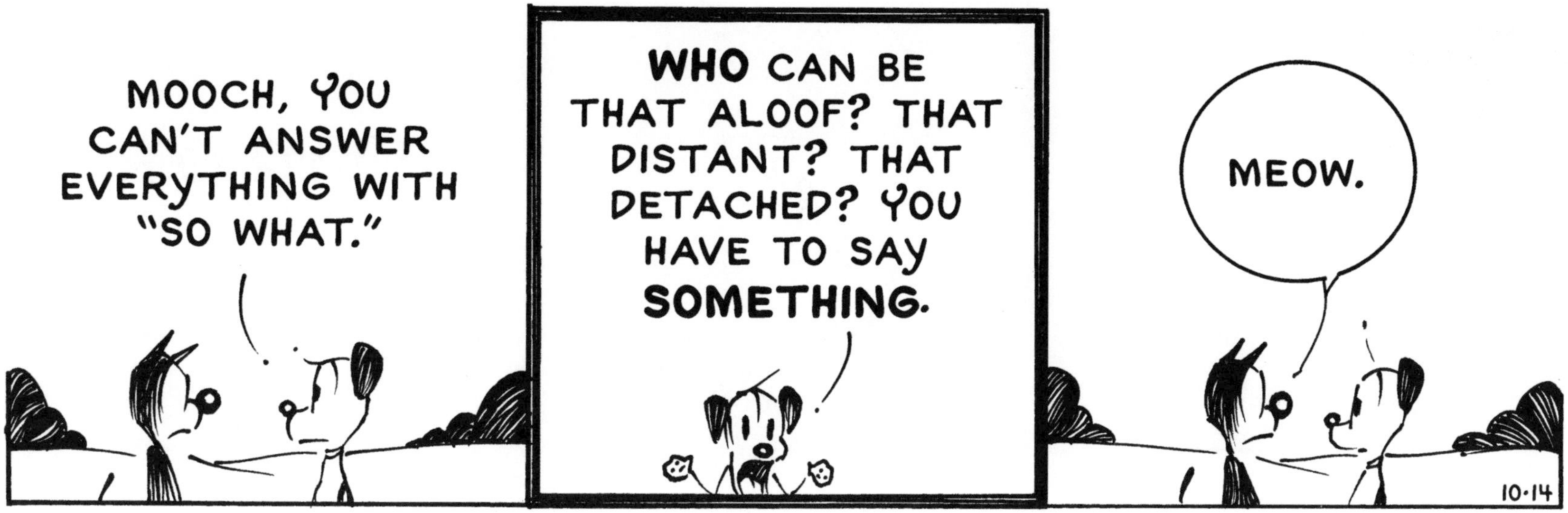
MOOCH, YOU CAN'T ANSWER EVERYTHING WITH "SO WHAT."
WHO CAN BE THAT ALOOF? THAT DISTANT? THAT DETACHED? YOU HAVE TO SAY SOMETHING.
MEOW.
10·14

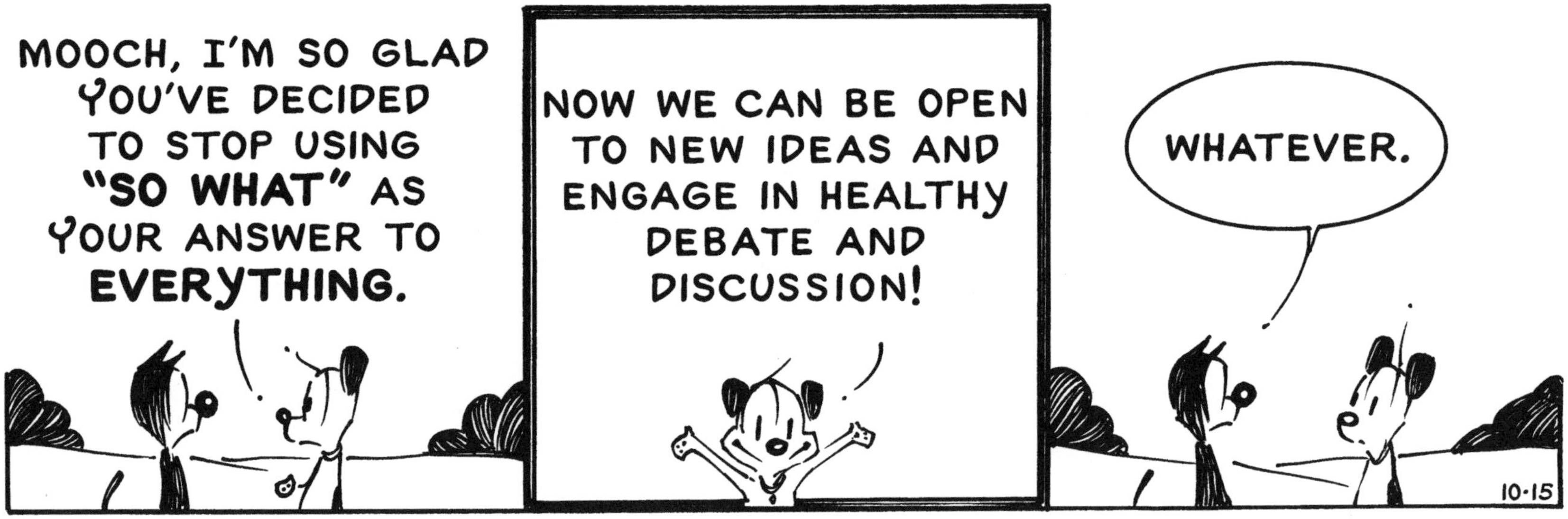
MOOCH, I'M SO GLAD YOU'VE DECIDED TO STOP USING **"SO WHAT"** AS YOUR ANSWER TO **EVERYTHING.**
NOW WE CAN BE OPEN TO NEW IDEAS AND ENGAGE IN HEALTHY DEBATE AND DISCUSSION!
WHATEVER.
10-15

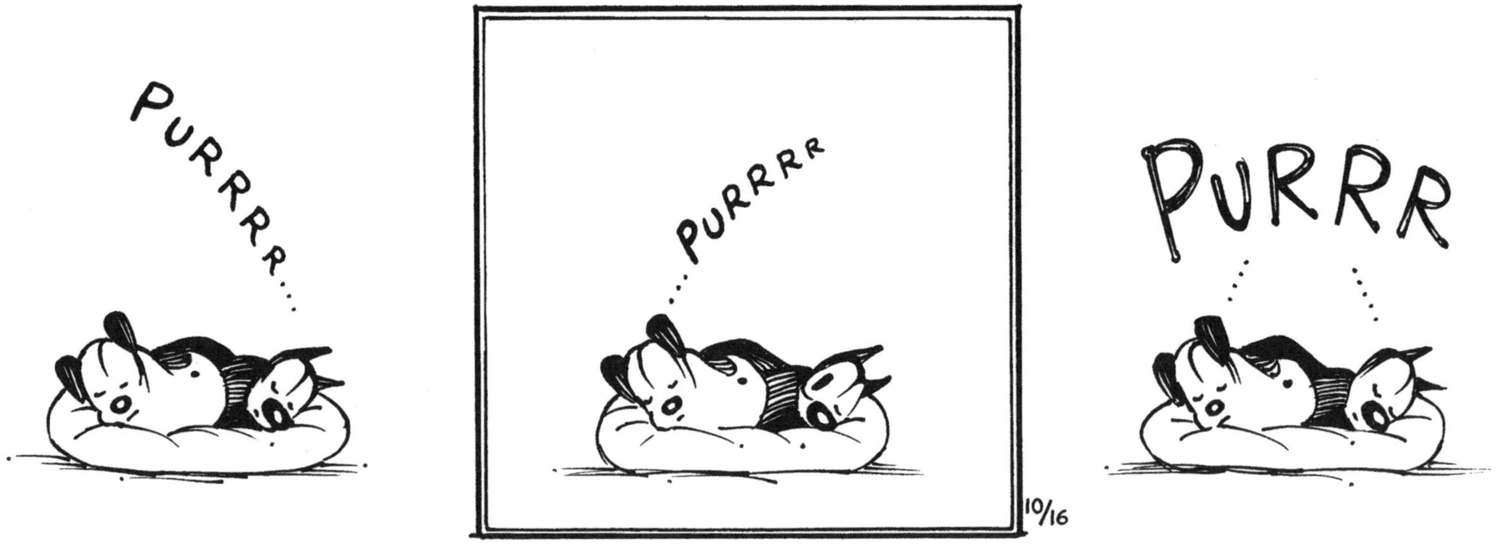
PURRRRR....
PURRRRR
PURRR
10/16

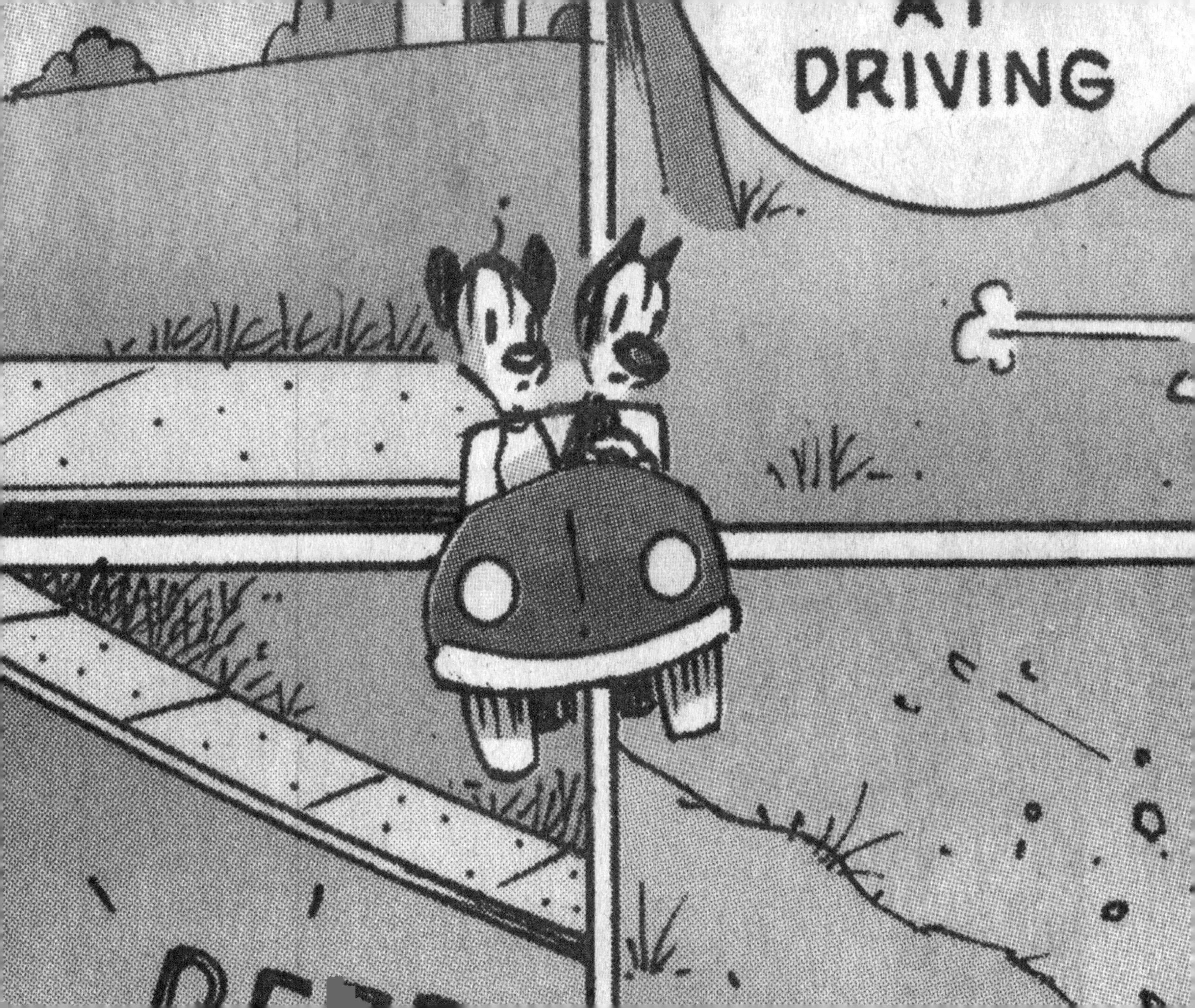
DRIVING

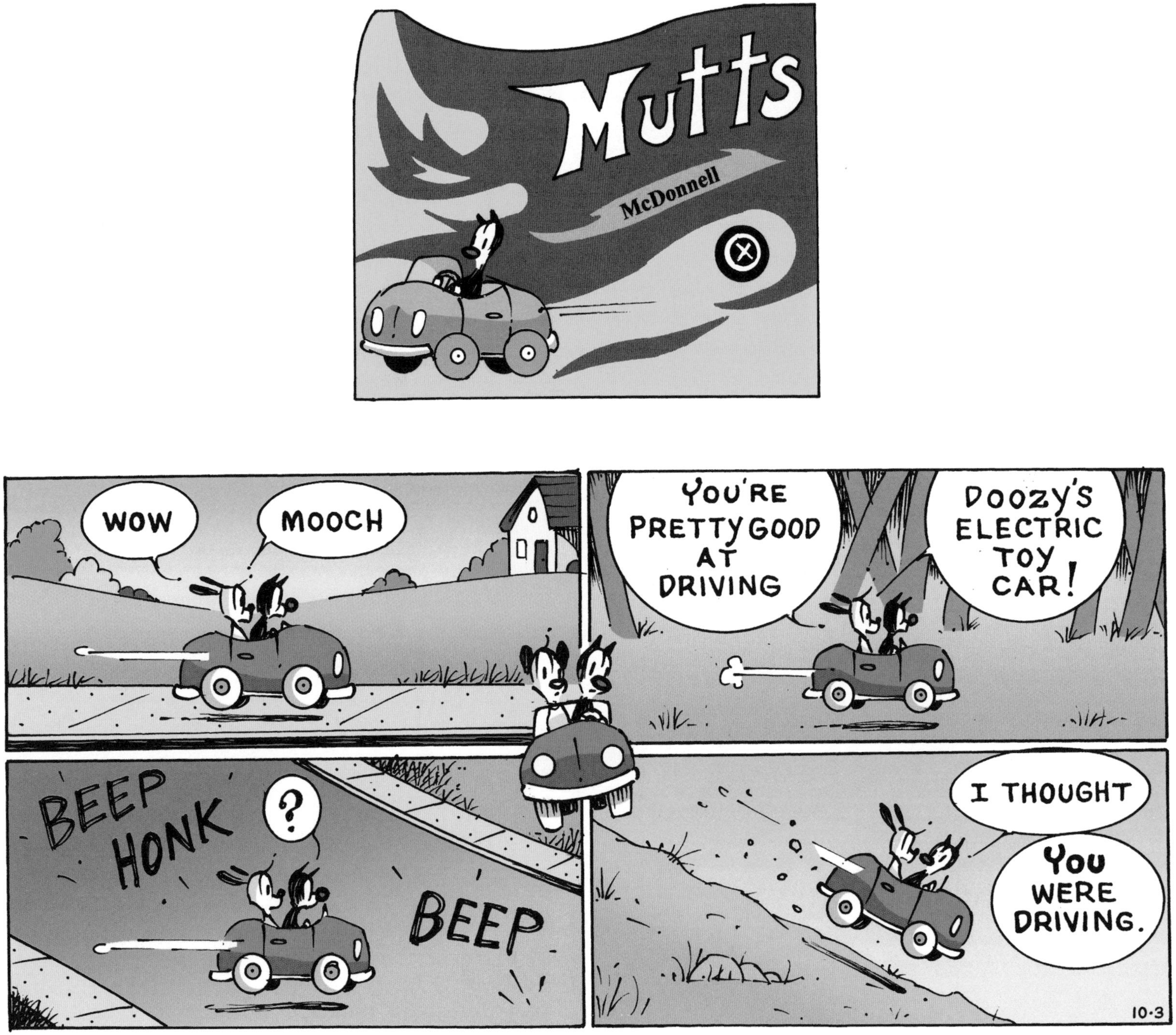
Mutts
McDonnell
WOW
MOOCH
YOU'RE PRETTY GOOD AT DRIVING
DOOZY'S ELECTRIC TOY CAR!
BEEP
HONK
?
BEEP
I THOUGHT
YOU WERE DRIVING.
10·3

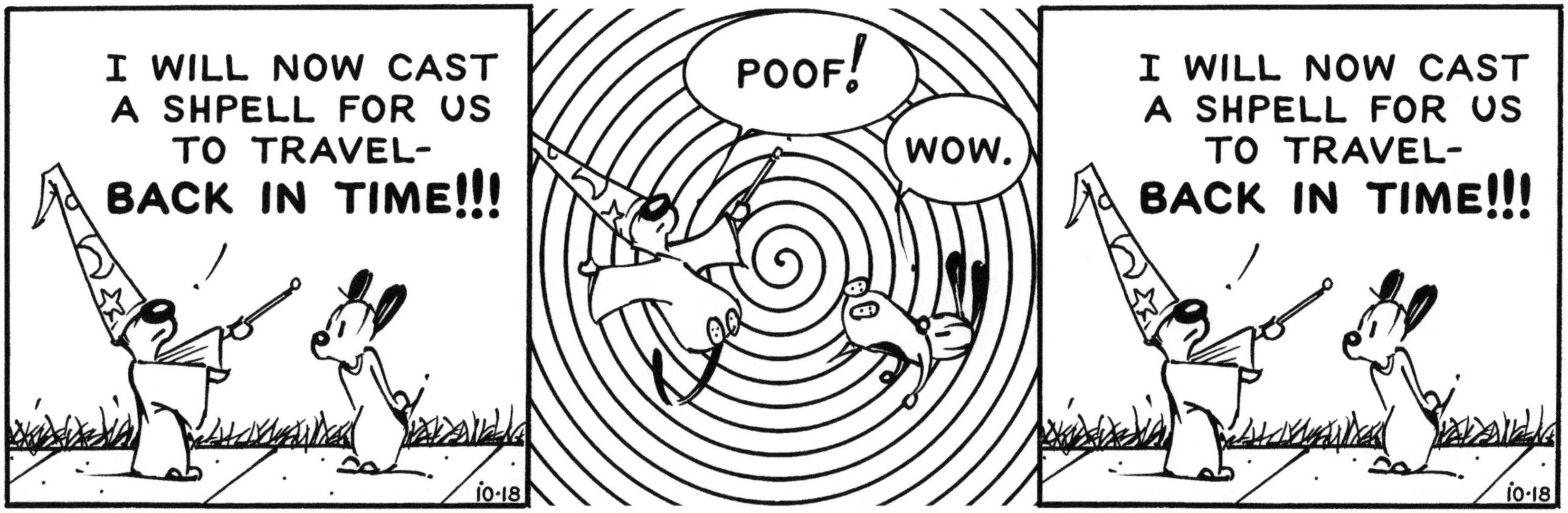
I WILL NOW CAST A SHPELL FOR US TO TRAVEL- BACK IN TIME!!!
10·18
POOF!
WOW.
I WILL NOW CAST A SHPELL FOR US TO TRAVEL- BACK IN TIME!!!
10·18

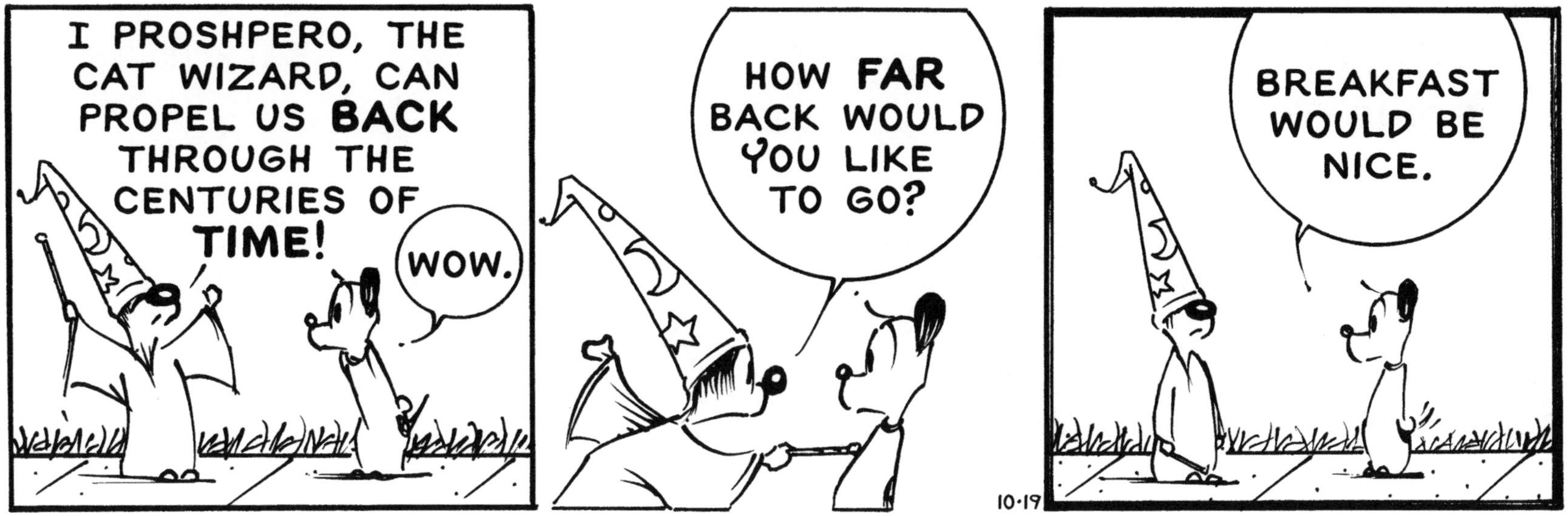
I PROSHPERO, THE CAT WIZARD, CAN PROPEL US BACK THROUGH THE CENTURIES OF TIME!
WOW.
HOW FAR BACK WOULD YOU LIKE TO GO?
10·19
BREAKFAST WOULD BE NICE.

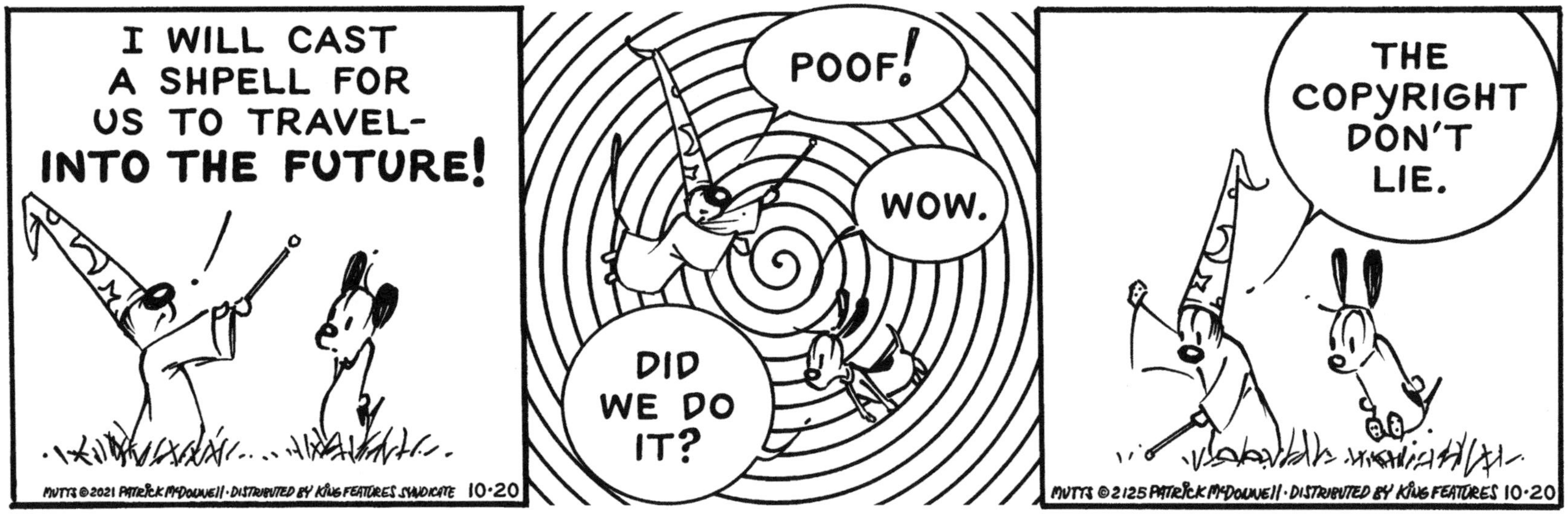
I WILL CAST A SHPELL FOR US TO TRAVEL- INTO THE FUTURE!
MUTTS ©2021 PATRICK McDONNELL · DISTRIBUTED BY KING FEATURES SYNDICATE 10·20
POOF!
WOW.
DID WE DO IT?
THE COPYRIGHT DON'T LIE.
MUTTS ©2125 PATRICK McDONNELL · DISTRIBUTED BY KING FEATURES 10·20

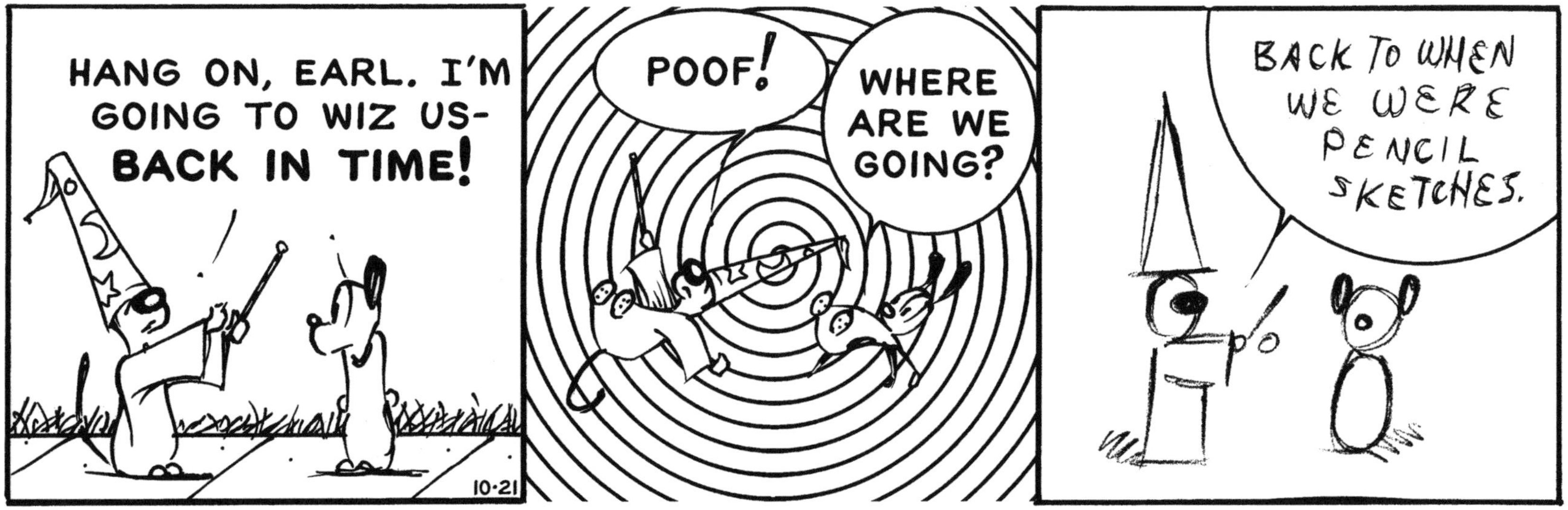
HANG ON, EARL. I'M GOING TO WIZ US- BACK IN TIME!
10·21
POOF!
WHERE ARE WE GOING?
BACK TO WHEN WE WERE PENCIL SKETCHES.

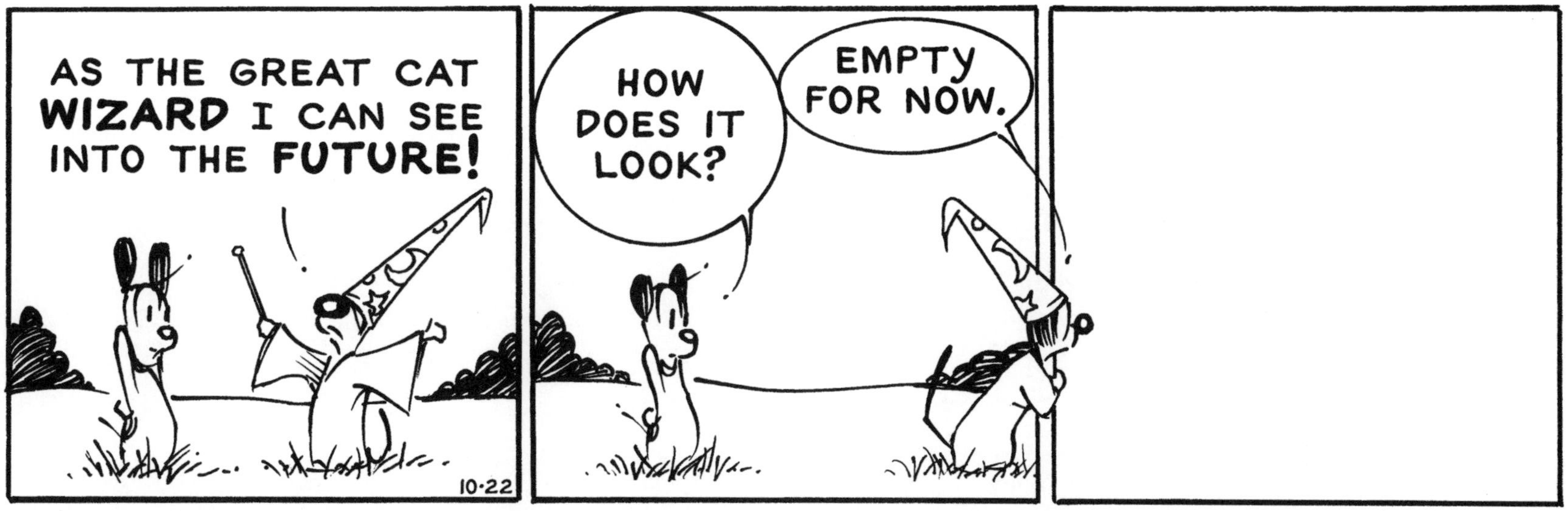
AS THE GREAT CAT **WIZARD** I CAN SEE INTO THE **FUTURE!**
HOW DOES IT LOOK?
EMPTY FOR NOW.
10-22

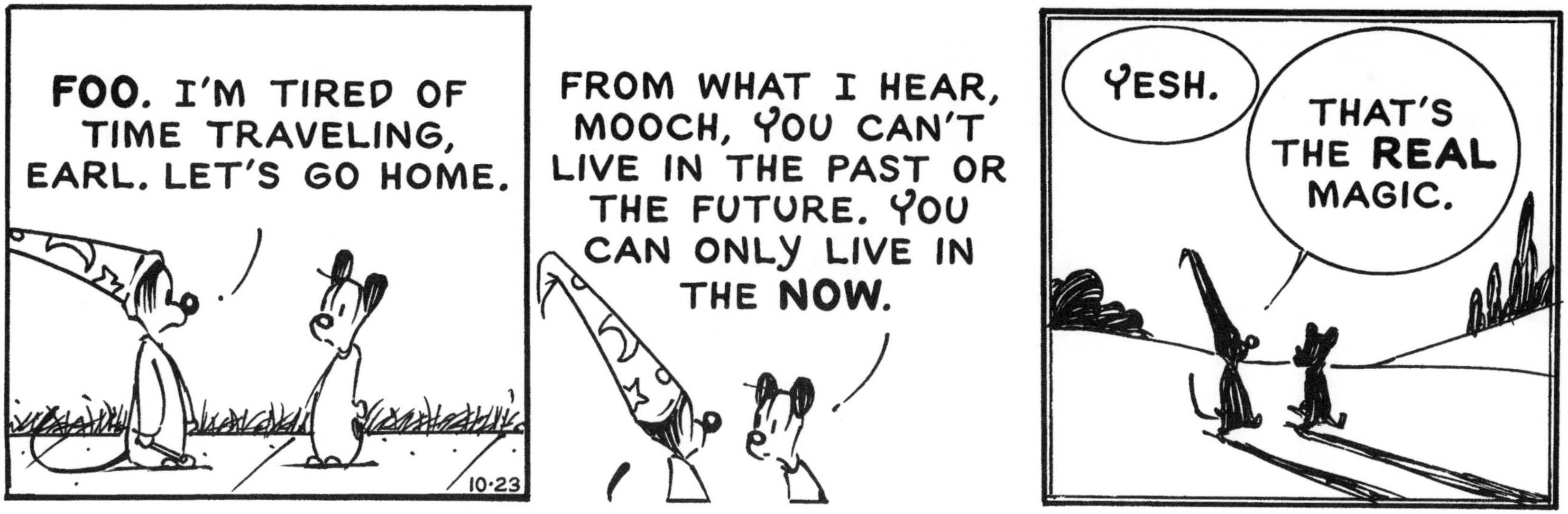
FOO. I'M TIRED OF TIME TRAVELING, EARL. LET'S GO HOME.
10-23
FROM WHAT I HEAR, MOOCH, YOU CAN'T LIVE IN THE PAST OR THE FUTURE. YOU CAN ONLY LIVE IN THE **NOW.**
YESH.
THAT'S THE **REAL** MAGIC.

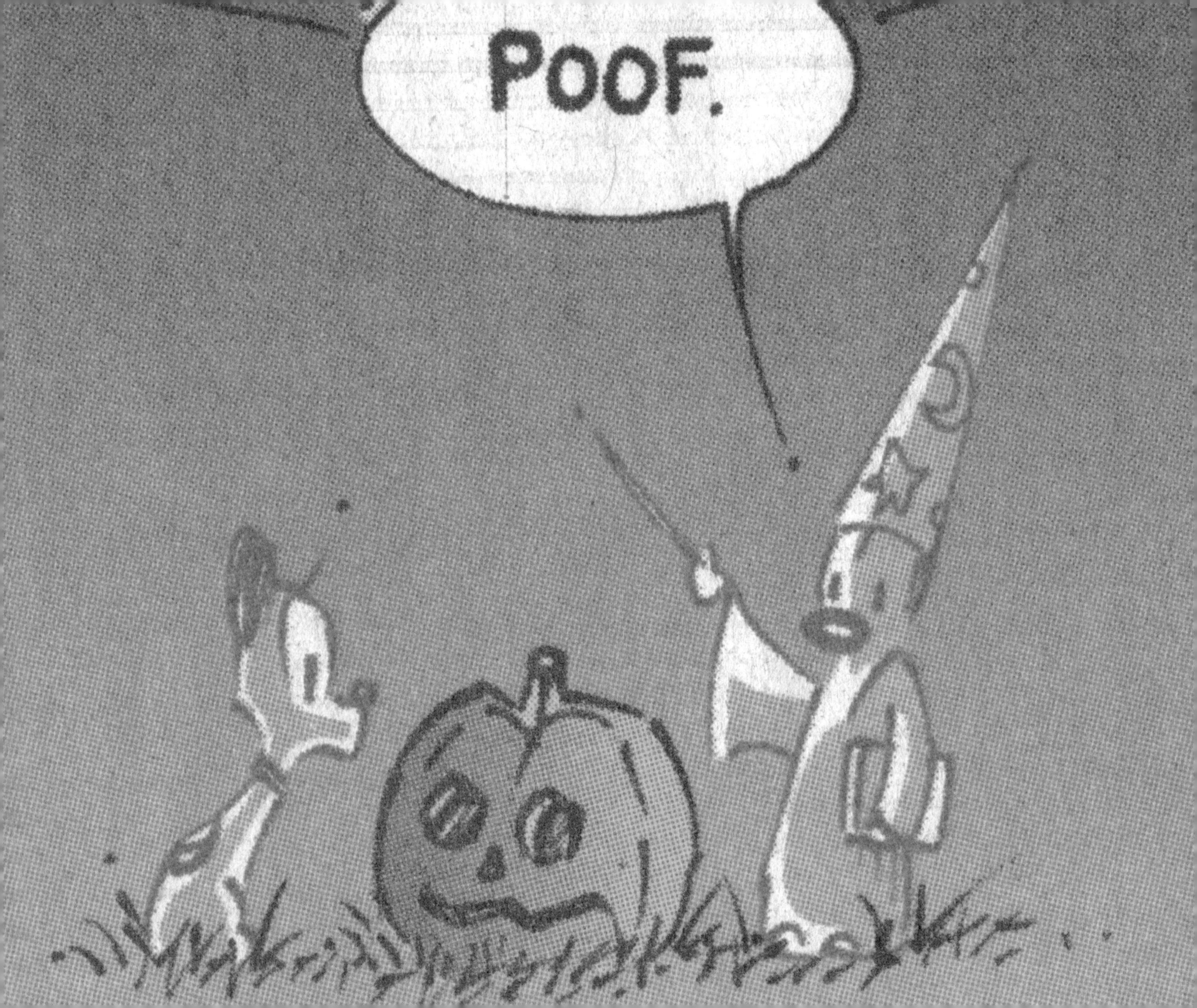
POOF.

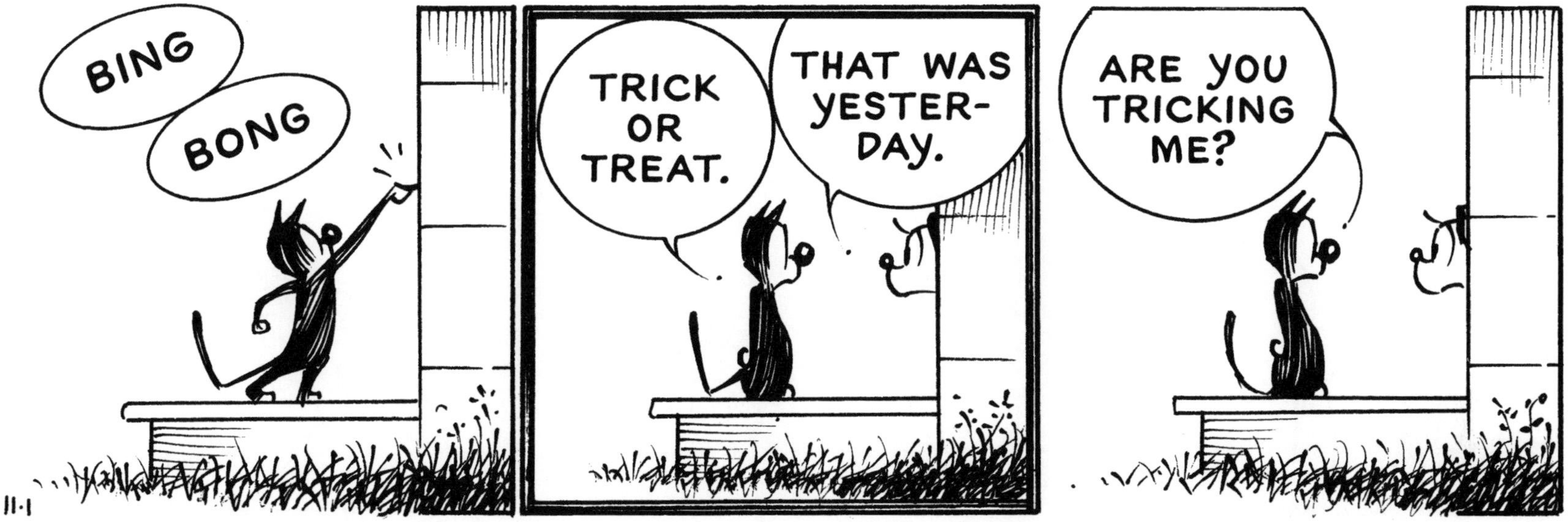
BING
BONG
TRICK OR TREAT.
THAT WAS YESTER-DAY.
ARE YOU TRICKING ME?

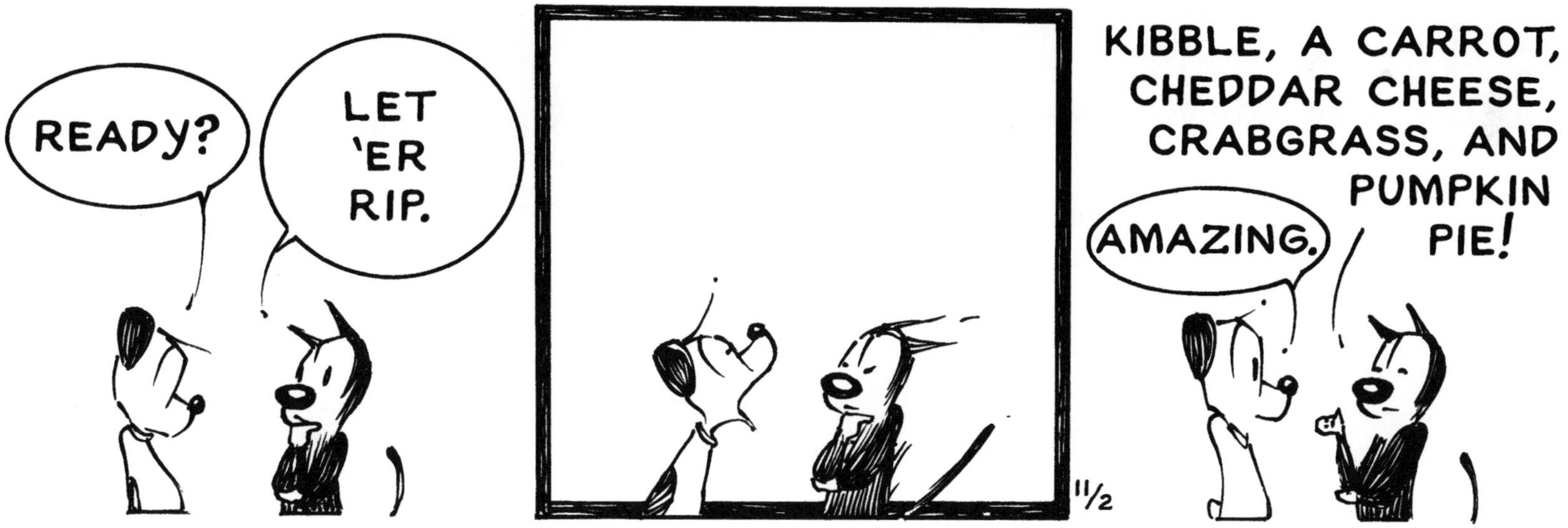
READY?
LET 'ER RIP.
KIBBLE, A CARROT, CHEDDAR CHEESE, CRABGRASS, AND PUMPKIN PIE!
AMAZING.

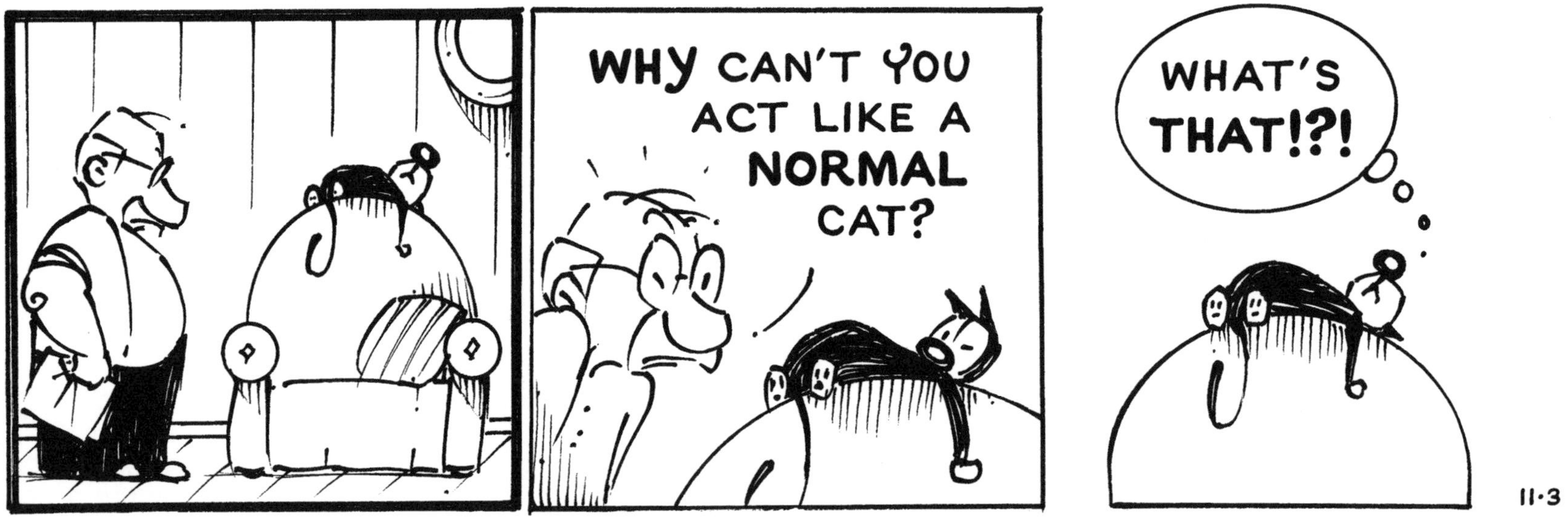
WHY CAN'T YOU ACT LIKE A NORMAL CAT?
WHAT'S THAT!?!
11·3

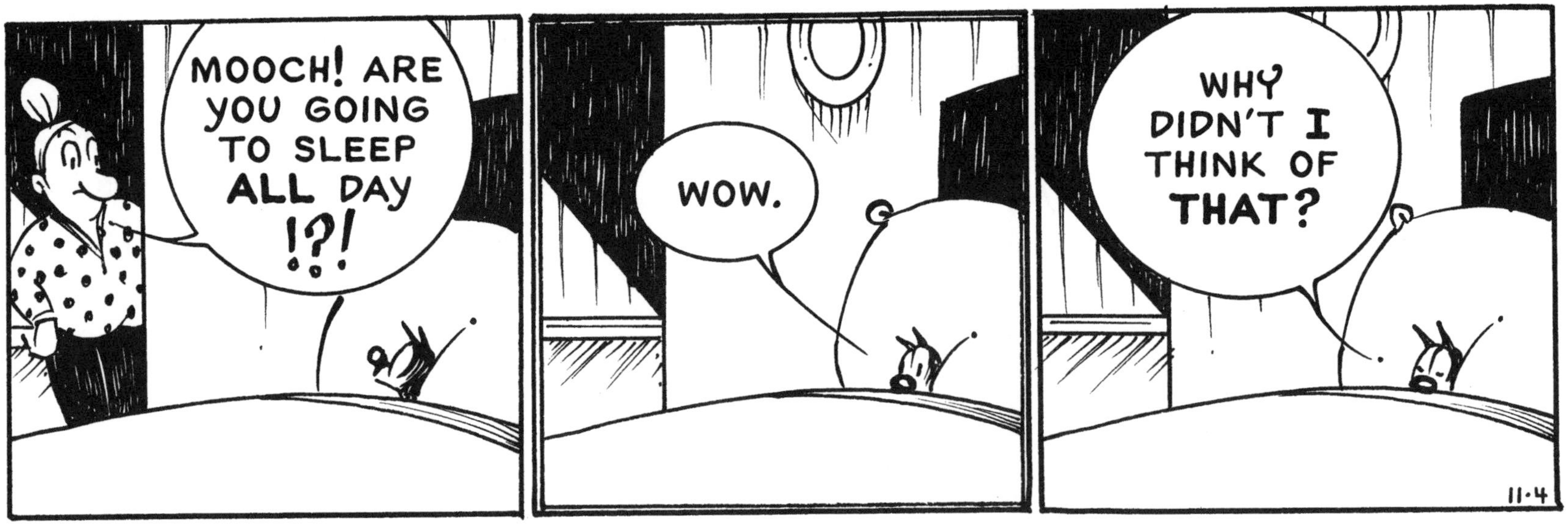
MOOCH! ARE YOU GOING TO SLEEP ALL DAY !?!
WOW.
WHY DIDN'T I THINK OF THAT?
11·4

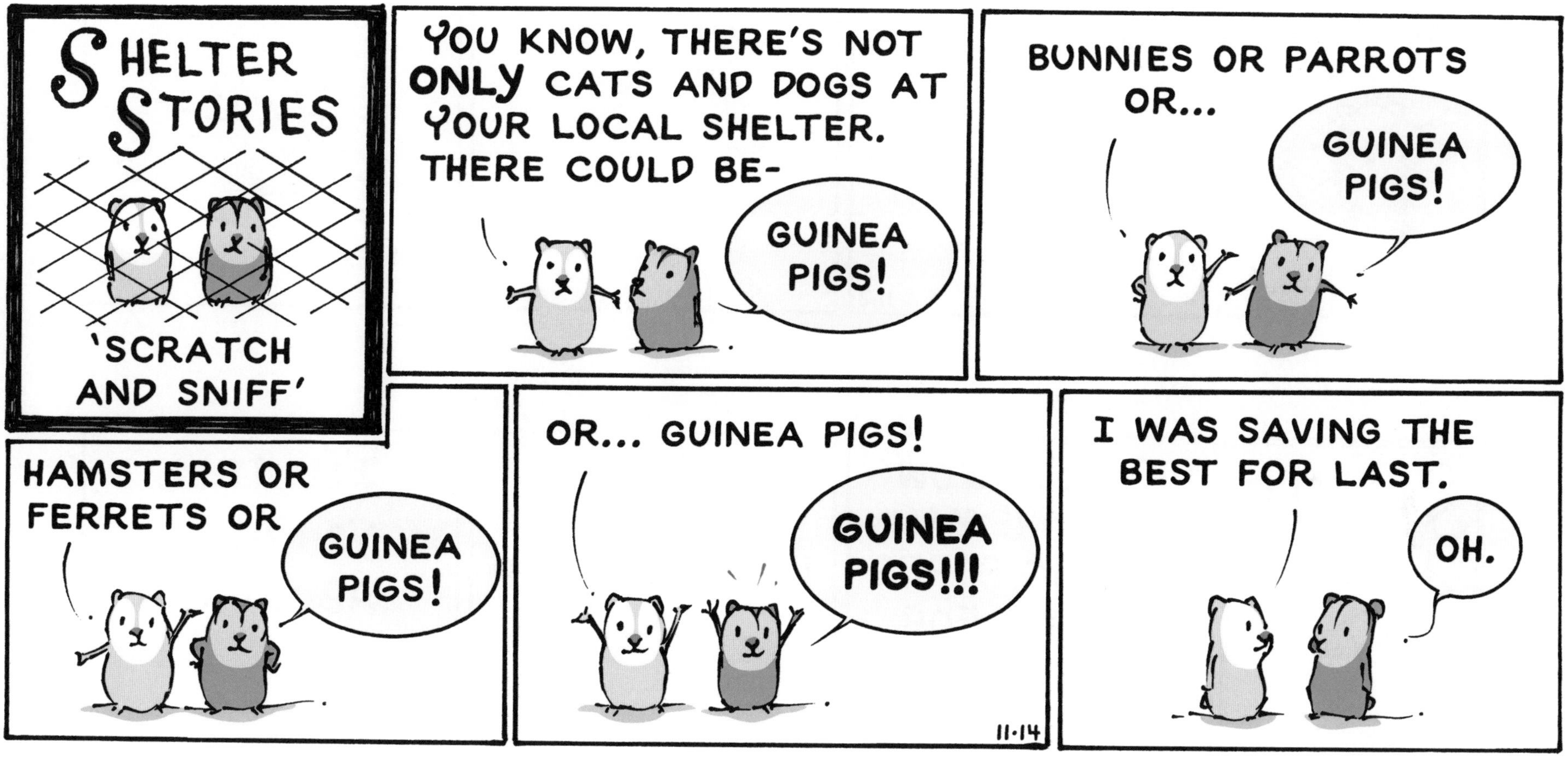
SHELTER STORIES
'SCRATCH AND SNIFF'
YOU KNOW, THERE'S NOT ONLY CATS AND DOGS AT YOUR LOCAL SHELTER. THERE COULD BE-
GUINEA PIGS!
BUNNIES OR PARROTS OR...
GUINEA PIGS!
HAMSTERS OR FERRETS OR
GUINEA PIGS!
OR... GUINEA PIGS!
GUINEA PIGS!!!
11·14
I WAS SAVING THE BEST FOR LAST.
OH.

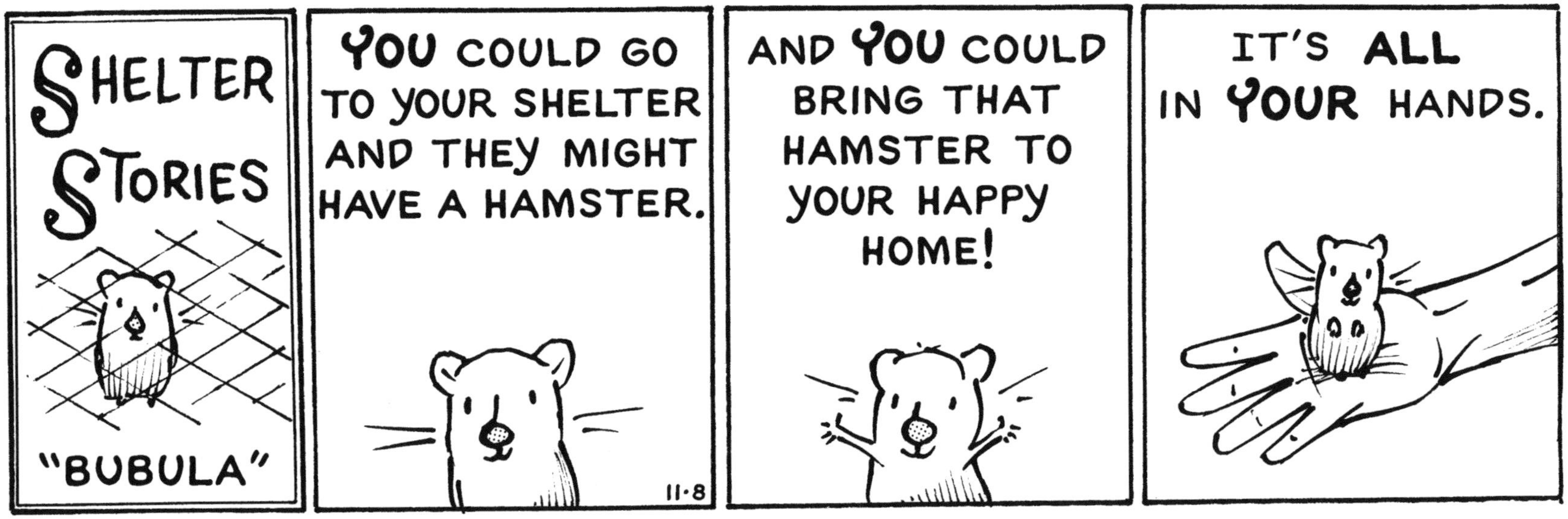
SHELTER STORIES
"BUBULA"
YOU COULD GO TO YOUR SHELTER AND THEY MIGHT HAVE A HAMSTER.
11·8
AND YOU COULD BRING THAT HAMSTER TO YOUR HAPPY HOME!
IT'S ALL IN YOUR HANDS.

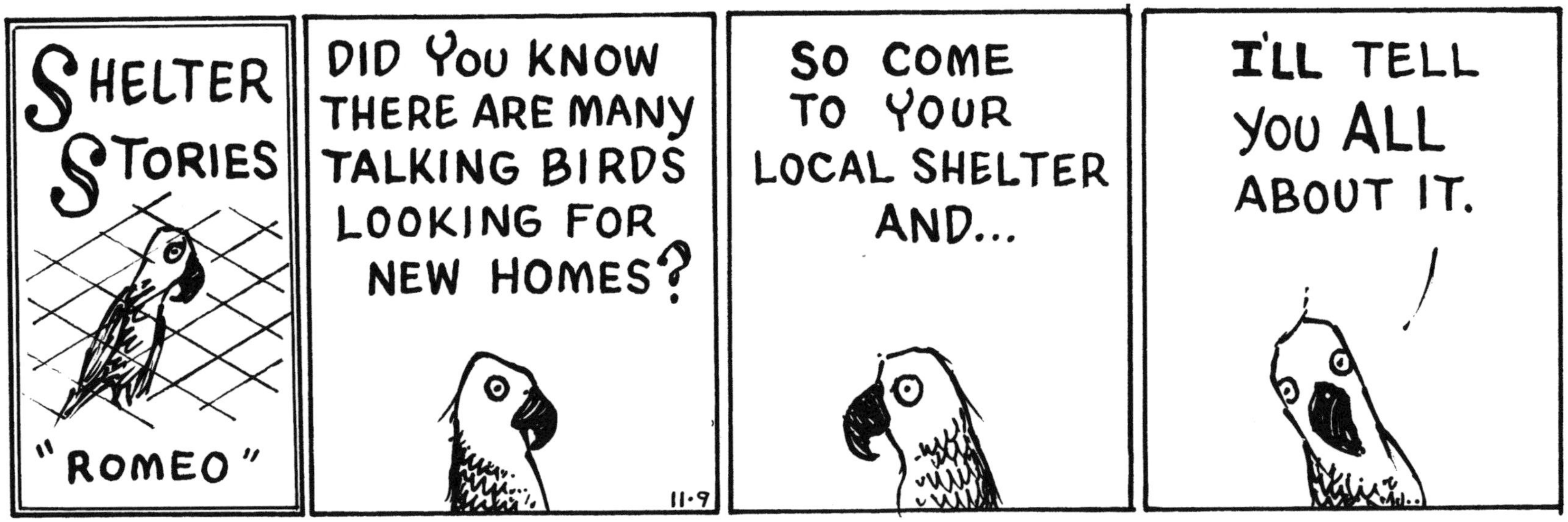
SHELTER STORIES
"ROMEO"
DID YOU KNOW THERE ARE MANY TALKING BIRDS LOOKING FOR NEW HOMES?
11·9
SO COME TO YOUR LOCAL SHELTER AND...
I'LL TELL YOU ALL ABOUT IT.

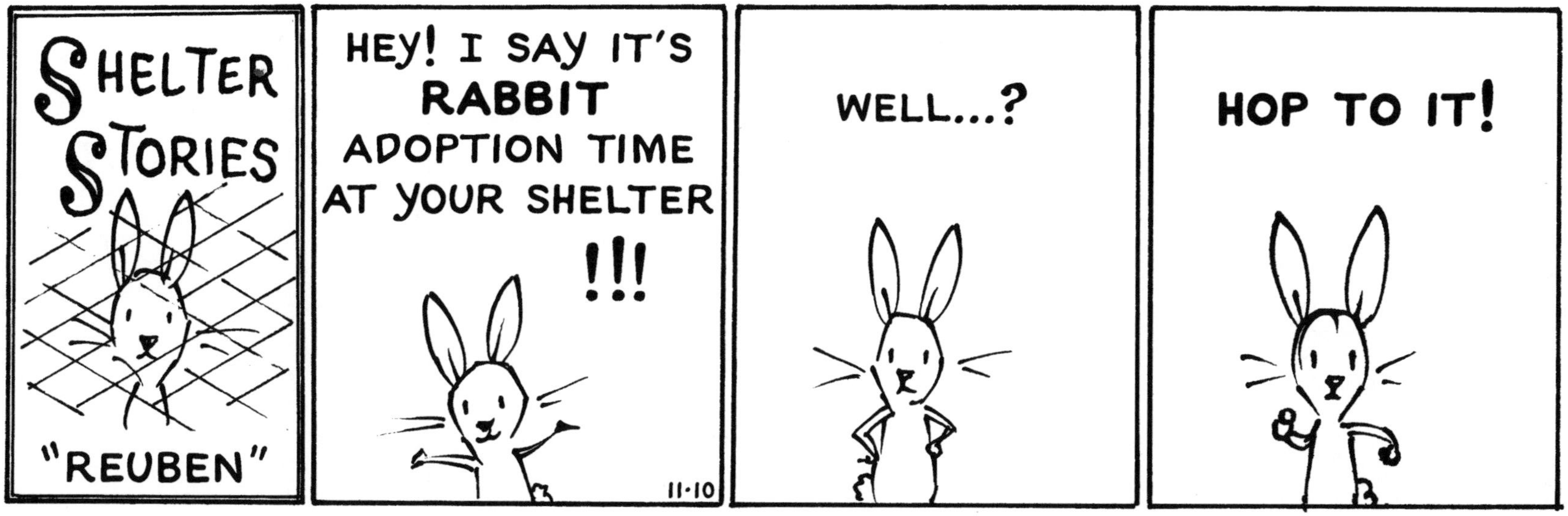
SHELTER STORIES
"REUBEN"
HEY! I SAY IT'S RABBIT ADOPTION TIME AT YOUR SHELTER !!!
11-10
WELL...?
HOP TO IT!

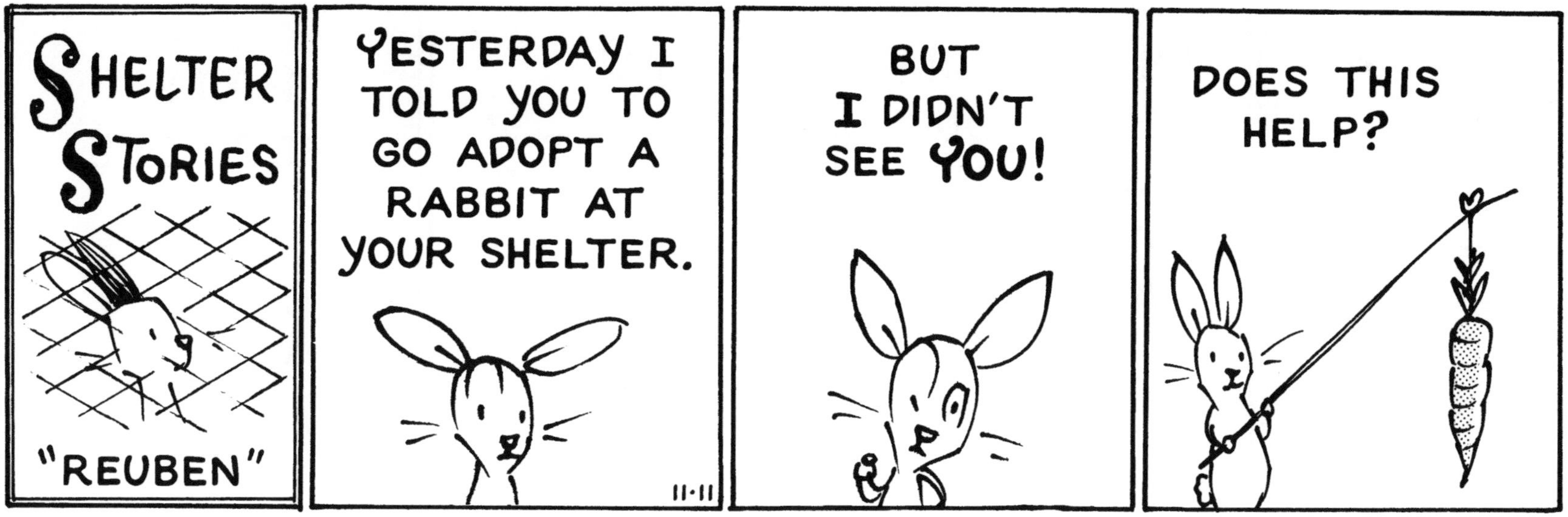
SHELTER STORIES
"REUBEN"
YESTERDAY I TOLD YOU TO GO ADOPT A RABBIT AT YOUR SHELTER.
11-11
BUT I DIDN'T SEE YOU!
DOES THIS HELP?

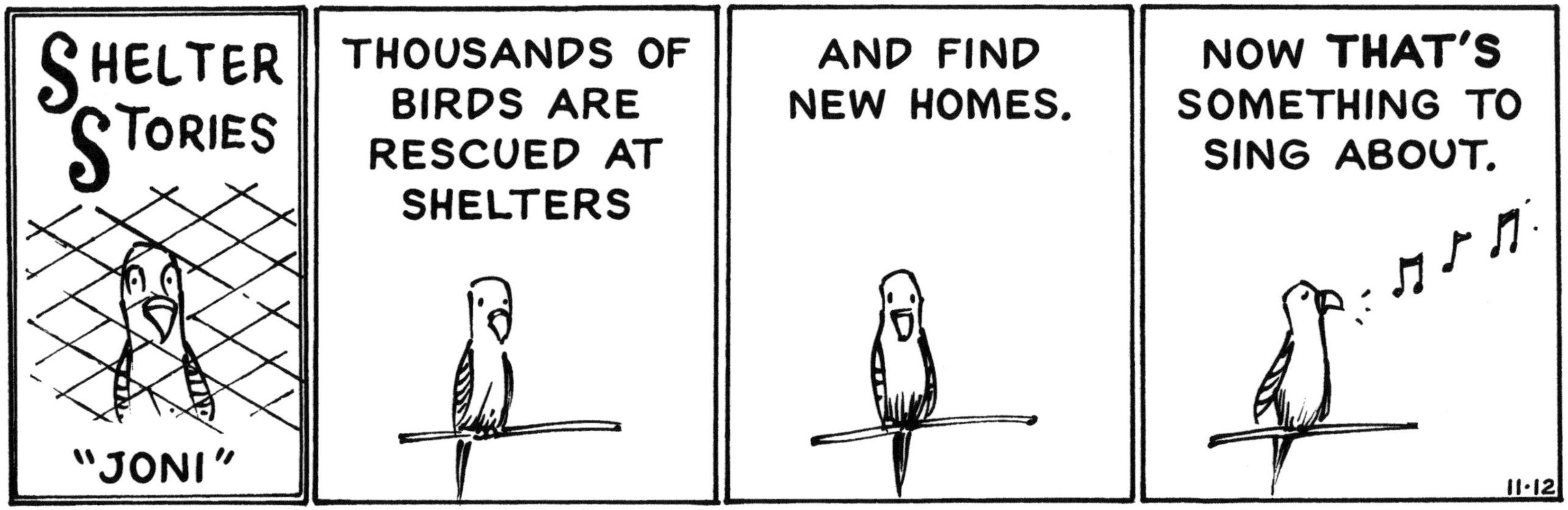
SHELTER STORIES
"JONI"
THOUSANDS OF BIRDS ARE RESCUED AT SHELTERS
AND FIND NEW HOMES.
NOW THAT'S SOMETHING TO SING ABOUT.
11·12

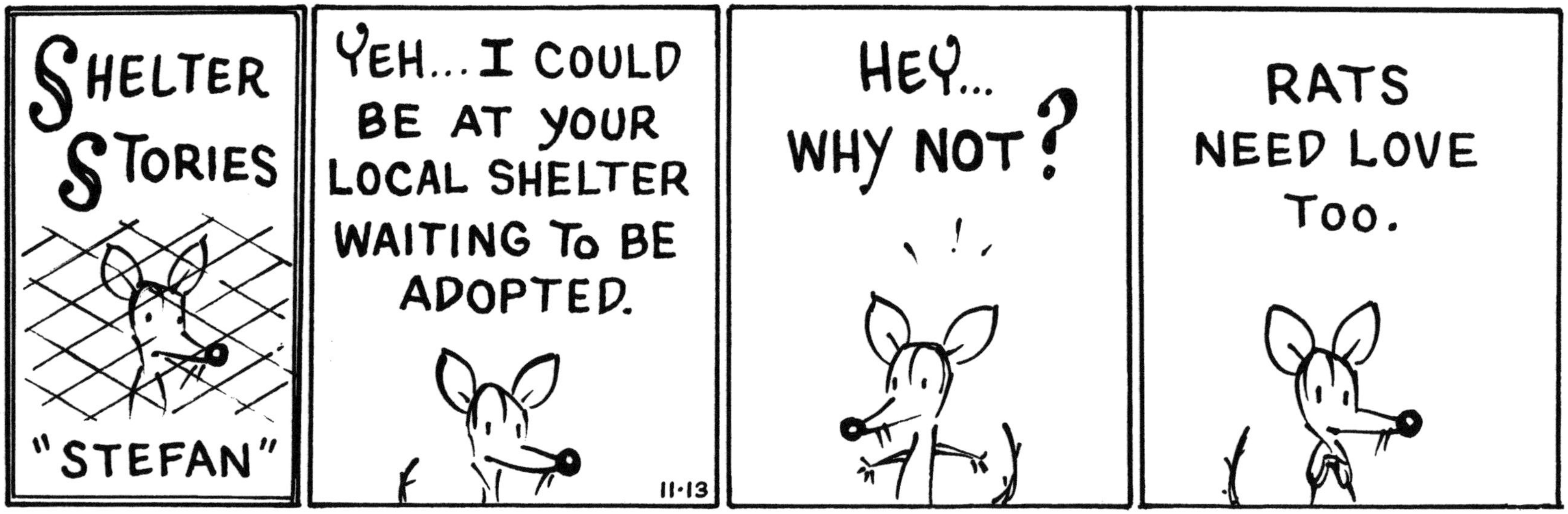
SHELTER STORIES
"STEFAN"
YEH... I COULD BE AT YOUR LOCAL SHELTER WAITING TO BE ADOPTED.
11·13
HEY... WHY NOT?
RATS NEED LOVE TOO.

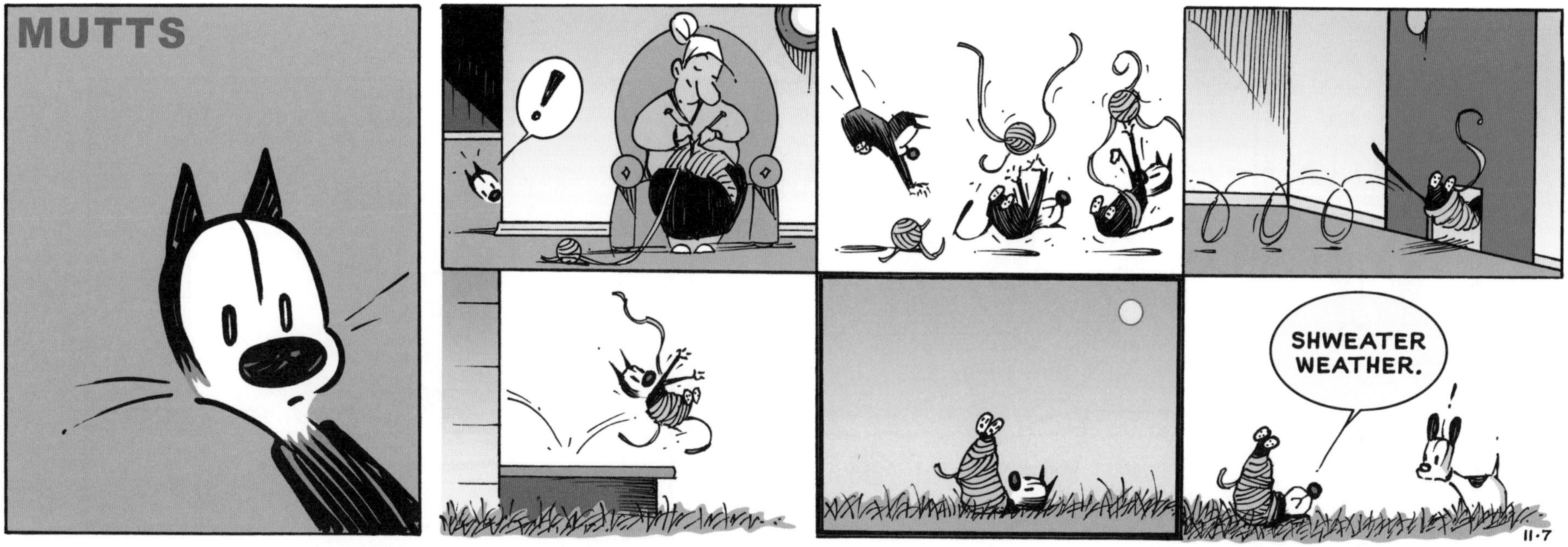
MUTTS
!
SHWEATER WEATHER.
!
11·7

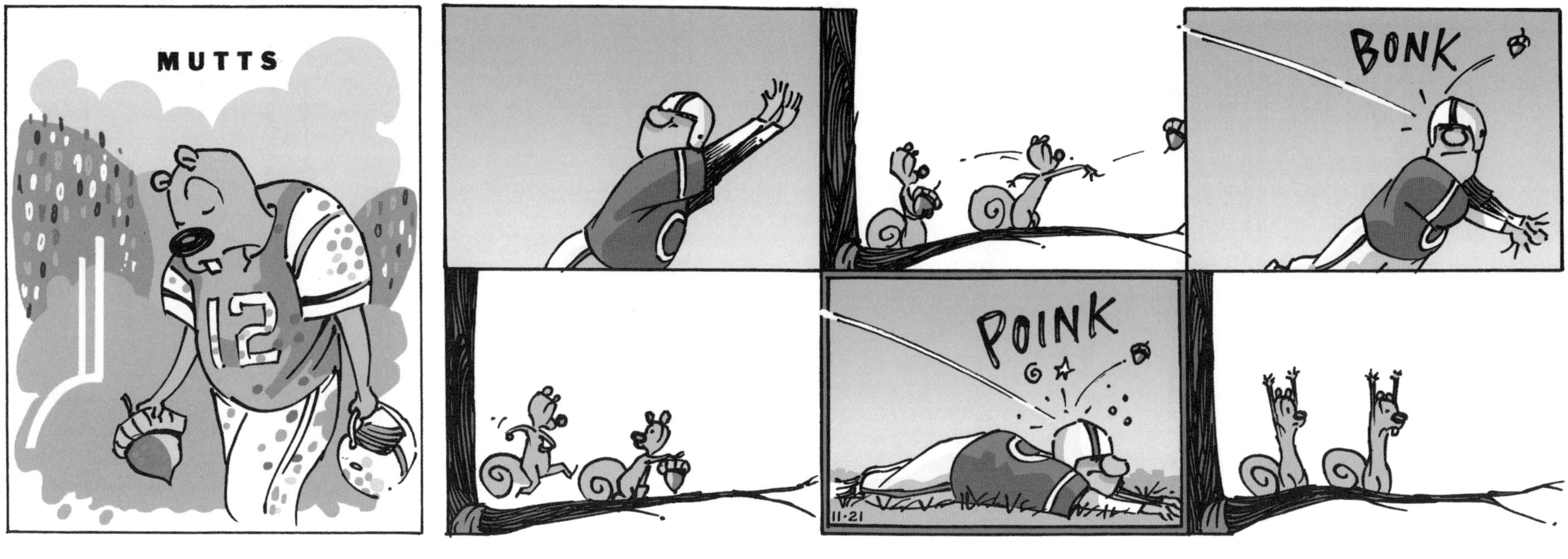
MUTTS
12
BONK
POINK
11·21

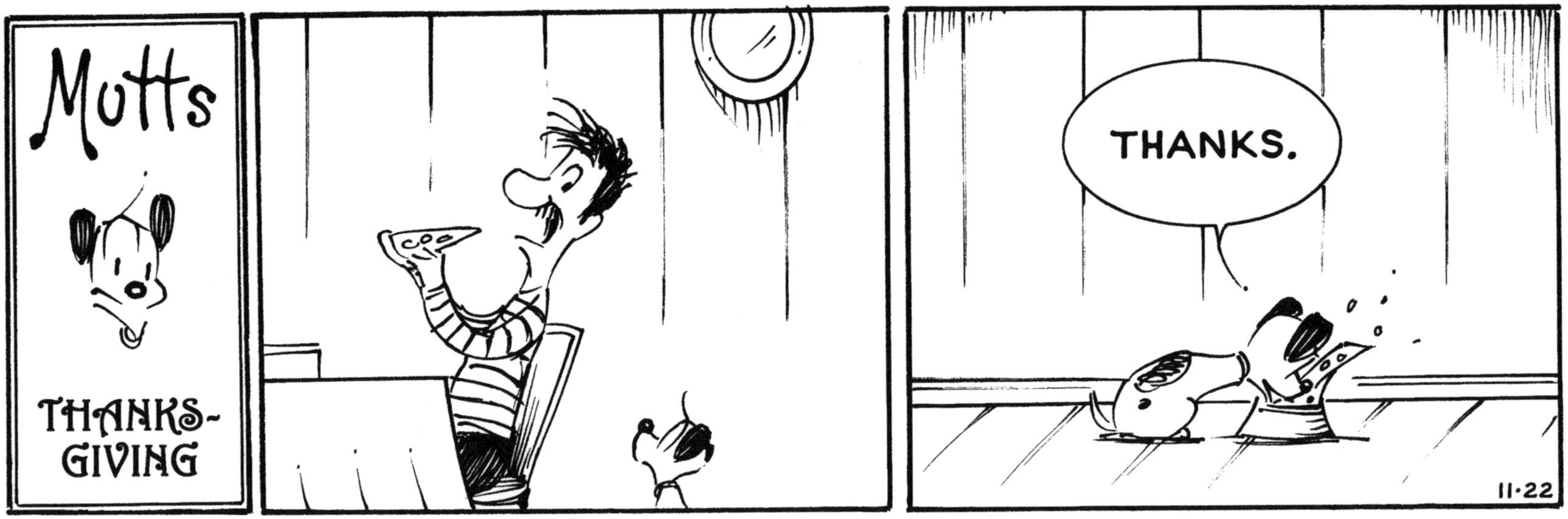
Mutts
THANKS-GIVING
THANKS.
11·22

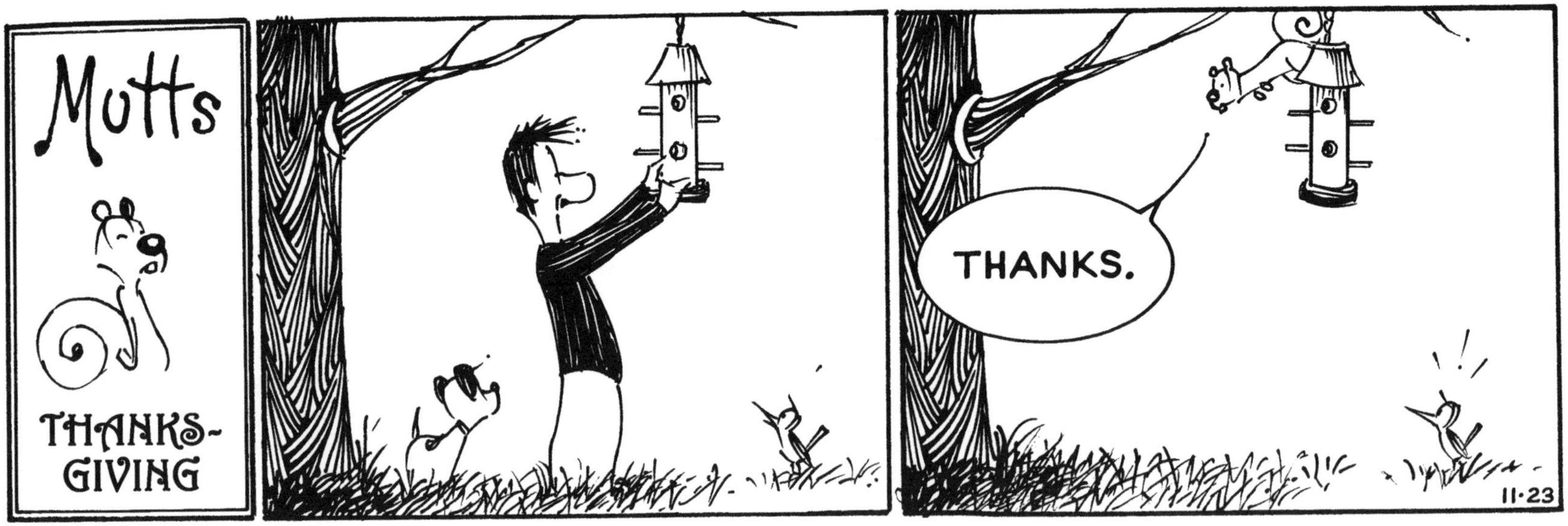
Mutts
THANKS-GIVING
THANKS.
11·23

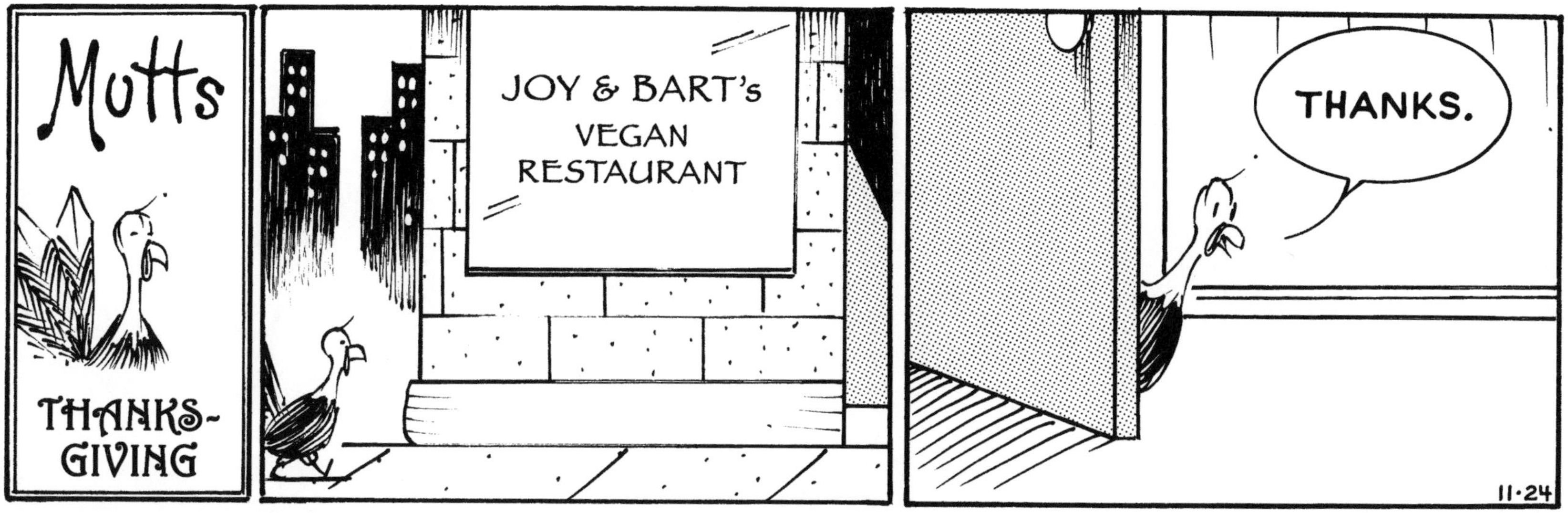
Mutts
THANKS-
GIVING
JOY & BART's
VEGAN
RESTAURANT
THANKS.
11·24

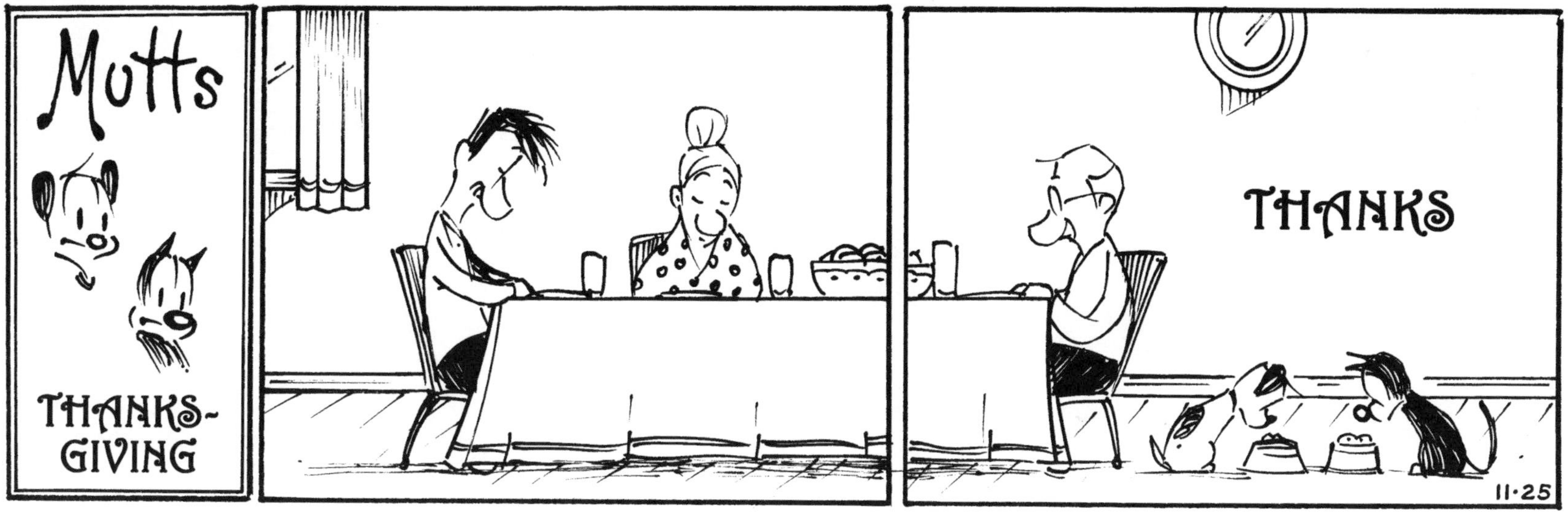
Mutts
THANKS-
GIVING
THANKS
11·25

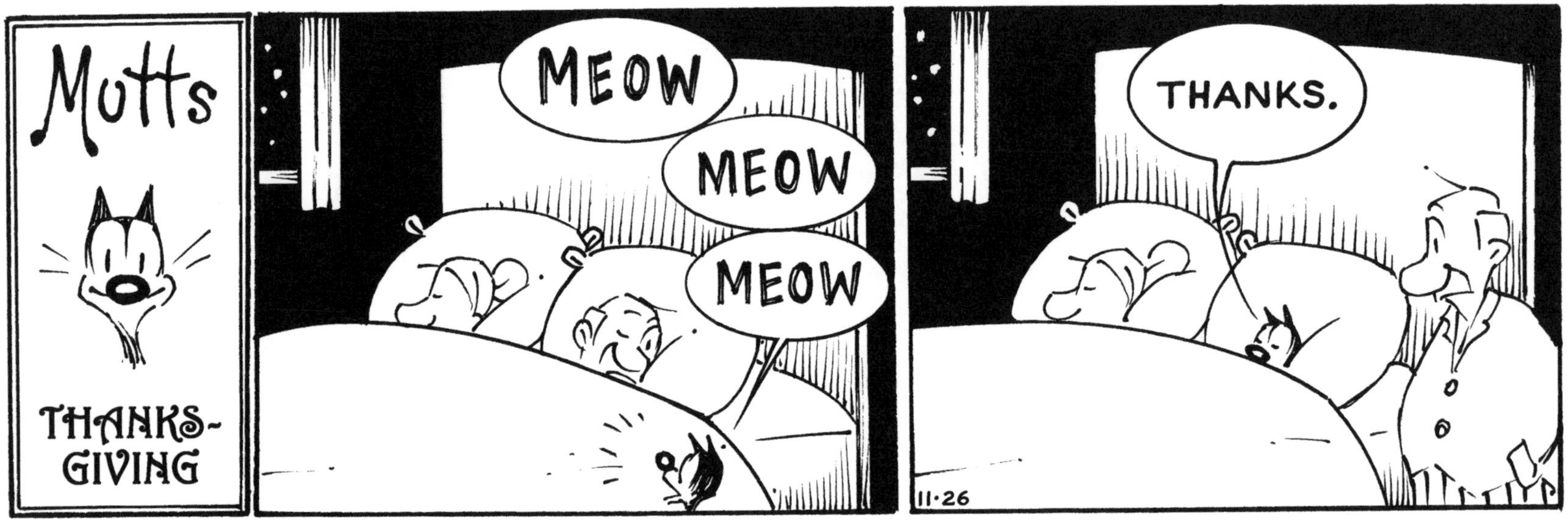
Mutts
THANKS-
GIVING
MEOW
MEOW
MEOW
11·26
THANKS.

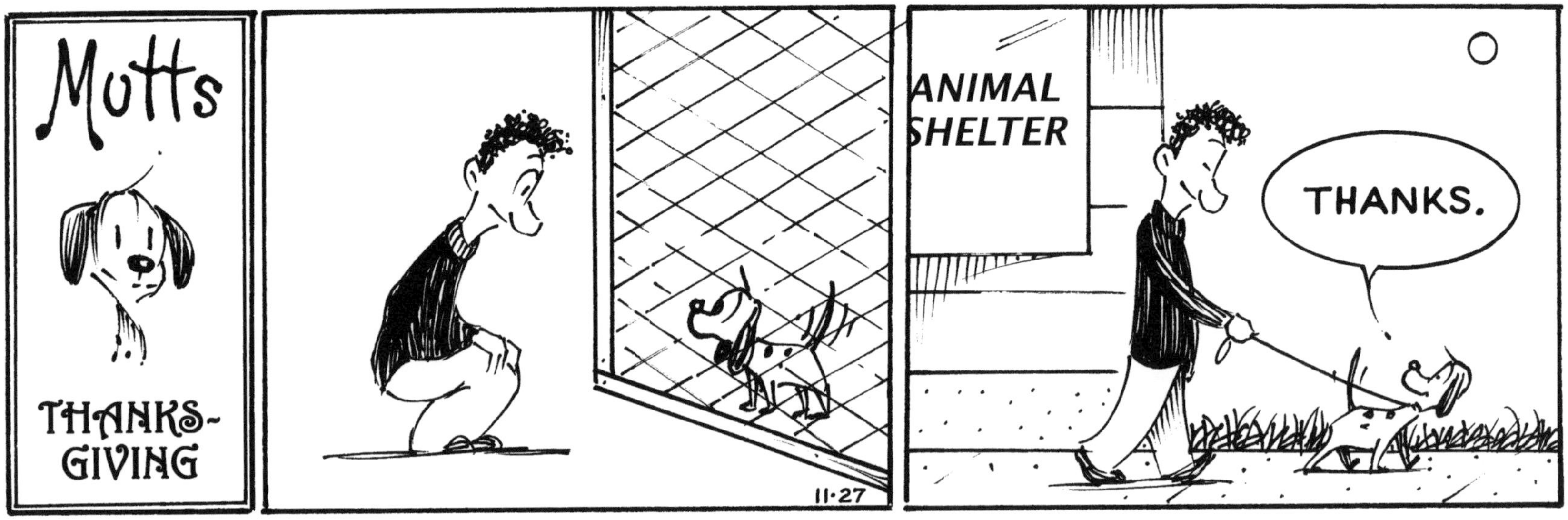
Mutts
THANKS-
GIVING
11·27
ANIMAL
SHELTER
THANKS.

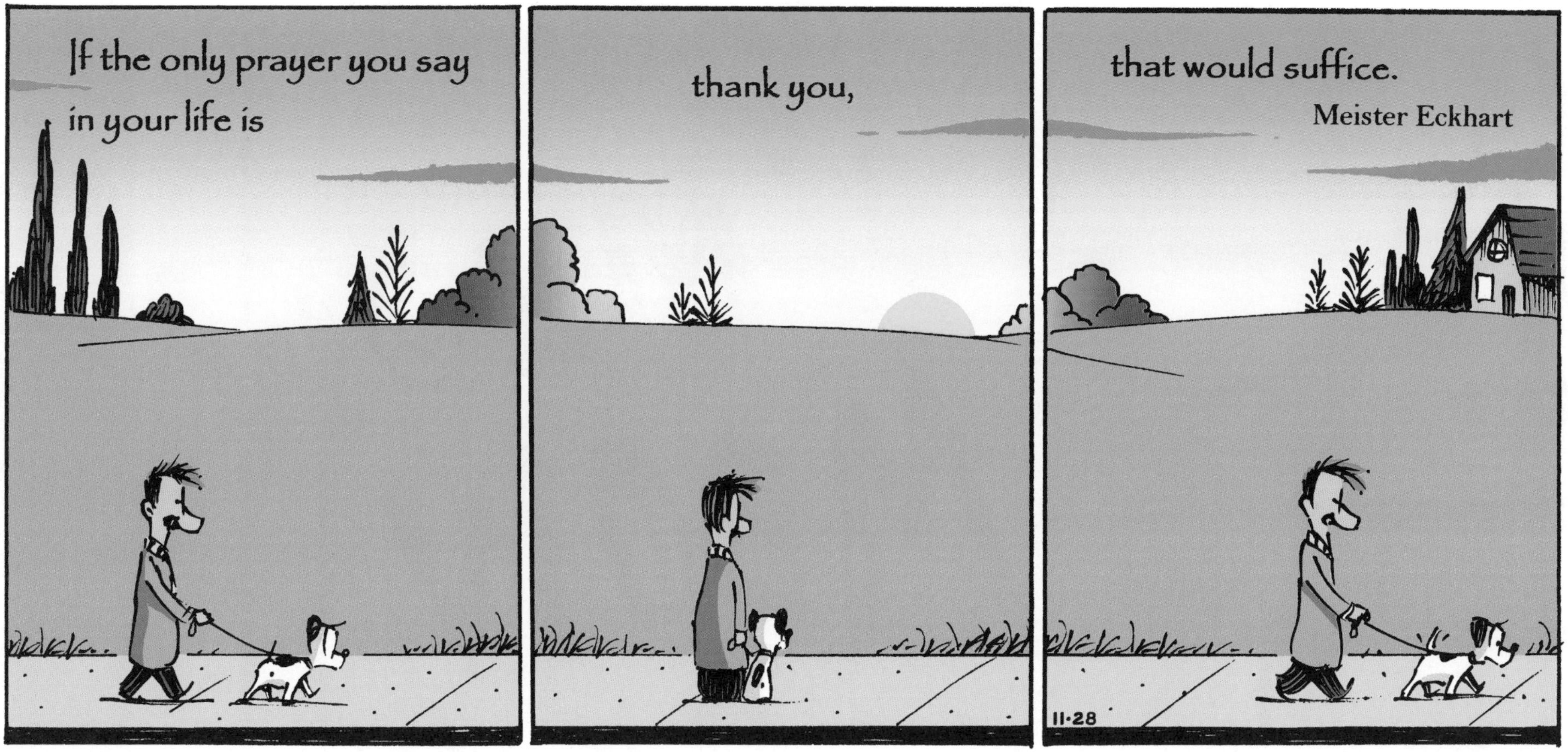
If the only prayer you say in your life is
thank you,
that would suffice.
Meister Eckhart
11·28

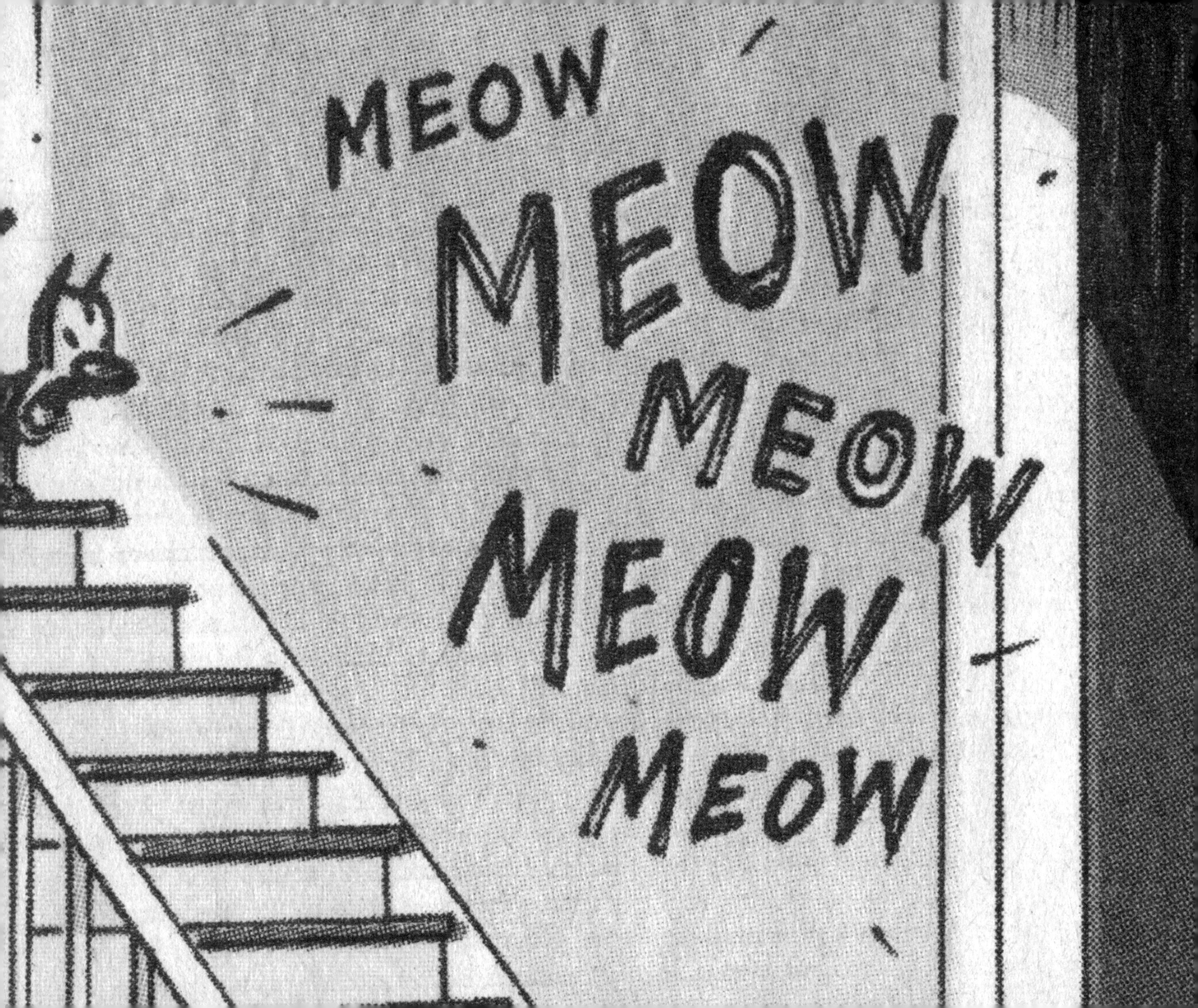
MEOW
MEOW
MEOW
MEOW
MEOW

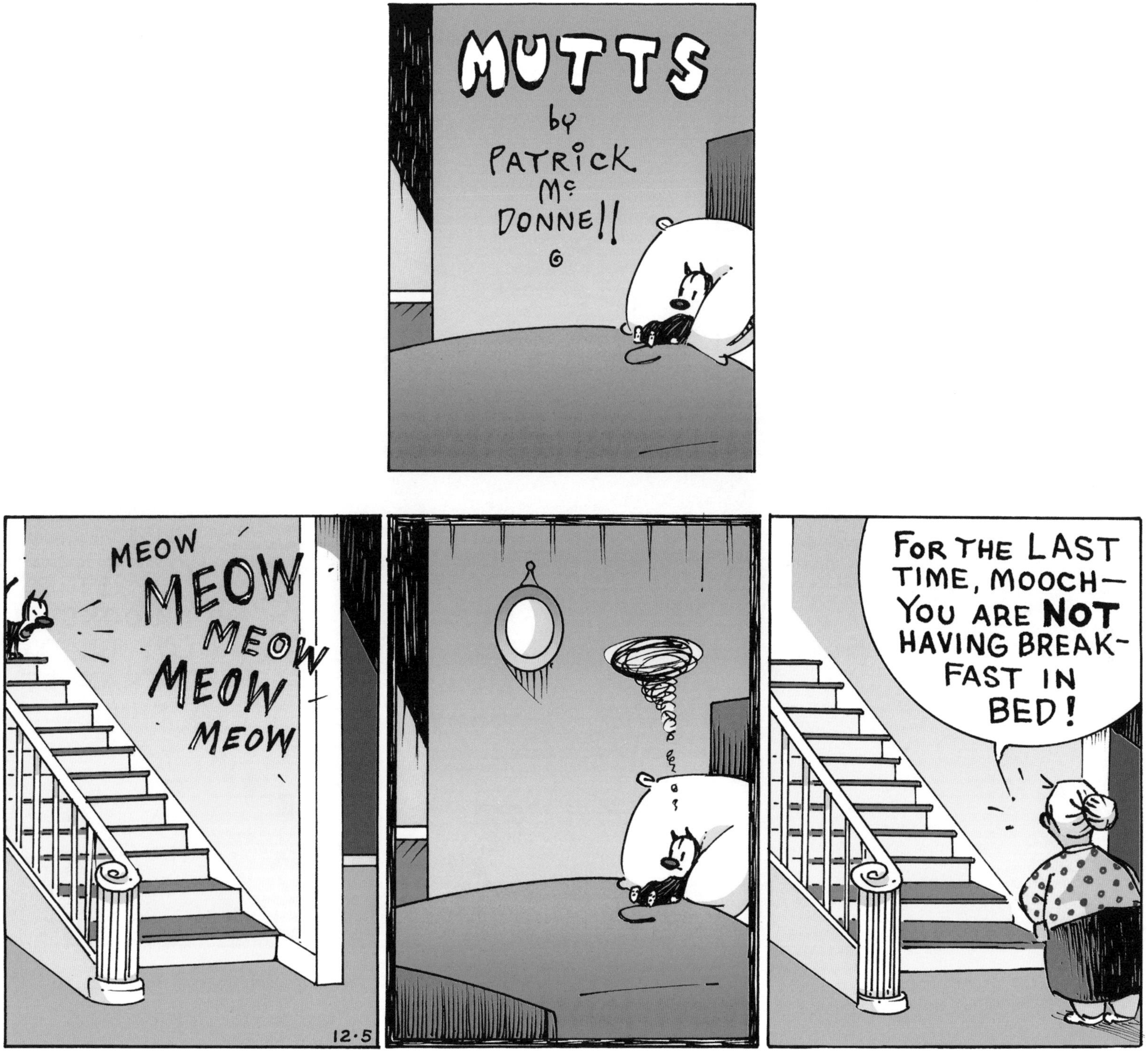
MUTTS
by PATRICK Mc DONNELL ©
MEOW MEOW MEOW MEOW MEOW
12·5
FOR THE LAST TIME, MOOCH— YOU ARE NOT HAVING BREAK-FAST IN BED!

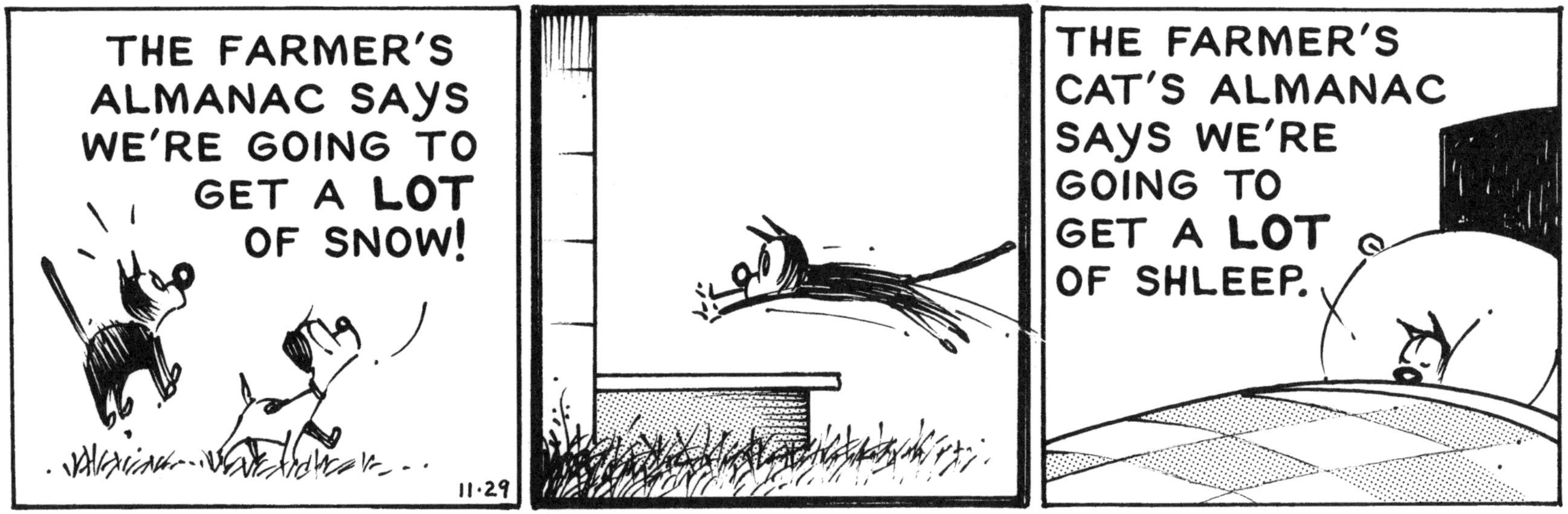
THE FARMER'S ALMANAC SAYS WE'RE GOING TO GET A **LOT** OF SNOW!
11·29
THE FARMER'S CAT'S ALMANAC SAYS WE'RE GOING TO GET A **LOT** OF SHLEEP.

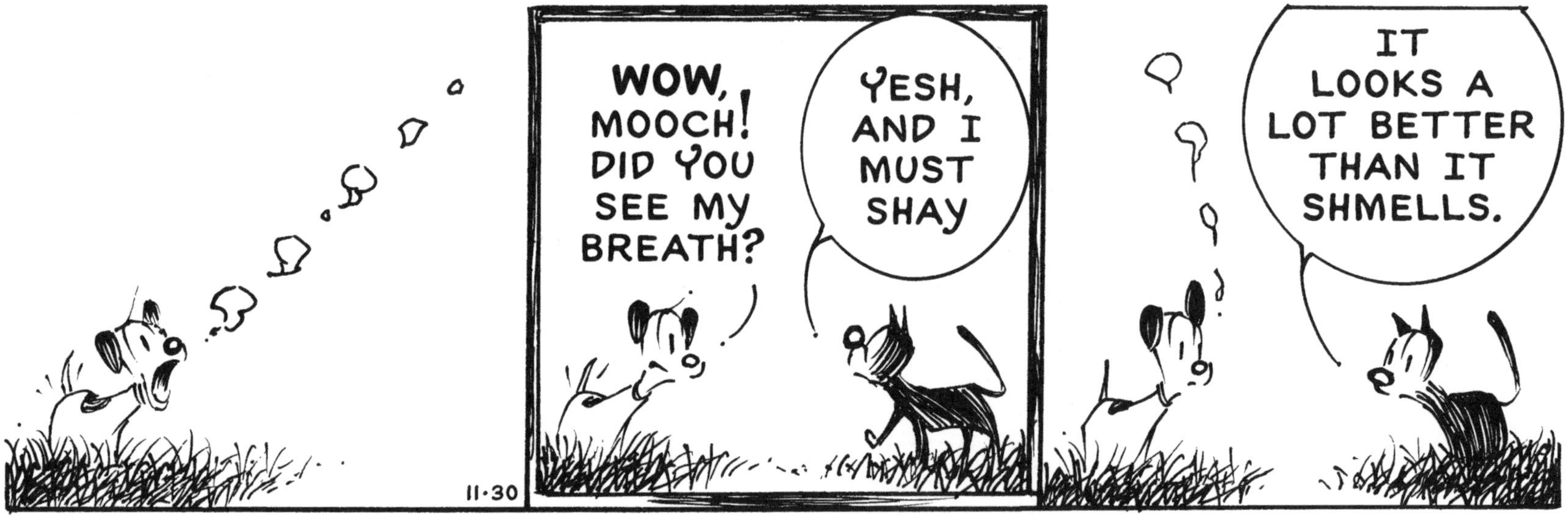
11·30
WOW, MOOCH! DID YOU SEE MY BREATH?
YESH, AND I MUST SHAY
IT LOOKS A LOT BETTER THAN IT SHMELLS.

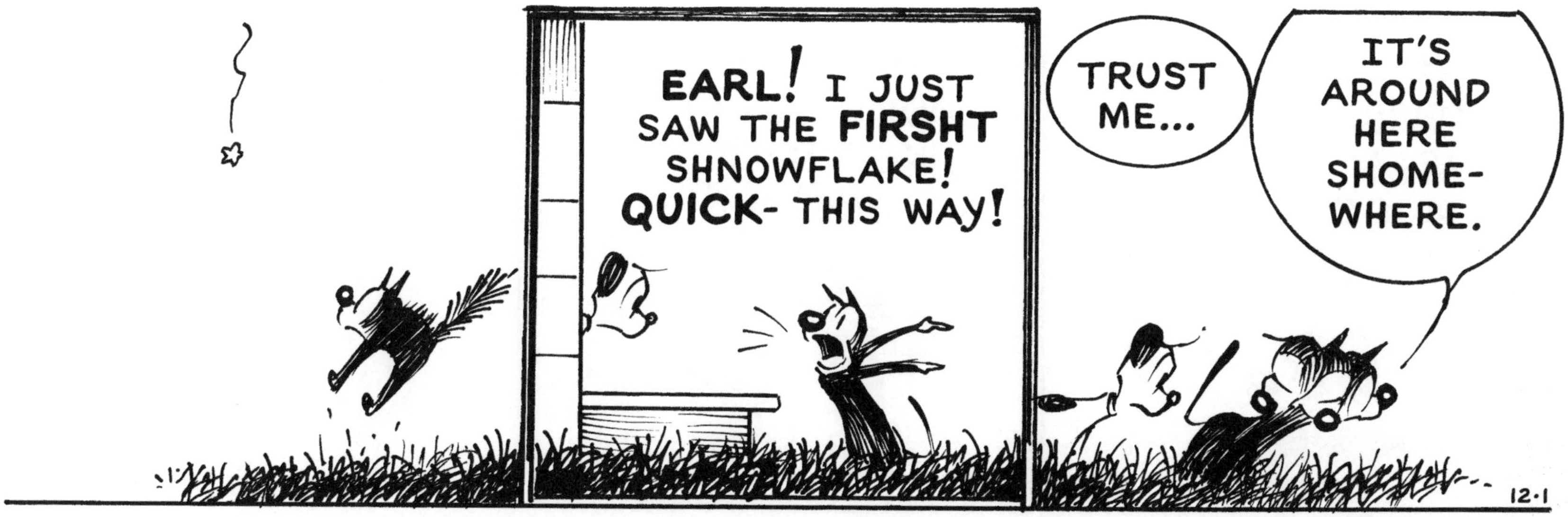
EARL! I JUST SAW THE FIRSHT SHNOWFLAKE! QUICK- THIS WAY!
TRUST ME...
IT'S AROUND HERE SHOMEWHERE.
12·1

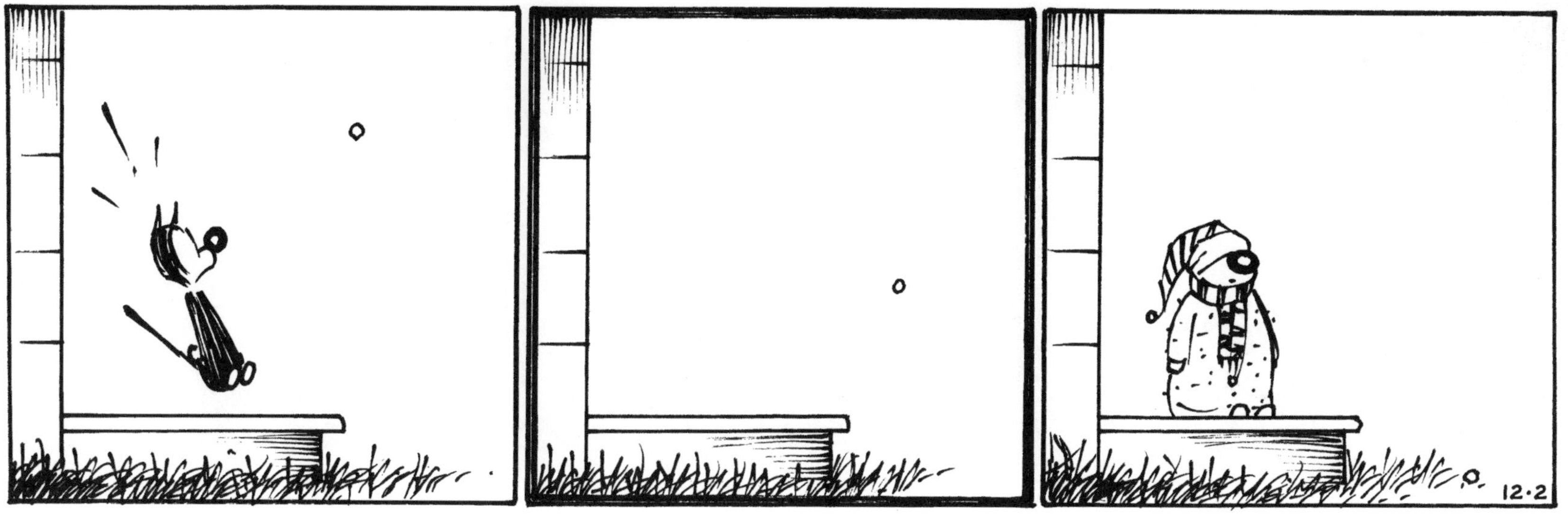
12·2

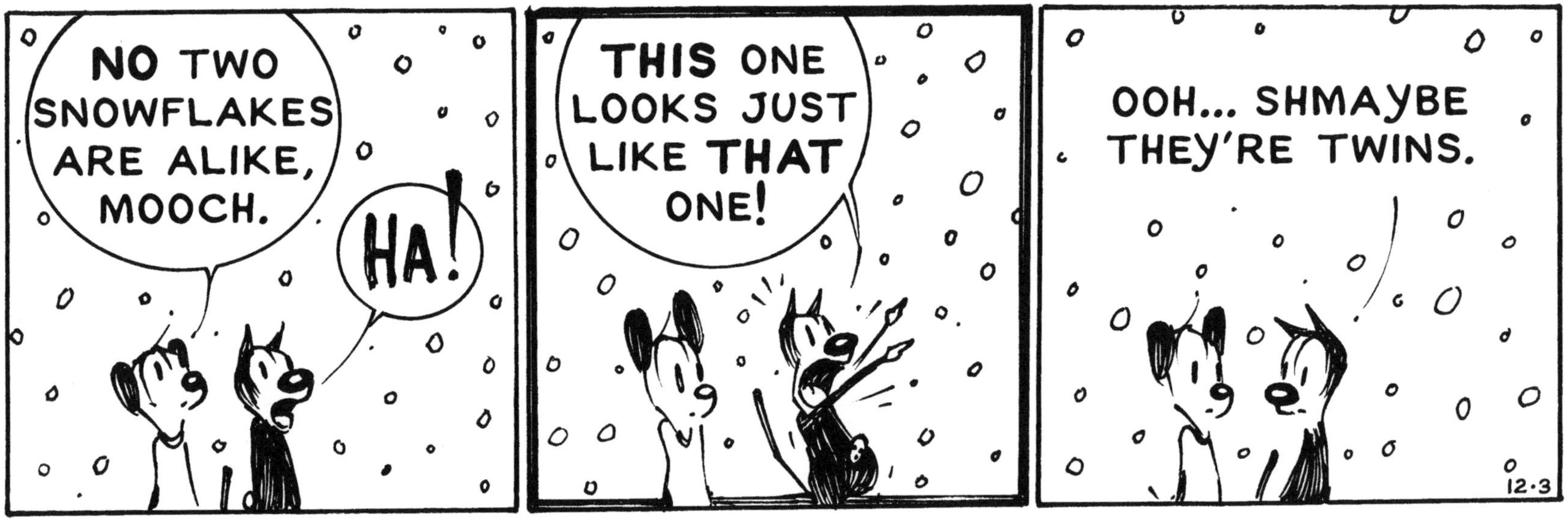
NO TWO SNOWFLAKES ARE ALIKE, MOOCH.
HA!
THIS ONE LOOKS JUST LIKE THAT ONE!
OOH... SHMAYBE THEY'RE TWINS.
12·3

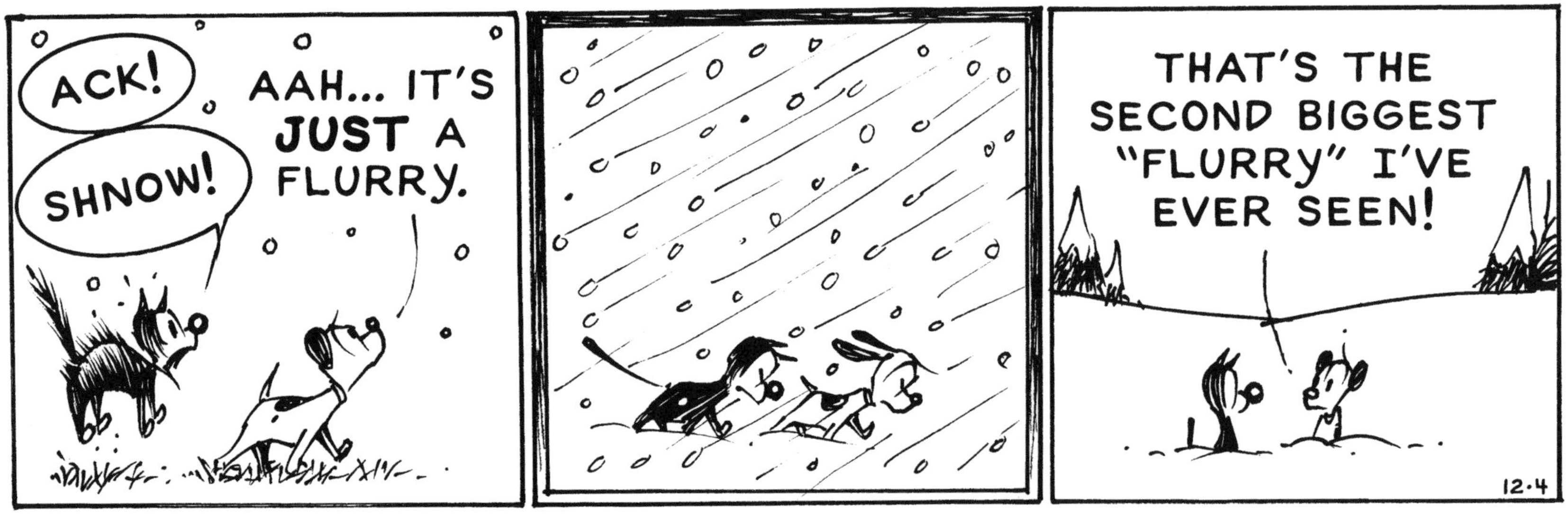
ACK!
SHNOW!
AAH... IT'S JUST A FLURRY.
THAT'S THE SECOND BIGGEST "FLURRY" I'VE EVER SEEN!
12·4

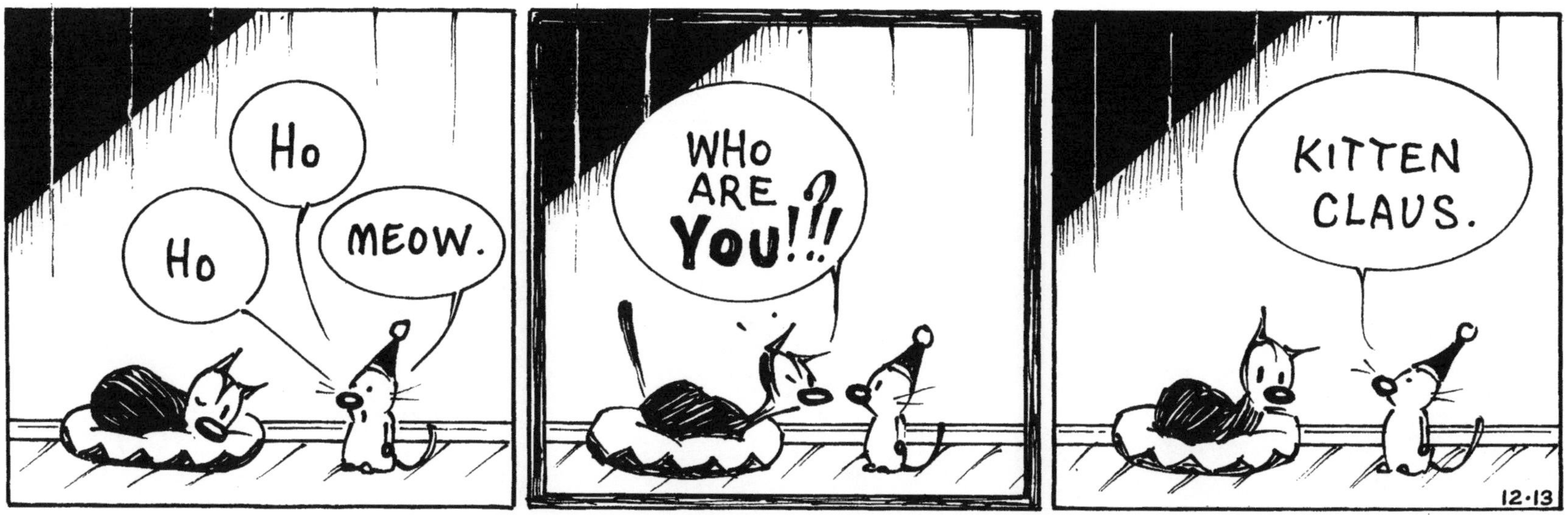
Ho
Ho
MEOW.
WHO ARE YOU?!!
KITTEN CLAUS.
12·13

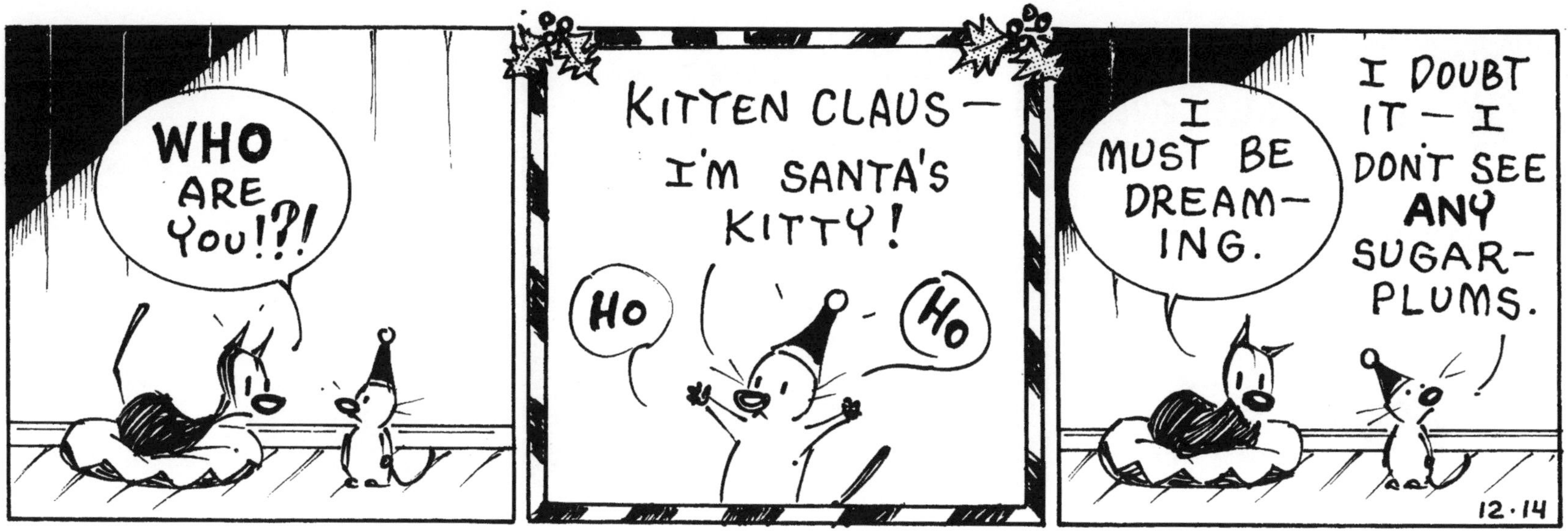
WHO ARE YOU!?!
KITTEN CLAUS— I'M SANTA'S KITTY!
HO
HO
I MUST BE DREAM-ING.
I DOUBT IT— I DON'T SEE ANY SUGAR-PLUMS.
12·14

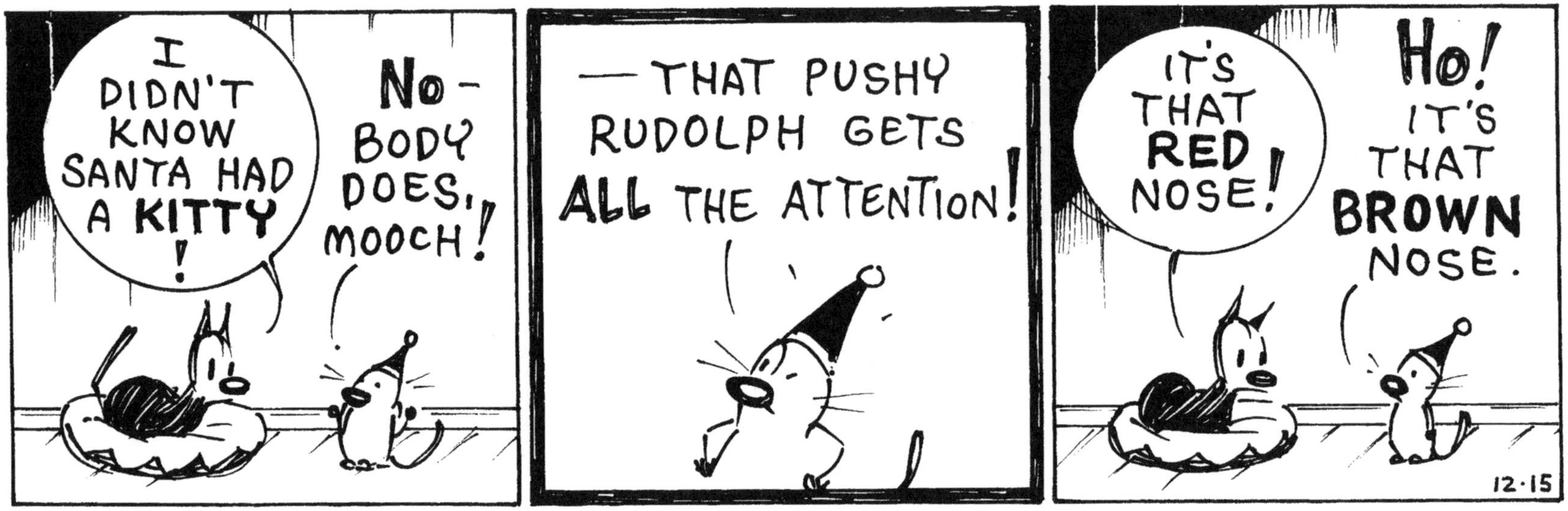

I DIDN'T KNOW SANTA HAD A KITTY!
NO-BODY DOES, MOOCH!
— THAT PUSHY RUDOLPH GETS ALL THE ATTENTION!
IT'S THAT RED NOSE!
HO! IT'S THAT BROWN NOSE.
12·15

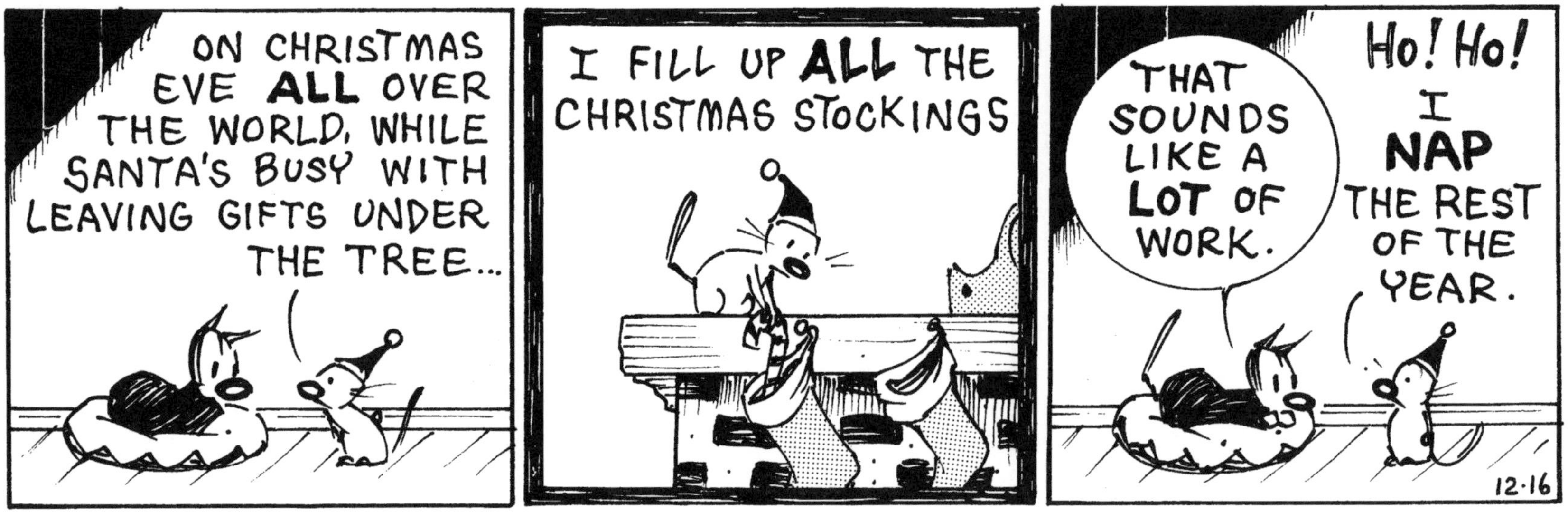

ON CHRISTMAS EVE ALL OVER THE WORLD, WHILE SANTA'S BUSY WITH LEAVING GIFTS UNDER THE TREE...
I FILL UP ALL THE CHRISTMAS STOCKINGS
THAT SOUNDS LIKE A LOT OF WORK.
HO! HO! I NAP THE REST OF THE YEAR.
12·16

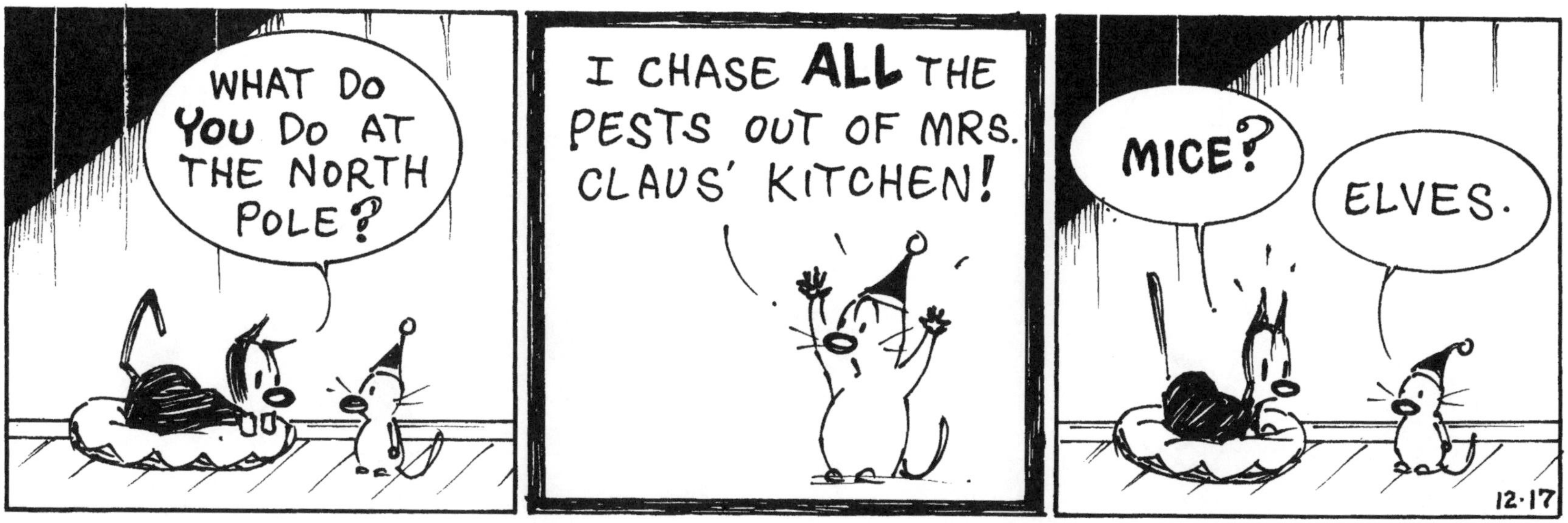
WHAT DO YOU DO AT THE NORTH POLE?
I CHASE ALL THE PESTS OUT OF MRS. CLAUS' KITCHEN!
MICE?
ELVES.
12·17

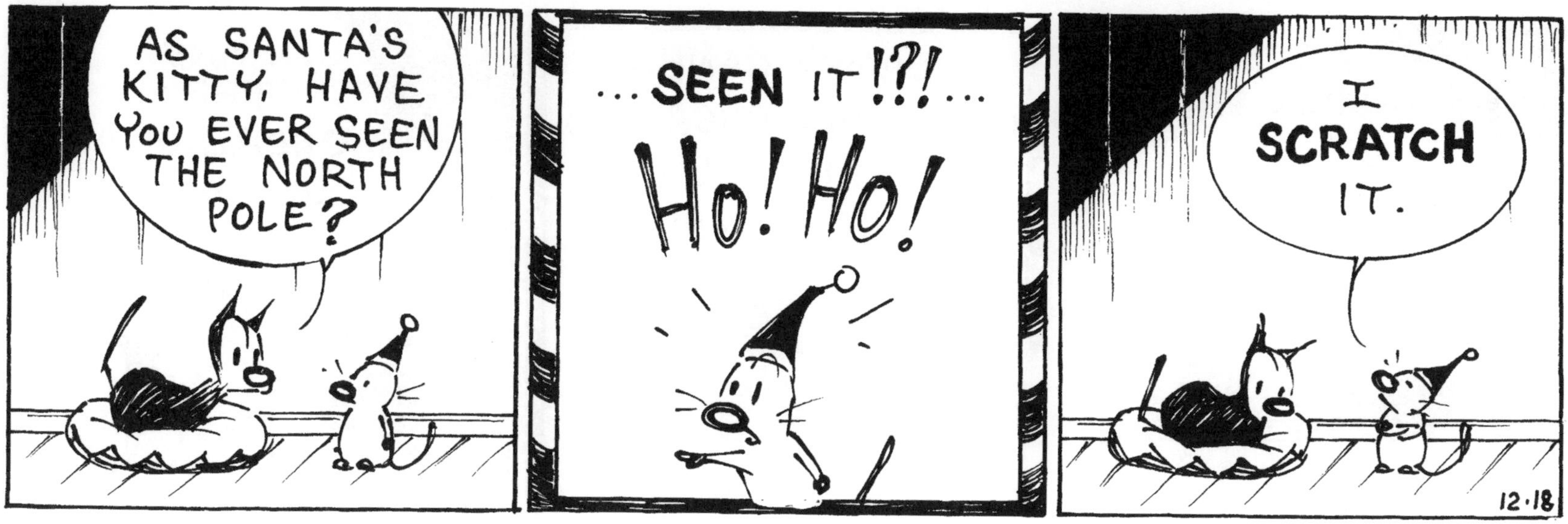
AS SANTA'S KITTY, HAVE YOU EVER SEEN THE NORTH POLE?
...SEEN IT!?!...
Ho! Ho!
I SCRATCH IT.
12·18

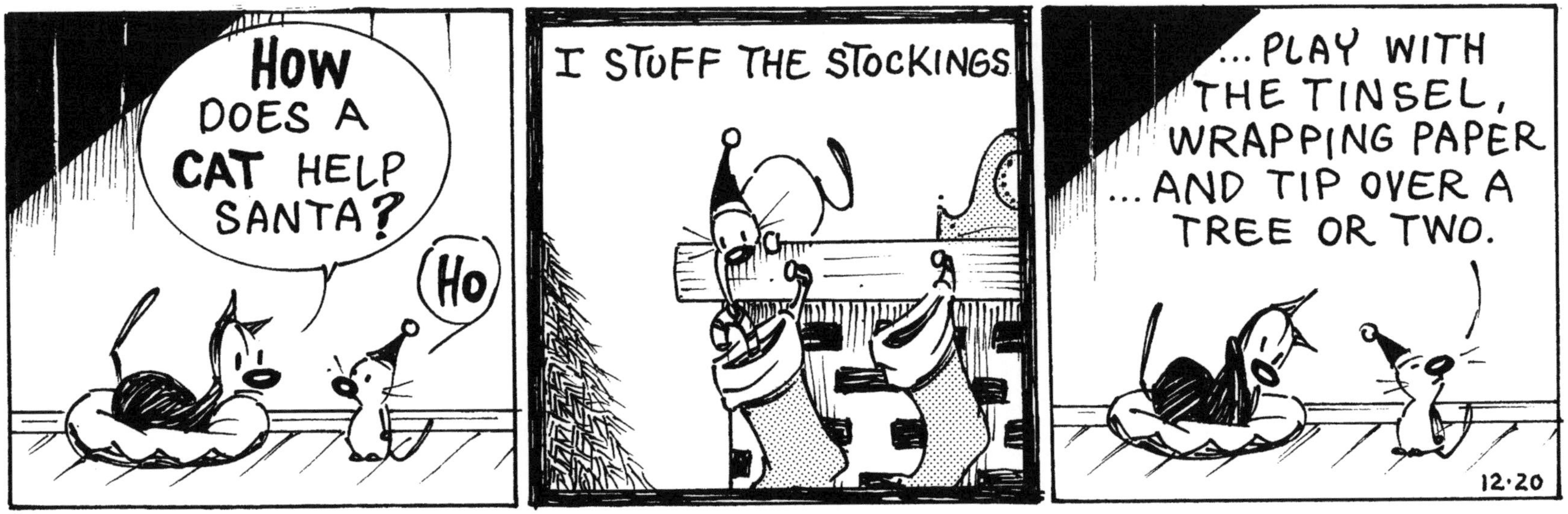
HOW DOES A CAT HELP SANTA?
HO
I STUFF THE STOCKINGS
...PLAY WITH THE TINSEL, WRAPPING PAPER ...AND TIP OVER A TREE OR TWO.
12·20

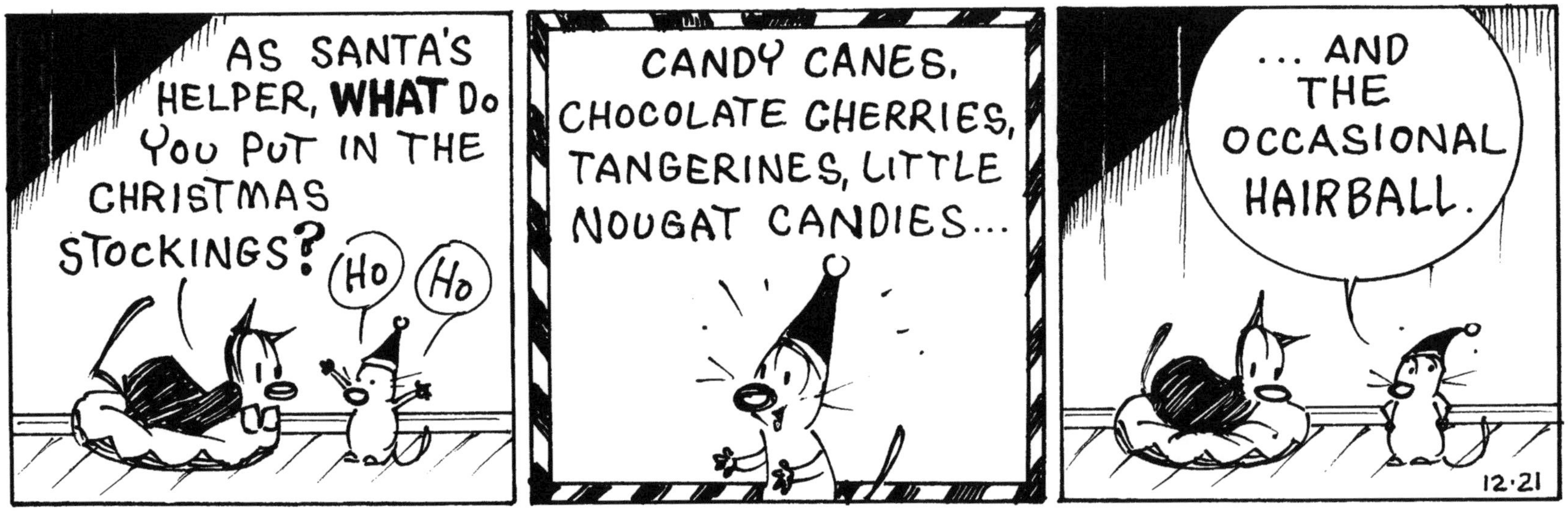
AS SANTA'S HELPER, WHAT DO YOU PUT IN THE CHRISTMAS STOCKINGS?
HO
HO
CANDY CANES, CHOCOLATE CHERRIES, TANGERINES, LITTLE NOUGAT CANDIES...
... AND THE OCCASIONAL HAIRBALL.
12·21

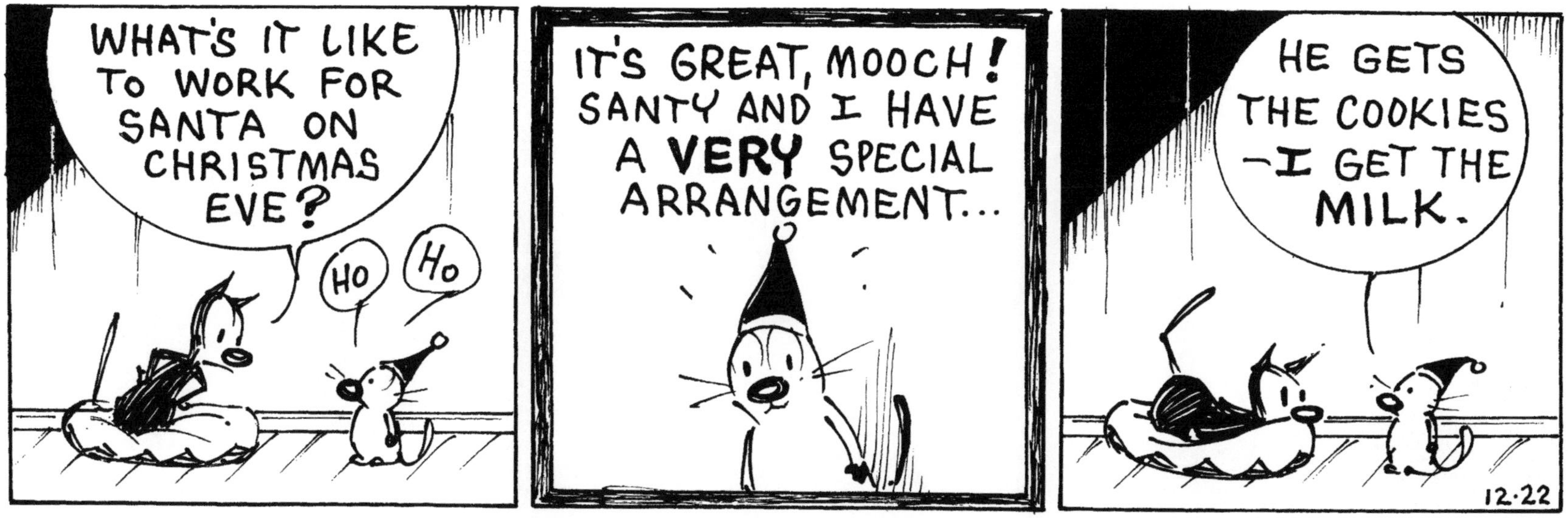
WHAT'S IT LIKE TO WORK FOR SANTA ON CHRISTMAS EVE?
HO
Ho
IT'S GREAT, MOOCH! SANTY AND I HAVE A VERY SPECIAL ARRANGEMENT...
HE GETS THE COOKIES —I GET THE MILK.
12·22

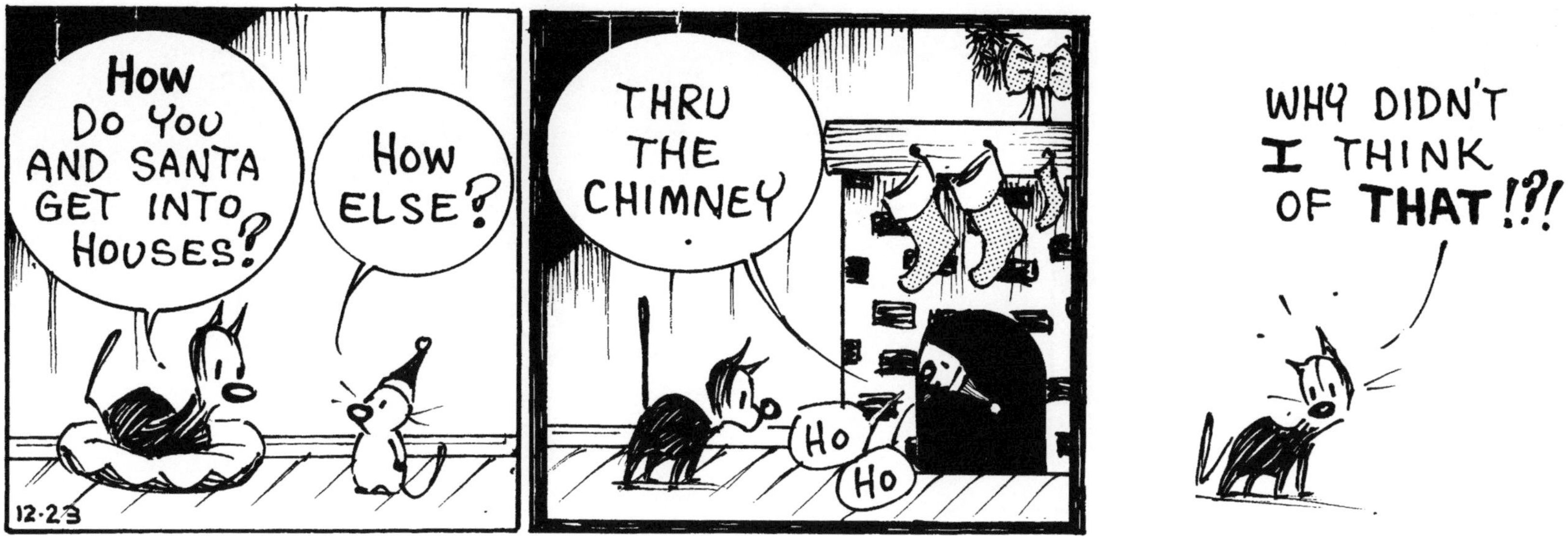
HOW DO YOU AND SANTA GET INTO HOUSES?
HOW ELSE?
12·23
THRU THE CHIMNEY.
Ho
Ho
WHY DIDN'T I THINK OF THAT!?!

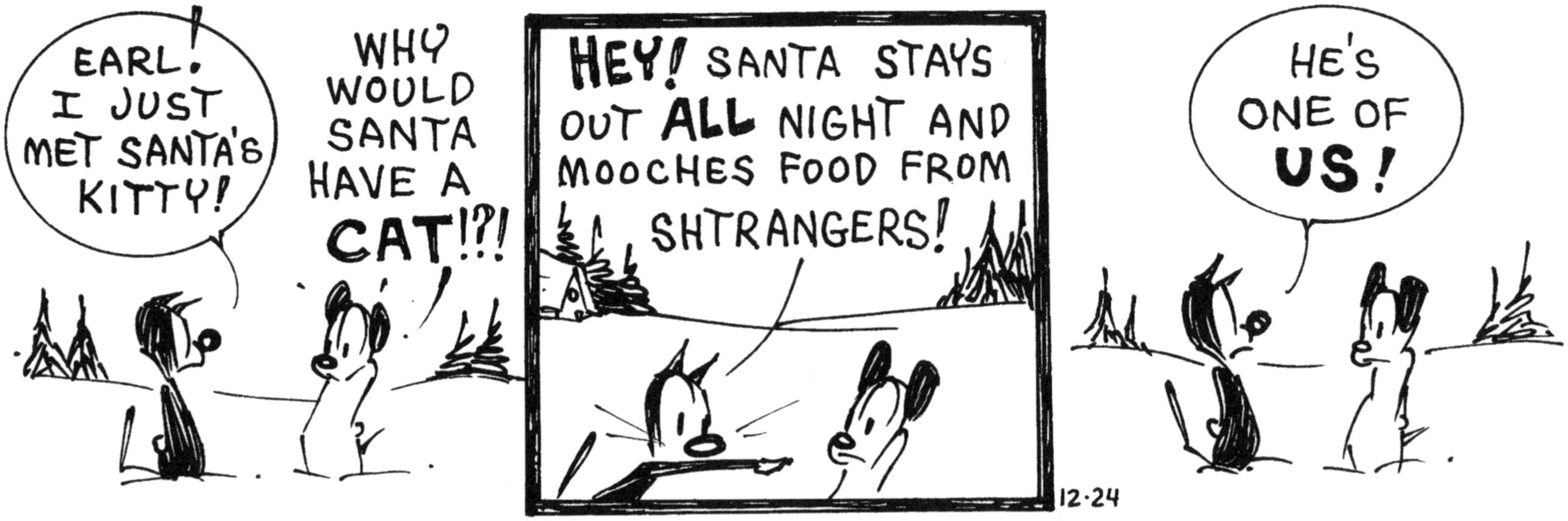
EARL! I JUST MET SANTA'S KITTY!
WHY WOULD SANTA HAVE A CAT!?!
HEY! SANTA STAYS OUT ALL NIGHT AND MOOCHES FOOD FROM SHTRANGERS!
HE'S ONE OF US!
12·24

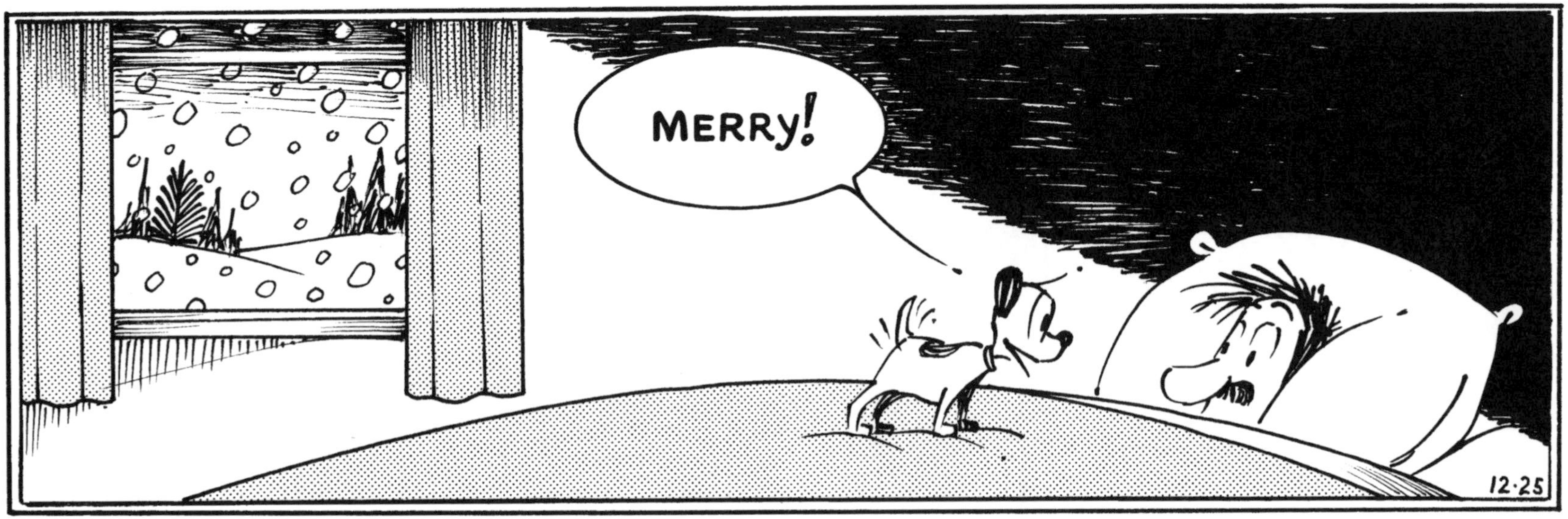
MERRY!
12·25

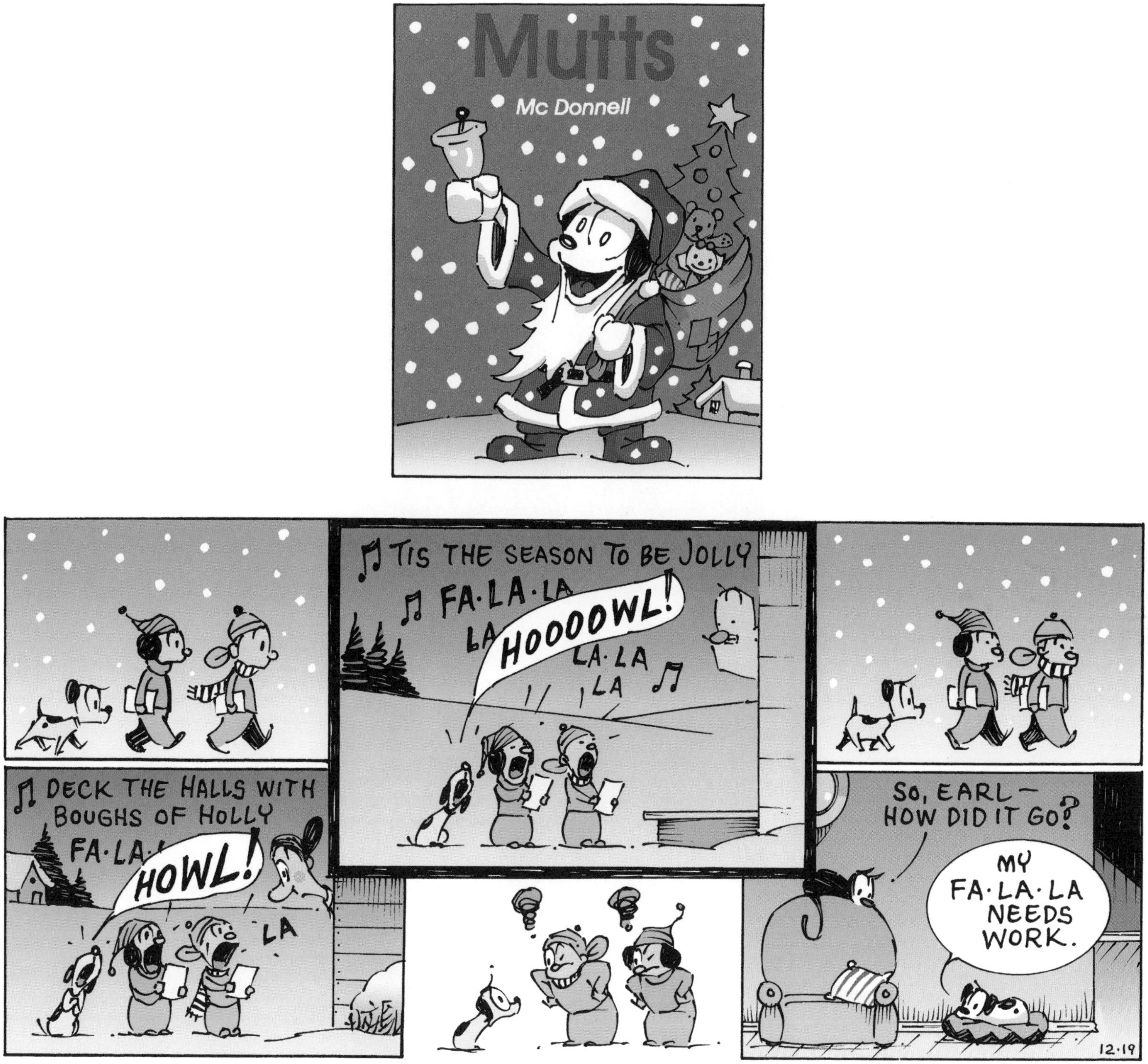

Mutts
Mc Donnell
♫ DECK THE HALLS WITH BOUGHS OF HOLLY
FA·LA·
HOWL!
LA
♫ TIS THE SEASON TO BE JOLLY
♫ FA·LA·LA LA
HOOOOWL!
LA·LA LA ♫
SO, EARL— HOW DID IT GO?
MY FA·LA·LA NEEDS WORK.
12·19

PEACE TO ALL BEINGS

12·26